global explorations

stage 4 geography

Grant Kleeman
Rod Lane
Raymond Pask
John Butler
Helen Rhodes
Peter Elliott

Heinemann
Harcourt Education

Heinemann
HARCOURT EDUCATION
20 Thackray Road, Port Melbourne, Victoria 3207
World Wide Web hi.com.au
Email info@hi.com.au
PO Box 460 Port Melbourne, Victoria 3207

First published 2004
2008 2007 2006 2005
10 9 8 7 6 5 4 3 2

Publisher: Mark Childs
Editor: Susan Lee
Designer: Rebecca Harrison
Text designer: Rebecca Harrison and Nikki De Leo
Cover designer: Rebecca Harrison
Illustrations: Guy Holt, Julie Knoblock, Ophelia Leviny, Pat Kermode, Bill Woods and Chris Cooke
Photograph researcher: Lara Artis

Typeset in 11/12 Goudy by Palmer Higgs
Prepress by Print + Publish, Port Melbourne
Printed and bound by Craft Print International Limited, Singapore
National Library of Australia
cataloguing-in-publication data:

Global explorations. Stage 4 : Geography.

Includes index.
Secondary school students.
ISBN 1 74081 336 7.

1. Geography - Study and teaching (Secondary). I. Kleeman, Grant.

910.712

(Pack ISBN: 1 74081 240 9; CD ISBN: 1 74081 339 1)
Reed International Books Australia Pty Ltd ACN 001 002 357

Acknowledgments
The publisher would like to thank the following Geography teachers for their assistance with the development of this project: Abby Jeffrey, Edward Codsi, Helen Rhodes, David Hamper, Dominique Marturia, Danielle Calman, Jane Lovett, Robyn Anderson, Elizabeth George and Elizabeth Stokes.

The authors and publisher would like to thank the following for permission to reproduce the copyright material in this book.

Photographs
AAP Images: pp. 133, 270, 276 (top and bottom right), 302 (bottom), 313 (centre left); Airbus 2004: p. 269; Auscape: (Kathie Atkinson) p. 234 (top left), (John Cancalosi) p. 148, (Kevin Deacon) p. 258, (Jean-Paul Ferrero) p. 231 (bottom), (D. Fleetham-OSF) p. 234 (bottom left), (Brett Gregory) p. 64 (bottom right), (P. Leroux-Explorer) p. 291, (John McCammon) p. 243 (middle left), (Colin Monteath) p. 125, (D. Parer and E. Parer-Cook) p. 235 (bottom), (Tom Till) p. 186; Australian Antarctic Division: p. 134; Australian Picture Library: pp. 131 (right), 141, 202 (top), 206(middle), 209, 231 (top), 260, (Corbis) pp. 79 (top left), 137, 318, (Robert Gill) p. 198, (Joseph Sohm) p. 203; Australian Red Cross: p. 308 (right); Bill Bachman: pp. 64 (bottom left), 280, 282 (right); Eric Berger: p. 188 (bottom); Digital Vision: pp. 4–5, 18–19, 22 (top), 41, 58–59, 67 (top left), 77 (top), 106 (middle and right second row from top, centre third row from top, middle and right bottom row), 107 (left second row from top, left bottom row), 118 (bottom), 122–123, 138–139, 140–141, 162–163, 194 (middle centre and right), 202 (bottom), 222 (top), 226–227, 228, 232, 235 (top), 254 (top and bottom), 257 (top), 320; Fairfax Photo Library/Jason South: p. 301; Great Barrier Reef Marine Park Authority: pp. 243 (middle right), 244; Great Southern Stock/K. Hopper: p. 233 (bottom); Greenpeace: pp. 10, 11 (top), 302 (top), 306, 307; Stavro Jabba: pp. 288 (top), 314; Grant Kleeman: pp. 13 (middle right), 64 (top), 66, 77 (bottom right), 180, 187, 188 (top), 194 (bottom far left), 196, 201, 243 (top centre and right, bottom left and centre), 265–266, 265 (top), 272, 274, 278–279, 321; Landcare Australia: p. 324; Lochman Transparencies: (Brett Dennis) p. 193, (John Kleczkowski) p. 324, (Jiri Lochman) p. 194 (bottom right), (Michiko Suzuki) p. 217 (bottom); Lonely Planet Images: (ABI) p. 219 (bottom), (Christopher P. Baker) p. 238 (bottom), (Ross Barnett) p. 323 (left), (Judy Bellah) p. 71, (Tom Boyden) p. 104 (top right), (Andrew Brownbill) p. 43, (Bob Charlton) p. 234 (bottom right), (Graeme Cornwallis) pp. 132, 136 (bottom), (Mary Daffy) pp. 83 bottom), 154 (bottom right), (Scott Darsney) pp. 183, 184, (Grant Dixon) p. 182 (bottom), (Krzysztof Dydynski) p. 313 (bottom left), (John Elk III) pp. 78 (bottom right), 104 (bottom left), (Lee Foster) pp. 83 (top), 216 (top), (Christer Fredriksson) p. 223, (Jerry Galea) p. 312 (bottom right), (Antony Giblin) p. 313 (top), (Manfred Gottschalk) p. 230, (Anthony Ham) p. 67 (bottom right), (Luke Hunter) pp. 105 (top second from left), 213, (Richard I'Anson) pp. 14 (bottom), 105 (top and bottom second from right), 281,282 (left), 294–295, (Michael Lawrence) p. 238 (top), (Chris Mellor) p. 78 (bottom left), (Mark Newman) p. 105 (bottom, second from left), (Andrew Peacock) p. 182 (top), (Steve Simonsen) pp. 239, 240, (Oliver Strewe) p. 293 (top), (Deanna Swaney) pp. 136 (top), 171, (David Tipling) pp. 130 (top), (Wayne Walton) p. 74 (bottom left), (Jim Wark) p. 169, (Christopher Wood) pp. 67 (top right), 259; NASA: pp. 216, 219 (top), (AIRS Science Team/JPL) p. 28; National Trust of Australia (NSW): p. 308 (left); Newspix: pp. 68, 172, 173, 236 (bottom), 299, 303, 327; Peter Nicholson: pp. 271, 279 (left), 239; Oxfam Community Aid Abroad: p. 304; Ray Pask: p. 155; Pepsi: p. 273; PhotoDisc: pp. 7, 12, 13 (top, middle left, bottom), 19 (inset), 39, 44, 57, 60–61, 65 (top), 67 (middle, bottom left), 69, 70, 74 (middle, bottom right), 75, 76, 77 (middle left, bottom left), 78 (top right), 79 (top middle and right, bottom), 82–83, 84–85, 104 (bottom right), 105 (top second from left and far right, bottom far left and right), 106 (top), 107 (right, third from top), 115, 117, 118 (top), 121, 124, 125, 126, 130 (bottom), 131 (left), 164–165, 175, 176, 181, 185 (bottom right), 190–191, 192–193, 194 (top, bottom left), 204, 206 (left and right), 208–209, 233 (centre), 243 (top left, bottom right), 248–249, 250, 251, 253, 256, 262–263, 264 (middle, bottom), 266 (bottom), 274, 288 (bottom), 289, 292, 310–311, 312–313, 312 (top and bottom left), 313 (bottom right), 323 (right), 328–329; Photolibrary.com: cover, pp. 40, 107 (top left, right second row from top, left third row from top, right bottom row), 135, 152, 185 (left), 199 (top), 298–299, 308–309; Reuters/Picture Media: p. 266 (top); Eric Sierans: p. 14 (top); Ski-Zermatt: pp. 178, 185 (top right); Sport the Library: (Icon SMI) p. 165, (Manny Millan/Sports Illustrated) p. 8; Sydney Freelance: p. 227; Ron Tandberg: p. 11 (bottom); UNESCO: p. 81; WaterAid: p. 293 (left); Cathy Wilcox: pp. 279 (right), 315; The Wilderness Society: p. 308 (middle); www.mcspotlight.org: p. 276 (centre and bottom left).

Extracts
Hallwag for map extract on p. 21; ITMB Publishing for map extract on p. 191; Land and Property Information NSW for map extract on p. 96; Ordnance Survey/Geographers' A-Z Map Company Ltd for map extract on p. 22 (bottom);

Contents

Part C Global change

Part D Global issues and the role of citizenship

Introduction

Global Explorations: Stage 4 Geography forms part of an exciting educational resource pack that introduces secondary school students to the study of geography. The text and accompanying Student CD highlight the interactions that exist within and between the earth's physical and human environments at a variety of scales. It explores the diversity of the earth's physical environments and the ways people cope with, impact on and manage these environments. The knowledge, understanding, attitudes, values and skills gained from using this text will help students to develop an informed perspective on a range of important global issues, and provide them with a view of the world that can enhance their understanding and enjoyment of life. The book should also contribute to a more active participation in community life and a greater commitment to ensuring that the environment is appreciated, improved and protected.

The text is divided into three parts: investigating the world, global environments and global change. The first of these parts introduces students to key geographical concepts and skills, with a special focus on fieldwork. The second focuses on the geographical processes that form and transform the earth's physical environments and the way in which communities interact with the environment. Part C focuses on the nature of global change and issues, global inequalities and the role of global organisations.

The book contains a range of material in the form of overviews and sample studies. The overviews are designed to develop the students' knowledge and understanding of the concepts, processes and issues central to the study of geography at this level. Sample studies, which illustrate these concepts, processes and issues within particular spatial contexts, are featured throughout the text. Care has been taken to provide sample studies that emphasise the importance attached to contemporary geographical issues. By emphasising such issues we not only make the subject matter interesting and relevant but provide students with comparisons of scale and context.

The language used in this book is clear and direct. As a result, the text is accessible to students with a wide range of language skills and abilities. The content operates on a variety of levels, providing a core of essential understanding for the less able students and more conceptually challenging material for talented students. Enhancing the literacy skills of students is a major focus of the text. The approach adopted is consistent with a functional view of language.

To further cater for the diversity of learners the various global environments addressed in Part B of the text have been differentiated according to level of difficulty. This differentiation is shown in the table below.

Level of difficulty	Chapter
Elementary	6 Polar lands
	7 Rainforests
Standard	8 Mountains
	9 Coasts
	10 Wetlands
Advanced	11 Coral reefs
	12 Deserts

The book contains a wealth of stimulus material, including photographs, diagrams, maps, cartoons, newspaper extracts and up-to-date statistical information. Activities based on these materials will enable students to develop the skills used by geographers. ICT-related skills are developed within context throughout the text.

The content of the text is organised into relatively short units to facilitate the planning of learning experiences. In addition to its explanatory text and stimulus material, each unit contains Understanding the Text questions and activities to guide students towards an understanding of the material covered, and Working Geographically activities that extend students beyond the text and involve them in a variety of learning experiences. The questions and activities have been carefully selected to cater for the full range of student abilities. The Working Geographically activities reinforce key geographical concepts and skills and extend students beyond the text. They include a focus on group work, interpretation of stimulus material, the development of literacy-based skills, library and Internet-based research, oral reports and multimedia presentations. Many of these activities are student-centred and contribute to the development of skills associated with active and informed citizenship. They also provide opportunities for students to explore the perspectives of men and women, indigenous peoples and various cultural, socioeconomic and lifestyle groups.

The inclusion of practical, skills-based units and Skills boxes is designed to facilitate the development of key geographical skills. Emphasis has also been placed on providing opportunities for collaborative learning and the development of oral and written communication skills.

Students using this book will gain a solid foundation for the study of Australian Geography in Years 9 and 10.

The following icons appear throughout the text.

- ICT-based activities
- Challenge activities
- Indicates websites are available on hi.com.au/globalexpl/
- Cross-references to Chapter 2 The geographer's toolbox
- Cross-references to the Student CD
- Cross-references to the Reflection box on page 17

The Student CD accompanying this text contains:

- a full copy of the text with active URLs
- computer-generated animations that illustrate selected geographical processes
- self-correcting, randomised multiple-choice questions
- self-correcting cloze passages and memory activities
- homework-based activity sheets that help students revise the concepts and skills developed in class
- extension activity sheets
- self-correcting chapter revision tests
- links to quality interactives, games, puzzles, virtual tours and stimulus material available via the World Wide Web
- map outlines
- text-type scaffolds and Excel and PowerPoint templates
- an ICT toolkit
- an e-glossary.

Grant Kleeman

Stage 4 Syllabus Outcomes matrix

Outcome	A student:	Focus area (chapters)			
		4G1 (1–4)	4G2 (5–12)	4G3 (13–15)	4G4 (16)
4.1	Identifies and gathers geographical information	✓	✓	✓	
4.2	Organises and interprets geographical information	✓	✓	✓	✓
4.3	Uses a range of written, oral and graphic forms to communicate geographical information	✓	✓	✓	✓
4.4	Uses a range of geographical tools	✓	✓	✓	✓
4.5	Demonstrates a sense of place about global environments	✓		✓	✓
4.6	Describes the geographical processes that form and transform environments	✓	✓		
4.7	Identifies and discusses geographical issues from a range of perspectives			✓	✓
4.8	Describes the interrelationships between people and environments		✓		✓
4.9	Describes differences in life opportunities throughout the world			✓	✓
4.10	Explains how geographical knowledge, understandings and skills combine with knowledge of civics to contribute to informed citizenship	✓	✓	✓	✓

Answers to selected textbook activities can be found at hi.com.au/globalexpl/

Stage 4 Geographical tools

Maps

Students learn to:	Unit
Use an atlas	2.6
Use various types of maps: physical, political, topographic and thematic	2.1
Identify and use elements of maps, including legend, direction, title, scale and border	2.2
Distinguish between different types of map projections	2.3
Locate features on a map using:	
• latitude and longitude	2.4
• area and grid references	2.5
Identify physical and cultural features on a map	2.5
Measure distances on a map using a linear scale	2.5
Identify scale as a written, linear or representative fraction	2.5
Calculate the area of a feature	2.5
Calculate the density of a feature	2.5
Use the points of a compass to determine direction	2.5
Identify and interpret relief using shading, spot heights, colour and contour lines	2.5
Construct cross-sections	2.5, 4.2
Identify the aspect of a slope	2.5
Describe and explain relationships on maps	2.5
Read and interpret synoptic charts	2.7

Photographs

Students learn to:	Unit
Construct a line drawing (photo sketch)	2.9
Distinguish between oblique, aerial, ground level photographs and satellite imagery	2.8
Collect and interpret photographic images	2.8
Collect and use digital images	2.11

Graphs and statistics

Students learn to:	Unit
Identify and calculate total, range, rank and average	2.12
Construct and interpret bar, column, line, climatic and proportional graphs	2.13
Construct and interpret climate graphs	2.7

ICT

Students learn to:	Unit
Create a desktop-published document for a specific audience	CD
Develop and refine search techniques using the Internet	2.11
Collect and interpret electronic information	2.11
Design and create a multimedia presentation	2.16
Use email for a specific geographical purpose	CD
Practice ethical behaviour when using email and the Internet	CD
Use a range of digital images, sound and other appropriate multimedia sources to develop a multimedia presentation or web page	2.16, CD

Fieldwork

Students learn to:	Unit
Use geographical instruments, including:	
• a compass to determine direction	2.5
• a clinometer and tape	4.2
• weather instruments, a Beaufort wind scale and cloud identification charts	4.1
Collect and record data in the field, including:	
• design and conduct interviews	4.4
• construct and implement surveys	4.4
• construct field sketches and diagrams	2.9, 4.2
• use fieldwork techniques to collect primary and secondary data	4.1–4.4

Chapter 1

PART A **Investigating the world**

The nature and role of geography

Introduction

Geography is the study of the interactions between people and their environment. Geographers study these interactions to learn more about the ways environments influence the activities of people and the impacts people have on environments. By developing these understandings we are better able to manage our environment. Good environmental management is important if we are to leave our children and grandchildren a better world in which to live.

In this chapter we will explore the nature and role of geography and be introduced to the elements of the earth's physical and human environments. We will also examine the factors that help define a community.

Learn about:

- the nature of geography
- the major physical and human elements of environments
- the tools and skills used by geographers
- geographical research
- global patterns of physical and human features
- World Heritage sites

Learn to:

- classify features of the environment as physical or human elements
- record patterns of physical and human elements of environments
- identify patterns resulting from the interaction of physical and human environments
- recognise continents using different map projections
- use latitude to describe the global pattern of climate
- use longitude to explain world time zones
- describe global patterns of physical and human features
- apply key geographical questions to a local environment
- use geographical tools to measure and record elements of the local environment
- identify and locate natural and cultural World Heritage sites
- use geographical questions to investigate a World Heritage site
- explain the importance of World Heritage listing
- outline the legal obligations of governments to the preservation of World Heritage sites
- outline the role of individuals, groups and governments in protecting World Heritage sites

Key questions

1. What is geography?
2. How do we distinguish between the physical and human environments?
3. How do geographers define communities?

Spaceship earth

Once a photograph of the earth, taken from the outside, is available ... a new idea as powerful as any other in history will be let loose.

Fred Hoyle (1948)

In 1968, *Apollo 8* became the first manned spacecraft to leave the earth's gravity and reach the moon. As it orbited the earth, the craft's camera was turned towards earth. The images it beamed back to mission control were to change forever the way people thought about the planet on which they live. Set against the vastness of space, the blue, pearl-like sphere—now home to more than 6 billion people—looked small and very vulnerable.

Since those first pictures arrived from space we have learned a lot about the earth. We now know that our actions have an impact on people elsewhere, and can even affect the global environment. When we drop a piece of litter someone has to pick it up, when we tip oil down a drain we pollute a waterway, and when we drive our cars or switch on the electricity we add to global warming.

The term 'spaceship earth' has been used to describe our planet. It reminds us that, like people on a spacecraft, we need to protect and carefully manage our life support systems—the environmental processes that provide the air we breathe, the water we drink and the food we eat.

The photograph that changed the way we think about our planet.

Glossary of key terms

Built environments The earth's human-altered landscapes. These include all those features that are normally associated with settlements, industries and farms.

Community A group of people who share a particular space (location), have a shared interest or share a particular form of social organisation.

Density The population or number of objects per unit area.

Distribution The spread or arrangement of geographical features on the earth's surface.

Ecosystem A community of plants and animals and their non-living environment.

Environment Our total surroundings, including the living and non-living features of the earth's surface as well as those features that are altered or created by people.

Geographical issues Topics of a geographical nature that are widely discussed and debated within the media and the wider community.

Geography The study of the interactions between people and their environment.

Human environments The elements of the environments created by people. These include the social, cultural, economic and political systems developed by humans.

Location The position of a place on the earth's surface.

Movement The flow of goods, people, information and energy from one place to another.

Perspective A way of viewing the world.

Physical environments Our natural surroundings, including soil, water, air, sunlight and all living things.

Quality of life (standard of living) People's economic, social and personal well-being.

Site The place where something is located, including its physical setting.

Situation The location of a feature or place relative to other features or places.

eGlossary

GeoToolkit

ICT Toolkit

Foundation worksheet 1.1

1.1 Geography: window on the world

NASA: keeping watch from space

ICT

Each day NASA posts a new satellite image on its website. The NASA website is linked to a library of satellite images. Use the site's search facility to locate images that illustrate the geographical processes you will study during Years 7–8. Each image is accompanied by a brief explanation.

Access the NASA website and select an image that appeals to you. Print a copy of the image and paste it into your workbook.

What is geography?

Geography is the subject that helps us to find answers to questions about the world around us—about where things are and how they got there. It seeks to explain the character of places and the **distribution**, or spread, of people, features and events on or near the earth's surface. It is concerned with the processes that shape the earth's surface and the way people interact with the environment. The study of geography helps us to better understand the world in which we live.

Geography: it's all around us

Those of us who live in cities are surrounded by change. How many of the changes shown in Figure 1.1a have you noticed?

Those of us living in rural communities are also surrounded by change. How many of the changes shown in Figure 1.1b have you noticed?

Geographers refer to the changes shown in Figures 1.1a and 1.1b as *changes over time and space*. The outcome of these changes are **locations** or places that are *spatially different*. The study of geography helps us to understand these changes and to predict what might occur in the future.

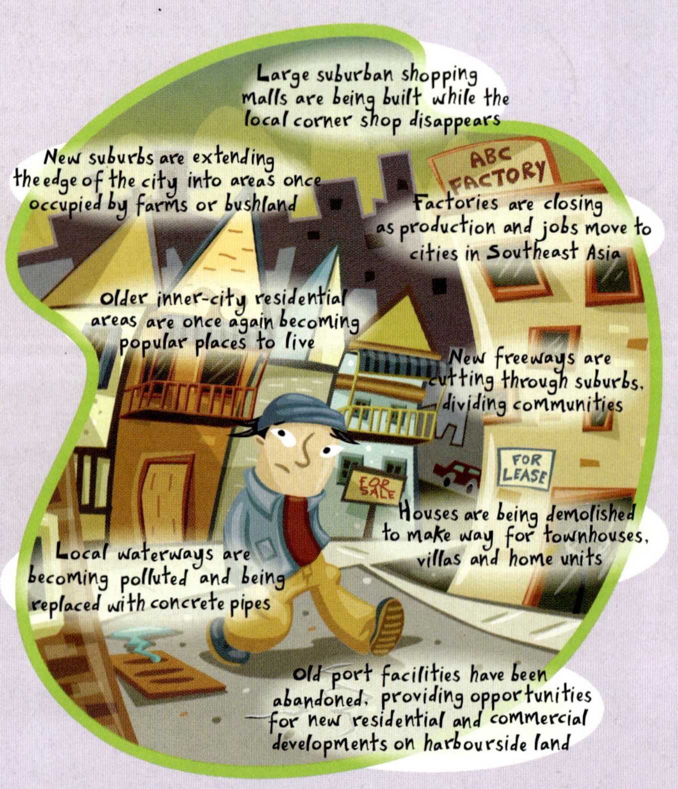

Figure 1.1a

Figure 1.1b

The role of geography

The role of geography is to promote:

- a greater understanding of the ways people interact with physical environments
- an appreciation of the ways in which the world's cultural diversity enriches our way of life
- a commitment to ecological sustainability—the idea that we pass on to future generations a world at least as good, if not better, than we found it
- a commitment to social justice and equity—the idea that everyone has a right to fundamental human rights and a fair share of the earth's resources
- active and informed participation in decision-making processes.

Figure 1.1c Yosemite National Park, California. Physical environments are those dominated by natural features, such as landforms and vegetation.

Figure 1.1d Singapore. Human environments are those dominated by the activities of people.

Different perspectives

A **perspective** is a way of viewing the world, the people in it and their relationship with each other and with their environments. This means that people will describe and explain **geographical issues**, features and processes differently. A trail-bike rider and conservationist, for example, may have quite different perspectives, or points of view, on the range of activities that should be allowed in National Parks.

Even though we may disagree with a particular point of view we must respect the right of someone to hold that view or opinion. The perspectives or points of view a person holds will be influenced by a range of factors. These factors include age, gender, level of education, cultural and ethnic background and socioeconomic status (class).

Why study geography?

The study of geography will help you to:

- make sense of a complex and rapidly changing world
- see yourself as part of a wider global community and understand how your actions can impact on it
- become informed about important social and environmental issues
- appreciate that people can have different points of view and ways of looking at the world
- become active and informed citizens
- develop knowledge and skills that will help you gain employment
- use your leisure time effectively
- better appreciate the wonder of the world around you.

Famous geographers

Mother Teresa (1910–97), Saint and Nobel Peace Prize winner, taught geography at Calcutta's St Mary's High School for Girls before devoting her life to helping the city's poor.

In 1948, Sister Teresa came across a dying woman lying in front of a Calcutta hospital. She stayed with the woman until the woman died. From that point on she dedicated her life to helping the poorest of the poor.

Sister Teresa also founded an order of nuns called the Missionaries of Charity. Today, this order has over 3000 sisters in 517 missions in 100 countries.

Michael Jordan (b. 1963), basketball legend and sporting icon, has a geography major from the University of North Carolina (UNC).

The legend of Michael Jordan started in 1982 when he sunk a 7-metre basket to give UNC a narrow victory in a National Collegiate Athletic Association championship. In 1984 Jordan's crowning achievement came when he led the Chicago Bulls to the first of six NBA titles. Jordan's 31.5 career-scoring average is the highest in NBA history. Jordan also played in two gold-medal-winning Olympic basketball teams. His popularity lifted the profile of NBA to new heights and helped him become a global marketing celebrity.

Figure 1.1e Michael Jordan.

Working geographically

1 **Group work** In small groups, list the changes taking place in your local environment. Share your group's list with other groups. Make up a class list and copy it into your workbook.

2 **Collage** Develop a photographic collage to show the difference between physical and built environments.

3 **Group work** In small groups, complete the following tasks:

a Identify the groups that might have an interest in gaining access to a local beach and its dune system.

b How might the perspectives of these groups vary?

c Compile a list of the points of view that might be typical of each group.

d Share your group's findings with the rest of the class.

Physical and human geography

Physical geography looks at how the earth was formed and how it continues to change. It includes the study of the atmosphere, hydrosphere, lithosphere and biosphere—the four parts of *physical environments* (see Unit 1.2).

Human geography looks at how people, individually or as members of a group or community, behave: where they live, work and play, and how they use or misuse the land. It includes the study of:

- urban, industrial and rural landuses
- the development of countries
- population, such as population movements
- how economic changes affect people
- issues such as global terrorism, human rights, global inequality, child labour and social justice.

The work of geographers

Geographers investigate the ways people interact with each other and with the environment. As they go about their work they create and record new knowledge. This adds to our understanding of the world.

The questions geographers ask

When studying, people, places and environments, geographers ask these questions:

- What is it?
- Where is it?
- Why is it there?
- How did it get there?
- How is it changing?
- How do people affect it?
- How does it affect people?
- Should it be like this?
- What may it be like in the future?
- What action is appropriate?

cd Foundation worksheet 1.2

cd Extension worksheet 1.1

Tools used by geographers

Geographers use tools and technologies, including maps, photographs, remotely sensed satellite images, computer-based geographical information systems (GIS), databases published on CD-ROMs, and information available via the Internet (see Unit 2.11).

Computers are important tools that allow geographers to store, analyse and reproduce huge amounts of information. They also allow geographers to study and present information more effectively than by using traditional forms of presentation, such as statistical tables and graphs.

Jobs for geographers

There are many jobs that use the knowledge and skills developed by geographers. Figure 1.1f shows some of the occupations in which study of geography plays an important role. Having studied geography you will have the following advantages:

- you will know about local, national and global issues and be able to talk about them
- you will have developed skills, such as explaining your ideas clearly to others and using maps, photographs and diagrams
- you will be aware of events around you and appreciate that people have different views and there are different solutions to issues.

Even if none of the careers shown in Figure 1.1f interest you, remember that the study of geography develops a range of skills that are highly valued by employers. These include:

- collecting, organising and analysing information
- communicating ideas and information
- planning and organising activities
- working with others in teams
- solving problems
- using mathematical ideas and techniques
- increasing your understanding of your own culture and the culture of others.

Figure 1.1f Jobs that use the knowledge and skills developed by geographers.

Geographical resources

Geographers use a variety of resources and data to study the earth. In your studies you are likely to use many of the resources listed below:

- *fieldwork*—observations, maps, sketches, diagrams and interviews
- *maps*—atlases, street directories, topographic maps, weather maps and road maps
- *written information*—books, newspapers, magazines and reports
- *computers*—databases, CD-ROMs, the Internet and webcams
- *statistics*—tables, graphs and diagrams
- *photographs*—ground-level photographs, aerial photographs and satellite images.

Understanding the text

1. What is geography?
2. Explain what is meant by 'change over time and space'.
3. What is meant by the term 'perspective'?
4. Explain the difference between physical and human geography.
5. What is it that geographers do?
6. List the questions geographers use to organise geographical knowledge.
7. List the work-related skills you will gain from the study of geography.

UTT worksheet 1.1

Working geographically

1 Challenge: Using the media Select one of the employment categories shown in Figure 1.1f (p. 9). Use the employment section of a daily newspaper to find at least two job advertisements that fit the category you have chosen and use the skills developed by geographers. Find out what training is required for the position and describe what a person doing the job would be required to do. Write this up in your workbook.

2 Classroom display Use the advertisements collected for activity 1 to develop a classroom display of 'Jobs for geographers.'

3 Library work Ask your school librarian to show you the resources available to help you in your study of geography. Write down the name and location of each resource. What library call numbers relate to the subject matter of geography?

4 Matching Which of the resources listed in the box 'Geographical resources' (p. 9) would help you to find out about the following?

- **a** a holiday destination
- **b** the landforms found in an area
- **c** changes in an area over time
- **d** the population of a country
- **e** material related to current events
- **f** the area affected by drought

Investigating contemporary issues

The study of geography covers some issues that are 'in the news'. These are issues that are discussed and debated widely in the community. They are generally called *contemporary issues*. This book discusses a number of important contemporary issues that involve the physical and built environments. Many of them affect our future well-being. Geography gives us a way of investigating and understanding these contemporary issues. This is one of the most important benefits of studying geography.

Figure 1.1g Making a statement about the wisdom of the decision to construct a new nuclear reactor in suburban Sydney.

Skills

Contemporary issues: research scaffold

When investigating a contemporary issue you may find that using the following points will help you develop your knowledge and understanding of the issue:

- Read or view the material dealing with the issue.
- Name and briefly outline the issue.
- Identify the main people involved in the issue.
- Identify the scale at which the issue is relevant. Is it a global, national, regional or local issue?
- Describe or map the area where the issue is relevant.
- Explain why the issue is of interest to geographers.
- List the main sources of information about the issue.
- State whether the sources used present different points of view about the issue.
- State whether the sources of your information are reliable.
- Outline the actions people could take to address the issue. What would be the likely outcome?
- Consider how the media have influenced your study of the issue.
- Explain how the study of the issue has affected your own views on the issue.
- Consider the actions you would take to address the issue.

Table 1.1a Contemporary geographical issues

Air pollution	Impacts of tourism
Algal blooms	Population growth
Catchment management	Poverty
Child labour	Refugees
Decline of country towns	Rights of indigenous people
Deforestation	Salinity
Drought	Soil erosion
Endangered species	Spatial inequality
Global climatic change	Sustainable development
Global inequalities	Unemployment
Global terrorism	Urban decay and renewal
Habitat destruction	Waste disposal
Human rights	Water quality
Immigration	Woodchipping

Figure 1.1h Greenpeace anti-whaling protest.

Working geographically

1 **Challenge: Research** Choose a contemporary issue (see Table 1.1a for ideas) and, using the media and other sources, collect material dealing with the issues. Using the approach in the box 'Investigating contemporary issues', prepare a presentation on the issue. Use one of the following formats: a three-minute oral report, a PowerPoint presentation of four slides, a written three-page report, a poster, a video or a three-minute audio recording.

2 **Group work** Study Figure 1.1g. In groups, discuss whether images such as this are effective in raising the community's awareness of important environmental issues.

3 **Class discussion** Study Figure 1.1h. As a class, discuss the reasons why organisations such as Greenpeace go to such elaborate lengths to highlight their environmental concerns.

4 **Internet research: Wall display** Access the Greenpeace website and investigate some of its recent campaigns. Download and print images that illustrate the range of issues they are concerned about. Mount a wall display with appropriate captions.

5 **Group work: Interpreting cartoons** Identify the issue being addressed in Figure 1.1i. In groups, brainstorm the issue the cartoon illustrates. Have a member of the group record the main points raised by the group. Use these to write a short outline of the issue.

6 **Wall display** Over time collect cartoons related to the issues listed in Table 1.1a and any others you can think of. Use them to develop a contemporary issues wall display.

Extension worksheet 1.5

Figure 1.1i Cartoonists often present complex issues in simple drawings that both inform and entertain.

Understanding the text

1 What is a contemporary issue?

2 What is the link between geography and such issues?

UTT worksheet 1.1

1.2 Elements of physical and human environments

Elements of physical environments

In geography the word **environment** is used to describe our total surroundings. This includes the living and non-living features of the earth's surface as well as those features altered or created by people. Geographers divide environments into two kinds: physical environments and human environments.

Physical environments are those dominated by natural features, such as landforms and vegetation. Physical environments, which are sometimes referred to as natural environments, include the earth's soil, water, air, sunlight and all living things. These are often referred to as the elements of physical environments (see Figure 1.2a). The world's physical environments are examined in more detail in Chapters 3 and 5.

Figure 1.2a Elements of physical environments.

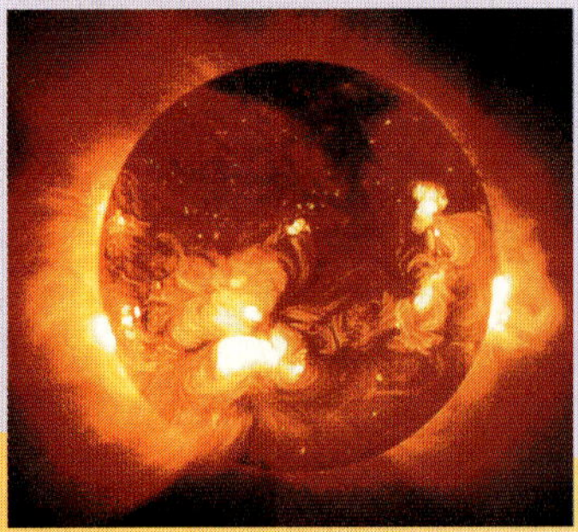

Sun

Solar energy: All life on earth depends on the energy (light and heat) produced by the sun.

Water

Hydrosphere: The earth's store of water and how it circulates. Geographers are interested in how people try to control and manage water resources to meet their needs.

Rocks and soil

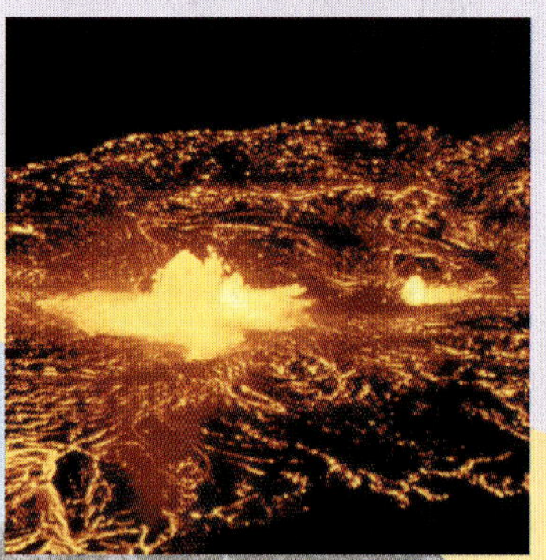

Lithosphere: The earth's solid outer shell. Geographers study the processes shaping the earth's crust and how these processes affect people.

Elements of the physical environment

Air

Atmosphere: The combination of gases that surround the planet. Geographers are particularly interested in weather and climate. They investigate:

- how climate determines where plants and animals can live
- how climate affects the activities of people
- how the activities of people affect climate.

Plants and animals

Biosphere: The surface zone of the earth in which all life exists. Geographers are particularly interested in how living things interact with each other and the non-living parts of the environment.

Elements of human environments

Human environments are best defined as all the elements of the environments created by people. They include the social, cultural, economic and political systems created by humans (see Figure 1.2b). Human environments are sometimes referred to as **built environments**. Built environments are all the human-altered landscapes. They include all those features normally associated with settlements, industries and agriculture (see Figure 1.2c).

It is important to note that the physical and human environments always interact. Physical environments are always affected by the activities of people; and built and human environments are always affected by events within physical environments.

Cultural: The beliefs, traditions and practices characteristic of a group of people.

Political: The manner in which a country, and society generally, is governed.

Figure 1.2b Elements of human environments.

Figure 1.2c Examples of built environments.

Foundation worksheet 1.1

Foundation worksheet 1.2

Understanding the text

1. Define each of the following terms: environment, physical environment, built environment and human environment.
2. List the elements of the physical environments.
3. List the elements of the human environment.

UTT worksheet 1.2

Working geographically

1. **Workbook task** Using photographs taken from magazines and travel brochures, reconstruct Figures 1.2a and 1.2b in your workbook.
2. **Group work** Select a partner to act as a timer. In three minutes, write down as many features of physical environments as you can think of. Swap roles with your partner. The student with the longest list is the winner.
3. **Challenge: Writing task** Write a paragraph describing how your local area might have looked before it was settled by people. Write a second paragraph, describing how people have transformed or changed the area.
4. **Fieldwork** Visit a local lookout. Construct a field sketch of the area being observed. Using two different colours, label features of both the physical and human/built environments.

1.3 Types of communities

Figure 1.3a Members of Australia's Italian community celebrating a soccer victory.

The word **community** is used a lot in geography. What does the term mean?

In the physical environment we often talk about a 'community of plants and animals'. This describes how a group of plants and animals interact with each other and with their environment. Many such communities are confined to particular locations. A rainforest community, for example, is confined to those parts of the world that are both hot and wet.

In the human environment, the use of the term 'community' is more complex. Sometimes a community is made up of people who *share the same space*; for example, people who live in the same neighbourhood, town or village. Sometimes a community is made up of people who belong to the same sporting club, have similar interests, belong to a particular profession, belong to a particular political party or interest group, speak the same language or have the same religion. Technological advances in communications allow communities to interact across the globe. Members of these communities have links beyond a particular loction. Their 'sense of community' is a product of their *shared social organisation* or interests.

Figure 1.3b Varanasi, a sacred place of pilgrimage for Hindus.

Each of the people shown in Figure 1.3c is making a statement about belonging to a particular community. Of course, each of them belongs to other communities as well.

Which community does each one of them belong to? Some possibilities are:

- an ethnic community
- an indigenous community
- a sporting community
- a religious community
- a community based on an interest, activity or profession.

Figure 1.3c Which community does each of these people belong to?

Understanding the text

1. What is meant by the term 'community' when we are talking about the physical environment?
2. Explain the difference between communities based on shared space and those based on shared social organisation.

UTT worksheet 1.3

Working geographically

1. **Classifying** Study the speech bubbles in Figure 1.3c, then complete the following tasks:
   a. Identify the type of community that each person belongs to.
   b. What do the members of each community have in common?
   c. State whether each community is based on shared space or shared social organisation.
2. **Class brainstorm** As a class, brainstorm the types of communities to which members of the class belong.
3. **Class discussion** As a class, discuss the following questions:
   a. Is your school a community?
   b. Are communities changing?

Extension worksheet 1.2

Extension worksheet ICT 1.3

1.4 Review and reflect

Chapter summary

In this introductory section of the text we were introduced to the nature and role of geography. We discovered that geography is the study of the interactions between people and the environment and we can now distinguish between the physical and human environments. We also know that communities can be defined in terms of both shared space and shared social organisation.

Activity 1

Thinking critically: Making choices—which future?

Humans as planetary masters

doing what they want and keeping control

Humans as partners

closely linked to every other part of the global system

Humans as pawns

at the mercy of the elements

Humans as polluters

a blight on the face of the earth

Figure 1.4a Alternative futures.

Look at Figure 1.4a. Which cartoon best fits your view of the relationship between people and their environment? Write a paragraph about each cartoon saying whether you agree with the view presented. Explain why. Return to this activity at the end of Year 8 and see whether you have changed your views.

Activity 2

Thinking geographically: Neighbourhood

1 Choose five features from Table 1.4a that you would value having in your neighbourhood.

2 Refer to the rating scale below and determine how close you would want them to your home.

Very close — Far away

1 2 3 4 5 6 7 8 9 10

3 List the features that you would value in your neighbourhood but not want too close to your home. Explain your answer.

4 Suggest three different groups of people in your neighbourhood who might disagree with your choices. How and why might their views differ?

Table 1.4a Neighbourhood facilities

Skateboard bowl	Motorway interchange
Public housing	Railway station
Indoor sports complex	Primary school
Church	High school
Youth club	Corner shop
Shopping mall	Factory
Aquatic centre	Internet cafe
Restaurant	Football field
Takeaway food outlet	Cinema complex
	Service station

GeoMatch GeoWords
GeoQuiz Chapter test

Activity 3

Reflective thinking: Communities

What influences your values and attitudes? How people think and feel about their neighbourhood and community depends largely on the different influences shown in Figure 1.4b. These influences also affect our values and attitudes towards our neighbourhood and the people who make up the communities with which we interact.

Make a large copy of the outline of Figure 1.4b. On the outline, add drawings of social, environmental and economic influences that affect your values and attitudes. Use examples from your own community and neighbourhood to make your diagram personal and unique.

Extension worksheet 1.4

Extension worksheet ICT 1.6

Environmental factors include housing type and condition, amount of open space and level of noise and air pollution

Social factors include family, friends and links with people and organisations

Neighbourhood The buildings and other landuses within which the local community lives. People usually belong to just one neighbourhood.

Community A group of people who live together in a neighbourhood or make up a common social or cultural group; for example, a religious community. People can belong to several different communities.

Economic factors include how people obtain money and how they spend it

Figure 1.4b Values and attitudes.

reflection

Working in groups

1 List the key ideas or concepts addressed in this chapter.
2 List the geographical skills developed in this chapter.

Working individually

3 Rate your understanding of the key ideas or concepts addressed in this chapter (select one).
basic satisfactory good excellent
4 Rate your understanding of the geographical skills developed in this chapter (select one).
basic satisfactory good excellent
5 What aspects of this chapter did you find the most interesting?
6 What aspects of this chapter did you find the least interesting?
7 Which one of the following illustrations best reflects your overall response to this chapter?

a b c

Chapter 2

The geographer's toolbox

Introduction

Geographers use many different tools and skills to create new knowledge about the world in which we live. Some of the most important of the tools used by geographers include maps, photographs, satellite images, statistical information, and data collected during fieldwork. Computer-based geographical information systems (GIS) are often used to analyse and interpret this information, which is then used in the decision-making processes of government, business and a range of non-government organisations. In this chapter we will be introduced to the skills and tools geographers use to investigate the world.

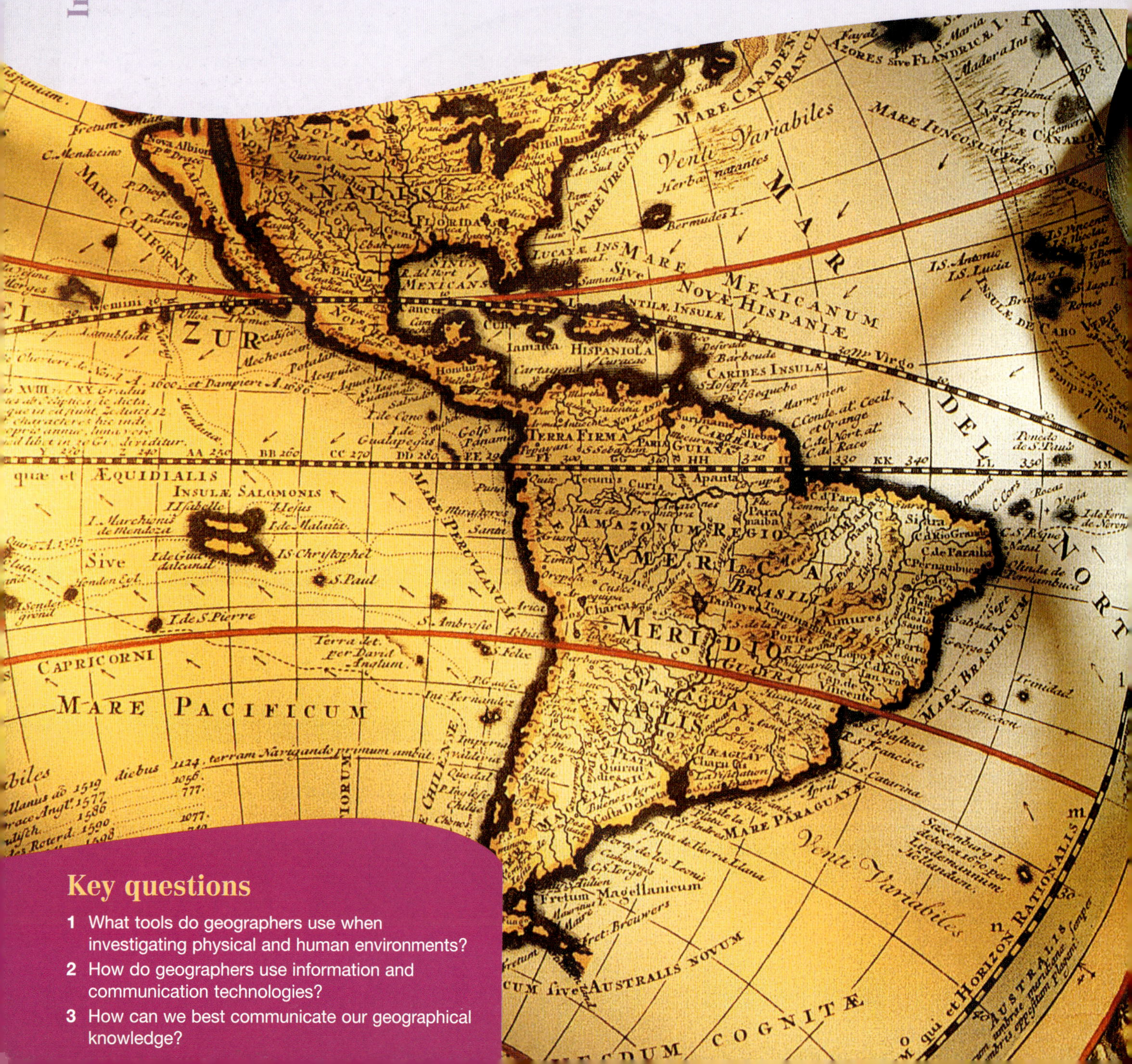

Key questions

1 What tools do geographers use when investigating physical and human environments?
2 How do geographers use information and communication technologies?
3 How can we best communicate our geographical knowledge?

Who made the first map?

The world's oldest known map was a clay tablet made in Mesopotamia around 2500 BC. It showed a settlement nestled in a river valley surrounded by mountains. The area covered by the map, like that of all early maps, was limited to people's everyday existence. As explorers and traders travelled farther from home and returned with stories of far-off places, maps started to cover more distant lands. The oldest existing map was made in Babylonia in about 600 BC; it located the kingdom of Babylonia at the centre of the world.

Early Greek cartographers, such as Hecataeus, also placed their homeland in the centre of their world maps. Around 250 BC, however, a Greek mathematician named Eratosthenes proposed that the earth was a sphere. Ancient map-making reached its peak in the second century AD, when Egyptian scholar Claudius Ptolemy wrote *Geography*, a manual on how to make maps of a spherical earth.

The Americas, a 1587 map by Abraham Ortelius.

eGlossary

GeoToolkit

ICT Toolkit

Glossary of key terms

Aspect The direction that a slope faces.

Bearing Direction given in terms of degrees from north.

Cartographer A person who draws maps.

Cartography The process of constructing maps.

Climate graph A graph showing average temperature and rainfall experienced at a particular place.

Contour interval The difference in height between two adjacent contour lines on a map.

Contour lines Lines joining places of equal height above sea level.

Density The population or number of objects per unit area.

Distribution The spread or arrangement of geographical features on the earth's surface.

Elevation The height of a point or place above mean sea level.

Geographical information systems (GIS) Computer-based systems that combine digital data (such as maps, aerial photographs and satellite images) with geographical information from other sources to create a variety of products that decision-makers use in the planning process.

Gradient A measure of the steepness of a slope.

Legend The part of a map that explains the meaning of the symbols used in the map.

Local relief The difference in elevation between the highest and lowest point in an area.

Location The position of a feature or place on the earth's surface.

Meridians of longitude Imaginary lines drawn around the earth from north to south.

Relief A general term describing the shape of the land, including height and steepness.

Scale The relationship between the distance on a map and the actual distance on the earth's surface.

Site The place where something is located, including its physical setting.

Situation The location of a feature or place relative to other features or places.

Spot height The exact altitude or height above sea level of a point on the earth's surface.

Thematic map A map designed to illustrate a particular theme; for example, annual rainfall, ethnic groups or the location of oil resources.

Topographic map A detailed, large-scale map of part of the earth's surface, illustrating selected features of the physical environment.

Topography The geographical features of landforms of an area.

Weather map A map that shows the weather conditions experienced over a particular area at a particular time.

Types of maps

Foundation worksheet 2.1

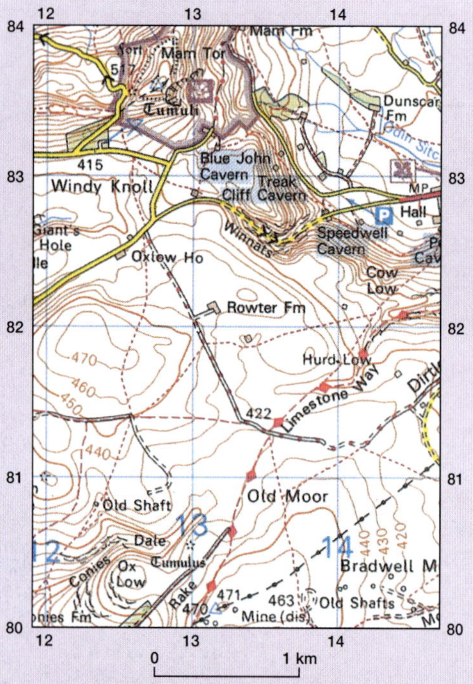

Figure 2.1a Topographic map extract, Castleton area, United Kingdom.

Figure 2.1b Landuse map of Africa. Source: *Heinemann Atlas*.

Geographers use many different types of maps. Of particular use are topographic maps, which show a small area of the earth's surface in great detail (see Unit 2.5). Geographers also use atlas maps of regions, countries, continents and the world (see Unit 2.6). Atlases, websites, textbooks, magazines, television and computer databases and even, at times, advertisements use all kinds of maps.

Topographic maps

Topographic maps, such as Figure 2.1a, show the shape of the land (topography) as well as a range of natural features (such as rivers and vegetation) and cultural features (such as landuse, settlement patterns and road and rail networks). These maps use a variety of symbols to represent these features.

Landuse maps

Landuse maps provide a summary of human activities in an area. A landuse map of your school, for example, would show the location of classrooms, playground areas, sports fields, car parking and the library and auditorium. On maps covering much larger areas many different landuses are often combined into broad categories. Figure 2.1b shows the pattern of agricultural landuse in Africa.

Landuse maps can be compared with maps showing the relief, or shape, of the land. In this way the links or associations between relief and landuse can be seen.

Thematic maps

Thematic maps show the pattern of a particular geographical theme or issue. They are often used to show the **distribution** of one or more of the following: climate, vegetation types, average rainfall, average temperature (see Figure 2.1c), population **density**, various development indicators (for example, population growth rates) and agricultural landuses. Thematic maps that use a graduated colour scale or shading to show a pattern are called choropleth maps.

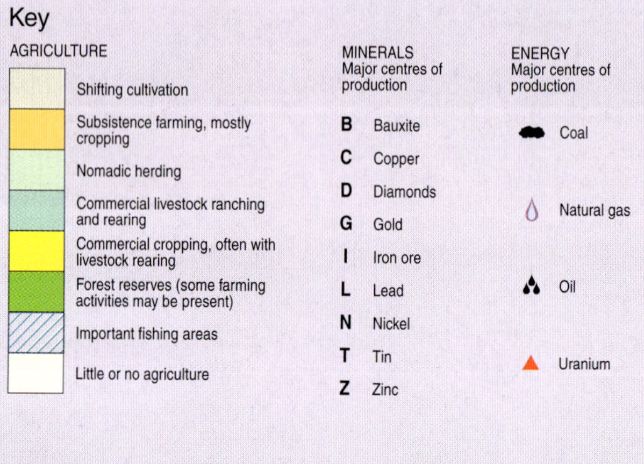

Weather maps

Weather maps, including Figure 2.1d, tell us about the weather conditions over particular areas of the earth's surface at a particular time. Figure 2.1d shows the condition of the atmosphere (including air pressure, rainfall and wind direction and strength) in the previous twenty-four hours. It also shows the location and direction of warm and cold fronts. From this information, predictions about the weather that places will experience can be made several days ahead.

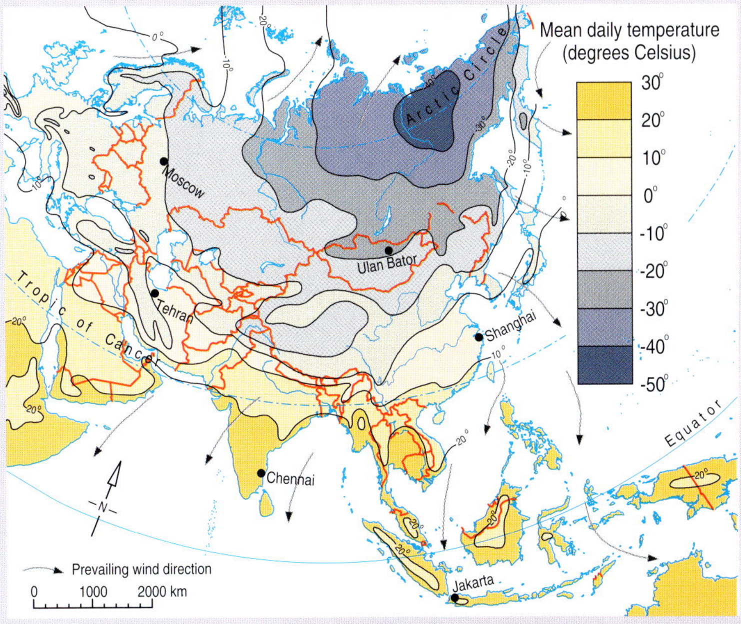

Figure 2.1c January temperature, Asia. Source: *Heinemann Atlas*.

Street maps

Street maps, such as Figure 2.1e, show parts of a city or town. Streets are named and important features are shown. These features include schools, police stations, religious buildings, shopping centres, parks and major landmarks. The larger the scale of the map, the greater the variety of information that can be shown. Grid lines are drawn over street maps so that the location of features can be easily recorded and found.

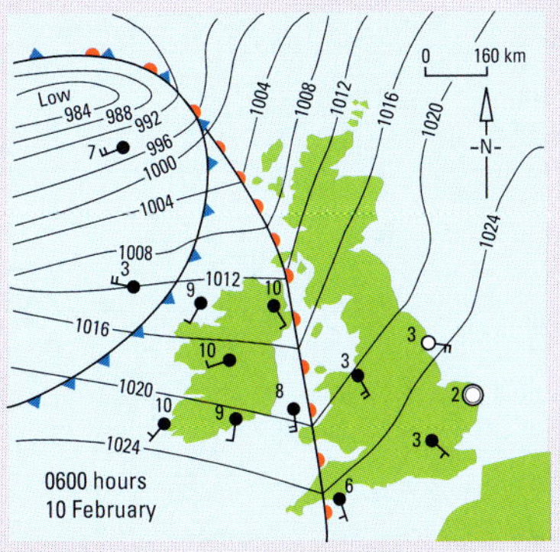

Figure 2.1d A weather map of the United Kingdom.

Foundation worksheet 2.1

Understanding the text

1. List the features shown on a topographic map.
2. Outline the purpose of landuse maps.
3. What are thematic maps?
4. What is a choropleth map?
5. Explain what weather maps show.
6. What do street maps show?

UTT worksheet 2.1

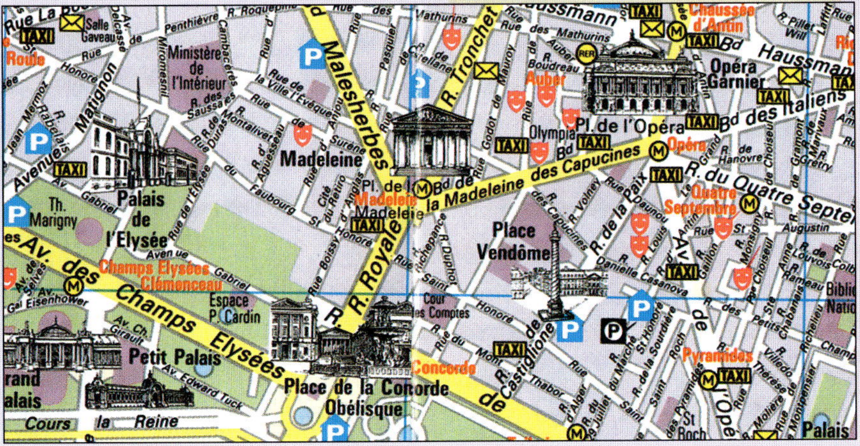

Figure 2.1e Street map of Paris, France.

Working geographically

1. **Interpreting topographic maps** Study Figure 2.1a. List at least three features of each of the physical and built environments shown on the topographic map extract.
2. **Using landuse maps** Study Figure 2.1b. Name the dominant type of landuse in northern Africa.
3. **Using thematic maps** Study Figure 2.1c. Which parts of Asia have the highest mean daily temperature in January?
4. **Challenge: Interpreting weather maps** Collect a series of weather maps from your local newspaper. Use the maps to describe the weather being experienced over three days. The information in Unit 2.7 will help you complete this task.
5. **Using street maps** Study Figure 2.1e. Locate the following famous landmarks: Av. des Champs Elysées, Opéra Garnier and Palais de l'Elysée.

2.2 Elements of maps

Figure 2.2a Maps provide geographers with valuable information about change over time.

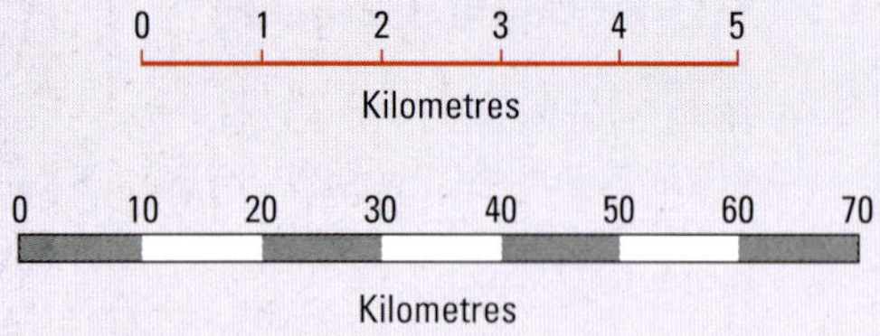

Figure 2.2b Examples of different line scales.

Maps play a very important role in the study of geography. They tell us about places and help us to identify patterns and changes in the landscape.

A map is a graphic representation of part of the earth's surface drawn to scale on a flat surface. The amount and type of detail shown on maps depend on the scale and purpose of the map. For example, a street map of London with a scale of 1:21 477 (see Figure 2.2c) can show a lot more information about the city than a world map with a scale of 1:80 000 000.

Maps range from the very simple to the very complex. No map can show every feature of the landscape. If it did it would be so detailed that it would be impossible to read and interpret. Maps, therefore, need to be selective in what they show. **Cartographers** (map makers) use symbols, shading and colour to simplify reality and show how the features of the earth's surface are arranged and distributed.

Map essentials include a title, a direction indicator, a grid, a scale, a legend, a border and an indication of latitude and longitude.

Title

A title tells us the purpose of a map. Usually the title has two parts: the name of the place and what is being shown on the map.

Direction indicator

To use a map, you need to know where the directions are on the map. Maps have an indicator to show the direction of north. Once you know where north is, you can work out other directions. This makes it easier to describe the location of places.

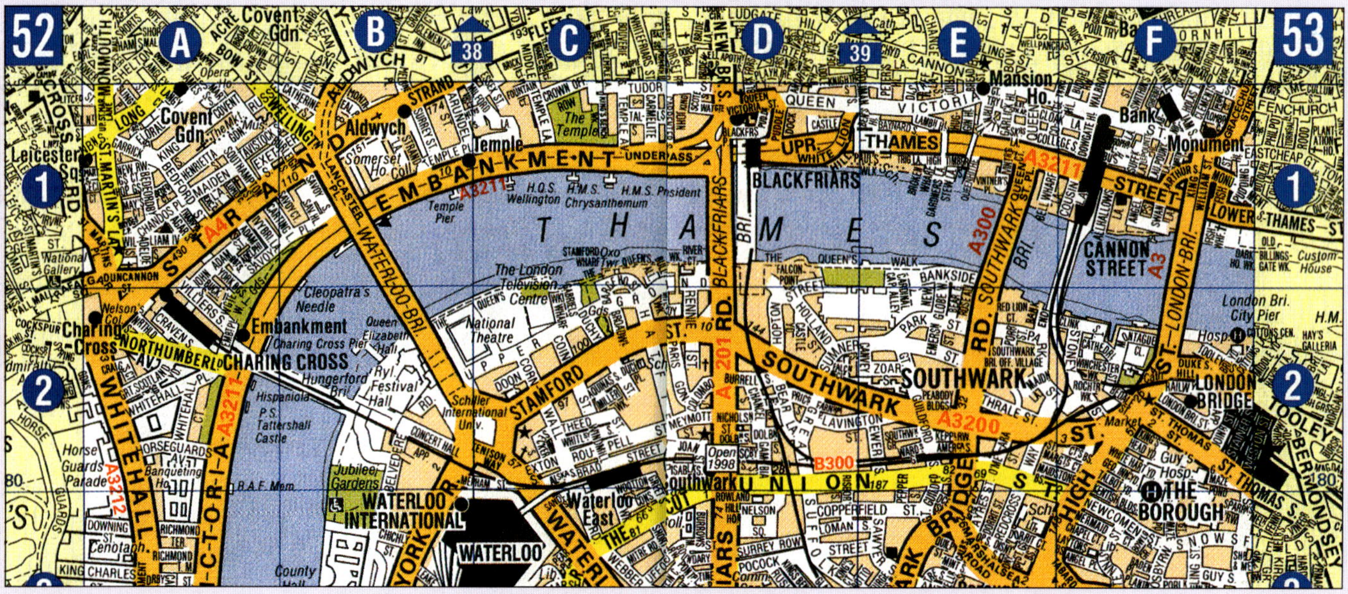

Figure 2.2c A street map of central London. Finding a street on a map in a street directory is easy with the use of a grid.
Source: *Ordnance Survey/Geographers' A–Z Map Company Ltd.*

Grid

A grid is a set of vertical and horizontal lines that are drawn on most maps. A grid makes it easier to find the location of a particular place on a map. A grid is used on street directory maps, such as the one shown in Figure 2.2c. You can find out more about grids in Unit 2.5.

Scale

Every map is smaller than the real area it represents. The **scale** on a map shows how much smaller the map is than the real area. Using a scale, you can measure distances on the map and calculate the distances they represent on the earth's surface. A scale on a map can be:

- a line scale (see Figure 2.2b)
- a description in words, such as 1 centimetre equals 1 kilometre
- a proportional scale (a ratio or representative fraction), such as 1:100 000 or 1/100 000.

Legend

The **legend** of a map is also called the key. It contains all the symbols, such as the ones in Figure 2.2d, that are used on the map and shows what each of them means.

Map symbols are used to show the location of selected features of the physical and built environments. Many symbols look like the features they represent. The colours used for a symbol may also provide a clue to its meaning (blue for water and green for vegetation, for example). The importance of a feature may be shown by the size of the symbol, the thickness of the line or the size of the printing used. Where features extend over large areas they are often identified by shading or colour.

Latitude and longitude

Including an indication of latitude and longitude (see Unit 2.4) helps us to locate a place on the earth's surface. It also helps us to work out the scale of the map and measure distance. One degree of latitude equals approximately 110 kilometres.

Foundation worksheet 2.1

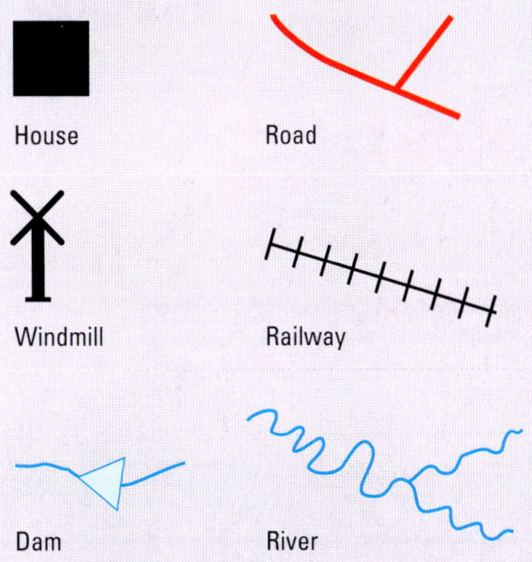

Figure 2.2d Some common map symbols.

Understanding the text

1 What is a map?
2 What role do maps play in the study of geography?
3 Explain why maps cannot show every feature of the landscape.
4 What is used to show how features of the earth's surface are arranged and distributed?
5 List the essential elements of a map.

UTT worksheet 2.2

Working geographically

1 **Using maps** Ask your teacher for a map of the school (or draw a sketch map). Add to it the essential elements of a map.

2 **Group work**
   a Working in groups, design map symbols for the following: bicycle track, bus stop, fast-food outlet, football field, swimming pool, playground, race course, school, skateboard park, lookout, telephone box and video shop.
   b Explain to other groups how your group came up with its symbols.
   c Are your symbols similar to or different from the ones used on a topographic map or street directory?
   d Make your map symbols part of a wall display under the banner 'Map symbols'.

3 **Using street maps** Using a street directory map of the city or town in which you live, locate your home and school.

2.3 Map projections

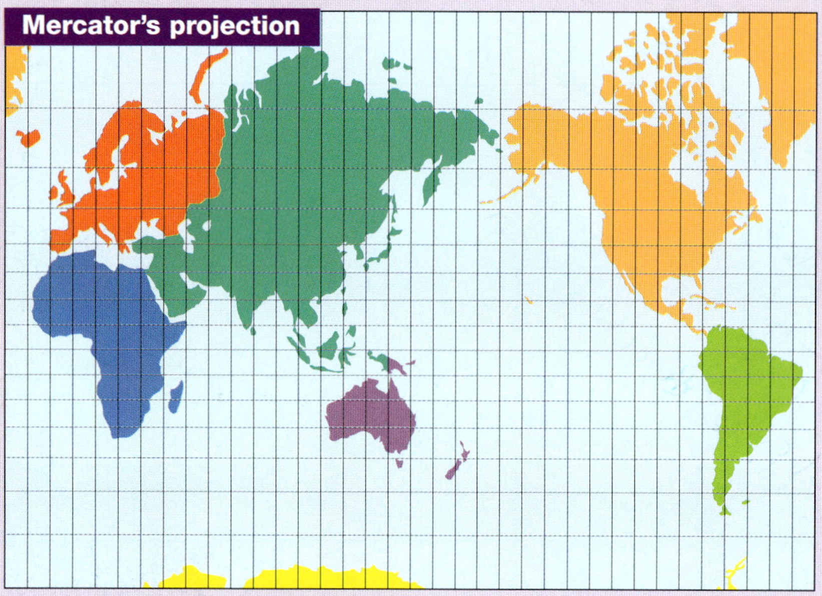

Figure 2.3a *Mercator's projection* was developed in 1569 to assist with sea navigation. This projection shows the correct shapes of landmasses and oceans but the relative size of landmasses is distorted. The farther the land is from the Equator, the larger it appears on a map. Greenland, for example, is less than one-twelfth the size of South America, but on a Mercator map Greenland appears to be much bigger than South America. Any straight line on the map is a line of constant compass bearing but it does not represent the shortest route between two points.

The search for the perfect map

More often than not, world maps are drawn on a flat surface. Because the earth is actually a sphere it is impossible to create flat maps without some distortion. It is not, for example, possible to draw a map that shows both the relative size and shape of continental landmasses correctly.

It would, of course, be ideal if we could always use a globe but there are some practical considerations to take into account. For example, at any one time, only half the globe can be seen. As well, there is a limit to the size that a globe can be and therefore a limit to the amount of detail that can be shown on it.

Over time there have been many attempts to turn the spherical shape of the earth into a two-dimensional flat map. These methods are called *projections*. They aim to minimise distortions in terms of the shape and size of continents as well as directions and distance.

The projections most commonly used are shown in Figures 2.3a to 2.3d. Two other popular map projections are the Peter's projection and the Lambert's conformal conic projection. The *Peter's projection* reduces the amount of exaggeration found in the high latitudes on other maps. The *Lambert's conformal conic projection* was developed by Lambert in 1772. This projection is used for maps of regions that cover a wide area from east to west. The distortion of landmasses is minimised. This projection is used for air navigation.

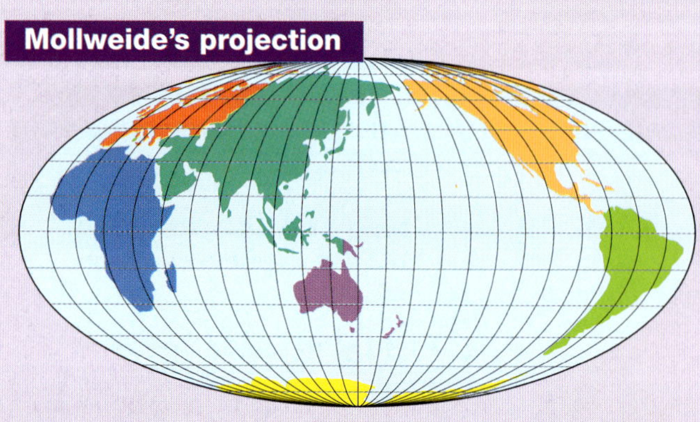

Figure 2.3b *Mollweide's projection* was developed in 1805. This projection accurately represents the relative size of landmasses but distorts their shape.

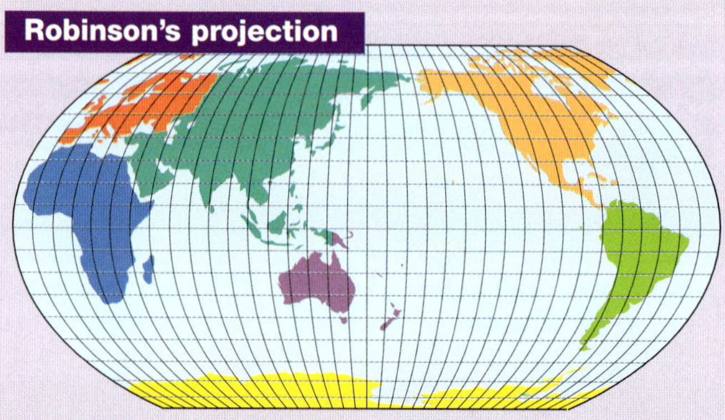

Figure 2.3c *Robinson's projection*. Many geographers believe this projection is the most accurate in terms of the shape and size of landmasses and oceans presented. Distances are also fairly accurate. However, the projection leads to distortions, especially around the edge of the map.

Interrupted projection

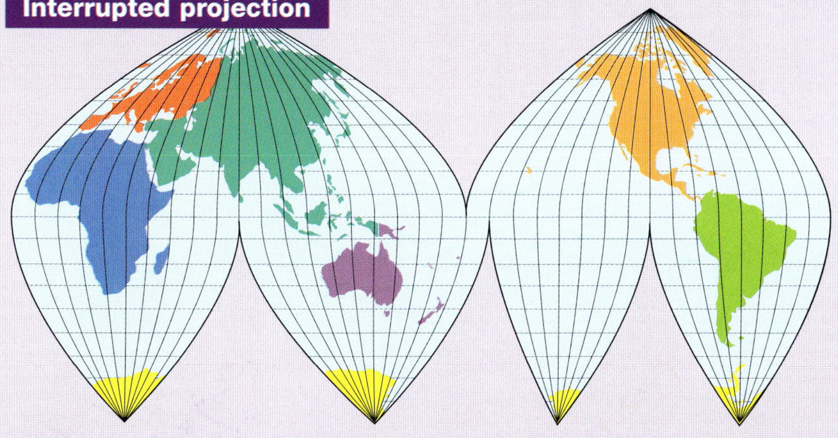

Figure 2.3d *Interrupted projection*. This projection likens the globe to a carefully peeled orange where the peel has been flattened. It features size and shape accurately, but gaps at the poles distort distance.

Computer-generated projections

Map projections can now be created with the aid of computers. This has led to the production of maps that can be 'centred' on any place in the world. In the past, projections such as the Mercator's and Mollweide's were 'Europe-centred'. European cartographers still favour these projections because the size of the smaller European countries is enlarged relative to the size of countries near the Equator so they look bigger. As well, they show Europe at the centre of the world.

Many of the world maps used in Australia are centred on Australia and the Pacific.

Understanding the text

1 Outline the advantages and disadvantages of the Mollweide's projection.
2 Explain why the Robinson's projection is favoured by geographers.
3 Outline the advantage of the interrupted projection.
4 Which map can be used for:
   a navigation at sea
   b air navigation?
5 Which projection is best suited for mapping regions that cover a wide area from east to west?
6 Which projection minimises the exaggeration found in high latitudes on some maps?

UTT worksheet 2.3

Map projections

ICT

Visit the National Geographic's map projection website and complete the following task.

You have been asked to develop maps for several clients with very different needs:

- an adventure travel company planning a tour to Antarctica
- a publisher of geography textbooks
- a non-government organisation mapping the global pattern of AIDS infections
- a company producing road atlases
- organisers of an around-the-world yacht race.

In groups, identify the type of map projection that would best meet the needs of each client.

Also access these great sites:

- *Online Map Creation*—This site allows you to construct your own maps. You can select a projection, decide what data you would like to map, and then watch the result appear on your computer screen. You can also read about different projections.
- *Picture Gallery of Map Projections*—Over 100 different projections are available on this very useful site. It is excellent for base maps for use in assignment work.

Foundation worksheet 2.2

Working geographically

1 **Interpreting maps** Locate North America on the Mercator and Mollweide map projections (Figures 2.3a and 2.3b, respectively). Compare the continent's shape and size on the two maps. Suggest why they are different.

2 **Using atlas maps** Study a number of atlases and find examples of as many different map projections as you can. Make a list of these projections.

2.4 Latitude and longitude

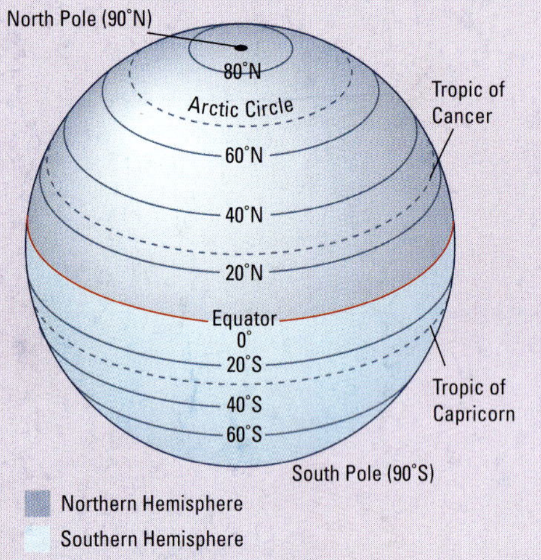

Figure 2.4a Parallels of latitude.

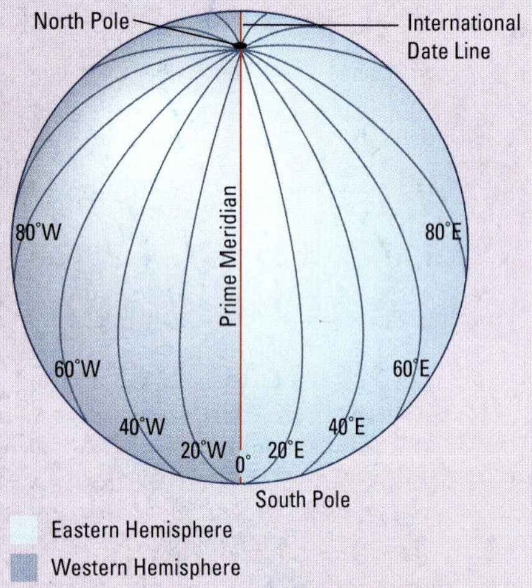

Figure 2.4b Meridians of longitude.

Most of the maps you will use in your study of geography include lines of latitude and longitude. These allow you to quickly and accurately locate places and features on the earth's surface. They also play an important role in determining times and dates.

Latitude

Lines of latitude (see Figure 2.4a) are imaginary lines that run in an east–west direction around the earth. Because the lines of latitude are parallel to each other they are often referred to as *parallels of latitude*.

The most important line of latitude is the *Equator* (0°). The Equator divides the earth into two halves: the Northern Hemisphere and the Southern Hemisphere. All other lines of latitude are either north or south of the Equator and are given a number between 0° and 90°. The North Pole is 90° north and the South Pole is 90° south.

Some of the other important lines of latitude are the Tropic of Cancer (23° 30′ N), the Tropic of Capricorn (23° 30′ S), the Arctic Circle (66° 30′ N) and the Antarctic Circle (66° 30′ S).

Latitude plays an important role in shaping the *global pattern of climate*. Figure 2.4d (p. 28), for example, shows the relationship between latitude and global temperatures. We will have a closer look at climate in Unit 5.3.

Longitude

Lines of longitude (see Figure 2.4b) run in a north–south direction. They are not parallel to one another, but pass through both the North and South Poles. Any number of these lines can be drawn but they all converge, or meet, at the poles. These imaginary lines are called **meridians of longitude**.

The most important line of longitude is the *Prime Meridian* (0°), which passes through Greenwich Observatory just outside London, England. All other lines of longitude are located either to the east or west of the Prime Meridian.

The Prime Meridian plays an important role in the determination of time. The earth's twenty-four time zones are organised according to Greenwich Mean Time (GMT). Places east of the Prime Meridian have sunrise before GMT. Locations to the west of the Prime Meridian have sunrise after GMT so their local times are behind GMT. Sydney, which is 115° east of Greenwich, has its sunrise before Greenwich. It is, therefore, ahead of GMT.

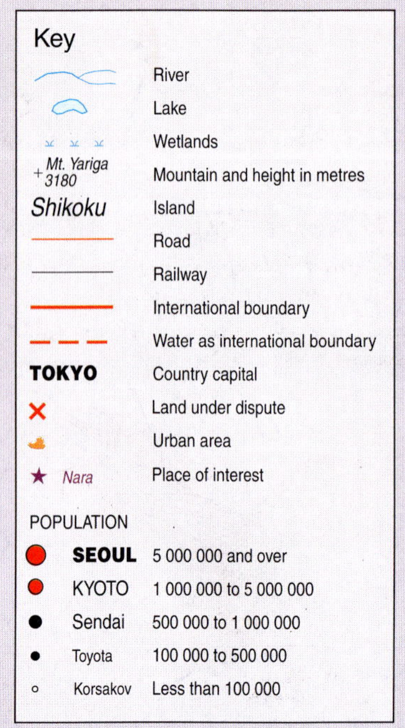

Understanding the text

1. Define the terms 'parallel of latitude' and 'meridian of longitude'.
2. Explain the difference between parallels of latitude and meridians of longitude.
3. Describe the location and significance of the Prime Median and the International Date Line.

UTT worksheet 2.4

Figure 2.4c Atlas map of Japan. Source: *Heinemann Atlas*.

Working geographically

1 Using an atlas
Study a map of the world's time zones in an atlas.
- **a** Calculate what time it will be in London, Singapore, Los Angeles and New York when it is midday in Sydney.
- **b** If you lived in Sydney and wanted to phone a friend in London at 8 a.m. before she leaves for school, what time of day would it be in Sydney when you call?

2 Using atlas maps Study Figure 2.4c (p. 27). Name the feature of the physical environment located at each of the coordinates below.
- **a** 36° 05′ N 133° 00′ E
- **b** 45° N 132° 30′ E
- **c** 35° 23′ N 138° 42′ E
- **d** 38° 20′ N 138° 30′ E
- **e** 43° 42′ N 142° 54′ E
- **f** 44° N 127° E
- **g** 42° 30′ N 142° 30′ E

3 Using atlas maps
Study Figure 2.4c. Name the feature of the human environment located at each of the following locations.
- **a** 35° 40′ N 139° 45′ E
- **b** 34° 23′ N 132° 27′ E
- **c** 39° 00′ E 125° 47′ E
- **d** 37° 30′ N 127° 00′ E
- **e** 43° 05′ N 141° 21′ E
- **f** 35° 02′ N 135° 45′ E

4 Interpreting satellite images
Study Figure 2.4d. Write a paragraph describing the relationship between latitude and the global pattern of climate.

Another important line of longitude is the *International Date Line* (IDL), which is on the opposite side of the world to the Prime Meridian, at 180°. Together, the Prime Meridian and IDL divide the earth into two halves: the Western and Eastern Hemispheres.

The IDL is the point at which the change of day takes place. When we travel from east to west across the IDL, we gain a day. When we travel from east to west we miss a day. Australians travelling to the United States often arrive at their destination before their departure time. On the way back, however, they miss a day.

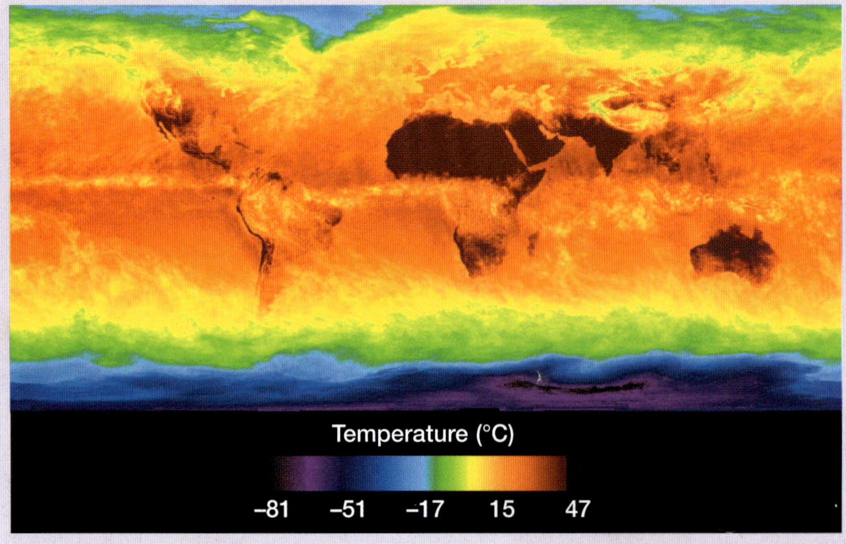

Figure 2.4d The temperature of the earth's surface measured by one of NASA's satellites.

Skills

Finding places using latitude and longitude

When put together, lines of latitude and longitude form a grid that allows us to pinpoint places and features on the earth's surface (see Figure 2.4e). Kobe, Japan (see Figure 2.4c, p. 27), for example, has a latitude of approximately 35° north of the Equator and a longitude of approximately 135° east of the Prime Meridian. To be even more accurate, each degree can be divided into smaller units, called minutes. There are 60 minutes in each degree. Kobe's location using degrees and minutes is lat. 34° 40′ north, long. 135° 12′ east.

When using latitude and longitude to describe the location of a particular place, give the latitude first and then the longitude.

If you are given the latitude and longitude of a place and asked to find it follow the steps below:

1. Using a world map, find the general location of the latitude and longitude you have been given.
2. Turn to a map of the region or continent and locate the latitude and longitude more accurately.
3. You can check your answer by locating the place name in the index of the atlas. Most atlases include the latitude and longitude of each place.

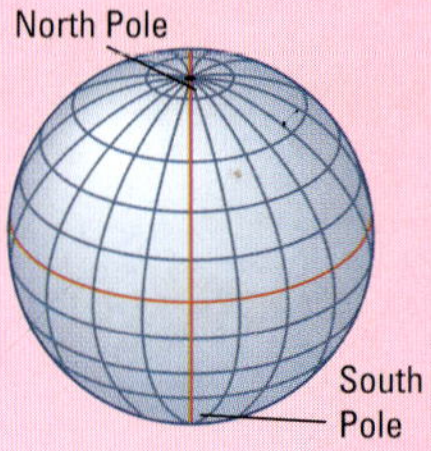

Figure 2.4e Grid pattern.

2.5 Topographic maps

Skills

Locating places on a topographic map using grid and area references

We can locate places easily on a topographic map by using the map's grid lines. On a topographic map the vertical lines are called *eastings* because they increase in value as we move eastwards. The horizontal lines are called *northings* because they increase in value as we move northwards.

Grid references

We can locate relatively small features on topographic maps by using a six-figure grid reference (GR). The first three digits refer to the eastings and the last three digits refer to the northings. Each set of figures is referred to as a *coordinate*. The first two digits of each coordinate refer to the eastings and northings that surround the map. The third digit needed to complete each coordinate is obtained by dividing each easting and northing into tenths. In Figure 2.5a, point A is located at GR335638.

Area references

Features such as a small lake, quarry or village are usually located by means of an area reference (AR). To find the AR of a feature, we use the coordinate in the lower left-hand corner of the grid square in which the feature is located. In Figure 2.5a, the quarry is located in AR3165.

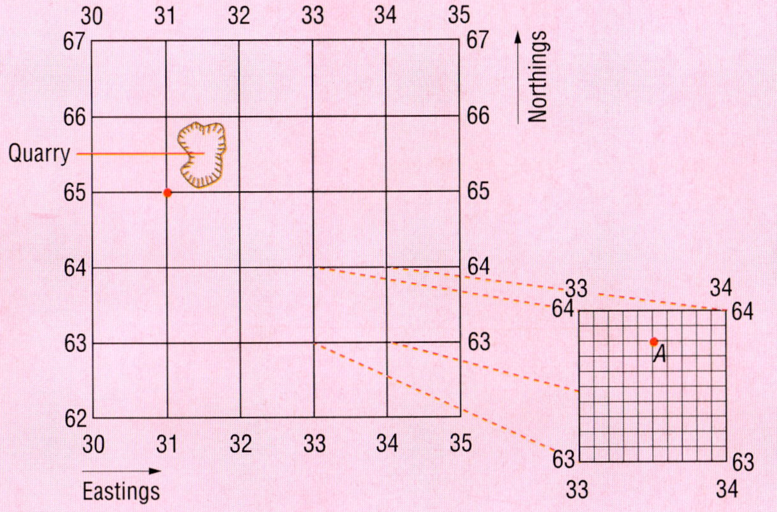

Figure 2.5a Finding grid and area references.

A **topographic map** is a detailed, large-scale map of part of the earth's surface, showing selected features of the physical and human environments: the height, relief and slope of the land; drainage patterns and vegetation; and a range of human features, such as settlements and transport linkages.

Being able to interpret topographic maps is an important geographical skill. It allows you to:

- locate features of the physical and human environments
- describe distributions and patterns
- identify relationships between features.

Scale

To draw a map of any part of the world, the area must be reduced in size, or scaled down, so that it can fit on to a sheet of paper. The **scale** on a map shows how the distance on a map relates to the actual distance on the earth's surface.

Scales allow you to work out distances between places as well as the size of large towns, lakes, forests and the map area.

Map scales can be expressed in three ways:

- as a statement; for example:
  - 1 centimetre (on a map) represents 100 000 centimetres (in reality) *or*
  - 1 centimetre represents 1 kilometre.
- as a ratio or representative fraction; for example:

  $1{:}100\,000$ or $\frac{1}{100\,000}$

- as a linear scale; for example:

Skills

Measuring distances on maps

The scale of a map can be used to calculate the distance between places on maps, vertical aerial photographs or satellite images.

To find the straight-line distance between two points follow the steps below (see Figure 2.5b):

1. Put the edge of a piece of paper along the distance to be measured.
2. Mark the starting and ending points on the piece of paper.
3. Place your paper against the linear scale and work out the distance between the two features.

To find the distance between two points along a railway line, road, track or river, follow the steps below (see Figure 2.5b):

1. Mark the location of one of the points on the edge of a sheet of paper.
2. Move the paper so that its edge follows the railway line, road, track or river.
3. Use pencil marks to help you position your paper as you move it around the curve of the line.
4. Place your paper against the linear scale and work out the distance between the two features.

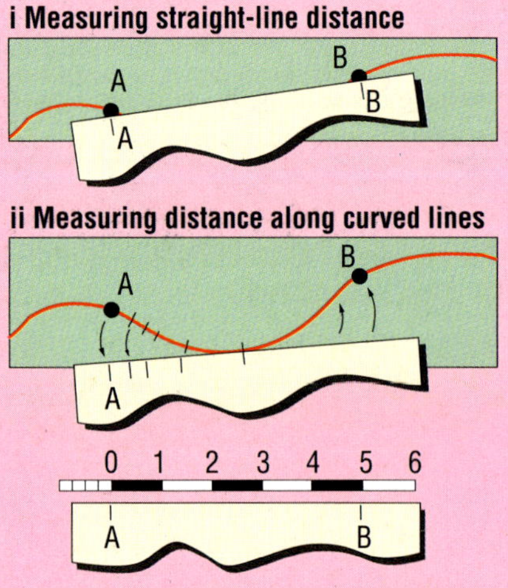

Figure 2.5b Measuring distances on maps.

Did U know?

More on scale

The most common scales used for topographic maps are 1:25 000, 1:50 000 and 1:100 000. Atlas maps use a variety of scales depending on the area of the earth's surface to be shown. To fit an atlas map of the world on to an A4 sheet of paper you would need to use a scale of approximately 1:135 000 000. To fit a map of Australia on to an A4 sheet of paper you would need to use a scale of approximately 1:20 000 000. At a scale of 1:250 000 (a relatively small scale), it takes 544 map sheets to cover Australia. At a scale of 1:25 000 (a larger scale) it would take 50 000 map sheets!

Because of their larger scale, topographic maps show a greater variety of information about places than most atlas maps. Their scales allow individual buildings, small rivers and creeks, and even dams, fences and telephone lines to be shown. In addition, they show contour lines, **spot heights** and hill shading. Generally, as the area shown on a map increases, the amount of detail decreases and the accuracy of the map becomes less reliable. You can see the difference in Figure 2.5c.

The terms 'large scale' and 'small scale' often confuse people. It is wrong to think that a large-scale map covers a large area and a small-scale map covers a small area.

A map scale of 1:100 000 is smaller than a map scale of 1:50 000.

- 1:25 000 means 1 centimetre represents 0.25 kilometres or 250 metres
- 1:50 000 means 1 centimetre represents 0.5 kilometres or 500 metres
- 1:100 000 means 1 centimetre represents 1.0 kilometre or 1000 metres.

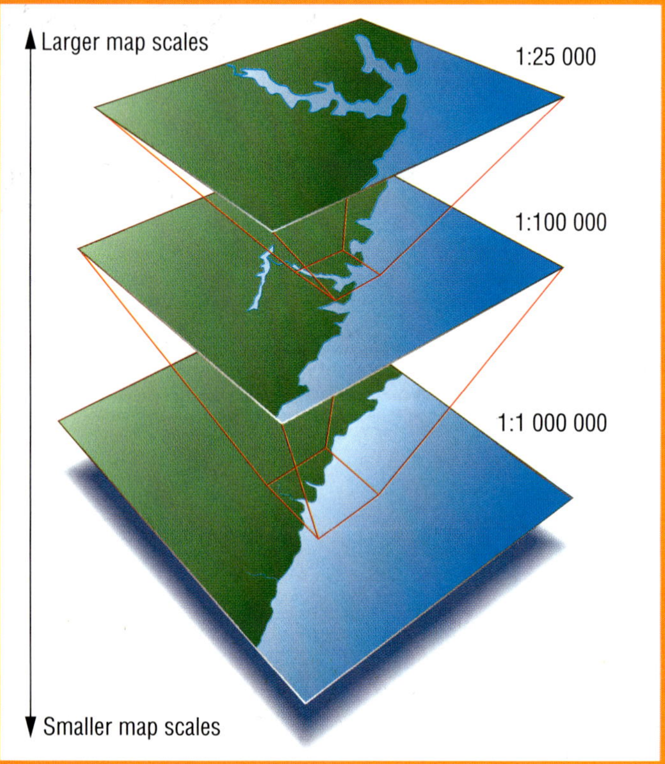

Figure 2.5c Different scales can show different details.

Skills

Measuring areas using scale

Sometimes you will need to know the area of features on a map, or even the total map area. The following techniques use scale to help you find map areas.

To measure the *whole area* covered by a map follow the steps below:

1. Use the straight edge of a piece of paper to work out the east–west length of the map.
2. Move your paper to the scale line and work out the distance in metres or kilometres.
3. Repeat steps 1 and 2 for the north–south length of the map.
4. Multiply the east–west distance by the north–south distance.
5. State your result in square metres (m^2) or square kilometres (km^2).

To measure an *irregular area* on a map (such as a lake, forest or built-up area) follow the steps listed below (see Figure 2.5d).

1. Trace the area to be measured.
2. Use the scale line to rule a grid over the area. Many topographic maps have grid lines 1 kilometre apart. In other words, the grid squares are 1 km^2.
3. Tick each grid square that is completely within the area you are measuring.
4. Put a tick in each grid square that is half, or more than half, enclosed by the area.
5. Add up your ticks. If you used a grid of 1 km^2 your answer will be in square kilometres.

Please note that neither technique is completely accurate.

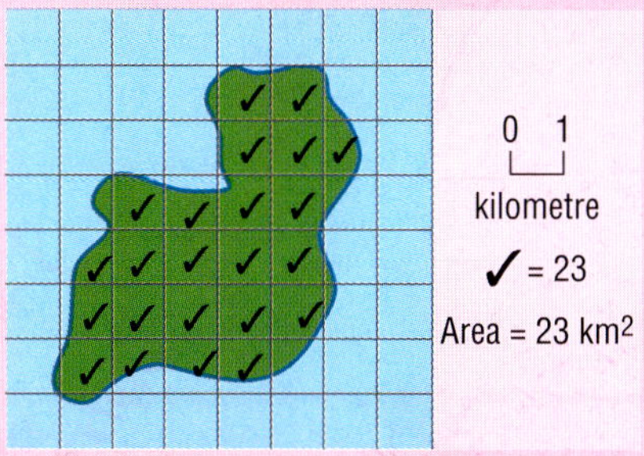

Figure 2.5d Measuring irregular areas.

Relief

Relief is a general term describing the shape of the land, including height and steepness. The main techniques used by cartographers to show relief are spot heights, contour lines and patterns, and layer colouring and landform shading.

Spot heights

Spot heights are shown on maps as a black dot with the height written next to it. You can see a spot height in Figure 2.5e. Spot heights give the exact height above sea level of the particular **location** or feature.

Contour lines

Contour lines join points of equal height above sea level. Thus, every point along the line has the same value (see Figure 2.5e).

Contour lines provide geographers with information about the shape and slope of the land and the height of features above sea level. The **contour interval**, or *vertical interval*, is the difference in height between two adjacent contour lines. This interval is normally stated in the map's legend or near the edge of the map (see Figure 2.5e).

Contour patterns

Each type of topographic feature is represented by its own distinctive *contour pattern*. A skilled user of topographic maps can visualise the shapes of particular features by studying the patterns created by the contour lines.

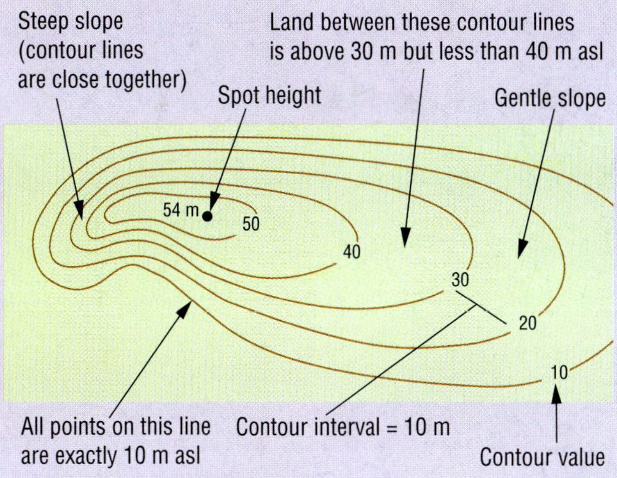

Figure 2.5e Contour line features.

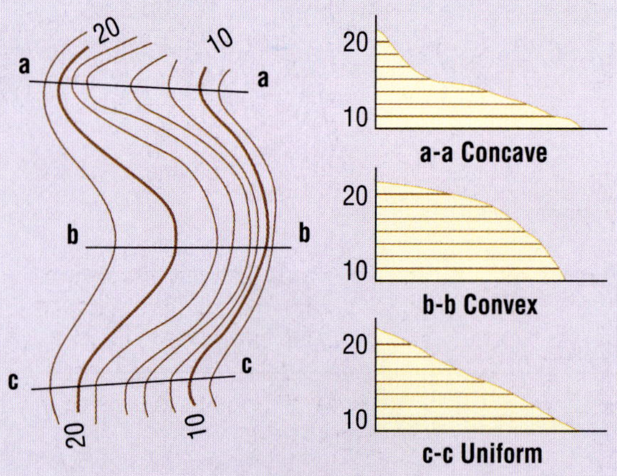

Figure 2.5f Contour lines and slopes.

Remember:

- The spacing of the contours on a map shows the steepness of slopes. Areas where contour lines are close together have steep slopes. Areas where the contour lines are widely spaced are very flat (see Figure 2.5e, p. 31).
- The spacing of contour lines on a map also indicates the shape of a slope. Evenly spaced contours indicate a uniform slope. When the spacing of contour lines reading from high to low decreases, the slope is convex; that is, curved like the outside shape of a circle. When the spacing of contour lines reading from high to low increases, the slope is concave; that is, like the inside shape of a circle (see Figure 2.5f).

With practice we can gain a visual impression of the shape of the land by interpreting the patterns made by the contour lines on a map. In Figure 2.5g, each of the eight block diagrams (1 to 8) matches one of the contour patterns (A to H). At the end of this unit you will be asked to try to match them.

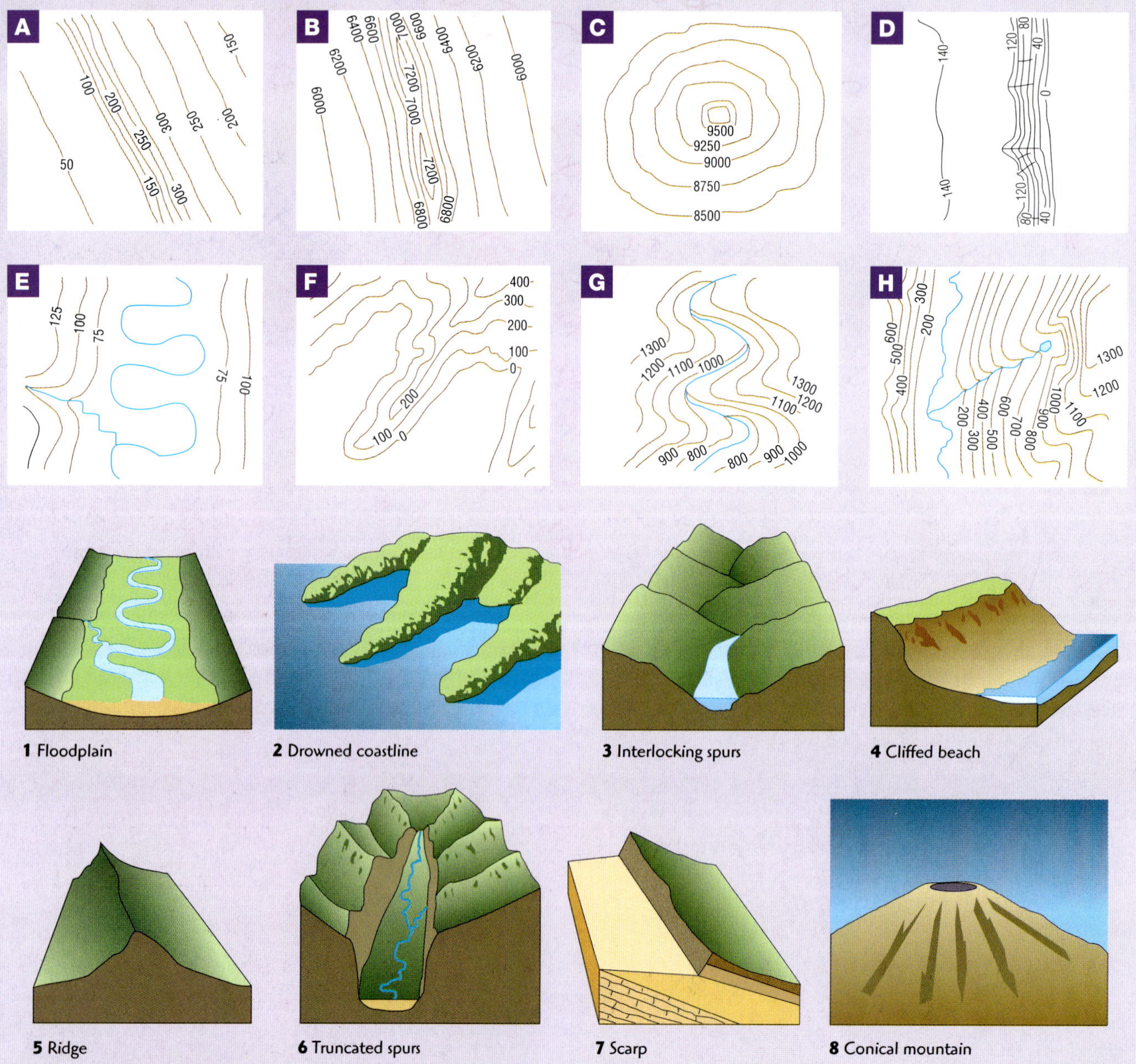

Figure 2.5g Landform features and their contour patterns.

Layer colouring

Layer colouring is a simple and effective way of showing relief on maps. It involves colouring the area between selected contours in different colours (see Figure 2.4c, p. 27). When it is used in combination with spot heights, and sometimes landform shading, it can tell you a good deal about the shape of the land. Remember always to use the key to help you interpret the colours used.

Landform shading

Shading may be applied to maps so that colours darken as **elevation** increases. Alternatively, shading may be applied as if the light was coming from one direction, so that one side of a hill is shown in a lighter shade than the other to give it greater definition. *Landform shading* is sometimes used in conjunction with contour lines.

Skills

Estimating heights of landform features

Sometimes you will need to know the height of a map feature, such as the top of a hill or a plain. If there is no spot height on the feature, it is possible to estimate the height by studying the contour lines of a map. Use the following examples as a guide.

Example 1

Estimate the height of the hill at point A in Figure 2.5h.

Point A lies more than 150 metres above sea level. However, it is obviously less than 200 metres above sea level. Your answer can be expressed in one of two ways:

- *as a statement*—point A is more than 150 metres, but less than 200 metres, above sea level
  or
- *as an estimate*—point A is 160 metres (any number between, but not including, 150 and 200 would be acceptable) above sea level.

Example 2

Now try to estimate the height of point B.

Point B lies between the 50 and 100 metres contour lines. Your answer can be expressed in one of two ways:

- *as a statement*—point B is more than 50 metres, but less than 100 metres, above sea level
  or
- *as an estimate*—point B is 75 metres (any number between, but not including, 50 or 100 would be acceptable) above sea level.

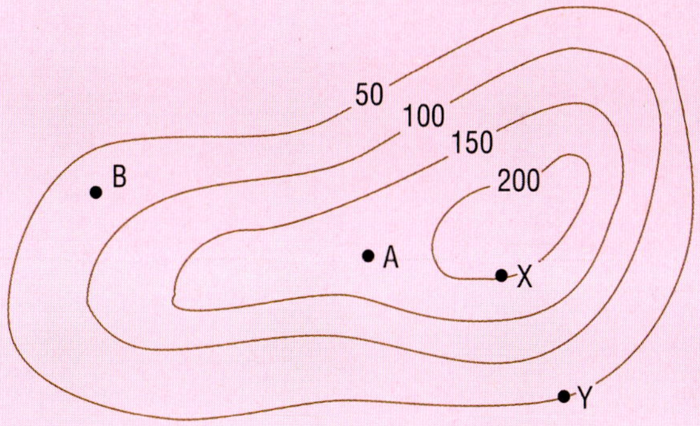

Figure 2.5h Contour heights.

Getting technical

Quadrants To help locate features on topographic maps, their location is sometimes expressed in terms of quadrants. Quadrants derive their name from the points of a compass (see Figure 2.5i).

Figure 2.5i The quadrants of a map.

Skills

Density

The density of a feature can be determined by counting their number within a specific area (see Figure 2.5j). Answers should be expressed as the number of features per square kilometre.

Example: The density of buildings in AR3178 is 6/km^2.

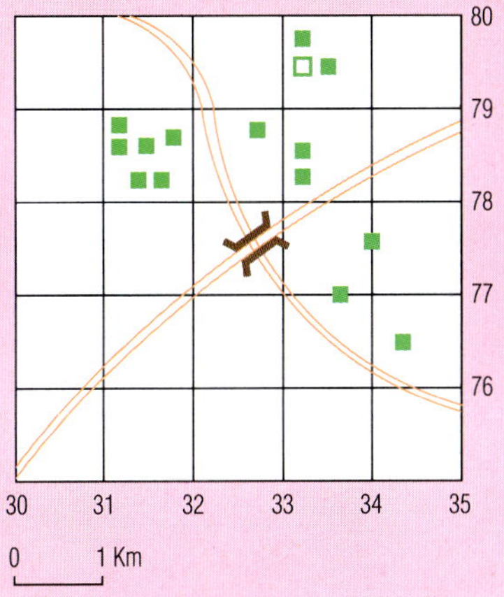

Figure 2.5j Density.

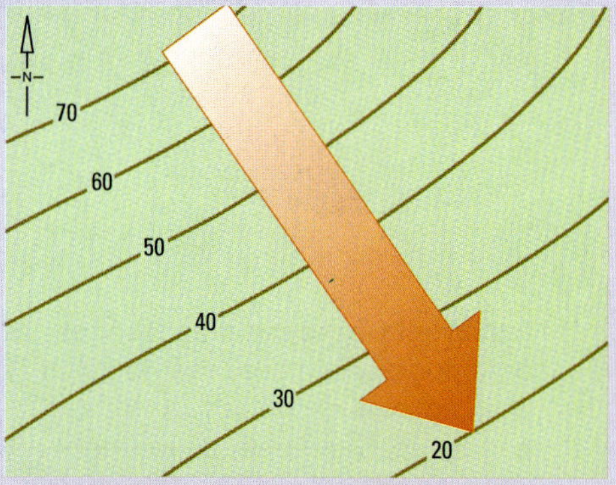

Figure 2.5k A slope with a southeasterly aspect.

Aspect

Aspect refers to the direction that a slope faces. The aspect of a particular slope can be determined by examining the height and pattern of contour lines. The slope shown in Figure 2.5k has a southeasterly aspect.

Compass direction

Geographers give directions and describe the location of places on maps and in the real world. They do this by using terms such as 'north' and 'southeast'.

Skills

Drawing a cross-section

A cross-section is a side view, or profile, of a landscape. Cross-sections drawn from topographic and atlas maps give an immediate visual impression of the shape of the land.

Information about landuse, settlement, drainage and vegetation can be added to cross-sections. This provides a means of seeing how the shape of the land influences these features.

To draw a cross-section, follow the steps below and refer to Figure 2.5l.

1. Locate the two points on the map between which the cross-section is to be made. Label these points 'A' and 'B' (see drawing i).
2. Place the straight edge of a piece of paper along an imaginary line joining points A and B. Mark points A and B on your paper (see drawing ii).
3. Mark the position where your paper crosses each contour line. Write the value of each contour line on your piece of paper (see drawing ii). You may have to estimate the height of your starting and finishing points.
4. On graph or squared paper draw the horizontal and vertical axes for your cross-section. The length of the horizontal axis should equal the distance between A and B. The vertical axis should use a scale that does not exaggerate your vertical scale too much. You don't want a range of low hills looking like the Himalayas!
5. Place your piece of paper along your horizontal axis. Lightly plot, in pencil, the contour points and heights as if you were drawing a line graph (see drawing iii).
6. Join the dots with a fine, single, smooth curved line.
7. Label any features intersected by your cross-section, such as rivers and major roads.
8. Finish off your cross-section by:
   a. shading in the area below the landform you have drawn
   b. labelling the scale on the horizontal and vertical axes
   c. giving it a title.

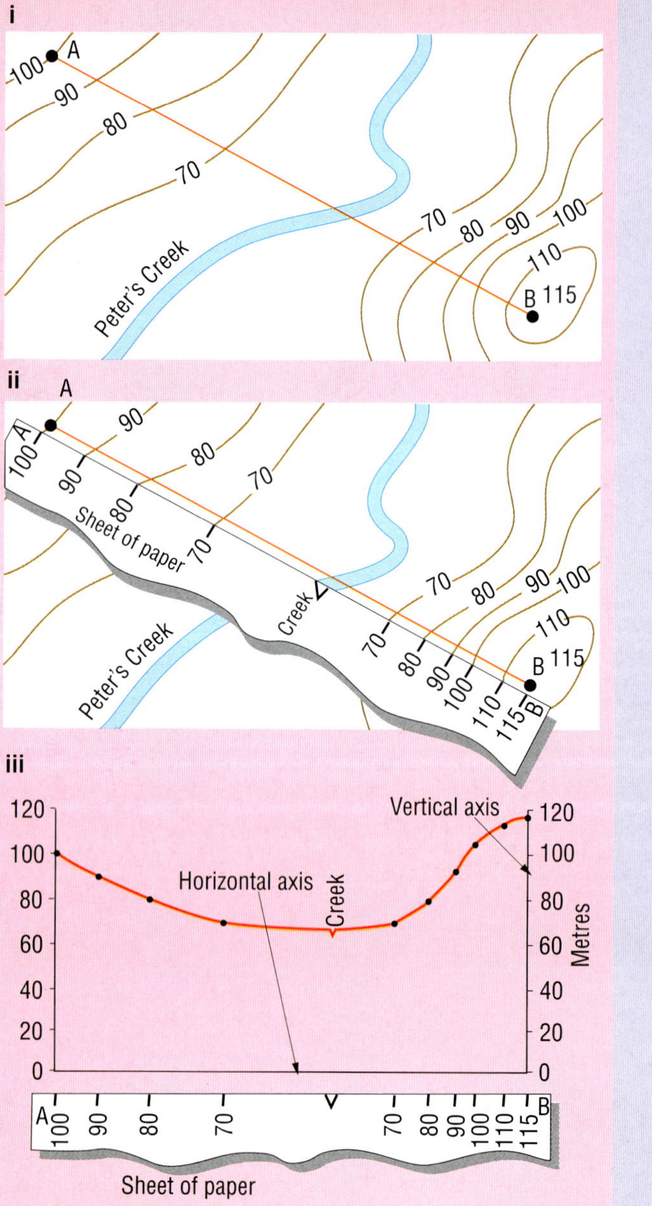

Figure 2.5l Drawing a cross-section.

Compass points

North, south, east and west are known as the *cardinal* (main) *points* of the compass. In between these points are the *intermediate points* (such as northeast, southwest and west-south-west), which give a more specific indication of direction (see Figure 2.5m).

Most maps have a directional arrow indicating where north is. Topographic maps are generally designed so that north is at the top of the map. Just to be sure, check the direction arrow, which is usually located near the legend or key. If there is no arrow, then north is at the top of the map.

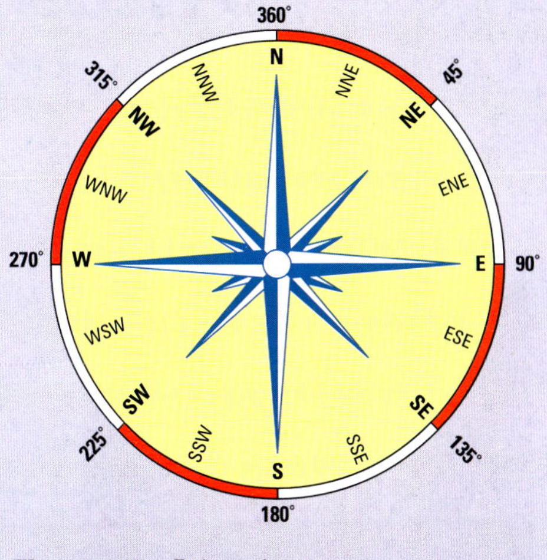

Figure 2.5m Points of a compass.

Skills

Locating a point using compass bearings

When **bearings** are used to give direction, they are given in terms of degrees from north. They are calculated by measuring the angle from north in a clockwise direction using a protractor. North is taken to be zero (see Figure 2.5n).

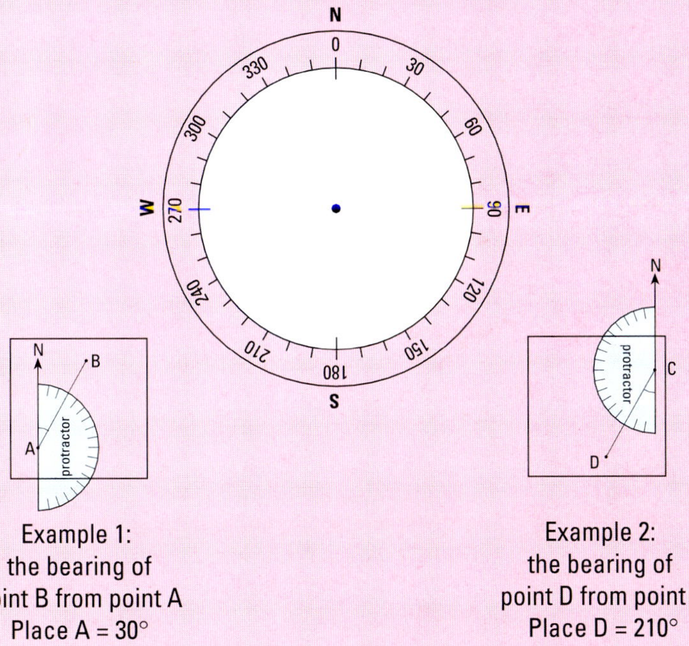

Figure 2.5n Finding compass bearings.

Understanding the text

1 What are topographic maps and what do they show?
2 What do we use grid and area references for?
3 What is scale used for?
4 List and explain the various ways relief is shown on maps.
5 Why do geographers construct cross-sections?
6 What is meant by the term 'aspect'?

cd UTT worksheet 2.5

Working geographically

1 **Matching** Study Figure 2.5g (p. 32) Write the numbers 1 to 8 down the left-hand side of a page. Give each landform feature its correct name. Next to each, write the letter of the contour pattern (A to H) that best matches the illustration of the landform feature.

2 **Using topographic maps** Study a topographic map, in particular its contour lines. Identify some of the landform features in Figure 2.5g.

2.6 Atlas maps

Figure 2.6a An atlas is an important source of information.

An *atlas* is a collection of maps. These maps show physical features, human features or a mixture of both. Atlases also contain world maps and regional maps showing particular themes, such as climate or wealth.

In an atlas there are usually maps of each continent, more detailed maps of regions showing particular countries, and even more detailed maps of some smaller areas, such as cities. Cities are usually represented on maps using dot symbols. Often, different symbols are used to distinguish a capital city from a large city, smaller city, town or village.

There are also many special atlases available. These atlases contain maps linked to a particular theme or place. There is probably an atlas of your state, and in the library there may be an atlas of population or agriculture or a historical atlas. Atlases can be viewed in print form and in electronic form on a computer. With developments in computer technology, electronic atlases are becoming increasingly sophisticated and interactive.

Contents page and index

Look at the *contents* page at the front of your atlas. If you want to find a general area, such as North America, or a theme, such as population, the contents page of your atlas will be useful. If you want to find a particular place, such as a town or mountain, you should use the *index* at the back of your atlas.

Every place that is shown on any map in an atlas is listed in the index. They are usually listed in alphabetical order, like a dictionary. This information allows you to locate places and features quickly and accurately. The entry for Singapore is shown below.

Page Number
Alphanumeric grid reference
Latitude
Longitude
Singapore **78** **C4** 1.16N 10.50E

Physical and human features maps

The maps in an atlas are often labelled with human (that is, cultural and political) features such as boundaries, countries and cities. Physical (that is, natural) maps show features such as rivers, mountains, plains and lakes. Figures 2.6b and 2.6c show these two types of maps.

Thematic maps

Atlases contain maps that are intended to illustrate particular themes. These maps may show annual rainfall, ethnic groups or the oil resources of a region or the whole world (see Figure 2.6d).

Figure 2.6b Part of a political atlas map. Source: *Heinemann Atlas*.

Figure 2.6c Part of a physical atlas map.
Source: *Heinemann Atlas*.

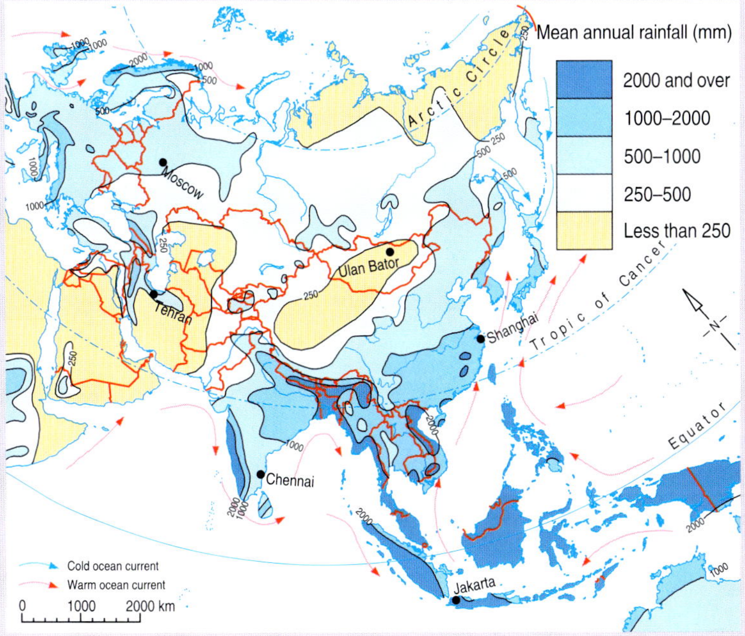

Figure 2.6d Annual rainfall across Asia.

Understanding the text

1. What part of an atlas would you refer to if you wanted to locate a general area, such as southern Asia or North America?
2. What part of the atlas would you refer to if you wanted to find a particular place?
3. What features are shown on physical maps?
4. What features are shown on political maps?
5. What are thematic maps?

UTT worksheet 2.6

Working geographically

1. **Interpreting maps** Study Figures 2.6b and 2.6c. List the types of information shown on each map.
2. **Selecting maps** Which kind of atlas map (physical, human or thematic) would be the best source of information on the following?
   - a the capital cities of Europe
   - b the names of Indonesia's main islands
   - c the mountains and rivers of China
   - d the shape of countries in South America
   - e the political divisions of Africa
   - f the population density of North America
   - g the landform features of Europe
   - h the temperature patterns of Australia and New Zealand

2.7 Climate graphs and weather maps

Skills

Constructing a climate graph

When constructing a climate graph, follow the steps below:

1. Transfer the relevant temperature and rainfall data from your data source into the table at the base of the climate graph. Table 2.7a shows the data used to create the climate graph in Figure 2.7a.
2. Study the data to identify the wettest month and the highest and lowest temperatures. Use this information to select a suitable scale for both temperature and precipitation.
3. Place the precipitation scale on the right-hand side of the graph and the temperature scale on the left-hand side of the graph.
4. Plot the rainfall figures. Then colour the columns blue.
5. Plot the average temperature data, making sure each dot is placed in the centre of each month. Use a red pen or pencil to join the points with a smooth, red curve.
6. Add a heading that includes the name of the place being graphed and its latitude, longitude and elevation.

Climate graphs

Climate graphs show the average temperature and rainfall experienced at a particular place throughout the year. They consist of a line graph showing average monthly temperature and a simple column graph showing average monthly rainfall figures.

Climate graphs are constructed using data collected by meteorologists. The main features of a climate graph are shown in Figure 2.7a.

Weather maps

A **weather map**, or synoptic chart, is a record of the weather conditions being experienced across part of the earth's surface at a particular point in time. It includes information about air pressure, wind speed and direction, and the distribution of rainfall. This enables us to predict the weather we are likely to receive over the next two to three days.

Being able to read weather maps is an important life skill to master. Farmers, for example, use weather maps to help them plan their farming activities. It also enables people to plan their recreational activities, such as going to the beach and playing sport. With the aid of weather maps and satellite photographs, meteorologists are able to identify hazardous weather conditions, including storms, gales, hail, temperature extremes and cyclones. Being aware of these dangers enables people to take precautions. To find out more about weather and climate go to Unit 5.3.

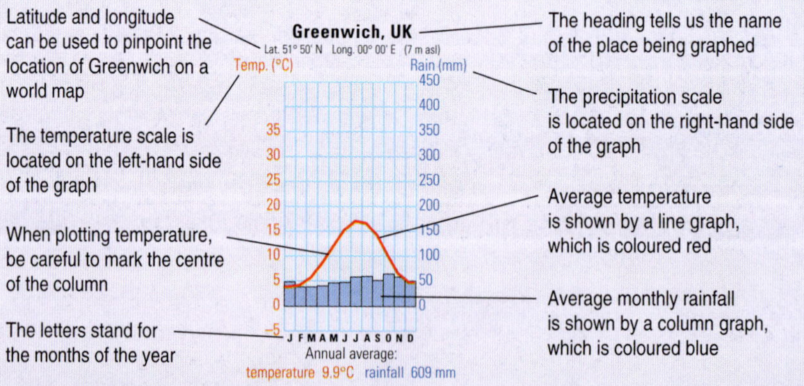

Figure 2.7a Climate graph for Greenwich, United Kingdom.

Table 2.7a Climate data for Greenwich, United Kingdom

Month	J	F	M	A	M	J	J	A	S	O	N	D	Year
Average temp. (°C)	3.9	4.2	5.7	8.5	11.9	15.2	17.0	16.6	14.2	10.3	6.6	4.8	9.9 av.
Rainfall (mm)	49	39	39	41	47	48	59	60	52	65	59	51	609 total

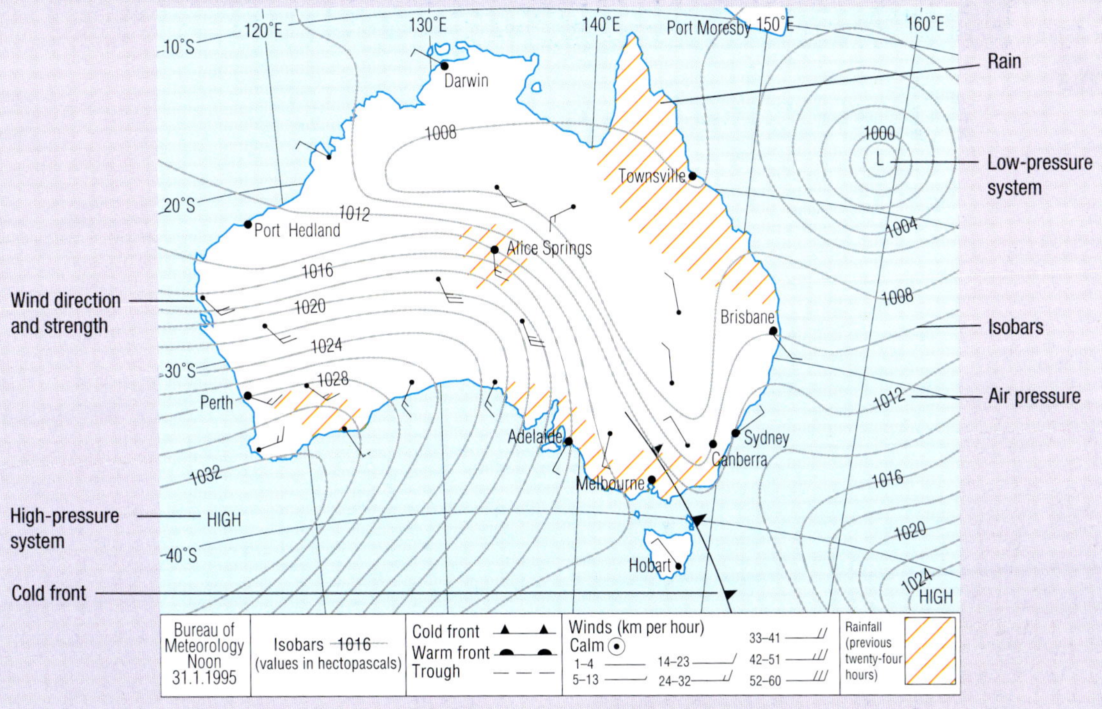

Air pressure (also known as atmospheric, or barometric, pressure) is the weight of air pressing down on the earth's surface. If air is warmed, it expands, rises and creates a low-pressure area on the earth's surface. If air is cooled, it contracts, descends and creates an area of high pressure on the earth's surface. Areas of high and low pressure determine much of the earth's weather.

Isobars are lines that join places of equal atmospheric pressure. Air pressure is measured in hectopascals (hPa). Isobars are usually drawn at intervals of 2 hPa.

High-pressure systems (or anticyclones, as they are sometimes known) are areas of stable atmospheric conditions: gentle winds, clear skies and little chance of rain. Air pressure increases towards the centre of the pressure system. Air flows out from the high-pressure system in an anticlockwise direction.

Low-pressure systems (or cyclones, as they are sometimes referred to) form when warm air rises. They are often associated with unstable weather conditions: cloudy skies, rain and relatively strong winds. Air pressure decreases towards the centre of the pressure system. Air flows in an anticlockwise direction of the low-pressure system in the Northern Hemisphere, and in a clockwise direction in the Southern Hemisphere.

Rain Areas that have received rainfall are shown by diagonal lines.

Warm fronts occur when a warm parcel of air overtakes a colder, denser parcel of air. As with a cold front, rain often results as air rises. However, rainfall resulting from the passage of a warm front tends to last for a longer period of time and to be less intense than that resulting from a cold front. Warm fronts are not common in Australia.

Cold fronts occur when a mass of cold, dense air pushes in under a mass of warm air, forcing it to rise. As the warm air rises, it cools and condensation takes place. Lower temperatures are experienced once the front has passed.

Wind direction and strength for selected locations are shown using lines with small barbs or tails. With the aid of the legend we can determine wind speed. Winds are named after the direction from which they blow. A southerly, for example, blows from the south. Winds are strongest where isobars are close together. It is useful to know that winds occur when air moves from areas of high pressure to areas of low pressure. We will explore this further in Unit 5.3.

Figure 2.7b A weather map, or synoptic chart, records the conditions in the atmosphere at a particular time. Source: Bureau of Meteorology.

Extension worksheet 2.13

Working geographically

1 Constructing climate graphs

a Use one of the websites listed in the ICT box on page 112 to find data dealing with your nominated city's climate. Use this data to construct a climate graph similar to the one shown in Figure 2.7a.

b Compare your graph with those drawn by your classmates. How does the climate of the two cities compare? For example: Which city has the coldest winter? Which receives the most precipitation?

2 Internet research

Each member of the class nominates a city they would like to visit when travelling overseas. Using one of the websites listed in the ICT box on page 112, investigate the weather conditions being experienced by the city. Write a brief report describing these conditions. Download any relevant weather maps and satellite images. Use these to illustrate your report.

3 Challenge: Investigating weather maps online

Using the Australian Bureau of Meteorology website, download a series of forecast maps over a five-day period.

a Study the maps to determine the general pattern of movements of the highs and lows.

b Study today's weather map. Predict what the weather will be like tomorrow. Review your predictions in your next geography lesson.

2.8 Photographs

Figure 2.8a An oblique photograph of the walled city of Dubrovnik, Croatia.

Photographs are very important to geographers. A photo of an area of the earth can provide an idea of what it looks like without visiting it. Photographs can record a landscape as it exists at a particular time. They can be used to record fieldwork observations (see Units 4.2 and 4.3, pp. 90–9) for later use. Photographs also record information that may not be present on a map, such as the location of people and motor vehicles.

Geographers describe photographs in four different ways, as Figure 2.8b shows.

Ground-level photographs

Ground-level photographs, such as Figure 2.8c, are taken from the ground. This means a horizon can be seen. Features in the foreground will appear larger than those in the background. Large objects in the foreground can often block out features in the middle and background.

Oblique photographs

Oblique photographs (such as Figure 2.8a) are similar to ground-level photographs in that features in the background will appear smaller than those in the foreground. Unlike ground-level photographs, oblique photographs are taken from above the ground. Often a horizon cannot be seen. The camera is pointed at an oblique angle to the ground.

Vertical photographs

Vertical photographs are taken from above the ground with the camera lens pointed directly down on the area being photographed. Features across the photograph will not be distorted, although it will be hard to estimate their height.

Understanding the text

1 Why are photographs important to geographers?
2 How are ground-level photographs different from oblique photographs?
3 Name one advantage and one disadvantage of vertical photographs.
4 How are satellite images produced?

UTT worksheet 2.8

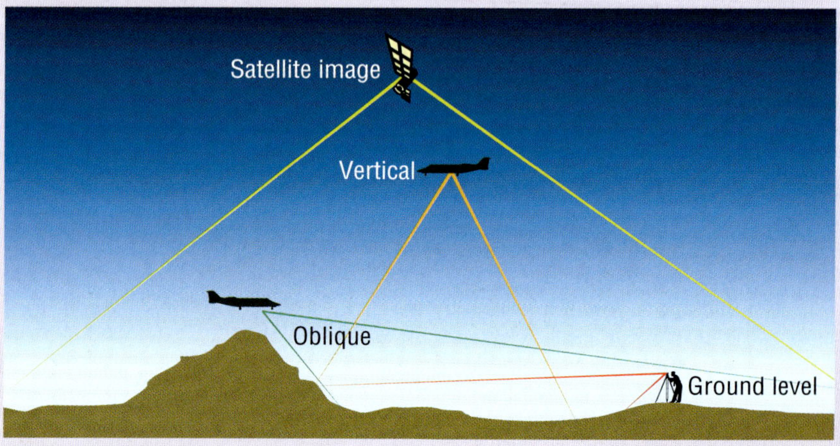

Figure 2.8b Ground-level, oblique and vertical photographs, and satellite images.

Figure 2.8c A ground-level photograph of part of Yosemite National Park, California, United States.

Satellite images

Satellite images are images, not photographs. They are recorded from satellites located hundreds of kilometres above the earth. As a result they can cover larger areas of the earth. Satellite images are widely used in many aspects of geography. Different landuses can be picked out and the movement of features (such as cold fronts and shipping) and the exact shape of landforms, can be discovered.

Skills

Interpreting photographs

When looking at photographs, remember to:

- look for the main features being shown
- note relevant information given with the photograph, such as written explanations of events or features depicted
- look for evidence of location and time
- look for clues for scale (such as people's height) and living conditions (such as building materials and open space)
- look for features that seem out of place as they may warrant further reading or investigation
- check whether anything seems to be missing.

Did U know?

Photographic images sourced from the Internet

A photograph, like all creative works, is the intellectual property of the creator. Using a photograph without the creator's permission is a breach of ethical standards. When using images sourced from the Internet always check their copyright status. If the image is protected by copyright you should not use it. Some sites will allow you to use images for non-commercial purposes.

Working geographically

1 **Constructing photo sketches** Study Figure 2.8a, then complete the following tasks:
  - a Construct a photo sketch (see Unit 2.9) of the image. Label Dubrovnik's harbour, marina and fort.
  - b Describe the site of Dubrovnik.

2 **Selecting photographs** Study Figure 2.8b, then complete the following tasks:
  - a Which type of photograph:
    - i covers the largest area
    - ii shows excellent detail about the foreground
    - iii eliminates any distortion to the shape of an area covered by features
    - iv best shows the shape of the landscape?
  - b Which type of photograph would be most suitable for showing:
    - i a plan view of your school
    - ii a crowded shopping centre
    - iii areas affected by flooding
    - iv the height of a new building?

3 **Challenge: Studying photographs** Study Figure 2.8c, then complete the following tasks:
  - a Describe the scene in the foreground.
  - b Explain how the foreground scene differs from the background scene.

4 **Using the media** Collect three photographs from the daily newspapers that would be of interest to geographers. Share these with others in the class. Explain why you selected each photograph.

Extension worksheet ICT 2.6

Extension worksheet ICT 2.7

2.9 Map and photo sketching

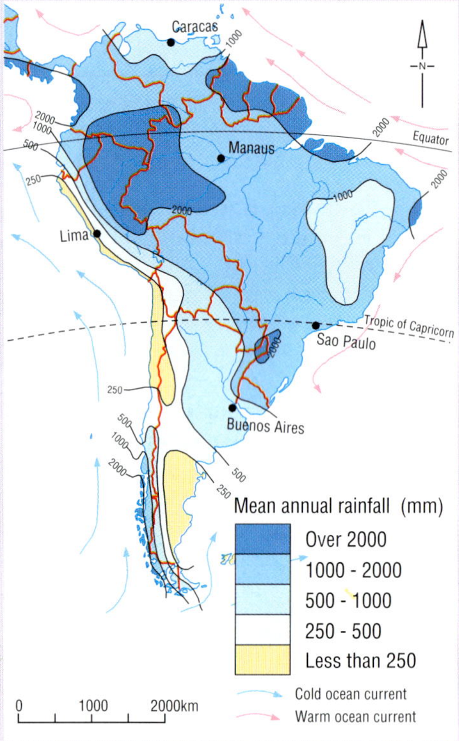

Figure 2.9a South America, annual rainfall. Source: *Heinemann Atlas*.

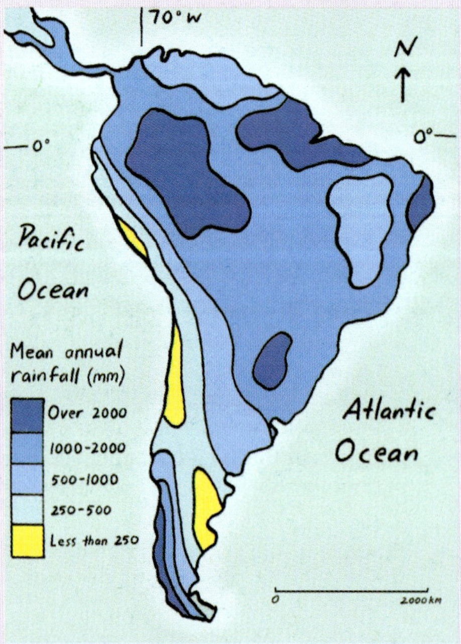

Figure 2.9b A sketch map of South America's annual rainfall, with annotations.

Sketching from maps and photographs is a valuable skill to have. It allows you to make a quick *summary* of a situation as well as *highlight* or annotate (or both) the key features of the situation. Sketch maps and photo sketches can both be used to illustrate reports and displays. They can also be scanned and used in PowerPoint presentations.

For both maps and photographs, sketches should not reproduce everything that is already there. Use a soft pencil (it makes it easier to erase errors) on blank paper. Pick out the main features of the map or photograph and sketch in their shape. Include, of course, the features you want to highlight. Always produce your sketch within a frame that is in the same proportion as the original. Annotate your sketch to point out the main features or indicate a changing feature or some important link between features. To avoid cluttering your sketch with labels you can use a key. Sketches need a title. At the bottom of your sketch, indicate the source of your photograph or map.

Sketch maps

Sketch maps can be made from maps of any size, scale or purpose. It may be a simple map showing where you live or it may be a more complex map that includes a number of features. Figure 2.9b is an example of a sketch map.

On a sketch map the scale can only be approximate, but it is an important feature to include on your map. This is because you need to give an idea of the distance between places and the area covered by features. On sketch maps, notes can identify and explain particular features.

Topographic maps, such as the map on page 191, can also be used for sketch maps. Sometimes photographs or sketches of features found on the topographic map can be put next to or on the sketch map. This helps to make your sketch map even more realistic.

Photo sketches

Photo sketches (or line drawings) can be made in the same way as sketch maps. For ground-level photographs (see Figure 2.9d) it may be useful to divide your photograph into three areas: foreground, middle ground and background. Before you begin sketching, lightly pencil these three areas into your frame. The features of the photograph can then be sketched in. Begin with the background, followed by the middle ground and then the foreground.

Like sketch maps, photo sketches can be annotated or coloured to highlight particular features. You can see this on Figure 2.9c, which has been drawn from Figure 2.9d.

Sketches can be produced from vertical photographs in the same way that sketch maps are made. The view in a vertical photograph has no distortion in the size of features. This means that a scale can be worked out and added to your sketch. As for a sketch map, your photo sketch needs a title and a source.

Figure 2.9c Stages in the development of a photo sketch.

Figure 2.9d Moraine Lake, Banff National Park, Canada.

Understanding the text

1 Of what use are sketch maps and photo sketches?

2 Distinguish between a sketch map and a photo sketch.

UTT worksheet 2.9

Working geographically

1 **Constructing sketch maps**
Plan a vacation to Asia. You can afford to visit five places. Show your destinations on a sketch map, together with the route you plan to take and what you want to see and do at each place. Make sure that you include a title and an approximate scale for your sketch map.

2 **Constructing photo sketches**
Select one of the photographs in Unit 3.3 (p. 67). Construct a photo sketch. Label the prominent features of the image.

2.10 GIS and information databases

Computers in geography

When computers were first introduced in the 1950s they were very large and expensive. Today, much faster and more powerful computers are available for a fraction of the cost. Many are now small enough to sit on your desk or lap. Others can fit in the palm of your hand. Internet-linked computers allow information, images and sound to be transferred across the globe in a fraction of a second.

Geographers use computers for a wide variety of tasks, including:

- writing reports using a word-processing program
- undertaking research via the Internet
- gathering information from online databases; for example, the archives of major newspapers and the Australian Bureau of Statistics
- using data entered on spreadsheets to construct graphs
- using tables and spreadsheets to record data collected in the field
- preparing PowerPoint presentations
- developing websites to share the fieldwork and other activities with a worldwide audience
- communicating with other geographers via email
- accessing the online catalogues of large public libraries
- locating places using online maps.

Geographical information systems

Geographical information systems (GIS) are changing the way geographers undertake their investigations. They are computer-based systems that enter, store, manage, analyse and present data. They

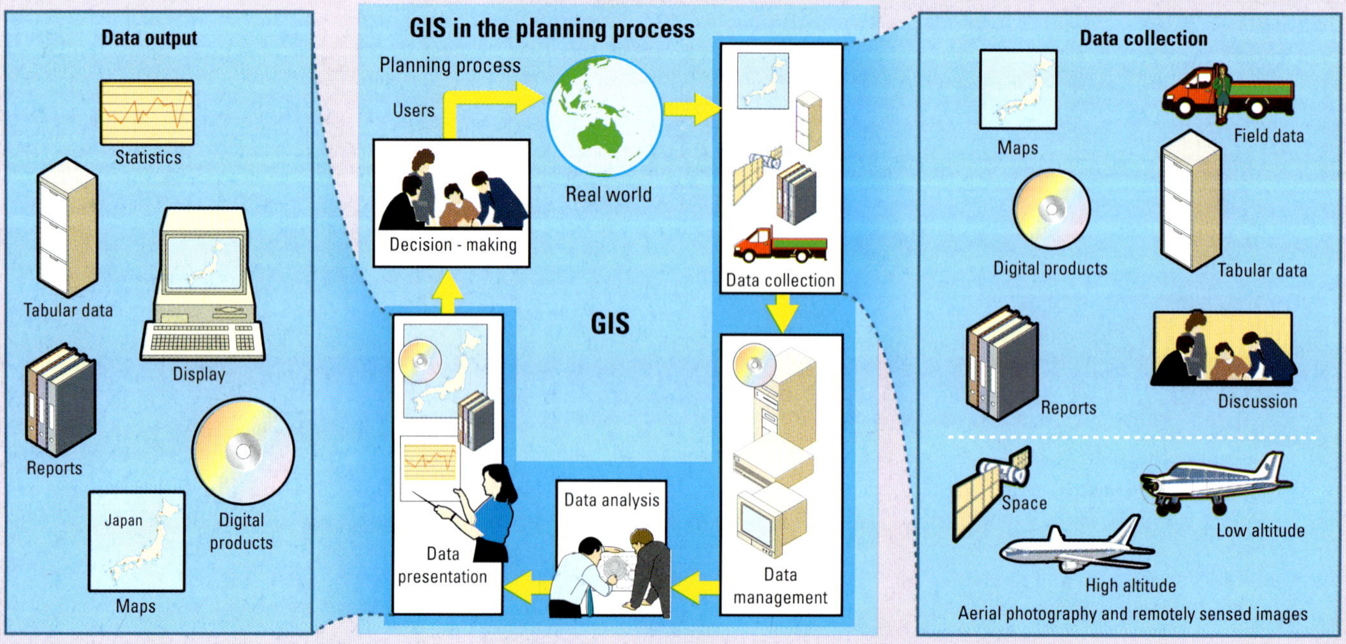

Figure 2.10a Geographical information systems (GIS) in the planning process.

combine digital data (such as maps, aerial photographs and satellite images) with geographical information from other sources to create a variety of products that decision-makers use in the planning process.

Businesses and individuals that use GIS include retailers, property developers, mining engineers, management consultants, military strategists, forecasters and environmental consultants.

The GIS process is explained in Figure 2.10a.

Information databases

An information database is computer software that typically consists of a database of information and tools to make the most out of that information. One of the best examples of this type of software is Census 2001 Explorer, published by PMP Software. The CD-ROM-based package contains the complete Census 2001 data collected by the Australian Bureau of Statistics. It also contains additional behavioural and lifestyle data supplied by Roy Morgan International, Australia's largest independent research company.

Census 2001 Explorer enables geographers to learn about people and their social environment and to make comparisons on a suburb, statewide or national scale. Sets of data taken from spreadsheets can be converted into maps using the built-in map generator (see Figure 2.10b). Data can also be presented in a graphic form (see Figure 2.10c).

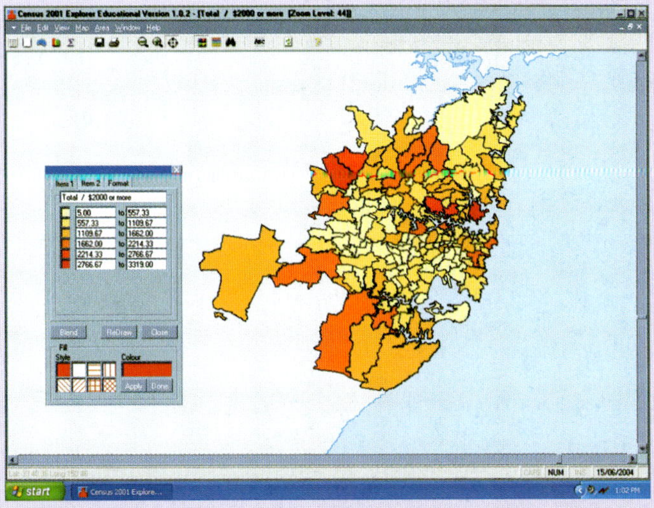

Figure 2.10b A map of Sydney showing the distribtution of people earning more than $2000 per week. Created by Census 2001 Explorer's built-in map generator.

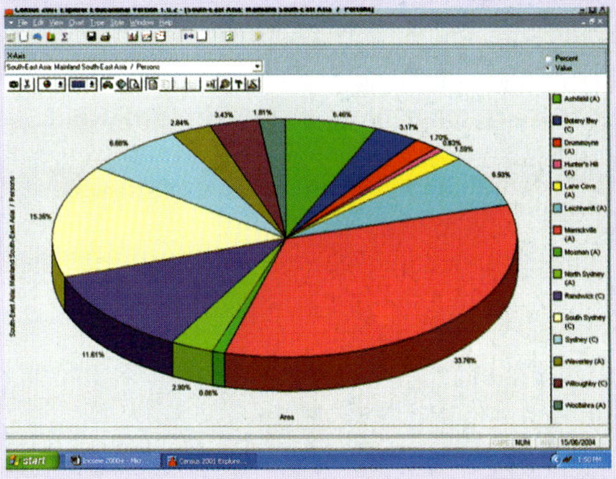

Figure 2.10c A pie graph showing the distribution at Asian–born residents in selected Sydney suburbs, generated from data available on Census 2001 Explorer.

Working geographically

1 **Thinking about technology** Study the list of tasks geographers use computers for. How many of these tasks are you familiar with? How many have you undertaken?

2 **Writing task** Use the information in Figure 2.10a to write a report on how GIS are used in the planning process.

3 **Library research** Investigate the range of databases available in your school library. Which ones are likely to be of interest to geographers? What types of geographical information do they contain?

Understanding the text

1 Explain what a geographical information system is.

2 What can databases, such as Census 2001 Explorer, be used for?

UTT worksheet 2.10

2.11 Using the Internet

Useful Internet sites ICT

There are hundreds of sites that geography students will find useful. The websites of the following organisations are just some of these.

- Australian Conservation Foundation
- Australian Bureau of Statistics
- Bureau of Meteorology
- Greenpeace
- New Internationalist
- NASA: Earth Observatory
- National Geographic
- News Limited
- New Scientist
- Sydney Morning Herald
- UNESCO
- World Bank
- World Resources Institute
- World Wide Fund for Nature

Cyber terrorism: key Internet servers hit by attack

Nine of the 13 computers servers that manage global Internet traffic were crippled by a powerful electronic attack this week.

An official described last Monday's attack as the most sophisticated and large scale assault against these crucial computers in the history of the Internet.

The 13 computers are spread geographically across the globe as a precaution against physical disasters and are operated by US government agencies, universities, corporations and private organisation.

CNN website, Washington (AP), 23 October 2002

The *Internet* is a worldwide computer-based information system. It consists of many interconnected computer networks, each of which may link tens, hundreds or even thousands of computers. The system allows us to access and share vast amounts of information. With the introduction of the Internet, finding up-to-date geographical information is easier than it has ever been. The term 'Internet' is derived from INTERnational NETwork.

The Internet has doubled in size every nine to fourteen months since it was developed in the late 1970s. In 1981 only 213 computers were connected to the Internet. By 2000 the number had grown to more than 100 million. The current number of people who use the Internet can only be estimated. One survey found that there were 61 million Internet users worldwide at the end of 1996, 148 million at the end of 1998, and 407 million by the end of 2000. The number of users had doubled again, to over 800 million, by the end of 2002.

Some of the main features of the Internet are discussed below.

The *World Wide Web* (WWW) is an information retrieval system linking Internet sites or documents. This is made possible by using a special coding language (HTML), which enables links to be placed within documents. These 'links' take the form of underlined or coloured location 'addresses'. For example, the address of the National Geographic website is <http://www.nationalgeographic.com>.

You can locate information on the World Wide Web in the following ways:

- If you already know the address of the site you wish to visit you can type it into your computer and then click on the Go button. If you have typed in the address correctly the selected site should appear on your screen. You can then 'navigate' the site by using your mouse and cursor.
- If you don't have an address you can find information by 'surfing the Web'; that is, using a search engine, such as Yahoo! or Sherlock. Enter the topic you wish to investigate and then click on the Search button. The search engine will list all the sites relevant to the selected topic. You can then work your way through these sites until you find the information you are looking for.

Each page of information has its own unique *uniform resource locator* (URL). You can then *download* the information; copy and print images; and send and receive text, images and sound. You can even publish your own web pages. Figure 2.11a outlines one model of Internet research.

Electronic mail (email) is a text-based message from one Internet user to another user, or group of users, on a mailing list. Documents and images can be sent with emails as *attachments*.

Newsgroups are the means by which information about specific topics or issues can be distributed to a group of subscribers. Examples are headline alerts from news organisations, such as CNN, and snow updates from your favourite ski resort.

Extension worksheet ICT 2.8
Extension worksheet ICT 2.9
Extension worksheet ICT 2.10
Extension worksheet ICT 2.11
Extension worksheet ICT 2.12

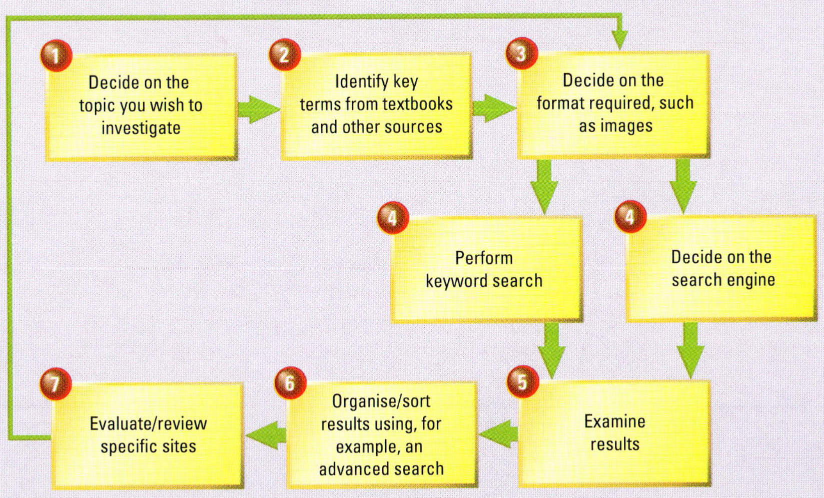

Figure 2.11a An example of an Internet search strategy.

Table 2.11a Classification of websites and the reliability of each type

Classification/meaning	Reliability
.org—Organisation	These sites are likely to reflect the perspective of the organisation they promote
.gov—Government	Generally reliable
.edu—Educational institution	Generally reliable
.com—Commercial	Variable—these sites are generally business-based, but .com can be used by almost any group or organisation and the site's reliability depends on the business itself

The Internet has made it possible for people all over the world to communicate with one another quickly and cheaply. Unlike radio and television, the Internet does not have a centralised distribution system. Instead, someone who has Internet access can communicate directly with anyone else on the Internet, make information available to others, find information provided by others, or sell products with a minimum of overhead cost.

The information divide

The revolution in information and communication technologies (ICT) has increased the divide between the world's rich and poor. Eighty-five per cent of Internet users live in the countries of the developed world.

Reliability of information

When using the Internet we need to keep in mind that the material we find may be unreliable or from biased sources. It is advisable to check sources and consider the extent to which you can have confidence in the information obtained.

Understanding the text

1. What is the Internet?
2. From what is the term 'Internet' derived?
3. List the main features of the Internet.
4. What is the World Wide Web? Identify the feature that enables a Web user to access different documents and websites.
5. Explain how the Internet differs from traditional broadcasting media.
6. Why is it important to check the source of the information you find on the Internet?

UTT worksheet 2.11

Working geographically

1. **Constructing graphs** Use the data describing the growth of the Internet to construct a simple line graph showing the rate of increase in Internet use (see Unit 2.13).
2. **Internet research** Study Figure 2.11a. Select a geographical concept or issue you wish to investigate and use the model to structure your research. Prepare a short oral report or PowerPoint presentation to communicate your findings.
3. **Thinking geographically** Study the box 'The information divide'. To what extent has the revolution in ICT increased the divide between the world's rich and poor?
4. **Group work** In groups, brainstorm the impact that a successful terrorist attack on the servers that manage global Internet traffic would have on the way the world operates. Share your group's findings with the rest of the class.

2.12 Using statistics

Table 2.12a World population growth, 1950–2050		
Year	Population (million)	Average annual rate of increase (%)
1950	2555	1.47
1955	2780	1.89
1960	3040	1.33
1965	3346	2.08
1970	3708	2.07
1975	4087	1.74
1980	4455	1.69
1985	4850	1.68
1990	5275	1.58
1995	5685	1.38
2000	6079	1.23
2005*	6449	1.12
2010*	6812	1.06
2015*	7172	0.98
2020*	7516	0.87
2025*	7835	0.77
2030*	8129	0.69
2035*	8401	0.61
2040*	8650	0.55
2045*	8878	0.48
2050*	9079	0.43

*Projection
Source: US Bureau of the Census, 2003

Useful websites ICT

The Internet is also a source of up-to-date statistical information. Some useful websites include those of the:

- World Resources Institute
- World Bank
- United Nations
- Australian Bureau of Statistics
- Bureau of Meteorology.

Statistics such as those in this unit and throughout this book are very useful to geographers. They can be used to help describe the location, size and distribution of the features that form patterns over the earth's surface. As Unit 2.13 shows, they can be converted into a graphic form.

Sources of statistics

Statistics can come from many different sources. *Fieldwork*, for example, can produce statistics from counts of traffic flows or housing types, or from responses to interviews of shoppers, residents or park users. *Weather observations* taken over a period of time are another source of useful statistics.

Many organisations publish statistics that geographers use. International bodies such as the United Nations and World Bank are a major source of information, as are organisations such as the World Resources Institute and the Population Reference Bureau. In Australia an important and reliable source of statistical data is the Australian Bureau of Statistics. Through a national *census* (conducted every five years) it collects data on population and other areas of interest, such as employment, manufacturing, agriculture, tourism and trade. The Bureau of Meteorology is another valuable source of statistics. It collects data on weather and climate in Australia.

Using statistics

Statistics can help describe features, situations and trends more exactly. See the following examples.

Table 2.12a outlines the growth in the human population since 1950 when there were just 2.5 billion people. In 2000 the world's population passed 6 billion. By 2050 the world's population is projected to exceed 9 billion. The rate of population increase peaked in the 1960s at over

Table 2.12b Distribution of the world's population		
Area	Population (million)	Percentage
World	6314	–
Developed world	1202	19.0
Developing world	5112	81.0
Region		
Africa	861	13.6
North America	323	5.1
South and Central America	540	8.6
Asia	3831	60.7
Europe	727	11.5
Oceania	32	0.5

Source: *2003 World Population Data Sheet*, Population Reference Bureau

Table 2.12c Climate statistics for New Delhi, India

Month	J	F	M	A	M	J	J	A	S	O	N	D	Year
Average temp. (°C)	14	17	22	29	33	34	31	30	29	26	20	15	25 av.
Rainfall (mm)	23	20	15	10	15	68	200	200	123	19	3	10	706 total

2 per cent a year. It has since slowed to 1.18 per cent and is expected to keep declining. This data is shown in graphic form in Figures 2.13b and 2.13c (pp. 50–1).

Table 2.12b shows the global distribution of the world's population. Only one in five people live in developed countries. Asia accounts for 60 per cent of the world's population. Africa accounts for 13.6 per cent. This data is shown in graphic form in Figure 2.13d (p. 51).

Table 2.12c shows key climate statistics for New Delhi, India. These figures have been processed to produce the average temperature and rainfall for each month. A yearly average for temperature has been calculated using the monthly averages. A total rainfall figure has been calculated by adding up all twelve months. A temperature range (that is, the difference between the highest and lowest monthly temperature) has been calculated. Presenting climate data in this way makes it easy to compare New Delhi with other places in the world. The climate graph for New Delhi is shown in Figure 2.13a (p. 50).

Table 2.12d shows the population of the world's twenty largest urban centres. With 31.2 million people Tokyo-Yokohama is the world's largest city. Thirteen of the cities are located in developing countries. This data is shown in a graphic form in Figure 2.13f (p. 52).

Table 2.12d The world's 20 largest urban centres, 2004

Metropolitan area/ country	Population
Tokyo-Yokohama, Japan	31.2
New York-Philadelphia, USA	30.4
Mexico City, Mexico	21.5
Seoul, South Korea	20.1
Sao Paulo, Brazil	19.2
Jakarta, Indonesia	18.2
Osaka-Kobe-Kyoto, Japan	17.6
Delhi, India	17.4
Mumbai, India	17.3
Los Angeles, USA	16.9
Cairo, Egypt	16.2
Calcutta, India	14.4
Manila, Philippines	14.0
Buenos Aires, Argentina	13.2
Moscow, Russia	12.6
Shanghai, China	12.2
Rio de Janeiro, Brazil	11.6
Paris, France	11.4
Rhine-Ruhr, Germany	11.4
Tehran, Iran	11.2

Source: World Gazetteer

Extension worksheet 2.2

Working geographically

1 **Interpreting statistics** Study Table 2.12a and then complete the following questions:
  - **a** What was the world's population in 1960?
  - **b** During what period of time did the world's population first exceed 5 billion and then 7 billion?
  - **c** Describe, using data, the trends in the average annual rate of population increase.

2 **Interpreting statistics** Study Table 2.12b and then complete the following questions:
  - **a** Which region of the world has the smallest share of the world's population?
  - **b** What is the combined share of the world's population found in North and South America?
  - **c** What proportion of the world's population live in developing countries?

3 **Challenge: Research task** Study Table 2.12c. Undertake research to locate the climate data for your local community. Write a paragraph comparing this data with that of New Delhi. Compare both temperature and rainfall. Which place is hotter and when? Which place is colder and when? Which place is drier and when?

4 **Interpreting data** Study Table 2.12d. Note which cities are located in the developed and developing worlds (see Unit 14.1). What conclusion can you draw from this data?

5 **Internet research** Use the Internet to locate the websites of at least one of the organisations listed in the ICT box on page 48. Describe and record in your workbook the types of statistical data available at each site you access.

2.13 Drawing graphics

Presenting statistical information in a graphic form often makes it much easier to interpret. It can, however, be difficult to select the type of graphic that best suits your information and the purpose for which it is intended. The following guidelines will help.

Line graphs

Line graphs are useful for showing values that change over time or distance. Figure 2.13b is an example of a line graph. It shows the growth in world population since 1950 and projected growth to 2020.

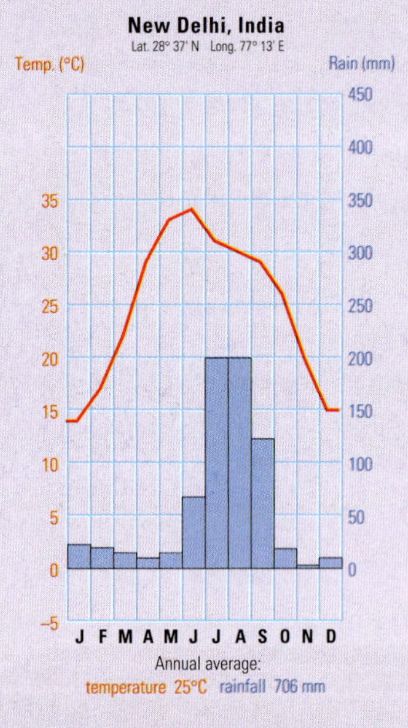

Figure 2.13a Climate graph. New Delhi, India.

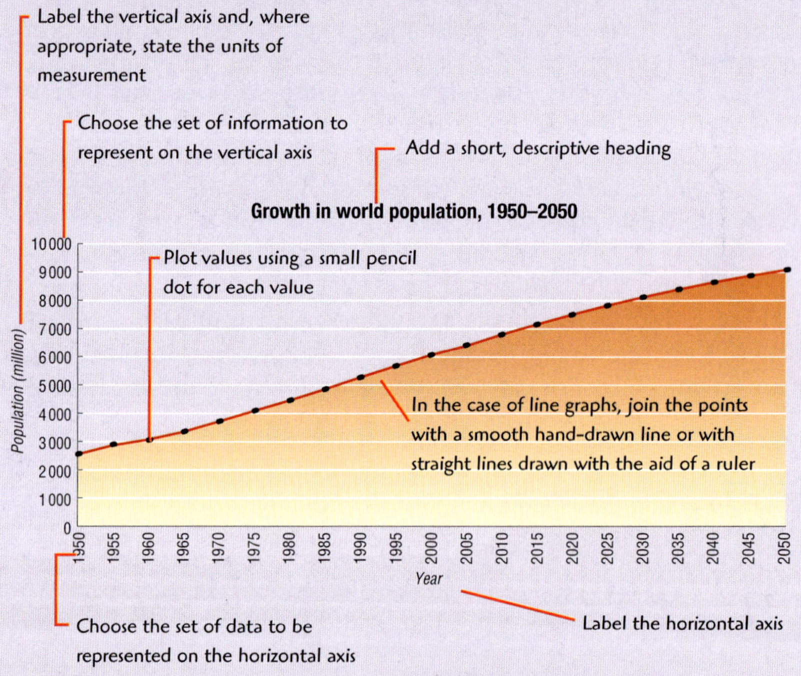

Figure 2.13b Line graph. Growth in world population, 1950–2050. Source: US Bureau of the Census, 2003.

Constructing graphs

ICT

Using Figure 2.13a as a model, construct a climate graph for New York (see the Skills box on p. 38). The data for this graph can be accessed at the WorldClimate website.

Using the statistics provided in Unit 2.12, use spreadsheet software (such as Excel) and the chart function of graphics or spreadsheet software to construct a variety of graph types. Make sure your graphs are correctly labelled and then paste them into your workbook. Compare your graphs with those constructed by other students.

Bar or column graphs

Bar or column graphs use horizontal or vertical bars to show information about the same feature. This information could come from several different places, as in Figure 2.13c which shows the average annual rate by which the world's population is increasing.

Sometimes column and line graphs can be combined, as in Figure 2.13a. Bars and columns can be given a three-dimensional effect to make their appearance more dramatic.

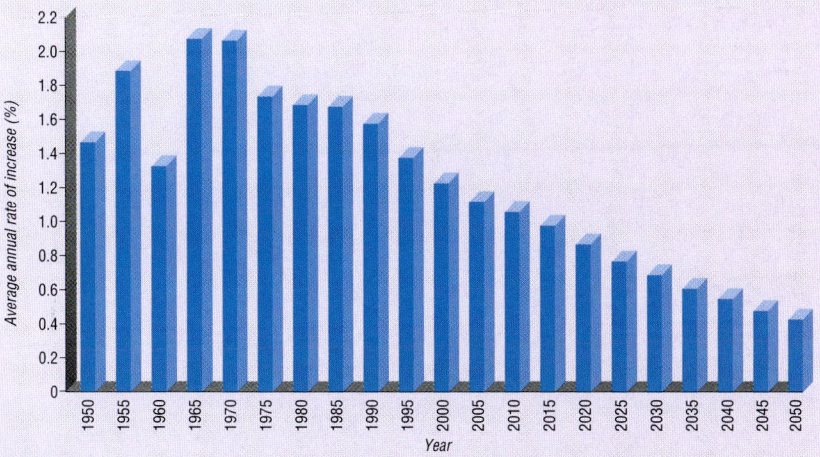

Figure 2.13c Column graph. World population: average annual rate of increase, 1950–2025. Source: US Bureau of the Census, 2003.

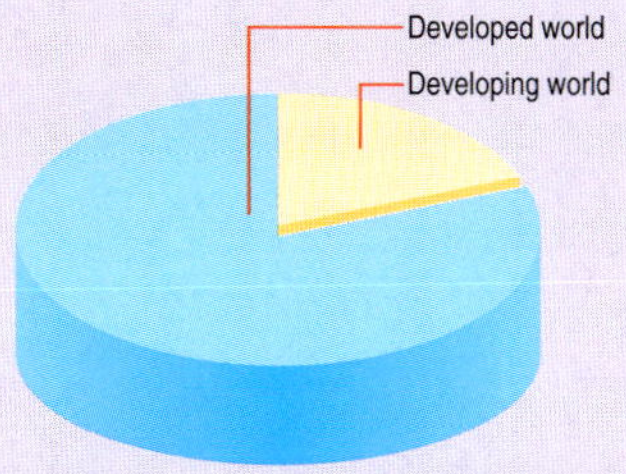

Figure 2.13d Pie graph. Distribution of the world's population: developed and developing countries, 2003. Source: *2003 World Population Data Sheet*, Population Reference Bureau.

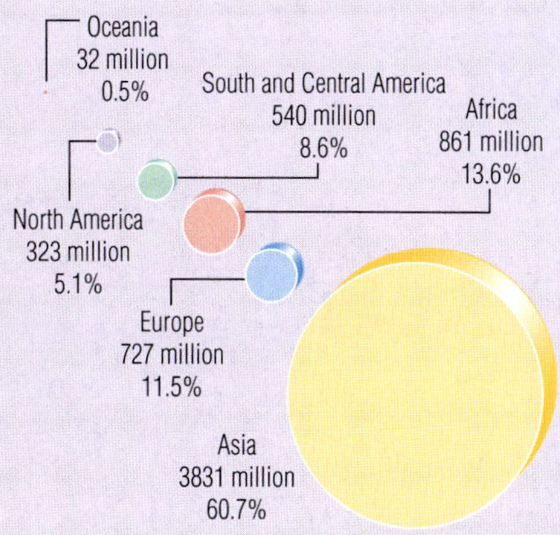

Figure 2.13e Proportional circle graph. Distribution of the world's population by region, 2003.

Pie graphs and proportional circles

Pie graphs, such as Figure 2.13d, are circles that are divided to show how separate parts make up a total amount. See the Skills box for instruction on how to construct a pie graph.

The size of circles can be varied to reflect the total amounts being drawn. These are known as *proportional circles*. Figure 2.13e is an example of a proportional circle graph. It shows the distribution of the world's population by region.

Skills

Constructing pie graphs

To construct a pie graph follow the steps below:

1 Draw a circle and then extend a line from its centre to the 12 o'clock position.
2 Convert the percentage value of each component to degrees by multiplying it by 3.6. For example, if the percentage was 10 per cent, this would represent 36 degrees on the pie graph; that is, $10\% \times 3.6 = 36°$.
3 List your converted values from the largest to the smallest. Categories that are not specific, such as 'others', should be placed at the end of your list.
4 Starting at 12 o'clock, mark in each segment using a protractor. Work in a clockwise direction, starting with the largest segment. The segment for a non-specific category (such as 'others') should be placed last even though it may not be the smallest segment.
5 Shade in and label each segment. It may be useful to provide a legend. If a legend is included it is not necessary to label the segments.
6 Add an appropriate title.

Computer-generated pie graphs

ICT

You can construct pie graphs using your computer (see the Skills box). Enter your data into spreadsheet software (such as Excel), highlight the information entered and select the appropriate chart type. Add the appropriate labels.

Note: You can construct a wide range of graph types using spreadsheet software and its graph creation function.

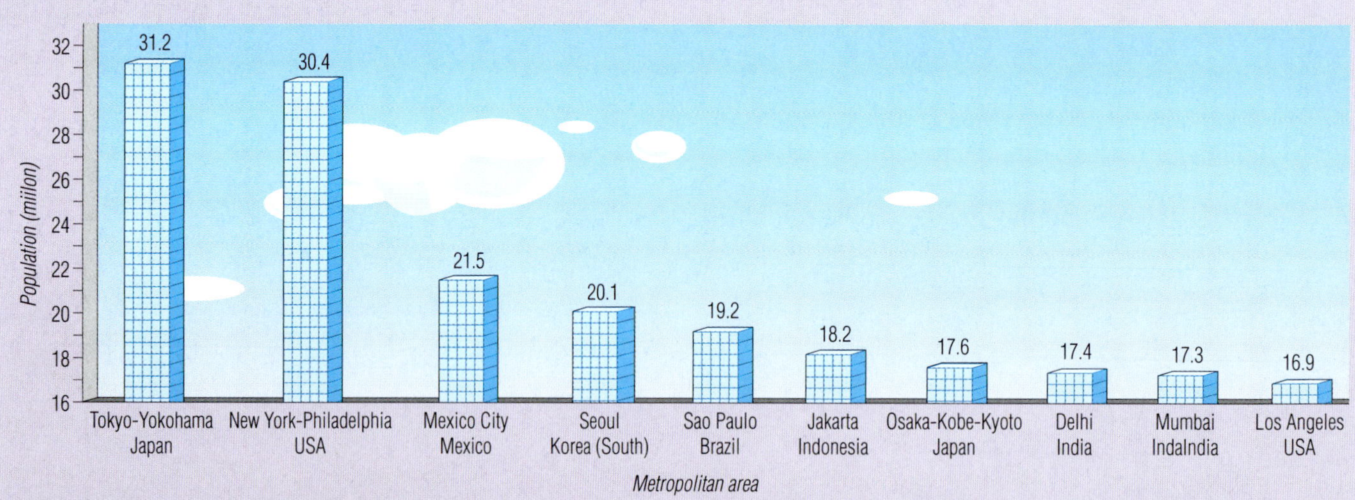

Figure 2.13f Picture graph. The world's largest urban centres, 2004. Source: World Gazetteer.

Understanding the text

1 Why do we choose to present statistical information in a graphic form?

2 What types of graphs are there?

UTT worksheet 2.13

Picture graphs

Picture graphs use *symbols* to represent values. The size of the symbol can vary according to the amount it represents. Alternatively, it may represent a set amount and be repeated to make up the required amount (see Figure 2.13f). Picture graphs can make reports and statistics very interesting since they attract attention.

Other graphics

Geographers use a large number of different types of graphics. These include *scattergraphs*, *flow maps* (see Figure 14.4b, p. 290) and *flow diagrams* (see Figure 2.11a, p. 47).

Graphics need to be drawn carefully with a pencil and ruler. Include printed labels, a title and, if possible, the source of the information. Computer-generated graphics can be very successful because they are sharp and have clear lines. These can be generated using spreadsheet software and can be 'pasted' into word-processed documents or PowerPoint presentations. Be sure your computer-generated graphics follow the guidelines shown in Figure 2.13b (p. 50).

Working geographically

1 **Investigating** Look through this book and identify at least three types of non-map graphics. Write a brief description of how information is presented in them.

2 **Presenting data** What would be the best method of presenting the following pieces of information?
   a the number of tourists visiting Bali between 1990 and 2003
   b the origin of tourists visiting Bali in 2002
   c the population of Australia, New Zealand, Papua New Guinea and Indonesia
   d the proportion of different types of motor vehicles using a busy street
   e the monthly average temperature and rainfall figures for Singapore

3 **Constructing graphs** Using data from Table 2.12d (p. 49), construct a graph comparing the population of Tokyo-Yokohama, Sao Paulo, Delhi, Los Angeles and Moscow.

4 **Constructing graphs** Study the Skills box on how to construct a pie graph (p. 51). Then construct a pie graph showing the known causes of animal extinctions since 1600 using the following data: species introduction 39 per cent, habitat destruction 36 per cent, hunting 23 per cent and other 2 per cent.

2.14

Communicating geographical information

Oral reports

During your study of geography, you may be asked by your teacher to present the findings of your research as an oral report. Your oral report may even be assessed. Developing and practising your public speaking skills will help you do well.

The fear of talking to a large group is very common, and there are ways of overcoming it. One way is to carefully plan and prepare your presentation.

1 Be sure that you understand clearly the purpose of the report you are presenting. The most common purpose of an oral report is to inform an audience.
2 Know your audience. The more you know about your audience the more appropriate and focused your oral report will be. For example, if your audience already has a good knowledge of the topic you may choose to leave out information they are already familiar with.
3 Ensure your information is well organised. The most successful oral reports have a structure similar to an extended response or essay; that is, they have an introduction, a body and a conclusion (see the box).

Using speaker's notes

Rather than simply reading a prepared speech, it is often more effective to use a series of words or phrases that act as cues for your presentation. Make sure, however, that the words and phrases are written in large print and that there are not too many points on a page. It is also a good idea to number the points so that you do not get out of sequence. Different colours and highlighter pens may prove useful as well.

Delivering your oral presentation

To avoid stagefright, check through these points before delivering your report:

- know your topic thoroughly
- use numbered points on speaking cards
- practise your speech several times
- visualise yourself as relaxed and calm
- do not rush your presentation
- use appropriate gestures and maintain good posture
- use a range of visual aids
- make eye contact with members of the audience
- vary your voice throughout your presentation
- stand still.

Structure of an oral report

Introduction
The first part of your oral report tells the audience what your topic is. Do this in a way that gains the audience's attention and relaxes you. A good way to do this is to make a formal opening statement that outlines the focus of your report. Show some visual material as you do this, such as a slide projection or a video extract. You could use humour to gain the audience's attention.

Body
The body of the oral report should be the focus of your presentation. Develop your main ideas and support them with examples, quotations, analogies and statistical information. These will make your presentation more interesting and memorable.

Conclusion
Let your audience know when you are nearing the end of your presentation by using words such as 'in conclusion' or 'to sum up'. In your conclusion, briefly highlight the main points you have made during your presentation.

Figure 2.14a Presenting an oral report.

2.15 COMMUNICATING GEOGRAPHICAL INFORMATION
Writing

The ability to communicate your knowledge and understanding of geography in writing is a very important skill that you need to practise. The *text types* most commonly used in geography include reports, explanations, expositions and discussions.

Reports

Purpose

A *report* is used to classify and describe a geographical feature or process. It usually contains facts about the feature or process.

Structure

The three parts of a report are:

- A general *introductory statement* introducing the subject of the report—it can be a short description or a definition.
- A *series of paragraphs* about the feature or process—each new paragraph usually describes just one aspect of the feature or process and begins with a topic (or preview) sentence. Use words or phrases that allow for comparisons.
- A conclusion that summarises the information presented.

Explanations

Purpose

An *explanation* is used to explain how or why something occurs.

Structure

The three parts of an explanation are:

- A *general statement* about the geographical feature or process being written about—the general statement serves as an introduction.
- A *series of paragraphs* that tell us how or why—these should be in sequence so that the reader builds up their understanding of the feature or process. Use words that show cause and effect.
- A *concluding paragraph*—this signals to the audience that the explanation is finished.

Discussions

Purpose

A discussion is used to present the different opinions on a particular issue or topic; that is, the arguments for and against.

Structure

The three parts of a discussion are:

- An *introductory paragraph* that introduces the issue or topic being discussed—it can contain a question or state the writer's view.
- A *series of paragraphs* that outline the *arguments for and against* the issue or topic. Use words that show a comparison or contrast and words that link arguments.
- A *conclusion* that sums up the issue and outlines the writer's own point of view or recommendation.

REPORT SCAFFOLD

Introductory statement: ______

Description: ______

Description: ______

Description: ______

Description: ______

Figure 2.15a Report scaffold.

EXPLANATION SCAFFOLD

General statement: ______

Explanation (how and why) sequence: ______

Figure 2.15b Explanation scaffold.

DISCUSSION SCAFFOLD

Introductory paragraph: ______

Arguments for: ______

Arguments against: ______

Summary and recommendation: ______

Figure 2.15c Discussion scaffold.

Expositions

Purpose

An *exposition* argues only one side of an issue. It is used to persuade the reader by presenting a particular point of view.

Structure

The three parts of an exposition are:

- An *introductory statement* that gives the writer's point of view and previews the arguments he or she will present to support his or her position—a question or emotive statement is sometimes used to gain the reader's attention.
- A *series of arguments* that aim to persuade the reader—a new paragraph is used for each new argument and each new paragraph begins with a topic sentence that introduces the new argument.

Use words that link cause and effect.

- A *conclusion* that sums up the arguments presented and reinforces the writer's point of view.

EXPOSITION SCAFFOLD

Introductory statement: ______

Argument 1: ______

Argument 2: ______

Argument 3: ______

Argument 4: ______

A summary of your view on this issue: ______

Figure 2.15d Exposition scaffold.

Writer's word bank

The following word lists will help you improve your writing.

Words that compare
also
as
as do
like
similar to
the same as

Words that contrast
alternatively
although
but
by constrast
differs from
however
instead
nevertheless
on the contrary
on the other hand
rather
whereas
yet

Words for presenting another argument
also
as well as
besides
furthermore
in addition to
likewise
moreover
not only

Words for introducing examples
as shown by
for example
for instance
including
such as
these include

Words that show cause and effect
an effect of
an outcome of
as a result of
because
brought about
caused by
consequently
contributed to
creates
despite this
due to
even though
gives rise to
leads to
otherwise
produced by
results in
so
therefore

Words that show time and sequence
after a while
afterwards
at this point
before
finally
first (second, etc.)
here
in the end
lastly
meanwhile
next
next time
now
previously
shortly
soon
then
when

Getting technical

Scaffolds help you organise your information in a way that makes your writing task easier. They help you to answer two important questions: Where do I start? What do I do next?

2.16 COMMUNICATING GEOGRAPHICAL INFORMATION
Multimedia presentations

Mastering ICT

ICT

To find out more about:
- developing a PowerPoint presentation
- constructing websites
- using email and searching the Internet

access the actden (Digital Education Network) website.

Working geographically

Using software Prepare a sample PowerPoint slide summarising the general guidelines for PowerPoint presentations given in Table 2.16a. Add appropriate images, graphics and/or sound effects.

Extension worksheet ICT 2.4

Multimedia presentations combine various types of media, including text, graphics, clip art, digital photographs, video, sound effects and music.

The most widely used multimedia presentation tool is PowerPoint. PowerPoint is a powerful software tool used for presenting information in a slide-show format. Text, charts, graphs, sound effects and video are just some of the elements you can incorporate into a PowerPoint

Table 2.16a A guide for successful PowerPoint presentations

General guidelines

- Plan your PowerPoint presentation carefully
- Use a common design template throughout your presentation
- Limit the number of slides you use—too many slides can bore and confuse your audience
- Include only essential information
- Standardise the position, colours and styles of headings, text and images
- Use colours that contrast; for example, yellow or white text on a dark blue background works well
- Be consistent with sound effects, transitions and animations

Text guidelines

- Generally, it is best to have no more than six lines of text per slide, with no more than six words a line
- Avoid long sentences
- Use a larger font to highlight key points
- Select a suitable font size—in the range from 18 to 48 point
- Avoid fancy fonts as they can be hard to read
- Be sure the text contrasts with the background
- Avoid words in all capital letters as they are hard to read
- Avoid abbreviations and acronyms; for example, approx. and WTO

Clip art, photographs and graphics

- Ensure these balance the slide and enhance and complement the text, not overwhelm it
- Present any data as a graphic
- Include no more than two graphics per slide

Presenting your PowerPoint presentation

- Practise and time your presentation
- Distribute a printout of your presentation with spaces for note-taking
- Speak confidently and clearly
- Make your presentation available on the World Wide Web. PowerPoint allows you to turn your presentation into a ready-made web page. Go to 'Save as'. In the 'Save file as type' list select 'web page' and then 'Save'

presentation. A PowerPoint display is usually supported by an oral presentation (see Unit 2.14). A PowerPoint presentation is a great way to communicate geographical information, including the results of a research assignment or your fieldwork.

Figure 2.16a shows the main features of a PowerPoint presentation. Guidelines for a successful PowerPoint presentation are shown in Table 2.16a.

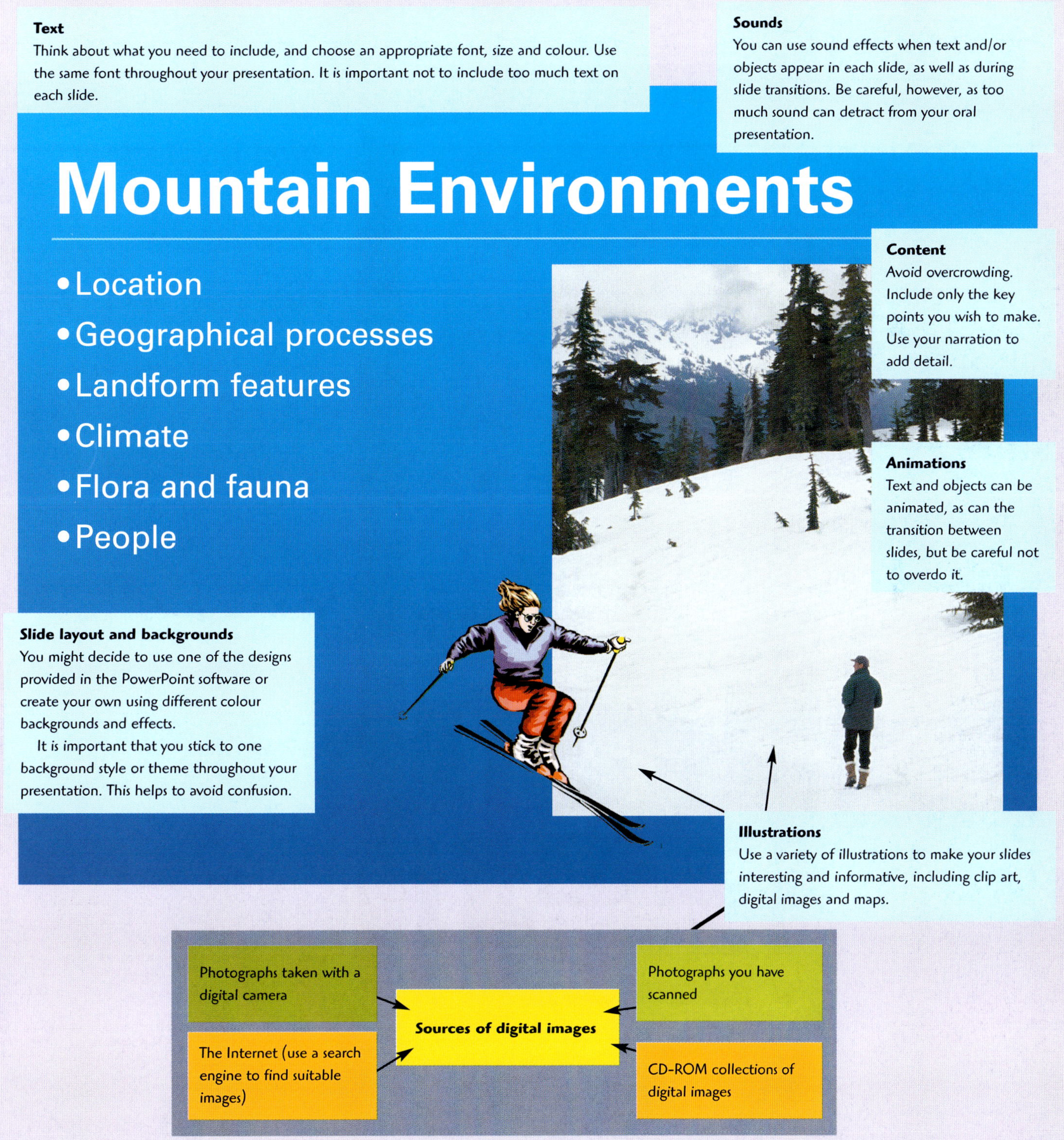

Figure 2.16a Key elements of a PowerPoint presentation.

2.17 Review and reflect

Chapter summary

In this chapter we have been introduced to many of the tools and skills used by geographers when they investigate the physical and human environment. We will have many opportunities to further develop and practise these skills as we work through the following chapters.

Activity 1

Geocrossword

Make an enlarged copy of the crossword. Then complete it using the clues below.

Across

1 The population of number of objects per unit area.

4 The flow of goods, people, information or energy from one place to another.

5 A set of questions used to gather information.

7 The general name given to maps showing borders of countries.

9 An essential feature of a map.

11 The air surrounding the planet.

13 The collection of data from the entire population.

14 A way of showing relief on maps (two words).

15 The spread or arrangement of geographical features on the earth's surface.

16 Atlas maps that illustrate a particular theme (two words).

Down

2 The height of a point or place above sea level.

3 The name given to a person who draws maps.

6 An essential feature of a map.

8 A book containing a collection of maps.

10 A place name associated with the Prime Meridian.

12 Shown on weather maps.

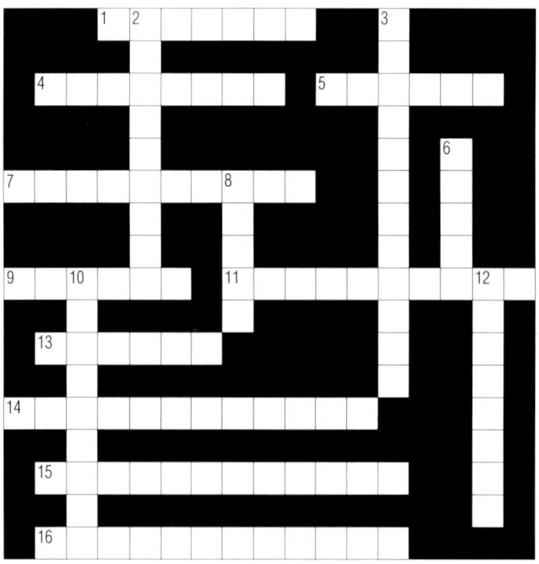

Activity 2

Using atlas maps

Using an atlas, complete the following tasks:

1 Locate and name ten thematic maps.

2 Name ten South American cities that have at least 1 000 000 people. In which countries are these cities? Are they mainly near the coast or are they inland?

3 Count the number of countries located in Africa. Name the largest of these countries.

4 Name the countries that share a common border with Russia.

5 Name the North American river that flows into the Gulf of Mexico.

6 Name a desert located in the state of California.

7 Name the five lakes that make up the Great Lakes of North America.

8 Name two land-locked seas located in Asia.

9 Name the continental landmasses divided by the Panama Canal and the Suez Canal.

10 Name the continent on which you would find the following:

- a the city of Bratislava
- b the Lina River
- c the Okavango Delta
- d Banff National Park
- e the Atacama Desert.

Foundation worksheet 2.2

Extension worksheet ICT 2.3

Extension worksheet 2.1

Extension worksheet ICT 2.5

Activity 3

Topographic mapping skills

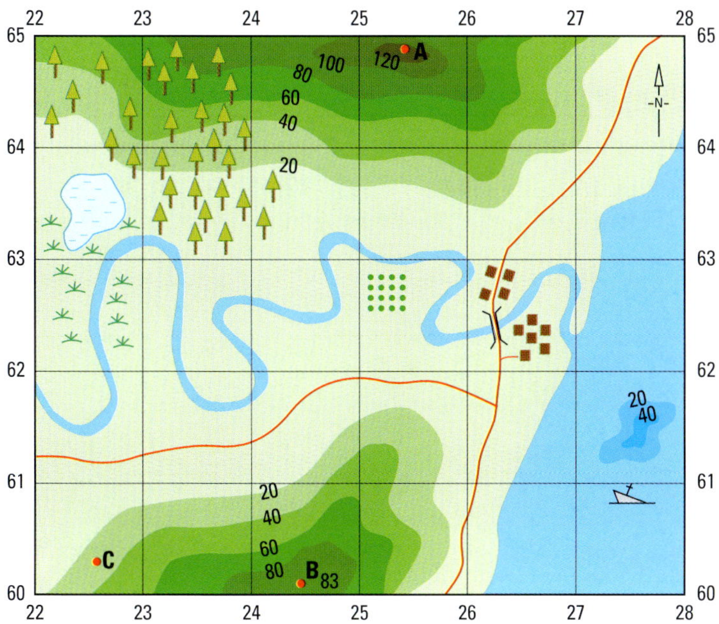

Legend

- Contours
- Road
- Bridge
- Building
- Pine plantation
- orchard
- lake
- wetland
- shipwreck

0 1 2 km

Contour interval 20 m

Study the map above and then answer the following questions:

1 What landform feature is found in AR2263?

2 In what area reference is the orchard located?

3 What is the grid reference of point C?

4 What features of the built environment are located at:
  a GR275608
  b GR263624?

5 What is the straight-line distance between point A and point B?

6 What is the direction of the bridge (AR2662) from the hill AR2460?

7 In what direction is the river flowing in AR2262?

8 What is the aspect of the slope in AR2564?

9 What is the height of the hill located in AR2564?

10 What is the height of point C above sea level?

11 What landuse activity is found in the northwest quadrant of the map?

12 What is the density of buildings in AR2662?

13 Estimate the area of the lake in AR2263.

14 Construct a cross-section between point A and point B. Use a vertical scale of 1 cm = 40 m.

Activity 4

Using ICT

Select one of the topics from the list below to research using the Internet and/or library. Produce a PowerPoint, or other type of multimedia, presentation providing a summary of the key points in the topic you have researched. (Unit 2.16 will assist you with this task.) Present your finished presentation to the class.

- types of maps
- latitude and longitude
- map projections
- showing relief on maps
- weather maps
- types of photographs

The following should be used as a guideline for your presentation.

- You have five minutes in which to give your presentation.
- Develop activities that you can use to teach your content. This may involve asking the audience questions or having them complete a worksheet. Avoid lecturing to your audience.
- Five to ten slides may be used in PowerPoint presentations but you are encouraged to integrate a range of multimedia resources.
- Use bullet points to provide a brief summary of each idea. Each point should be no more than two lines long.
- Use your talk to provide further detail on each point. Do not read from your presentation; it should only be used as a guide.
- Rehearse your oral presentation.
- Use pictures and animations sparingly so that they have an impact.

GeoMatch

GeoWords

GeoQuiz

Chapter test

Refer to the Reflection box on page 17.

Chapter 3

Our world

Introduction

Our world is incredibly complex. For this reason geographers often talk about the natural and human environments. The physical environment includes our natural surroundings: the earth's soil, water, air, sunlight and all living things. The human environment includes the social, cultural, economic and political systems created by people. In this chapter we focus on the key features of the physical environment and some important aspects of our human environment, including countries, large cities and agricultural landuses. We also consider the role of the World Heritage Convention in protecting the world's physical and cultural heritage.

Key questions

1 In what ways do the physical and human environments interact?
2 What are the forces shaping the earth's crust?
3 How many countries are there in the world today?
4 Why are people moving to large cities?
5 What is the difference between subsistence and commercial agriculture?
6 What is the role of the World Heritage Convention?

eGlossary

ICT Toolkit

GeoToolkit

Foundation worksheet 3.1

Big foot, small world

The rate at which people are using the earth's natural resources is unsustainable. Global warming, deforestation, soil erosion, species loss and declining water quality are the results of this overuse. At present humans overuse the earth's resources by 20 per cent. By 2050, if this trend continues, we will need two planets the size of earth to live **sustainably**.

Every person has a 'footprint'. The *ecological footprint* measures people's dependence on natural resources. It includes the total area of productive land and sea used to:

- grow food
- supply energy
- build roads and buildings
- grow forests for wood and paper
- dispose of waste.

We can reduce our footprint (and save money) by:

- switching off electrical appliances when they are not in use
- having shorter showers
- turning off lights when we are out of the room
- walking or cycling for short trips, such as going to school
- using public transport for longer trips
- recycling paper, cans and plastic containers
- promoting the use of wind power and solar energy
- buying a fuel-efficient car
- using a clothes line rather than a clothes dryer
- using double-glazing and insulation so less energy is used to heat and cool buildings.

The world's average citizen has an ecological footprint of 2.3 hectares. An Indian's footprint is 0.8 hectares compared to a Western European's 5, a North American's 10 and an Australian's 9.

Glossary of key terms

Alluvium Fine particles of silt deposited by rivers.

Commercial agriculture The use of energy, water and chemicals to produce food and other agricultural products for sale to other people.

Deforestation The large-scale removal of trees.

Desertification The process by which semi-arid areas become more arid due to inappropriate landuse.

Developed world The world's rich countries. Most are industrialised. Incomes are high. After fulfilling their everyday needs of water, food and shelter, most people have money left over for buying consumer goods and luxury items.

Developing world The world's poor and middle-income countries. In many of these countries the majority of people depend on subsistence farming. Although industry is increasing in some countries, in others it only makes a small contribution to the economy. For all but the few people who are very rich, there is a constant struggle to satisfy the basic necessities of life.

Erosion The wearing down, transportation and deposition of material by water, wind and ice.

Extensive agriculture The production of crops and animals for sale, rather than use by the producer.

Intensive agriculture Agricultural landuses that use relatively small areas of land farmed by large numbers of people with only limited use of machinery; or small areas of land used to produce crops and/or livestock using factory-like methods.

Landform A natural feature of the earth's surface; for example, a mountain, valley, lowland or volcano.

Landscape The overall appearance of an area resulting from the interaction of landforms, vegetation and soils together with human elements of the environment, such as transport networks, settlements, farms and factories.

Megacity A city with more than 10 million inhabitants.

National identity A population's view of itself, as well as the way people in other countries view that population.

Sovereignty A country's power to govern its own affairs and make its own decisions.

Subsistence agriculture Crops grown to meet the immediate needs of the producer's family.

Sustainable Meeting the needs of the present generation without affecting the ability of future generations to meet their needs.

Urbanisation The process by which an increasing proportion of a population lives in towns and cities.

Weathering The physical or chemical breakdown of rocks into smaller pieces.

World city A city that has developed into a centre of global economic and cultural significance.

World Heritage sites Sites of universal natural and cultural significance that are protected by an international agreement between nations.

3.1

USING ATLAS MAPS

Our physical world

Table 3.1a	Earth's dimensions
Surface area: 510 066 000 km^2	
Land surface: 148 326 000 km^2	
Water surface: 361 740 000 km^2	
Equatorial circumference: 40 075 km	

Table 3.1b Continent areas

Continent	Area
Asia	44 391 162 km^2
Africa	30 244 049 km^2
North America	24 247 038 km^2
South America	17 821 028 km^2
Antarctica	13 338 500 km^2
Europe	10 354 636 km^2
Australia	7 682 300 km^2

Table 3.1c Ocean and sea areas

Ocean/sea	Area
Pacific Ocean	165 384 000 km^2
Atlantic Ocean	82 217 000 km^2
Indian Ocean	73 481 000 km^2
Arctic Ocean	14 056 000 km^2
Mediterranean Sea	2 505 000 km^2
South China Sea	2 318 000 km2
Bering Sea	2 269 000 km^2

Table 3.1d River lengths

River	Length
Nile	6695 km
Amazon	6570 km
Mississippi–Missouri	6020 km
Chang	5471 km
Irtysh	5410 km
Huang	4840 km
Congo	4630 km

Working geographically

1 **Constructing graphs** Study Tables 3.1b–d, then complete the following tasks:

- **a** Construct a pie graph showing the relative size of the earth's continental landmasses.
- **b** Construct a pie graph showing the relative size of the oceans listed in Table 3.1c.
- **c** Construct a picture graph showing the length of the rivers listed in Table 3.1d.
- **d** On which continent would you find each of the rivers listed in Table 3.1d?

2 **Interpreting maps** Study Figure 3.1a. Construct a three-column table to show the elevation of the highest mountain on each continental

Extension worksheet 3.10

Figure 3.1a A physical map of the world.

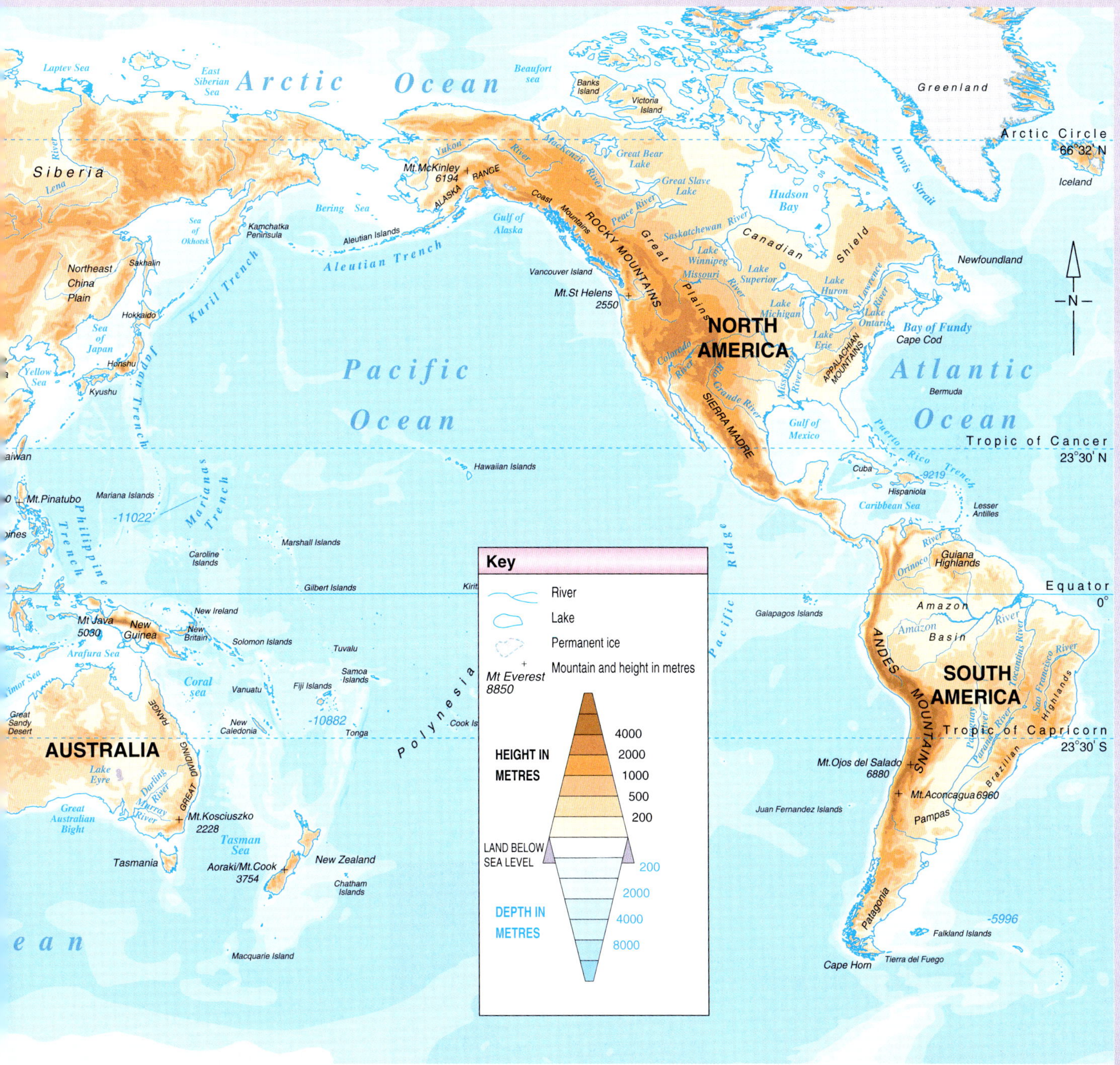

landmass. Use the following headings: 'continent', 'mountain' and 'elevation'. Using the information in the table you developed, construct a picture graph showing the relative size of the mountains listed in the table.

3 **Using atlas maps** Study Figure 3.1a, then complete the following tasks:

a Name the continent on which each of the following deserts is located: Sahara, Kalahari, Gobi and the Great Sandy Deserts.

b Name the continent on which each of the following mountain ranges is located: the Andes, Atlas, Appalachian, Ural, Alps, Rocky, Tian and Kunlun Mountains and the Sierra Madre, Himalayas and Alps.

c Name the oceans separating Africa from Australia, North America from Asia, and Europe from North America.

4 **Mapping** Locate and label all the physical features noted in activities 1–3 on an outline map of the world.

3.2 Processes shaping landforms

Figure 3.2a Changes in temperature have caused the outer layer of these rocks to crack and break away.

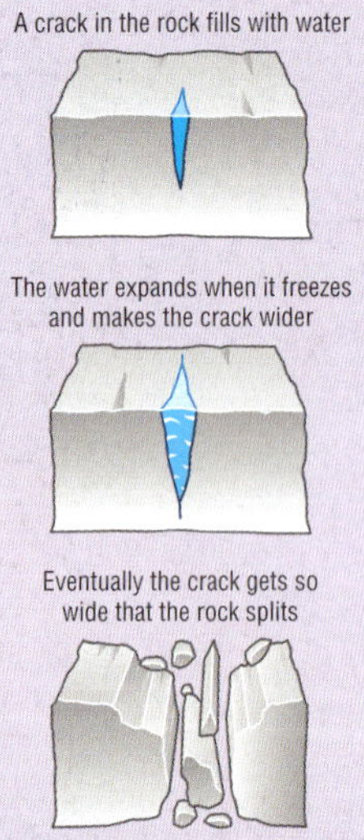

Figure 3.2b Freeze–thaw weathering.

Figure 3.2c Organic weathering.

The shape and appearance of the earth's **landforms** are constantly changing. The processes responsible for these changes are known as **weathering** and **erosion**.

What is weathering?

Weathering involves the physical or chemical breakdown of rocks into smaller pieces.

Physical weathering

There are three main types of physical (or mechanical) weathering. These are discussed below.

Temperature change

Rocks are heated by the sun during the day. At night, as temperatures fall, the rocks contract. Over time, this expansion and contraction causes cracks to appear and the rock begins to break down. This is called *exfoliation* and is common in deserts where daily differences in temperature are great (see Figure 3.2a).

Freeze–thaw action

Water collects in the cracks of rocks and when the water freezes it expands. This exerts pressure that is strong enough to widen and deepen the cracks. It may eventually cause fragments of rock to break off (see Figure 3.2b). This type of weathering is common in mountainous areas where large amounts of frost-shattering material, called scree, are found at the base of steep slopes.

Organic action

The roots of plants can force cracks in rocks to widen (see Figure 3.2c). Gradually the rock breaks down into smaller pieces.

Figure 3.2d When rainwater mixes with carbon dioxide it forms a weak acid that attacks limestone. This process formed these spectacular cave formations at Jenolan in New South Wales.

Active and passive agents of change

Weathering is sometimes called the *passive*, or *inactive*, agent of erosion because weathered material usually remains in place. Erosion and deposition (the laying down of transported material), on the other hand, are known as *active processes* because the material is moved from its original position or location.

Chemical weathering

When rainwater mixes with carbon dioxide (which is present in the atmosphere), it forms a weak acid that attacks many of the minerals contained in rock. It is especially effective in dissolving limestone. Limestone caves (including the Jenolan Caves in New South Wales—see Figure 3.2d) are a result of this type of weathering.

Rocks that contain iron are affected by a process known as *oxidation*. When oxygen and water come into contact with the iron in rock it changes its chemical make-up—it takes on a rusty appearance. The surface of the rock gradually decays.

Organic acids are produced when water mixes with decaying vegetation. These acids help to break down minerals in rocks.

What is erosion?

Erosion is the wearing down, transportation and deposition of material by water, wind and ice. The processes of erosion are:

- *attrition*—Rocks collide as they are transported and are worn into smoother, rounded stones.
- *abrasion/corrasion*—Material rubs against river banks or valley sides as it is transported, or is thrown against cliffs by the sea. This acts like sandpaper on the **landscape**, gradually wearing it away.
- *corrosion*—Some rocks, especially limestone, are dissolved by the natural acids in water and are carried away, suspended in the water.
- *hydraulic action*—River banks or cliffs can be worn away by the sheer force of water hitting them, or blasted apart as air is forced into cracks.

Agents of erosion

The agents of erosion are water, wind and ice.

Water

Running water

Running water is the most powerful agent of erosion, transportation and deposition. It is especially effective in very dry areas and where people have damaged the protective cover of vegetation that binds the soil together. When rain falls on exposed earth it erodes deep channels called gullies (see Figure 3.2e).

Rivers

Rivers shape the land by eroding, transporting and depositing material. In mountainous areas, rivers erode downwards, creating narrow, V-shaped valleys. Away from the mountains, valleys become wider and some of the river's load of sediment is deposited. Closer to the sea, the river meanders across a wide, flat plain, depositing fine particles of soil called **alluvium**. These alluvial soils are usually very fertile and are often used for agriculture.

Waves

Coastlines are constantly changing. Some are eroded by storm waves and are dominated by erosional landform features, such as headlands, cliffs, rock platforms and arches. Others advance towards the sea as waves deposit large amounts of sand. Such coasts are dominated by depositional features, such as sand dunes, sand bars and spits. Coastal procesess and landform features are examined in more detail in Chapter 9.

Understanding the text

1 Write a definition of 'weathering' using your own words.

2 Explain the difference between physical and chemical weathering.

3 Outline the three processes of physical weathering.

4 Explain how chemical weathering helps to weaken and break up rock.

5 Explain why weathering is described as a passive, or inactive, agent of landform development.

cd UTT worksheet 3.2

Figure 3.2e Death Valley, United States. A landscape deeply scarred by running water.

Figure 3.2f Wind-borne sand grains wear away the base of a desert rock leaving this pedestal-shaped feature.

Figure 3.2g Findel Glacier, Zermatt, Switzerland.

Wind

Wind is a very effective agent of erosion especially in areas where there is little or no vegetation. These include the world's deserts and those areas where people have damaged the land and destroyed the vegetation.

Close to the ground the wind picks up weathered rock material and 'sandblasts' larger rock features. This process is known as *abrasion*. It results in the formation of sculptured rock formations such as that shown in Figure 3.2f (p. 65).

On a larger scale, rock-strewn desert surfaces form when strong winds sweep away finer materials. This process is known as *deflation*. Landform features shaped by wind are examined in more detail in Chapter 12.

Ice

Glaciers are slow-moving rivers of compacted snow (glacial ice). They form when the compacted snow, which has gathered over many years, gradually moves downhill under the influence of gravity. Glaciers are very effective at eroding the land and transporting rock. Glacial processess and the landforms they produce are examined in more detail in Chapter 8.

Understanding the text

1. What is erosion?
2. Under what conditions is water the most effective agent of erosion?
3. Describe how the shape of a river valley changes as the river flows towards the sea.
4. Explain each of the following terms: attrition, abrasion, corrosion and hydraulic action.
5. Explain the difference between erosional coasts and depositional coasts.
6. What are glaciers?

UTT worksheet 3.2

Table 3.2a Weathering and erosion in summary

Weathering	
Physical weathering	*Chemical weathering*
• Temperature change • Freeze–thaw action • Organic action	• Weak acids (when rainwater and carbon dioxide mix) • Organic acids
Erosion	
Erosional processes	*Agents of erosion*
• Attrition • Abrasion/corrasion • Corrosion • Hydraulic action	• Running water, rivers and waves • Wind • Ice

Foundation worksheet 3.2 | Extension worksheet 3.1 | Extension worksheet ICT 3.4

Working geographically

1. **Constructing diagrams** Construct a series of diagrams like those in Figure 3.2b (p. 64) to explain how organic weathering occurs.
2. **Constructing diagrams** Construct a series of block diagrams to illustrate the development of the landform feature shown in Figure 3.2f (p. 65).
3. **Geographical drawing** Use an overhead projector to enlarge a selection of landform sketches from the text and other suitable sources. Make copies of them and add descriptions of how these features are formed.
4. **Challenge: Fieldwork** Do some fieldwork in an area with interesting landforms. Make field sketches or use photography to record your observations. Investigate and make notes on the processes responsible for the development of the different features observed. Mount a display of your completed work. See Chapter 4 for information relating to fieldwork.
5. **Developing a collage** Develop a collage of pictures illustrating the variety of landforms mentioned in this unit.

3.3

Using photographs

What landform is that?

1

2

3

4

5

6

Did U know?

- The world's largest gorge is the Grand Canyon in the United States. Carved by the Colorado River, it is 349 kilometres long and 20 kilometres wide at its widest point. It is more than 1.5 kilometres deep.
- The world's deepest canyon is the El Canon de Colca, in Peru, South America. It is 3 kilometres deep.
- With a length of 515 kilometres, the Lambert-Fisher Ice Passage in Antarctica is the world's longest glacier.
- The world's fastest-moving glacier is Greenland's Quarayaq Glacier. It moves 20 to 24 metres per day.

Working geographically

1 **Matching photographs and captions** Match the following captions with the photographs:
- **a** Mt Fuji, Japan
- **b** Atlantic coast, United States
- **c** fjord, Norway
- **d** Sahara Desert, Northern Africa
- **e** Grand Canyon, United States
- **f** Yellowstone National Park, United States.

2 **Interpreting photographs** Identify the photographs that best match each of the following statements:
- **a** landscape shaped by wind
- **b** landform shaped by ice
- **c** landform shaped by wave action
- **d** landform feature produced by volcanic action.

3 **Writing task** Write a sentence describing the type of landform shown in each photograph.

4 **Challenge: Writing task** Select one of the photographs and write a paragraph explaining the processes responsible for the formation of the landform features.

5 **Photo sketching** Select the photograph that appeals to you the most and construct a photo sketch of the landform features. (See Unit 2.9.)

3.4 Countries of the world

Getting technical

Sovereign countries are those that are self-governing.
Dependent territories are those that are ruled by another country.
Disputed territories are those where more than one country claims to exercise control over the territory.

The world is divided into many different countries. Each country has its own name, territory and borders. It also has a government that has the power or **sovereignty** to govern its own affairs, make and enforce laws, and control the movement of people and goods across its borders. Governments also have the power to declare war, sign treaties, exchange diplomatic representatives and join the United Nations. In mid-2003 there were 193 *sovereign countries*, sixty-one *dependent territories* and six *disputed territories*.

The definition of a country, then, is political not geographical. It depends on political independence and whether other countries recognise it as a country. It does not depend on geographical factors, such as size or location.

Identity and symbols

Like individuals, all countries are different. Each has its own history, institutions and culture.
A country's identity may consist of a population's view of itself, as well as the way people in other countries view that population. A country's identity is also created by a sense of belonging and pride felt by the population, and the symbols that are shared by all.

Each country has symbols that help to define its identity. Among the most common symbols are flags, emblems and coats of arms. Other common symbols include a country's unique plants and animals; its prominent landform features; its postage stamps, coins and banknotes; and any distinctive architectural achievements. Examples of symbols that define countries are France's Eiffel Tower, Australia's kangaroo and Sydney Opera House and the USA's 'stars and stripes' and Statue of Liberty.

Territories and borders

Each country exercises control (sovereignty) over the territory within its borders. These borders are usually recognised by other countries. There is a general agreement that people do not cross another country's borders without permission. To control these borders, countries have passport checks, border controls and sometimes even fences and gates at the busiest entry points. Some countries impose strict controls on people wishing to enter by only offering entry permits (called visas) with a strict time limit or for a specific purpose.

Borders are usually drawn up in one of three ways. First, they may follow a landscape feature, such as a river, coast or mountain range. The border between Spain and France, for example, is defined by the Pyrenees Mountains. Second, the border may be a straight line on a map following a line of latitude or longitude, such as the border between the United States and Canada. The third and most complex type of border may be based on historical or cultural factors. These borders may divide races, religions and languages. Disputes over territory or the location of borders are one of the most common forms of conflict between countries. For example, there is an ongoing territorial dispute between Israel and the Palestinians.

Figure 3.4a Israel's controversial 'security' wall is designed to isolate Palestinian communities.

Growing UN roll call

Since the United Nations was established in 1945, its membership has grown from just fifty-one countries to more than 190. The two biggest growth spurts occurred in the early 1960s, when more than two-dozen African countries declared their independence from their former colonial rulers, and the early 1990s, when the Soviet Union and Yugoslavia broke apart. In 2004 the United Nations had 191 members. The most recent to join were East Timor, which secured its independence after 450 years of foreign control, and Switzerland, which finally agreed to join the organisation following a national referendum in 2002.

The only two countries that are not members of the United Nations are Vatican City, which chose not to join, and Taiwan, which was replaced by the People's Republic of China in 1971.

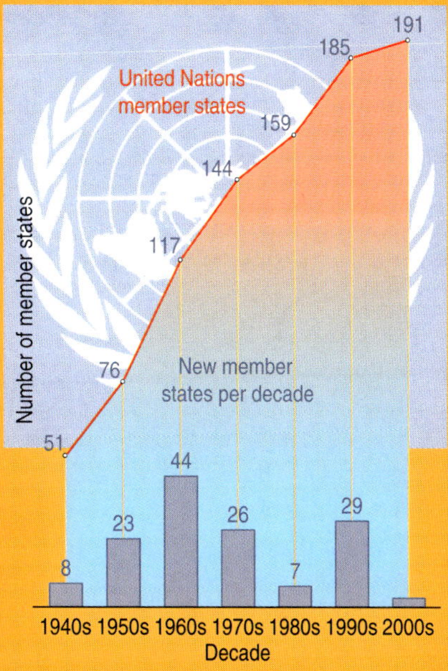

Figure 3.4b UN member states, 1945–2004.

Did U know?

- Africa is the continent with the most countries: fifty-four.
- Australia is the only continent occupied by just one country.
- Russia is the world's largest country. It has an area of 17 075 400 square kilometres.
- Vatican City is the world's smallest country. It has an area of just 0.44 square kilometres.

Understanding the text

1 What does the term 'sovereignty' mean?
2 What factors affect the way borders are determined?
3 What is meant by a 'country's identity'?
4 List the types of symbols that help define a country's identity.

UTT worksheet 3.4

Foundation worksheet 3.2

Extension worksheet ICT 3.5

Extension worksheet ICT 3.7

Extension worksheet ICT 3.6

Extension worksheet ICT 3.8

Working geographically

1 **Internet research** Access an online database, such as the US CIA's World Factbook. Select a country that interests you and undertake research. Prepare a short oral report and/or PowerPoint presentation on the country (see Units 2.14 and 2.16). Use the following headings: 'geography', 'people', 'government' and 'economy'. Other useful websites include:
- Infoplease
- Fact Monster
- Countries.com.

2 **Identifying national symbols** Identify the symbols that help define the country you selected in activity 1.

3 **Mapping an itinerary** Select an itinerary from a European travel brochure. On an outline map of Europe, mark the countries and cities visited. Repeat this activity using travel brochures from other parts of the world.

4 **Atlas activity: Writing task** Locate an atlas published in the 1930s or 1940s. Compare the political maps of Africa and Europe with those published in a recent atlas. Write two paragraphs outlining how the political maps of the two continents have changed over this period.

5 **Challenge: Internet research** Study the box 'Growing UN roll call'. Access the UN's website and write a paragraph about the role of the organisation. Make a list of its various agencies and explain what each is responsible for.

3.5 Large cities

Table 3.5a	The process of urbanisation

Pull factors

- Employment opportunities and the promise of higher standards of living
- Entertainment
- Medical facilities
- Educational opportunities

Push factors

- Landlessness and rural poverty
- War and civil disorder
- Intolerance of alternative lifestyles
- Desertification
- Lack of medical facilities
- Rapid population growth
- Lack of educational opportunity
- Transfer of land from subsistence to commercial (export-orientated) production

Large cities are one of the biggest impacts people have on the environment:

- Between 1950 and 2000 the number of people living in towns and cities increased from 200 million to 3 billion. By 2025, this number will have increased to 5.5 billion.
- The share of the earth's population living in towns and cities increased from just 14 per cent in 1900 to 50 per cent in 2000. By 2025 this will have increased to 61 per cent.
- In 1970, there were 109 cities with populations of more than 1 million. Today, there are 290.

The changes outlined above and illustrated in Figure 3.5a are the result of a process known as **urbanisation**: people moving from rural areas to large cities because of a number of push and pull factors. These factors are outlined in Table 3.5a.

Rates of urbanisation are highest in the countries of the **developing world** (see Figure 3.5c, p. 72). Poverty, overcrowding, pollution, traffic congestion and squatter settlements are often the result of this process. Authorities often find it impossible to meet the basic needs of new urban dwellers (see Table 3.5b). The urban poor experience both a low *quality of life* and a low *standard of living*.

The drift to cities also affects the rural areas from which people have moved. Usually the people who migrate are men between the ages of 15 and 45. This splits up families but, if the family goes too, it can have an even more severe effect. Often the elderly people who are left in the countryside are those who are least able to look after themselves (see Figure 3.5d).

Getting technical

Quality of life The happiness, well-being and satisfaction of a person. Among the many factors that influence quality of life are a person's family, health, income and access to services. To some people, these are more important than possessions.

Standard of living Many measures of a person's standard of living are to do with possessions, such as a house, a car or computers. These indicate a high standard of living but cannot guarantee a high quality of life.

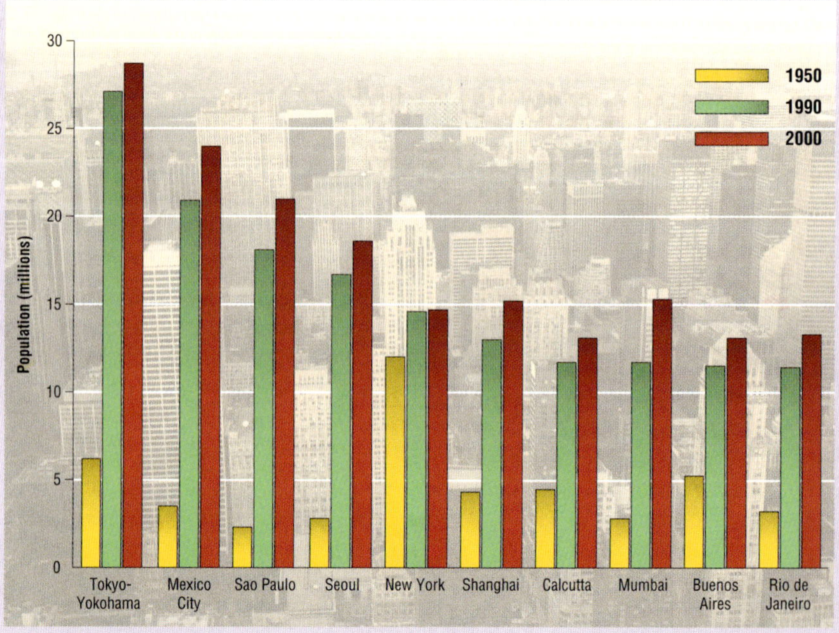

Figure 3.5a Large cities.

Sao Paulo, Brazil

One hundred years ago Sao Paulo was home to some 265 000 people; today there are more than 18 million people, nearly half of whom weren't born there.

Twenty per cent of the city's population live in its sprawling favelas (slums). Elsewhere, in the richest suburbs, the wealthy live in houses protected by fortress-like walls and security guards. For the rich and poor alike, daily life focuses on traffic congestion, crime and housing: three issues that highlight the problems that accompany rapid urbanisation. To avoid the city's congested roads the rich have taken to the air: Sao Paulo now having the second largest helicopter fleet in the world. Crime is a major problem. The city's murder rate of more than 9000 a year (compared with fewer than 700 in New York) results from slum violence and drug-related gang wars.

Sao Paulo's favelas are built on unclaimed land. Examples include steep hillsides, which are especially dangerous after heavy rain, and low-lying, mosquito-infested wetlands. Elsewhere, favelas have been built under motorway flyovers, in rubbish dumps and next to heavily polluted industrial areas.

Life in the favelas

- *Housing*—Usually this consists of simple, one-roomed shacks made out of scrap materials. They are crammed together as space is in short supply.
- *Sanitation*—There is no clean running water and no sewerage pipes. Streams flowing in and around the favela serve as a source of drinking water and a convenient place to dump rubbish and human waste. Water-related diseases spread quickly.
- *Disease*—This spreads quickly, and diseases such as dysentery and typhoid are common. Infant death rates are high.
- *Lack of security*—Crime rates are high. Because the squatters have no right to be on the land, it is not uncommon for authorities to bulldoze the shacks.
- *Employment*—Jobs are difficult to find. Wages are low and the journey to and from work can be a long one.
- *Education*—There are few formal schools, so literacy rates are low. Very young children are encouraged to earn money by street selling and shoe cleaning. Some beg on the streets. Many are exploited and subject to abuse.

Figure 3.5b Sao Paulo favelas.

Table 3.5b	Problems of large cities in the developing world
High unemployment	
Poverty	
Poor quality, overcrowded housing	
Failing transport, water supply and sewerage systems	
Too little water; water is often contaminated	
Overcrowded education and health facilities	
Loss of open space in urban areas to squatter settlements; felling of trees for firewood	
Inadequate enforcement of laws protecting the environment and public health	

Getting technical

Megacity A city with more than 10 million inhabitants. In 1950 there was just one megacity: New York. By 2000 there were fourteen such cities; based on current trends, in 2015 there will be twenty-one. Much of this growth has occurred in developing countries; those least equipped to meet the needs of their rapidly growing populations: employment, housing, transport, clean water, electricity and sewerage systems. The world's four largest cities are Tokyo-Yokohama, Mexico City, Sau Paulo (see box) and Seoul.

World city A city that has developed into a centre of global significance. Such cities exercise a level of economic and cultural control that extends well beyond the country in which they are located. Decisions made in these cities affect the well-being of people throughout the world. The most important of these cities include New York, London, Paris and Tokyo.

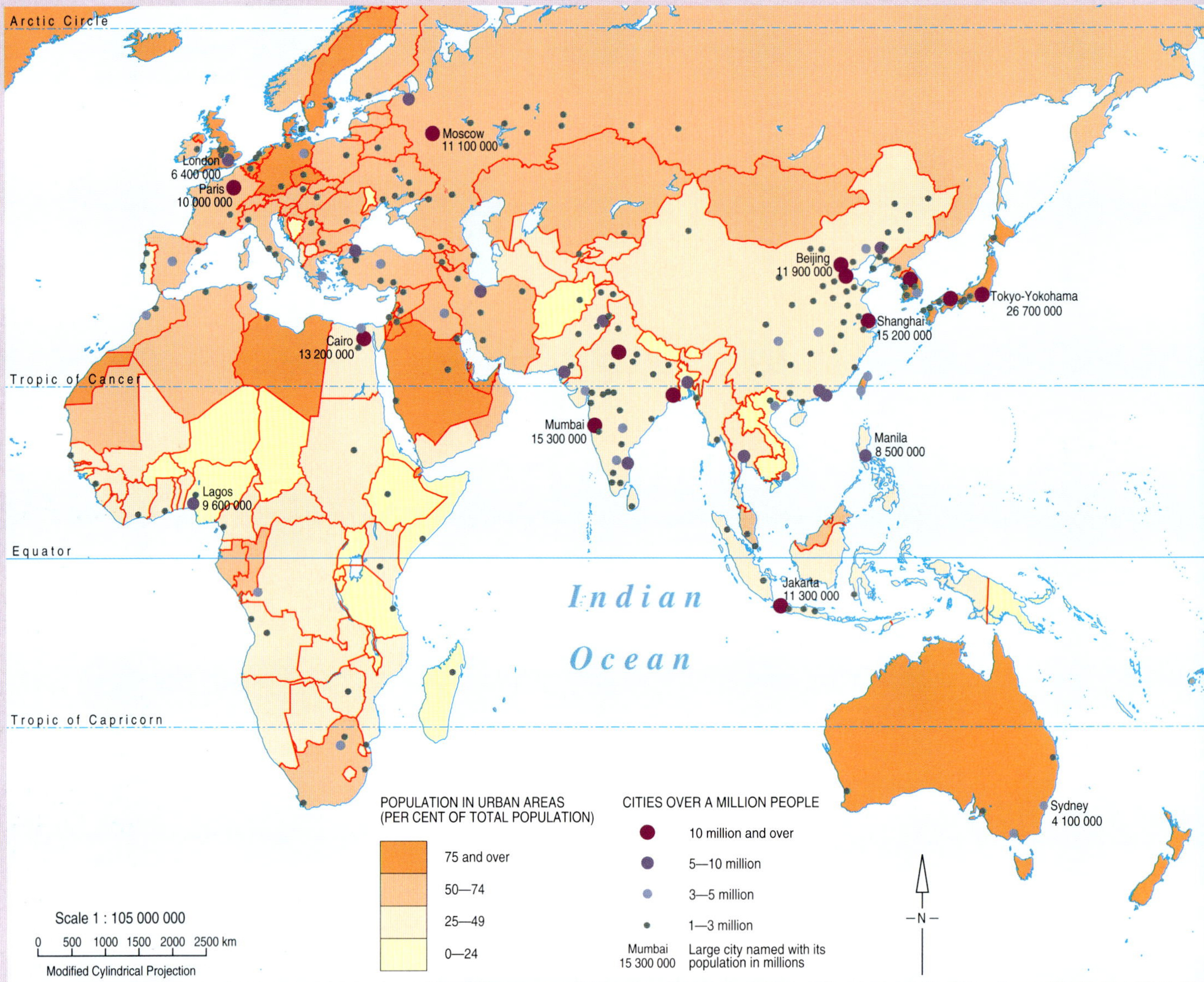

Figure 3.5c Population living in urban centres (source: *Heinemann Atlas*). In developing countries authorities find it difficult to cope with the impact of rapid urbanisation.

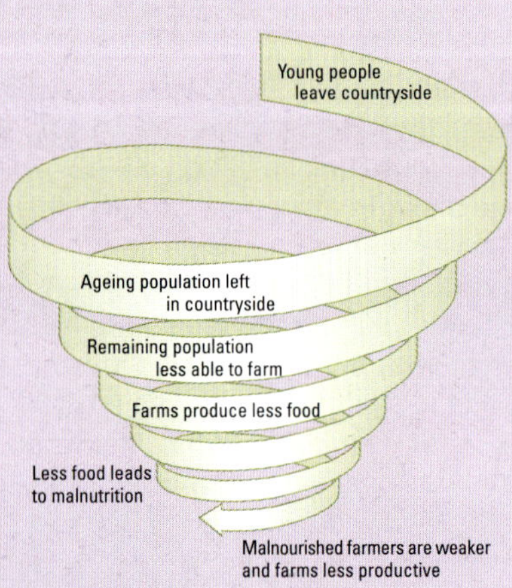

Figure 3.5d The effects that migration into cities has on rural communities.

Working geographically

1 **Writing task** Study Table 3.5a (p. 70). Write a report outlining the process of urbanisation and the push and pull factors that bring it about.

2 **Writing task** Study Figure 3.5d. Write a paragraph outlining the effects that migration into cities has on rural communities.

3 **Interpreting graphs** Study Figure 3.5a (p. 70). List the world's six largest cities in 1950, from the largest to the smallest. Then write down the names of the six largest cities in 2000, from the largest to the smallest. For each of the cities you have listed, state whether it is located in the developing or developed world. Compare the two lists. What differences do you notice?

4 **Writing task** Write a paragraph outlining the problems faced by large cities in the developing world.

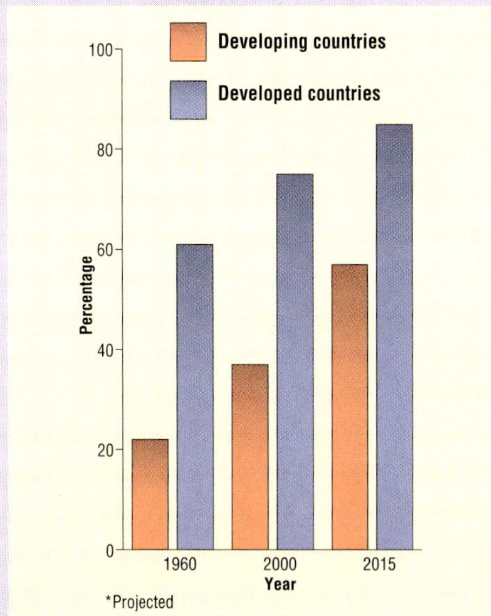

Figure 3.5e Population in urban areas.

Understanding the text

1. Explain the process of urbanisation in your own words.
2. Where are rates of urbanisation greatest? What problems does this create?
3. Explain the difference between quality of life and standard of living.
4. Outline the impact that urbanisation has on rural areas.
5. Explain the difference between a megacity and a world city. Give examples of each.

UTT worksheet 3.5

5 **Challenge: Writing task** Study the box 'Sao Paulo, Brazil' (p. 71), then complete the following tasks:
   - a Outline the problems resulting from Sao Paulo's rapid population growth.
   - b What are favelas? Where are they often located?
   - c Adopt the perspective of a teenager living in a Sao Paulo favela. Write a paragraph describing what it is like to live there.

6 **Interpreting maps** Study Figure 3.5c and, with the aid of an atlas, complete the following tasks:
   - a List the countries with more than 75 per cent of their population living in urban areas.
   - b Name ten countries with 0–24 per cent of their population living in urban areas. Where are the majority of such countries located?
   - c Name the countries with two or more cities with more than 10 million people.
   - d Name the two countries that have three cities with 10 million or more people but whose overall rate of urbanisation is just 25–49 per cent.

7 **Interpreting photographs** Study the photograph in Figure 3.5c. What impacts of rapid urban growth can you see in this photograph?

8 **Writing task** Study Figure 3.5e. Write a paragraph comparing the rate of urbanisation in the developed and developing worlds.

3.6 Our human world: agriculture

Figure 3.6a Nomads grazing their livestock in the African Sahel: an example of traditional subsistence agriculture.

Figure 3.6b The production of flowers under glass is an example of intensive commercial agriculture. High levels of capital investment and technology are used to produce flowers for domestic and international markets.

Agriculture is the world's most important industry because it provides us with our essential supplies of food and many other raw materials. Agriculture takes up more land than any other human activity and has a great impact on the physical environment. Soils, water, plants and other natural elements are important factors affecting the operation of a farming system. Farming makes use of these physical inputs and changes natural ecosystems controlled by nature into agro-ecosystems controlled by the farmer or grazier.

Some farming activities have more impact on the physical environment than others. The more commercial agriculture becomes, the more technology and chemicals are used. This is certainly the case in **developed countries**. Large-scale machinery and chemical fertilisers and pesticides are used to reduce the demand for expensive labour, increase yields and control pests. In most developing countries, however, less technology is used, productivity (output per worker) is lower and more people depend on farming as a source of food and employment. Agriculture has spread into areas of less reliable rainfall as a result of growing populations. The spread of agriculture into these areas is a major cause of problems, such as deforestation, soil erosion and desertification. Where population densities are lower, farmers can farm in a more sustainable way, causing minimal damage to the environment. Traditional forms of shifting agriculture, for example, are sustainable while population densities remain low.

Types of agriculture

Agriculture is an economic activity found in almost every country on earth. The type of agriculture depends on physical, human and economic factors. Agriculture is often classified as either commercial or traditional and as either intensive or extensive.

Figure 3.6c Rubber plantations are an example of commercial agriculture. Most plantation crops are found in the tropics. Other plantation crops are cacao, copra, coffee, tea, pineapples and bananas.

Figure 3.6d The cultivation of rice is an example of traditional subsistence agriculture. It involves farmers using human and draft labour, fertiliser and water to maximise the amount of food produced.

Commercial agriculture uses energy (mainly fuel oil for machinery), water and chemicals to produce huge amounts of food and other agricultural products, including fibres (such as cotton).

Traditional agriculture consists of two types:

- *Traditional* **subsistence agriculture** involves people producing just enough food to meet their family's needs. Subsistence farmers rely on human labour and animal power. Examples include shifting agriculture in tropical forests (see Chapter 7) and nomadic herding.
- *Traditional* **intensive agriculture** involves farmers using increased amounts of human and draft (animal) labour, fertiliser and water to increase the amount of food produced. If there is more food produced than can be used by the family, some may be sold at market. The intensive production of rice is an example of this type of agriculture (see Figure 3.6d). Traditional subsistence agriculture is practiced by almost half the people on earth.

Extensive agriculture involves a large area farmed with limited use of labour and capital (for example, cattle grazing in developing countries) or a large area of land with limited labour and high investment of capital and technology (for example, cotton growing in New South Wales).

Intensive agriculture refers to the farming of a small amount of land by a large labour supply with limited technology and investment (for example, rice growers in Bali) or a large amount of capital, labour and technology used in a relatively small area, as in horticulture.

Figure 3.6e The grazing of cattle in the United States is an example of extensive commercial livestock production.

Figure 3.6f Grain production is an example of extensive commercial agriculture using high levels of capital investment and technology.

Working geographically

1 **Classifying** Classify each of the following types of agriculture:
  - a the growing of rice in terraced paddy fields
  - b the combination of wheat and sheep production in Australia
  - c battery hen production
  - d dairying in Western Europe
  - e shifting agriculture in the Amazon Basin
  - f rubber plantations in Malaysia
  - g viticulture (the growing of grapes for wine production)
  - h cotton growing in northwest New South Wales.

2 **Research task** Select one of the plantation crops listed in the text. Undertake research to find out where the crop is produced, what it is used for and its main markets. Outline the growing or production process. Present your findings as an oral report (see Unit 2.14).

3 **Challenge: Using an atlas** Find an atlas map showing the distribution of the main types of agriculture. Then describe the global distribution of:
  - a shifting agriculture
  - b nomadic herding
  - c commercial cropping often with livestock rearing
  - d subsistence farming mostly cropping.

4 **Photo sketching** Select one of the photos in this section of the text. Construct a photo sketch (see Unit 2.9). Label the main features of the physical and human (built) environments.

Extension worksheet 3.2

Understanding the text

1 Why is agriculture defined as a primary industry?

2 Explain why agriculture is considered to be the world's most important industry.

3 Identify the impact of agriculture on natural ecosystems.

4 What impacts result from the overuse of land?

5 Use the glossary to define the following terms: deforestation, erosion and desertification.

6 What is meant by the term 'commercial agriculture'?

7 Distinguish between traditional subsistence agriculture and traditional intensive agriculture.

8 Explain the difference between extensive and intensive agriculture.

UTT worksheet 3.6

3.7

Using photographs
Human environments

Figure 3.7a Terraced rice fields in Bali, Indonesia.

Figure 3.7b Crops growing in a vast glasshouse.

Figure 3.7c Port facilities, United States.

Figure 3.7d Hong Kong, China.

Figure 3.7e Boeing aircraft factory, Seattle, United States.

Figure 3.7f Ridge-top village, Papua New Guinea.

Figure 3.7g Oil drilling platform.

Figure 3.7h Parthenon, Greece.

Working geographically

Study the photographs on pages 76 and 77, and then complete the following tasks:

1 **Matching** Match the photographs with the features of the built environment listed below:
   - **a** transport systems
   - **b** large urban centres
   - **c** industrial complexes
   - **d** exploiting natural resources
   - **e** traditional agricultural landuse
   - **f** centres where services are provided
   - **g** the heritage of our built environment
   - **h** traditional settlements
   - **i** modern intensive agricultural landuse.

2 **Interpreting photographs** Rank the photographs according to the impact they may have on the physical environment. Start with the aspect of the built environment that you think would have the most significant impact. Compare your ranking with a partner's to determine an agreed ranking. Then, working in groups of four, compare rankings. Discuss the reasons for the decisions you made and reach a group consensus on a ranking.

3 **Photo sketching: Writing task** Study Figure 3.7a, then complete the following tasks.
   - **a** Construct a photo sketch of the image.
   - **b** Write a paragraph outlining how the people of Bali have transformed their physical environments to meet their needs.

Figure 3.7i Ski and snowboard resort, Whistler–Blackcomb, Canada.

3.8 World Heritage

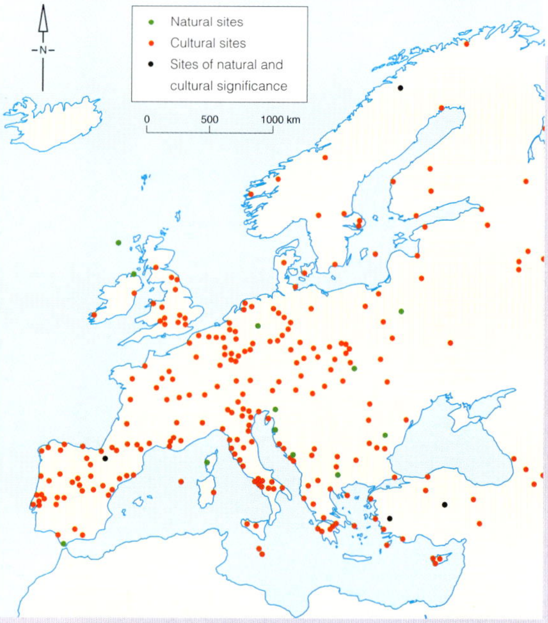

Our common heritage

The rocks of the Grand Canyon record 2 billion years of the earth's history. Africa's Serengeti National Park is famous for its wildlife. Peru's Machu Picchu and Egypt's pyramids are archaeological treasures. The Galapagos Islands inspired Charles Darwin's theory of evolution. Germany's Volklingen Ironworks tell the story of industrialisation. Italy's Venice and India's Taj Mahal are architectural masterpieces. Auschwitz Concentration Camp and the Hiroshima Peace Memorial remind us of the horrors of war. The Statue of Liberty is a symbol of freedom and hope. All these places are very different, yet they all have something in common. What is it?

These special places are just a few of the natural and cultural sites that have been identified as having international significance. They are special because they represent the common heritage of all the world's people: treasures to be protected for the benefit of present and future generations. These special places are referred to as **World Heritage sites**.

Making the grade

To be included on the World Heritage List a site must have global natural or cultural significance and satisfy the strict criteria adopted by the *United Nations Education, Scientific, and Cultural Organization (UNESCO)*. A *cultural* site could, for example, be a masterpiece of creative genius or have great architectural merit. It may be associated with ideas or beliefs of universal significance or be an outstanding example of a traditional way of life representative of a particular

Venice, Italy
Listed: 1994 **Criteria:** cultural
Description: Founded in the second century BC in northern Italy, Venice prospered from the early fifteenth century to the end of the eighteenth century as a major trading power.

Salzburg, Austria
Listed: 1996 **Criteria:** cultural
Description: Salzburg has managed to preserve its rich architectural heritage, developed over the period from the Middle Ages to the nineteenth century.

Château de Chambord, France
Listed: 1981 **Criteria:** cultural
Description: Located in a vast forest in the Loire Valley, the château is considered an architectural masterpiece.

Auschwitz Concentration Camp, Poland
Listed: 1979 **Criteria:** cultural
Description: The former concentration and extermination camp of Auschwitz-Birkenau, the largest in the Third Reich. One and a half million people, many of whom were Jews, were put to death in the camp. Protected as a reminder of humanity's cruelty to its fellow human beings.

The Great Wall, China
Listed: 1987 **Criteria:** cultural
Description: In c. 220 BC, sections of earlier fortifications were joined together to form a united defence system against invasions from the north. Construction continued up to the Ming dynasty (1368–1644).

Grand Canyon National Park, Arizona, United States
Listed: 1979 **Criteria:** Natural
Description: Carved by the Colorado River, and nearly 1500 metres deep, the Grand Canyon is the most spectacular gorge in the world.

Figure 3.8a Distribution of World Heritage sites.

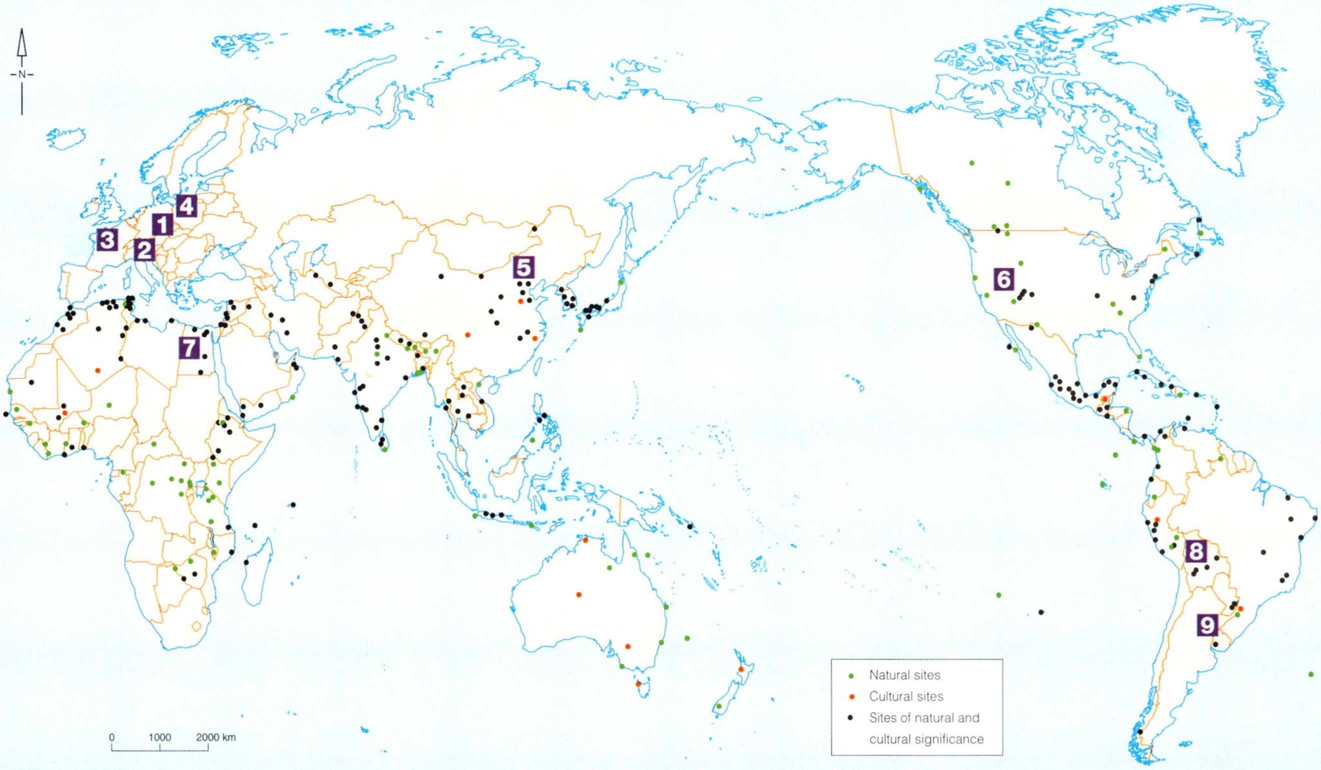

The Pyramids of Giza, Egypt
Listed: 1979 **Criteria:** cultural
Description: Built to house the remains of Egypt's rulers, these vast structures are considered one of the Seven Wonders of the (ancient) World.

Machu Picchu, Peru
Listed: 1983 **Criteria:** cultural
Description: Machu Picchu is the most amazing urban creation of the Inca Empire.

Iguazu National Park, Argentina
Listed: 1984 **Criteria:** natural
Description: One of the world's most spectacular waterfalls.

Table 3.8a UNESCO's World Heritage Endangered list, July 2003

Afghanistan: Minaret and archaeological remains of Jam; cultural landscape archaeological remains of the Bamiyan Valley

Albania: Butrint

Algeria: Tipasa

Azerbaijan: Walled City of Baku with the Shirvanshah's Palace and Maiden Tower

Benin: Royal Palaces of Abomey

Cambodia: Angkor

Central African Republic: Manovo-Gounda St Floris

Democratic Republic of the Congo: Virunga National Park, Garamba National Park, Kahuzi-Biega National Park, Okapi Wildlife Reserve, Salonga National Park

Ecuador: Sangay National Park

Egypt: Abu Mena

Ethiopia: Simien National Park

Honduras: Rio Platano Biosphere Reserve

India: Manas Wildlife Sanctuary; Group of Monuments at Hampi

Iraq: Ashur (Qal'at Sherqat)

Ivory Coast: Comoé National Park

Ivory Coast/Guinea: Mount Nimba Nature Reserve

Jerusalem: Old City of Jerusalem and its Walls

Mali: Timbuktu

Nepal: Kathmandu Valley

Niger: Air and Ténéré Natural Reserves

Oman: Bahla Fort

Pakistan: Fort and Shalamar Gardens in Lahore

Peru: Chan Chan Archaeological Zone

Philippines: Rice Terraces of the Philippine Cordilleras

Senegal: Djoudj National Bird Sanctuary

Tunisia: Ichkeul National Park

Uganda: Rwenzori Mountains National Park

United States: Everglades National Park

Yemen: Historic Town of Zabid

culture. A *natural site* may represent a significant stage in the earth's history or represent ongoing ecological and biological processes. It may contain the natural habitat of endangered species or be a place of great scenic beauty.

The first places were put on the UNESCO World Heritage List in 1979. By early 2004 there were 754 such sites spread across 125 countries: 149 natural sites, 582 cultural sites and twenty-three sites of natural and cultural significance. Fifteen of these sites were in Australia. When a country nominates a site it must agree to conserve it for future generations.

What does World Heritage listing achieve?

The main benefit of putting a site on the World Heritage List is the attention it focuses on the place. Listing it means that people are aware of how special the place is. It puts pressure on governments to protect the site. When a problem arises there is enough public interest to make it an issue for community debate and action.

At certain times, particular sites are endangered by war, pollution, poachers, lack of maintenance, the damming of rivers, illegal logging or similar activities. These sites are often placed on a temporary endangered list and assistance is given to help protect the site. Examples of places that have been listed in recent years are the Old City of Jerusalem because of the Israeli–Palestinian conflict, and the Ngorongo Crater in Tanzania because of lack of controls on landuses. The crater was taken off the list when management plans were put in place to protect it.

Getting technical

UNESCO The United Nations Educational, Scientific, and Cultural Organization's role is to contribute to peace and security in the world by promoting cooperation between nations through education, science, culture and communication. Its aim is to increase respect for justice, for the rule of law and for the human rights and freedoms to which everyone is entitled without discrimination based on race, gender, language or religion.

Treaties, conventions and agreements A *treaty* is a general term used to describe a legally binding agreement between governments (and/or international organisations). A *convention* is a formal multilateral treaty between a large number of countries. They are normally open for participation by the international community as a whole. *Agreements* are usually less formal than conventions and deal with a narrower range of concerns.

Legal status of international treaties When the Australian Government signs an international agreement it becomes enforceable under Australian law. This principle was confirmed in 1983 when the High Court of Australia ruled that the federal government had the power to overrule the Tasmanian Government's decision to dam the Franklin River.

Extension worksheet 3.3

Extension worksheet ICT 3.9

The Everglades National Park in Florida, United States, was added to the List of World Heritage in Danger in 1993 after the park's superintendent informed the committee of extensive damage to the Everglades' ecology. The Everglades has been called 'a river of grass' because it flows very slowly from the hinterland into the sea. The exceptional variety of its water habitats has made it a sanctuary for a large number of birds and reptiles, as well as for threatened species, such as the manatee. The Everglades' ecology has been damaged by nearby urban growth, pollution from fertilisers, mercury poisoning of fish and wildlife and a fall in water levels caused by flood protection measures. The Everglades are examined in more detail in Unit 10.3.

Listing, however, does not always guarantee protection. Historic Dubrovnik (Figure 2.8a, p. 40) in Croatia, for example, was partially destroyed during the war in former Yugoslavia.

Role of governments

Governments who sign up to the World Heritage Convention agree to protect listed cultural and natural sites located within their borders. This includes:

- developing community-based planning programs that protect the site
- establishing a body whose responsibility it is to protect a site
- developing scientific and technical studies and research that help to protect sites against potential dangers
- putting in place the appropriate legal, scientific, administrative and financial measures to protect sites
- recognising that the protection of sites is the responsibility of the international community and, in this respect, there is a loss of national sovereignty
- undertaking not to damage directly or indirectly any World Heritage site.

ICT — World Heritage Internet investigation

Access UNESCO's World Heritage website, then complete the following tasks:

1. Outline the 'objective' and 'mission' of the Convention Concerning the Protection of the World Cultural and Natural Heritage. How many countries have signed this international agreement?
2. Outline the role of the World Heritage Committee.
3. Study the criteria used to determine whether a site is to be included on the World Heritage List.
4. Select five World Heritage sites, each from a different country. Name each site and identify the criteria used to justify its placement on the list. In brief, explain why the site is special.
5. Draw up a list of the sites added to or deleted from the list since 2003.
6. Work out which country has the largest number of World Heritage sites.
7. Access UNESCO's list of endangered World Heritage sites. Compare the sites listed to those in Table 3.8a. Which sites have been added since 2003? Which sites have been deleted? Select one of each and find out why they have been added or deleted.
8. List Australia's World Heritage sites. Locate these on a map of Australia. Identify the most recent addition(s) to the list.

Figure 3.8b UNESCO's World Heritage logo.

Understanding the text

1. Explain the factors that determine whether a site qualifies for World Heritage listing.
2. Explain why World Heritage sites are special.
3. Outline the responsibilities governments have regarding the sites they nominate.
4. What happens when a site is added to the World Heritage endangered list?

UTT worksheet 3.8

Working geographically

1. **Challenge: Writing task** Write a report, design a newsletter or develop a poster outlining the role of governments in protecting, conserving and presenting World Heritage sites.
2. **Internet-based task** Use the World Heritage website to identify Australia's World Heritage sites. Locate and label these on an outline map of Australia.
3. **Group work** In groups, select a feature of the world's natural and cultural heritage. Brainstorm the actions you could take to protect the feature. Share your group's suggestions with the rest of the class.
4. **Class discussion** Should the Sydney Opera House receive World Heritage listing? What selection criteria would it meet? Undertake research to find out why it has not yet been listed.

3.9 Review and reflect

Chapter summary

In this chapter we were introduced to some of the distinctive features of the world's physical and human environments. We saw how the processes of weathering and erosion are constantly working to change the shape and appearance of landforms. We discovered that a country is defined by the ability of its government to exercise sovereignty: the power to govern its own affairs and to make and enforce laws. We then studied two of the most important ways in which people have had an impact on the physical environment: the development of the large city and the use of land for agriculture. Finally, we examined the role of the World Heritage Convention in protecting the world's most important natural and cultural sites.

Activity 1

True and false

Select 'true' or 'false' for each of the following statements.

1. Exfoliation occurs when the roots of plants force cracks in rocks to widen.
2. Attrition occurs when rocks collide and are worn into smoother, rounded stones.
3. The wind blasting sand against a cliff face is an example of abrasion.
4. Running water, rivers, waves, wind and ice are all agents of weathering.
5. Rock-strewn desert surfaces are the result of a process known as deflation.
6. A country's national identity is created by a sense of belonging shared by the population.
7. The growing of rice in irrigated paddy fields in an example of extensive agriculture.
8. The production of sheep and wheat in Australia is an example of extensive agriculture.
9. To be included on the World Heritage list a site must have global natural or cultural significance.
10. Governments are under no obligation to protect sites given World Heritage status.

Activity 2

Internet research: What is your footprint?

Calculate your ecological footprint by going to one of the following websites:

- earthdaynetwork
- Powerhouse Museum: Bigfoot Interactive.

Activity 3

Challenge: Internet research—World Heritage

Undertake Internet research. Investigate a World Heritage site that is of interest to you. Use the following geographical questions to structure your research:

- What is it?
- Where is it?
- Why is it classified as a site of international importance?
- How has it changed over time?
- How do people affect it?
- Who is responsible for protecting the site?
- How is it being protected?
- What can individuals do to protect the site?

Present your findings as either a desktop-published document or a multimedia presentation. Use the image-capture facility of your computer to insert visual images into your document or presentation.

As a class, develop a World Heritage web page incorporating each of the desktop-published documents or multimedia presentations developed as part of this research task.

Foundation worksheet 3.1
Foundation worksheet 3.2

Activity 4

Interpreting photographs: Agriculture

Study Figures 3.9a and 3.9b. Write two paragraphs describing the type of agricultural activity taking place in each photograph. Make sure that you use the appropriate terms; for example, intensive or extensive agriculture; and commercial or subsistence agriculture.

Figure 3.9a

Figure 3.9b

Activity 5

Media-based task: World Heritage

Study the extract below, then complete the following tasks:

1 a Describe the impact of snowmobiles on Yellowstone National Park.
  b Why are local communities resisting attempts to limit snowmobiles in the park?
  c As a class, discuss whether such recreational activities are consistent with the park's World Heritage status.
  d Conduct a class debate. Topic: Snowmobiles should be banned from Yellowstone National Park.

Smog-choked Yellowstone mulls snowmobile ban

By Natalie Pawelski

A lawsuit brought by environmental groups has Yellowstone National Park [in Wyoming, United States] re-examining one of its most popular recreational activities.

The snowmobile has joined hot springs and wildlife as a common sight in Yellowstone, the nation's first national park.

'When you can't hear the wind and the trees and the chirping of birds because it sounds like the Indy 500,' said John Catton of the Greater Yellowstone Coalition, 'the park is going downhill and we need to turn that around.'

But snowmobile devotees consider the activity a fun way to see the park…

[While] cars and other vehicles outnumber snowmobiles 16-to-1 in Yellowstone during the course of a year … studies show snowmobiles are responsible for most of the air pollution in the park.

About 55 000 snowmobiles enter the park each winter at the West Yellowstone entrance. When employees working there reported getting sick, the park found high carbon monoxide levels and had to start pumping fresh air into the entrance booths.

The pollution levels at the west entrance at times range as high as famously smoggy cities like Denver and Atlanta.

It may be hard to believe the small machines could broadly affect the air in Yellowstone…

The environmental protection agency said the park should ban all snowmobiles until the air quality situation improves.

A snowmobile ban would mean serious problems for the gateway community of West Yellowstone, which calls itself the snowmobile capital of the world.

'If you cut off snowmobiles in Yellowstone tomorrow or for next season, it would devastate our community'… said West Yellowstone Mayor Jerry Johnson … Like many in Yellowstone, Johnson's family depends on the snowmobile economy for a living.

'They matter because it's our winter economy. It is how we make a living. It's why the town can be open in the wintertime,' he said.

Some are pinning their hopes for a solution on a new generation of cleaner, quieter snowmobiles…

CNN website, 6 March 2000

GeoMatch

GeoWords

Refer to the Reflection box on page 17.

GeoQuiz

Chapter test

Chapter 4

Geographical research

Introduction

Fieldwork is an important part of the study of geography because it enables us to develop our understanding of geographical processes that form and transform environments. It also allows us to explore different perspectives or points of view on geographical issues. When undertaking fieldwork we develop a 'research action plan' to guide our investigation. We then observe, map, measure and record geographical information in a real-world setting. Information and communication technologies (ICT) are used to help organise, present, interpret and communicate information collected during fieldwork.

In this chapter we explain how to use fieldwork to record weather data, investigate a local river, measure water quality in a local waterway and develop a community profile.

Key questions

1. What geographical tools and skills are needed to gather information in the field?
2. How do we go about collecting weather data in our local area?
3. What tools and skills do we need to investigate a local waterway?
4. How can we tell if a local waterway is healthy?
5. How can we develop a community profile using census data?

Research action plan

When interplementing a **research action plan** you need to follow the steps below.

Identify the aim, or purpose, of the investigation: what are you going to investigate?

↓

Develop a series of questions that you want to answer during your investigation

↓

Identify the primary and secondary data you need to answer your questions

↓

Select the geographical tools needed to collect the data

↓

Collect your primary and secondary data

↓

Process and study the data collected

↓

Select the best form of presentation to communicate your research findings; for example, a word-processed report, an oral presentation, a PowerPoint presentation or a wall display

↓

Outline and, where appropriate, take individual or group action to address the issues raised in your investigation

Glossary of key terms

Air pressure The weight of a column of air pressing down on the earth's surface. Also known as atmospheric pressure.

Catchment The drainage basin of a river and its tributaries.

Census A count of the entire population conducted every five years.

Humidity The amount of atmospheric moisture.

Meteorologist A person who uses atmospheric data to make predictions about weather.

Point bar The accumulation of sediment on the inside of a river bend.

Primary data Data collected in the field.

Questionnaire A set of survey questions.

Research action plan A strategy for approaching a research task. It involves identifying an aim, asking specific geographical questions and identifying the data needed and the time and resources available.

River discharge The amount of water flowing from a river catchment.

Secondary data Information and data collected by others and published in newspapers, magazines, journals and government reports or on the Internet, for example.

Survey The collection of information from a sample of the population.

Tributary A river that flows into a larger river.

Turbidity The cloudiness of water. High turbidity occurs when there are high levels of suspended sediment in water.

Watershed The boundary between catchments.

Weather The condition of the atmosphere at one place and time.

eGlossary

GeoToolkit

ICT Toolkit

4.1

USING FIELDWORK

Measuring and recording weather data

Getting technical

What is weather? Weather is the day-to-day condition of the atmosphere at a particular place. It includes all the daily changes in temperature, precipitation, wind, sunshine, air pressure and humidity (the amount of moisture in the atmosphere).

What is air pressure? Air has weight. It exerts pressure on us and on everything around us. The pressure of the atmosphere on our body would crush us if it were not counterbalanced by the equal internal pressure of the fluids inside our body.

What is wind? Heat from the sun warms the air near the earth's surface and makes it rise. This occurs mainly in tropical regions, near the Equator, where the sun's energy is at its most intense. As warm air rises, cool air rushes in to take its place. We feel this movement of air as wind.

Did U know?

Low-cost thermo-hygrometers are readily available and are used widely in greenhouses and nurseries. These pocket-sized digital instruments can be used to measure temperature and humidity.

The steps below explain how to measure and record **weather** data. You will need to follow these steps when completing the fieldwork activity on page 89.

Step 1: measuring temperature

Use a thermometer to record air temperature. If the temperature needs to be recorded at a specific location over a certain number of days, the thermometer reading should be taken at the same time and place over the period. It is best to hang or hold the instrument for five minutes before measuring the air temperature. You must also remember not to hold the 'red' end of the thermometer as that would give a false reading.

If you have a maximum–minimum thermometer housed in a Stevenson screen (see the box 'Instruments used to record weather data') it is possible to record the maximum and minimum temperatures experienced at this particular location in the previous twenty-four hours.

Step 2: measuring relative humidity

Use a wet–dry bulb thermometer (or thermo-hygrometer; see the Did U Know? box) to measure and record the relative **humidity** at the same time and place as you measured the temperature.

Step 3: measuring air pressure

Use an aneroid barometer to measure **air pressure**, or atmospheric pressure. To check the accuracy of your observations compare them with the weather maps published in the daily newspapers or the readings taken by the Bureau of Meteorology (see the ICT box 'Bureau of Meteorology', p. 88).

Step 4: measuring rainfall

Use a rain gauge to measure the amount of rainfall received in the preceding twenty-four hours. Refer to the scale (in millimetres) on the glass cylinder contained within the rain gauge. If you catch hail or snow, wait for it to melt before taking a reading.

Step 5: determining wind direction

Use a wind vane to determine the direction *from* which the wind is blowing.

Step 6: measuring wind speed

Use an anemometer to measure wind speed (velocity). If you don't have an anemometer, estimate the approximate wind speed by observing surrounding conditions and comparing these with the descriptions provided in the Beaufort Scale (see column 4 of Table 4.1a, p. 89). This will give you the approximate wind speed (see column 3 of Table 4.1a).

Instruments used to record weather data

1. Rain gauge

Official forecasters have used rain gauges for over 100 years. A rain gauge is shown in drawing 1 in Figure 4.1a. It consists of a large cylinder with a funnel and a smaller measuring tube inside. The funnel collects the rainfall and directs it into a measuring tube, which has exactly one-tenth the cross-sectional area at the top of the funnel. The smaller measuring tube allows more precise measurements to be made because it exaggerates the height of the water in the tube. The graduations used on the side of the measuring tube take into account this exaggeration. This allows **meteorologists** to make very precise measurements.

The rain gauge should be positioned where there will be no runoff of rainwater from trees, roofs or signs, for example. There is a minimum distance that official rain gauges must be from such obstructions. For example, if a nearby tree is 5 metres tall, the rain gauge must be at least twice the distance (10 metres) away.

During periods of heavy rainfall the measuring tube may overflow into the larger cylinder. If this happens the tube needs to be emptied and the additional water needs to be carefully poured into the measuring tube. The total rainfall should be tallied.

When measuring precipitation in the form of hail or snow, the inner tube and the funnel are removed. The ice or snow collected by the outer cylinder is melted and then measured using the inner measuring tube.

2. Wind vane

A wind vane tells the direction of the wind. Remember that winds are named after the direction *from* which they are blowing. A wind blowing from the south, for example, is called a southerly.

3. Anemometer

An anemometer revolves in the wind. The faster the wind speed, the faster it revolves. Wind speed is calculated by counting the number of revolutions per unit of time.

7. Aneroid barometer

An aneroid barometer contains a sealed box with most of its air removed. Any change in pressure will make the box shrink or expand. Levers magnify these changes, causing a pointer to move on a dial. Air pressure at sea level fluctuates around 1013 hectopascals (hPa). It can drop to 970 hPa during severe storms. In a high-pressure system it can reach 1040 hPa. A drop in air pressure, measured over a day or two, will indicate the approach of unsettled weather.

5. Maximum–minimum thermometer

A maximum–minimum thermometer is a special type of thermometer that can record both the maximum and minimum temperature experienced over twenty-four hours. It needs to be reset daily.

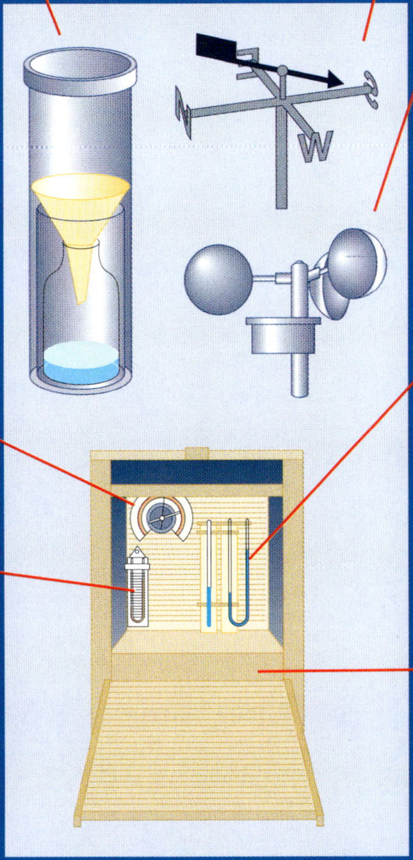

Figure 4.1a Instruments used to record weather.

6. Wet–dry bulb thermometer

A wet–dry bulb thermometer is a standard mercury-in-glass thermometer, with the thermometer bulb wrapped in muslin, which is kept wet. The evaporation of water from the thermometer has a cooling effect, so the temperature indicated by the wet–dry bulb thermometer is less than the temperature indicated by a normal thermometer. The rate of evaporation from the wet–dry bulb thermometer depends on the humidity of the air: evaporation is slower when the air is already full of water vapour. For this reason, the difference in the temperatures indicated by the two thermometers gives a measure of atmospheric humidity.

4. Stevenson screen

A Stevenson screen is used to house various instruments. Air can move freely through the slats, the white colour reflects the worst of the heat, and the roof keeps out the rain. Because the screens are built to a standard design, data collected from anywhere in the world can be compared.

Skills

Make your own simple barometer

Use a glass jar, balloon, rubber band, wooden skewer, adhesive tape and a ruler to construct a simple instrument to measure fluctuations in air pressure.

Procedure

1. Stretch a piece of balloon membrane over the jar and secure it with a rubber band.
2. Tape the end of a wooden skewer to the centre of the balloon (see Figure 4.1b)
3. Use adhesive tape to support an upright ruler behind the end of the pointed end of the skewer (see Figure 4.1b). Note: Place the 'zero' at the bottom.
4. At the same time each day note the height on the ruler aligned to the end of the skewer. As air pressure rises, it forces the balloon down into the jar, making the end of the skewer rise.
5. Draw up a table to record your observations. Alternatively, enter your data into a spreadsheet and use the graph creation function to show your data as a graphic.

Note: The movement of the skewer can also be caused by variations in temperature. As air warms it expands, which puts upward pressure on the rubber balloon membrane.

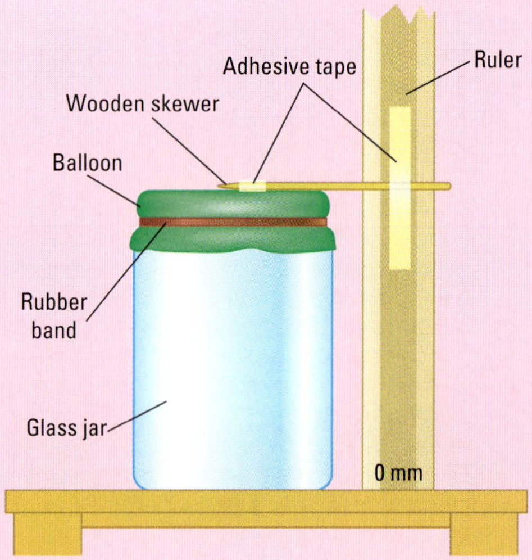

Figure 4.1b A simple instrument to measure variations in air pressure.

Did U know?

- The Beaufort Scale is named after the British Admiral Sir Francis Beaufort. In 1805 the admiral devised a scale of twelve wind forces for use in sailing. For many years this scale has been used on land as well as at sea, although winds of scale 10, 11 and 12 rarely occur over land.
- Air pressure was discovered and measured by Evangelista Torricelli, an Italian scientist and pupil of Galileo, in 1643. Torricelli measured air pressure using a mercury barometer he had invented.
- The first thermometer was made in about 1600 by the Italian scientist Galileo Galilei (1564–1642).

Extension worksheet 4.1

Extension worksheet ICT 4.2

Australian Bureau of Meterology

ICT

The Australian Bureau of Meteorology has a website that will assist you in your study of weather and climate. In addition to weather charts and forecasts the site contains:

- long-term climatic data for most Australian communities
- weather warnings
- radar and satellite images
- material for projects on weather and climate
- information relating to major weather events; for example, droughts.

You might like to check out the bureau's radar images showing the intensity of rainfall. The radar loops allow you to track rainfall across much of Australia. Students in New South Wales can access radar images centred on Canberra, Grafton, Mildura, Moree, Newcastle, Norfolk Island, Wagga Wagga and Yarrawonga. Sydney-based students can focus on the Sydney metropolitan region (using the 128-kilometre loop) or observe much of southeast New South Wales via the 256-kilometre loop. Different colours are used to show the intensity of rainfall. Try tracking the path of storms across the Sydney region following the passage of a cold front.

Satellite images showing the extent of cloud cover over the continent can also be located on the bureau's Satellite Image Home Page.

Identifying clouds

Access the Bureau of Meteorology website, then complete the following tasks:

1. a Name the four primary cloud groups. Give a brief description of each group.
   b Group the ten principle cloud forms according to the height at which they occur.
2. Complete the site's cloud quiz.
3. Use digital photography to record different cloud types. Use these images to develop your own cloud identification chart.

Table 4.1a Beaufort Scale

Beaufort number	Category	Speed (km/hour)	Effects
0	Calm	0–2	Smoke rises vertically
1	Light air	2–5	Smoke drifts
2	Light breeze	5–10	Leaves rustle, vane moves
3	Gentle breeze	10–20	Leaves and small branches move
4	Moderate breeze	20–30	Small branches move, dust and paper lifted
5	Fresh breeze	30–40	Large branches move, wave crest on water
6	Strong breeze	40–50	Large trees move, umbrellas difficult to use
7	Moderate gale	50–60	Large trees sway
8	Fresh gale	60–75	Branches break off trees
9	Strong gale	75–90	Large branches come down
10	Full gale	90–100	Trees uprooted, structural damage to buildings

Construct an instrument to measure wind speed

ICT

Access the 'Measuring wind speed' worksheet for students at the Bureau of Meteorology's website.

Following the instructions provided, construct your own instrument to measure wind speed, Use your instrument to measure wind speed at five-minute intervals for thirty minutes. Enter your data into a spreadsheet and then generate a graph showing the variation in wind velocity over the thirty minutes.

Working geographically

1 **Fieldwork** To better understand weather and climate, study Units 2.7 and 5.3 before you undertake this fieldwork-based activity. Select a suitable site in the school grounds or local community and, following the steps outlined on page 86, collect weather data on temperature, relative humidity, air pressure, rainfall (precipitation), wind speed and wind direction over a five-day period. Copy the fieldwork data table below and record your findings in your copy of the table.

Fieldwork data

Date: ___________ **Time:** ___________ **Location:** _________________

	Day 1	Day 2	Day 3	Day 4	Day 5
Temperature (°C)					
Relative humidity (%)					
Air pressure (hPa)					
Precipitation (mm)					
Wind speed (km/hour)					
Wind direction					

2 **Constructing graphs: Internet research** When you have completed activity 1, graph your results and compare them with the Bureau of Meteorology's average monthly data for the area.

3 **Challenge: Investigating weather** Follow the procedure below to investigate the extent to which weather varies within an area:

a In pairs, record weather data at or near the place where you live.

b Compare the data you collected with the data collected by others in the class.

c What do the results of this activity tell us about weather conditions in an area?

4.2

USING FIELDWORK

Investigating a river

A fieldwork investigation of a length of river provides us with an opportunity to learn more about these important features of the physical environment. It also allows us to practise a range of geographical skills.

Step 1: asking questions

The first step in a geography fieldwork investigation is to ask questions. What, for example, do you want to find out about a local river? Your title for this investigation could be 'Investigating a local river'. Some of the questions you might like to investigate are shown in Figure 4.2a.

Figure 4.2a Questions for investigation.

Getting technical

Catchment A **catchment** or drainage basin is the area drained by a river and its **tributaries**. Its boundary is marked by a ridge of higher land. Beyond the ridge, any precipitation will drain into another catchment. The boundary is called a **watershed** (see Figure 4.2c).

Tributary A river system flowing into a larger river is known as a tributary.

Water velocity The velocity, or speed, of water within river channels is influenced by:

- *the shape of the channel*—the rate of flow is faster in channels that are as deep as they are wide compared with channels that are wide but very shallow or very deep and narrow
- *the roughness of the channel's bed and banks*—water flowing through a channel full of large rocks is more turbulent, but slower, than water flowing through a channel lined with fine silt
- *the gradient or slope of the river*—as a river approaches the sea its gradient decreases, but because more water is added to the channel, the velocity of the river actually increases.

Figure 4.2d shows how the velocity of water within a river channel can vary. The slowest flow occurs where the water comes into contact with the river bed and banks.

River discharge Discharge is the amount of water that flows from a river catchment and into another river system, the sea or a lake.

Turbidity **Turbidity** refers to the cloudiness of water, which is caused by suspended sediment.

Figure 4.2a The velocity of water in a river is determined by the shape of the channel, the roughness of the river bed and the gradient of the river.

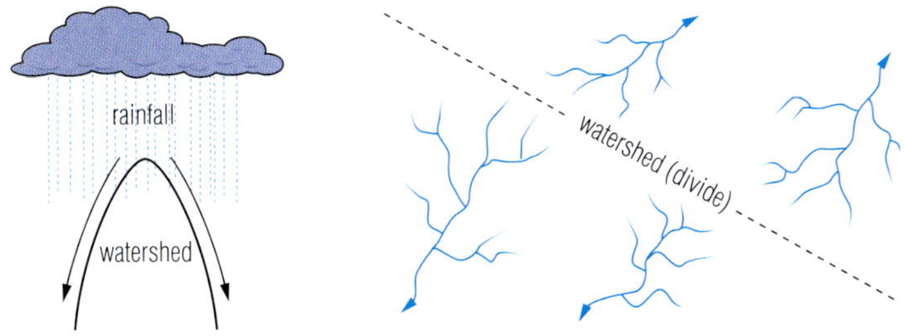

Figure 4.2c A watershed or divide.

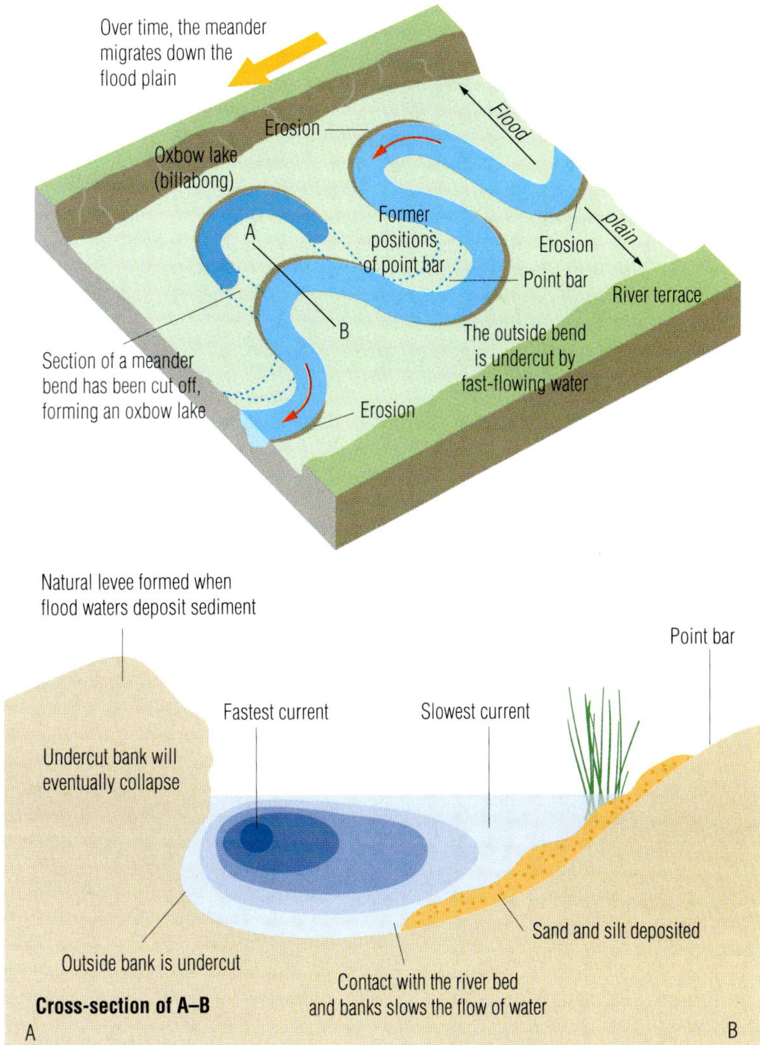

Figure 4.2d Landform features of a river and its floodplain.

Why do rivers meander?

Meanders are most likely to develop where rivers flow across relatively flat land with deep alluvial deposits (soils consisting of fine sediment deposited by rivers). Because water tends to flow in a wave-like pattern, alternating *pools* and *riffles* tend to develop on the floor of the river channel (see Figure 4.2e). As water travels through a riffle it is deflected onto the outside of the bank at the next bend by centrifugal forces (the outward force of matter moving from the centre). As the river undercuts the outside bank, the meander migrates outwards. **Point bar** deposits build up on the inside of the loop.

During flloods, meander loops can be cut off, forming a billabong or oxbow lake.

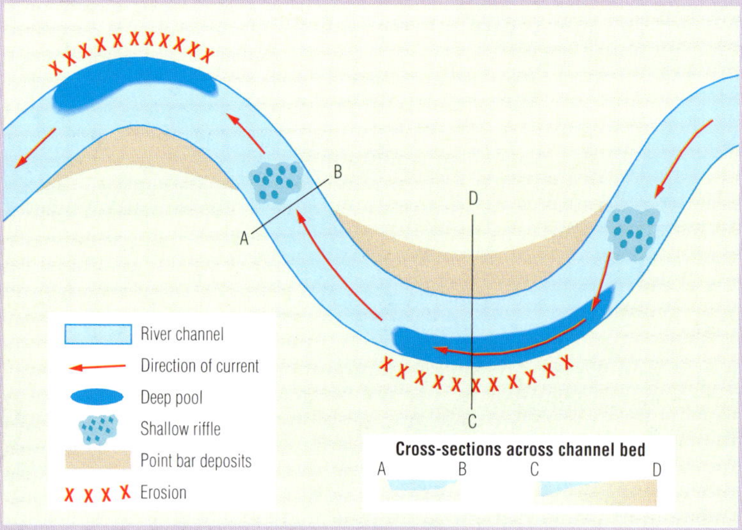

Figure 4.2e Features associated with a meander loop.

How do the activities of people affect rivers?

- *Reduced water flow*—Water used for irrigation and household and industrial use reduces river discharge.
- *Change in seasonal flows*—Increases in the consumption of water in summer can reduce the amount of water available to support life in the river.
- *Temperature change*—Storing water in large dams causes a drop in temperature (especially when the dam is very deep). Industries and thermal power stations can pollute rivers with very warm water.
- *Disruption to migratory patterns*—Dam walls can prevent fish from moving upstream to breed.
- *Siltation*—Increased siltation, resulting from land clearing and careless landuse practices, fills deep pools and dams and destroys the habitats of aquatic plants and animals.
- *River improvements*—The removal of logs and other material from rivers may destroy fish habitats.
- *Overfishing*—This results in a decrease in fish populations.
- *Pollution*—Pesticides can kill aquatic plants and enter the food chain, causing genetic damage. Fertilisers can encourage excessive plant growth, including toxic algal blooms.
- *Introduced species*—Introduced fish compete for food and habitat with native species. Introduced plants can choke waterways and crowd out native species.

Figure 4.2f The impact of people on river systems.

Step 2: collecting information

First, decide which questions shown in Figure 4.2a (p. 90) you are going to investigate. You may like to add additional questions, but they must be relevant to your study. Now decide on how you are going to collect the information. It is important to measure and record your data accurately.

Most of the data you will collect during a river investigation will be **primary data**; that is, data you actually go out and collect through measuring, sketching and observing. The equipment you might use to collect this data is shown in Figure 4.2g.

You could collect **secondary data** about the river you are investigating by contacting the NSW Department of Infrastructure, Planning and Natural Resources. You could then compare this secondary data with your own data.

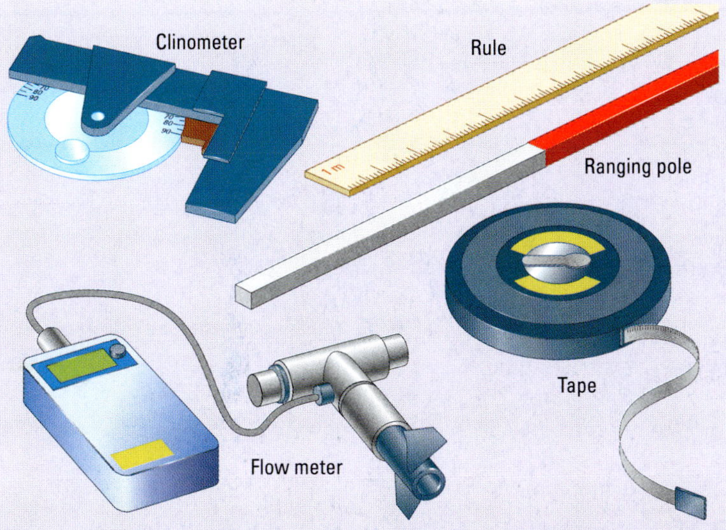

Figure 4.2g Tools used to collect data in the field.

Skills

Calculating cross-sectional area

To find out the cross-sectional area of a river complete the following steps:

1. Use a long tape measure to determine the width of the river.
2. Measure the depth of the water at regular intervals across the width of the river (for example, every 100 centimetres). A 2-metre pole marked with 10-centimetre intervals will assist you in this task. It may be easiest to measure the depth of the river where there is a low bridge for you to stand on.
3. Record your measurements on your data record sheet (see Figure 4.2h, p. 94).
4. Calculate the average depth by adding all the depth readings and divide by the number of readings. Using the data shown in Figure 4.2h, the average would be (20 cm + 25 cm + 35 cm + 45 cm + 30 cm + 20 cm)/6 = 29 cm.
5. Multiply the average depth by the average width of the river to give the area. Using the data shown in Figure 4.2h, the area would be 29 cm (or 0.29 m) × 15 = 435 cm^2 (or 4.35 m^2).

Skills

Calculating water velocity

The most accurate way to measure water velocity is to use a flow meter (see Figure 4.2g). If you don't have a flow meter you can use the following procedure:

1. Select a straight section of the river that is free of pools and/or shallow, fast-flowing sections.
2. Measure out a distance of 50 metres.
3. Find an object that will float on the surface of the river. The object should be brightly covered and it is best if it is heavy enough to be partly submerged in the water.
4. With the aid of a stopwatch, measure how long it takes for the floating object to cover the 50 metres.
5. Take at least three readings. For greater accuracy take readings on both sides of the river and in the middle. Record your readings on your data record sheet (see Figure 4.2h, p. 94). Average the readings to determine the water velocity.

Skills

Calculating discharge

The amount of water flowing down a river is known as **discharge**. The discharge can be calculated by using the formula below.

Discharge = velocity × cross-sectional area

Skills

Recording data

Before you go on your field trip, you need to construct data collection sheets to record your data. Figure 4.2h shows a data collection sheet for one measuring site along the course of a river. The group using this sheet decided to record the depth of the river at three different sites in the river valley. They took six depth readings at regular intervals across the river at each of the three sites. Figure 4.2h shows their data for site 1.

Always double-check your measurements and the information you add to your data collection sheet.

Table 4.2a Sample fieldwork data

Site	Depth of river Readings (cm): starting on the left bank					
	1	2	3	4	5	6
Site 1	20	25	35	45	30	20
Site 2						
Site 3						

Data record sheet

River: Sandy Creek — Location: Site 1 — Date: 23 May 2004

A. Water velocity

Length of river section:	50 metres
Measurement 1	75 seconds
Measurement 2	90 seconds
Measurement 3	85 seconds
Average	83.3 seconds
Average velocity: (50/83.3)	0.6 metres per second (i)

B. Cross-sectional area

Average width of the river	15 metres
Channel depth at various points (in centimetres)	
Point 1	20
Point 2	25
Point 3	35
Point 4	45
Point 5	30
Point 6	20
Average depth: (175/6)	29 centimetres

Cross-sectional area: average river width × average depth

15 × 0.29 = 4.35 square metres (ii)

C. Discharge

Velocity (*i*) × cross-sectional area (*ii*)

0.6 metres per second × 4.35 square metres = 2.61 cubic metres per second

Figure 4.2h Sample data record sheet.

Step 3: showing your results

Once you have collected your data, you can start to write up your investigation and show what the data means. You will have collected a lot of measurements at different points along the river. You can use some of these measurements to draw cross-sections of the river channel. You can also work out the speed of flow and the changes in volume, erosional processes and landforms as you move to different sections of the river. Use a variety of maps, graphs and written work to show this information. The next three pages show you how to analyse and present your data.

Drawing a field sketch and sketch plan

When you are out collecting data in the field you might like to sketch the river valley at different locations. See Unit 2.9 for instructions on how to draw field sketches.

When you return to school you can draw neater versions of your field sketches. Annotate the completed sketches to highlight the main features and processes. Use the completed sketches to illustrate your fieldwork. An example of a field sketch (Figure 4.2i) and a sketch plan (Figure 4.2j) appear on the following page.

If you have taken images with a digital camera, you could load them onto your computer, annotate them and print them to illustrate your field report.

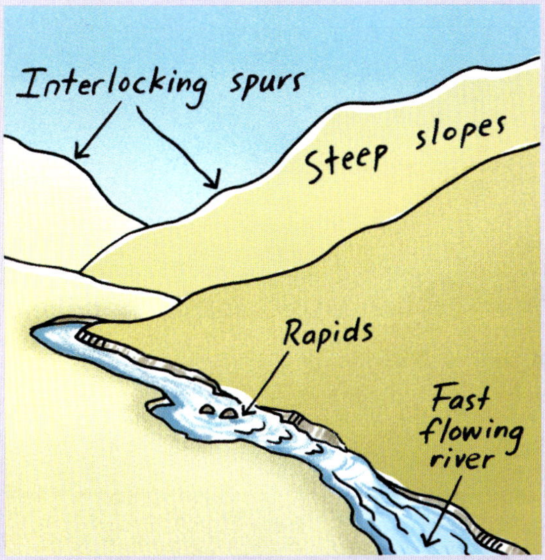

Figure 4.2i Annotated field sketch of the upper reach of the river being studied.

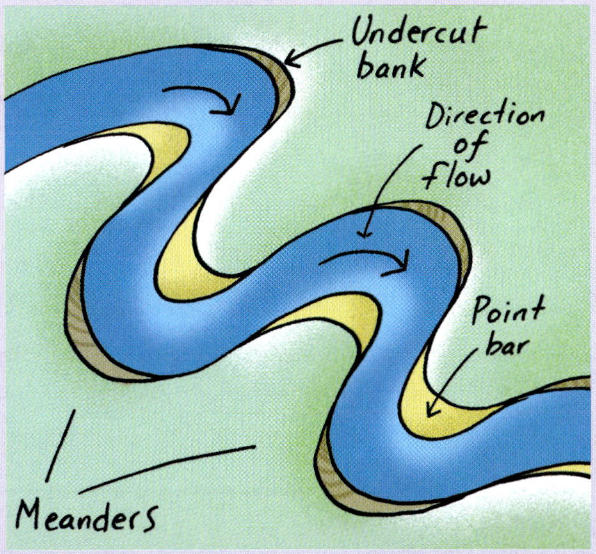

Figure 4.2j Sketch plan of the mid reach of the river being studied.

Graphs and proportional lines

Some of the data you have collected may be best shown by constructing bar graphs or proportional line graphs. Examples include the speed, or velocity, of flow in different sections of a river (see the graph on the left in Figure 4.2l, p. 96) and changes in velocity across the river (see the graph on the right in Figure 4.2l).

Skills

Drawing a river channel cross-section

To draw a cross-section of a river, you need measurements of the:

- depth of the river
- width of the channel
- width of the river from bank to bank
- height of the bank above the river.

Using these measurements, construct your cross-section by following the steps below:

1. Study the measurements you have collected and select a scale that will fit on your paper.
2. Start your cross-section by drawing a line representing the width of the river. Make sure you have enough room to draw in the river channel below it.
3. Look at the measurements for the height of the bank above the river level on both sides and mark the position of both banks.
4. Measure the width of the channel from bank to bank. Now draw in the banks.
5. Mark in the river bed by using your measurements of the depth of the river from the surface. Join the points together to show the shape of the river bed.
6. Add a scale and a heading.

Data for sample cross-section

Width of channel (bank to bank): 18 metres
Width of river: 16 metres
Height of bank above the river:

- Left side: 50 centimetres
- Right side: 75 centimetres

Depth of river:

	Left bank				Right bank
Reading	1	2	3	4	5
Depth	1.2 m	1.4 m	1.5 m	1.3 m	1.0 m

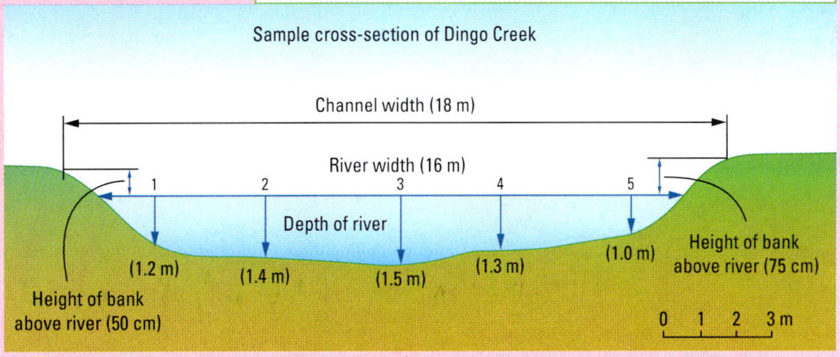

Figure 4.2k Sample cross-section of a river.

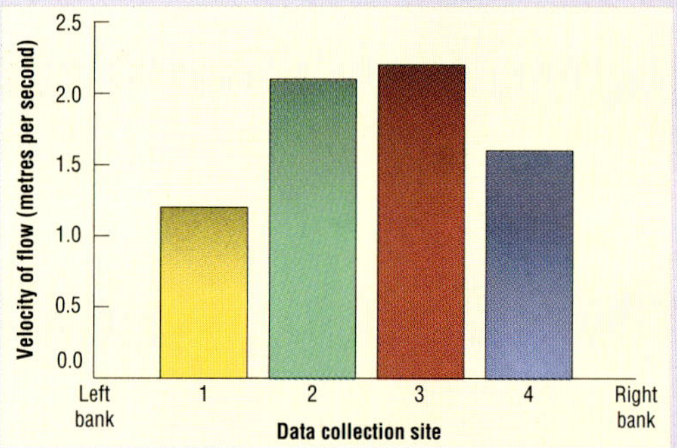

Data collection site	Velocity of flow (m/second)
1	1.2
2	2.1
3	2.2
4	1.6

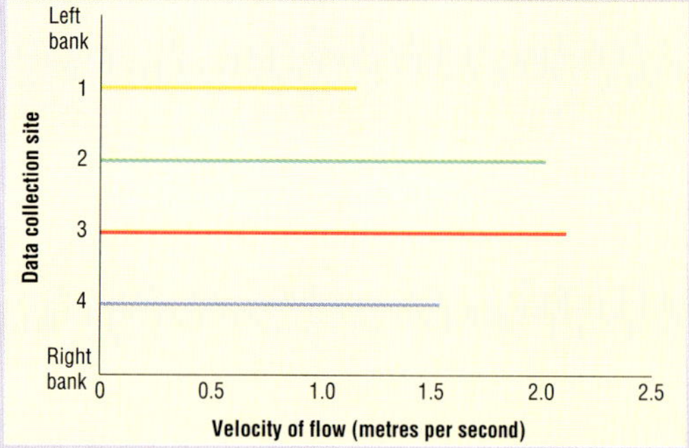

Figure 4.2l The bar graph on the left shows the changes in the velocity of flow in different sections of the river. The proportional line graph on the right shows the changes in velocity of flow across the river.

Skills

Drawing a river profile

To draw a river profile you will need a topographic map of the area you are studying. Follow the steps below:

1. Use the edge of a piece of paper to measure the length of section of river you are investigating on the map (see Figure 2.5l, p. 34). This will be the length of the river profile for the horizontal axis.
2. Use the map's contour lines to determine the height of the river at the point where you began your river study. Now estimate the height of the point at which you completed your river study. Use this information to determine the vertical scale of your river profile.
3. Place a straight edge of paper along the length of the river and carefully mark each point where the river crosses a contour line. Write the height of the contour line next to each mark. Put your paper along the bottom of the profile. Mark off the changes in height. Join up the points and draw your profile.
4. Label the profile with the information you have collected at your various study sites, including the measurements and main features.

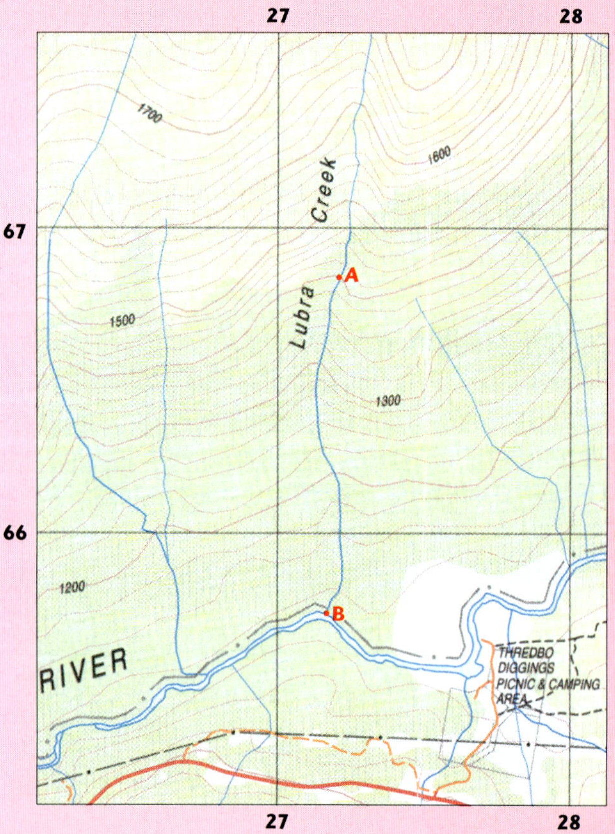

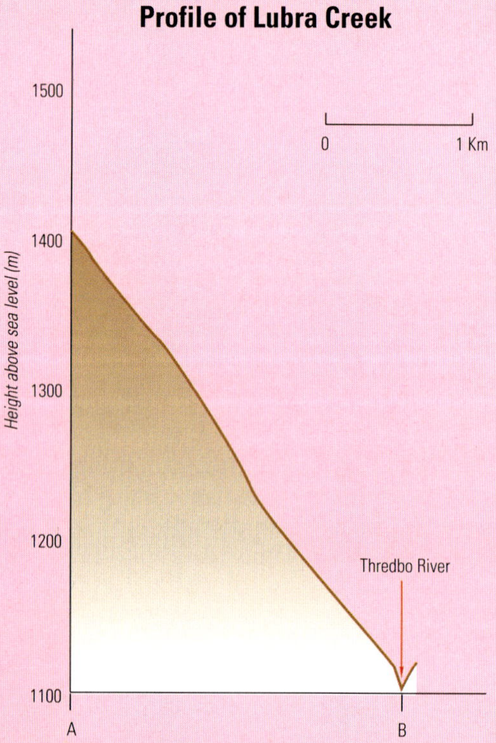

Figure 4.2m A sample river profile drawn using a topographic map.

Step 4: drawing conclusions

Once you have collected enough data and displayed the results using a range of techniques, you must now draw some conclusions about your investigation and evaluate your work.

Conclusion

As part of your conclusion you should give a general statement about what you found from your investigations. You could start your conclusion by writing:

From my study of the different sections of the ... River I found that the river landscapes and processes did change as it moved downstream. The main changes were...

Then give details, including measurements, and refer to the diagrams, maps and graphs you have drawn.

Evaluation

Your evaluation should finish off your enquiry. It refers to the whole study and you should make a note of the strengths and weaknesses of the project. You should mention what went well and what didn't go so well. Then suggest how it could be improved next time. You also need to suggest ideas for further investigation of the same topic.

You could start your evaluation by writing:

I learned a lot about river landscapes and processes from doing this inquiry. I also learned now important it was to...

You could then go on to say:

We had some difficulty collecting information because...

Finally, give suggestions about how you could extend your study:

It would be good to do some further study on...

Skills

Documenting the results of your fieldwork

When writing up your fieldwork report use the following subheadings:

- *introduction*—Outline the purpose of the fieldwork.
- *fieldwork methods*—Outline the way you gathered your data.
- *results*—These could be shown in a graphic form using line, pie, bar and column graphs and/or presented in tables.
- *explanation of results*—Outline what your results show.
- *conclusions*—Propose individual or group action that can be implemented to address any findings that concern you.
- *evaluation*—What worked well and what did not? How would you improve the effectiveness of the fieldwork if you were to repeat it?

Working geographically

1 **Calculating velocity** Students from a local high school measured the velocity of Runaway River at five points down its length. They took three readings at each point. Their results are shown in the table below. Copy the table and work out the average speed of flow at each of the five locations.

2 **Constructing graphs** Using the data in activity 1, draw a bar graph or proportional line graph to show how the speed of flow changes along the course of the river.

3 **Writing task** Look at the graph you have drawn for activity 3 and write a statement about what is shown. You may like to use the following writing frame as a starting point.

Comment on the changes in speed of flow along a river's profile

The fastest-flowing section of the river is at study point _____ , recording an average velocity of _____ metres per second. The slowest section is at study point _____ , which records an average speed of metres per second.

This shows that...

The reasons for this pattern/these results may be...

Velocity (metres per second)

Nearest the source	Site 1	Site 2	Site 3	Site 4	Site 5	Nearest the mouth
Reading 1	4.5	3.5	3.2	5.4	6.4	Reading 1
Reading 2	4.8	4.1	2.8	5.0	5.5	Reading 2
Reading 3	4.1	3.8	3.4	4.3	6.2	Reading 3
Average						Average

4.3

USING FIELDWORK

Measuring water quality

Water quality results

Name of waterway: ____________ Date: ____________

Location: ____________

Site number: ☐

Test	1	2	3	Comments
Turbidity				
Smell				
pH				
Ammonia				
Organisms				
Site observations				

Figure 4.3a Water quality results sheet.

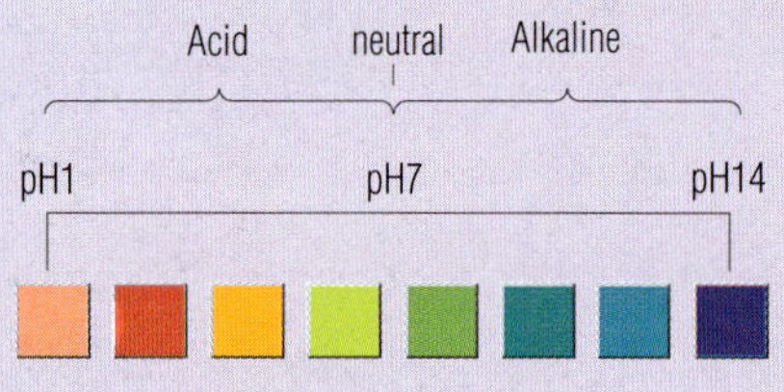

Figure 4.3b A pH chart.

Many communities are concerned about the quality of water in local creeks and rivers. What is the state of the waterways in your local area? This fieldwork activity will enable you to make a judgment about how clean they are.

You can measure water quality without expensive equipment. One simple method involves looking at the kinds of animals that are found in creeks and rivers. The health of a river ecosystem can be measured by the variety of animal species present. If the water is polluted, many species find it almost impossible to survive.

The aim of this fieldwork task is to investigate water quality in one or more creeks or rivers in your local area.

Step 1: selecting a suitable site

You can approach the task in one of two ways:

- you can compare pollution levels in two or more rivers or creeks
- you can measure how pollution levels change down the course of one river or creek.

Step 2: gathering equipment

You will need the following equipment:

- a white dish or tray
- a magnifying glass
- bottles and jars with lids for collecting water samples
- a pond dipping net
- tumeric paper (which turns brown in ammonia)
- pH paper (which measures acidity)
- a clipboard, pencil and recording sheet.

Step 3: drawing up a results sheet

Figure 4.3a shows a results sheet that will help you record your observations and measurements.

Step 4: taking measurements and making observations

At each of the selected sites complete the following experiments. Repeat each experiment three times at each site to make sure the results are reliable.

Turbidity

Fill your jar with water. Is the water clear or is it muddy? Allow the water to stand for ten minutes. How clear is the water now? How much sediment has settled on the bottom of the jar?

Filter another sample of the same water through some filter paper or blotting paper. Observe what remains on the paper.

Smell

Using the same jar of water, smell the contents. Does the water smell? Record your observations on the results sheet.

pH test

Fill your dish with water taken from the river or creek. Place a piece of indicator paper in the water. Estimate the pH by comparing the test strip with the indicator chart (see Figure 4.3b). If recordings taken at different sites within the same river vary significantly, this may indicate pollution.

Ammonia test

Use the tumeric paper to test a sample of water taken from the creek or river. If the paper turns brown, ammonia is present in the water. Ammonia is a poisonous chemical that builds up in water when it is polluted by sewage, rotting vegetation and carbon-based chemicals.

Organism survey

Scientists have found that the number and variety of water bugs found in a stream can indicate the amount of pollution present. Sampling the water bugs in a local stream will give you an indication of the quality of the water.

Water bugs live in many different parts of the stream. Some live on the water's surface, while others live on or in the bottom of the river or creek, in the surrounding vegetation or among the rocks.

Scoop your net through the weeds growing on the river bed, through the plants growing on the water's edge, and through the water at various depths. Wash off the excess mud by dunking the base of the net into the water. Empty the contents of the net into your white tray and, with the aid of a magnifying glass, look for bugs similar to those shown in Figure 4.3c. List the organisms present in your sample.

If you can identify bugs from groups 1 and 2, the quality of the water is quite good. If bugs from only groups 3 and 4 are present, the creek or river probably has quite high levels of pollution.

Site observations

Record any additional observations about the sites selected. Identify any possible sources of pollution. Use photographs to illustrate your notes.

Step 5: using the results of your fieldwork

If you find that your local creek or river is polluted, you may like to do something about it. In small groups, discuss the actions you could take. You could consider:

- writing to the Environment Protection Authority and your local council
- mounting a public information campaign using posters and leaflets warning of the dangers of water pollution.

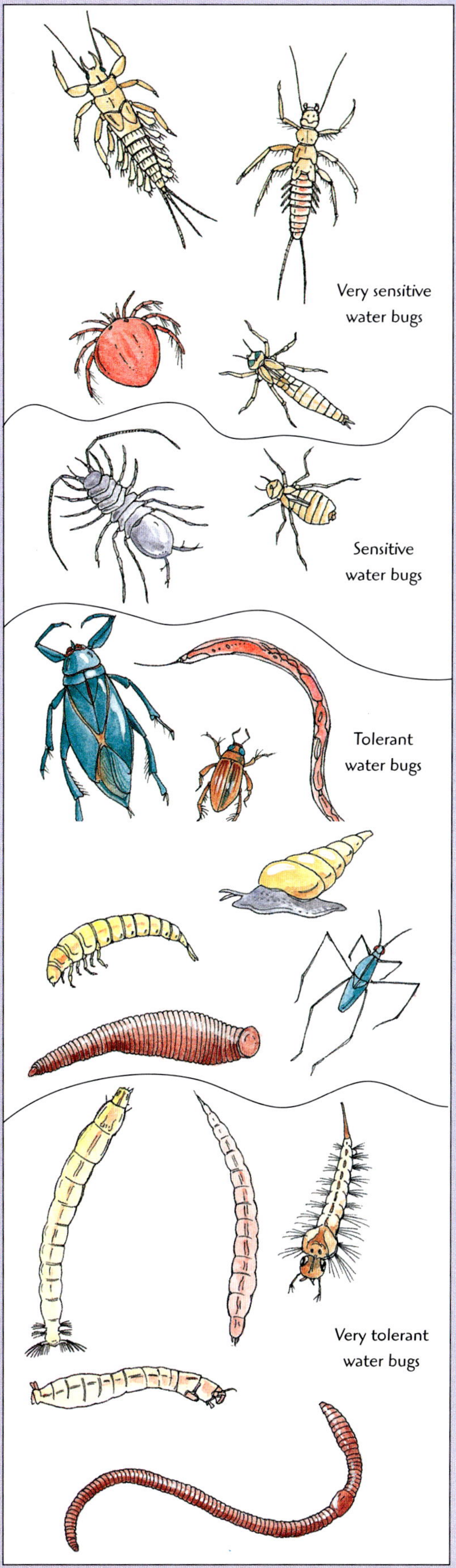

Figure 4.3c Some of the small aquatic animals found in rivers and creeks.

4.4

USING STATISTICS

Developing a community profile

Many of the characteristics of your local community cannot be observed during fieldwork. Looking at the type and size of homes, the general streetscape and the range of shops and restaurants serving the area may suggest some features of the community, but actual statistics are often needed before firm conclusions can be made.

The best source of statistical data for any area of Australia is the *Australian Bureau of Statistics* (ABS), which is recognised throughout the world as one of the best gatherers of statistical data. This government agency conducts a **census** of each Australian household every five years. During the census, a range of data is obtained, including details of people's occupations, ages, families, religion, education and ethnic background.

At other times the ABS uses **surveys** to gather information from a sample of the population. All this information is available to the public. Many public libraries and some school libraries keep a range of ABS publications. Others can be obtained directly from the ABS or from government bookshops. Some data, including that shown in Table 4.4a, is available via the Internet and the range of CD-ROM databases produced by the ABS. Newspapers often use ABS data in a graphic form to illustrate stories.

Before you begin your search for data, determine what statistics you need and what information about your local area you hope to gain from them. Some suggestions are given in the box 'Developing a local area profile'.

Developing a local area profile

Who lives in the local area?
The ABS can provide you with information about age, birthplace, family size and ethnic background.

What can we learn about how people live in the local area live?
The ABS can provide you with information about income, home ownership, education and occupations.

How does the local community compare with other areas?
The statistics mean more when they are compared with those of other areas (see Table 4.4a).

How does my local area compare with other places?
Comparing statistics helps us to understand more about our own community. In activity 1 at the end of this unit you will use information from the ABS to find statistics for your own local government area (LGA). This will allow you to construct a table like Table 4.4a to show statistical data for your own community. You can then compare the statistics with the information that the table provides about other communities in Australia.

The statistics in Table 4.4a give only a limited set of information, but you can draw a number of conclusions from them. What else would you like to know about your community?

Remember that statistics such as these often mask significant differences within communities. Care should always be taken when making generalisations based on statistical data.

Table 4.4a A comparison of statistics for selected communities

Demographic and social characteristics	Woollahra	Penrith	Bankstown	Port Macquarie
Population	50 897	172 397	165 604	38 288
Population aged <15 years (%)	14.2	24.5	21.6	19.0
Population aged >65 years (%)	15.1	7.0	14.2	23.4
Median age (years)	37	30	35	43
Population born outside Australia (%)	31.7	21.2	35.3	11.7
People unemployed (%)	3.6	5.9	7.9	10.2
Median weekly family income ($)	1500–1999	1000–1199	800–999	600–699

Based on Statistical Local Areas
Source: ABS, 2001

Collecting statistical data

Geographical research often depends on information and data collected in surveys. Being able to develop a survey is an important geographical skill. Because it is very expensive to survey the whole population, often just part of the population is surveyed. This part of the population is called a sample.

Sometimes, the findings of a survey need to reflect the views of the whole population. Specific groups then have to be surveyed so that the sample reflects the make-up of the whole population. This is how public opinion polls are taken. Points to consider when developing a survey **questionnaire** are listed in the box below.

Skills

Developing a questionnaire

Developing a questionnaire requires careful thought and some testing,. the aim being to obtain clear answers from those being questioned. The views of those being surveyed should not be influenced by confusing questions or the views of the interviewer. Keep the following points in mind:

- Make sure the information you collect meets your needs.
- Keep the questionnaire short.
- Use clearly worded, simple questions.
- Test your questionnaire on a small sample group before conducting your survey. Change any questions considered confusing.
- Present your questionnaire in a professional way. Include a short introduction explaining its purpose. Have it neatly typed and well spaced.
- As the interviewer, behave in a way that encourages people to answer your questions. Be friendly and polite and explain the survey's purpose.

A sample questionnaire is given in Figure 4.4a.

Working geographically

1 **Research** Copy column 1 of Table 4.4a. Add a second column where you can record the statistical data for your own local area. Research the data for your area and add this to your table.

2 **Interpreting statistics** Study Table 4.4a. Name the community that has the:
   - **a** the highest proportion of its population under 15 years
   - **b** the community with the lowest and highest median age
   - **c** the highest proportion of its population born outside Australia
   - **d** the highest level of unemployment
   - **e** the highest and lowest median weekly family income.

3 **Challenge: Interpreting statistics** Based on the statistical data provided in Table 4.4a, identify the communities enjoying the highest and lowest overall level of economic well-being. What criteria did you use to make these judgments?

4 **Challenge: Writing task** Write a report comparing your local community with those shown in Table 4.4a. Use statistics from the table to illustrate your report.

Using statistical databases to investigate your local community

ICT

Australia's census data is available on a number of commercially available CD-ROM databases. Use a database, such as Census 2001 Explorer, to investigate the town or city in which you live or go to school.

1 Use the inbuilt map generator to construct a choropleth map (see Unit 2.1) showing:
   - **a** the income of households
   - **b** unemployment levels
   - **c** the percentage of people with tertiary education
   - **d** the proportion of Australian-born residents

2 Construct a pie graph (see Figure 2.13d, p. 51) showing the ethnic composition of the town or city.

3 Place the data for the town or city into a spreadsheet. Print the spread-sheet and paste it into your workbook.

Sample questionnaire about enviromentally friendly practices

1 Sex: male ☐ female ☐

2 Age group: 15 - 19 ☐ 20–39 ☐ 40–59 ☐ 60+ ☐

3 Which of the following would you be prepared to do to help the environment?
- recycle waste ☐
- use energy-efficient lighting ☐
- turn down the heating ☐
- use the car less ☐
- buy 'green' products ☐
- buy goods that use ☐
- less packaging ☐
- avoid using plastic bags ☐
- buy products made ☐
- from recycled products ☐
- plant more trees ☐
- join a conservation group ☐
- don't know ☐
- none of the above ☐

4 What household wastes do you recycle?
- paper ☐
- glass ☐
- aluminium cans ☐
- plastic drink containers ☐
- vegetable waste ☐

5 Why do you recycle?

____

____

Figure 4.4a Surveying community attitudes to environmental protection.

Chapter 5 PART B Global environments

Introducing physical environments

Introduction

In this chapter we will begin to develop our understanding of the geographical processes that form and transform global environments and identify human interactions within environments. We pay particular attention to global distribution of earth's terrestrial (land-based) environments. Many of these environments will be examined in greater detail in Chapters 6–12.

Learn about:

- the types of global environments and their location
- the spatial distribution of selected global environments
- the major geographical processes within selected environments
- the ways humans, including indigenous groups, interact with selected environments
- the way the environment influences communities
- the ways the relationships between communities and environments are changing
- strategies and processes that individuals, groups and governments use to influence change
- the ways communities are responding to these changes

Learn to:

- locate different global environments
- outline the basic characteristics of different types of global environments
- recognise the spatial distribution of a global environment
- describe the geographical processes that shape the selected environment
- draw and describe the operation of a simple ecosystem
- describe the interaction of humans with the environment
- describe the interrelationship of the environment and a specific community
- explain how individuals, community organisations and government actions are contributing to the current management of the environment
- identify the responsibility of government to the community and its environment
- describe current use of the environment and suggest strategies for future ecological sustainability

Key questions

1 How do we classify global environments?
2 What is the difference between weather and climate?
3 Why does temperature vary with latitude?
4 What drives the earth's water cycle?
5 How do the animals within an ecosystem interact?

Why is it so?

Why is the sky blue? Blue light is scattered (spread) much more than all the other colours contained in the light coming from the sun. This causes the sky to appear blue.

Why are clouds white? The water and ice particles found in clouds scatter wavelengths of all colour by the same amount. Because all colours are represented in this scattered light the clouds appears white. White light is made up of all colours, such as red, blue and violet.

Why are sunsets red? At sunset, light from the sun has to travel through much more atmosphere compared with when the sun is directly overhead. Blue light, and all the other colours, are scattered and diluted. As a result, only red, orange and yellow light remain visible in the atmosphere.

Why do we see rainbows? The bending of sunlight by raindrops is the key to the formation of rainbows. To see a rainbow, the sun must be behind you and rain falling in front of you. As sunlight enters a raindrop it is dispersed, or spread out, into its various colours, creating a spectrum.

Why do we see rainbows?

eGlossary

GeoToolkit

ICT Toolkit

Glossary of key terms

Air mass A large body of air with similar temperature and moisture characteristics.
Aquatic ecosystems Water-based communities of plants and animals.
Aquifer A layer of rock in which water is found.
Atmospheric pressure The weight of the air pressing down on the earth's surface.
Biome A vegetation community occupying a large area of the earth's surface.
Carnivores Animals that eat only meat.
Climate The long-term weather pattern for a place or region.
Condensation The conversion of water vapour into droplets of liquid water.
Consumer An organism that gains its energy requirements by eating plant or animal matter.
Decomposers Organisms that break down the remains of other living things.
Ecological sustainability Using, conserving and enhancing the earth's natural resources so that ecological processes, on which life depends, are maintained and the total quality of life, now and in the future, can be increased.
Ecosystem A community of interacting plants and animals and their physical surroundings.
Evaporation The conversion of liquid water into water vapour.
Front The boundary between two air masses.
Groundwater Water stored beneath the earth's surface.
Herbivores Animals that eat only plants.
Infiltration The movement of water down through the soil.
Omnivores Animals that eat both plants and meat.
Orographic rainfall Rainfall that occurs when warm, moist air is forced to rise by a mountain barrier. The rain falls on the mountain's windward side.
Percolation The movement of water down through the soil to become groundwater.
Photosynthesis The process by which green plants trap the energy from sunlight and use it to make food (such as sugars) from water and carbon dioxide.
Porous The ability of some rock types to store air or water in small spaces between the material from which it is made.
Precipitation Any moisture reaching the surface of the earth, such as rain, snow and sleet.
Producers Organisms (plants) that produce their own food via the process of photosynthesis.
Runoff The movement of surface water down slopes.
Terrestrial ecosystems Land-based communities of plants and animals.
Transpiration The loss of water vapour from the leaves of plants.
Water table The level to which an aquifer is filled.
Weather The day-to-day condition of the atmosphere.

5.1 Locating and classifying physical environments

Physical environments are those dominated by natural features, such as landforms and vegetation. The elements of the physical environment include the rocks and soils, vegetation, animals, water and climate. The ways these elements interact result in the development of distinctive physical environments. In this unit we examine the classification and global distribution of these physical environments.

One way to classify physical environments is to look at the different types of ecosystems found on the earth's surface. An **ecosystem** is a community of living plants and animals that have adapted to the conditions within a particular environment. The many ecosystems that exist can be divided into two groups: aquatic ecosystems and terrestrial ecosystems.

- **aquatic ecosystems**—These water-based ecosystems include open oceans, river estuaries (the part of a river influenced by the sea), coastal wetlands (see Chapter 10) and coral reefs (see Chapter 11).
- **terrestrial ecosystems**—These land-based ecosystems include the tundra and polar lands (see Chapter 6), tropical rainforests (see Chapter 7), tropical savannas, temperate grasslands, mountains (see Chapter 8), broadleaf forests, coniferous forests and deserts (see Chapter 12). The earth's major terrestrial ecosystems are shown in Figure 5.1a.

The earth's terrestrial ecosystems are usually named after the type of vegetation that dominates the area. The type of vegetation, in turn, depends mainly on climate. The different combinations of temperature and rainfall found in different places determine what types of plants can grow there. Compare Figure 5.1a with the world pattern of climate (Figure 5.3j, p. 112).

Foundation worksheet 5.1

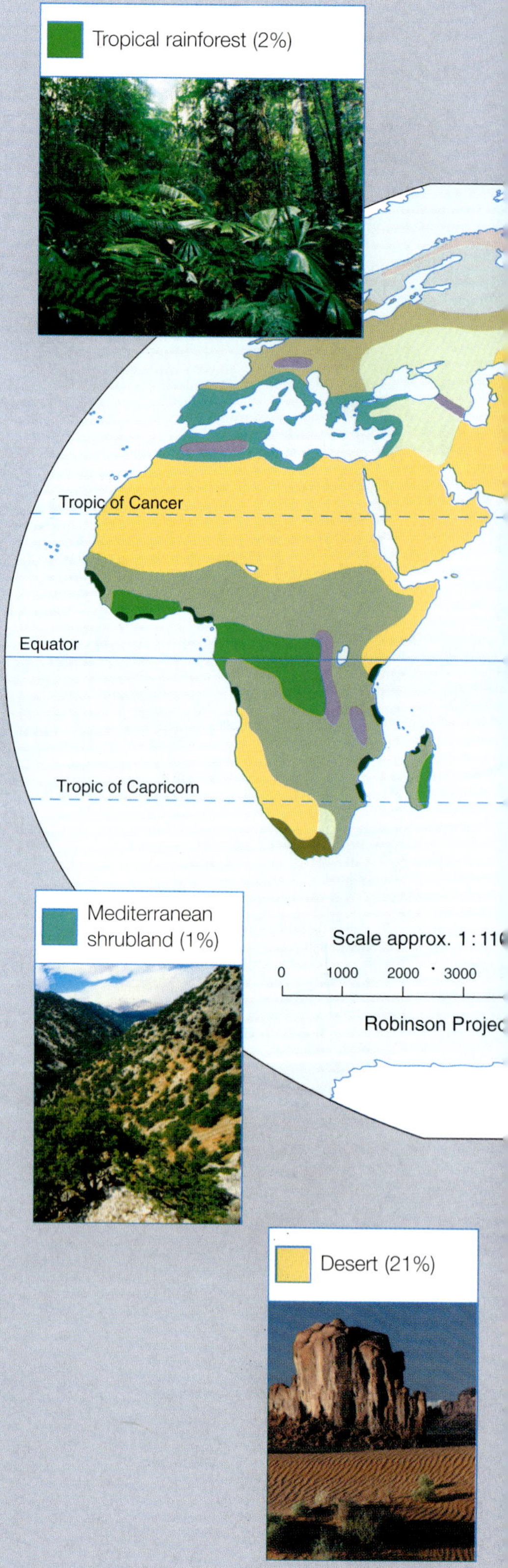

Understanding the text

1. Define the term 'ecosystem'.
2. Distinguish between aquatic and terrestrial ecosystems.
3. After what are most terrestrial ecosystems named?
4. What important role does climate have in determining the type of ecosystems that exist in an area?

UTT worksheet 5.1

Activity 2

1. **Writing task** Study Figure 5.1a. With the aid of an atlas write a report describing the distribution of the earth's major terrestrial ecosystems.
2. **Interpreting maps** Study Figure 5.1a and the map showing the world pattern of climate (Figure 5.3j, p. 112). Comment on the relationship between the world pattern of climate and the location of the earth's major terrestrial ecosystems.

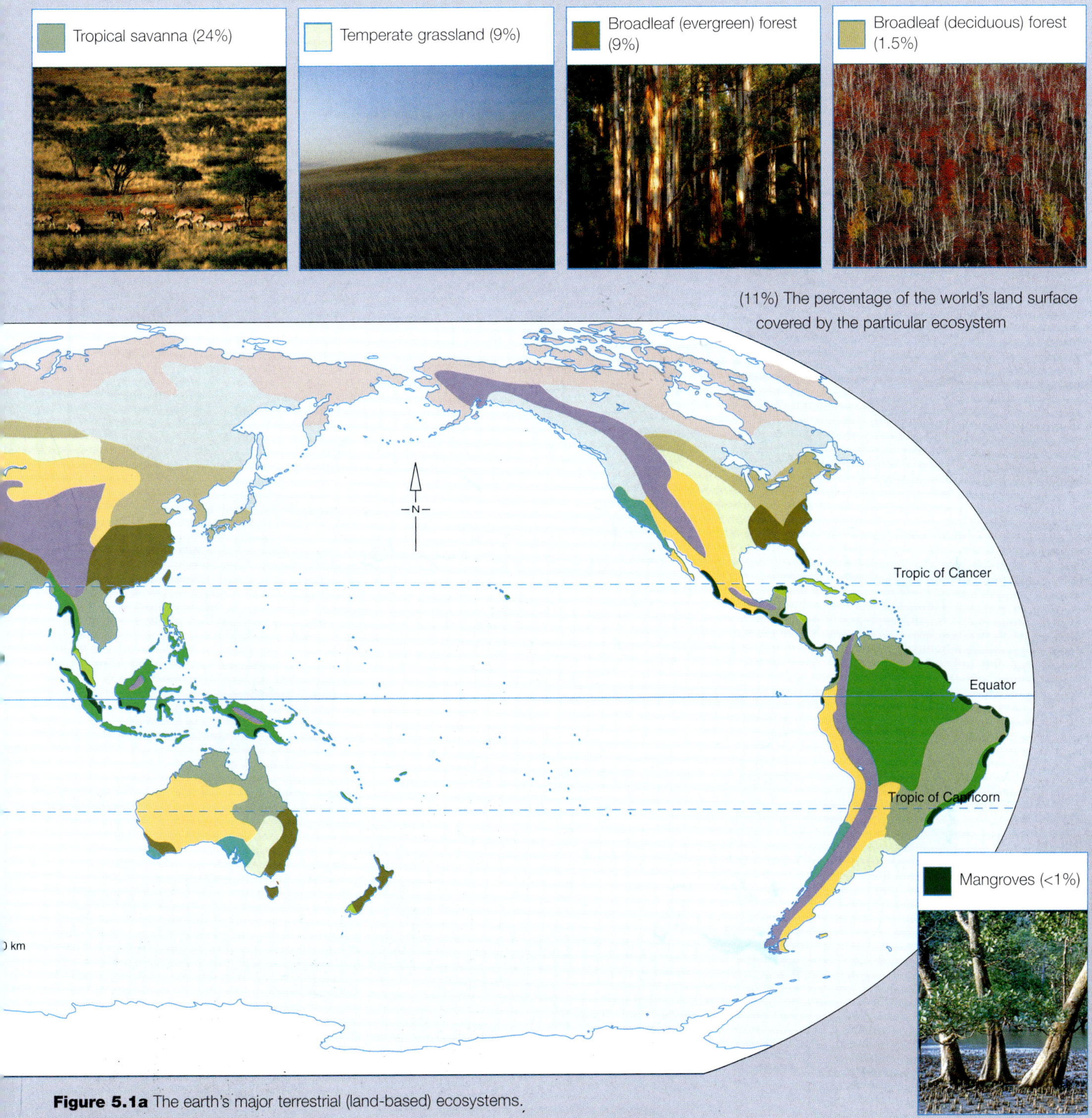

Figure 5.1a The earth's major terrestrial (land-based) ecosystems.

5.2

USING PHOTOGRAPHS

What physical environment is that?

The photographs on this page illustrate the great diversity of the earth's physical environments. Each physical environment or ecosystem has its own complex community of plants and animals. The amazing diversity of life forms shows how these organisms have adapted, through evolution, to the different environmental conditions that exist within particular ecosystems.

1

2

3

4

5

6

7

8

9

10

Bison

Llamas

Siberian tiger

Polar bear

Brown bear

Alligator

Orang-utan

Goanna

Giraffe

Fallow deer

Activity 2

1 **Interpreting photographs**
Look at page 106.
- a Divide a page in your workbook into four columns. Label them with the following headings:
  - photograph number
  - type of physical environment or ecosystem
  - dominant features
  - climate.
- b In the second column, write the name of the physical environment or ecosystem shown in each of the photographs (see Unit 5.1).
- c In the third column, describe the main features of each physical environment.
- d In the fourth column, use evidence from the photographs to describe the climate of each physical environment.

2 **Research: Report** Study the photographs on page 107 and match each animal with the physical environment on page 106 that is its natural habitat.
Now choose two of the animals shown on page 107. Do some library research on each of the animals to find answers to the following questions:
- a Where in the world is the animal found?
- b What type of animal is it?
- c What is its natural habitat?
- d What does it eat?
- e Has it any special adaptations that help it survive?
- f Does it have any predators?
- g Is it endangered? Why?

Present an oral report on the findings of your research (see Unit 2.14).

Extension worksheet 5.1

5.3 Weather and climate

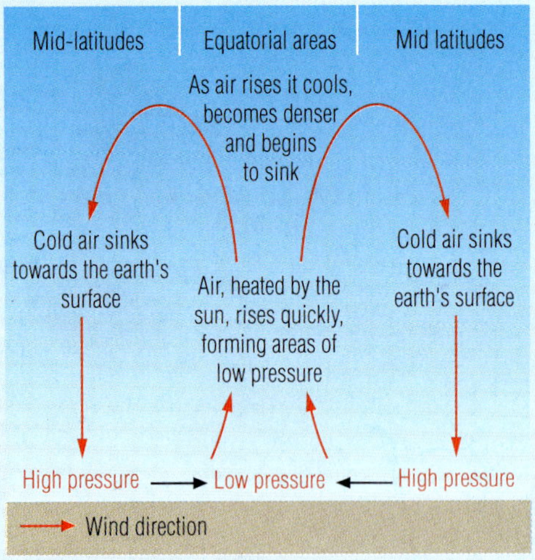

Figure 5.3a When air near the earth's surface is heated rapidly, it rises, forming areas of low pressure. As the air cools, it sinks, forming areas of high pressure.

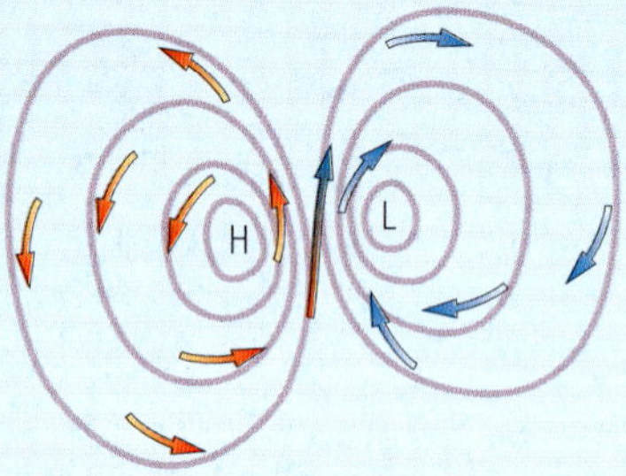

Figure 5.3b Air moves from areas of high pressure to areas of low pressure. The closer the isobars, the stronger the wind.

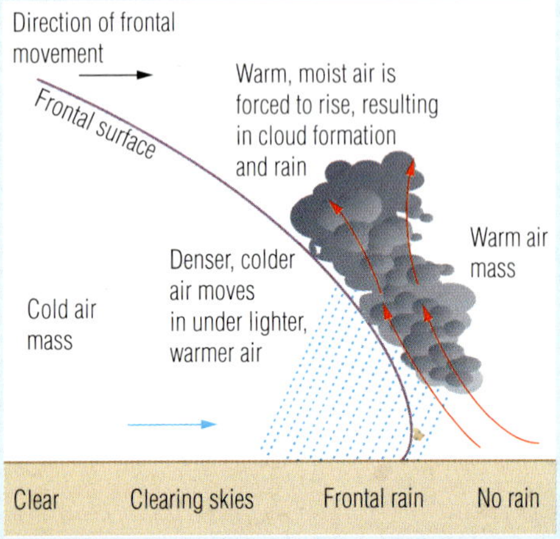

Figure 5.3c The passing of a cold front often results in rainfall and a drop in temperature.

What is the difference between weather and climate?

The words 'weather' and 'climate' do not mean the same thing. **Weather** is the day-to-day condition of the atmosphere at a particular place. It includes all the daily changes in temperature, precipitation, wind, sunshine, humidity (the amount of moisture in the air) and atmospheric pressure. Weather maps, or *synoptic charts*, use symbols to show the pattern of these changes (see Unit 2.7).

Climate is the long-term weather pattern for a place or region. The climate of a place depends on its latitude, the season, its aspect, how close it is to the sea, ocean currents and its height above sea level (elevation).

Weather and climate affect the type of clothing we wear, our activities, the food we grow, the kinds of houses we live in and the types of transport we use. It also affects the types of plants and animals living in an area. Weather and climate are important indications of changes in the earth's geographical processes. This is because a change in the atmosphere can quickly change the weather. For example, a volcanic eruption can affect weather around the world in a matter of days.

Weather

How does the weather we experience happen? To understand weather, we need to understand atmospheric pressure. **Atmospheric pressure** is the weight of the air pressing down on the earth's surface. When air is heated by the energy of the sun, it rises. This forms areas of low pressure. When air cools, it sinks towards the earth's surface. This forms areas of high pressure. The location of high-pressure and low-pressure systems helps us predict the weather for a particular place. High-pressure systems are usually associated with settled, or fine, weather. Low-pressure systems are generally associated with unsettled weather. Figure 5.3a shows how high-pressure and low-pressure systems form.

We can also use pressure systems to read and predict wind direction. Moving air, known as *wind*, always moves from areas of high pressure (highs) to areas of low pressure (lows). In the Southern Hemisphere, the air moves out from the centre of a high in an anticlockwise direction. It moves into the centre of a low in a clockwise direction (see Figure 5.3b).

Pressure systems are not the same as air masses. **Air masses** are large bodies of air with similar temperature and moisture content. The line along which two air masses meet is known as a **front**. Figure 5.3c shows how the passing of a *cold front* can result in rainfall and a sudden drop in temperature. The passing of a *warm front* results in a rise in temperature and more widespread rainfall. Warm fronts are very rare in Australia.

Precipitation is any moisture reaching the surface of the earth. Forms of precipitation include rain, sleet, snow, hail, dew and frost.

Climate

Climate is the weather experienced by a place over many years. The factors that contribute to this long-term pattern are discussed below.

Factors affecting temperature

Latitude

As Figure 5.3e shows, solar energy has twice the area to heat at 60° north and 60° south as it does at the Equator. Therefore, average temperatures are lower at higher latitudes (see Table 5.3a).

Length of day and night

Because the earth's axis is tilted at an angle of 23.5°, there are seasonal differences in the number of daylight hours. The shorter the day, the less opportunity there is for the earth and its atmosphere to absorb heat. The differences in the length of day and night at different latitudes is shown in Table 5.3b.

Seasonal differences

The changing seasons not only determine the length of the day but also the angle at which the sun's rays reach the earth's surface. Figure 5.3d shows that from November to January the Southern Hemisphere is tilted towards the sun. From May to July, the Northern Hemisphere is tilted towards the sun. This is why the Northern Hemisphere has its summer in the middle of the year while Australia is having its winter.

Elevation (height above sea level)

Because of their height, mountain areas are cooler than areas at lower elevations. Mt Kilimanjaro is Africa's highest mountain. At 5894 metres its top is permanently covered with snow, even though it is

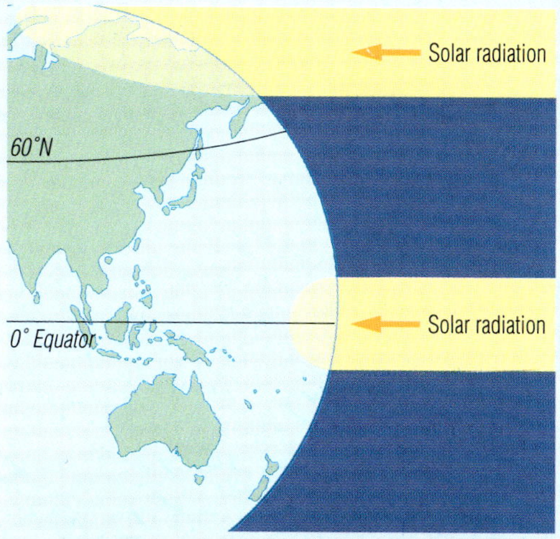

Figure 5.3e The impact of latitude on the heating of the earth's surface.

Table 5.3a Amount of incoming solar energy reaching the earth's surface at different latitudes

Latitude	Incoming solar energy (%)
0°	100.0
10°	98.6
20°	94.5
30°	88.0
40°	79.2
50°	68.5
60°	57.0
70°	47.4
80°	43.0
90°	41.6

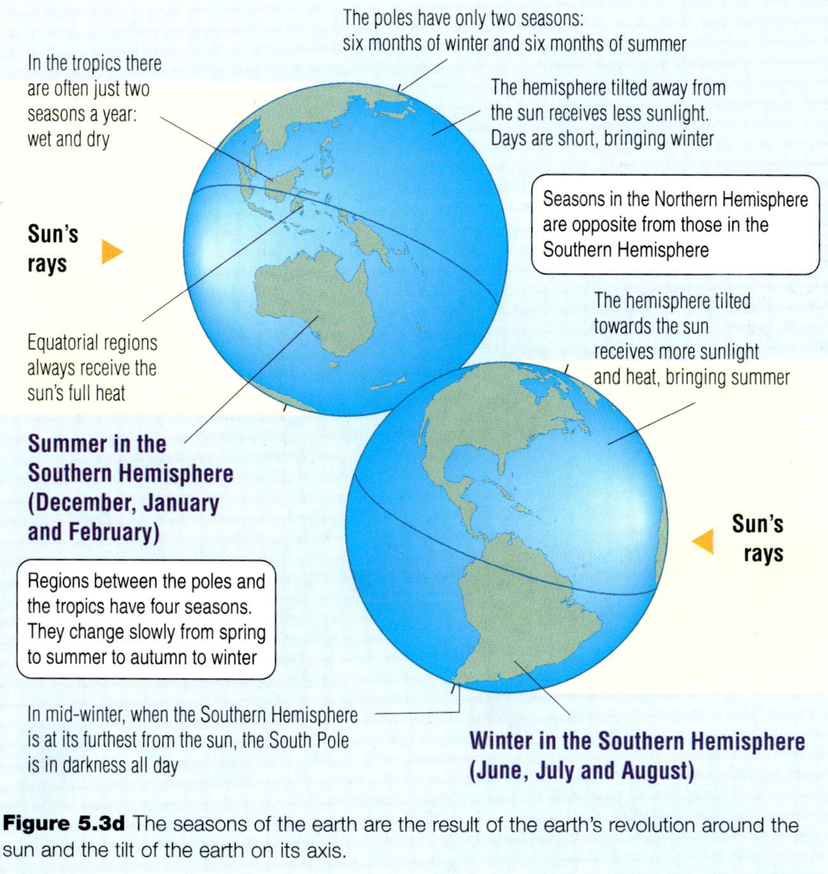

Figure 5.3d The seasons of the earth are the result of the earth's revolution around the sun and the tilt of the earth on its axis.

Table 5.3b Length of day and night at different latitudes

Latitude	Length of the longest day and night
0°	12 hours 0 minutes
10°	12 hours 35 minutes
17°	13 hours 0 minutes
20°	13 hours 12 minutes
30°	13 hours 56 minutes
40°	14 hours 52 minutes
50°	16 hours 18 minutes
60°	18 hours 27 minutes
63°	26 hours 0 minutes
66.5°	24 hours 0 minutes
67.5°	1 month
70°	2 months
80°	4 months
90°	6 months

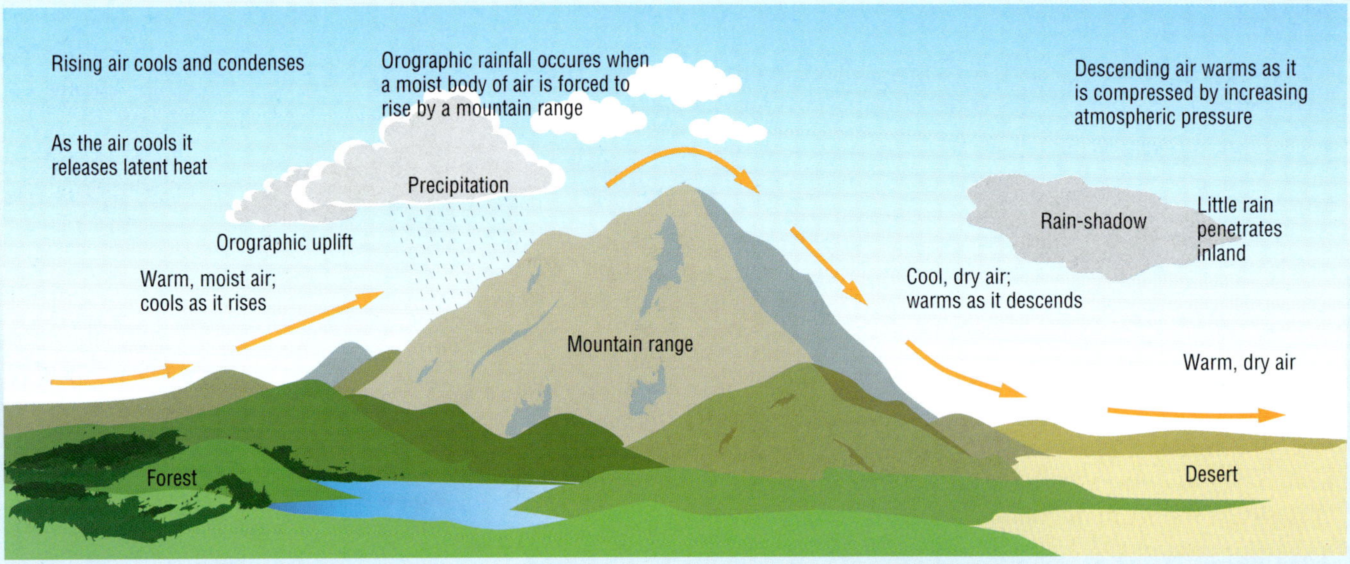

Figure 5.3f The impact of topography on rainfall and temperature.

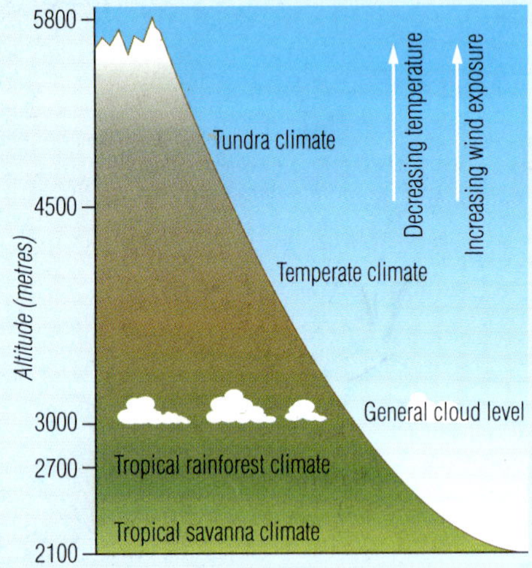

Figure 5.3g Many of the changes in climate that occur with latitude are mirrored as you go up mountains.

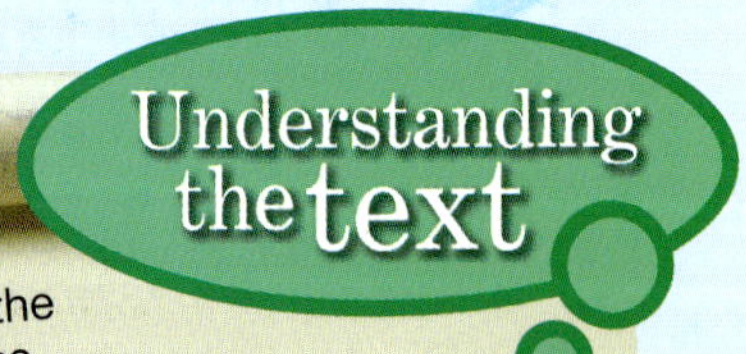

1. Explain the difference between weather and climate.
2. Explain how high-pressure and low-pressure systems develop. Describe the type of weather usually associated with each.
3. What are air masses?
4. What is precipitation? Name the various types.

just south of the Equator. On average, the temperature drops by approximately 6.5°C for every 1000 metres of elevation (see Figures 5.3f and 5.3g).

Factors affecting both temperature and rainfall

Mountain barriers

Mountains also act as barriers to the movement of moisture-laden air. As shown in Figure 5.3f, when warm, moist air is forced to rise, it cools and the water vapour in the air turns into droplets of water. These water droplets fall on the mountain's windward side (the side facing directly into the wind) as either rain or snow. This is known as **orographic rainfall**. The air flowing over the mountain is much drier. Deserts are often found on the leeward (sheltered) side of large mountain ranges. This is known as the *rain-shadow effect*.

Distance from the sea

Distance from the sea influences both temperature and rainfall.

Temperature

The sea gains and loses its heat much more slowly than the land—the sea maintains more even temperatures. Places near the coast therefore have less variation in temperature than inland places. Places away from the coast can have higher temperatures during the day and lower temperatures at night because of the speed at which land gains and loses heat.

Rainfall

Winds blowing off the sea carry a lot of moisture. Because of this, places near the coast often receive higher rainfall than those further inland. By the time the winds reach inland areas, they have lost most or all of their moisture.

Ocean currents

The temperature of ocean currents influences both air temperature and rainfall.

Temperature

Oceans absorb heat during the day and release it slowly during the night. This helps keep coastal areas much warmer than inland areas.

Rainfall

Water evaporates much more quickly from oceans affected by warm ocean currents. As a result, nearby coastal areas are likely to have higher levels of rainfall. Areas affected by cold ocean currents have much lower **evaporation** rates. As Figure 5.3j (p. 112) shows, the world's deserts are located in areas affected by cold ocean currents.

Prevailing winds

The prevailing wind is the direction from which the wind blows most often. The temperature of the prevailing wind is affected by the area it blows from and over. When prevailing winds blow from over warm bodies of water they often bring rain.

World climate pattern

World climate patterns are quite complicated. The best way to understand them is to begin with very broad differences and add detail, step by step, to build up the whole picture.

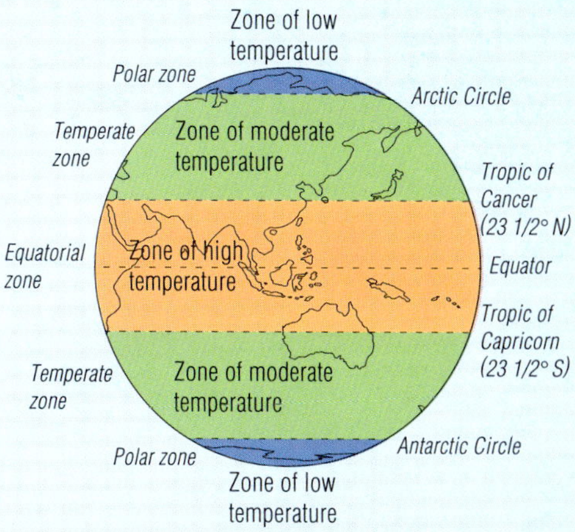

Figure 5.3h The broad temperature zones of the world.

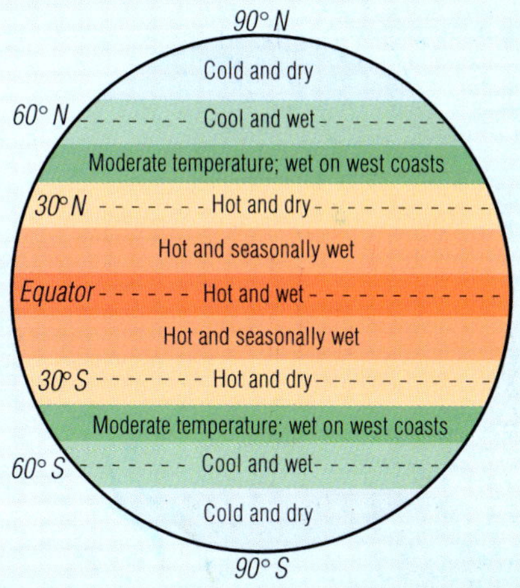

Figure 5.3i The broad rainfall zones of the world.

Did U know?

- Raindrops fall to earth at 11–29 kilometres per hour in still air. The speed of the raindrop depends on its size.
- The weight of a cloud depends on its size and type. A typical cumulus cloud, with a volume of 1 cubic kilometre, will weigh about 635 million kilograms.
- Thunderstorm clouds (cumulonimbus clouds) reach the highest elevation—often more than 10 kilometres above the earth's surface. As much as 140 000 tonnes of water can be contained inside a cumulonimbus cloud. That is enough to fill a lake 1.6 kilometres long, 91 metres wide and 1.5 metres deep.
- The average evaporation rate across the planet is 2.84 millimetres per day.
- The explosive forces unleashed by a large thunderstorm equals 12 000 tonnes of dynamite.
- The sound of thunder is created when lightning heats the air to 25 000°C.
- A bolt of lightning creates light equal to 10 million 100-watt light bulbs.
- The weight of all the rain falling to earth each day is approximately 10 billion tonnes.

Using the Internet to investigate weather and climate

ICT

The sites listed below provide information about weather and climate. Some of these sites have a detailed database that provides climate data for locations around the world.

- World Meteorological Organization
- UK Meteoroligcal Office
- US National Oceanic Atmospheric Administration: National Weather Service
- Australian Bureau of Meteorology
- BBC Weather
- WorldClimate
- World Weather

Activity 2

1 **Interpreting diagrams** Study Figures 5.3f and 5.3g. Write an explanation of the impact that topography has on climate.

2 **Internet research: Constructing graphs** Use the Bureau of Meteorology website to find climate statistics for the area in which you live. Construct a climate graph similar to Figure 2.7a (p. 38). Use your graph to write a description of your local climate.

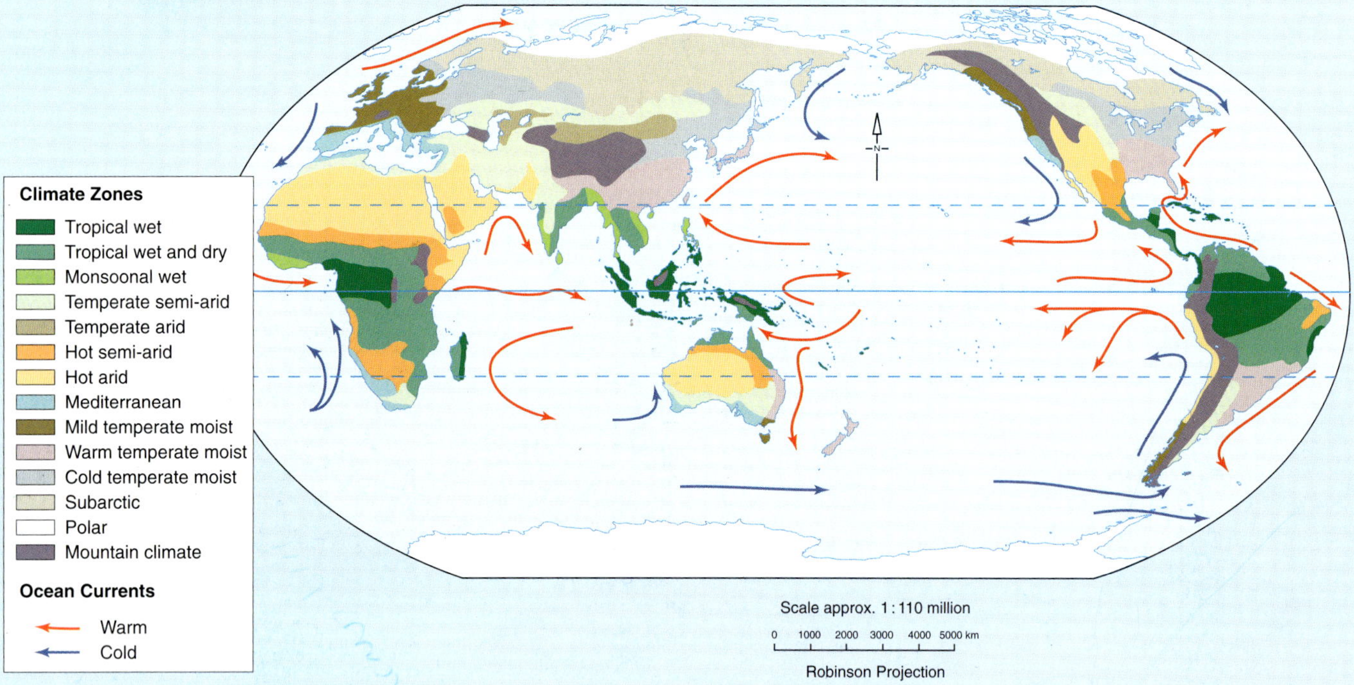

Figure 5.3j World climate zones.

Understanding the text

1. Explain why temperatures are lower at higher latitudes.
2. Explain how seasonal differences affect climate.
3. Describe how elevation affects climate.
4. Outline the ways in which mountain ranges affect climate.
5. Explain how distance from the sea affects climate.
6. Describe the impact that warm and cold ocean currents have on climate.

UTT worksheet 5.3

There are three very broad zones of climatic differences across the world. They are shown in Figure 5.3h (p. 111). These zones are caused by the difference in the amount of heat received from the sun. The zone of high temperature (equatorial zone) is in the tropics, the zones of low temperature (polar zones) are near the North and South Poles, and the zones of moderate temperature (temperate zones) are located between the two, in the mid-latitudes.

These three broad zones are only a general indication of climatic difference. A more specific indication can be made by adding rainfall patterns. Broad groupings of rainfall patterns can be used. Figure 5.3i shows these.

The pattern of climate now shows:

- hot, wet regions
- hot, dry regions
- moderate temperature, moderate rainfall regions
- cool, wet regions
- cold, dry regions.

Figure 5.3j shows the world's major climate zones.

Working geographically

1 **Class discussion** As a class, make a list of all the ways weather and climate affect people.

2 **Using an atlas** Study Figure 5.3j. Using an atlas, describe the global distribution of tropical climates; temperate arid and semi-arid climates; and Mediterranean climates.

3 **Challenge: Interpreting maps** Study Figure 5.3j. Describe the relationship between the location of cold ocean currents and regions that have an arid climate.

Foundation worksheet 5.1 | Foundation worksheet 5.2 | Extension worksheet ICT 5.2 | Extension worksheet ICT 5.4

5.4 The water cycle

The *water cycle* describes how water is collected, purified and distributed over the earth in an endless cycle. The water cycle is a closed system because the same water has been circulating since the earliest days of the planet. No water is added and none is taken away. Within the system, water is always moving and always changing—it changes its form (such as ice and snow, liquid water and water vapour) and its geographical location. The main processes involved in the water cycle are shown in Figure 5.4a.

The water cycle is powered by the sun's energy and by gravity. Solar energy evaporates water from the oceans, rivers, lakes, soil and vegetation. Water changes from a liquid to a gas. About 84 per cent of the water vapour in the atmosphere comes from the oceans. The oceans cover about 71 per cent of the earth's surface.

The amount of water vapour that can be held in the air depends on its temperature. Warm air is able to hold more water vapour than cold air. This means that the warmer tropical regions near the Equator generally have more precipitation than the colder areas near the poles. Winds, particularly those coming from over warmer ocean areas, can transport moisture-laden air over long distances. This means that even those areas with very little surface water will sometimes receive precipitation.

As warm, moist air rises, it cools. This causes the water vapour to condense into tiny droplets that form clouds or fog. For precipitation to occur, air must contain small particles of dust, smoke, sea salt or pollutants from factories and cars. It takes millions of tiny water

Figure 5.4b Snowflakes magnified.

Getting technical

water cycle The transfer of water between various stgorages (such as oceans, lakes and the atmosphere) through a variety of processes (such as evaporation, condensation, precipitation and runoff)

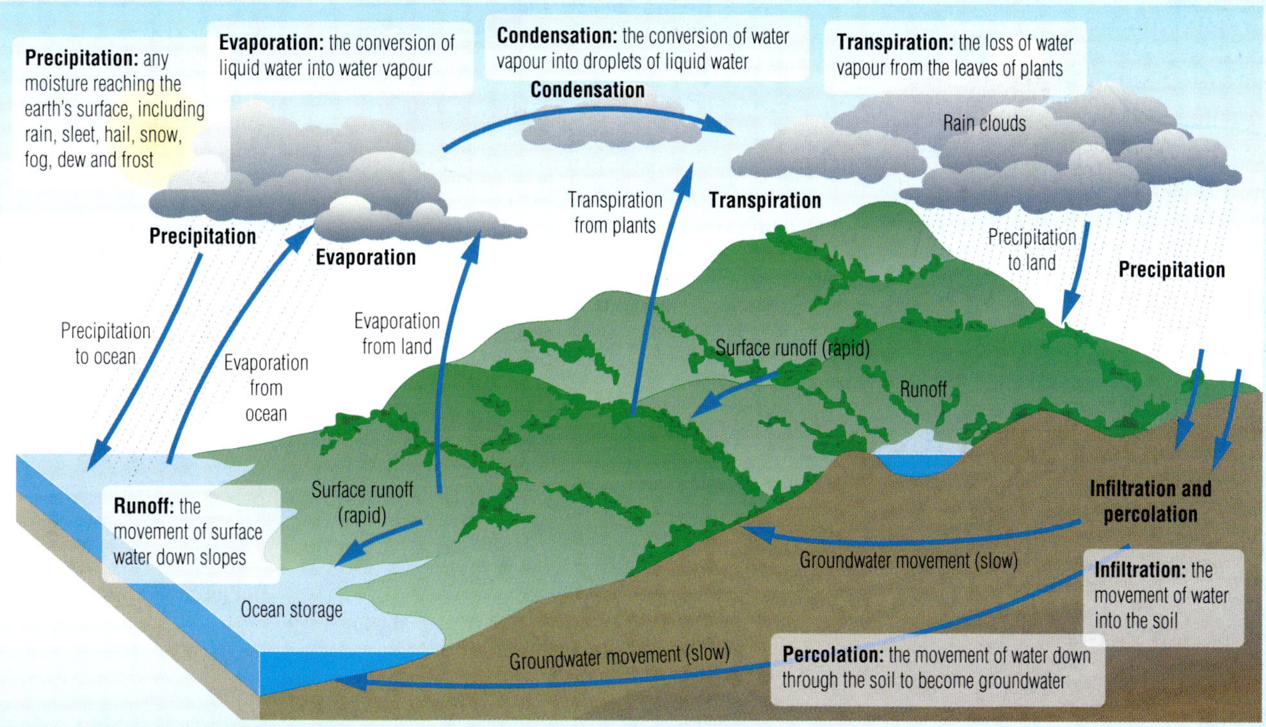

Figure 5.4a The water cycle.

Human interactions with the water cycle

Humans interact with the water cycle in a variety of ways:

- building structures, such as levee banks, to protect farmland and settlements from flooding
- storing water in dams in areas where rainfall is unreliable
- using canals and pipelines to transport water from one area to another
- sinking wells and bores to extract groundwater
- using water and gravity to generate hydroelectricity
- using large bodies of water to dilute various pollutants, such as dumping sewage into oceans
- clearing land for agriculture, mining and urban development.

Foundation worksheet 5.2

Did U know?

- The total amount of water on earth is 1385 million cubic kilometres.
- The amount of water vapour in the atmosphere represents just 1/10 000 of the total volume of the earth's surface water but is enough to cover the earth's land surface to a depth of 2.5 metres.
- The amount of water vapour transferred to the atmosphere by plants (in a process called evapotranspiration) is enough to meet the annual water needs of 200 million people.
- Water covers 70.8 per cent of the earth's surface, or 360 million square kilometres, with an average depth of 4 kilometres. Only 1.4 per cent of the earth's water is fresh. Most of this is trapped in the polar ice caps and glaciers.
- Eighty-seven per cent of the world's precipitation falls over the oceans. Only 17 per cent reaches the land.
- Australia receives less precipitation than any other continent with the exception of Antarctica. Australia receives an average of just 47 centimetres, compared with 163 centimetres in South America and more than 60 centimetres on the other continents. Most of this evaporates. Only 10 per cent actually flows into the continent's rivers.
- Although the salinity of the sea varies there are, on average, 25 grams of salt in each litre of seawater.
- Antarctica's massive ice fields hold 70 per cent of the earth's freshwater supplies.
- More than 30 per cent of the earth's surface is covered by snow during at least part of the year. About 10 per cent is permanently covered by ice and snow.
- The amount of water stored in polar ice and glaciers is 4.7 million cubic kilometres.

droplets clinging to these small particles to produce a single drop of rain or a snowflake heavy enough to fall to the earth's surface. About 77 per cent of all precipitation falls back into the sea. The rest falls on land.

Some of the fresh water returning to the earth's surface becomes locked in glaciers and ice sheets. The rest either flows into lakes, rivers and streams, which eventually carry it back to the sea, or seeps into the ground, where it can be stored in layers of **porous** rock for thousands of years as **groundwater**. Saturated porous rock is called an **aquifer**. The level to which the aquifer is filled is called the **water table**.

Understanding the text

1. What is the water cycle?
2. Why is the water cycle referred to as a closed system?
3. What powers the water cycle?
4. What is evaporation?
5. What determines the amount of water vapour in the air?
6. Why do regions near the Equator receive more rainfall than other areas?
7. What name is given to the process by which water vapour is converted into droplets of liquid water?
8. Describe what happens to precipitation once it reaches the earth's surface.

UTT worksheet 5.4

Working geographically

1. **Constructing diagrams** Construct your own drawing of the water cycle. On your drawing, label the main processes involved in the operation of the water cycle.
2. **Writing task** Write a short story titled 'A day in the life of a water molecule'. Be creative. The water molecule must take on at least three different forms; for example, liquid, solid and vapour.
3. **Writing task** Write a report outlining the ways people alter the water cycle (see Unit 2.15).

5.5 Ecosystems and food webs

Living organisms interact with each other and their non-living environment. The nature of these interactions determines the variety of ecosystems that we studied in Unit 5.1. Each ecosystem has its own characteristic community of plants and animals that are adapted to a particular set of environmental conditions. Ecosystems can exist at a variety of scales. On a local scale, for example, an ecosystem could be a small area of wetland. On a global scale, an ecosystem could, for example, be a forest community dominated by a particular type of tree, such as conifers or eucalypts. Global ecosystems are often referred to as **biomes**.

The variety of ecosystems on the earth's surface depends mostly on climatic differences. The main types of ecosystems on land are forests,

Figure 5.5a The major elements of an ecosystem and the interactions between them.

Interactions in an ecosystem

Ecosystems get their energy from the sun. The sun gives light and warmth to plants and powers the processes that give us our weather and climate. Figure 5.5a shows the links between climate, plants, animals and soil, as well as their links with solar energy and the earth's surface. Each arrow in this illustration represents one set of interactions, and shows the effect that one element has on another. For example, plants influence the type of soil found in an area. In turn, the soil type found in an area may favour certain plants and particular plant communities. An ecosystem may also include birds that distribute seeds of a plant, which, in turn, provides food and shelter for other species of birds.

Getting technical

Food chain The relationship between living organisms where one organism is dependent on another as a food source.

Food web The series of inter-connected food chains within an ecosystem.

Understanding the text

1 What does each ecosystem have?

2 Outline the factors that interact to produce the variety of ecosystems on earth.

UTT worksheet 5.5

Extension worksheet 5.3

grasslands and deserts. In general, areas of high rainfall have forest, areas of medium rainfall have grasslands and areas of low rainfall have deserts. Figure 5.5b shows how rainfall and temperature interact to produce different types of ecosystems. Figure 5.5c shows how latitude and height above sea level influence ecosystems.

Figure 5.5b Temperature and rainfall interact to produce different types of ecosystems.

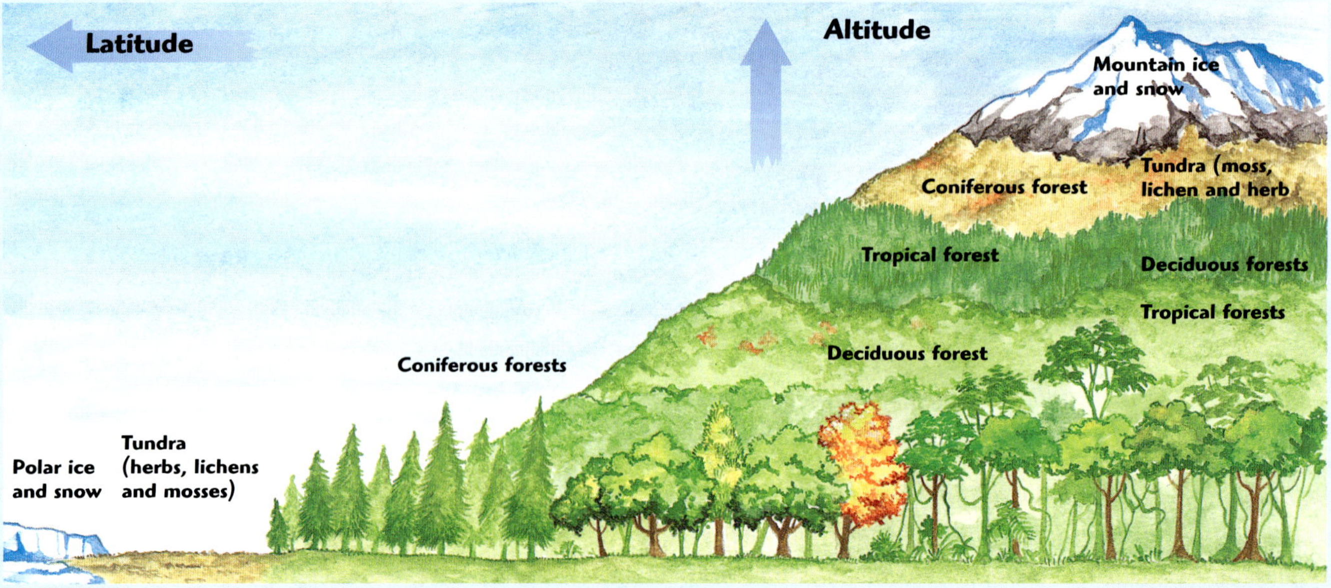

Figure 5.5c Latitude and height above sea level are important factors in producing different ecosystems.

This unit looks at the operation of ecosystems and the types of relationships that exist within them.

What are food chains?

Within every ecosystem there are *food chains*, made up of **producers**, **consumers** and **decomposers**. A food chain (see Figure 5.5d) indicates the flow of energy from the sun through to the various kinds of animals in the ecosystem.

Producers

Plants are called the producers in an ecosystem because they produce their own food. They do this by **photosynthesis**. They use energy from the sun to convert carbon dioxide and water into sugars, starches and cellulose (carbohydrates), producing oxygen as a byproduct.

Only plants and a few bacteria can produce their own food. All other organisms are either consumers or decomposers. Animals and humans are the most obvious examples of consumers.

Consumers

Herbivores are *primary consumers*—they eat only plants. Herbivores include animals that graze on grass, birds that eat seeds, and animals that browse on leaves. These herbivores are eaten by the *secondary consumers*—**carnivores** (meat eaters). Some carnivores eat only herbivores; others eat only other carnivores. Those animals and birds that feed on other carnivores are called higher-level, or *tertiary, consumers*. Examples of these are sharks, hawks and lions. They are said to be at the top of the food chain. This is because the energy from the sun has

Figure 5.5e Caterpillar, an example of a herbivore (primary producer).

Figure 5.5f Fungi, an example of a decomposer.

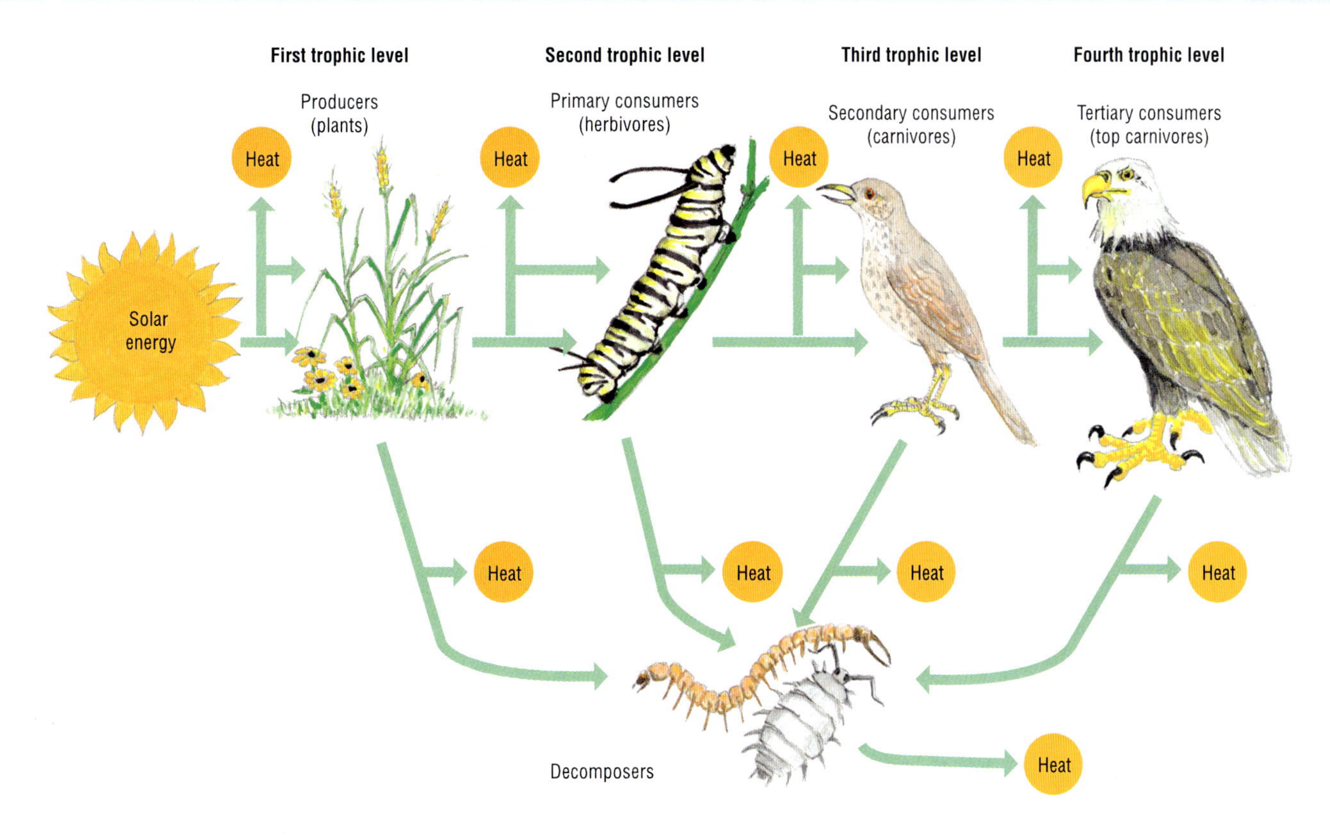

Figure 5.5d This food chain shows the transfer of energy and nutrients. The sun is the source of energy for all the levels of the biosphere, including the decomposers that return the minerals to the producers.

Figure 5.5g Lions are at the top of the savanna grassland food chain. They are a tertiary consumer.

Figure 5.5h Wood owls.

worked its way through the producers, the herbivores and the lower-order carnivores before it reaches them.

Some animals (including pigs, cockroaches and humans) are both herbivores and carnivores. They eat a mixture of plants and animals and so are called **omnivores**.

Decomposers

Decomposers include many kinds of bacteria and fungi. Their function in the food chain is to break down (decompose) the wood, leaves and dead bodies of other living things, so that every living thing is recycled.

This recycling means that there is no waste in an ecosystem. For example, a mouse eats grain; an owl eats the mouse; a fox eats the owl. Other grain, owls and foxes die naturally and their remains are broken down by decomposers.

What are food webs?

Although a food chain shows in a simple way how energy moves through different feeding levels in an ecosystem, it does not show all the relationships. Each animal does not eat one type of plant or one type of animal only. A *food web* shows the more complex interactions between different food chains within an ecosystem (see Figure 5.5i).

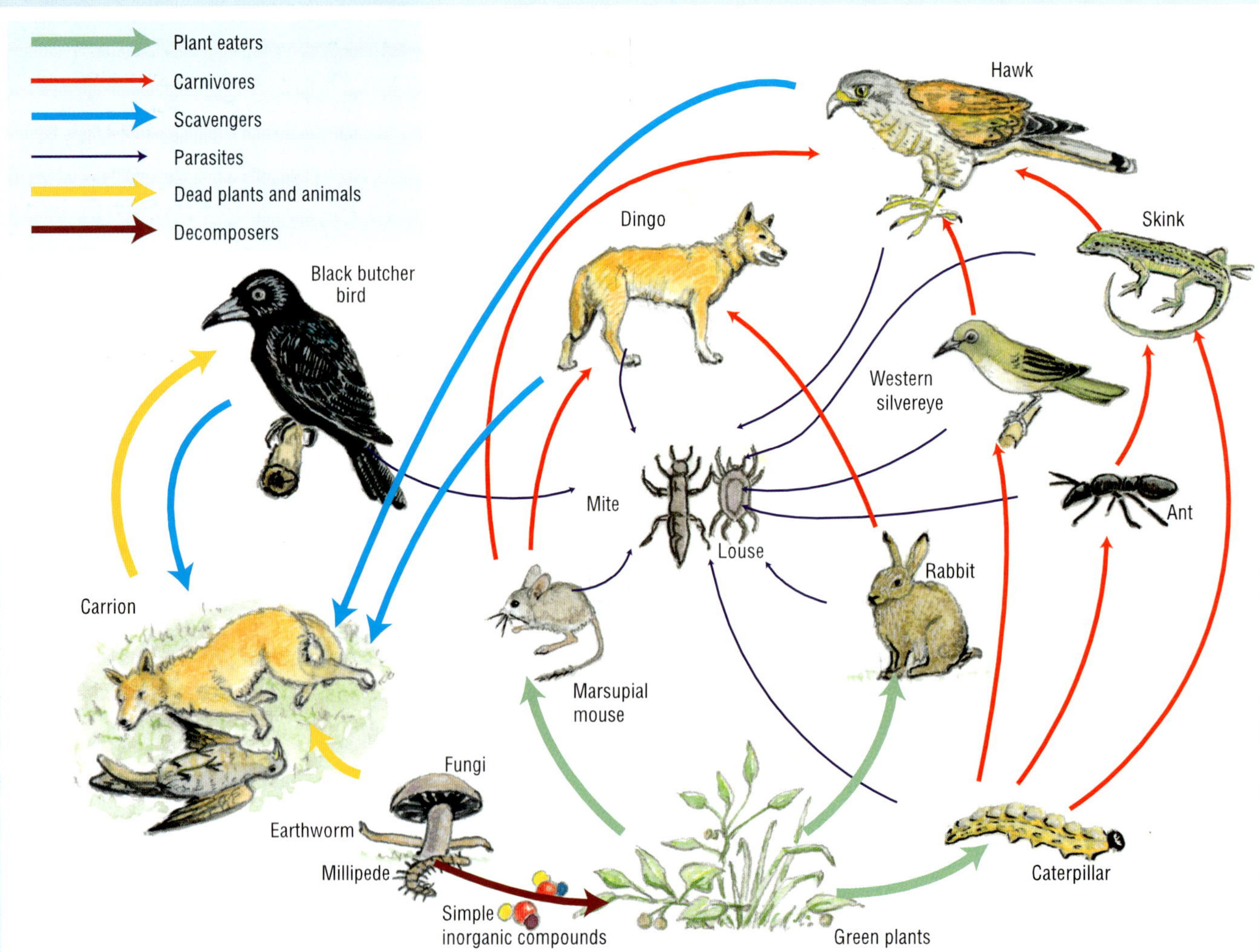

Figure 5.5i A simplified model of a food web. Real food webs are often much more complex and involve the interaction of smaller food chains. Food webs also overlap, blurring the edges of an ecosystem.

Energy flows

At each level of the food chain or food web, energy passes from one organism to another. The energy for plants comes from the carbohydrates produced by photosynthesis; the energy for animals comes from eating plants and other animals. Most of the energy taken in by an animal is used in the process of living, but a small percentage is passed on to the next-level consumer when the animal is eaten, or to the decomposers when the animal dies.

At each level of the food chain, most of the energy is used up in living; only a little goes to the next level. This means that less energy is available at each higher level of the food chain. For example, of 100 units of energy produced by plants, only 0.1 unit is available to humans, who are at the top of the food chain and have eaten carnivores that have eaten herbivores that have eaten plants. More people can be supported by eating grains and vegetables than by feeding grains and vegetables to animals and then eating the animals (see Figure 5.5j).

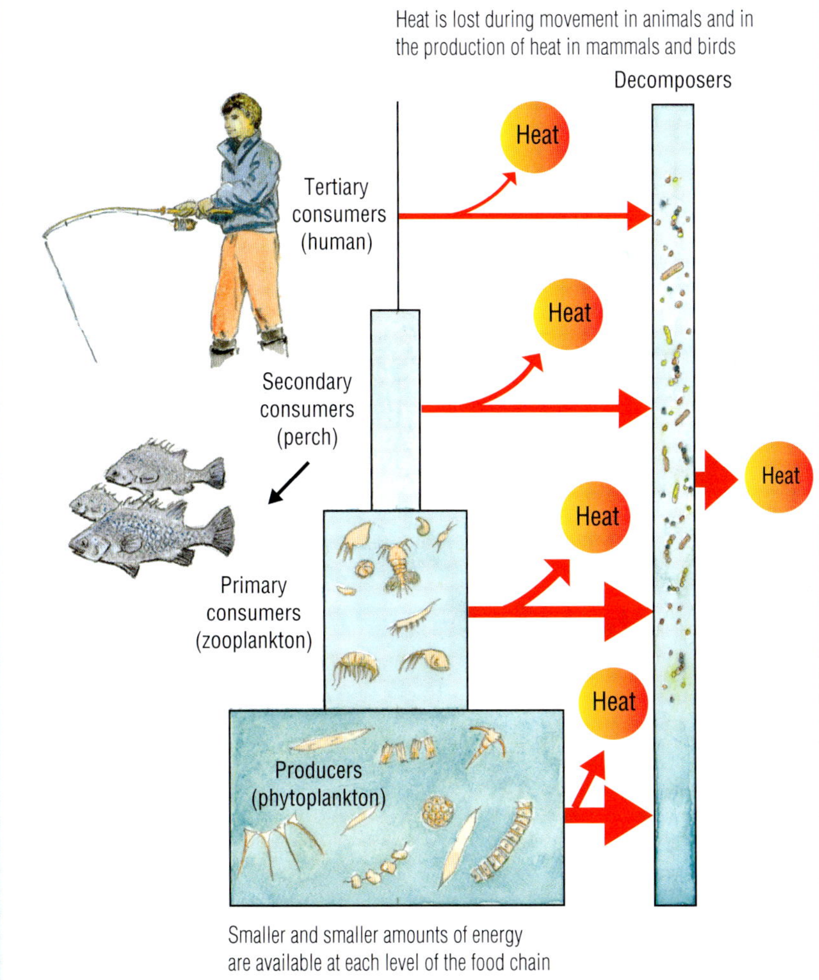

Figure 5.5j Pyramid of energy transfers within an ecosystem. Energy is lost from the system at each level in the food chain.

Working geographically

1. **Challenge: Interpreting diagrams** Study Figure 5.5a (p. 115), then write a paragraph explaining how plants, animals, soil and climate interact.
2. **Library research: Classroom display** Do some library research to find examples of food webs for each of the main ecosystems shown in Figure 5.5b (p. 116). Use a photocopier to enlarge the food webs. Display them on the classroom wall.
3. **Challenge: Writing task** Study Figures 5.5b and 5.5c (p. 116). Write a report describing how rainfall, temperature and altitude interact to produce different ecosystems.
4. **Library research** Do some library research to investigate the work of decomposers, such as bacteria, dung beetles or fungi.
5. **Writing task** Study Figure 5.5j. Write a report describing the flow of energy within an ecosystem.

Understanding the text

1. Explain how ecosystems get their energy.
2. Explain the difference between a producer and a consumer in a food chain.
3. Outline how green plants manufacture their own food.
4. Explain the difference between a herbivore and a carnivore. What is an omnivore?
5. Outline the role of decomposers in the food chain.
6. Explain why there is no waste in an ecosystem.
7. Identify what a food web shows that a food chain does not.
8. What happens to the energy that is taken in by an animal when it eats some grass?

UTT worksheet 5.5

5.6 Review and reflect

Chapter summary

In this chapter we were introduced to the geographical processes common to all the ecosystems presented in Part B of the text. We began by classifying the earth's physical environments. We noted, for example, that it is possible to distinguish between aquatic and terrestrial ecosystems. We were then introduced to weather and climate, the processes of the water cycle, and the functioning of ecosystems and food webs. Knowledge of the ways these processes interact helps us to better understand the global distribution of the earth's distinctive physical environments.

Activity 1

Using an atlas: For the record books

Use an atlas to locate each of the places mentioned below. Annotate (label) the map with the climatic record for which each place is known.

Climatic record	Location
Highest recorded temperature: 57.7°C	Al Aziziyah, Libya
Lowest recorded temperature: –88.3°C	Vostock, Antarctica
Most sunny days: 768 consecutive days (1967–69)	St Petersburg, Florida, USA
Highest average annual rainfall: 11 430 mm	Cherrapunji, Assam, India
Lowest average annual rainfall: 0.88 mm	Arica, Chile
Most rainy days: 350 days a year	Wai-'ale-'ale, Hawaii
Most rainfall in one day: 1870 mm	Cilaos, La Reunion, Indian Ocean
Most rainfall in one year: 26 461 mm	Cherrapunji, Assam, India
Most thunder in one year: 322 days	Bangor, Java, Indonesia
The world's driest place: the first rain for 400 days fell in 1971	Atacama Desert, northern Chile
Highest recorded wind speed: 317 km/hour	Mt Washington, USA

Activity 2

Using satellite images to study weather

The UK's Meteorological Office has an excellent satellite imagery site that you can access from its home page. The site features a Mercator's projection satellite image of the entire globe that is updated every six hours. Also available are 'full earth disc' images for different regions of the globe, including Asia/Australasia.

Use the image-capture function of your computer to copy a selection of these images and glue them into your workbook. Repeat this activity over three to four days to observe the movement of weather systems from west to east.

Activity 3

Using software: Terrestrial ecosystems

Select one of the terrestrial ecosystems shown in Figure 5.1a (pp. 104–5) and prepare a PowerPoint presentation highlighting the distinctive features of the selected ecosystem. Using the following points to help structure your presentation:

- location
- relationship to climate
- distinguishing characteristics
- distinctive flora and fauna
- human interactions.

Unit 2.16 will assist you with this task.

Activity 4

Ecosystem terms and definitions

List the term that matches each of the definitions below.

- The name given to a community of living plants and animals
- A name used to describe water-based ecosystems
- A name used to describe land-based ecosystems
- The day-to-day condition of the atmosphere
- The long-term weather pattern for a place or region
- The weight of air pressing down on the earth's surface (two words)
- The line along which two air masses meet
- The type of rainfall that occurs when warm, moist air is forced to rise by a mountain barrier
- Any moisture reaching the surface of the earth
- A word meaning height above sea level
- The name given to saturated porous rock
- The level to which an aquifer is filled (two words)
- The conversion of liquid water into water vapour
- The loss of water vapour from the leaves of plants
- The conversion of water vapour into droplets of liquid water
- The movement of water down through the soil
- The movement of water down through the soil to become groundwater

GeoMatch
GeoWords
Refer to the Reflection box on page 17.
GeoQuiz
Chapter test

Activity 5

Challenge: Using software—Why protect the environment?

Working in groups, produce either a short PowerPoint presentation (see Unit 2.16) or a poster titled 'Why protect the environment?'. Your presentation/poster must:

a Persuade the audience that it is in all our interests to protect the environment.
b List all the reasons why we should protect the environment.
c Tell people why sustainability is so important.
d Outline what will happen if we don't protect the environment.

Remember, your arguments need to be convincing. The more you can refer to real places and real cases, the better. Don't just use emotional arguments.

Chapter 6

Polar lands

Introduction

The polar lands of the Northern and Southern Hemispheres are among the earth's harshest environments. Extreme cold, frozen landscapes, wild storms, long hours of darkness (and daylight) would, you think, discourage plants and animals and human settlement. Yet these lands are home to a variety of people and they support an amazing range of plants and animals that have been able to adapt and use the environments around them. The polar lands are important to us all. Buried in layer upon layer of ice and snow are clues that tell us a great deal about the history (and perhaps the future) of our planet.

Key questions

1 What are the geographical processes that operate in polar lands?
2 How do polar plants and animals cope with their harsh environment?
3 How do scientists working at the South Pole and the Inuit of Greenland interact with the polar environment?

Rescue at the South Pole

Living at the South Pole would be a great adventure for some people. Dozens of researchers and other personnel spend anything from a few weeks to twelve months at probably the remotest place on earth: Amundsen-Scott South Pole Station. During winter, temperatures fall to –78°C and skies remain dark all day. This is not a place to become seriously ill. Yet this has happened twice in recent years. The most recent of these events happened in April 2001 when the station's Dr Ronald Shemenski developed pancreatitis, a potentially life-threatening condition.

The 'dash' to the South Pole to bring out Shemenski was in fact a long ten-hour flight from Britain's Rothera Station. A small aircraft called a Twin Otter had to be used because its hydraulic fluid was less likely to clog in the cold air. Visibility in the almost dark conditions was further reduced by strong coastal winds and blowing snow. Drums of burning rubbish on the ice served as landing lights for the plane. Fortunately, all went well. Shemenski was soon being treated back in the United States.

The central dome of the Amundsen-Scott South Pole Station.

Glossary of key terms

Antarctic Circle Latitude 66° 32′ south of the Equator.

Arctic Circle Latitude 66° 32′ north of the Equator.

Blizzard A snowstorm accompanied by strong winds.

Crevasse A crack in the surface of a glacier, ice sheet or iceberg.

Glacier A moving mass of ice formed from the accumulation of snow on higher ground.

Iceberg A mass of floating ice that has broken from an ice sheet or ice cap.

Ice cap A mass of ice that is smaller in volume than an ice sheet.

Ice floe A mass of floating ice formed from the frozen surface of the sea.

Ice sheet A mass of ice covering the landscape.

Ice shelf An extension of a glacier or ice sheet onto the ocean.

Krill Small crustaceans that provide food for larger sea creatures.

Lichens Simple plants that colonise bare rocks.

Nunatak The peak of a mountain protruding through an ice sheet or ice cap.

Ocean current A flow of water in the ocean with a different temperature or salinity from the water it is passing through.

Pack ice Numerous, separate pieces of sea ice that have been packed together in dense concentrations.

Permafrost Permanently frozen ground; although a few centimetres of the surface may thaw during the brief summer period.

Precipitation Water from the earth's atmosphere falling as rain, snow, hail or sleet.

Sustainable development Development that meets current needs without destroying the ability of future generations to meet their needs.

Tundra Natural vegetation of low shrubs and grasses surviving in thin soil in areas of permafrost.

cd eGlossary

cd GeoToolkit

cd ICT Toolkit

6.1 The earth's polar lands

Figure 6.1a The earth's polar lands are among the planet's most spectacular but harsh environments.

The earth's polar lands are among the planet's coldest places. The lowest temperature ever recorded on earth was –89°C at Vostok Station in Antarctica. Temperatures of –50°C are often recorded throughout the Arctic and Antarctic.

These cold, white, often dark places are also some of the earth's least inhabitated places. Huge areas are without plants and animals, even birds and insects. Life forms are found in some locations but in each case the plants and animals have developed special adaptations that allow them to cope with the harsh conditions.

Where are the polar lands?

The earth's polar lands are the most northern and the most southern regions of our planet. They are much larger than just the immediate area around the North Pole and the South Pole. One way to locate the polar lands on maps is to find the areas polewards of the **Arctic Circle** (latitude 66° 32′ north) and the **Antarctic Circle** (latitude 66° 32′ south). You can see these locations on Figures 6.1b and 6.1c.

Figure 6.1b The Arctic.

Figure 6.1c The Antarctic.

Figure 6.1d Adelie penguins on the Antarctic coast.

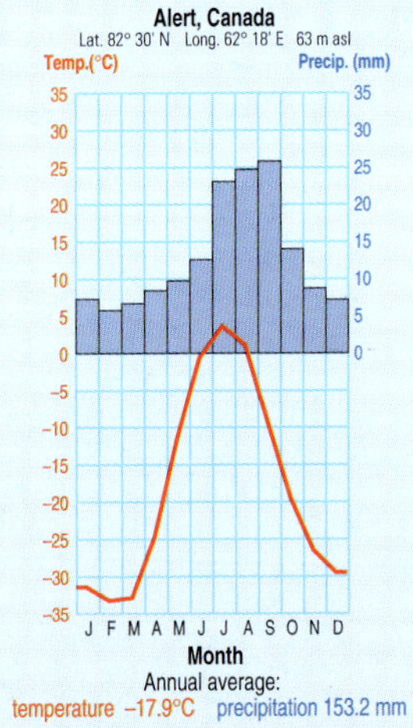

Figure 6.1e Climate graph for Alert, Canada.

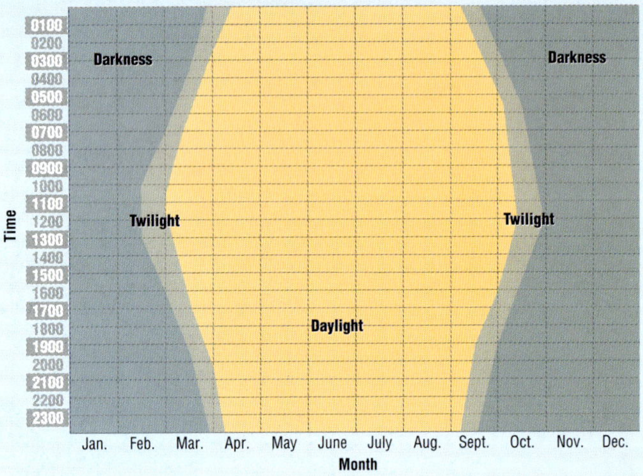

Figure 6.1f Daylight–darkness graph for Alert, Canada.

Climate of the polar lands

Around 21 June of each year, areas north of the Arctic Circle experience twenty-four hours of daylight, while areas south of the Antarctic Circle experience twenty-four hours of darkness. Around 21 December each year, there are twenty-four hours of continuous darkness north of the Arctic Circle and twenty-four hours of continuous light south of the Antarctic Circle. This pattern of light and darkness greatly affects the heating and cooling of these lands.

Generally, as you move north and south of the Equator, the climate of the earth becomes cooler. Polewards of latitudes 60° north and 60° south, the sun's rays are very weak. The information on page 109 explains why this is so. For large parts of the year, the extreme northern and southern regions of our planet receive very little light and heat. As a result, the atmosphere in these regions is cold. Look at the climate data in Figure 6.1e to get an idea of the low average temperatures experienced in these regions. Precipitation falls as snow, not rain. Over many thousands of years, snow has built up on the Antarctic landmass to form a massive **ice sheet** that is several kilometres thick (see Figure 6.1h). You can learn more about this on page 130.

It is so cold, even the sea freezes over. The areas of frozen sea can be seen on Figures 6.1b and 6.1c (pp. 124 and 125). These areas of frozen sea can also be regarded as parts of the polar lands.

In the Northern Hemisphere the area of frozen sea is distorted by the shape of the land as well as by ocean currents. In the Southern Hemisphere the area of frozen sea is more regular, roughly following the shape of the Antarctic landmass.

In the Northern Hemisphere, huge land areas surrounding the Arctic Ocean are also frozen. Large areas of ground in northern Canada and Siberia in Russia are permanently frozen to depths of up to 600 metres. This type of land is called **permafrost**. Ground temperatures are constantly below 0° C. In the brief summer period, the top few centimetres of the permafrost

Figure 6.1g The polar landscape

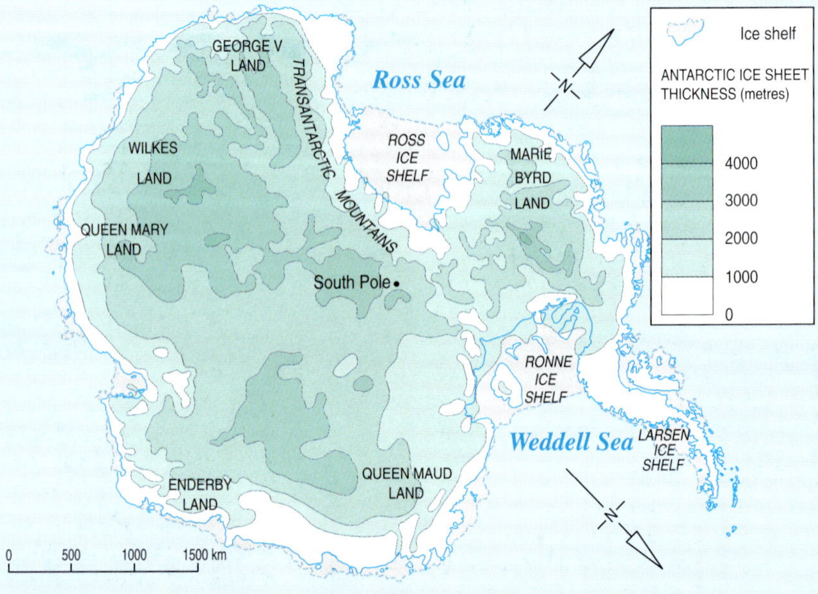

Figure 6.1h Ice-sheet thickness, Antarctica. Source: *Heinemann Atlas.*

may thaw. On flat land this can cause problems of waterlogging. In some places, low shrubs, grasses and herbs may survive, growing and flowering only in the brief summer. The term **tundra** is applied to these polar lands.

Because they have so much snow and ice we often think of the polar lands as wet places. In fact, they are large, cold deserts. Despite layers of thick ice covering much of the Antarctic and parts of the Arctic, these lands have low annual **precipitation**: as low as the amount of rain that falls in the Sahara Desert of Africa or the Great Victoria Desert of Australia. Cold, descending winds over both polar regions carry little moisture. The cold air of the polar lands means the precipitation that does fall is unlikely to evaporate. As a result, snowfalls accumulate and become compressed as ice. Away from the North and South Poles, winds can be very severe. **Blizzards**, a mixture of snow and strong winds with speeds over 100 kilometres per hour, can last several days and lead to total 'white outs' of the landscape.

Understanding the text

1. Name three features of polar lands that are different from the area where you live.
2. Polewards of which lines of latitude are there large areas of polar lands?
3. Why are these lines of latitude critical in deciding where cold, often dark, conditions of polar lands begin?
4. Name two differences and two similarities between the polar lands of the Arctic and the Antarctic.
5. Explain why the polar lands often have long periods of darkness.
6. What is permafrost?
7. Name two places where large areas of permafrost can be found.
8. Why are the areas of frozen sea so different in shape in the Arctic and the Antarctic?
9. Why can polar lands also be called desert lands?

UTT worksheet 6.1

Did U know?

- The Antarctic has about 90 per cent of the earth's ice: equivalent to about 80 per cent of the earth's freshwater reserves.
- The Arctic is ice-covered ocean surrounded by land while Antarctica is ice-covered land surrounded by ocean.
- It is possible to travel under the North Pole: by submarine. This was first done in 1958.
- The highest point of Antarctica, the Vinson Massif at 4897 metres, is almost the same measure in reverse as the deepest part of the Arctic Ocean.
- No country 'owns' any part of Antarctica.
- Both the Arctic and Antarctic have whales, seals, fish, **krill** and birds but only the Arctic has polar bears and only the Antarctic has penguins.

Foundation worksheet 6.1

Extension worksheet 6.1

Working geographically

1. **Interpreting photographs: Group work** Make a photo sketch of Figure 6.1a (p. 124) or 6.1g in the centre of a blank piece of paper, leaving room around your sketch for some notes. In groups, discuss what labels you can put onto your sketch that will help describe and explain the features of the landscape.
2. **Interpreting climate graphs** Study Figures 6.1e and 6.1f, then complete the following tasks:
   - a What do you think are the three main characteristics of Alert's climate?
   - b Which are Alert's four warmest months?
   - c How much daylight per day do these months average?
   - d Suggest why Alert is not warmer.
   - e Which months of the year have days of twenty-four hours of darkness?
   - f What are the average temperatures of these months?
   - g Suggest why Alert is so cold.
   - h Collect data from your own region and make a comparison with Alert's climate.
3. **Challenge: Research** Windmills are replacing diesel oil as the preferred source of energy in the Antarctic. Research the advantages of wind energy over other types of energy, the costs and the problems involved. How widespread has been this change to wind energy?
4. **Interpreting maps** Study Figure 6.1h. Identify the parts of Antarctica that have ice greater than 3000 metres thick. Where does the ice sheet exceed 4000 metres?

6.2 Plants and animals of the polar lands

Figure 6.2a The highly specialised plants of the tundra have a brief but rapid cycle of growth.

The polar lands are cruelly cold environments. The plants and animals that live there have had to adapt to survive these harsh conditions.

Plants

In the Antarctic, most land is under ice. However, there are a few places where plants can grow. There are bare, rocky areas as well as some valleys near the coast that are ice-free. Antarctica's severe climate of very low temperatures, strong coastal winds and limited water supply can support only a few species of plants. These plants are **lichens**, mosses, algae and fungi.

No trees, shrubs or flowers can survive in Antarctica. The continent's lichens and mosses grow very slowly: perhaps only 15 millimetres every 100 years. Some lichens freeze-dry in the long winter and revive when there is some liquid available during the Antarctic summer.

Figure 6.2b The musk ox of the tundra.

The Arctic's land areas are further away from the North Pole than their counterparts in the Southern Hemisphere. As a result, the polar lands of the Northern Hemisphere have areas with short, cool summers with temperatures averaging above freezing.

With the sun above the horizon for most of the day, many plants have a brief but rapid cycle of growth. Near areas of permanent ice, mosses and lichens grow on rocks, as in Antarctica. Further away from the permanent ice, grasses and heaths can appear on the permafrost (see p. 126). In sheltered areas, stunted trees and shrubs can survive (see Figure 6.2a).

These polar ecosystems are fragile. If disturbed by explorers, tourists, miners and animals they may be permanently damaged or only recover very slowly.

Animals

The waters surrounding Antarctica are a habitat for the southern polar land animals and birds. There are no land-based mammals or reptiles on Antarctica. Penguins, seals and seabirds may breed and raise their young on land, but their food sources are found in the adjoining waters. The less severe climate of the Antarctic peninsula and sub-Antarctic islands near southern South America are more densely populated with animal and bird life.

Figure 6.2c Polar bears play-fighting in the Arctic.

Essential to the survival of life in the Antarctic is the presence of phytoplankton and krill. Phytoplankton grow on the water's surface in the warmer months of the year. It is the source of food for krill, a tiny crustacean (less than a few centimetres long). Krill is the staple food of many species of fish, seals, whales and birds. You can see their key role in the Antarctic food chain in Figure 6.2d. As this diagram shows, krill is not the only source of food for some creatures. Smaller penguin species, such as the Adelie (Figure 6.1d, p. 125), are a favourite food of the leopard seal and killer whale.

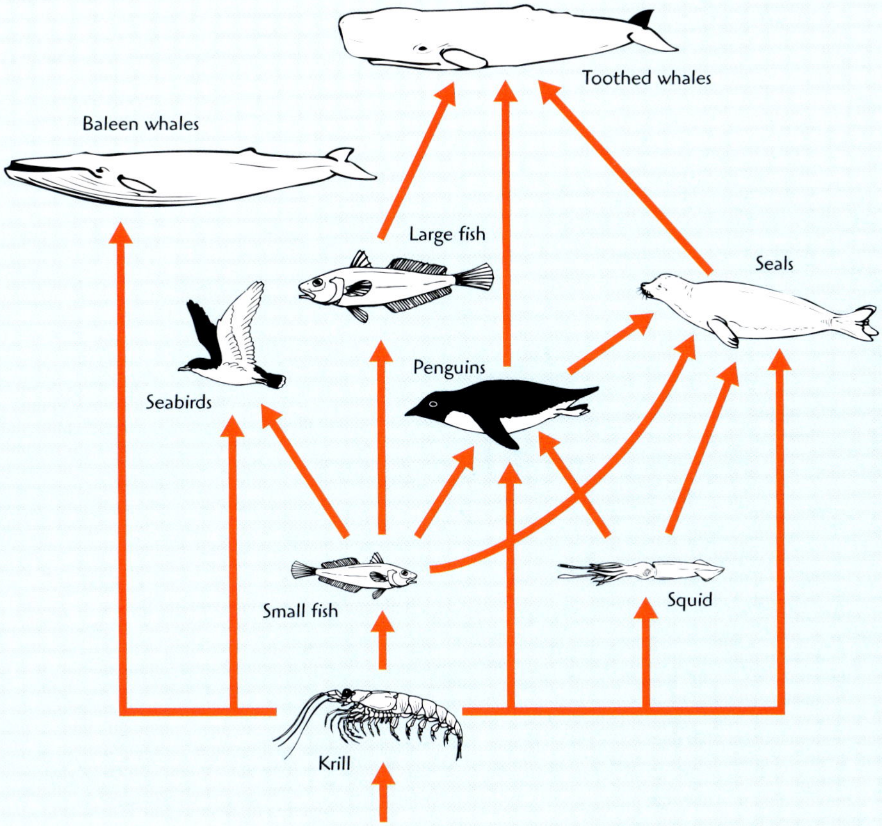

Figure 6.2d An Antarctic food chain.

Antarctica's animals have adapted in remarkable ways to their harsh environments. Penguins are unique to the Southern Hemisphere (see Figure 6.1d, p. 125). They are unable to fly, but they are excellent swimmers with their webbed feet, powerful flippers and rudder-like tail. Their waterproof feathers trap the air close to their skin. Their bodies are further insulated by the amount of fat they carry. On land, when their parents are away searching for food, chicks gather together for protection against storms and predators. In water, penguin vision is particularly sharp and clear, whereas on land it is blurred.

In the Arctic there are extensive land areas not permanently covered by ice (see Figure 6.1b, p. 124). Mosses, lichens and even shrubs and grasses allow certain land animals to exist. These animals include the caribou (or reindeer), arctic fox and polar bear. All these animals are unique to the polar lands of the Northern Hemisphere.

Polar bears are found in the icy northern regions of Alaska, Canada, Greenland and Russia (see Figure 6.2c). The bears, with their thick fat layer and dense fur coat, are well insulated against the cold. When winds are fierce they will dig out a shelter in the surface snow and curl into a tight ball. A major food source for the bears is ringed seals. These are hunted from ice platforms in the water. The bears wait for the seals to rise from the water for air, and then quickly grab the seals.

Polar bear numbers are somewhere between 20 000 and 30 000. In recent years harvesting by indigenous groups, the effects of pollution and a warming climate are believed to be responsible for a decline in their numbers.

Foundation worksheet 6.2

Extension worksheet 6.2

Understanding the text

1 a Name one animal found in polar lands in the Southern Hemisphere but not in the Northern Hemisphere.
  b Name one animal found in polar lands in the Northern Hemisphere but not in the Southern Hemisphere.
2 Give two reasons why plants grow slowly in polar lands.
3 Why are there no land-based plants, animals or birds at the South Pole?
4 Which Northern Hemisphere polar land animal might eat lichens and mosses?
5 In winter, the waters around the Antarctic landmass freeze. What problems could this create for penguins seeking food?
6 Name two ways the bodies of polar bears or penguins have adapted to their harsh environments.

UTT worksheet 6.2

Working geographically

1 **Interpreting food chains**
Study the food chain in Figure 6.2d and answer the following questions:
  a What does the krill eat?
  b For which animals is the penguin a food source?
  c Name two food sources for penguins.
  d What is the main food source of baleen whales?
  e Suggest what could happen in the food chain if humans harvested so much krill that it became scarce.

2 **Challenge: Internet research**
Polar bears may soon become an endangered species. Use the Internet to investigate the reasons why this is happening. What has been done about the problems and how successful have these measures been? An excellent starting point is the website for Polar Bears International.

6.3 Polar landscapes

Figure 6.3a Antarctica's vast ice sheet is up to 4 kilometres thick.

Ice dominates the landscapes of the polar lands. This ice varies from slabs several kilometres thick, which cover most of Greenland and Antarctica, to metres thick ice shelves that form over the ocean and are joined onto landmasses. In addition, much of the water that makes up the Arctic Ocean and surrounds Antarctica is frozen. There are other landscape features apart from ice: mountains, valleys, hills and rocky coastlines, for example. But it is ice that affects or has affected all these features.

Ice sheets and ice caps

Without ice, only 60 per cent of the Antarctic mass you see in Figures 6.3a and 6.3c would be above sea level (see Figure 6.3d). Mountain ranges such as the Transantarctic Mountain range (see Figure 6.1c, p. 125), which is approximately 4800 kilometres long, would remain as a central spine. Today, Antarctica is a large, frozen wilderness covered by a huge ice sheet that moves a few centimetres a year outwards from the centre of the continent. Nearer the coast, fingers of the ice sheet move faster as **glaciers**, such as the Byrd Glacier in Figure 6.3e.

Antarctica's dome-shaped ice sheet measures 4.7 kilometres at its thickest point. As Figure 6.1h (p. 126) shows, there are large areas where the ice is more than 4000 metres (or 4 kilometres) thick. Figure 6.3d is a cross-section through Antarctica where the ice sheet's thickness is over 2 kilometres. The weight of Antarctica's ice sheet is so immense that it pushes some of the land down below sea level.

Figure 6.3b An icebreaker making its way through ice floes.

Figure 6.3c Antarctica with and without its ice sheet.

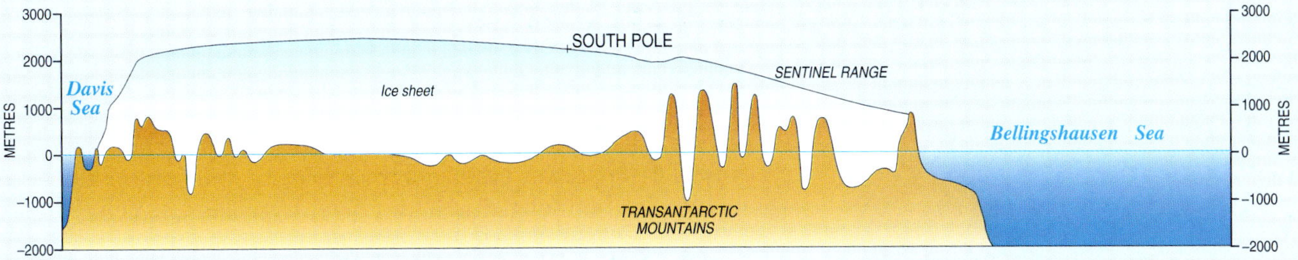

Figure 6.3d A cross-section through Antarctica along the 90° east and west line of longitude. (Vertical scale is exaggerated 250 times the horizontal scale.)

If ever Antarctica's ice sheet were to melt, this land would slowly rise up; perhaps by several centimetres every 100 years. In the meantime the world's coastal areas would be drowned as the sea level would rise by tens of metres.

In the Northern Hemisphere's polar lands, a smaller ice sheet or **ice cap** covers about 85 per cent of Greenland. Parts of this ice cap are up to 3 kilometres thick. Like the ice sheet on Antarctica, the weight of the ice has pushed much of Greenland's rock mass below sea level. In some places, mountain peaks remain uncovered by ice. These peaks are called **nunataks**.

These masses of ice appear smooth and even on small-scale maps and cross-sections (see Figure 6.3d). In reality, as these masses of ice slowly move over the land, pressure develops, creating cracks and **crevasses**. A crevasse is shown in Figure 6.3f. Crossing ice masses is obviously not an easy matter. Snowfalls frequently cover these crevasses, making another hazard for people trying to cross the ice.

Figure 6.3f Crossing an ice sheet is no easy matter.

Figure 6.3e The Byrd Glacier emerges from the Antarctic ice sheet.

Did U know?

- Icebergs can be a great danger to ships, especially when the iceberg rolls over. The 'unsinkable' *Titanic* is probably the most well-known victim of an iceberg.
- In 1987 a 6350 square kilometre iceberg broke off from the Ross Ice Shelf in the Antarctic. Its 1.4 trillion tonne mass would provide 240 tonnes of pure drinking water for every person in the world.
- Greenland's glaciers produce about 10 000 icebergs every year.
- People in the Middle East, Australia and California have investigated towing icebergs from Antarctica to help overcome local water shortages.

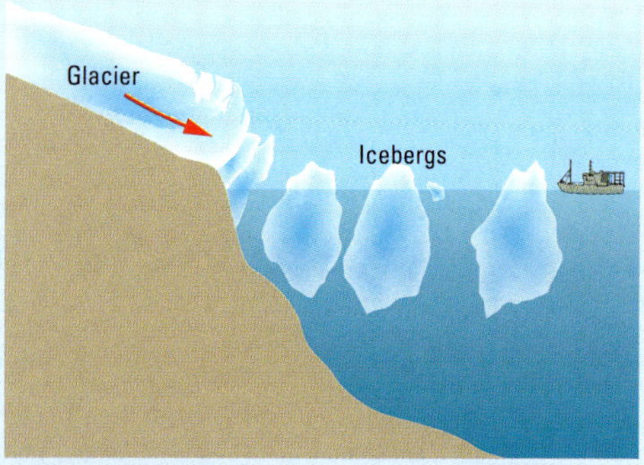

Figure 6.3g The formation of an iceberg from a glacier.

Figure 6.3h An iceberg in the North Atlantic Ocean.

In Antarctica, parts of the ice sheet have flowed onto the sea and formed extensive **ice shelves**. The Ross Ice Shelf (see Figure 6.1c, p. 125) covers an area twice the size of Victoria. In summer, parts of these ice shelves weaken and break, or calve, into the sea. In this way, thousands of **icebergs** are created. In the Antarctic, icebergs are typically flat-topped, or tabular. This is because they originated from ice shelves. In the Northern Hemisphere, large icebergs calve from the Greenland ice sheet as well as from mountain glaciers that reach the sea. As a result, they have an irregular shape. You can see how they form in Figure 6.3g. Many of these icebergs are jagged and peaked, like a floating mountain. Figure 6.3h shows one of these icebergs.

Only about one-ninth of the total mass of an iceberg is above sea level. Ocean currents can move icebergs away from their points of origin at a rate of 10 to 20 kilometres a day. Icebergs have an average life of several years, eventually breaking into smaller bergs and melting in warmer waters.

Large areas of water in the polar lands of both the Northern and Southern Hemispheres freeze. You can see the extent of this sea-ice on Figures 6.1b and 6.1c (pp. 124 and 125). Sea-ice can be up to several metres thick. In the warmer summer, parts of the sea-ice break up, forming **ice floes** (see Figure 6.3b). Ice floes are lower than icebergs but often cover hundreds of square metres. As temperatures fall, these ice floes build up as **pack ice** and can eventually refreeze as sea-ice.

Understanding the text

1. What is the difference between an ice sheet, an ice shelf and an ice floe?
2. What is a glacier? Check page 179 to see what changes a glacier can make to the landscape it passes over. List these changes.
3. What effect does the weight of the ice sheet have on polar landscapes?
4. If an iceberg is 20 metres in height above sea level, how far under water will the rest of it be?
5. Which polar land has more ice: the Antarctic or the Arctic?
6. Describe how icebergs are formed. Why are Northern Hemisphere icebergs different from most Southern Hemisphere icebergs?

UTT worksheet 6.3

Working geographically

1. **Challenge: Interpreting photographs** Draw a photo sketch of Figure 6.3e (p. 131) on a blank piece of paper (see Unit 2.9). Add the following labels in the appropriate places: ice sheet, glacier, nunatak, crevasses. Add an arrow to indicate which way the Byrd Glacier is moving. Make up a title for your sketch that includes all these words: ice, landscape and edge.
2. **Writing task** Study Figure 6.3g. Write a paragraph outlining how icebergs are formed.
3. **Research: Mapping** Where did the *Titanic* sink? (Hint: The *Heinemann Atlas* will help you.) If the iceberg that struck the *Titanic* came from Greenland, approximately how far would it have travelled? Show your findings on a sketch map complete with title, north indicator and approximate scale.
4. **Challenge: Research** Investigate the proposals made to tow icebergs from Antarctica to places with water shortage. Why have these proposals never become reality?
5. **Challenge: Research** 'Ice in the polar regions is climatic history.' Investigate this statement to decide what it means. What evidence can you find to support the statement?

6.4 SAMPLE STUDY
Life at the South Pole

Humans in Antarctica

People do live at the South Pole. The total population is small and nearly everyone stays for only short periods of time. In winter, between twenty-five and fifty people might live at the South Pole. During the summer as many as 120 to 150 people might be found there. These people are mostly researchers in astrophysics, geophysics, meteorology, glaciology and biomedicine. The population also consists of doctors, cooks and electricians.

A team led by the Norwegian explorer Amundsen was the first to reach the South Pole. They reached their destination in 1911. A month later, a British expedition led by Scott also reached the pole. Unfortunately Scott's team perished on the return journey to the coast. A permanent base at the South Pole was first set up by a US team in 1956. In the following years, the complex seen in Figures 6.4a and 6.4b has developed. By 2005 further extensions will have been completed to house more equipment and people.

Figure 6.4b Aerial view of Amundsen-Scott South Pole Station.

Challenges of living at the South Pole

Life at the South Pole has its problems, many of which are caused by the harshness of the physical environment and the isolation.

New arrivals suffer altitude sickness because the South Pole is 2900 metres above sea level and the air is not as oxygen-rich as at lower altitudes. There are oxygen supplies in the station's medical centre.

In summer, temperatures climb to –21°C. The sunlight is very intense and can cause temporary blindness and eye irritation if precautions are not taken. The brightness is because skies are clear and there is a strong reflection from the snow and ice.

Amundsen-Scott South Pole Station ICT

Check out the Amundsen-Scott South Pole Station live camera, which you can access via the South Pole Observatory link at the US Climate Monitoring and Diagnostics Laboratory website.

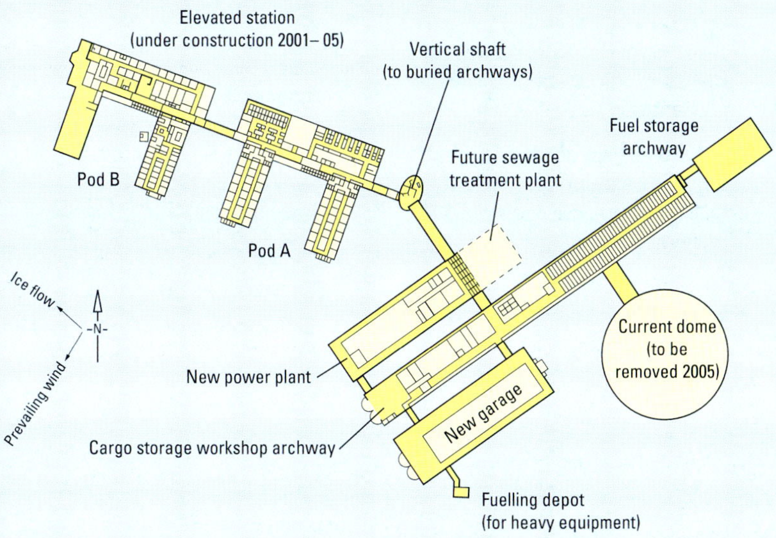

Figure 6.4a Plan of the facilities of the Amundsen-Scott South Pole Station.

Figure 6.4c A scientist at work at Amundsen-Scott South Pole Station.

In winter, temperatures can fall to –78°C and the remaining crew move into the central dome to work and live. Power cords, drills and machinery can freeze in the South Pole's winter temperatures. During winter there is no sun and little light. This is great for astronomical observations but can prove depressing and frustrating for some residents.

Winds at the South Pole average only a few kilometres an hour. Despite this, the central dome of the station (see p. 123) is slowly being buried by drifts of snow. Some bulldozing has been necessary. In fact, little snow falls here—on average fewer than 4 millimetres a month.

The isolation of the South Pole can also cause difficulties. Workers do not always have the same backgrounds or similar viewpoints, and so differences of opinion can arise. All supplies (including food, medicines, fuel, entertainment and building equipment) must be airlifted into the station, usually during summer. The station's small greenhouse grows fresh herbs for the kitchen.

The nearest station to Amundsen-Scott is McMurdo Station, which is 1350 kilometres away. Satellite communication does not cover the South Pole region. A 2000 kilometre long fibre-optic cable is being laid across the polar ice to allow data to be transmitted. It will also keep the station's population in touch with other parts of the world through emails and chatlines.

Understanding the text

1. Name five jobs people do at the South Pole.
2. Suggest why no-one lives permanently at the South Pole.
3. How did the permanent station at the South Pole get its name?
4. List at least three health problems workers at the South Pole may develop during their stay.
5. Why is winter better than summer for astronomical studies carried out at the South Pole?
6. a What benefits will the new fibre-optic cable link bring to people at the South Pole?
   b What problems could there be in laying this cable?

cd UTT worksheet 6.4

cd Foundation worksheet 6.2

cd Extension worksheet 6.3

Working geographically

1. **Challenge: Hypothetical** Write a job description for a twelve-month stay at Amundsen-Scott South Pole Station. Be sure to include the advantages and disadvantages of such a position. Show your job description to a class group and see how many might be interested in applying. What were the reasons why people did not want to apply? Would the number of applicants be different if the position were for just three months?
2. **Interpreting data** Suggest why Amundsen-Scott South Pole Station has not opted for solar or wind power as a major fuel source.
3. **Internet research** Amundsen-Scott South Pole Station is one of many stations on Antarctica. Use the Internet to look at another station, such as Mawson (Australia), McMurdo (United States), Halley (United Kingdom) or Vostok (Russia). Compared with Amundsen-Scott, what differences are there in the appearance of the station, its weather and climate, landscapes, links with the outside world and jobs undertaken?
4. **Internet research** Take a virtual tour of the South Pole using the University of Chicago website. Make a summary of what you learn. Compare your summary with that of another student in your class. What differences and similarities were there in your discoveries?

6.5 SAMPLE STUDY The Inuit of Greenland

Unlike the Antarctic, parts of the polar lands of the Northern Hemisphere are permanently inhabited. This sample study looks at the Inuit of Greenland.

Greenland's physical environment

Greenland has a harsh polar environment. As you can see from Figure 6.5a, more than two-thirds of its land area is located north of the Arctic Circle. This gives Greenland its severe polar climate of long and dark, very cold and fairly dry winters as well as brighter, longer and milder days in summer. Greenland's climate is less severe further south where the relatively warm **ocean current** creates an ice-free coast and harbours. The coastal areas not covered by ice are typically mountainous and bare of soil and vegetation. Figure 6.5c (p. 136) is typical of Greenland's landscape.

Most of Greenland is covered by a huge ice cap, equivalent to 10 per cent of the world's total fresh water. Yet these environments have supported people for about 5000 years. Greenland's Inuit population today numbers around 45 000 with another 15 000 people from Europe, mainly Denmark. Approximately 100 000 Inuits are found in other polar lands: Russia, Canada and Alaska.

Figure 6.5a Greenland's geography.

Did U know?

- After Australia, Greenland is the world's largest island, measuring more than 2.5 times the area of New South Wales.
- Around 85 per cent of Greenland is covered by ice.
- Fewer than 60 000 people live in Greenland.
- Greenlanders are Danish: Greenland is a self-governing part of Denmark.
- Greenland's capital is Nuuk.

Figure 6.5b A baby harp seal.

Figure 6.5c Greenland's coastal landscape.

Figure 6.5d Greenland's interior landscape.

The Inuit

Traditional Inuit communities were based around hunting Greenland's animal resources: polar bears on land and, from the sea, whales and seals as well as fish. These resources provided the Inuit with food as well as raw materials for their clothing, weapons, boats and heating.

By the late twentieth and early twenty-first centuries, Inuit life had changed significantly. Only a few small communities to the north of Greenland follow what could be called a traditional lifestyle. Seal skin kayaks, which were traditionally used for fishing, sealing and whaling, have been replaced by motorboats. Rifles are used instead of whalebone harpoons. Inuits wear modern clothing instead of animal skin garments and live in wooden houses rather than traditional ones of earth and/or ice. They speak Danish as well as Inuit and most are now Christian. Many Inuit work in shops, offices, tourist facilities and in fish-processing centres for wages. Payments from the government have become the major source of income for most Inuit households. Severe problems of unemployment, alcoholism and drug use have emerged in the last fifty years.

Some features of traditional life have taken on a new form. Fishing is now more commercially based, especially with large-scale shrimp catching and processing. The processing centre on Disko Island (see Figure 6.5a, p. 133) employs several hundred Inuit. Smaller-scale hunting of whales and seals continues, despite international pressure for it to stop. Greenlanders argue that the minke, pilot, humpback and other whales they hunt and kill each year are less than 1 per cent of the total numbers in nearby waters. All the crew share in the whale catch with the balance of meat being sold in shops and markets.

Around 50 000 harp seals are killed each year from a stock estimated at around 4 million. International bans on the imports of seal skin products have hit sales to the once lucrative North American and European markets.

The number of whales, seals (see Figure 6.5b, p. 135) and polar bears that can be hunted for food and skins is regulated by the Greenland Government. For example, only 150 polar bears can be killed each year. The government has been careful to only allow harvesting so future stocks will remain largely unaffected. This is an example of **sustainable development**. However, these restrictions have had their impact on Inuits. According to Greenland's finance minister there are no other possibilities for the Inuits to exist because they are unable to harvest crops or farm the land. The minister has commented that preventing Greenland from exporting seal skin is like cancelling out the Inuit's culture.

Figure 6.5e An Inuit man fishing in a frozen lake.

Working geographically

1 **Interpreting maps** Study Figure 6.5a (p. 135). Describe Greenland's location in relation to:
   a the Arctic Circle
   b the landmass of North America.

2 **Class discussion** Discuss why Greenland has not become more widely settled despite 5000 years of occupation.

3 **Challenge: Comparing perspectives** In groups, discuss the statements made by Greenland's finance minister. Do you agree with his comments? What can be done about the situation? Would independence from Denmark help or hinder the problems Greenland's Inuits face?

4 **Research** Carry out research to find answers to the following questions:
   a How might tourism help Greenland's Inuits?
   b Could there be any problems tourism might bring to Greenland?
   Try this search term if you are using the Internet: Greenland tourism.

5 **Research: Using presentation software** As a class, discuss where else in the world traditional communities have been greatly affected by changing technology and events. Each student should then select one of these communities to investigate. Your investigation should include research into:
- the location of the group
- the type of environments the group lives in
- the features of their traditional life
- how and why their lifestyles have changed.

Present your findings using presentation software, such as PowerPoint (see Unit 2.16).

Foundation worksheet 6.2

Understanding the text

1 Name five features of Greenland's physical environments.
2 Apart from Greenland, in which other polar lands do Inuit live?
3 How did hunting whales, seals, fish and polar bears support traditional Inuit lives?
4 Make a list of five key changes that have occurred to Inuit life in the last fifty years.
5 Outline the main sources of income for today's Inuits in Greenland.
6 Explain what has restricted the amount of whale and seal hunting taking place in Greenland's waters.

UTT worksheet 6.5

6.6 Review and reflect

Chapter summary

In this chapter we have investigated some of the earth's most extreme environments. We have learned that they occupy extensive regions around the North and South Poles. We have studied the distinctive characteristics of these environments: their very cold temperatures, long hours of darkness and daylight at different times of the year, as well as their extensive areas of permanent ice. It probably came as a surprise to learn that geographers call these environments deserts because of their very low precipitation. We have seen how plants, animals and fish have had to adapt to these harsh environments in order to survive.

Using the two sample studies, we have been able to gain an understanding of how some people live and use the environments of the polar lands. The Inuit occupy extensive areas of the polar lands of the Northern Hemisphere using the limited resources around them to build a distinctive way of life. We saw how modern influences have undermined this culture, replacing it with new characteristics. In the Southern Hemisphere's polar lands, people are relatively new arrivals with individuals visiting for only short periods of time. Their roles as researchers and visitors may significantly affect our life in the future.

Activity 1

Mystery words: Polar land

Make an enlarged copy of the grid below. Then find fifteen words linked to the study of polar lands. These words cover topics such as the weather, landforms, life forms and places. Lightly shade these words to reveal sixteen unshaded letters that make up two words describing a weather phenomenon that can occur in the polar lands.

I	C	E	S	H	E	E	T	V	I
O	K	L	E	N	T	P	U	K	C
S	R	S	E	A	L	O	N	A	R
L	I	C	H	E	N	L	D	Y	A
A	L	A	S	K	A	A	R	A	C
G	L	A	C	I	E	R	A	K	K
N	O	W	I	C	E	B	E	R	G
S	T	W	H	A	L	E	S	O	O
R	M	C	R	E	V	A	S	S	E
P	E	R	M	A	F	R	O	S	T

Activity 2

Group work: Plan a tour of the polar lands

Work in groups to develop an itinerary for a tour of either a part of the Northern Hemisphere polar lands (such as Greenland, northern Alaska or northern Siberia) or part of the Antarctic.

Visit a travel agent to get some ideas and information about how tours are organised and the best places to go.

Research on the Internet the places located in brochures obtained from the travel agent.

Interview anyone who has been to a part of the polar lands. What questions could you ask them?

Decide on the best time to go, what to see and what to do. Present your findings as a travel brochure, produced using suitable software. Make your brochure as appealing as possible. Include digital photographs sourced from the Internet, but ensure they are copright-free.

Activity 3

Group research: Using presentation software—Polar animals

In groups, select one of the following polar land animals for investigation: emperor penguin, minke whale, humpback whale, killer whale, elephant seal, toothfish, wandering albatross, skna, Arctic fox or caribou (reindeer). What are the animal's characteristics (for example, its appearance, numbers and location)? How is it adapted to its environment? What are its main food sources? Wha natural and human-made hazards does the animal face? Are there any working solutions to these problems? Present your findings using presentation software, such as PowerPoint (see Unit 2.16).

Activity 4

Cloze passage: Polar life forms

Test your knowledge and understanding about animal, bird, fish and plant life in the polar lands. Copy and complete the following passage using the words and phrases below.

arctic fox, bans, caribou (reindeer), fish, food chain, hunted, international protests, krill, lichens, life forms, mosses, penguins, plants, polar bears, seals, short growing season, shrubs, trees, warmer, warming, whales

There are many differences and similarities between the type of ________ found in polar lands in the Northern Hemisphere and the Southern Hemisphere. In the Southern Hemisphere's polar lands, ________ are found, but not ________ ________ . In the polar lands of the Northern Hemisphere are ________ ________ and ________ ________ , but these are not found in the Southern Hemisphere. In the waters of both the Arctic and the Antarctic there are various species of ________ and ________ . Both are still ________ to a limited extent despite ________ ________ and ________ on products made from these creatures. In addition to these creatures, ________ are found in the waters of the polar lands of the Northern and Southern Hemispheres. In the Antarctic there are no ________ or ______ growing, only very limited areas of ________ and ________ near the coast. In the polar lands of the Arctic, landmasses are further away from the pole and temperatures can be ________ ________ than in the Antarctic. This allows a ________ ________ for a limited range of ________ to grow. These plants are a key part of the ________ ________ for life forms, such as insects, birds and caribou (reindeer). In the polar lands of the Southern Hemisphere the food chain has close links to sea creatures, especially the tiny crustacean called ________ .

Perhaps the greatest threat facing the future of the polar lands is global ________ . Projected increases in average global temperatures will reduce the annual accumulation of snow and ice. The melting of the ice caps will result in rising sea levels.

Activity 5

Reflection: An Antarctic world park?

Antarctica is the earth's last great wilderness, still largely untouched by people. Should activities such as research, exploration, mining, tourism and fishing be controlled by a body such as the United Nations or left to the countries that have an immediate interest in the icy continent? Should mining take place? Should there be controls on where tourists can go and where scientific stations can be set up? Should this wild, beautiful part of the earth be kept just as it is?

Conduct a class debate on the cases for and against making Antarctica into a world park. Be sure to:

- base your arguments on researched information as well as information from the text and other sources
- look into existing agreements, such as the Antarctic Treaty and the Protocol on Environmental Protection.

Once you hold your debate, discuss what you can do about letting more people know about your conclusions.

cd GeoMatch

cd GeoQuiz

cd GeoWords

cd Chapter test

cd Extension worksheet ICT 6.4

Refer to the Reflection box on page 17.

Chapter 7
Rainforests

Introduction

Tropical rainforests are located near the Equator where it is hot and wet all year. These dense, damp environments are found in Central and South America, and in Africa and Southeast Asia. While tropical forests cover just 6 per cent of the Earth's surface, they are home to between 50 and 70 per cent of the planet's plant and animal species.

Tropical rainforests once covered 14 per cent of the earth's land surface. The main cause of rainforest loss is land clearing. Huge areas have been cleared for farming, ranching and logging. These activities threaten to destroy the home and traditional way of life of some of the world's indigenous people.

In this chapter we study the geographical processes that created and sustain the rainforest ecosystem. We will also look at the ways indigenous people interact with the rainforest environment.

Key questions

1 What are the geographical processes that operate in tropical rainforests?
2 Why are tropical rainforests so important?
3 How do humans, including the Dyak and Penan people of Borneo and the Indians of the Amazon, interact with the rainforest environment?

Glossary of key terms

Aerial roots A type of plant root that absorbs moisture and nutrients from the air and falling debris rather than growing in the ground.

Buttress roots A special type of root system, most of which is found above the ground.

Canopy The uppermost layer of the forest which allows little light to pass through.

Deforestation The large-scale clearing of vegetation.

Ecosystem A community of interacting plants and animals.

Emergent A tall tree extending above the canopy of the rainforest.

Endangered species Species of plants and animals that are under threat from the activities of people.

Epiphytes A plant that grows on another tree using the tree to anchor itself.

Germinate To sprout or shoot.

Indigenous people People who are native to an area.

Leaching The removal of nutrients from the soil by the downward movement of water; common in areas of high rainfall.

Lianas Climbing plants found in rainforests.

Microclimate The climate of a very small area; for example, on the floor of a forest. It is smaller in scale than the local climate.

Parasites Plants and animals that live off a host organism (another plant or animal). Many parasites eventually kill their host.

Pollination The spread of pollen; required for the fertilisation of plants.

Shifting cultivation A farming system that involves moving from site to site as soil fertility declines as a result of leaching.

Species A group of plants or animals of the same type. Members of the same species are able to reproduce fertile offspring.

Water cycle The recycling of water between bodies of water, land and the atmosphere by the processes of evaporation, condensation and precipitation.

Headhunters and cannibals

When Europeans first visited the rainforests they brought home fantastic stories of headhunters and cannibals. By the time these stories made it into the newspapers they had been so exaggerated that they bore little resemblance to reality. Nevertheless, headhunting and cannibalism were still practised in some remote areas of the Malaysian state of Sarawak, in Peru in South America, and in New Guinea until as recently as the 1950s.

Such activities were part of the forest dweller's spiritual world; a victim's severed head kept close to the victor was thought to protect him from the spirit of the victim seeking revenge. But the victim's strength and courage were honoured by the victor eating some of his flesh—usually the thigh and his brains. When a young boy took part in a ceremony to mark his initiation into manhood, a victim's head was placed between his legs. It was believed that this would make him grow faster.

In some places it was the practice for people to eat parts of a dead relative's body. This was an act of affection and allowed the good qualities and life forces of the dead person to survive.

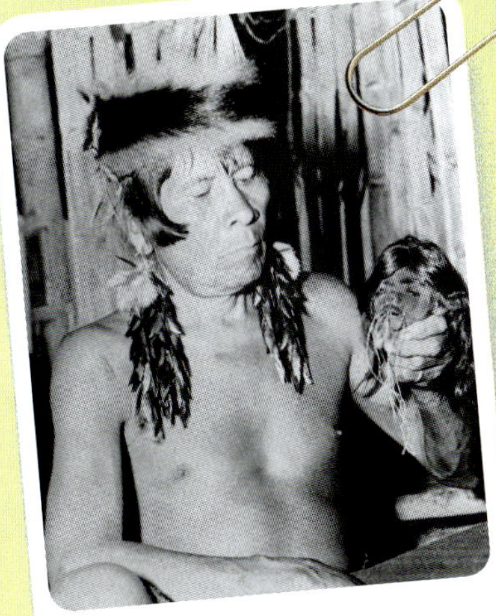

Peruvian headhunter.

eGlossary

GeoToolkit

ICT Toolkit

Foundation worksheet 7.1

7.1 Rainforest environments

Imagine trying to walk through a rainforest area like the one in the photograph or sketch opposite. Enormous trees, some over 40 metres above the ground, are a feature of rainforests. Where light can reach to the ground, rainforests have a dense undergrowth of bushes, young trees and creepers. Elsewhere, below the **canopy**, where the light does not easily penetrate, it is likely to be darker, cooler (perhaps 28°C to 30°C) and with less undergrowth. The canopy, the undergrowth and the forest floor (see Figure 7.1a) are home to some of the world's most incredible life forms.

Rainforests are important for their influence on the world's climate, our health and as a supply of valuable resources. They are home to more than 50 million indigenous people and countless **species** of birds, fish, reptiles and insects. Yet, parts of many rainforests remain unexplored while others are being destroyed by human activity. Rainforests are often described as the 'lungs of the earth' because of their ability to store carbon dioxide and release oxygen. In this chapter we will investigate many of these features of rainforests.

A rainforest can develop in an area that has high rainfall all year round. Tropical, or equatorial, rainforests have evolved in areas between the Tropic of Cancer and the Tropic of Capricorn (see Figure 7.1e, p. 145), where the climate is hot and wet for most of the year. In cooler regions of the world, such as southeast Australia and New Zealand, temperate rainforests are found.

A rainforest is a community of plants and animals. This means that trees, shrubs, herbs, creepers, ferns and mosses, as well as insects and other

Figure 7.1a The profile of a rainforest.

Figure 7.1b Tropical rainforests are among the world's most fragile ecosystems.

Understanding the text

1 Under what climatic conditions can rainforests develop?
2 Explain the main difference between tropical rainforests and temperate rainforests.
3 Explain what is meant by the term 'community'.
4 Why is the canopy of a rainforest like an umbrella?
5 How do the conditions found on the forest floor differ from those among the emergents?

UTT worksheet 7.1

animals, live together. Each plant and animal is dependent on other members of the community to survive. As you can see in Figure 7.1a, the rainforest is made up of distinct layers.

Why are rainforests hot and wet?

In the equatorial regions of the earth the sun is almost directly overhead throughout the year. This means that it has a smaller area of the earth's surface to heat than at locations further north or south of the Equator. As a result, rainforests have a hot climate throughout the year (see Figures 5.3a and 5.3d, pp. 108 and 109).

The *diurnal range* (the difference between the highest and lowest temperature experienced in a twenty-four-hour period) and seasonal range of temperatures is very small. Nights are not much cooler than daytime temperatures and the coolest month of the year may be only 1°C cooler than the hottest month. Singapore, for example, which is only 1° of latitude north of the Equator has a seasonal range of just 1.5°C (see Table 7.1a).

The high level of rainfall received near the Equator is mainly due to convectional rainfall. Convectional rainfall occurs when warm, moist air is heated by the earth's surface. As a body of air increases in temperature it expands and becomes lighter than the surrounding air. This causes it to rise and cool. Condensation takes place and precipitation occurs usually on a daily basis. Afternoon thunderstorms are common near the Equator (see Figure 7.1c).

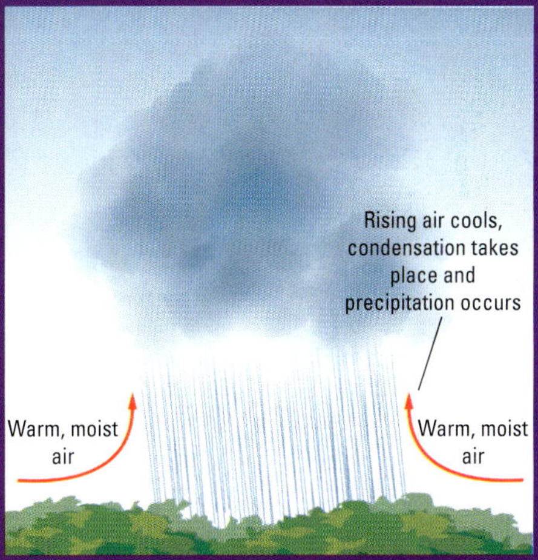

Figure 7.1c Convectional rainfall.

Table 7.1a shows that Singapore receives 2273 millimetres of rainfall a year. This is almost twice as much as Sydney's average annual rainfall of 1223 millimetres.

Table 7.1a Climate statistics for Singapore

Month	J	F	M	A	M	J	J	A	S	O	N	D	Year
Average temp. (°C)	26.0	26.6	27.0	27.3	27.5	27.5	27.1	27.0	27.0	27.0	26.6	26.2	26.9 av.
Rainfall (mm)	239	165	174	166	171	163	150	171	164	191	250	269	2273 total

Working geographically

1 **Writing task** Develop a postcard to send to a friend after you have visited a rainforest. Sketch part of a rainforest on one side. Describe a brief walk in one on the other side.

2 **Comparing heights** What is the tallest part of your school building? Estimate its height. Using an accurate scale, make a sketch of this part of the building and next to it sketch an emergent. Give your sketch an appropriate title and vertical scale.

3 **Applying knowledge** Copy the following statements into your workbook. Next to each statement, write the name of the rainforest layer that:
- a receives the greatest amount of sunlight
- b receives the least amount of sunlight
- c has the highest humidity
- d receives the strongest winds
- e records the highest temperatures
- f records the lowest temperatures.

4 **Challenge: Writing task** Using the information on pages 142–6, write a paragraph explaining why rainforest vegetation along river courses is much denser than other areas of rainforest.

5 **Challenge: Group work** Working in groups of two or three, list the factors that plants would have to adapt to in the different layers of the rainforest. Put this information on a sketch or copy of the rainforest profile in Figure 7.1a (p. 142).

6 **Constructing climate graphs** Using Table 7.1a, construct the climate graph for Singapore (see Unit 2.7, p. 38).

7 **Internet research** Use the WorldClimate website to gather climate data for at least one other city located in an area of the world where tropical rainforests are found (see Table 7.1b). Construct the climate graph for the city selected (see Unit 2.7, p. 38). Write a paragraph comparing the climate of this place with that of Singapore.

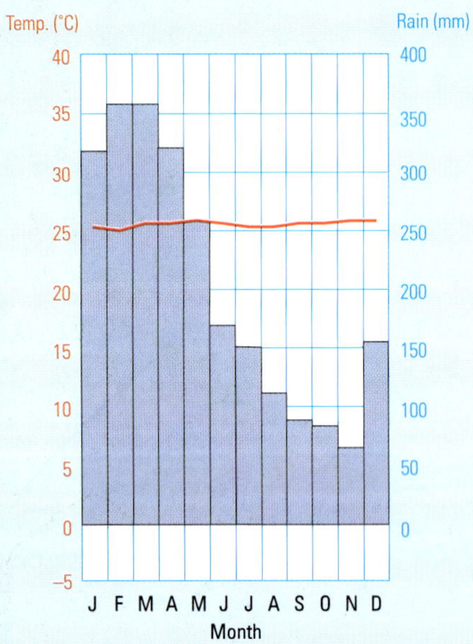

Figure 7.1d Climate graph for Belem, Brazil.

Where are the rainforests located?

Rainforests only develop in particular regions on our planet. They need heat, light and, as their name suggests, large amounts of rain or moisture. Figure 7.1e shows where the world's remaining natural rainforests are located. This distribution is changing as rainforests are cleared by people or are burned during natural disasters.

Map boundaries suggest that rainforests start and finish abruptly. However, this is not usually the case. Trees in rainforests become

Table 7.1b Distribution of the world's tropical rainforests

Region	Millions of hectares	Percentage of the world's rainforests
West Africa	162	9.2
Central Africa	204	11.6
Southern Africa	162	9.2
South Asia	64	3.6
Southeast Asia	211	12.0
Pacific	36	2.1
Central America, Caribbean	115	6.5
South America	802	45.8
Total	**1756**	**100.0**

Source: Food and Agriculture Organisation, 1993

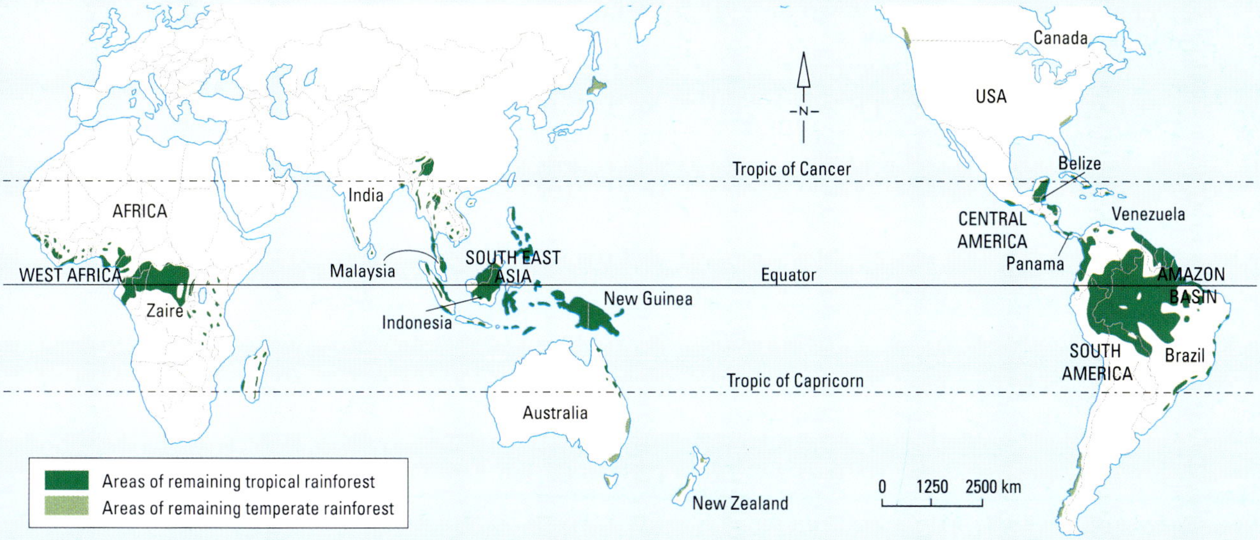

Figure 7.1e The world's remaining rainforests.

shorter and further apart as the amount of rainfall that places receive becomes less and less. Grasses and smaller trees become more common in these drier areas. In the shallow waters of some coastlines, mangrove forests can develop.

All the rainforest locations shown in Figure 7.1e have some elements in common. The most important of these elements are those essential for the growth of plants: heat, water and light.

Heat

Areas located between the Tropic of Cancer and the Tropic of Capricorn (see Figure 7.1e) receive the most direct rays from the sun. As a result, these regions of the earth heat up faster than other areas. For places near the Equator, such as Belem (see Figure 7.1d), average temperatures remain high throughout the year. This allows plant growth to occur all year; as long as there is sufficient water.

Water

The sun provides light and heat for plant growth. Its energy causes massive evaporation from seas and rivers as well as from plants. Evaporated moisture rises, cools and condenses into clouds. Winds, particularly from warmer oceans, may be moisture laden and will add to the atmosphere's store of moisture. If hills or mountains force these winds to rise, the air may cool and condensation may quickly occur.

Rain, often very heavy, will occur once the atmosphere cannot hold any more moisture. The amount of moisture that the atmosphere can hold depends on its temperature. The higher the temperature, the greater the amount of moisture that can be held and that may be released as rain. Figure 7.1d shows the huge amounts of rainfall received by Belem, which is in the Amazon Basin.

With high temperatures and water all year, plant growth in the tropical rainforests can be very rapid. The atmosphere is usually very humid—like that inside a greenhouse. The rainforest taps into the **water cycle** by making use of the large amount of rainfall and humidity. Plants absorb water as it rains. The rain trickles down leaves, branches and trunks, allowing the roots of plants to take up the water that has soaked into the soil. Water absorbed by plants circulates

Did U know?

- Rainforests are the most diverse ecosystems on earth. A single hectare of Kenya's Kakamega Forest hosts between 100 and 150 different tree species, compared with approximately ten species in other forest types.
- While the canopy of the rainforest might look like a tangle of branches, the branches of trees never actually touch each other. Scientists refer to this as 'crown shyness'.
- The canopy can prevent as much as 99 per cent of the light reaching the forest floor.
- Many species of rainforest trees have drip-tip leaves, which help drain off excessive moisture.
- Twenty per cent of the nutrients of the rainforest are in the soil; 80 per cent of the nutrients remain in the trees and plants.
- The rainwater of the forest is recycled by evaporation. Clouds above the forest's canopy help reflect sunlight. This keeps temperatures within the forest more stable.
- Rainforest soil is only suitable for rainforest plants; crops may not grow well in it. When forests are cut down, the soil can erode quickly and soon only a degraded landscape remains.

Understanding the text

1 Outline the factors that have contributed to the changing distribution of rainforests.
2 Explain why most rainforests are located between the Tropic of Cancer and the Tropic of Capricorn.
3 Explain why areas close to the Equator receive large amounts of rainfall.
4 Why is plant growth in tropical rainforests so rapid?
5 How do rainforest plants use the rainfall available?
6 Define the following terms: evapotranspiration and humidity.

cd UTT worksheet 7.1

Did U know?

- Tropical rainforests are the biggest genetic library in the world with at least half the Earth's life forms on less than 5 per cent of its land surface.
- Seventy per cent of identified cancer-fighting plants come from rainforests.
- One-third of the world's bird species nest in rainforests.
- Teak, rosewood, mahogany, ebony, balsa and bamboo are all valuable rainforest timbers.
- We eat rainforests: bananas, sugar cane, pepper, ginger, pineapples, mangoes, vanilla, chocolate and the gum in most chewing gums originated from rainforests.

cd Extension worksheet 7.1

cd Extension worksheet 7.2

through all the cells of each plant, carrying food to the cells. Eventually the excess water is released back into the atmosphere from the leaves of plants in a process called evapotranspiration.

Light

The world's hot and wet areas are not always the brightest areas. Long periods of cloud cover, because of high evaporation and condensation, reduce the amount of light that an area receives. However, the combination of heat, water and light received in the area between the Tropic of Cancer and the Tropic of Capricorn produces the luxuriant growth common to all tropical rainforests.

Working geographically

1 **Mapping task** Study Figure 7.1e (p. 145). On a blank map of the world, locate and name the remaining regions of tropical rainforests. Use an atlas to assist you. Label the map using the region names given in Table 7.1b (p. 144).

2 **Constructing graphs** Study Table 7.1b. Construct a pie graph showing the distribution of the world's tropical rainforests (see Unit 2.13).

3 **Writing task** When you have completed activities 1 and 2 above, write four or five sentences summarising what you see. Include in your account:
   a the location of the world's tropical rainforests
   b why they occur in these areas.

4 **Using an atlas** Study Figure 7.1e (p. 145). Name five countries in which temperate rainforests are located. Use an atlas to help you identify these countries.

5 **Interpreting maps** The average temperatures of temperate rainforests are lower than those in tropical rainforests. Use Figure 7.1e to help you explain why this is so.

6 **Interpreting graphs: Internet research** Study the climate graph for Belem (Figure 7.1d, p. 144), then complete the following tasks:
   a What is the average annual temperature of Belem (see Unit 2.7)?
   b Estimate the total average annual rainfall received by Belem.
   c Describe the seasonal distribution of rainfall.
   d Explain why Belem is so hot and wet all year round.
   e Construct a table to make a comparison of the climate of Belem to that of your own area. Visit the Bureau of Meteorology website to help you locate the data for your area.

7.2 Life in the rainforests

Plants

Tropical rainforests, with their hot and wet conditions, have rapid plant growth. They also support an enormous number of plant species. For example, an average hectare in a Malaysian rainforest can support as many as 180 different tree species. In Brazil, an average hectare of rainforest support about 40 000 species of flowering plants.

Rainforest plants are valuable resources in so many ways. Some plants are the basis for valuable medicines. Quinine (used to treat malaria) and reserpine (used to treat high blood pressure) are just two medicines in wide use that have come from rainforest plants. Indigenous forest people have used many local plants for medicinal purposes for generations. Many rainforest plants probably remain to be 'discovered' for use in treating a wide range of illnesses.

Rainforest plants have provided many of our food sources and industrial raw materials, including rubber. Look at the Did U Know? box opposite for some examples.

Conservationists argue that the known and potential value of rainforests is so high that we should not be clearing them at such a fast rate. Pages 151 and 160 look at this issue in greater detail.

Figure 7.2a Buttress roots support tall trees and search for nutrients in the soil.

Amazing plants

Tropical rainforests are always green. With constant high temperatures and rainfall there is continuous growth. Plants shed their leaves, grow new ones, and flower and fruit alongside one another. No single species dominates the tropical forest landscape.

Fungi are just one of the amazing plants of the tropical rainforest. Fungi play an important role in the maintenance of the rainforest ecosystem. They break down dead organic matter, making nutrients available for the ongoing operation of the nutrient cycle. In addition, most plants would not be able to grow without the fungi that inhabit their roots and help the plants absorb nutrients from the soil (see Figure 7.3b, p. 150).

Rainforest plants have adapted to their environment in a number of ways. These are discussed below.

Tree trunks

Many rainforest trees have straight trunks with no branches under 20 metres. This adaptation helps the trees maximise their access to light. The bark of the trunks is usually smooth, which allows water to run down to their roots. Flowering can take place directly on tree trunks as well as on thick branches.

Buttresses

Some rainforest trees, such as the one shown in Figure 7.2a, develop wide buttresses. These buttresses appear to be part of the trunk but are really roots that can develop 6 metres up from the base of a tree. **Buttress roots** provide support for the tree.

Soil nutrients are greatest near the surface of the soil, so few rainforest plants have deep roots. Instead, most have fine feeding roots near the surface.

Understanding the text

1. Explain why the plants of tropical rainforests are such an important natural resource.
2. How are the trunks of rainforest trees adapted to the conditions in which they grow?
3. Why do some trees develop buttress roots?
4. How have lianas, vines and creepers adapted to the conditions that exist in tropical rainforests?
5. What is an epiphyte? Describe the relationship between epiphytes and the plants they grow on.
6. List the features developed by the leaves of plants that enable them to cope with the conditions found in rainforests.
7. Explain the role played by fungi in the rainforest ecosystem.

UTT worksheet 7.2

Working geographically

1 **Constructing diagrams**
Locate an example of a tropical plant in your home or local area. Sketch the plant you are studying. Annotate (label) your sketch with the appropriate features from the list below:
- shiny leaves
- drip tips
- large leaves
- attached to another plant
- fast growing
- aerial roots.

Suggest how the plant's features would allow it to survive in the rainforest environment.

2 **Constructing diagrams**
On the left-hand side of a page in your workbook make a sketch of a large rainforest tree. Refer to the text and Figures 7.1a (p. 142) and 7.1b (p. 143) to assist you. On the right-hand side of the page, annotate your sketch to indicate and explain the reasons for the following features:
- **a** the shape of the tree trunk
- **b** buttress roots
- **c** shallow roots
- **d** lianas, vines and creepers
- **e** the shape of the leaves.

3 **Challenge: Internet research**
Become a chemical prospector! Investigate at least one rainforest plant that has potential use in the health field. Present an oral report on the latest findings available (see Unit 2.14).

Foundation worksheet 7.1

Foundation worksheet 7.2

Extension worksheet 7.1

Extension worksheet 7.2

Lianas, vines and creepers

About 90 per cent of the earth's climbing plants originate from the tropics. Typically, they attach themselves to trees by tendrils or roots and spread their leaves in the canopy where light is available. **Lianas**, such as those in Figure 7.1b (p. 143), hang from the trees to which they are attached. Some lianas reach the ground and anchor themselves in the soil or around other trees. **Epiphytes** are plants that grow on branches of other plants without harming them.

Leaves

The leaves of many rainforest plants are often dark and waxy to reduce water loss but also to help water run off quickly. Some have drip tips on their leaves, which are another efficient way for the leaves to rid themselves of water. Often the leaves of the rainforest plants at the lower levels of the forest are very large. This allows as much light as possible to be absorbed in the dark environment near the forest floor.

Animals

The world's tropical rainforests are the habitats of thousands of different species of animals, including reptiles, birds, fish and insects. Anacondas, piranhas, komodo dragons, orang-utans, gorillas, jaguars, vampire bats and tapirs are all rainforest creatures. A few are pictured on these two pages. Most of these lifeforms can be put into several main categories: fruit and seed eaters, leaf eaters and predators.

Fruit and seed eaters

Rainforest plants can produce fruit and many seeds, especially in the canopy layer (see p. 142). Fruit attracts birds and animals, which deposit the seed as waste matter. This allows seeds to **germinate** elsewhere in the forest. Birds with bills or beaks that are long, such as the bird of paradise of New Guinea, or strong or both long and strong, such as the South American toucan (see the box below), can search for fruit and break it open. Larger creatures, such as the lowland gorillas of the Congo Basin in Africa and the orang-utans of Borneo, are fruit, seed and leaf eaters.

Toucans

Toucans with beaks as bright as rainbows are the showy residents of the tallest rainforest trees. The bird's large beak—which is often longer than the bird's body—enables it to harvest berries from thin branches that would not be strong enough to support its weight. The beak may also serve as a 'flag' to assist in species and mate recognition. When sleeping, the toucan lays its huge bill along its back and covers the bill with its tail.

Toucans make their nest in high natural tree holes, which they enlarge by removing rotten wood. The toucan is a very social bird. They move about in groups of a dozen or so. They are weak fliers and merely glide short distances between trees.

Figure 7.2b A toucan's beak is often longer than the bird's body.

Leaf eaters

One square metre of some tropical rainforests can produce almost 1 kilogram of new foliage every year: a valued source of food for the forests' leaf eaters. Leaf eaters range from small ants and caterpillars to monkeys, such as the proboscis monkey of Borneo, which lives in mangrove forests.

Leaf-cutter ants (see Figure 7.2c) cut up leaves with their scissor-like jaws. The cut leaves are carried back to their nests and stored underground. Here the ants chew the cut leaves and add fungus spores. A fungus grows on the leaf pulp, providing food for the ants.

Many plants have developed defences against attack from leaf eaters. These defences include tough leaves, thorns, sticky gum and toxins that can prove poisonous to many leaf eaters.

Figure 7.2c Leaf-cutter ants at work.

Predators

Predators, such as those shown in Figure 7.2d, are life forms that feed on other insects, birds, reptiles and animals. They range in size from moths and spiders to hawks, deer and forest pigs, as well as tigers in Asia and jaguars in South America.

Rainforests support many insect eaters, especially birds. They can seek insects, including ants and butterflies, among the leaves of plants, in the bark of trees and on the forest floor. To avoid capture some insects camouflage their appearance, or sting or bite their attackers. Frogs and the eggs of many species provide some snakes with a rich food source. Snakes can be found in the canopy of tropical rainforests, along with birds and apes. At the other end of the size scale, jaguars in South American rainforests feed on monkeys, birds, fish, lizards, peccaries (a pig-like mammal) and wild pigs.

Figure 7.2d Pythons are a predator of the rainforest floor.

Working geographically

1 **Challenge: Internet research** Select a tropical rainforest animal and research the following information:

- **a** a sketch or copyright-free downloaded image of the selected animal
- **b** the region of the world in which it is found
- **c** any adaptations that assist the animal's survival in the rainforest
- **d** its place within the food chain—its sources of food and any predators
- **e** other threats to its survival.

Develop a PowerPoint presentation of your research findings to present to the rest of the class (see Unit 2.16). Be sure to include a locating map, images of the animal selected and its habitat.

2 **Group work: Research** Working in groups, do some library research to compile a list of endangered rainforest animals. Identify the main source of habitat destruction threatening the survival of the species. Pin your list to the noticeboard. Over time, add newspaper and magazine articles dealing with these endangered animals.

Understanding the text

1. Explain why there is such a large variety of animals in tropical rainforests.
2. Outline how fruit and seed eaters assist in the germination and spread of plants in the rainforest.
3. What adaptations do birds, such as the bird of paradise and the toucan, have to help them obtain their food?
4. Explain why the rainforest is able to support such a large variety of leaf eaters.
5. Explain how leaf-cutter ants use the leaves of plants as food.
6. Outline the defences that some rainforest plants have developed to defend themselves against attack.
7. What are predators?
8. What adaptations have some insects developed to avoid capture?

UTT worksheet 7.2

7.3 Rainforest ecosystems

In any area of the world there is a link between plants and animals and between plants and soil. These connections form an **ecosystem**. Within all ecosystems there is a flow of energy and nutrients. Figure 7.3a shows the main processes in the nutrient cycle of the rainforest—a cycle vital for their existence.

The ecosystems of tropical rainforests are the most complex on earth. This is because rainforests are very rich in the number of species they can support. On the slopes of one volcano in the Philippines there are more plant species than in the entire United States. The links between the species are very involved. If these links are broken by natural disasters or the actions of people, all parts of the ecosystem are quickly affected. The removal of a plant species could result in the removal of a food source or a habitat for other plants and animals. Many different types of plants and animals play their part in the working of the ecosystem and help keep its delicate balance undisturbed.

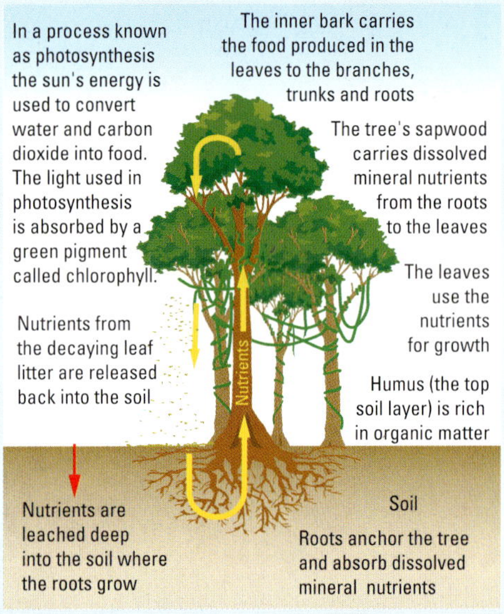

Figure 7.3a The nutrient cycle of tropical rainforests.

Recycling in the rainforest

Huge amounts of plant material exist in rainforests because of the hot temperatures and high rainfall (see p. 143). In these conditions, plants grow very fast and in large numbers. They rely on the rain falling regularly and often, as well as temperatures remaining high.

With so many plants in the forest there is, of course, a large amount of dead plant material. When a leaf falls to the ground or when a tree or animal dies, it is pounced upon by termites, ants and worms. Thousands of these tiny creatures eat the decaying matter and recycle it into the soil. Figure 7.3a shows how these nutrients are used by forest plants. The remains of the rainforest tree shown in Figure 7.3b are evidence of this process. In this way, rainforest soils help provide nutrients for plants to grow densely, rapidly and, for some, to great heights. The speed of nutrient recycling is very important. If the nutrients aren't recycled quickly they will be **leached** out of the soil by the heavy rainfall.

Figure 7.3b A rainforest tree rots away in the humid conditions of the forest floor.

Links in the rainforest ecosystem

There are many examples of links within tropical rainforests. One example is how trees depend on insects, birds and other animals for **pollination**. Some trees are only pollinated by bats that feed on the nectar of flowers. Because each tree in the rainforest comes into flower at different times, the bats move from tree to tree for food. As they move, the bats carry pollen from one tree to the next. This, in turn, allows trees to produce fruit and seeds.

Imagine if two of these tree species in an area of rainforest were cut down for timber. There could be a two-month period of no flowers and therefore no food for the bats in this area. This may cause the bats to die out or go elsewhere. As a result, other trees would not be pollinated. Thus, cutting down one or two types of trees could have far-reaching consequences for the working of the rainforest.

Once the nutrient cycle is disrupted by clearing, the fertility of the soil declines rapidly. In addition, if the forest's canopy of leaves is removed, the harsh tropical sun can penetrate into the lower layers of the forest. This will alter the **microclimate** of the forest floor and kill off the shade-loving vegetation. Soil becomes hard and infertile as it is baked in the hot sun. In such conditions, it is unlikely that the forest will ever recover.

Destroy or save?

Half the world's rainforests have been lost and much of what remains could be lost in the near future. There are a number of reasons for this loss:

- clearing of forest to create new agricultural land
- logging to produce an export income. Many developing countries, such as the Solomon Islands, have little else to trade
- the collection of fuel wood. For many millions of the world's poorest people, wood is the main source of energy for heating and cooking.

On the Indonesian island of Sumatra, the rate of rainforest clearance has been very rapid. Elsewhere on the planet there are encouraging signs for the future of the rainforests.

Over 3000 sites, representing about 4 per cent of all tropical rainforests, are now protected areas. Protected areas are designed to assist the preservation of rainforest species, such as the tigers of India and orang-utans of Malaysia and Indonesia (see Figure 7.3c, p. 152), as well as plants. Many governments are setting quotas on the percentages of rainforests that must forever remain as rainforests.

The Tropical Forestry Action Plan was developed in 1985 by the UN Food and Agriculture Organization (FAO), the UN Development Programme (UNDP), the World Bank and other interested bodies. This plan aims to promote:

- sustainable yields of timber
- better use of forest lands
- a sustainable supply of fuel wood for a growing population
- conservation of species and forest ecosystems
- sharing of knowledge in the area of forest management.

Did U know?

- Tropical rainforests continue to be cleared at a rate of around 86 000 square kilometres per day—an area half as big again as the size of Tasmania.
- At the current rate of deforestation, 4 to 8 per cent of rainforest species will be extinct or endangered by 2015 and between 17 and 35 per cent by 2040.
- Rainforests cover less than 2 per cent of the earth's surface, yet they are home to some 40 to 50 per cent of all life forms on our planet—as many as 30 million species of plants and animals.
- Rate of loss:
  - 2.4 acres (1 hectare) per second (equivalent to two football fields)
  - 31 000 000 hectares per year—an area larger than Poland
- Scientists estimate an average of 137 species are driven into extinction every day; or 50 000 each year
- The economic value of 1 hectare of Peruvian rainforest: US$6820 per year if intact forest is sustainably harvested for fruits, latex and timber; US$1000 per year if clear-cut for commercial timber (not sustainably harvested); and US$148 per year if used as cattle pasture.

Understanding the text

1. Explain what an ecosystem is.
2. Why is the ecosystem of the tropical rainforest so unique?
3. Explain what happens when the complex links between rainforest species are broken by natural disasters or the actions of people.
4. Outline why the recycling of nutrients is so important in rainforests.
5. Describe one link in the rainforest ecosystem.
6. Use the glossary to help you define leaching. Explain its role in the nutrient cycle.

cd UTT worksheet 7.3

Working geographically

1. **Challenge: Interpreting diagrams** Study Figure 7.3a. Describe how the nutrient cycle of the rainforest operates. Be sure to identify the sources of nutrients and how plants are able to use them.
2. **Constructing diagrams** Create a series of diagrams with captions and/or annotations to explain what would happen to the soil in a tropical rainforest if most of the trees in an area were cut down. Consider soil erosion and the changes to nutrient recycling and soil fertility.
3. **Library research** Do some library research to find examples of rainforest food chains and food webs. Copy one into your workbook.

Figure 7.3c Once captive and orphaned orang-utans are encouraged to live as wild animals in the rainforests of Borneo.

Conservation groups, such as Greenpeace and the World Wide Fund for Nature, have successfully educated many people about the need to conserve rainforests. The World Bank no longer grants loans to projects such as dam construction if the danger of destruction to habitats is likely to be large. Another scheme encourages richer countries to cancel debts owed to them by poorer countries with rainforests, on the condition that these countries create protected areas of rainforest. This strategy has been used to save some of Costa Rica's remaining rainforests.

Investigating indigenous rainforest dwellers

ICT

Select one of the websites listed below and compile a list of the types of information available on the site:

- *National Geographic*—this site takes you on a virtual expedition to meet the Korubo tribe in the depths of the Amazon
- *Cultural Survival*—a good site for news and information on the human rights of indigenous peoples
- *Indigenous Environmental Network*—a great site focusing on environmental threats to indigenous communities
- *Native Web*—this site has a wealth of resources on indigenous cultures from around the world
- *Penan*—a site dedicated to the Penan's struggle for survival as one of the world's few remaining nomadic peoples of the rainforest
- *Rainforest Action Network*—learn how to protect the earth's rainforests and support the rights of their inhabitants.

Understanding the text

1. What proportion of the world's rainforests have already been lost?
2. Outline the reasons for this loss.
3. What problems does the loss of rainforests create?
4. How much of the world's rainforest has been included in protected areas?
5. What is the Tropical Forestry Action Plan? What does it aim to promote?
6. Outline the role that groups such as Greenpeace and the World Wide Fund for Nature play in efforts to protect rainforests.

UTT worksheet 7.3

Working geographically

1. **Challenge: Civics and citizenship** Which of the following actions do you think would be the most realistic and effective in stopping the destruction of rainforests in Sumatra?
   - a writing a letter to your local member of parliament
   - b writing a letter to the Indonesian President
   - c refusing to buy Indonesian products
   - d joining Greenpeace
   - e visiting Sumatra
   - f joining a 'friends of the Sumatran rainforest' group

   Give reasons for the option you chose. Explain why you think the others would not be so effective.
2. **Internet research** Investigate biosphere reserves as a way to save rainforests and their species of life forms. Find answers to the following questions: What are biosphere reserves? Who promotes them? Where do biosphere reserves exist? How do they work? Will they work in rainforests?

Extension worksheet 7.3

Extension worksheet ICT 7.4

7.4 SAMPLE STUDY
The Dyaks of Borneo

The world's rainforests are home to over 50 million indigenous people. Some of these people are the Dyaks in Borneo, the Yanomani in Brazil, Papuans in Papua New Guinea and the Mbuti of the Congo Basin. As well as these groups, there are increasing numbers of non-indigenous people. These people have moved, or are moving, into rainforest areas to exploit the forests' natural resources of timber, water, minerals and potential agricultural land.

This sample study focuses on how change is affecting the Dyak people of Borneo and their rainforest environment.

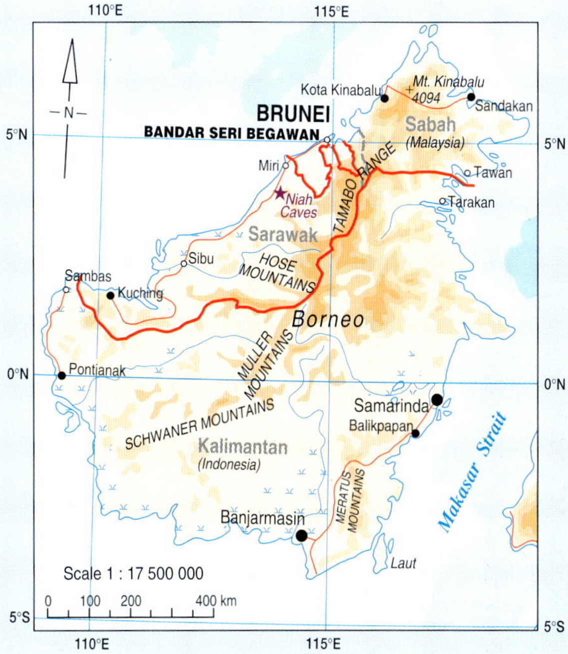

Figure 7.4a Borneo and the east Malaysian states of Sarawak and Sabah. Source: *Heinemann Atlas.*

The Dyaks

Borneo is a large island in Southeast Asia. As Figure 7.4a shows, the island is divided politically by three countries. Part of Indonesia, part of Malaysia and all of Brunei are in Borneo.

Borneo's location either side of the Equator (0° latitude) means all but its highest peaks have high temperatures all year round. Rainfall totals are high but there is a less wet season in the second half of each year. During this time, plant growth slows and river levels drop. Overall the climate is hot and mostly very wet and humid. These conditions can produce dense rainforest vegetation of the type seen in Figure 7.4b. It is also responsible for creating Borneo's rivers, like the one in Figure 7.4b. Rivers are an essential part of life in this part of the world—for transport, a source of food as well as for domestic needs.

The indigenous people of Borneo probably arrived on the island 50 000 years ago. The name Dyak is given to these people. It originates from the Malay word for 'up-country', suggesting where the indigenous people were found. In fact, they are distributed along the coast, in valleys and in remote highland regions.

There are many Dyak groups, including the Iban, Bidayuh and Penan.

In the Malaysian state of Sarawak (see Figure 7.4a), Dyaks make up around 47 per cent of the total population. In the northern state of Sabah, ethnic groups such as the Dusun and Bajan also make up around half the total population.

Figure 7.4b Trading stations on rivers provide contact points for a range of services for the Dyaks of Borneo.

Table 7.4a Climate data for Kalimanatan, southern Borneo

Month	J	F	M	A	M	J	J	A	S	O	N	D	Year
Average temp. (°C)	22	22	25	30	30	27	27	27	30	31	25	22	26.5 av.
Rainfall (mm)	300	260	200	120	110	100	70	60	80	100	120	180	1700 total

Figure 7.4c A Penan tribesman using a blowpipe.

Figure 7.4d A Penan tribesman climbing a forest tree to obtain fruit.

The Penan

All Borneo's ethnic groups have used the resources of the rainforest to provide for their everyday needs. The Penan, for example, developed a nomadic lifestyle within the rainforest. They collected edible fruits and seeds to supplement their main source of food, wild sago palm. In addition, the Penan hunted wild boar, monkeys, deer, fish and birds. Over thousands of years the Penan destroyed little of the rainforest. Instead they used it in a sustainable way.

While the totally nomadic Penan now number only around 1000, many thousands of other Penan still know how to use the rainforest resources. They can predict when edible plants will flower and when the fruit will ripen. They can identify fifty medicinal plants, over 100 fruiting trees and ten toxic plant substances that will kill fish. The Penan can also identify eight dart poisons for blowpipes, such as the one shown in Figure 7.4c. The rainforest provided materials to build temporary shelters. Importantly, the rainforest plants and animals were part of the Penan's spiritual wealth.

Disturbing any of the forest's characteristics can be devastating to a lifestyle based on maintaining the forest in its original condition. Unfortunately, much of Borneo's forests have been disturbed. Large-scale logging of the rainforest, damming rivers for hydroelectricity and introducing new cash crops have permanently altered the Penan way of life. Thousands have been resettled to new and permanent villages. Loss of traditional homelands, erosion of cleared hillsides and the siltation of lowland rivers have occurred throughout areas once occupied only by the Penan.

These changes have brought widespread protests from among the Penan community and overseas groups.

Cultivating the forest lands

Elsewhere in Borneo, Dyaks were **shifting cultivators**. Small areas of forest were cleared every year or two and food crops, such as sago and bananas, were grown for the family. After a few years, as soil fertility declined and these gardens became less productive, these areas were invaded by weeds and the regrowth of forest plants. New areas in the forest were then cleared. Family groups lived in permanent longhouses,

Figure 7.4e The traditional longhouse consists of many apartments.

Figure 7.4f Interior of a longhouse, the location of many communal activities and the sleeping area for children and single adults.

Figure 7.4h A newly constructed longhouse. Concrete, aluminium and glass replace timber but the plan is the same.

like those in Figures 7.4e and 7.4f. Generally, living conditions were poor with little access to health facilities. Dietary standards, however, were good.

The Malaysian Government has helped to improve the living conditions of the Dyaks. It recognised that this improvement would be best achieved through more commercial farming and other activities, as well as the development of health and education programs. It was also anxious to have rural communities, such as the Dyaks, become part of modern Malaysian society and identify themselves as Malaysians.

The results of these policies are very noticeable. Government and local money has led to many longhouses either being upgraded or rebuilt, such as the one in Figure 7.4h. Most housing now has electricity, although often from generators. Some villages have town water supplies, especially where the traditional river water supply has become heavily silted from logging and road construction. School-age

Figure 7.4i Pepper has become an important crop to inland Dyaks of Borneo.

Figure 7.4g Steep, cleared land is planted with hill rice using simple tools, including a digging stick.

Understanding the text

1 Describe Borneo's location in relation to the Equator. What effect does this location have on the climate?

2 What does the name Dyak mean?

3 Outline the ways in which the Penan use but do not destroy the rainforest.

4 Identify the changes that have disrupted traditional Penan lifestyles.

5 Use the glossary on page 141 to help you define the following terms: indigenous people and shifting cultivation. Write the definitions in your own words.

6 What is a longhouse?

7 How has farming and everyday life changed for many Dyaks?

UTT worksheet 7.4

children live at boarding schools for most of the year. Health services have become available at central locations.

In many areas, there has been a change in farming practices. Forest land is still cleared by villagers, but instead of using axes, chain saws are common now. Large trees are easily cut and the long trunks are used to mark out family gardens. Food crops, such as hill rice, are widely planted (see Figure 7.4g, p. 155). Commercial crops of pepper, palm oil and fruit have become commonplace. Pepper, in particular, has been a very successful crop for families. Plots such as the one in Figure 7.4i (p. 155) dot the landscape near longhouses. It is often planted as a semi-permanent crop on land that has been used for hill rice for a few years. These crops provide a cash income, allowing families to buy clothes, furniture, farming equipment and improve their housing. The cash income also gives people access to health and education facilities not paid for by government agencies.

Life has changed, but some things have stayed the same for many Dyak groups. As one longhouse village head said:

> For us Dyaks, the forest still has everything. We have freedom to do what we like. We pay no taxes. The government gives us basic education and health care. We have all the food we want: fruit, vegetables and fresh fish from the river. We have the closeness of our family and friends in the longhouses. Life is good.

Foundation worksheet 7.2

Working geographically

1 **Photo sketching** Make a photo sketch of Figure 7.4b (p. 153). (See Unit 2.9.) In one colour label the main characteristics of Borneo's environment (for example, 'many rivers'). Using another colour, label the probable causes of these characteristics (for example, 'heavy rainfall').

2 **Writing task** 'Every time a tree falls in the forest a star falls from the sky.' Write an exposition supporting the cause of the Penan people.

3 **Internet research** Use the Internet to investigate events concerning logging and displacement of Dyaks from their traditional lands in Borneo. Key search words and phrases could include the following: Dyaks, Bakun Dam, Borneo rainforest, Borneo logging, and Malaysian government logging policy.

4 **Interpreting the text** Suggest two major reasons why the Malaysian Government was keen to change the way most rural people in Borneo lived.

5 **Interpreting photographs** Look at the longhouse photographs in Figures 7.4e, 7.4f and 7.4h (pp. 154–5). What advantages might there be for members of a community to live so close to one another? Would you have recommended individual farmhouses or a traditional longhouse for all new Dyak housing? Give reasons for your answer.

6 **Class discussion** Discuss the following statement: 'Improvements in living conditions for Dyaks have come at a cost to Borneo's environment.' Do you agree or disagree with this statement? Give reasons for your answer.

7 **Challenge: Futures wheel or flow line** Draw a futures wheel or flow line to suggest the consequences of a collapse of world pepper prices on rural communities in Borneo. Include in your diagram such changes as new farming products, a drift to towns in search of work and a change in new building plans.

8 **Constructing climate graphs** Using the data in Table 7.4a, construct the climate graph for Kalimantan (see Unit 2.7).

9 **Interpreting graphs** Using the data in the graph you constructed in activity 8, complete the following tasks:
   a Name the wettest and driest months.
   b Describe how temperature and rainfall change throughout the year.
   c Compare Kalimantan's climate with the climate of the town or city in which you live. If necessary, visit the website of the Bureau of Meteorology to find the climate data for your town or city.
   d Which climate is more suitable for all-year-round tree growth: Kalimantan or the town or city in which you live? Justify your answer.

7.5 SAMPLE STUDY

The Amazon Basin

The Amazon Basin of South America supports about one-third of the world's remaining tropical rainforests. The landscapes, vegetation and animals in this region of the world have many spectacular and unusual features.

The Amazon Basin is a huge area of land that takes its name from the major river that drains water from it: the Amazon. Figures 7.5a and 7.5c (p. 158) show the sources of the Amazon River and its tributaries, the direction of their flow and the point where they empty into the ocean.

Traditional landuses

For perhaps 20 000 years, areas such as the one shown in Figure 7.5d have been able to support people. At one stage, there were more than 2 million people living in the basin. There were more than 200 tribes, often referred to as Indians or Amerindians. These people farmed

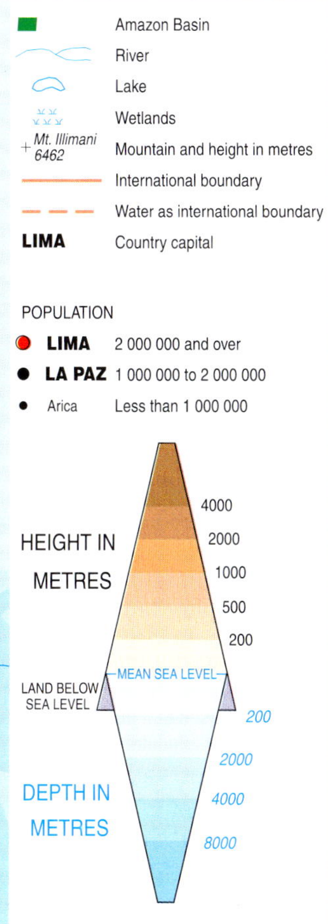

Figure 7.5a The Amazon Basin contains the earth's largest river system.

Did U know?

- The Amazon Basin is drained by one of the world's longest rivers: the Amazon River. This river is approximately 6280 kilometres long and is fed by over 1000 tributaries. Many of the tributaries are large rivers in their own right.
- Ocean-going vessels can reach the town of Iquitos on the Amazon River. Iquitos is 3700 kilometres inland from the Atlantic Ocean.
- The Amazon Basin covers an area almost the size of Australia.
- There may be up to 30 million different species of insects in the Amazon Basin, with each type of tree supporting over 400 insect species.
- The Amazon Basin contains one-fifth of the world's fresh water.
- The Amazon River discharges so much water that the Atlantic Ocean can be fresh water as far as several hundred kilometres from the river's mouth.

patches of land, hunted animals and collected fruit. Traditional farming was the practice of shifting cultivation in small gardens, such as the one in Figure 7.5b. Shifting cultivation in the Amazon Basin was, and is, similar to the methods carried out by the Dyaks of Borneo (see Unit 7.4).

Traditional Indians regard the rivers and trees of the rainforest as a spiritual source and something that should not be overexploited. Their way of farming was one that cared for the rainforest over a long period of time without destroying the forest environment.

The number of tribes and people living traditional lifestyles in the Amazon has fallen dramatically. At the same time, the basin is now supporting several million more people on farms, at mining sites and in towns and cities.

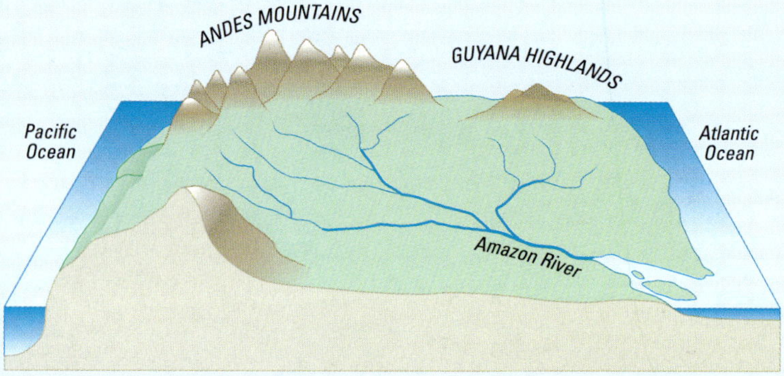

Figure 7.5c A block diagram of the drainage system of the Amazon Basin.

Figure 7.5d The Amazon Basin supports about one-third of the earth's remaining tropical rainforest.

Figure 7.5b In the hot, humid environment of the Amazon Basin, the gardens of shifting cultivators require frequent weeding.

Working geographically

1 **Interpreting maps and illustrations** Study Figures 7.5a (p. 157) and 7.5c, then complete the following tasks:
  a In which mountains do many of the Amazon's tributaries begin?
  b State the general direction in which the Amazon River flows.
  c Does the Amazon River flow over mainly flat or steep ground for most of its course?
  d Name the ocean into which the Amazon River empties.

2 **Integrating knowledge** Which of the features described in the text and illustrations best tells you that the Amazon Basin is:
  a large
  b drained by a huge river
  c supporting a large amount of vegetation?

3 **Internet research** Use the Internet and an atlas to gather information to make a comparison of the Amazon Basin and the Murray–Darling Basin. Summarise this information in your workbook. Be sure to include at least two maps and two annotated photos or sketches in your report.

4 **Interpreting photographs** Study Figure 7.5b, then complete the following tasks:
  a Describe the scene. Be sure to mention the shape of the farming land, how well cleared it is and the type of work that is being done.
  b Suggest why this scene will look very different in five years' time and even more different in fifteen years' time.

5 **Interpreting photographs** Study Figure 7.5d, then answer the following questions:
  a How can you tell that the area is likely to be very wet and humid?
  b Is the forest dense or thin?
  c What may be the best way to travel from one part of the area shown to another part?

Did U know?

Since the 1960s a series of ambitious plans to develop and colonise the Amazon have taken a heavy toll on the forest environment. An area of forest more than twice the size of Victoria has been cleared. Since 1988 new policies designed to protect the environment and the rights of the indigenous forest dwellers have slowed the annual rate of loss from 2.2 million hectares to 1.4 million hectares.

Understanding the text

1 Summarise the changes that have occurred to the population of the Amazon Basin.

2 Outline the relationship between traditional Indians and the environment of the Amazon Basin.

3 What is the advantage of the traditional form of farming used by the Amazon Indians?

UTT worksheet 7.5

Changing landuses

Investors from the United States, Japan and Europe, as well as from South America, have poured millions of dollars into large-scale projects hoping to gain large profits from the huge resources of the Amazon Basin. But modern development has not always been successful.

Roads and settlers

Since the 1960s, government planners in Brazil, Bolivia, Peru, Colombia and Venezuela have wanted many settlers to move into parts of the Amazon Basin and establish farms. These land-settlement schemes have required the building of a road network. Brazil, with the largest share of the Amazon Basin, has built an extensive network of roads, including the Trans-Amazonian Highway. Roads have often been built straight through rainforests. The road shown in Figure 7.5e is an example. These gravel or dirt roads are extensions of main highways built across the basin. Around these roads, many thousands of settlers were given land for farming. Often this land had been occupied and used by Indian tribes for centuries.

Did U know?

It is estimated that there are about 1000 groups of indigenous people living in what remains of the earth's rainforest. Like many of the plants and animals of the rainforest, many of these groups face extinction. In 1900, Brazil had 1 million Indians. Today, there are fewer than 200 000.

Debt and rainforest destruction

Most of the world's remaining rainforest is located in countries with huge national debts. This drives these countries to exploit their forest resources. To slow, and eventually halt, the rate of rainforest destruction requires international cooperation. If the debt crisis can be addressed the need to destroy the rainforests will be eliminated.

Extension worksheet 7.5

Extension worksheet 7.7

Land-settlement schemes have displaced thousands of Indians. Once the rainforest is burned and cleared, the key resource of traditional Indian life is gone. Violent clashes with new settlers have been common. Diseases brought with the new settlers have killed thousands of Indians. One-third of all known Amazonian tribes died out in the twentieth century. With them has gone the knowledge of plant and animal species that could have added to the world's medicine and agriculture.

Small farms, such as the ones shown in Figure 7.5e, were carved out of the rainforests to grow rice, coffee, maize and other crops, as well as to raise cattle. The farmland soon lost its fertility, however, and few farmers could afford to buy chemical fertilisers. The millions of cattle raised on the new ranches compacted large areas of soil. Runoff increased and erosion spread, especially on newly cleared land. Many unsealed roads became unusable because of the heavy rains. In Figure 7.5e you can pick out the beginning of a serious erosion problem near one of these roads.

Minerals and energy

The Amazon Basin is rich in mineral deposits. Its enormous rivers have considerable capacity to produce a huge amount of hydro-electricity. One project to develop the Amazon's resources was the US$70 billion Great Carajas Development Project (see Figure 7.5f). Since the 1980s it has involved the construction of:

- iron ore mines (there are unexploited deposits, or reserves, of 17.8 billion tonnes of high-grade ore)
- new towns for miners and transport workers
- forestry projects
- a huge dam across the Tocantins River to produce electricity for aluminium smelters and refineries
- a 900-kilometre-long railway to connect iron ore mines with a port
- a deep-water port at Sao Luis to handle exports.

Figure 7.5e A new road penetrates the Amazon rainforest.

Figure 7.5f Part of the large Carajas iron ore mine in northern Brazil.

As the world price of iron ore dropped, Brazil decided to smelt pig iron to gain more export income. This resulted in even more rainforest destruction as huge areas were cleared to provide fuel for the charcoal burners used to smelt the iron ore.

Unfortunately, the development of the Carajas Project had negative aspects. Huge areas of rainforest were cleared and 40 000 people, including local Indian tribes, were displaced by the lake that formed behind the newly dammed Tocantins River. The huge lake drowned thousands of rare plant and animal species. In addition, Brazil went further into debt as the prices received from other countries for its exports became lower.

Any large-scale clearing of the rainforest between Carajas and the coast has the potential to disrupt the region's climate by interrupting the flow of 'recycled' rain (the almost constant evapotranspiration and precipitation) right across the Amazon Basin. Clearing the rainforesst would result in a dying out of what remained of the rainforest ecosystem.

Understanding the text

1 Describe the impact that road construction has had on the Amazon rainforest.
2 What crops are grown on the small farms that have been carved out of the rainforest by settlers?
3 What impact have cattle had on the land?
4 List the benefits and disadvantages of the Carajas Project.

UTT worksheet 7.5

Working geographically

1 **Group work** Working in groups, complete the following task. From the perspective of an Indian tribe living in the Amazon, discuss why you might object to the Brazilian Government's land-settlement scheme for the Amazon Basin. Would you see any advantages in the scheme? Share the main points raised in your group's discussion with the rest of the class.

2 **Writing task** Imagine that you are a settler living in the farmhouse shown at the top of Figure 7.5e. Write a letter to a friend in the city who wants to buy a nearby farm. Your friend particularly wants to know about the soil's fertility and any environmental problems that exist in the area.

3 **Photo sketching** Construct a photo sketch of Figure 7.5e (see Unit 2.9). Write a comment about the link between the roads and the new settlement.

4 **Group work** Working in groups, discuss the following questions:
a What value could damming some of the rivers of the Amazon Basin bring to new industry and the local Indian inhabitants?
b What disadvantages could damming the rivers bring to the Amazon?

5 **Writing task** A new mining project is planned for an area south of Manaus (see Figure 7.5a, p. 157). Write a discussion outlining the cases for and against its development based on the experience of the Carajas Project. Use this material to prepare a class debate on the issue.

6 **Group work** Work in groups to research and then debate the following ideas:
a The experience of the Dyaks of Borneo (see Unit 7.4) is much like that of the Amazon Indians.
b The Dyaks and the Indians must adapt to change or face extinction.

7 **Research** Undertake library or Internet-based research. Select a rainforest environment other than the Amazon and Borneo. Develop a display poster featuring information about:
a the location of the rainforest environment (include a map)
b the climate of the region (include a climate graph)
c a description of the plants and animals found in the forest
d a description of the way indigenous people interact with the environment
e existing and potential threats to the environment
f strategies being used to protect the selected rainforest environment.

Mount a classroom display of your posters.

7.6 Review and reflect

Chapter summary

In this chapter we have investigated the world's tropical rainforests: where they are found, their main characteristics and how plants and animals interact to produce unique interrelationships.

Traditional users of the rainforests, including the Dyaks of Borneo and the Indians of the Amazon, have inflicted only minor disruptions to the ecological balance of the rainforests. Over a long period, perhaps more than 20 000 years, forms of sustainable agriculture and hunting and gathering evolved. However, the arrival of people armed with high technology and the ability to clear massive areas of forests, exploit the mineral wealth, dam rivers and put thousands of settlers onto 'new' farm land, has led to many of the world's rainforests becoming threatened. Such threats have the potential to change the world's weather, and lead to the loss of a huge genetic storehouse with potential medical treasures as well as the extinction of so many unique species.

Activity 1

Challenge: Explaining the nutrient cycle of the rainforest

1 Match the following captions with the numbers on the nutrient cycle shown in Figure 7.6a.
   - **a** Sun's energy used to convert water and carbon dioxide into food
   - **b** Infertile rainforest soil
   - **c** Surface layer rich in organic matter
   - **d** Nutrients absorbed by shallow roots
   - **e** Leaves use nutrients for growth
   - **f** Nutrients released into soil by decaying leaf matter
   - **g** Nutrients transported via inner bark to leaves and branches
   - **h** Nutrients leached from soil by downward movement of water

2 Use the information above and on page 150 to write a one-page explanation of the nutrient cycle of the rainforest.

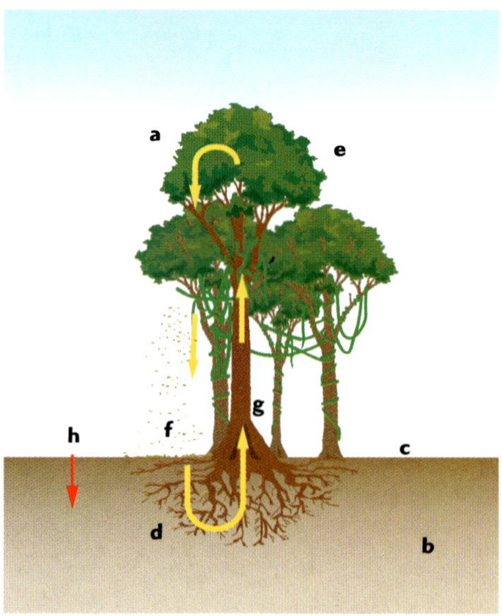

Figure 7.6a The nutrient cycle of the rainforest.

Activity 2

Class-based reflection and writing task: Protecting rainforests

As a class discuss the following statement: 'People have cleared the natural vegetation from other areas of the earth. Why are the tropical rainforests so special that they should be saved?'

Build up a whiteboard summary of the key points raised in this discussion. Write a one-page report outlining the reasons why it is important to protect what remains of the world's rainforests.

Activity 3

Interpreting maps: Changing landuses in the Amazon Basin

Study the information in the key and map that make up Figure 7.6b. Completing the following tasks will test and extend your understanding about tropical rainforests:

1. Use an atlas to locate Rondonia. Where is Rondonia within Brazil?
2. Suggest what the various landuses might be.
3. What approximate proportion of the land is being farmed: one-quarter, one-half or three-quarters?
4. What evidence is there on the map to suggest that the farming area will expand in the future?
5. Describe in one word the pattern of minor roads marked on the map. On what type of landuse are they located? What purpose could the roads have?
6. Two towns are marked on the map. Both have between 7000 and 10 000 people. What services might they offer to people living in the established farming area?
7. Thirty years ago this area had only a minor road from the north to Ariquemos. There was a small patch of cleared land around this town. The rest of the area was forest land occupied by several Amazon Indian tribes who cleared fewer than ten patches of land for small gardens. Produce a map that shows these landuses. Add an appropriate title and key.
8. Now produce a map as you might expect the area to be in thirty years. You could go one of two ways: more roads, more clearances and perhaps another town or a reversal of the trend. Annotate (label) your map with an appropriate title and key. Add a brief explanation as to why the changes have occurred.

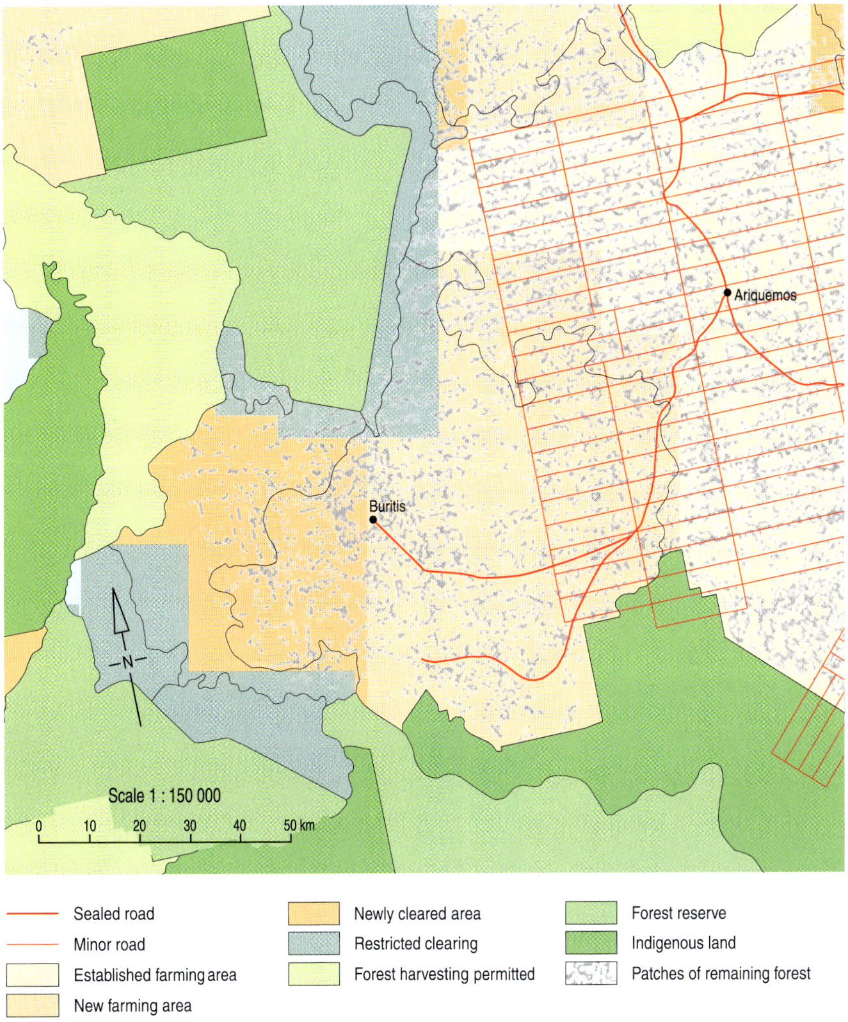

Figure 7.6b Landuse in part of the Brazilian state of Rondonia.

Extension worksheet ICT 7.6

GeoMatch

GeoWords

Refer to the Reflection box on page 17.

GeoQuiz

Chapter test

Chapter 8

Mountains

Introduction

Mountain ranges, such as the Andes of South America, the Himalayas of Asia, the Rockies of North America and the Alps of Europe, are among the world's most spectacular landscapes. Mountains are formed when forces working deep within the earth's crust push up and create new landforms. Without these new landforms, the earth's surface would have long ago been reduced to a flat, featureless plane—worn down by the processes of weathering and erosion.

In this chapter we study the forces that form and shape mountain landscapes and the ways people interact with such a difficult environment. We look at how the Sherpa people of Nepal interact with the mountain environment of the Himalayas and the impact that the growing popularity of sports-related tourism is having on the communities of Zermatt in Switzerland and Whistler in Canada.

Key questions

1 What are the geographical processes that form and shape mountain environments?
2 How do humans, including the Sherpa people of Nepal, interact with the mountain environment?
3 What impact has the growing popularity of sports-related tourism had on the mountain communities of Zermatt and Whistler?

Snowboarding

Snowboarding developed in the United States in the 1960s. Over the next decade, different pioneers refined the design of boards and promoted interest in the sport. Surfers and skateboarders became involved and, by the late 1980s, snowboarding had become hugely popular.

International competition began in the 1980s. The United States hosted the first World Championships (1983) and a four-stop World Cup tour was established (1987). Snowboarding first featured in Olympic competition in 1998. There are two snowboarding events: the halfpipe and the parallel giant slalom. In the first, using speed gained on the slope, snowboarders come up over the rim of the pipe and perform aerial manoeuvres. The second event features head-to-head matches on the mountain, where competitors battle it out on two side-by-side courses until there is a winner.

For many young winter sports fans, snowboarding is seen as being 'cooler' than traditional skiing. But skiing enthusiasts are fighting back. Many skiers now dress like snowboarders, ski in their terrain parks, use snowboarding terms to describe their aerial and on-snow manoeuvres and ski 'switch' (backwards) like snowboarders. Skiing has transformed itself into an X-Game sport that millions of people watch on television. Skiing is again 'cool'.

Snowboarding is one of the most popular winter sports.

Glossary of key terms

Alpine The area above the tree line in mountainous areas.

Block mountain A landform feature that has been uplifted by earth movements along fault lines.

Continental drift The idea or theory that the earth's continents broke apart and drifted away from an original large landmass or supercontinent called Pangaea.

Crust The thin outer layer of the earth; the lithosphere.

Earthquake Sudden movements within the earth's crust caused by plate movements.

Epicentre The point on the earth's surface that is directly above the centre (focus) of an earthquake.

Fault mountains Formed by the large-scale fracturing of the rock strata (layers). Resulting landforms include block mountains and rift valleys.

Focus The point at which a sudden movement in the earth's crust occurs.

Fold mountains Formed when layers of sedimentary rock, located near the margins of the earth's continental plates, are slowly compressed into folds.

Landslide The rapid, downhill movement of rock and soil under the influence of gravity.

Magma The hot molten rock found under the earth's crust.

Mantle The layer found between the earth's core and its crust.

Mid-ocean ridge An underwater ridge formed when plates move apart allowing molten material to fill the gap created.

Ocean trench An underwater depression created when oceanic plates are drawn down into the earth's mantle.

Plate margins The area where the earth's plates meet.

Plate tectonics The movement of the earth's plates by currents deep within the earth's liquid mantle.

Plates The segments of the earth's crust that are slowly moving due to convection currents in the mantle.

Richter scale A scale used to measure the strength (intensity and severity) of an earthquake.

Rift valley A valley formed as a result of plate movements. They are usually long and narrow, with steep-sided valley walls.

Sea-floor spreading The separation of oceanic plates.

Soil creep The slow, downhill movement of soil under the influence of gravity.

Volcano An opening in the earth's crust through which molten rock, lava and ash erupt.

Weathering The physical, biological or chemical breakdown of rock into smaller fragments.

Foundation worksheet 8.1

GeoToolkit

eGlossary

ICT Toolkit

8.1 The restless earth

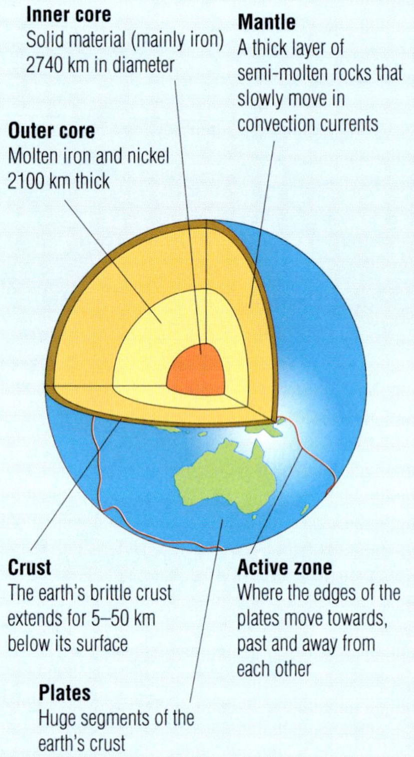

Figure 8.1a The internal structure of the earth.

Continents on the move

Scientists believe that all the earth's continents were once part of one large supercontinent, known as Pangaea (a Greek word meaning 'all lands'). Pangaea consisted of two main areas: Gondwanaland (Australia, Antarctica, Africa, India and South America) and Laurasia (Asia, Europe, Greenland and North America). These two main areas began to move apart and break up about 200 million years ago. Over time they 'drifted' to their present locations.

Forces deep within the earth push up and create new landforms. Without these new landforms, the earth's surface would have long ago been reduced to a flat, featureless plain—worn down by the processes of *weathering* and *erosion*.

Movement of the earth's crust

The earth's thin **crust** is broken into eight vast segments or **plates** (and several smaller plates) that travel slowly across the face of the planet. This movement is caused by currents deep within the earth's liquid **mantle**. The name given to this process is **plate tectonics**. Figure 8.1b shows the location of the earth's plates and the direction in which they are moving.

Although the earth's plates move very slowly—generally less than 15 centimetres a year—the results can be dramatic. The location of the earth's great mountain ranges, its deep ocean trenches, and its volcanic and earthquake activity can all be linked to the movement of the earth's plates.

Types of plate movements

The earth's plates move in different ways:

- some plates move towards each other
- others move apart
- some slide past each other.

The places where the plates meet are known as **plate margins**. These are often areas of great crustal stress and activity. The different types of plate margins shown in Figure 8.1b give rise to many of the earth's earthquakes, volcanoes and major structural features, such as **fold mountains**.

There are four different types of plate margins. These are discussed below.

Destructive plate margins

Destructive plate margins occur where a plate made of heavier (dense) oceanic crust moves towards a plate consisting of lighter (less dense) continental crust. Because it is heavier the oceanic crust is forced down under the lighter continental crust, forming a *deep-sea trench* (see Figure 8.1c).

As the oceanic crust pushes beneath the continental crust, it melts. This is partly due to the friction that builds up between the two plates and partly due to the increase in temperature as it reaches the earth's mantle. This creates magma, which can escape to the surface along lines of weakness in the earth's crust, called *faults*, to form a **volcano**. Volcanic eruptions at destructive plate margins can be very violent. Volcanic activity is examined in more detail in Unit 8.3.

Because the plates do not slide smoothly past each other, there is often an enormous build up of pressure. If the crust breaks, shock waves are sent out in all directions causing an **earthquake**. Earthquakes are examined in more detail in Unit 8.2.

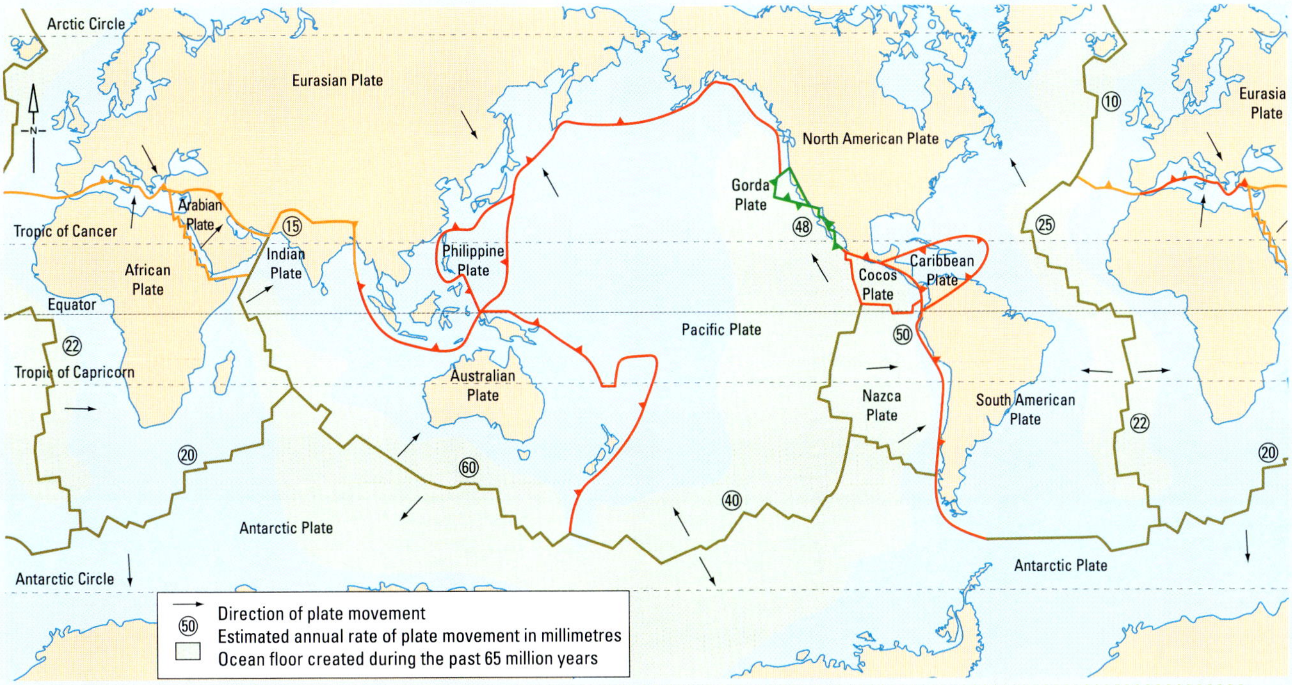

Type of plate margin	What happens at this margin
Destructive margin	Oceanic crust moves towards continental crust. Oceanic crust is heavier than continental crust, so the oceanic crust sinks below the continental crust and is destroyed.
Collision margin	Plates made up of continental crust move towards each other. They cannot sink so they crumple upwards to form fold mountains.
Constructive margin	Two plates move away from each other. Magma rises to the surface to form new crust.
Conservative margin	Two plates move past each other. Crust is neither formed or destroyed.

Figure 8.1b Continental plates of the world and the boundaries between them.

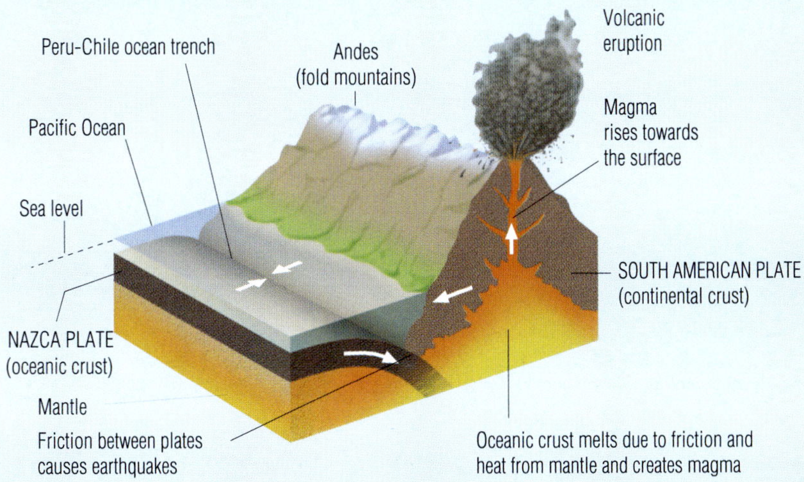

Figure 8.1c An example of a destructive plate margin.

Figure 8.1d The Strait of Mandeb links the Gulf of Aden with the Red Sea (background). The Red Sea is formed by the separation of the African and Arabian Plates.

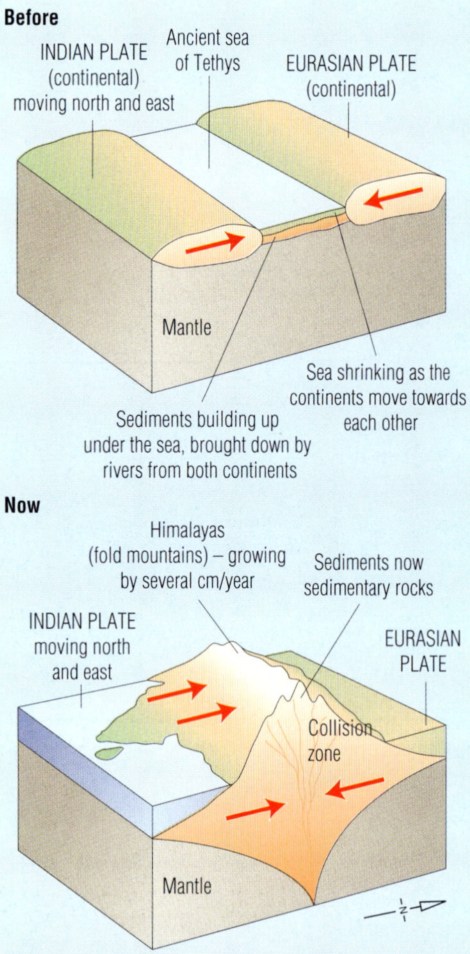

Figure 8.1e The Himalayan Mountains are still increasing in height as the Indian Plate moves into the Eurasian Plate at a rate of about 5 centimetres a year.

Collision plate margins

When two plates made of continental crust move towards one another they create a *collision zone*. Because neither plate can sink beneath the other, their crust is crumpled upwards to form fold mountains. The Himalayas—formed as a result of the collision between the Indian and Eurasian Plates—are an example of a fold mountain system. Sometimes, as with destructive margins, pressure builds up over time. Eventually, the crust breaks, sending out shockwaves—an earthquake (see Figure 8.1e).

Constructive plate margins

When two plates move away from each other magma rises from the mantle to form new crust. This creates a line of underwater volcanoes along what is called a **mid-ocean ridge**. Sometimes these volcanoes become large enough to emerge above sea level as volcanic islands. The Mid-Atlantic Ridge—formed by the separation of the North American and Eurasian Plates—is an example of a constructive zone (see Figure 8.1g).

Constructive margins can also be found on land. The East African Rift Valley continues to widen, with new land being created on the floor of the valley.

Conservative plate margins

Conservative plate margins occur where two plates move past one another. The San Andreas Fault in California, for example, marks the point at which the North American and Pacific Plates meet. Although the two plates are moving in the same direction, the Pacific Plate is moving faster, causing the plate margins to 'grind' past each other. The tensions between the two plates build up over time. When this tension is suddenly released an earthquake occurs. Minor earthquakes occur almost daily along the fault, but major earthquakes, causing loss of life, are less frequent. The last major earthquake was the 1994 Northbridge earthquake. It measured 6.6 on the **Richter scale** and killed sixty people (see Figure 8.1h).

Figure 8.1f The Strait of Gibraltar and Mediterranean Sea (background) mark the boundary between the African and Eurasian Plates.

Did U know?

- Eurasia is the world's largest landmass. It covers almost 54 million square kilometres. Only the human-made Suez Canal separates it from Africa.
- With a peak 8850 metres above sea level, Mt Everest is the highest point on the earth's surface. It is not, however, the world's highest mountain. When measured from base to peak, Mauna Kea on Hawaii totals 10 023 metres, 5818 metres of which is below the Pacific Ocean.
- The world's longest mountain range (excluding those found under the sea) is the Cordillera de Los Andes (the Andes) in South America. It is 7200 kilometres long.
- The deepest part of the ocean is the Marianas Trench, south of Japan. It is 10 900 metres deep.
- Mauna Loa, on Hawaii, is the world's largest active volcano. It rises 4170 metres above sea level, but its base is 5180 metres below sea level. It erupts about every 3.5 years.
- The biggest volcanic eruption occurred in 1883 when much of the island of Krakatau, in Indonesia, was blown to bits. Rocks and volcanic ash were hurled 55 kilometres into the atmosphere. Tidal waves (tsunami) caused by the eruption killed 36 000 people.

Foundation worksheet 8.1

Global distribution of earthquakes and volcanoes

The distribution of the world's main earthquakes and volcanoes is shown in Figure 8.1i (p. 170). Note the relationship between earthquake and volcanic activity, the location of the world's great mountain ranges, and the margins of the earth's plates (see Figure 8.1b, p. 167).

A comparison of Figures 8.1b and 8.1c shows, for example, that:

- earthquakes occur in narrow belts along all types of plate margins; are found near volcanoes; occur on land and at sea; and are particularly concentrated around the Pacific Ocean
- volcanoes also occur in long, narrow belts; are most commonly associated with destructive plate margins, especially around the Pacific Ocean ('The Pacific Ring of Fire'); and coincide with constructive margins.

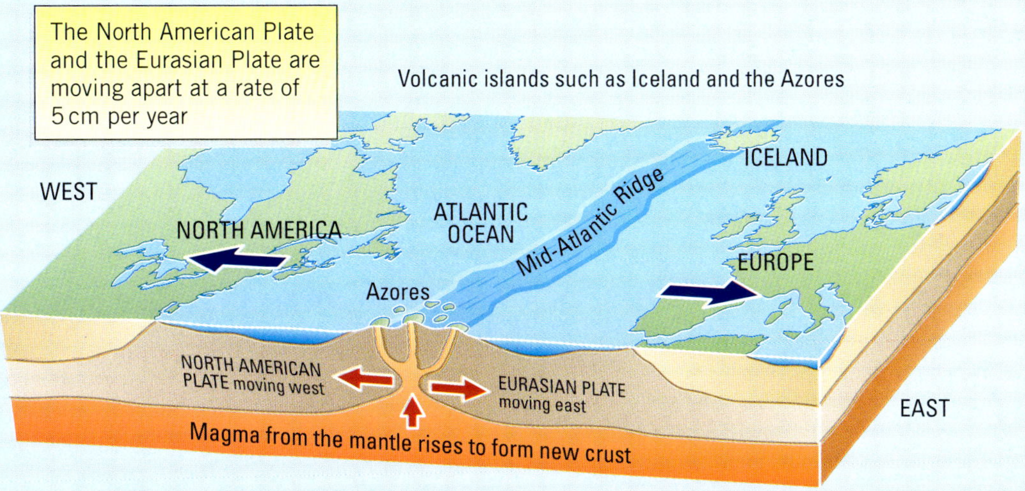

Figure 8.1g The Mid-Atlantic Ridge has been formed by the separation of the North American and Eurasian Plates. Each year the Atlantic Ocean widens by about 3 centimetres.

Mountains

The world's great mountain ranges are found along the active margins of the world's plates. As the plates press against each other, the earth's crust thickens in an effort to absorb the impact. As it does so, the pressure increases and layers of rock are compressed and forced upwards, folding and faulting as they move.

Because the movement of the plates tends to be very slow, the mountain chains they produce are dominated by folded layers of rock. They can, however, include landform features that are the result of faulting and volcanic activity. Folds are wave-like patterns in the earth's crust (see Figure 8.1k, p. 171). Faults are fractures in the rock structure. Figure 8.1j (p. 170) shows both these features. **Rift valleys** and **block mountains** are examples of large-scale landform features associated with faulting (see the Getting Technical box on p. 171).

As plates move apart (a process known as **sea-floor spreading**), molten material fills the gap, forming a mid-ocean ridge. These ridges extend for 65 000 kilometres through all the earth's oceans. **Ocean trenches** are formed when plates are drawn down into the earth's mantle, where they melt.

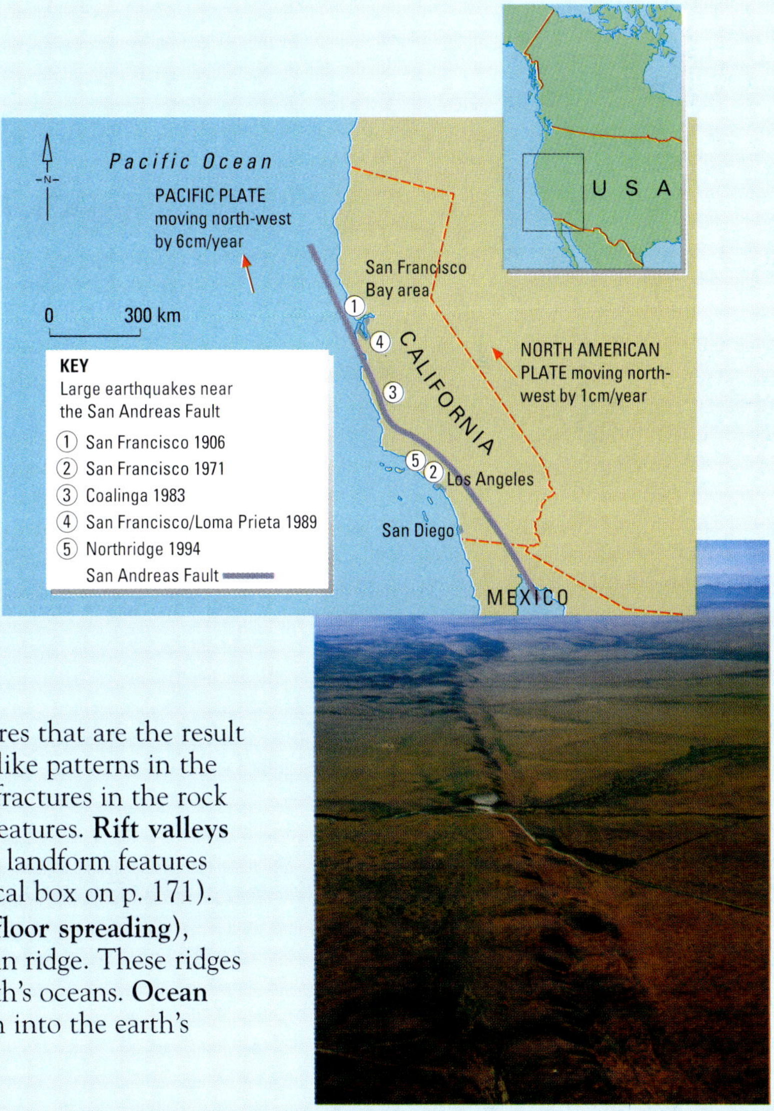

Figure 8.1h California's San Andreas Fault: a conservative margin.

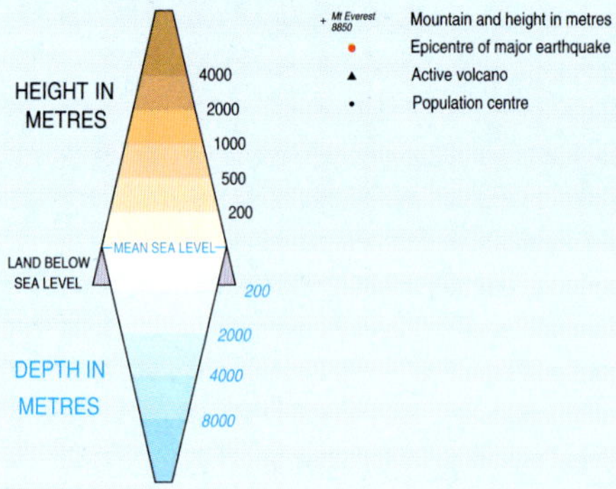

Figure 8.1i Location of earthquakes, volcanoes and the great mountain ranges.

Getting technical

The landforms characteristic of **fault mountains** include:

- **block mountains (horst)**—An elevated area of land that has been uplifted between two or more parallel normal faults (see Figure 8.1j). The edges of many block mountains may be distinguished by the presence of an escarpment.
- **rift valley (graben)**—a long valley area formed by the sunken land between two or more parallel normal faults. A series of sinkings at different rates may produce a series of step-like landform features.

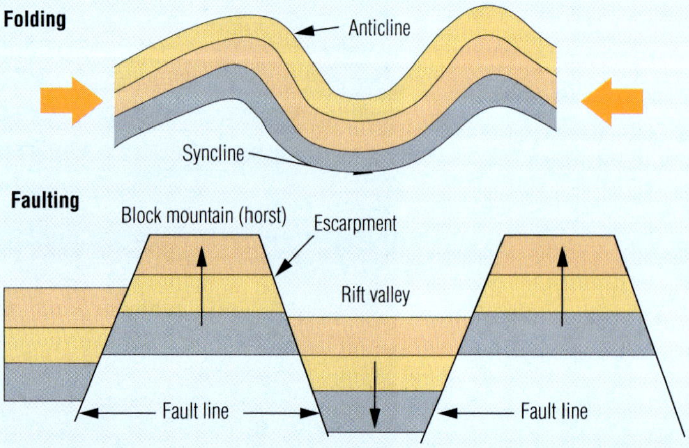

Figure 8.1j Folding and faulting of rock layers.

Working geographically

1 **Challenge: Writing task** Write a short statement that describes the relationship between plate tectonics and the distribution of the earth's great mountain ranges, its ocean ridges and trenches, and the regions subject to volcanic and earthquake activity.

2 **Interpreting diagrams** Study Figure 8.1c (p. 167). Write a paragraph explaining the formation of the Andes Mountains and the Peru-Chile ocean trench.

3 **Interpreting diagrams** Study Figure 8.1e (p. 168). Write a paragraph explaining the formation of the Himalayan mountain range.

4 **Observing** The next time you travel through a large road cutting, look at the rock to see if you can observe the layers of rock (rock strata), any fault lines, and any evidence of folding.

5 **Interpreting maps and photographs** Study Figure 8.1h (p. 169). Write a paragraph explaining why parts of California experience earthquakes.

6 **Interpreting maps** Study Figure 8.1i. Write a paragraph outlining the global distribution of earthquakes and volcanoes.

7 **Interpreting diagrams** Study Figure 8.1j. Outline the landform features associated with faulting. Using diagrams, explain how these features develop.

8 **Interpreting maps** Compare the map of the earth's major landform features (Figure 8.1i) with the map showing the distribution of its plates (Figure 8.1b, p. 167), then complete the following tasks:
   - **a** Name the mountain ranges formed by the collision of the following plates.
     - **i** Nazca and South American Plates
     - **ii** Indian and Eurasian Plates
   - **b** Name the landform feature formed by the separation of the South American and African Plates.
   - **c** Name the landform feature formed by the collision of the Pacific and Philippine Plates.
   - **d** Explain what is happening to the Atlantic Ocean.
   - **e** In which direction is the Australian Plate moving?
   - **f** Along the edge of which plates are the following landform features located?
     - **i** Puerto Rico Trench
     - **ii** Alps
     - **iii** Tian Mountains
     - **iv** Rocky Mountains
     - **v** Mt Pinatubo
     - **vi** Mt St Helens
   - **g** In which ocean are the following landform features located?
     - **i** Tonga Trench
     - **ii** Mid-Indian Ridge
     - **iii** Kuril Trench
     - **iv** Java Trench

Extension worksheet ICT 8.4

Figure 8.1k Folded layers of rock.

Understanding the text

1 What is the name given to the processes involved in the movement of the earth's crust? Explain the causes of this movement.

2 Explain the relationship between the earth's great mountain ranges, its deep ocean trenches and its volcanic and earthquake activity.

3 List the three types of crustal movement.

4 What is meant by the term 'crustal movement'?

5 Outline the features of destructive plate margins.

6 Describe what happens to the earth's crust in a collision zone.

7 Explain why the great mountain ranges are called fold mountains.

UTT worksheet 8.1

8.2 Earthquakes

Figure 8.2a The devastation caused by the 1999 Turkish earthquake.

Earthquakes occur when pressures, which build up in the earth's crust, are suddenly released. While they are most commonly associated with the movement of the earth's plates, smaller, often less destructive earthquakes can occur well away from plate margins. These are usually associated with faults (lines of weaknesses) in the rock strata.

When the built-up energy within the crust is released, shock waves are sent out in all directions. The point at which the sudden movement occurs is called the **focus**. The place where the shock waves reach the earth's surface is called the **epicentre** (see Figure 8.2c).

Measuring earthquakes

The intensity of an earthquake can be recorded on an instrument called a *seismograph* (see Figure 8.2b). The strength of an earthquake is measured on the *Richter scale* (see Table 8.2a). It is important to note that each point on the scale is ten times greater than the point below. This means, for example, that the Mexico City earthquake of 1985 (measuring 8.1 on the Richter scale) was ten times stronger than the one that struck San Francisco in 1989 (7.1).

Investigating earthquakes ICT

A great place to start any research on earthquakes is the 42eXplore website. Access this website and investigate the range of information available. Use this information to enhance your notes on this topic or to improve the quality of any assessment task.

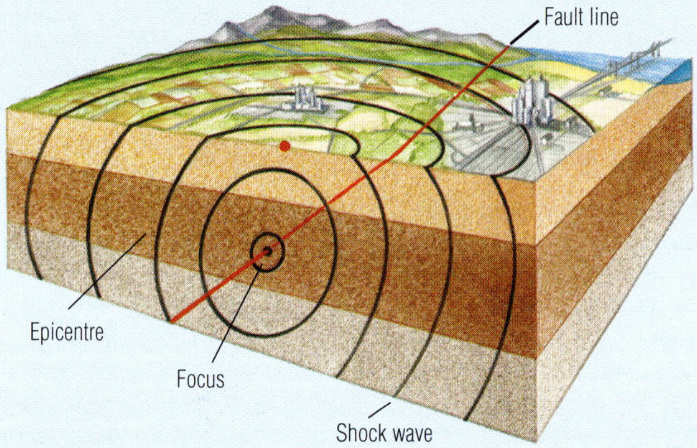

Figure 8.2c The focus, epicentre and shock waves of an earthquake.

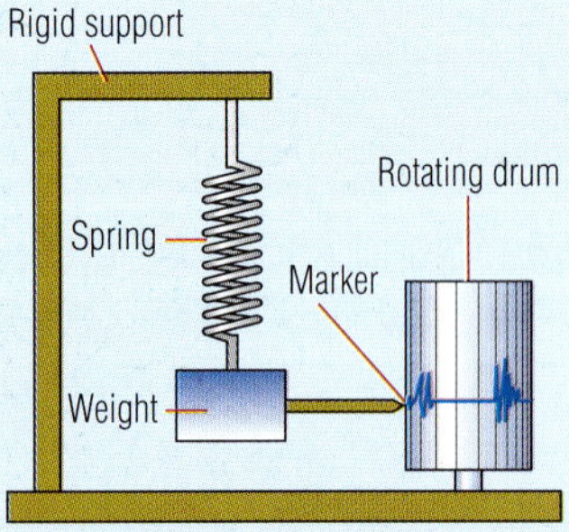

Figure 8.2b The seismograph is used to measure the intensity of an earthquake. Earth tremors cause the spring-mounted weight to go up and down. As it does so, an ink marker leaves a record of its vertical movements on a piece of graph paper attached to a rotating drum. When there are no tremors the marker leaves a straight line.

Table 8.2a The Richter scale

Magnitude on the Richter scale	Effects	Average number per year worldwide
Less than 2.5	Rarely felt by people	1 million
2.5–3.9	Minor earthquake felt by some people	100 000
4.0–4.9	Light earthquake felt by all	10 000
5.0–5.9	Moderate earthquake and some damage	1000
6.0–6.9	Strong earthquake with much damage	180
7.0–7.9	Major earthquake—very destructive	18
8.0–8.8	Great earthquake—widespread devastation	1 every few years
8.9 +	The 'Big One'	?

Case study: Bam earthquake, Iran, December 2003

At 5.27 a.m. on 26 December 2003 an earthquake measuring 6.3 on the Richter scale devastated the 2000-year-old city of Bam (population 220 000). Within a matter of seconds an estimated 45 000 people had been killed—most crushed as they slept in their beds. A further 30 000 were injured and tens of thousands were left homeless.

Iran straddles one of the world's most geologically complex regions. It is where three vast blocks of the earth's crust—the Arabian, Eurasian and Indian Plates—push and grind against each other. The Arabian Plate is constantly pushing northwards against the Eurasian Plate, producing frequent earthquakes along the northern side of the Persian Gulf. The Eurasian Plate, in turn, is pushing against a landmass known as the Central Iranian Block. This huge segment of crust is moving to the northeast. The Bam earthquake resulted from the sudden, jolting movement in the southeastern section of the Iranian Block.

Figure 8.2e The desperate search for survivors of the Bam earthquake.

The hours following the earthquake were dominated by a desperate attempt to save thousands of people trapped in collapsed buildings. Seventy per cent of the city's building—the majority of which were built of mud bricks—were reduced to piles of rubble. Electricity and telephone services were cut and the city's two hospitals destroyed. Specialist search and rescue teams, airlifted from around the world, searched the worst hit areas of the city using sophisticated listening equipment and sniffer dogs. Non-government organisations mounted a major relief effort, supplying much needed food, shelter and medical supplies.

The staggering death toll of the Bam disaster can be traced to the failure of authorities to enforce building codes and regulations. Had an earthquake of this magnitude occurred in a developed country few people would have died.

The Bam earthquake is not the first such disaster to strike Iran. In June 1990, 35 000 people were killed, 100 000 injured and 500 000 left homeless when an earthquake devastated an area adjacent to the Caspian Sea.

Figure 8.2f One of the world's great architectural treasures, the Arg-e Bam Citidal, was reduced to a pile of rubble by the Bam earthquake. The 2000-year-old World Heritage site covered almost 6 square kilometres and was built of mud bricks, straw and the trunks of palm trees.

Figure 8.2d The Bam earthquake, December 2003.

Understanding the text

1. What is an earthquake? Explain why and where they occur.
2. Define the terms 'focus' and 'epicentre'.
3. Identify the instrument used to measure the intensity of earthquakes.
4. What is the Richter scale? Describe an earthquake measuring between 7.0 and 7.9 on the Richter scale.
5. Differentiate between the primary and secondary effects of earthquakes.
6. Outline the reasons why some places are more seriously affected by earthquakes than others.

cd UTT worksheet 8.2

Working geographically

1 Internet research: Writing task Use the Internet to gather information about a recent earthquake. Write a report outlining the human costs of the disaster.

2 Challenge: Writing task
Study the box 'Case study: Bam earthquake, Iran, December 2003' (p. 173). Using the information contained in the box, write a report on the disaster from the perspective of someone directly affected by the earthquake. In your report explain why the death toll was higher than it could have been.

cd Foundation worksheet 8.2

cd Extension worksheet ICT 8.5

Effects of earthquakes

The *primary effects* of an earthquake are the immediate effects associated with the earthquake itself. People are killed or injured, and buildings and infrastructure are damaged (see Figure 8.2a on p. 172 and Table 8.2b).

Secondary effects are the indirect effects resulting from the earthquake's primary damage. They include people being made homeless, business losses, interrupted communications, broken sewage pipes, loss of water and electricity supplies, fires caused by broken gas pipes, and the sense of fear created by such events. Often these last longer than the primary effects.

Why are some places affected more than others?

Table 8.2b show the effects of some recent earthquakes. While the strength of the earthquake is important, other factors can also influence the extent of damage and loss of life. These include:

- *distance from the epicentre*—energy waves lose their intensity over time
- *level of preparation*—having structures designed to withstand earthquakes greatly reduces the number of deaths from collapsing buildings
- *population density*—densely settled urban centres are worse hit than rural areas
- *time of day*—early morning and late evening earthquakes cause fewer casualties because fewer people are moving about
- *season*—the secondary effects of earthquakes are much worse if it strikes during winter
- *type of land that cities are built on*—silt and reclaimed land tends to magnify the effects of earthquakes.

Table 8.2b Effects of some recent earthquakes

Year	Place	Size (Richter scale)	Impacts
1976	Tangshan, China	7.8	250 000 people dead; 650 000 homeless
1985	Mexico City, Mexico	8.1	10 000 dead; 1000 large buildings collapse
1989	San Francisco, USA	7.1	62 dead; further 81 die when freeway collapses
1993	Latur, India	6.4	24 000 dead; 150 000 homeless
1994	Los Angeles, USA	6.7	57 dead; 20 000 homeless; over 100 fires
1995	Kobe, Japan	7.2	5500 dead; 310 000 homeless
1998	Northeast Afghanistan	6.1 6.9	February: 4000 dead June: 3000 dead; 28 villages destroyed
1998	Papua New Guinea	7.0	Earthquake at sea triggers a tidal wave; 3000 dead
1999	Turkey	7.8	17 127 dead; 43 953 injured; 20 000 buildings destroyed

8.3 Volcanoes

Volcanic eruptions occur when molten material (*magma*) forces its way to the earth's surface through cracks or faults in the earth's crust. The molten material that flows from a volcano is called **lava**.

Over time, layers of lava and volcanic ash build up a **volcanic cone** (see Figure 8.3c) or *shield*. A **caldera** crater forms when a violent eruption blasts away the top of an existing volcanic cone or shield (see the box 'Classifying volcanoes', p. 177). The most active volcanoes lie in belts that coincide with the collision zones of the earth's plates (see Figure 8.1i, p. 170).

Volcanic eruptions can produce landforms in a rapid and spectacular manner. Some eruptions, however, are explosive while others are not. It depends on how sticky the magma is. If the magma is thin and runny it can flow easily out of the volcano (see Figure 8.3a). These lava flows are rarely a threat to humans because they move slowly enough for people to escape; but they can destroy towns and villages in their path.

If the magma is viscous (thick), gases cannot escape easily. Pressure builds up until the gases escape violently and explode. In this type of eruption, the magma blasts into the air and breaks apart into pieces called *volcanic bombs* (see Figure 8.3b). Explosive volcanic eruptions can be deadly. Molten material can shower down on the surrounding countryside. When hot volcanic material mixes with water from streams, **lahars** (mudflows) form. These can bury whole villages.

Some of the world's great mountains and many of the islands that dot the world's oceans are the result of past volcanic activity. There are 550 known active volcanoes on earth. Recent major eruptions have occurred at Mt St Helens' in the United States (1980), Mt Pinatubo in the Philippines (1991) and at Rabaul in Papua New Guinea (1994). Large eruptions may result in short-term climatic change because millions of tonnes of volcanic ash and smoke are released into the atmosphere, reducing the amount of sunlight reaching the earth's surface.

Figure 8.3a A lava flow.

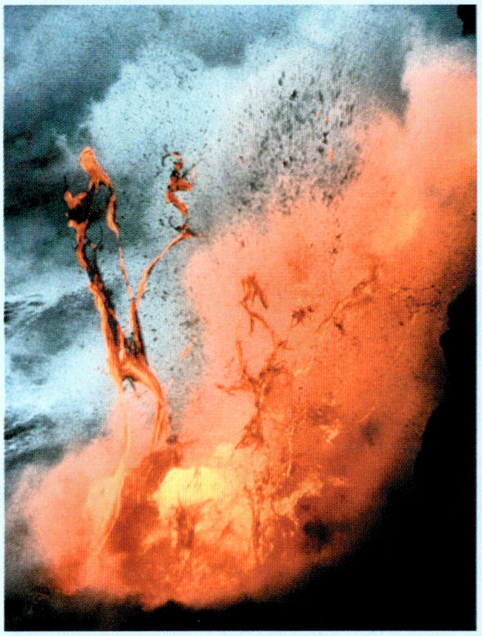

Figure 8.3b Volcanic bombs.

Table 8.3a Volcanic eruptions causing great loss of life

Year	Place	Impacts
1815	Tambora, Indonesia	92 000 people died, mostly because of starvation caused by the loss of crops and livestock
1883	Krakatau, the Sunda Strait	The resulting tsunami between Java and Sumatra killed 36 000
1902	Pelee, Martinique	Poisonous volcanic gases killed 36 000
1985	Nevado del Ruiz, Colombia	A wave of mud smothered 23 000
1991	Mt Pinatubo, the Philippines	900 were killed

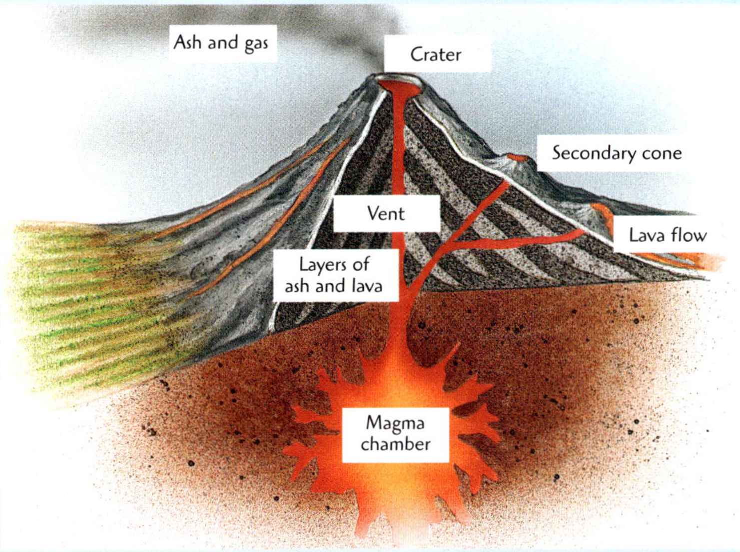

Figure 8.3c A cross-section through a volcano formed of layers of lava and ash.

Mt St Helens' eruption

One of the most spectacular volcanic eruptions of recent times was the Mt St Helens' eruption of 18 May 1980. The volcano, located in the Cascade Mountains of Washington State in the United States, had been dormant for over a century. At 8.32 a.m. an earthquake measuring 8.1 on the Richter scale rocked the earth directly beneath the mountain. The earthquake started an avalanche, which was followed by a massive blast of gas, rock, ash and ice. The effects were devastating:

- One hundred and twenty metres of the summit had vanished, leaving in its place a crater 2 kilometres wide, 4 kilometres long and 1.5 kilometres deep.
- Three hundred and eighty square kilometres of land to the north of the mountain was stripped of its vegetation.
- Volcanic ash, carried by the wind, spread 1500 kilometres to the west.
- Sixty-two people died.

Figure 8.3d The Mt St Helens' eruption, 1980.

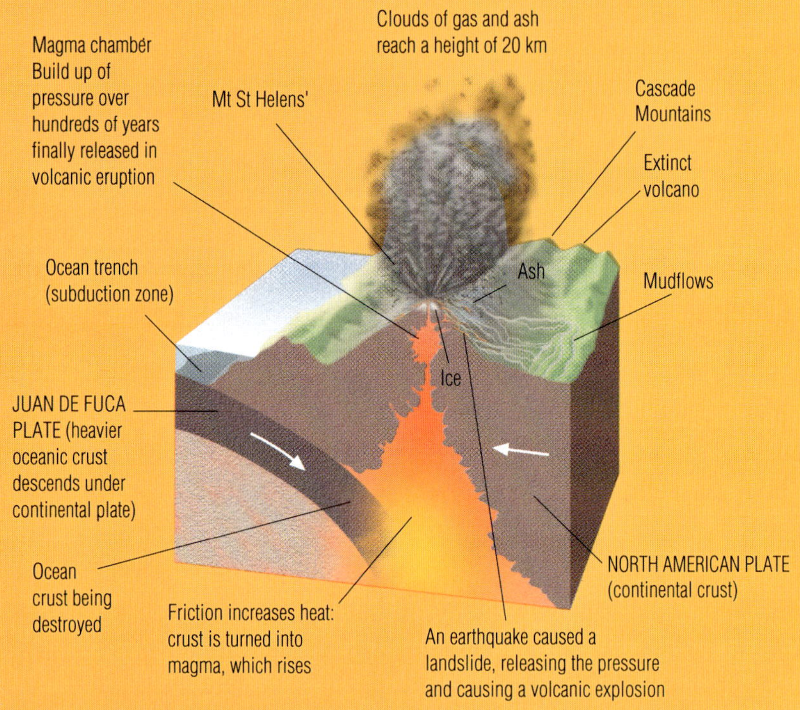

Figure 8.3f Causes of the Mt St Helens' eruption.

Figure 8.3e Location of Mt St Helens'.

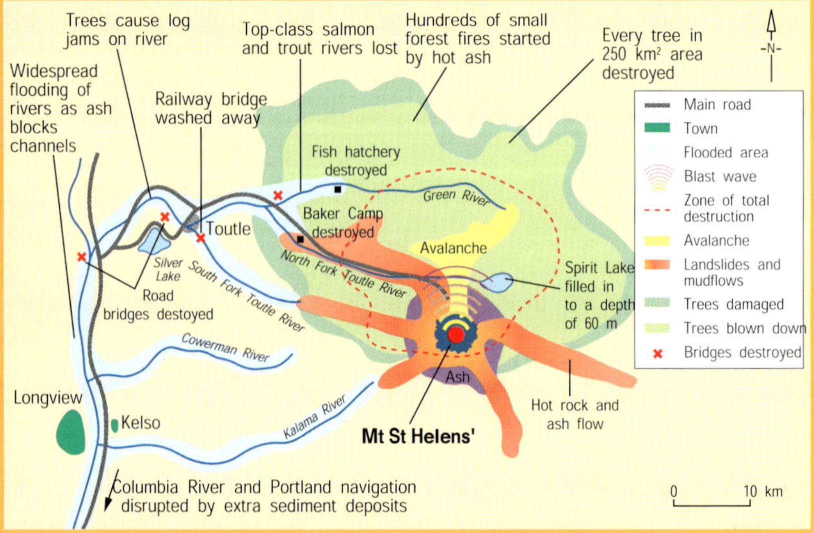

Figure 8.3g Effects of the Mt St Helens' eruption.

Classifying volcanoes

Volcanoes can be classified according to their shape. The most common types are discussed below.

Strato volcanoes

Strato volcanoes are the most common type of volcano and are formed from layers of lava and ash. Their lava tends to be viscous (thick) and flows very slowly. This causes them to form steep-sided volcanic cones, Examples include Mt St Helens' (see Figure 8.3d), Mt Pinatubo, Mt Fuji in Japan, and Mt Taranaki in New Zealand.

Shield volcanoes

Shield volcanoes are among the world's largest volcanoes. They develop a broad base because the very fluid lava from which they are made runs downhill rather than piling up. Examples include the Likauea and Mauna Loa volcanoes of Hawaii.

Calderas

While calderas are the least common form of volcano, they are often huge and potentially very explosive. When they erupt they tend to collapse in on themselves and so they don't build up a cone. Famous calderas include Yellowstone in the United States and Rabaul.

Figure 8.3h A strato volcano.

Getting technical

Caldera A volcanic landform feature formed when a violent eruption blasts away the top of an existing volcanic cone or shield.

Lahars Mudflows formed when volcanic material mixes with water.

Lava Molten rock; magma.

U-shaped valley A valley with a flat floor and steep sides; a result of glacial erosion.

V-shaped valley A valley eroded by a river.

Volcanic cone A cone-shaped volcanic landform made up of layers of lava and volcanic ash.

ICT

Mt St Helens' eruption

A series of excellent satellite images taken before and after the Mt St Helens' eruption can be found on the US Geological Survey's Earthshots website.

Working geographically

1. **Constructing diagrams** Copy Figure 8.3c (p. 175) into your workbook. Label the main features.
2. **Challenge: Interpreting maps and diagrams** Study the box 'Mt St Helens' eruption'. Write a one-page report outlining the causes and impacts of the Mt St Helens' eruption.
3. **Internet research: Oral report** Using the Internet, investigate a recent volcanic eruption. Prepare a short oral report outlining the information collected. Make mention of the volcano's location, the scale of the eruption and the eruption's impact on people and the physical environment.
4. **Internet research: Wall display** Access the NASA: New Images website. Use the site's search facility to locate satellite images of volcanic activity. Print the images and develop an annotated wall display.

Understanding the text

1. Outline the conditions under which volcanic eruptions occur.
2. Where are most of the world's volcanoes located?
3. Explain why some volcanic eruptions are violent while others are not.
4. What are volcanic bombs and lahars?
5. Explain how volcanic eruptions can bring about short-term climatic change.
6. Outline the various types of volcanoes.

UTT worksheet 8.3

Foundation worksheet 8.2

Extension worksheet ICT 8.1

Extension worksheet ICT 8.7

Extension worksheet 8.3

Extension worksheet ICT 8.6

8.4 Processes shaping mountain environments

Mass movement

Mass movements occur when weathered material moves downhill under the influence of gravity. These movements may be rapid (as in the case of rock falls, **landslides**, earth flows, mudflows and slumps) or slow (as in the case of **soil creep**). Figure 8.4a shows an earth flow with slump features in the upper section.

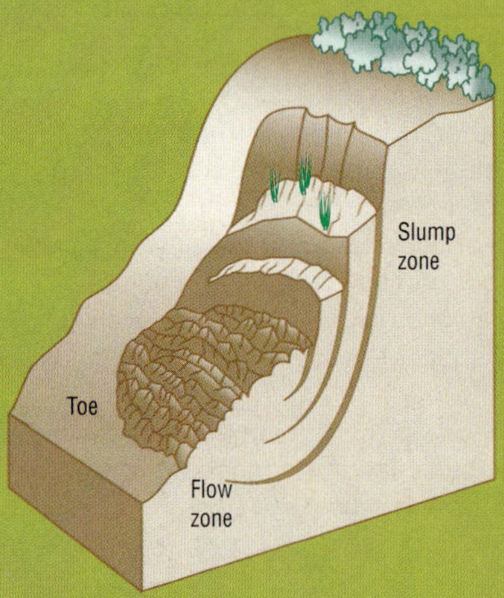

Figure 8.4a An earth flow with slump features well developed in the upper section.

As soon as new land is created by the mountain building processes outlined in Units 8.1–8.3, the agents of *weathering*, **mass movement** and *erosion* start wearing them away. Exposed rock surfaces are broken down by physical and chemical weathering, detached by mass movement and the agents of erosion, and then deposited (by rivers and glaciers) at lower elevations as **sediment**. (The processes of weathering and erosion are examined in greater detail in Unit 3.2.)

The work of rivers

Running water is the most powerful agent of erosion, transportation and **deposition** in mountain environments. In mountainous areas, rivers erode downwards, creating narrow, **V-shaped valleys**. Away from the mountains, valleys become wider and some of the river's load of sediment is deposited. Eventually, this material finds its way to the sea where it is deposited in layers. (The landform features associated with rivers are examined in more detail in Unit 4.2.)

Glaciers: rivers of ice shaping mountain environments

Many of the world's great mountains have been shaped by glacial processes. **Glaciers** are slow-moving rivers of compacted snow and ice. They form when compacted snow, which has accumulated over many years, gradually moves downhill under the influence of gravity.

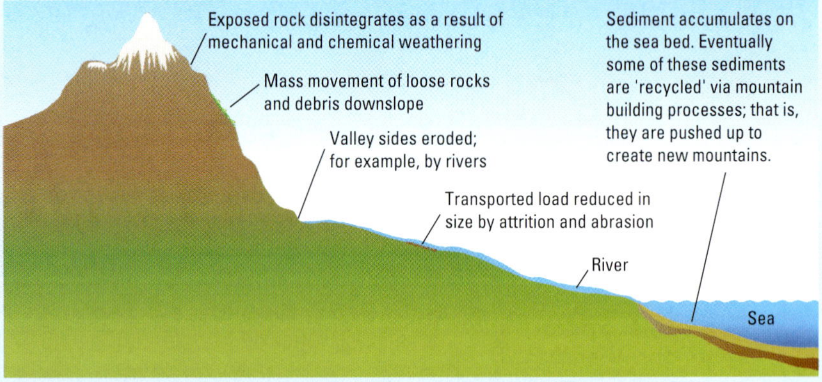

Figure 8.4b From mountains to the sea: processes of weathering, erosion, transportation and deposition. Sediment accumulates on the sea bed.

Figure 8.4c Swiss glaciers viewed from Gornergrat, just above Zermatt, Switzerland. The Matterhorn is on the far right.

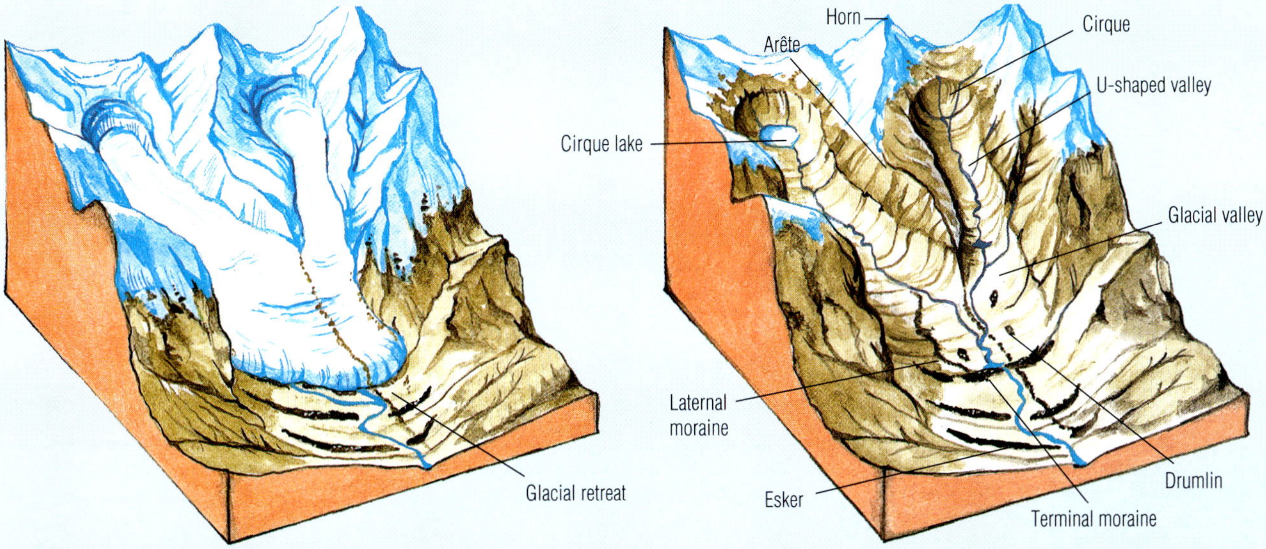

Figure 8.4d The development of glacial landform features.

Glaciers are very effective at eroding and transporting rock. The surface of the land is scratched and worn down by rock fragments that have been plucked from the ground and frozen into the base of the glacier. This process is known as *abrasion*. The most spectacular landform features of glacial landscapes are **U-shaped valleys**. During periods of glacial activity, glaciers deepen and widen the valleys once occupied by rivers. *Hanging valleys* form where smaller (tributary) glaciers join a larger glacier. Other erosional features include *cirques*, *arêtes* and *horns* (pyramidal peaks). *Fjords* are formed when rising sea levels flood the valleys once occupied by glaciers.

The rocks that are picked up and transported by the ice can be carried long distances before they are deposited, forming features known as **moraines**.

Glaciers are found in the Himalayas, the South American Andes, the European Alps, the North American Rockies and New Zealand's Southern Alps.

Getting technical

Deposition The process of sediment being laid down by water, wind or ice to create new land.

Glacier Slow-moving 'river' of compacted snow (glacial ice).

Mass movement Downhill movements of soil, loose stone and rock under the influence of gravity. It does not include movement of material carried by ice, water or wind.

Moraine Sediments that have been transported and deposited by a glacier.

Sediment Fine particles of soil deposited by rivers.

Working geographically

1 **Research: Writing task** Select one of the types of mass movement listed in the text. Undertake library research. With the aid of annotated diagrams, write two to three paragraphs explaining the process.

2 **Challenge: Interpreting diagrams** Study Figure 8.4b. Write a report outlining the work of rivers in the cycle of mountain building.

3 **Constructing diagrams** Sketch a glacial landscape. Label the main glacial landforms mentioned in the text. Select one of these features and undertake additional research to explain their formation.

Foundation worksheet 8.1

Understanding the text

1 Name the processes responsible for wearing away the land created by mountain building.

2 What is mass movement? How does it differ from weathering and erosion?

3 Outline the work of rivers in shaping the mountain environment.

4 What are glaciers? How do they erode the landscape?

UTT worksheet 8.4

8.5 Mountain ecosystems

Figure 8.5a The flowering plants of alpine areas have a brief and intense life. Above the treeline, the growing season is often as short as thirty days. During this time, the plants must race through the processes of germination, growth and reproduction.

The factors helping to shape the nature of mountain ecosystems include altitude, slope and aspect.

Altitude

With increasing elevation (or altitude), air temperatures decrease and wind speeds increase. These changes have a major impact on the growth of plants. As you go up mountains you notice very distinct zones of vegetation. These zones are much like the changes you would see when travelling from the Equator towards the poles. Figure 5.5c (p. 116) shows both these patterns. In the case of altitude, tropical and deciduous forests give way to a zone of coniferous forests. At even higher altitudes tundra-like plants dominate. Above this there is no plant life. Figure 8.5b shows a coniferous forest on the slopes of Canada's Whistler Mountain.

Slope

Slope is important because it influences both soil depth and moisture content. Rates of erosion are higher on steep slopes and moisture drains away quickly. This makes it difficult for steep slopes to support plant life.

Aspect

The *aspect* of a slope affects both light and temperature conditions. South-facing slopes in the Northern Hemisphere are more favourable for plant growth than those facing north (especially in winter). This is

Figure 8.5b Coniferous forest on the slopes of Canada's Whistler Mountain.

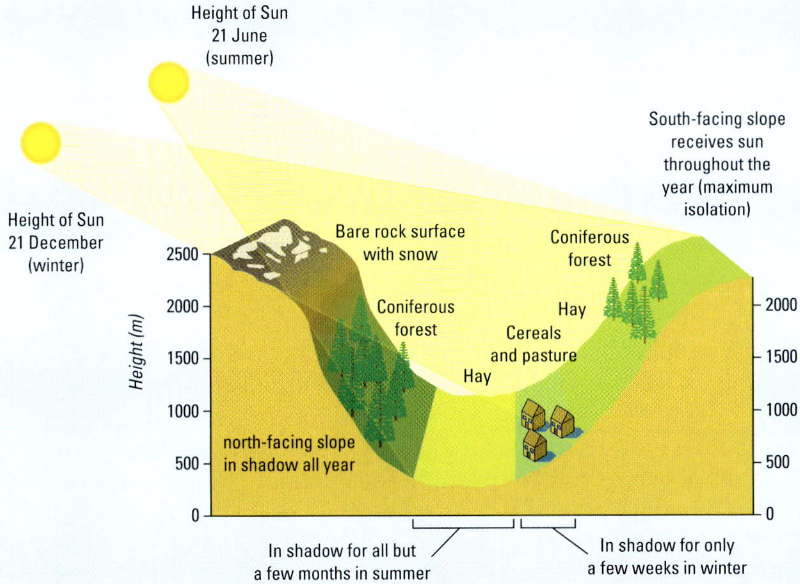

Figure 8.5c Impact of climate in a Northern Hemisphere valley.

because north-facing slopes receive less direct sunlight (see Figure 8.5c). In the Southern Hemisphere, north-facing slopes receive more direct sunlight.

In the Northern Hemisphere, ski resorts are located on slopes with a northerly or easterly aspect. Because these slopes receive less direct sunlight the snow cover remains in place longer.

Animals of the mountain environment

The animals that make their home in mountain environments have, over many generations, developed characteristics that allow them to cope with what can be quite a harsh environment. Many, for example, have large lungs and extra blood cells that help them cope with the thin air found at high altitudes. Others hibernate during the cold winter months. Some animals of the mountain environment are capable of living in a landscape that is covered by metres of snow for up to six to eight months of the year.

Each mountain system has its own distinctive fauna. The Himalayas are home to the yak, tahr, markhor, bharal and the largest of the living sheep, the argali. In mountainous Szechwan, just east of the Himalayas, is found the giant panda, which lives at altitudes of 1800–2500 metres. To the north of the Himalayas can be found the snow leopard and Siberian ibex. The Andes of South America is the home of the llama, alpaca, tapir and various species of deer. In the Rocky Mountains of North America are found cougars, lynx, the marmot, beavers, bighorn sheep and various species of bear.

Figure 8.5d Mountain goat.

Understanding the text

1 Explain how altitude affects plant growth.

2 Outline how slope affects the potential for plant life in mountain environments.

3 Outline how aspect affects the pattern of vegetation in mountain environments.

4 Explain how aspect affects the location of ski resorts in the Northern Hemisphere.

UTT worksheet 8.5

Working geographically

1 **Photo sketching** Construct a photo sketch of Figure 8.5b and undertake research to find out how conifers are adapted to the mountain environment. Use labelling to annotate your sketch with the information you have gathered.

2 **Challenge: Interpreting diagrams** Study Figure 8.5c. Explain the impact that aspect has on the valley shown in the diagram. If you were going to build a house, where would you build it? Justify your answer.

3 **Library research: Report** Identify at least three animals found in mountain environments. Select one of the animals for more detailed study. Prepare a short written report outlining the characteristics of the animal that allow it to survive in the mountain environment.

8.6 SAMPLE STUDY

The Sherpa people of Nepal

Figure 8.6a Sherpas and their yaks returning from Everest Base Camp.

Short of breath

At high altitudes the body is unable to cope with the thinning air and decreasing atmospheric pressure. At 8600 metres, atmospheric pressure is only 30 per cent of that at sea level. The heart pounds even at rest and people experience hallucinations. Blood plasma leaks through capillary walls, increasing pressure inside the skull. The lungs fill with bodily fluids, drowning the victim.

There are no permanent settlements above 5000 metres because people are unable to adjust to the state of the atmosphere at this altitude. At this elevation the lungs expel so much carbon dioxide that it affects the blood's pH balance and the kidneys discharge more water to try to correct this imbalance. This causes dehydration.

At 2500 metres, people begin to feel the effects of the thinning atmosphere. They start to breathe faster because the body senses that there is less oxygen in the blood. The brain swells, causing headaches and nausea.

The Sherpas, an ethnic group of devout Buddhists, live in northeastern Nepal in the shadow of Mt Everest, the world's highest mountain (see Figure 8.6b). Traditionally, the Sherpa people have followed a subsistence way of life based on yak herding and potato growing on steep, terraced hillsides. Within the Khumbu Valley, their traditional home, the Sherpa people went everywhere on foot, with their belongings strapped to their back. Those who could afford them had yaks to carry their belongings. Today, about 10 000 Sherpas live in the Khumbu Valley. The rest, some 60 000, live in neighbouring valleys and further afield (see Figure 8.6c). Because of their association with Everest, and those who seek to conquer it, the Sherpa people are the best known of the more than thirty ethnic groups that make up Nepal's population.

Scientists believe that over many generations the Sherpa people have developed genetic characteristics that enable them to thrive at an altitude of more than 3 kilometres above sea level. Because they have adapted to living in low-oxygen conditions they are able to cope with the thin Himalayan air. They breathe faster and take in more air per minute compared with those living at lower altitudes.

Tourism: transforming the Sherpa's way of life

Since Sir Edmund Hillary and Tenzing Norgay (a Sherpa) became the first climbers to reach the summit of Mt Everest in 1953, hundreds of thousands of international tourists have travelled to Nepal to hike among the earth's tallest peaks. This influx has transformed the Sherpa way of life. Their subsistence lifestyle has been replaced by tourism-based economy. Many Sherpas now work as high-altitude porters for climbing parties and guides for the 20 000 trekkers who flock to the region each year. In addition, they own most of the 300 plus lodges

Figure 8.6b Mt Everest (left, 8850 metres), Khumbu ice fall, and Mt Nuptse (right, 7879 metres).

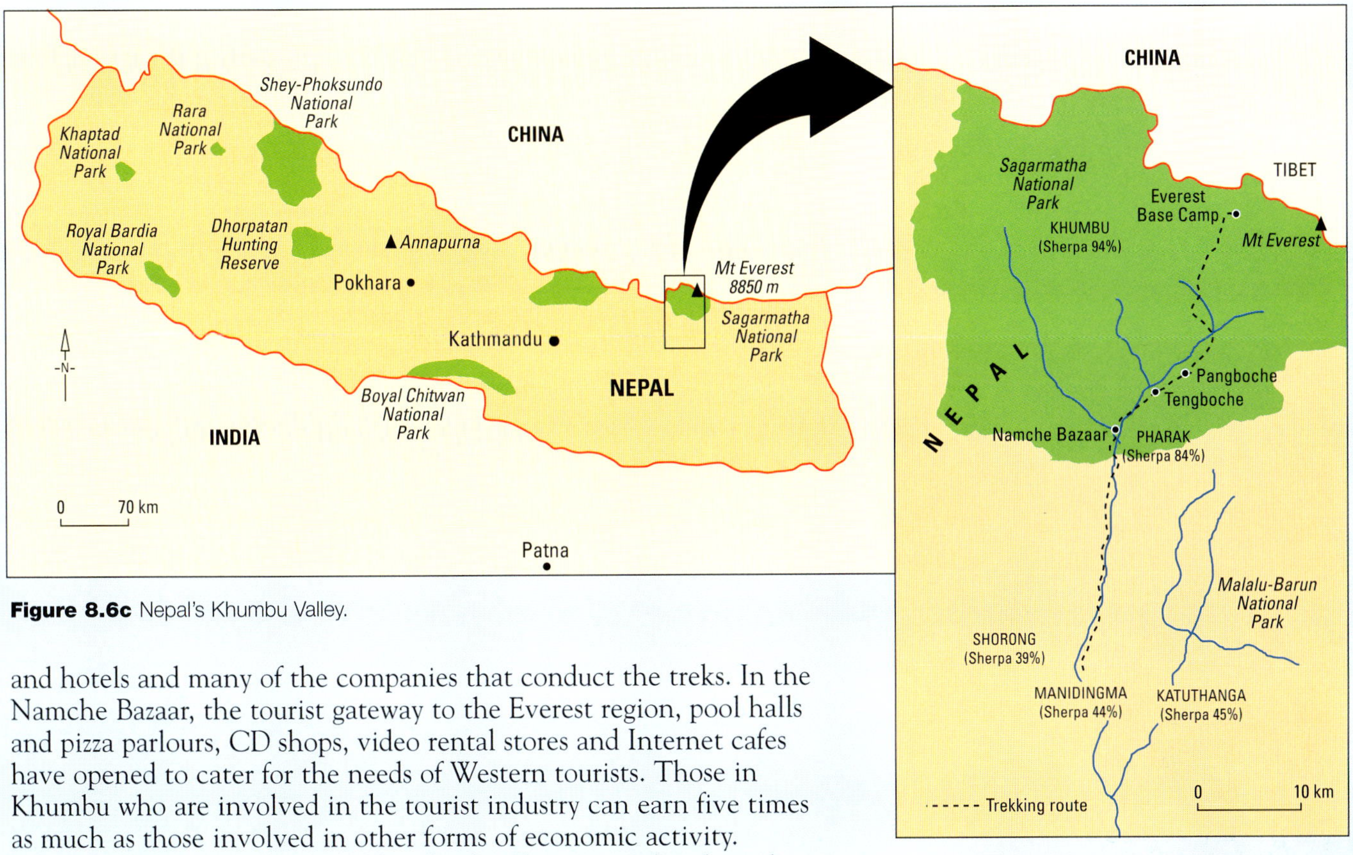

Figure 8.6c Nepal's Khumbu Valley.

and hotels and many of the companies that conduct the treks. In the Namche Bazaar, the tourist gateway to the Everest region, pool halls and pizza parlours, CD shops, video rental stores and Internet cafes have opened to cater for the needs of Western tourists. Those in Khumbu who are involved in the tourist industry can earn five times as much as those involved in other forms of economic activity.

Tourism, therefore, has helped make the Sherpa people relatively wealthy and has helped link the region into the global community. Unfortunately, the industry is not a reliable source of income. Concerns about global terrorism and civil unrest within Nepal have had an impact on tourist numbers. As a result, fewer trekkers and climbers are now visiting Khumbu. After reaching a peak of 25 292 tourists in 2000, numbers fell to below 16 000 in 2002, causing economic hardship for the Sherpa community. Guesthouses stood empty, goods remained unsold and mountain guides sat idle.

Fears that tourism would destroy the local Sherpa culture have not been realised. The people of the Khumbu Valley have been able to blend the old with the new. The Sherpa's perspective or world view continues to be shaped by their Buddhist beliefs. The availability of Western medicine has been used to complement, rather than replace, herbal medicines and faith healing.

Investigating Mt Everest ICT

Access the Everest page of the National Geographic Magazine website to investigate Mt Everest and the Sherpa people. Features of the site include:

- a 3-D model of Mt Everest
- downloadable wallpaper
- a site dedicated to those who have climbed the mountain
- links to other Everest-related sites
- a link to the National Geographic's Everest SuperSite, which features a virtual climb, a 360° view from the summit, photographs, maps, travel tips, games, quizzes and lesson plans.

Figure 8.6d A group of trekkers set up camp at the Everest Base Camp.

Investigating mountains ICT

You can find out the height of the world's highest mountains by going to the Lingtren Mountain Database.

Figure 8.6e Mountaineer sitting on the summit of Mt Everest.

Understanding the text

1. What is the traditional home of the Sherpa people?
2. Describe the traditional lifestyle of the Sherpa people.
3. Outline the genetic characteristics that enable the Sherpa people to cope with the thin air of the Himalayas.
4. Explain how international tourism has affected the Sherpa's way of life.
5. Explain why tourism is described as 'an unreliable source of income'.
6. What impact has tourism had on the culture of the Sherpa people?

UTT worksheet 8.6

Foundation worksheet 8.2

Did U know?

Everest fact sheet

At 8850 metres, Mt Everest is the world's tallest mountain. It is the highest of the peaks that make the Himalayas the most spectacular of the world's great mountain ranges. All twenty of the world's highest peaks can be found in the Himalayas. Of these, none is more than 100 metres lower in elevation than Mt Everest.

The Himalayas were formed 55 million years ago as a result of the collision between the Indian and Eurasian continental plates. This makes it the world's youngest mountain range. The processes of mountain building continue with the range being pushed up by a few centimetres each year.

- *Location:* latitude 27°59′ longitude 86°56′—the summit ridge separates Nepal and Tibet
- *Nepalese name:* Sagarmatha (meaning 'goddess of the sky')
- *Tibetan name:* Chomolungma (meaning 'mother goddess of the universe')
- *Named after:* Sir George Everest, British Surveyor-General of India
- *First ascent:* 29 May 1953 by Sir Edmund Hillary of New Zealand and Tenzing Norgay of Nepal

Working geographically

1. **Photo sketching** Construct a photo sketch of Figure 8.6b (p. 182). Label Mt Everest, Khumbu icefall and Mt Nuptse.
2. **Group work: Research** In groups, brainstorm the challenges associated with travelling to the Everest region. Compile a list of the equipment you would need to travel to the region. Share your list with other groups in your class. Then compare it with the equipment recommended in a Lonely Planet travel guide or similar publication. Use the Internet to investigate the range of trekking tours available. Share these with others in your class.
3. **Constructing diagrams** Study the box 'Short of breath' (p. 182). Using an annotated diagram, describe the impact of increasing altitude on the human body.
4. **Research** Use the Internet or library resources to research the Sherpa people. Identify three interesting pieces of information not included in this unit. Share this information with the rest of the class.
5. **Challenge: Research** Using this unit as a model, investigate the impact of tourism on one other indigenous mountain community. Present your findings using software, such as PowerPoint (see Unit 2.16).

8.7 *SAMPLE STUDY*

Zermatt: European alpine wonderland

The growth in sports-related **alpine** tourism has transformed the small mountain village of Zermatt, Switzerland, into one of the world's most desirable and fashionable tourist destinations.

Location

Zermatt is located at the head of a deep glacial valley in southern Switzerland. The village is surrounded by spectacular alpine scenery featuring several glaciers and twenty-nine mountains, whose summits all exceed 4000 metres. At 4478 metres, the Matterhorn is the most distinctive and best known of these peaks.

Development as a tourist destination

Zermatt can trace its origins back more than 700 years to 1280. For much of this time it was home to a small community of alpine farmers who lived in sun-baked wooden and stone slab houses lining narrow lanes and alleyways. Each summer they would graze their cattle in the high alpine pastures before retreating to the valley floor in winter.

Given its location at the base of the spectacular Matterhorn, Zermatt became a popular destination for mountain climbers. The village's first guesthouse was opened in 1838.

Figure 8.7a The village of Zermatt and the Matterhorn.

Zermatt live cameras and alpine panoramas ICT

Check out the great photograph of the Matterhorn available at the Topin: Zermatt Webcam site. Access this site over a period of nine to twelve months. Print off the image at regular intervals over this time to illustrate the changing nature of the alpine environment.

Other Zermatt live cameras are available at the Zermatt Live Cameras site.

Great alpine panoramas can be found at the Zermatt Photo Panoramas site.

Figure 8.7b Zermatt's logo.

Figure 8.7c Zermatt is one of the world's most famous ski resorts.

Climbing the Matterhorn

In July 1865, a party of seven climbers, including the English mountaineer Edward Whymper, were the first to climb the Matterhorn. On the descent, one of the party slipped and fell, pulling three others to their death. News of the triumph and tragedy was flashed around the world, and Zermatt and the Matterhorn have held a special fascination with people ever since. Whymper was not among those killed.

Figure 8.7d The world famous Matterhorn, first climbed in 1865.

Virtual Matterhorn climb

ICT

You can undertake a virtual Matterhorn climb at the Ski-Zermatt website.

Today, Zermatt is a popular summer and winter holiday destination where the hospitality industry dominates the economic life of the community. The majority of its 5500 permanent inhabitants work in tourism-related activities. The village's 116 hotels and 1800 apartments can accommodate 14 000 guests and there are more than 100 restaurants plus a wide range of retail outlets. There is even a McDonald's.

To help protect Zermatt's unique way of life and culture, only Swiss nationals are allowed to purchase property in the village.

Summer tourism

A ride to one of the summits surrounding Zermatt is just one of the activities that summer tourists can participate in. Other activities include walking the alpine trails, visiting a glacial grotto (ice cave), mountaineering and summer skiing and snowboarding.

Winter tourism

In winter, snow skiing and snowboarding dominate. Each year thousands of winter sports enthusiasts flock to Zermatt from around the world. The ski season extends from late November to early May. The longest ski run, from the summit of Klein Matterhorn to the village, is 13 kilometres long and involves a vertical decent of 2200 metres.

The infrastructure required to support snow-based sports is enormous. The resort's cog railway, a high-speed underground cable railway, seventeen aerial cable cars, six gondolas, fourteen chair lifts and thirty-four T-bars are capable of transporting 64 500 skiers and boarders an hour. Building and maintaining this infrastructure in such extreme conditions is very costly.

Decades of devastation ahead as global warming melts the Alps

A mountain of trouble as Matterhorn is rocked by avalanches

By Robin McKie

Mountain guide Victor Saunders and his companion Craig Higgins had reached … the Matterhorn's Hornli ridge last week when their balmy morning climb turned into a nightmare.

'An enormous avalanche hurtled down the mountain's east face,' said Saunders, one of Britain's leading climbers. 'I have never seen so much rock falling at one time.' The pair survived by cowering under an overhang as a rain of boulders ricocheted past them.

…within a couple of hours, another massive rockfall thundered down the Matterhorn—this time from its north face.

In the end more than 70 climbers had to be hauled from the slopes of the Matterhorn, … one of the biggest mass rescues in mountaineering history… Those climbing its slopes could have been forgiven for thinking the crown jewel of the Alps had started falling apart under their feet.

And they would not have been far wrong—for scientists now believe global warming is melting the Alps, threatening widespread devastation over the next two decades.

The great mountain range's icy crust of permafrost, which holds its stone pillars and rockfaces together, and into which its cable car stations and pylons are rooted, is disappearing…

The Observer, 20 July 2003

Making snow

When nature fails to deliver snow, the operators of ski resorts can always call on snow-makers to produce that much-needed snow cover. Snow-making systems are becoming an increasingly common sight at alpine resorts around the world. In many places they are used to extend the length of the ski season and to ensure that the runs are in the best possible condition.

There are two main types of snow-making machines:

- The *traditional snow gun* (see Figure 8.7f) produces water droplets by combining cold water and compressed air. The water and compressed air are delivered to the gun via separate hoses. The compressed air atomises the water (breaks it into minute particles) and blasts it into the cold air where it turns into snow and then settles onto ski runs.
- The *airless snow gun* (see Figure 8.7e) uses a nozzle to atomise water into a fine mist. The water droplets are then blown up into the air by a powerful fan.

Good snow-making conditions occur when temperatures fall to about –1°C and relative humidity is about 30 per cent. If the temperature drops to –6.7°C snow can be made even if relative humidity is 100 per cent. Temperatures below –10°C are ideal for snow-making. Sometimes a natural protein called snowmax is added to increase the amount of snow produced.

Figure 8.7e An airless snow gun.

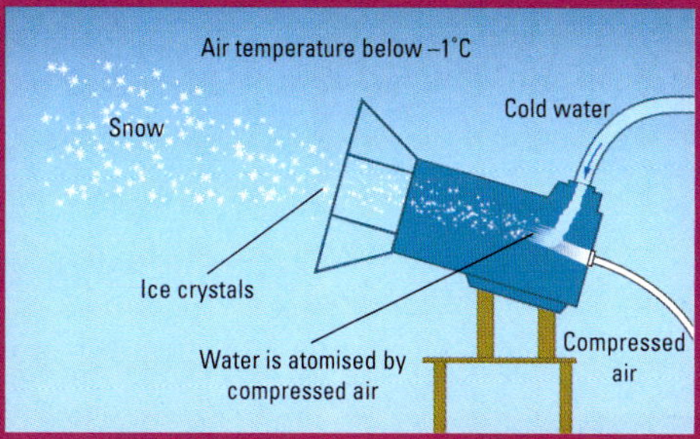

Figure 8.7f How a traditional snow gun works.

Working geographically

1 **Photo sketching** Construct a photo sketch of Figure 8.7a (p. 185). Label the prominent features of the physical and human environments.

2 **Class discussion** Study the article 'Decades of devastation ahead as global warming melts the Alps', then write a paragraph outlining the impact of global warming on the European Alps. As a class, discuss the long-term impacts of global warming on communities such as Zermatt. How might such communities adapt to these changes?

3 **Challenge: Internet research** Use the Internet to investigate the geological processes responsible for the formation of the Alps. Write a report describing these processes.

4 **Internet research** Access the Tourist Office of Zermatt and Ski-Zermatt websites. Using an appropriate software package, and the information and images on the sites, develop a travel brochure about Zermatt. Include information about:

- location
- how to get there
- climate
- attractions of the physical environment
- seasonal activities
- accommodation types and costs
- tourism-related facilities available in the village.

Investigating snow-makers ICT

Access the HowStuffWorks website and conduct a search for 'snow-maker'. Write a report outlining how nature makes snow, the conditions necessary for snow-making and how a snow-maker makes snow.

Understanding the text

1 Describe the community of Zermatt before it became a popular tourist destination.

2 Describe the impact that tourism has had on Zermatt.

3 Outline the outdoor recreational activities available to tourists in both summer and winter.

UTT worksheet 8.7

Extension worksheet ICT 8.8

8.8 SAMPLE STUDY

Whistler-Blackcomb: alpine resort

Figure 8.8a Whistler Mountain ski slopes.

Unlike Zermatt, Whistler is a relatively new community whose very existence has been based on the popularity of alpine tourism and the investment decisions of a large transnational corporation.

Whistler is a popular tourist destination for Australians. Thousands visit the resort each year and many young Australians travel to Whistler in search of work and adventure.

Location

Whistler is located in the Coastal Mountains of British Columbia on Canada's west coast. Moisture-laden winds from the Pacific Ocean are forced to rise by these mountains, resulting in annual snowfalls exceeding 9.14 metres. The resort is approximately 115 kilometres to the north of Vancouver.

Development as a tourist destination

Before the 1960s the only tourists to come to Whistler were those staying at the Rainbow Lodge on Alta Lake. In 1960 a group of businesspeople formed a company to develop a ski area on nearby Whistler Mountain. A separate company opened a second ski area on the adjacent Blackcomb Mountain in 1980. In 1997 Whistler Mountain Ski Corporation (which owned Whistler) merged with Intrawest Corporation (the owners of Blackcomb) to create one of the largest mountain resort complexes in the world. In just over forty years Whistler-Blackcomb has been transformed into one of North America's top ski resorts.

Today, the twin-mountain resort has nearly 3000 hectares of skiable terrain serviced by thirty-three ski lifts with a capacity of 59 000 people per hour. The longest run is 11 kilometres from top to bottom—a vertical descent of 1600 metres. The resort also offers a wide range of terrain parks and pikes for snowboarders and skiers.

Winter Olympics

In July 2003 the International Olympic Committee selected Vancouver as Host City for the 2010 Winter Olympic and Paralympic Games. Alpine skiing (the downhill, giant slalom and super G), nordic sports (cross-country skiing, ski jumping and biathlon) and sliding sports (bobsled, luge and skeleton) are to be held in and around Whistler. Freestyle skiing, snowboarding and all the ice sports (such as ice hockey, figure skating, curling and speed skating) will be held in Vancouver.

Figure 8.8b The Whistler-Blackcomb twin-mountain alpine resort.

Like Zermatt, the majority of Whistler's 10 000 permanent residents are involved in tourism-related economic activities. The resort has more than 115 hotels, including many of the major international hotel chains (such as Westin Hotels and Resorts and Four Seasons). There are also a wide range of restaurants and shops. And, yes, there is also a McDonald's.

To maximise the return on the money invested in the resort's infrastructure a wide range of activities have been developed to attract tourists during summer. These include alpine walks, mountain biking, mountaineering, fishing and golf.

Environmental management

Ski resorts can have a major impact on the fragile alpine environment. The clearing of vegetation for ski runs and lift lines exposes the soil to erosion and can reduce the visual appeal of the mountains. Silt-laden runoff can affect water quality in local waterways.

Whistler's environmental programs include Operation Green Up, which is a program designed to improve the valley's visual appeal and to protect its waterways and fish habitats. This involves a large-scale revegetation program and the use of land management practices that reduce the amount of silt washing into local waterways. These practices include the building of retention ponds, barriers and silt fences. Other environmental programs at Whistler include:

- the use of low-impact design principles for any new buildings to minimise tree loss and keep the mountain looking as natural as possible
- the work of a community-based group of volunteers (known as the Habitat Improvement Program) who undertake local projects to improve the environment
- the use of various strategies to manage solid waste and conserve energy and water.

Plans are being developed to build an environmentally clean hydro plant capable of producing enough electricity to match the power needs of the resort. The ultimate plan is to make Whistler-Blackcomb the world's first ecologically sustainable resort.

Investigating Intrawest: challenge task

ICT

Access the Intrawest website and complete the following tasks:

1. Briefly outline the nature of the Intrawest business.
2. Access the Quick Facts section of the site. With the aid of an atlas, map the location of Intrawest's resorts by category.
3. Construct a flow diagram to illustrates Intrawest's 'success formula'.
4. Develop a corporate fact sheet. Include information such as number of employees and total skier visits.

Extension worksheet ICT 8.2

Understanding the text

1. Outline the similarities and differences between Zermatt (see Unit 8.7) and Whistler.
2. Briefly outline the development of Whistler-Blackcomb as a tourist destination.
3. Outline the strategies that resort operators use to protect the alpine environment.

UTT worksheet 8.8

Working geographically

1. **Planning a vacation: Internet research** Access the Whistler-Blackcomb website and plan a vacation. Consider issues such as how to get there, accommodation choices (including type and cost), equipment hire and lift tickets, and the range of non-skiing/boarding recreational activities available to tourists. Prepare a detailed itinerary.
2. **Internet research: Using software** Access the website of the International Olympic Organization and complete the following task. Select one of the sports featured in the Winter Olympic Games. Use presentation software (such as PowerPoint) to develop a presentation highlighting the history and features of the sport, the various events within the sport, and the leading personalities associated with the sport. Include copyright-free photographs.

8.9 Review and reflect

Chapter summary

Mountains have challenged and inspired humans for thousands of years. Today, they are a major tourist attraction. The growing popularity of trekking, in places such as the Himalayas and New Zealand, and snow-based sports, in the mountains of Europe, North America, Japan, New Zealand and Australia, has transformed, and in some cases created, mountain communities.

In this chapter we have focused on the physical processes that form and shape the mountain environment. We have also seen how tourism has transformed the way of life of the Sherpa people of Nepal and the people of Zermatt. We have also seen how new communities (in this case Whistler) are developed to satisfy people's desire to engage with nature and meet the personal challenges associated with mastering an alpine sport.

Activity 1

Challenge: Using ICT—Investigating glaciers

Use presentation software (such as PowerPoint) to develop a presentation on glaciers. (Unit 2.16 will assist you with this task.) A good source of information is the All About Glaciers section of the National Snow and Ice Data Center website. Use the following questions to structure your presentation:

1. How is a glacier formed?
2. Why do glaciers move?
3. What are the components of a glacier?
4. Where are glaciers located?
5. What types of glaciers are there?
6. How do glaciers affect the land?
7. Are glaciers dangerous?
8. How do glaciers reflect climate change?

The site's Image Gallery can be used to add photographs to your presentation.

Activity 2

Topographic mapping skills

Study the topographic map extract of Whistler-Blackcomb opposite, then complete the following tasks:

1. What is the scale of the topographic map extract?
2. What feature of the physical environment is located at each of the following grid references?
   a 678319 **b** 724275
   c 677248 **d** 662241
3. What feature of the human environment is located at each of the following grid references?
   a 705295 **b** 662293
   c 664322 **d** 673243
4. What recreational activity takes place in each of the following area references?
   a 6530 **b** 6725
   c 6827 **d** 6729
5. Name the type of ski lift linking Whistler Village (AR6630) with the Roundhouse Restaurant and Ski Lodge (GR669257).
6. State the length of the Whistler Village Gondola.
7. What is the straight-line distance between the summit of Whistler Mountain (AR6624) and Blackcomb Peak (AR7226)?
8. Identify the main landuse in AR6428.
9. What is the direction of Whistler Village from the summit of Whistler Mountain?
10. In what direction does Harmony Creek flow in AR6825?
11. Name the creek that joins Fitzsimmons Creek at GR705248.
12. What is the aspect of the slope in:
    a AR7025?
    b AR6828?
13. What is the difference in elevation of Whistler Mountain and Blackcomb Peak?
14. Describe the topography between Whistler Mountain and Blackcomb Peak.
15. Explain how relief is shown on the map extract.
16. Use area references to identify at least three examples of recreational activities tourists could participate in during summer.
17. Use area references to identify the range of winter recreational activities available to visitors to Whistler.

Refer to the Reflection box on page 17.

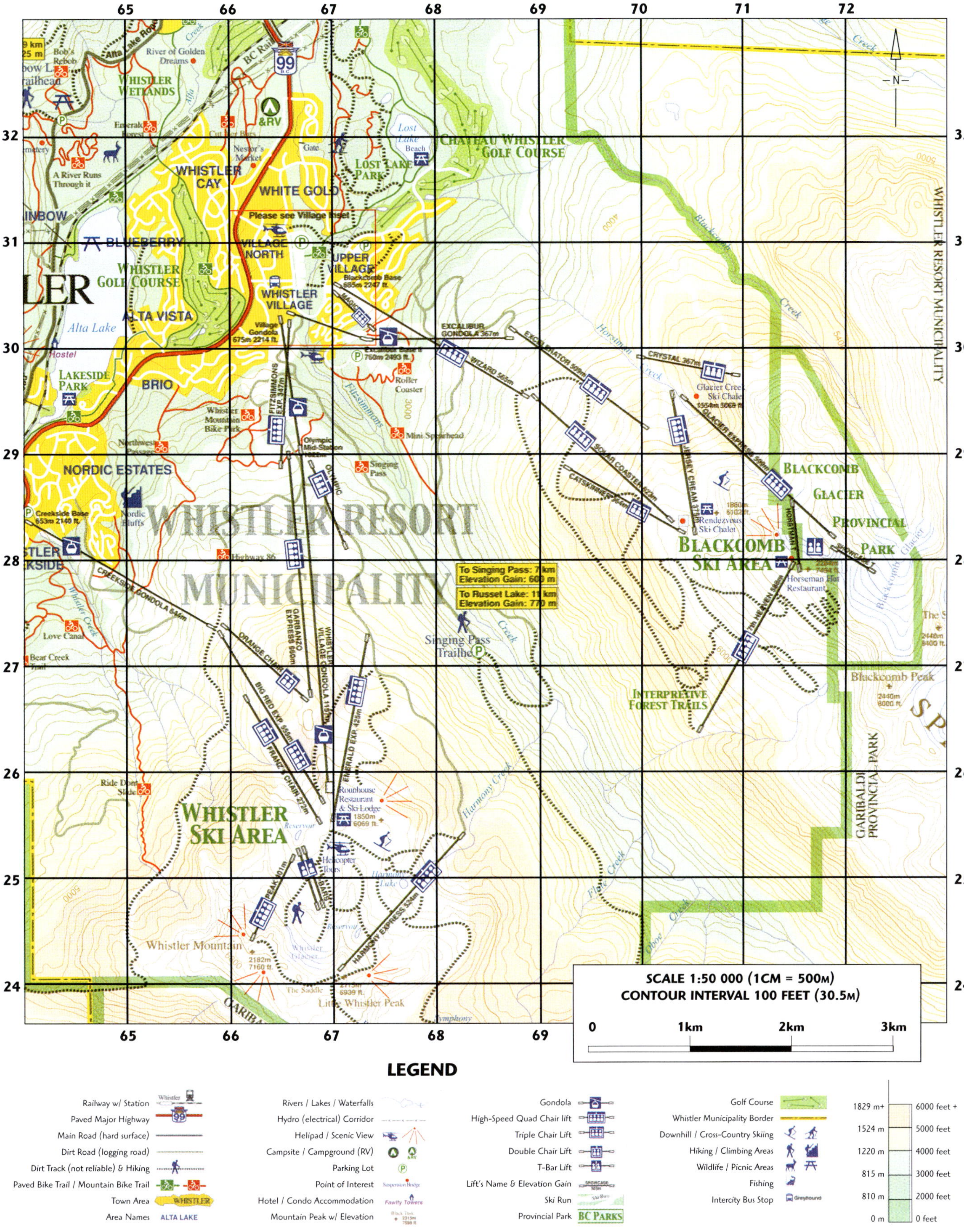

Chapter 9

Coasts

Introduction

Australians love the coast. Eighty per cent of the population lives within an hour's drive of it. They swim there, surf there and build houses there. The pattern is much the same throughout the developed world. In developing countries, small coastal communities, which rely on the resources harvested from the sea, are still a common feature of the coastal environment.

Coasts may consist of sandy beaches, rocky cliffs or muddy flats. Each of these exists because of the interaction of a set of physical forces.

In this chapter we study the forces that form and shape coastal landscapes, and the ways people manage and use the environment.

Key questions

1. What are the processes that shape coastal environments?
2. How do the activities of people affect coastal environments?
3. What strategies are used to manage the impacts people have on environments?
4. How does the west coast of the United States differ from its east coast?

Surfing

Surfing is one of the most popular ways of using coastal areas. It first developed in Hawaii, where long wooden surfboards were used to ride the waves rolling in from the Pacific Ocean. In the 1960s these surfboards were modified in Australia and the United States into lightweight fibreglass boards that could be manoeuvred more easily.

Surfing at high levels of skill requires a detailed knowledge of the formation, power and behaviour of the waves experienced. Surfers know that before a wave breaks, it is only the shape that is moving, not the water, but once it begins to break, a huge volume of water is sucked up from below and falls off the top of the wave. Surfers learn that waves break more slowly on coasts with gentle slopes, and that the slope beneath the sea has an enormous influence on which end of the wave breaks first.

Surfers also learn about offshore and onshore winds and their influence on waves, and about the differences in swell waves arriving from far-off storms. They know about the ways that local winds interfere with these desirable swell waves, and they learn which kinds of weather conditions produce the best waves.

Surfing is a very popular recreational activity in Australia, the United States and South Africa.

ICT Toolkit

GeoToolkit

eGlossary

Foundation worksheet 9.1

Glossary of key terms

Abrasion The erosion that occurs when rocks are thrown against a cliff face by breaking waves.

Arch Formed when waves undercut and undermine a headland.

Attrition Erosion of small rocks as they come into contact with each other.

Blowout A gap, or break, in the dune system formed by the inland movement of sand. Often caused by the destruction of dune vegetation.

Cliff A vertical or near-vertical slope.

Coastal barriers Long sand islands located parallel to the coast.

Corrasion The process by which surging water bombards the cliff with rock fragments and drags other fragments backwards and forwards over rock surfaces, wearing them away.

Deposition The accumulation of sediment by the action of waves and wind.

Development permit Permission to build on or alter land granted by an authority.

Erosion The breaking down and carrying away of rock.

Fetch The distance a wave travels without disruption.

Groynes Walls of rocks or timber built to trap sand on a beach.

Hydraulic action The action of waves crashing into cracks in a cliff face. The pressure exerted eventually leads to the breakdown of the rock and the collapse of part of the cliff.

Joints Gaps in layers of solid rock.

Lagoon A body of water separated from the sea by deposited sand.

Landuse zoning Plans outlining how land should be used in an area.

Notch A small undercut at the base of a cliff.

Outcrop Rock protruding from the rest of the rock structure.

Runoff Water flowing across the earth's surface.

Sand bars Areas of sand deposited in shallow water.

Sand replenishment Transferring sand to a beach that has had is own store depleted.

Sand spits Long fingers of sand bars rising to just above sea level.

Stack An isolated rock feature that once formed part of a retreating cliff face/headland.

Undermining Erosion at the base of a cliff.

Wave-cut platform A flat rock surface found at the base of a cliff or headland.

Weathering The physical, chemical or biological breakdown of rock.

9.1 The changing coast: waves, winds and tides

Figure 9.1a Erosion by waves.

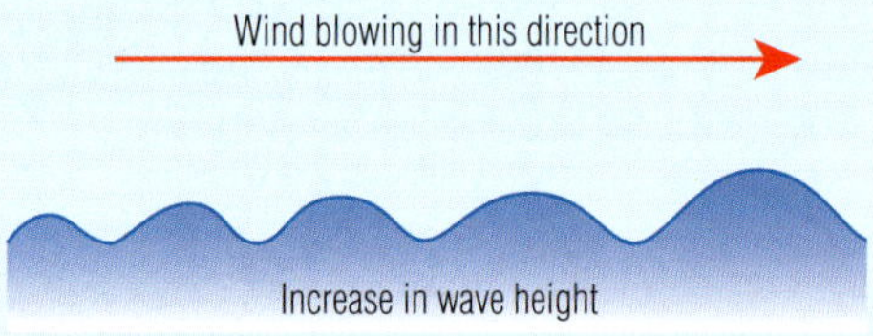

Figure 9.1b Formation of waves. Waves increase in height when the wind blows strongly, for a long time and over a long distance.

Why are coasts so varied?

The coast is the meeting place of land and sea. Because of the different characteristics of land and sea, coasts can vary greatly in their appearance. They can be rocky, sandy, muddy, steep, or gently sloping. The four photographs in Figure 9.1c show coastlines that contrast in appearance. What are the similarities and differences between them?

The appearance and characteristics of a coast depend on the interaction between **erosion** by waves (see Figure 9.1a), weathering by agents such as salt spray, shellfish and seaweed, deposition of material by waves and currents, the effects of tides, and rock type and hardness.

Forces of the sea

Waves

The sea is a very powerful force and has huge effects on the land. At the coast, some of the effects of the sea can be seen most clearly. The most powerful influence on the coast is that of waves. These are caused by the wind blowing across the sea surface. The stronger the wind, and the longer the distance over which it blows, the larger the waves (see Figure 9.1b).

Storm waves are very strong and have the power to shift large rocks and to erode extensive sections of rock from the coast.

Figure 9.1c Contrasting coasts.

Weathering

Although the waves are the most obvious sign of the effects of the sea, there is another set of influences that prepares the coast for erosion. These are the different types of **weathering**—the gradual decay and disintegration (breakdown) of rock:

- *Salt-spray weathering* gradually breaks up the surface of rock because the salt particles expand and contract as they dry out in the sun.
- *Plant weathering* breaks up rock as plants send tiny roots into **joints** within the rock.
- *Animal weathering* breaks up rock when sea creatures anchor themselves to rock. The animals produce chemicals that attack minerals in the rock.

Deposition

Many of the features we see at the coast (such as beaches, **sand bars** and **sand spits**) are built up by **deposition**. Waves and currents move sand along the coast and deposit it in large piles or strips. Beaches are the best known of these features and are formed only where there is a good supply of sand and some form of protection to prevent the sand from being eroded away (see Unit 9.3).

Tides

Tides are caused by the gravitational pull of the moon and sun on the oceans. They vary greatly in height from one place to another. While most places have an average of a few metres between high and low tides, there are places where the height of the tide rises by 20 or 30 metres in six hours.

Rock type

Because the coast is the meeting place of land and sea, the rock type and relief (the shape of the land) have an important influence. They can influence the shape of **cliffs**, the location of beaches, the occurrence of islands and the human uses to which the coast can be put. Different rocks erode at different rates and in different shapes.

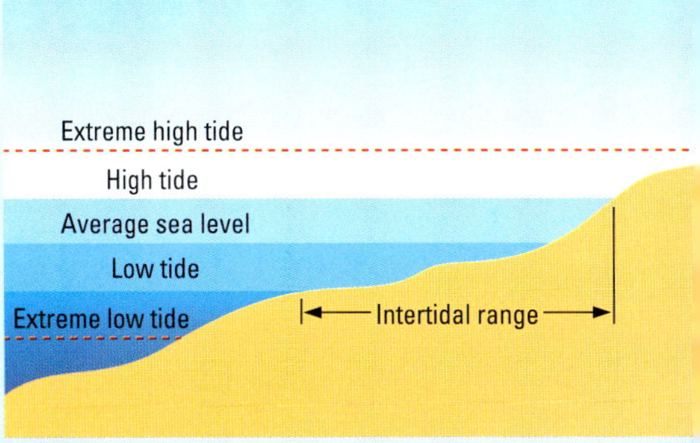

Figure 9.1d The effects of gravitational pull by the moon and the sun cause the daily and monthly pattern of tides.

Understanding the text

1. Explain how waves form.
2. What is weathering?
3. Outline the various forms of weathering that shape the coastal environment.
4. Name three landform features associated with the process of deposition.
5. Explain why rock type is considered so important.
6. Outline the factors that interact to determine the appearance and characteristics of the coastal environment.

UTT worksheet 9.1

Working geographically

1. **Interpreting photographs** Look carefully at the four photographs in Figure 9.1c. Make two lists: one of similarities and one of differences between the coastal landscapes shown in the photographs.
2. **Presenting photographs** Collect a set of copyright-free photographs of coasts from various sources, such as magazines, websites and calendars. Incorporate them into a presentation, a chart or collage, showing the variety of features. Be prepared to describe these contrasting features to the class.
3. **Challenge: Writing task** Write a paragraph describing an area of coast that you have visited. Describe the physical features (such as cliffs, beaches, rivers, islands and dunes) and uses of that location. Also describe the human constructions at the location.
4. **Research** Find out more about the causes of the tides. Most encyclopedias (book and electronic) contain diagrams explaining the causes. Look for explanations of spring tides, neap tides and tidal range. Write a report outlining your research findings.

Foundation worksheet 9.1
Extension worksheet 9.1
Extension worksheet 9.3
Extension worksheet ICT 9.4

9.2 Rocky coasts

Stacks and arches

Sometimes there are more erosion-resistant sections of rocks within the cliff face. As the cliff retreats, the softer rock around these more resistant rocks is eroded more quickly. The harder rock may then be left as an **outcrop** along the coast. The sea may eventually erode the less resistant rock on all sides of this outcrop. Then the resistant rock is left as a small island or **stack**.

Occasionally, the stack may be left linked to the headland by an arch. Eventually the arch will fall as more weathering and erosion occurs.

Figure 9.2a Formation of sea caves, arches and stacks.

Many coastlines are made up almost entirely of rock. Clearly, wave erosion dominates on these coasts. Storm waves undermine cliffs and gradually wear away headlands. Sometimes the largest waves that break on coasts are caused by storms hundreds of kilometres away. The wind may be so strong there that it builds up huge waves which travel uninterrupted across the sea. This distance is called the **fetch** of the waves. Coasts facing the open ocean have long fetches and, therefore, the largest waves.

Figure 9.2b Cliff face, notch and wave-cut platform.

Understanding the text

1. What is meant by the fetch of waves?
2. Explain why rocks erode at different rates.
3. How does weathering help the process of coastal erosion?
4. Outline the process by which rock platforms, stacks and arches are formed.

UTT worksheet 9.2

The power of waves

As waves move from the deep ocean towards the shallower waters of the coast their circular motion **(1)** becomes affected by the frictional drag of the ocean floor. This causes the bottom of the wave to move more slowly than the crest. The circular motion is increasingly distorted **(2)**; the wave increases in height until it finally plunges forward as a breaker **(3)**. The energy of the wave is released and the work of erosion, transportation and deposition takes place. On exposed coasts these are the dominant processes in the area between low and high tides **(4)**. They are most active during storms, when high wind speeds create large, high-energy waves.

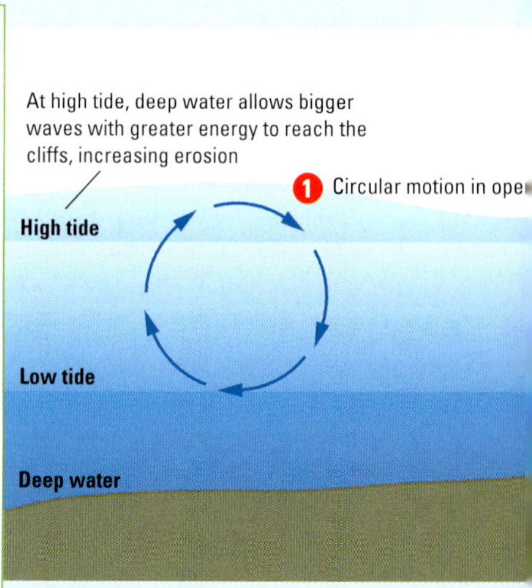

1 The power of the waves can break open the joints of rocks by **hydraulic action**.

2 Rocks thrown against the coast wear it away by **abrasion**.

3 Rocks hitting against each other are gradually worn away by attrition.

Figure 9.2c Processes of wave erosion.

Foundation worksheet 9.1

Working geographically

1 **Writing task** Study Figure 9.2a. With knowledge gained from the text and your own research, write a report explaining the events and processes responsible for the formation of cliffs, stacks and arches.

2 **Interpreting diagrams** Study Figure 9.2d. Write an explanation outlining how storm waves erode cliffs. Make sure that the correct terms for the processes of erosion are used.

3 **Photo sketching** Construct a photo sketch of Figure 9.2b. Annotate your sketch with the names of coastal landform features mentioned in this unit; for example, notch and cliff face.

4 **Classifying** Which of these activities would most likely be found along coasts with rocky cliffs:
swimming, hang-gliding, fishing, sunbaking, surfing, abseiling, boating, sightseeing, walking and team sports?

Coastal erosion on rocky coasts

On coasts with cliffs, wave action will be concentrated at the base. A wave-cut **notch (5)** will be eroded, which will eventually result in the cliff above collapsing **(6)**. The cliff face will retreat, leaving a sloping rock face called a **wave-cut platform**, which is covered with water at high tide **(7)**. The speed of erosion will, of course, depend on the strength of the rock from which the cliff is made. Processes of weathering, such as root penetration and salt crystal expansion, may loosen rock fragments on the upper cliffs, which will then fall away **(8)**. The eroded rock will fall on to the wave-cut platform, where it will be used in the process of abrasion **(9)**. Gradually **attrition** will reduce the size of the fallen rock and it will be transported away. This will happen very quickly when the cliffs are formed from softer rock, such as sandstone.

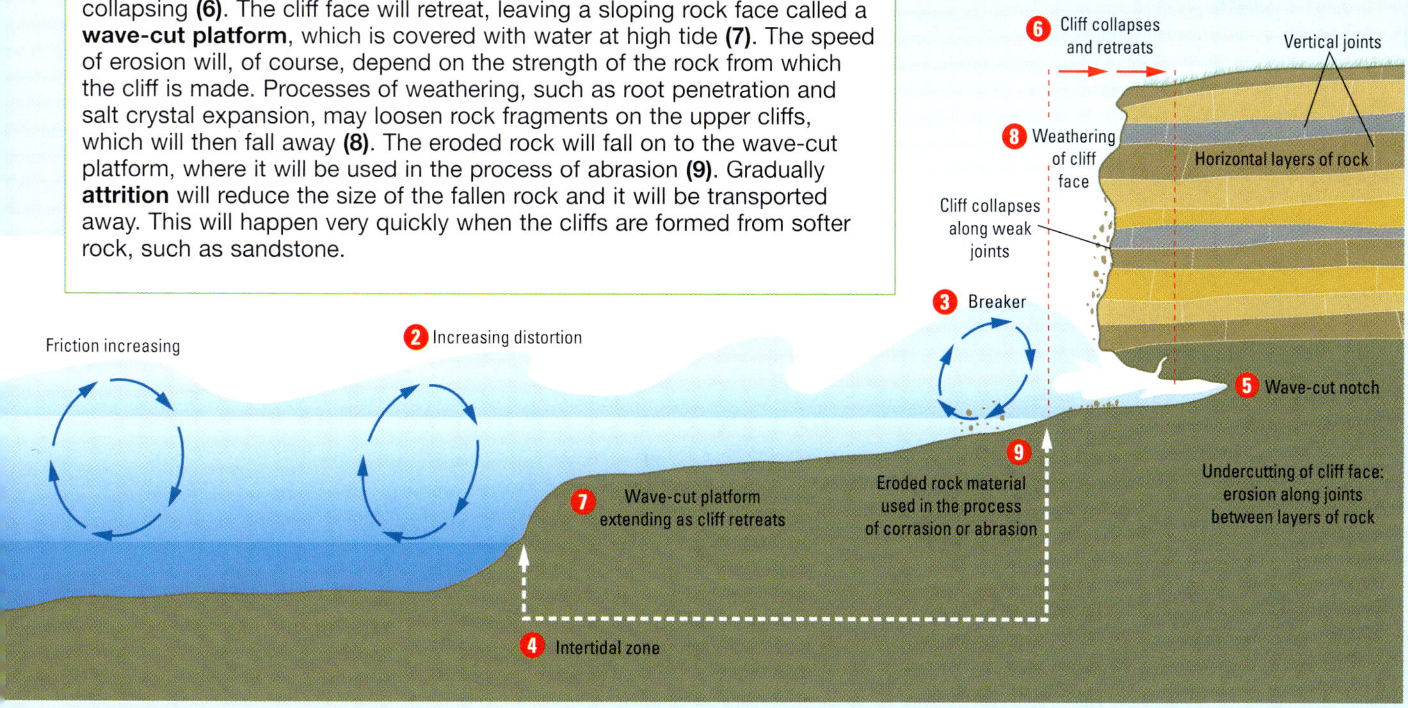

Figure 9.2d Coastal processes and landform features on a rocky coast.

9.3 Sandy coasts

Getting technical

Colonise Establish of new colony of plants and/or animals.
Sand dunes Hills of sand shaped by the wind.

Why do beaches only occur on certain coasts?

Beaches are familiar landforms seen on many coastlines. Beaches can be made up of any deposited material, including shingle (small, rounded pebbles), but most beaches consist of sand. The sand comes to the beach from elsewhere, and is distributed along the beach by wave movements. It may be brought to the coast by rivers, or it may come from eroded rock material along the coast.

Behind the beach there are often **sand dunes**. These are built by the wind blowing loose, dry sand from the beach inland where it accumulates to form a number of dunes called the *foredune* (or *primary dune*), *secondary dune* and *backdune*. The sand in the dunes is anchored, or stabilised by plants, such as those shown in Figure 9.3b.

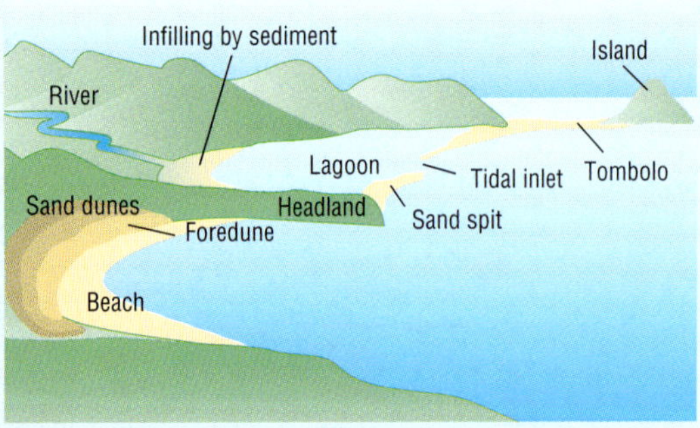

Figure 9.3a Depositional features of the coastal environment.

How are beaches formed?

Because beaches are made up of loose material, their location depends on the actions of the waves. Sand is continuously being deposited on beaches or taken away from beaches by the waves.

Figure 9.3b Sand dune, beach and sand-binding vegetation.

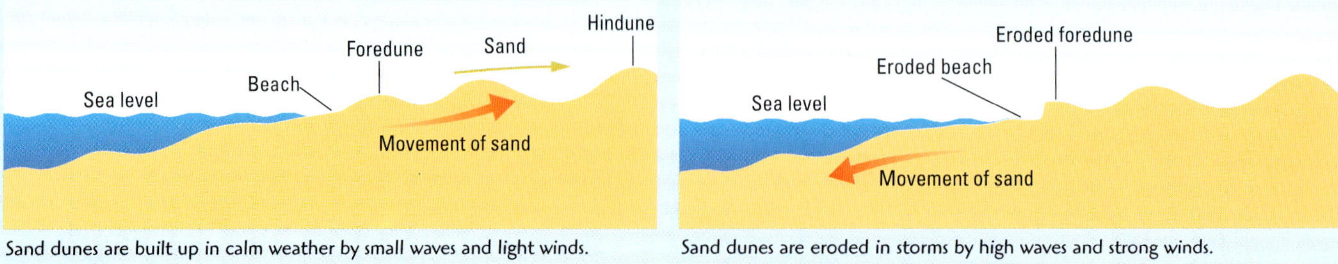

Figure 9.3c Sand erosion and deposition.

Beaches will only form in a place where there is a good supply of sand, and where are they protected enough to give the sand a chance to build up. On most beaches there is a continuous cycle of erosion and deposition. In seasons of strong winds and storms, the sand is taken from the beach. In seasons of calmer seas and light winds, the sand is gradually deposited on the beach. In the next storm period, the sand is taken from the beach again and is stored in the offshore sand bars.

This cycle of erosion and deposition affects not only the size and shape of the beach but also the dunes behind the beach. When storm waves are very large, they erode the beach and may also eat into the dunes. Sand taken from the dunes and the beach is moved offshore and deposited as sand bars in shallow water, where it remains until the calmer season of waves moves it back onto the beach.

Dunes

Many beaches are backed by a system of dunes. Dunes are very important parts of the sand cycle described opposite. They prevent storm waves from penetrating into low-lying areas behind the beach. For a sand dune system to exist there has to be a large supply of sand, long periods of dry weather and frequent onshore winds.

As sand begins to accumulate in a dune, plants start to **colonise** it. The first colonisers anchor the sand with their roots. This creates a more stable environment in which more and different plants can grow. Each succeeding group of plants is taller and more complex as the conditions are gradually improved by the earlier plants. Over time, a soil develops.

Dunes are found along many coasts in Australia. They have been used for recreation (see Figure 9.3d), mined for sand and rare minerals, used as rubbish dumps, built over for housing and, in many areas, completely removed. People now are much more concerned about conserving dunes in their natural state. There is more public understanding of how easily dunes can be damaged. Planning rules now protect dune systems in many coastal areas.

Figure 9.3d Dune bikes can have a destructive effect on sand dunes.

Figure 9.3e Beach erosion threaten's urban development on coastal dunes.

Working geographically

1. **Challenge: Constructing diagrams** Study Figure 9.3a. Select one of the depositional features and undertake research to find out how such features are formed. Use a series of annotated diagrams to explain the formation of the feature.
2. **Constructing diagrams** Draw a diagram to show how a dune system builds up. Use labels to name each dune in the system.
3. **Class discussion** Some of the human activities that are carried out on or near dunes are mining, building houses, walking, boating, planting trees. As a class, discuss which of these would have destructive effects on sand dunes.
4. **Proposing strategies** What advice would you give to people on a camping holiday at the beach to help them do little damage to the sand dunes?

Foundation worksheet 9.2

Extension worksheet 9.2

Understanding the text

1. Identify what conditions are necessary before a dune can be built.
2. Outline how plants anchor the surface of sand dunes.
3. Explain what causes the changes in erosion and deposition on a beach.

UTT worksheet 9.3

9.4 Managing coasts: how do we prevent destruction?

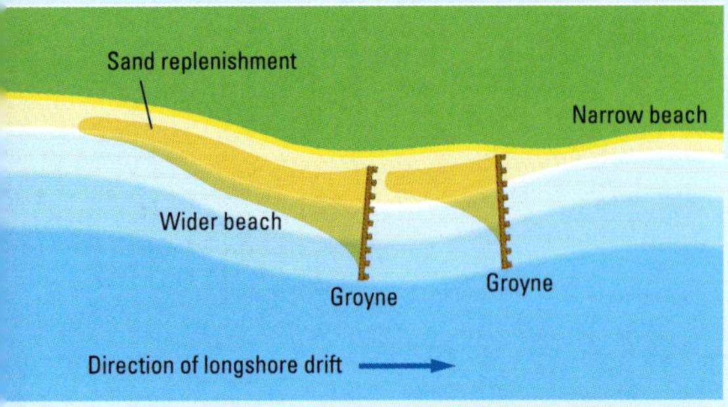

Figure 9.4a The natural movement of sand along a coast by longshore drift can be altered by constructing groynes or replenishing beaches with sand.

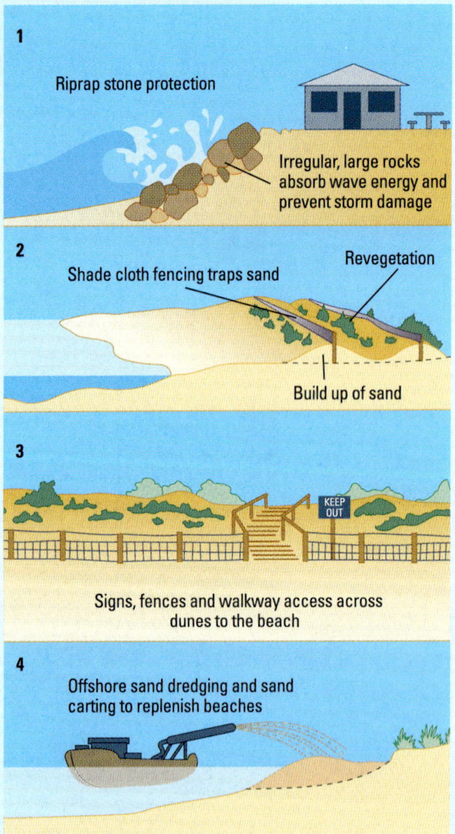

Figure 9.4b Some of the strategies used to manage coastal environments.

Because coasts are highly valued by people they come under great pressure. At the same time, parts of the coast are very fragile and are easily changed and damaged by human use and abuse. This means that individuals, communities and governments must be very careful in managing coastal areas.

Managing rocky coasts

Coasts with cliffs and rocks may seem very stable, but they may be eroding at different rates in different sections. Undermining at the base may threaten the landuses at the top of a cliff. Walls can sometimes be built at the base of cliffs to prevent undermining.

Managing beaches

Beaches are remarkably self-repairing. After a day of heavy human use, the tide gradually washes away most of these signs and redistributes the sand. However, humans can permanently damage beaches in more indirect ways.

Longshore drift is a natural process that shifts sand along the beach. If interruptions to this movement are built along the beach, the sand piles up against them, while other parts are deprived of sand. If the supply of sand is reduced (for example, by building on the dunes or by damming rivers, which stops the supply of sand from rivers) the longshore drift may not be able to replenish beaches naturally. As a result, sand is stripped away at a faster rate than it can be replaced.

To overcome these problems, management schemes may use **groynes** to slow down longshore drift (see Figure 9.4a). These trap sand so that it piles up on one side of the groyne. This, however, means that on the other side of the groyne the sand level is lower.

If the sand supply is limited, a scheme of artificial **sand replenishment** of specific beaches may be undertaken. This involves sand being taken from a beach with plenty of sand, or dredged from offshore, and transported to a depleted beach by truck or by pipeline. Shifting and dumping sand by truck is reasonably effective and inexpensive in the short term. Building pipelines to bring sand from other beaches or from offshore is a more expensive approach but is often much more effective. Figure 9.4b shows a range of coastal management strategies.

Managing dunes

Dunes are the most fragile part of the beach and dune system. Erosion of sand dunes is a major problem in many areas. It occurs whenever the vegetation is removed, allowing the sand to blow away and the dune to shift. If a large section of a dune is blown away, a large, bare depression, called a **blowout**, forms. Strategies used to manage blowouts include planting of new stabilising groundcover plants in disturbed areas. To prevent the destruction of plant cover, walkways are often built through the dunes to keep people on set paths. The remainder of the dunes are then fenced off.

Managing coastal landuses

The coast is an area that is in high demand. To ensure that the best use is made of these places, planning has to be done carefully and management has to be maintained continually. In the past, most coastal areas were developed without any overall plan. Only when problems arose and it was recognised that the coastal land was under pressure was a plan developed. Therefore, any plans developed had to accept and take into account many of the existing landuses. Planners could only slowly change landuses due to the rights that owners had to their land.

Management now involves instruments such as large-scale **landuse plans**, together with day-to-day administration of **development permits** to make sure that anything that is built or altered fits into the overall planning aims. Local councils usually administer these processes. Usually, their aim is to make sure that new developments do not interfere with existing landuses and residents, and to make sure that whatever is built is for the future benefit of the area.

In addition, there is sometimes an overall management plan for the whole coast. This may be administered by the state government, and aims to make sure that the physical and environmental character of the coast is not damaged. In some areas, coastal parks or national parks have been declared to control the use of the coast. The achievement of *sustainable development* and high environmental quality are among the main aims of coastal management.

Understanding the text

1. Explain how natural longshore drift can be altered by building structures on beaches.
2. Why is artificial sand replenishment used on some beaches?
3. Describe the sequence of events that lead to a dune blowout.
4. Why are development plans and permits necessary for coastal areas?
5. List the strategies that are used as part of coastal management.

Extension worksheet UTT 9.4

Management options for the coast

- *Use hard engineering*—Build sea walls, groynes, riprap and other hard structures. These are very expensive and often unsightly.
- *Use soft engineering*—Build up beaches with sand replenishment schemes (see Figure 9.4c). This can be expensive and must be maintained over the long term. It does not have as much visual impact as hard engineering.
- *Discourage building and development of part of the coast*—This is a long-term measure. It needs the cooperation of local, state and national governments. It is often unpopular with local residents or developers.
- *Do nothing*—This can be done in sparsely populated areas but is increasingly impossible in highly populated areas.

Figure 9.4c Sand replenishment.

Working geographically

1. **Challenge: Group work** In groups, make a list of the desirable characteristics of your ideal coastal location. Then discuss the management strategies that would be needed to keep that piece of coast forever desirable and ideal.
2. **Group discussion** In groups, discuss the controls that should be put on coastal development. Do you agree that governments and councils should be able to control all building and development along all coastal areas?
3. **Fieldwork: Wall display** If you live near the coast, visit a local beach and, using a digital camera, record local coastal management strategies. Develop an annotated wall display highlighting the findings of your investigations.

9.5

SAMPLE STUDY

Contrasting coasts in the United States

Figure 9.5a The west coast of the United States.

The long coastline of the United States is used for a wide range of activities. It has large cities and ports as well as areas that remain in their natural state. Both the east and west coast have a variety of natural landscapes but there are major differences between them.

West coast

The physical landscape of the west coast is dominated by cliffs and rocky coastlines. There are dramatic outcrops; forested mountains; small, rocky islands; and stacks. There are also beaches, stretching between rocky outcrops or contained in bays.

Cliffs and stacks

In California, the cliffs of the Big Sur area make this one of the most spectacular coastal drives in the world. A major highway is carved into the cliffs. It crosses canyons with high bridges, allowing views of the cliffs and sea from high above (see Figure 9.5c). This drive is very popular with tourists.

Figure 9.5b Oregon's coastline.

Figure 9.5c California's Big Sur coastline.

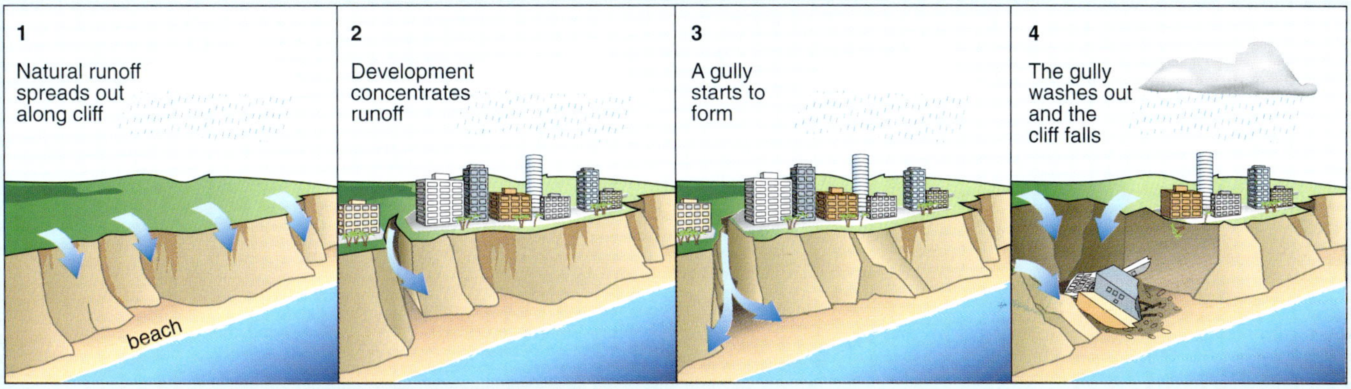

Figure 9.5d Concentrated urban runoff can cause gully erosion in coastal areas.

Further north, in Oregon, the rocky coast features many stacks scattered among the numerous bays (see Figure 9.5b). These stacks are remnants of ancient cliffs, left standing in the sea as the rest of the coast retreated because of erosion. Like Big Sur, communities in this area rely on its natural attractions as the basis of its tourist industry.

A particular threat to cliff coasts in the highly populated coastal areas of California is the change in water **runoff** caused by buildings and roads on top of the cliffs. Runoff of stormwater often becomes concentrated by hard surfaces, causing new gullies to form in the cliff face (see Figure 9.5d).

Beaches

The beaches of California also attract thousands of visitors. Famous beaches (such as Malibu, Santa Barbara and Santa Monica) are used for surfing, swimming, boating and sunbaking. Each of these beaches exists only because it is supplied with sand from rivers bringing silt from the coastal mountains. The natural longshore drift causes sand to move southwards along the coast. The sand that is lost from the

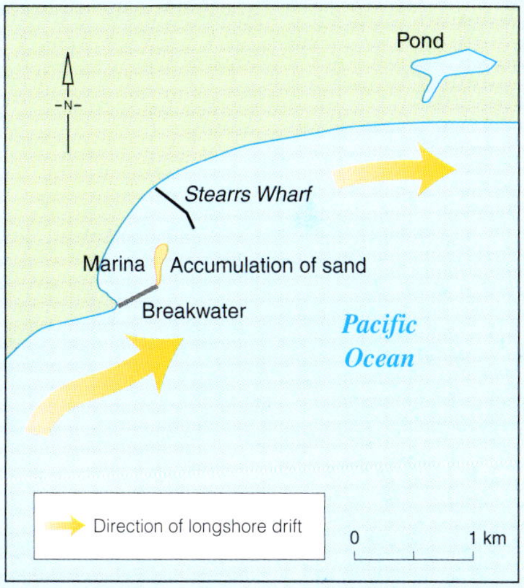

Figure 9.5f Santa Barbara's marina and beaches.

Figure 9.5e Santa Barbara and its harbour and beaches.

Figure 9.5g The barrier islands and cities of the east coast of the United States.

system is replenished by sand from the north. However, every time a dam is built across a river, some of the sand is trapped by the dam and never reaches the sea. This means that beaches are short of sand in some areas and need artificial replenishment.

The continual movement of sand caused by natural longshore drift causes problems in human-built harbours and marinas. At Santa Barbara the entrance to a marina has been partly blocked by sand forming a spit at the end of the breakwater (see Figure 9.5f, p. 203). The longshore drift is natural, but human constructions such as this marina have been built without taking it into account.

Resources and population

There are other valuable resources along the west coast—not just surf beaches and spectacular scenery. The region also has exploitable resources, such as oil, timber, fish and fertile soil. Oil has been found within a few hundred metres either side of the high-tide mark, and near Santa Barbara rows of oil wells pump oil from beneath the sea, leading to fears of an oil spill. Residents are aware of the devastation that could be caused by such a spill; previous small spills have alerted them to the risks.

North of Santa Barbara, between two heavily visited beaches, is the Diablo Canyon nuclear power plant. It is built over a geological fault line and, although the plant has been designed to take this into account, there are local fears about its safety, and concerns about the storage of nuclear wastes.

California has the largest population of all the US states, and its coast is lined with large cities, such as Los Angeles, San Francisco and San Diego. The vast numbers of people who live and visit there puts great pressure on this coast. In between these large cities are hundreds of smaller settlements clinging to cliffs or sheltered in bays. Management of this coast involves a complex system of laws and controls, backed up by continual research.

East coast

The natural landscape of the east coast of the United States differs from that of the west coast. In common with the west coast, it has large cities and a string of small settlements. The east coast was settled by European immigrants 200 years before the west coast, so many of the cities and developments are much older. However, on both coasts it is the last 100 years that have brought the most pressures on natural coastal systems.

Figure 9.5h Urban development on a barrier island, Miami Beach, Florida.

Barrier islands

The east coast of the United States has the longest and most continuous series of barrier islands in the world. For about 4000 kilometres along the east coast stretching into the Gulf of Mexico there is an almost continuous line of sandy islands, offshore sand bars and spits. Together these are called **coastal barriers**.

Coastal barriers are highly changeable. These long, sandy islands stretching along the coast are continually changed by wave action, winds and storms. They migrate backwards and forwards from the shore, and the sand drifts to and from them. Storms break through bars to form new inlets, and then drifting sand slowly seals up these inlets over time. Figure 9.5i shows how barrier islands were formed by rising sea levels and then moved towards the shore by the constant action of waves. Behind the barriers are systems of wetlands and **lagoons**.

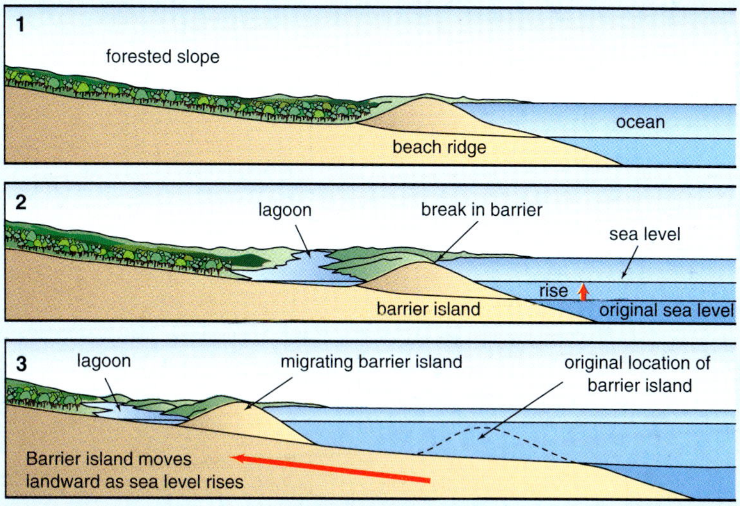

Figure 9.5i Stages in development of barrier islands.

Human settlement

Left to itself the coastal barrier system of the east coast would not be a problem. The islands would move slowly, the beaches would restore themselves and the wetlands would remain protected by the natural barriers. But houses and towns have been built along many of these coastal barrier islands, and houses do not migrate with the sand. Storms breaking through the sand bars threaten homes, roads and other features of the built environment.

The first houses on the dunes and beaches were simple holiday homes, but these were followed by towns and even cities of larger and more expensive houses. Now there is a clear conflict between the natural movement of the barrier islands and the large amounts of money invested in houses.

Working geographically

1 Mapping: Internet research

a On an outline map of the United States, locate and mark the places mentioned in the text. Add some sketches and notes about the issues affecting these particular coasts.

b Use the Internet to find copyright-free photographs of the places mentioned in the text and other coastal locations of the United States. Add these to your map.

2 Challenge: Group work Discuss the conflicts between uses of the coasts and the natural physical environments described in this sample study. What management procedures would you suggest could be used to help resolve these conflicts?

3 **Writing task** Using information in this sample study, write a report describing the influences that increasing population and settlement have on coasts.

Understanding the text

1 Summarise the main physical differences between the east and west coasts of the United States.

2 Make a list of the coastal landforms that can be found along both coasts of the United States.

3 Which natural processes are affected by human activities on the west coast?

4 Why are there conflicts in opinions about how the west coast should be developed?

UTT worksheet 9.5

9.6 Review and reflect

Chapter summary

This chapter introduced us to the main features of the coastal environment: cliffs, beaches and sand dunes. Next time we visit the coast we should have a better understanding of the power of the waves, the changing nature of the cliffs, beaches and dunes, and the processes affecting the appearance of the coast.

Through this study we should have developed an understanding of how people interact with the coastal environment. We should, for example, be able to identify the ways people's activities impact on the coast and be able to suggest strategies for the management of these impacts. We may even decide to join a community group that helps to protect the coast.

Activity 1

Coastal processes and features

In your workbook, write each of the words in column A. Match each of the words in column A with one of the words in column B to form a pair. Then write the meaning of each pair.

Columna A	Column B
Hydraulic	Cliff
Salt-spray	Platform
Vertical	Bars
Coloniser	Out
Fore	Action
Sand	Plant
Wave-cut	Weathering
Hard	Dune
Blow	Permits
Development	Engineering

Activity 3

Interpreting topographic maps

Study the Oregon topographic map extract opposite, then complete the following tasks:

1 Identify the feature of the physical environment located at each of the following grid references:
a 112032 **b** 114038 **c** 112042

2 What is the direction of Captain Cook Point (AR0211) from the Cape Perpetua Recreation Area (AR0311)?

3 What is the direction of the lookout at GR117042 from Devils Churn (AR1103)?

4 Copy the two cross-section grids opposite. Construct the cross-section from Point A to Point B and the cross-section from Point C to Point D.

5 Study the section of the Oregon coastline shown on the topographic map extract. Determine whether the coastline is dominated by erosional or depositional landform features. Justify your answer by making reference to the map extract.

6 Write a report outlining the geographic processes responsible for the formation of this section of coastline. Use annotated sketches to explain these processes.

7 Use the Internet to investigate the promotion of Oregon's coastline as a tourist attraction. Use copyright-free photographs to help inform and illustrate your response to activities 5 and 6.

Activity 2

Interpreting photographs

Look at these three photographs of coasts. Write a description of the main features of each location, using some of the key words and ideas you have learned from this chapter.

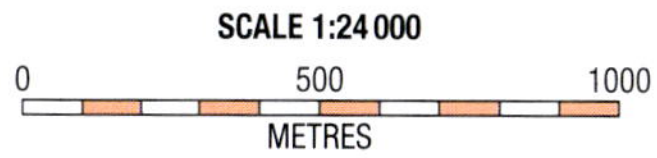

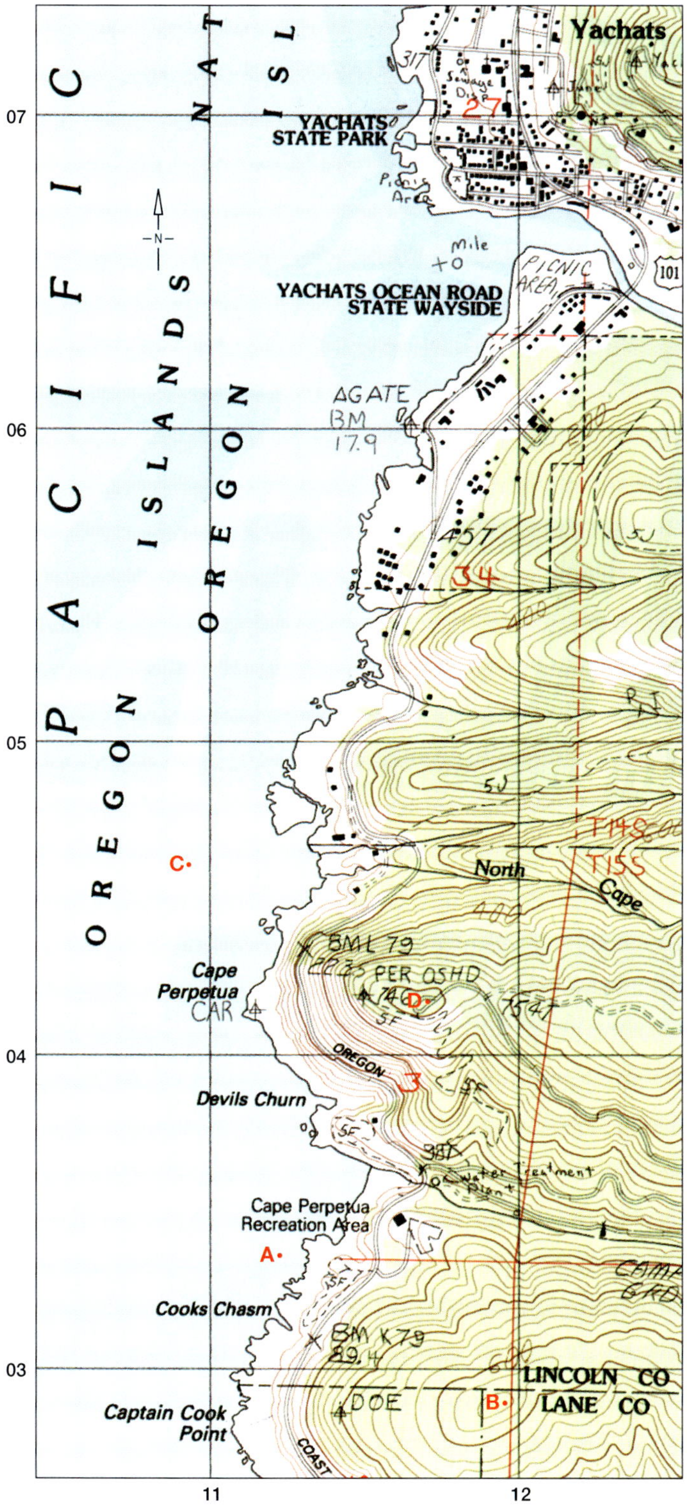

Topographic Map Symbols

Primary highway, hard surface
Other road or street; trail
Built up area; locality; elevation
Cemetery; building
Windmill; water well; spring
Mine shaft; adit or cave; mine, quarry; gravel pit
Campground; picnic area; U. S. location monument
Contours: index; intermediate; supplementary
Land subject to controlled inundation; woodland
Scrub; mangrove

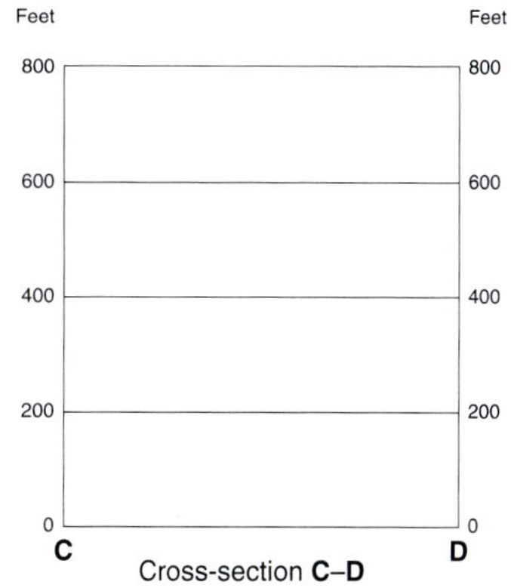

Cross-section **C–D**

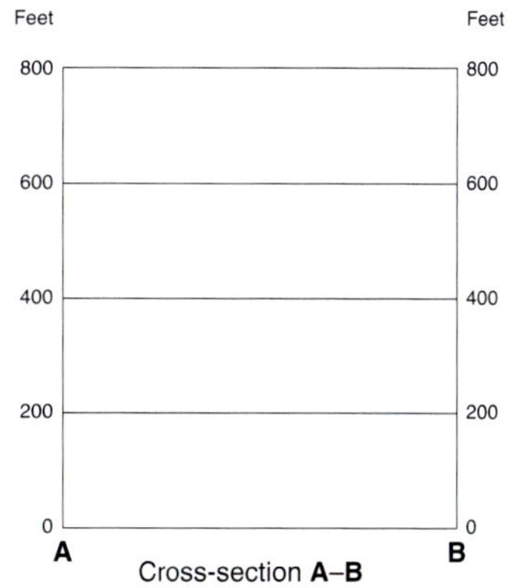

Cross-section **A–B**

GeoMatch

GeoWords

GeoQuiz

Chapter test

Foundation worksheet 9.2

Refer to the Reflection box on page 17.

Chapter 10

Wetlands

Introduction

Wetlands are among the most important of all environments because they provide a breeding ground for numerous fish species and other life forms. Destroy the wetlands and you degrade the fisheries that people rely on as a source of food.

There are many different types of wetlands. In this chapter we focus on inland freshwater wetlands. Two inland waterways—the Everglades of the United States and the Okavango Delta in Botswana, Africa—are examined in detail. In these sample studies we look at how communities interact with these fragile and unique environments.

Key questions

1 What are wetlands?
2 What are the geographical processes that operate in wetland environments?
3 How do the people of the Florida Everglades and the Okavango Delta interact with the wetland environments?

Swamp monsters

Stories about monsters feature in every culture and are often associated with the unknown and unexplained. Why swamps and why monsters? Monsters are often thought to exist in unexplored territory: rugged mountains, dense forests, remote islands and the depths of lakes and oceans. Swamps can be added to this list because they are often inaccessible and remote.

In North America, stories of swamp monsters have been inspired by traditions that go back to the days when the American Indians were the only people to roam the lands of North America. One of the most common of these is that of the Big Foot, or sasquatch, a giant hair-covered, man-like creature. While the major domain of Big Foot is the Pacific northwest, there have been many reported sightings in low-lying and/or swampy lands of the lower Mississippi and other major river basins. Other mythical swamp-dwelling 'beastmen' and 'manimals' said to live in America's wetlands include the smelly Skunkape and the Gatorman of the Florida Everglades; the Scape Ore Swamp Lizardman of South Carolina; and Momo, the Missouri Monster.

This photograph, taken in Florida, is believed to show Big Foot.

Glossary of key terms

Algal blooms High concentrations of microscopic aquatic plant life.

Coastal wetlands Low-lying coastal areas that are periodically covered with salt water.

Delta Extensive deposits of alluvial material (sediment) at the mouth of a river.

Ecotourism Travel to natural areas that are largely undisturbed by the activities of people. It is nature friendly. Sometimes referred to as ecologically sustainable tourism.

Environmental flow The minimum amount of water required to maintain a wetland ecosystem.

Estuary The area near a river's mouth where the tide ebbs and flows.

Exotic plants and animals Non-native plants and animals; those introduced from elsewhere.

Inland wetlands Areas covered with fresh water permanently or periodically.

Mangrove A salt-tolerant tree that can cope with being partly submerged under water.

Phytoplankton Aquatic plants; mainly single-celled algae.

Plankton Small plant and animal organisms that float or drift in great numbers in fresh or salt water.

Ramsar Convention The international convention or agreement that protects some of the world's most important wetlands.

Reclamation The conversion of an unsuitable site into a land suitable for commercial or residential landuses.

Sediment Fine particles of soil deposited by rivers.

Tide The alternate rise and fall in the level of the sea, caused by the gravitational pull of the sun and moon.

Wetlands Areas of land covered by water for all or part of the time.

Zooplankton Small aquatic animals; mainly small crustaceans and fish larvae.

cd eGlossary

cd Extension worksheet 10.4

cd GeoToolkit

cd ICT Toolkit

10.1 Wetland environments

Figure 10.1a The flood plain wetland of Kakadu National Park is a popular tourist attraction.

Figure 10.1b A freshwater wetland: cypress swamp, United States.

Wetlands are areas of land covered by water for all or part of the time. The water can be still or flowing, salty or fresh.

In the past, wetland ecosystems were seen as worthless, mosquito-infested wastelands. This attitude has changed. A growing number of people realise that wetlands are among the most important and productive life support ecosystems on earth. They support complex communities of plants and animals, help to maintain water quality and provide people with an important recreational resource. They are also important for the survival of the coastal fishing industry—a major supplier of food. Some, including Australia's Kakadu National Park (see Figure 10.1a), are a major tourist attraction.

Types of wetlands

Although there are many different types of wetlands they are usually identified as either coastal or inland wetlands.

Coastal wetlands

Areas of land covered with salt water for all or part of the year are called **coastal wetlands**. **Mangrove** swamps are the main type of coastal wetland found in the tropical parts of the world.

The types of coastal wetlands found in the more temperate parts of the world include bays, lagoons, salt flats, mud flats and salt marshes. Grasses are the main type of vegetation found in these ecosystems.

Coastal wetland ecosystems protect the coastline from erosion; reduce damage from cyclones and storms; trap **sediment** washed from the land; absorb nutrients and other pollutants; and provide breeding, nursery and feeding grounds for fish, invertebrates and plants.

Inland (freshwater) wetlands

Areas covered with fresh water permanently or periodically are called **inland** (or freshwater) **wetlands**. They include marshes, prairie potholes (depressions carved out by glaciers), swamps (dominated by trees and shrubs), mud flats, river flood plains, oxbow lakes (billabongs), bogs (peat-rich areas), wet meadows and the wet arctic tundra in summer. Some inland wetlands, such as the Everglades (see Unit 10.3), are huge, while others are quite small.

Some inland wetlands are covered with water throughout the year; others, including flood plain wetlands, are seasonal wetlands that are usually under water for only a short time each year. Some may remain dry for years before filling again.

Inland wetlands provide food and habitats for fish, insects, water birds, wading birds and other wildlife. They improve water quality by filtering, diluting and absorbing toxic wastes, nutrients, sediments and other pollutants. Wetlands are sometimes called 'nature's kidneys' because they filter out waste products, performing the same function as kidneys in the human body.

Inland wetlands also reduce flooding and erosion by absorbing excess runoff and releasing it slowly; they replenish groundwater supplies, provide a refuge for wildlife and stock during droughts and provide

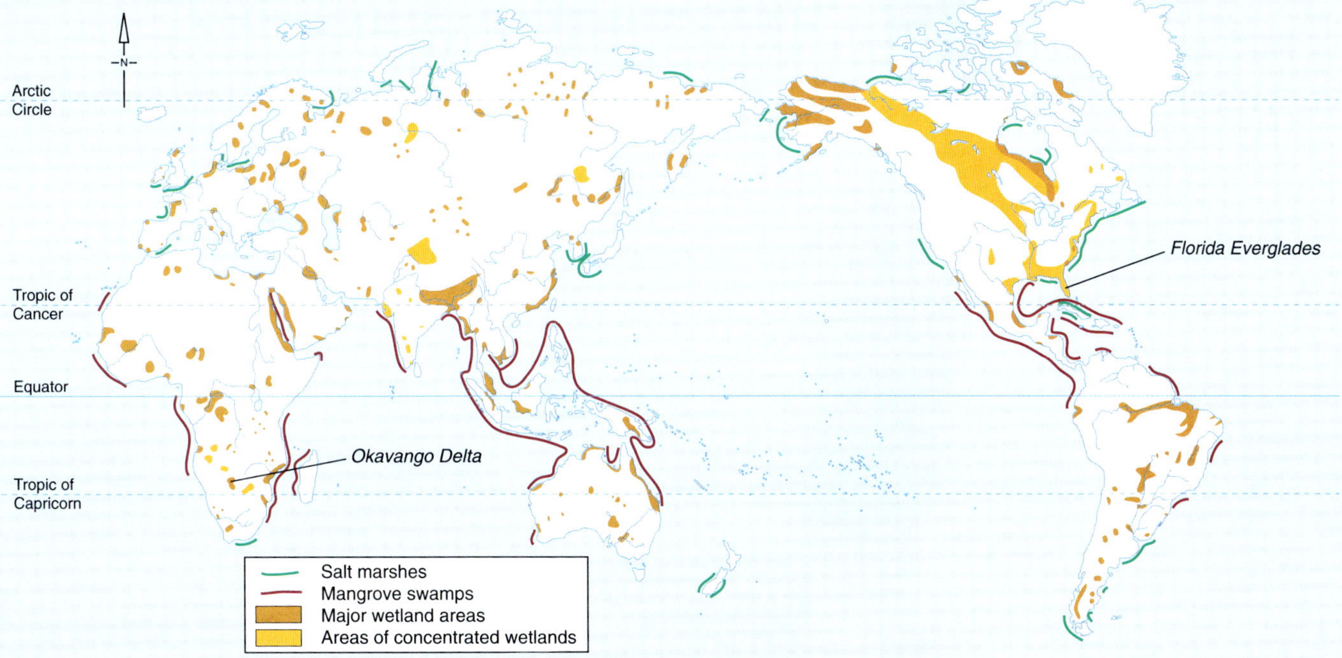

Figure 10.1c The locations of the world's wetlands.

places for a range of recreational activities, including swimming, boating and fishing. The world distribution of wetlands is shown in Figure 10.1c.

Foundation worksheet 10.1

Foundation worksheet 10.2

Extension worksheet 10.1

Extension worksheet 10.2

Human use of wetlands

Despite the environmental and economic importance of wetlands, many have been drained, dredged, filled in or covered over. Most have been used for agriculture; the rest for mining, forestry, industry, port facilities, highway construction and urban expansion (see Figure 10.1d).

This process has been taking place for centuries. In the Netherlands, where land is a scarce resource, wetland **reclamation** has been occurring for 500 years. The United States has lost half its wetlands over the last 200 years. The damming of rivers and the use of wetlands as landfill sites (rubbish dumps) also contributes to this loss.

Figure 10.1d Coastal developments, such as these on Australia's Gold Coast, have destroyed coastal wetland ecosystems.

Web quest: Ramsar wetlands

ICT

Visit the Ramsar website. Select two Ramsar listed wetlands: one from a developed country and one from a developing country. One should be an inland wetland, the other a coastal wetland.

Use the following geographical questions to structure a word-processed report:

1 What is it?
2 Where is it?
3 Why is it there?
4 What is it like?
5 How do people affect it?
6 How does it affect people?
7 What can people (governments, groups and individuals) do to protect the wetland?

Illustrate your report with copyright-free photographs downloaded from the Internet.

The protection of wetlands

Wetlands are the only ecosystem for which there is a special international convention or agreement: the **Ramsar Convention** on Wetlands (1971). By mid-2003 more than 136 countries had signed the convention, which now covers 1289 wetland sites with a total area of 109 million hectares. Examples of NSW coastal wetlands protected by the Ramsar Convention include the Hunter River estuary wetlands, Myall Lakes and the Towra Point Nature Reserve at Botany Bay. Internationally, more sites are added each year. Unfortunately, relatively few countries from Africa, south and Southeast Asia and South America have signed the convention. It is in these parts of the world where the rate of loss has been greatest.

The convention includes guidelines for the wise use of wetlands, encouraging practices that benefit the present generation while protecting food webs and other environmental processes, such as the recycling of nutrients.

Understanding the text

1 Explain what is meant by the term 'wetlands'.
2 Explain why wetlands are so important. Consider both coastal and inland wetlands.
3 List the different types of wetlands under two headings: coastal wetlands and inland wetlands.
4 What is the Ramsar Convention? How does it help protect wetland ecosystems?
5 Explain why the convention is likely to have only limited success.

UTT worksheet 10.1

Working geographically

1 **Internet research: Written report** Use the Internet to locate organisations concerned about the protection of wetlands. Select one of the sites and prepare a short written report outlining the group's aims and its strategies to protect wetlands.

2 **Challenge: Using the media** Collect media reports dealing with wetland issues. Use the framework to analyse geographical issues provided in Chapter 1 (p. 10) to investigate one of these issues. Present your findings as an oral report to the class. Mount a wall display of these media reports.

3 **Group work** In groups of four, discuss how our lifestyle contributes to the destruction of wetlands. Select a spokesperson to outline your group's discussion to the class.

4 **Interpreting maps** Study Figure 10.1c (p. 211). With the aid of an atlas and the information contained in the text, copy and complete the table below.

5 **Challenge: Research** Select two of the wetland types listed under the heading 'Inland (freshwater) wetlands'. Do some research to find out the conditions under which these wetlands develop. What are their special characteristics?

6 **Photographic collage** Use copyright-free phototographs collected from magazines, travel brochures or the Internet (using your computer's screen-capture facility) to construct a collage of wetland ecosystems. Display the collages in your classroom.

7 **Photo sketching** Select a photograph of a wetland featured in this chapter. Construct an annotated photo sketch highlighting the key characteristics of wetlands (see Unit 2.9).

Wetland type	Characteristics	Climate	Location (name specific countries)
Coastal wetlands (tropical)			
Coastal wetlands (temperate)			
Inland wetlands			

10.2 Wetland ecosystems

Wetland ecosystems

There is no typical wetland ecosystem. They can vary greatly in size and they can be forested, grassed or almost bare of vegetation. Some stay wet all year, while others dry out for a few months or a few years. Some are frozen during winter. There are three characteristics they all share:

- the periodic presence of water
- the lack of oxygen in the soil (because it is saturated)
- the special adaptations of plants that live there.

As we saw in Unit 10.1, wetland ecosystems can be divided into saltwater coastal wetlands and freshwater wetlands, but this distinction is artificial. Wetlands near the coast may receive their water from both the sea and rivers, and are influenced by a mix of both of these waters.

Wetland ecosystems are among the most productive on earth. Figure 10.2a shows they are as productive as **estuaries** and tropical rainforests.

Life in the wetlands

Many wetland ecosystems are dominated by birds and reptiles rather than mammals. This is because the combination of water and land acts as a barrier to land-based mammals, but not to birds and reptiles, such as the crocodile and alligator. The plant life includes submerged and floating vegetation, such as duckweed; grasses, sedges, rushes and reeds; and, in some areas, taller trees, such as coastal mangroves.

Small invertebrates, such as insects, are the main species at the lower level of the food chain. The insects feed on grasses and mosses

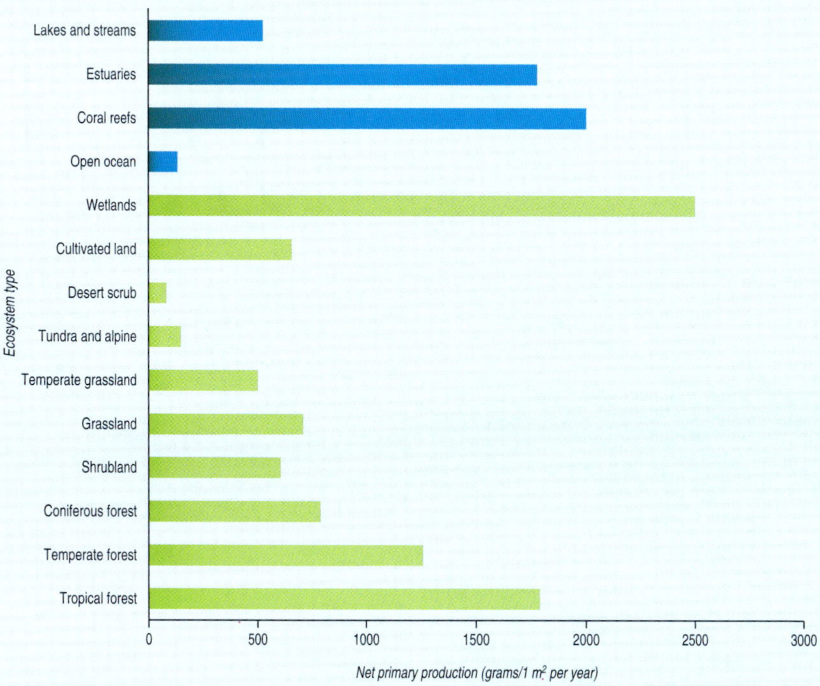

Figure 10.2a Average net primary production of selected ecosystems.

Figure 10.2b Wetlands support thousands of different species of waterbird. Each species has developed its own specialised way of gathering food.

Getting technical

Primary production is the rate of energy accumulation, usually through photosynthesis.

Figure 10.2c The giant saltwater crocodile seizes its prey and swallows it whole.

Activity 2

1. **Challenge: Constructing food chains** Using the information in the text and in Unit 5.5, construct your own wetland ecosystem food chain. Clearly identify which organisms are producers and which are consumers (herbivores, carnivores and omnivores).
2. **Interpreting graphs** Study Figure 10.2a (p. 213). Compare the productivity of wetlands with that of the other ecosystems shown in the graph. For example, which ecosystems are as productive as wetlands? Which are the least productive ecosystems?
3. **Challenge: Interpreting food chains** Write a half-page description of the flow of energy through the food chain shown in Figure 10.2d. Use the information in Unit 5.5 to assist you.
4. **Internet research** Using the Internet, conduct research to find out the difference between crocodiles and alligators. Write a paragraph explaining the difference.

and, in turn, provide a good food supply for many small birds. There are also many species of larger wading birds that live on small worms, snails and molluscs found in the water. Birds such as the yellowbilled stork have bills specially adapted to probe through the mud in search of food. Their large feet help support them on the marshy ground.

At the top of the food chain are the predatory birds. They prey on other birds. Falcons and hawks are typical members of this group. Figure 10.2d shows a sample food chain.

The largest reptiles living in wetlands are alligators and crocodiles. Alligators are found in the wetlands of southeastern United States (especially Florida). The Chinese alligator, which is much like the American alligator in its habits and appearance, lives in the wetlands of the lower Yangtze River. Freshwater and saltwater crocodiles are found throughout the tropical world. The giant saltwater crocodile (see Figure 10.2c) lives in coastal wetlands from India to northern Australia. Crocodiles are also found in southern Florida, the West Indies and Central America. The Nile crocodile is found throughout much of Africa. Crocodiles and alligators are also at the top of the food chain. They eat fish, birds and mammals that they seize and swallow whole.

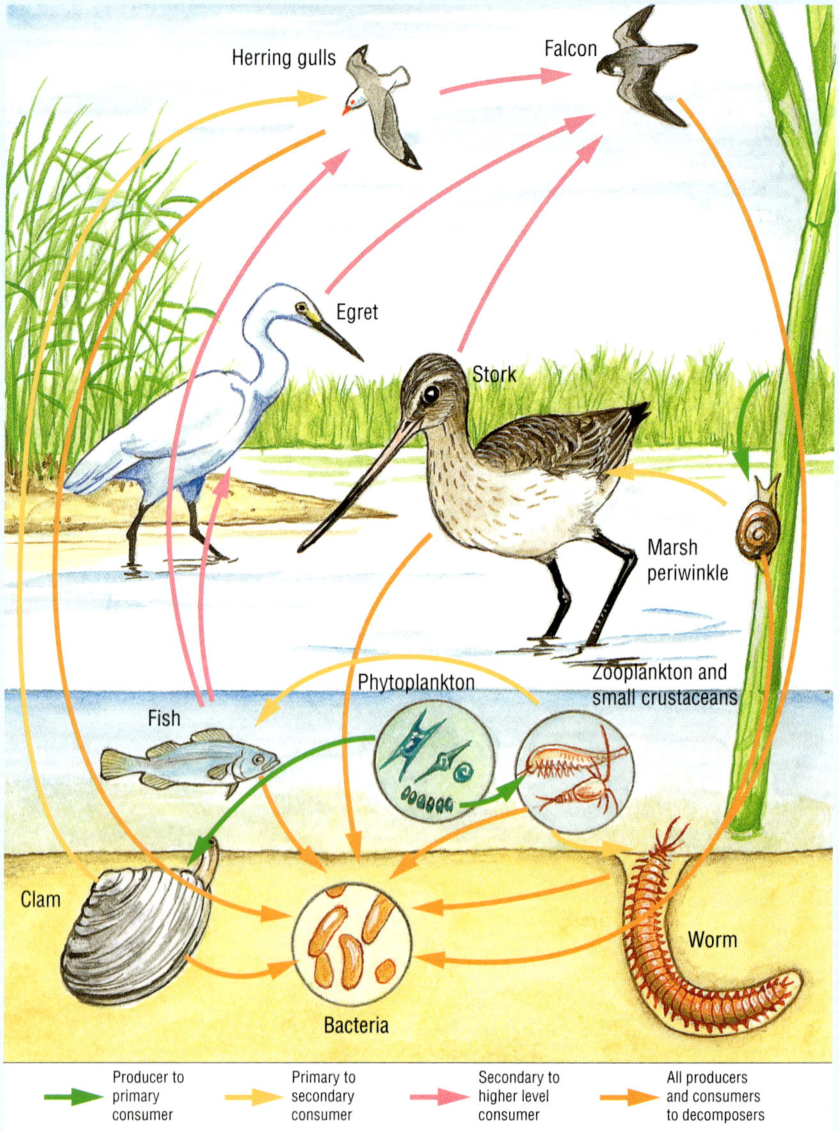

Figure 10.2d An example of a coastal (saltwater) wetland food chain.

While most mammals are not well-suited to wetland ecosystems, some have managed to adapt to the environment. In the mangrove forests of Borneo, for example, live populations of langurs, silver leaf monkeys, proboscis monkeys and crab-eating macaques.

Managing wetland ecosystems

How do we manage and protect wetlands so that they survive as functioning ecosystems? This question is being asked around the world as people begin to appreciate the value and importance of wetlands. There is now a general agreement that management designed to protect wetlands needs to take into account the following principles:

- The protected area needs to be large enough to allow the ecosystem to continue operating naturally. If the area is too small, surrounding activities (such as farming or mining) could disrupt the flow of water to the wetland and the flow of energy within food webs.
- The amount of water entering the wetland needs to be enough for the ecosystem to function. This is known as **environmental flow**. Where there is a conflicting demand for water, such as for irrigation or urban uses, a certain amount of water within a river system needs to be reserved for wetlands.
- The quality of the water entering wetlands needs to be protected. A buffer zone around the wetland where human activities are carefully managed would achieve this. The use of fertilisers and pesticides, for example, would need to be controlled.
- Sewage needs to be treated to a high standard to remove nutrients before it finds its way into wetlands.
- Introduced species of plants and animals need to be controlled in wetland ecosystems.
- Access of people (including tourists) and livestock needs to be restricted.
- The interests of local people need to be considered. If ignored they may resort to activities that damage wetlands.
- Governments must be willing to pass and enforce planning laws that manage landuse activities and protect wetlands.
- Funding levels need to be high enough to support the implementation of effective management strategies.

Figure 10.2e Controlling the access of people is one factor to take into account when managing wetlands.

Understanding the text

1. Explain why is it difficult to describe a typical wetland ecosystem.
2. List the three characteristics that all wetland ecosystems have in common.
3. Explain why wetland ecosystems are dominated by birds and reptiles rather than mammals.
4. Describe the animals found on the lower levels of the wetland food chain.
5. Outline the ways wading birds have adapted to the environment of the mangrove swamp.
6. Name the types of animals you would find at the higher levels of the wetland food chain.

UTT worksheet 10.2

Working geographically

1. **Library research** Choose one of the following animals: alligator, barramundi, crocodile, crab-eating macaque, flamingo, harrier, hawk, jabiru, langur, proboscis monkey, sandpiper and silver leaf monkey. Do some library research to find the following information about the animal you chose:
   - **a** habitat and distribution
   - **b** how the animal gets its food
   - **c** any special adaptations the animal has developed that enable it to live in its habitat.

   Include a photograph or sketch of the animal. Present your work as a poster. Display it on the classroom wall.
2. **Challenge: Fieldwork** Conduct research to find out if there are any wetlands near where you live. If there are no wetlands nearby, select one you are interested in. What type of wetland is it? Why is it there? Is it artificial or natural? Name the animals that inhabit the wetland. Find out if the wetland is managed. If it is, explain how it is managed.
3. **Group work** In groups, develop a set of rules to protect a local wetland ecosystem. Share your group's rules with others in the class. Develop a class list.
4. **Poster presentation** Using the rules listed in the task above, develop a poster with the title 'Protecting our wetlands'. Use illustrations to communicate the activities that are allowed and those that are prohibited.

Foundation worksheet 10.2

Extension worksheet 10.1

Extension worksheet ICT 10.6

10.3 SAMPLE STUDY

North America's 'river of grass': the Florida Everglades

Figure 10.3a Florida's 'river of grass'. The Everglades is the world's largest freshwater marshland.

The Florida Everglades has an area of more than 20 000 square kilometres. It is the world's largest freshwater marshland (see Figures 10.3a and 10.3d). This vast wetland is actually a slow-moving river measuring 80 kilometres wide and, on average, only 15 centimetres deep. It flows south down the Florida peninsula, through the Everglades National Park and into Florida Bay (see Figure 10.3b). The Florida peninsula is very flat and low-lying. Drainage is poor and rainfall is quite high; the rainfall averages 1300 millimetres per year. The region's unique environment is dominated by its 'river of grass' and thousands of small islands covered with trees, orchids and ferns. The Everglades is a World Heritage site and in 1993 it was placed on UNESCO's List of World Heritage in Danger (see Unit 3.8).

The Everglades ecosystem supports a variety of habitats and a staggering number of plant and animal species. There are 300 species of birds, 600 kinds of mammals and forty-five plants that are unique to or originate in the area. The area is the home of fourteen endangered or threatened species, including the American alligator and Florida panther (see Figures 10.3e and 10.3f).

Figure 10.3b The Florida Everglades.

Figure 10.3c Satellite photograph of southern Florida.

What impact have people had?

During the last 200 years, more than half the original wetland ecosystem has been lost to development and water-management projects. Today, the region is crisscrossed with 2250 kilometres of canals, levees, spillways and pumping stations. Large areas have been drained and the pattern of flooding in the area has been changed.

The most controversial of the water-management projects was the 1960s conversion of the meandering 165 kilometre long Kissimmee River into a straight 90 kilometre long canal. The canal helped to control flooding by speeding the flow of water, but in the process it drained water from the wetlands north of Lake Okeechobee. Farmers converted most of the land into pasture. Nutrients from cattle manure now represent a major source of pollution. They promote the growth of algae and reduce oxygen levels in the water. Lake Okeechobee is now heavily polluted. These pollutants eventually find their way into the wetlands.

South of Lake Okeechobee, large areas of wetland were drained and planted with crops, such as sugarcane and vegetables. These activities rely on the use of fertilisers and pesticides, which are washed into the wetlands. Once they reach the wetlands, the fertilisers and pesticides encourage the growth of introduced plant species and disrupt food chains.

Another major problem, throughout the wetlands, has been the introduction of **exotic plants and animals**. Introduced plants, in particular casuarinas from Australia, have invaded large areas of the Everglades and changed habitats. Introduced animals, such as the droll armadillo, are modifying the woodlands by their different eating habits.

The increasing demand for water in the region's rapidly growing cities has also had an impact on the ecosystem. Groundwater is being used faster than it can be replaced. As the water table drops, salt water moves inland, contaminating water supplies. Urban expansion has also meant vegetation has been cleared, wetlands have been drained, and marinas and canal estates have been developed.

Florida Bay has become saltier and warmer because there is less fresh water reaching it. These conditions, combined with the increased nutrients flowing into the bay, have led to the growth of vast **algal blooms**. These threaten the nearby coral reefs and the local tourist and fishing industries.

Figure 10.3d The Everglades meets the sea.

Figure 10.3e The endangered Florida panther.

Figure 10.3f An American alligator in the Everglades.

The Everglades National Park

The US Government established the Everglades National Park in 1947 in an effort to protect the lower end of the catchment. The park covers just 20 per cent of the remaining wetlands. It is not large enough to protect the wetland community properly. The park suffers from the management problems typical of parks that are incomplete parts of larger ecosystems. The diversion of water from the river system in the north, for example, restricts the water flow needed to support the park's wildlife. The number of birds in the park has declined by more than 90 per cent.

Can the Everglades be saved?

The environmental impacts of people have been recognised for at least twenty-five years. But it is only since the early 1990s that attempts have been made to undo the damage. In 1993, the US

The Everglades: endangered World Heritage site

ICT

Access the World Heritage Convention website and read UNESCO's List of World Heritage in Danger notice concerning the Everglades. Then answer the following questions:

1 What are the threats to the Everglades National Park? Which threats are the result of human activity and which are a part of natural processes?
2 What has been the US Government's response to the listing of the site as endangered?
3 Why must the views of the area's indigenous people be taken into account?

Understanding the text

1 Describe the physical environment of the Florida Everglades.
2 Outline the various ways in which people have had an impact on the Everglades ecosystem.
3 Explain what is being done to repair some of the damage people have caused to the ecosystem of the Florida Everglades.

UTT worksheet 10.3

Foundation worksheet 10.2

Extension worksheet ICT 10.5

Government announced that the Kissimmee River would be restored to its natural state at a cost of more than US$400 million. An additional US$2 billion will be spent on turning reclaimed land back into wetlands in a protective zone between agricultural areas and the Everglades National Park. The restored marshes will help to increase the flow of water through the Everglades. They will also help filter phosphorus and other nutrient runoff from sugarcane and vegetable fields, and reduce the amount of nutrients flowing into the park and bay.

Local community-based conservation groups are also playing a role. One group successfully stopped the urban centres of Marco and Naples (see Figure 10.3b, p. 216) from developing into a continuous urban strip. The group used funding provided by the Audubon Society (a non-government body committed to the conservation of habitats for birdlife) to buy private land between the two towns. This land is now the Rookery Bar Sanctuary.

These projects will not restore the Everglades to their natural state, but they will repair some of what has been damaged.

Working geographically

1 **Interpreting photographs** Study Figures 10.3a (p. 216) and 10.3d (p. 217). Write a paragraph describing the physical environment of the Everglades.

2 **Photo sketching** Construct a photo sketch of either Figure 10.3a (p. 216) or 10.3d (p. 217). Annotate the photo sketch to identify the characteristics of wetlands.

3 **Interpreting maps and satellite photographs** Study Figures 10.3b and 10.3c (p. 216), then complete the following tasks:
   - a Name the features numbered 1 to 6.
   - b In what direction does the water flow in the Everglades National Park? Justify your answer using evidence from the satellite photograph.

4 **Research** Study Figures 10.3e and 10.3f (p. 217). Do some research to find out more about the Florida panther and American alligator. Why are they endangered?

5 **Challenge: Writing task** Write a report on how the activities of people have modified the Everglades ecosystem.

6 **Designing posters** Take on the role of an advertising consultant for a travel agency. Design a poster for the Everglades, showing some of its main natural features. Emphasise the unique nature of the environment.

7 **Group work: Using graphics software** The wilderness areas of the Everglades is close to some of the most popular tourist destinations in the United States, including Orlando, Miami, Disney World and the reefs and beaches of Florida. Use a group discussion to suggest ways in which the tourists could see and appreciate the natural ecosystem without disturbing it. Present your findings as a mindmap created using graphics software.

10.4 SAMPLE STUDY

The Okavango Delta, Botswana

Deep in the heart of southern Africa lies one of the world's great wetlands, the Okavango Delta. This delta is not the point at which a river enters the sea. In this case, water drains towards a large inland depression where the water and its sediment spreads out over the Kalahari Desert. The result is a unique wetland ecosystem within a desert environment (see Figure 10.4a).

On an atlas map, the Okavango Delta appears to be a large lake in Botswana. It is actually a complex maze of channels flowing from the Okavango River. The waters from the river move slowly through the channels and flood large areas, before evaporating quickly in the high temperatures of this semi-arid area. The processes responsible for the formation of this delta are discussed in Figure 10.4e (p. 220).

Okavango has an unusual mixture of wetlands and drylands. The drylands are islands within both the permanent and seasonal wetlands. Many of the islands only exist when the water level is low and are only a fraction of a metre above the surface. Some islands are big enough to hold only one tree. Between the islands, the channels wind around, some of them so narrow that the plants on each side almost touch, and others so wide that they open into great expanses of lakes.

The whole area provides a habitat for a unique collection of wildlife. The numerous fish provide food for 400 species of birds, such as kingfishers, cormorants, fish eagles and fishing owls. Large mammals, which have adapted to life in the swamps, are found in abundance. Examples include the hippopotamus and the red lechwe antelope.

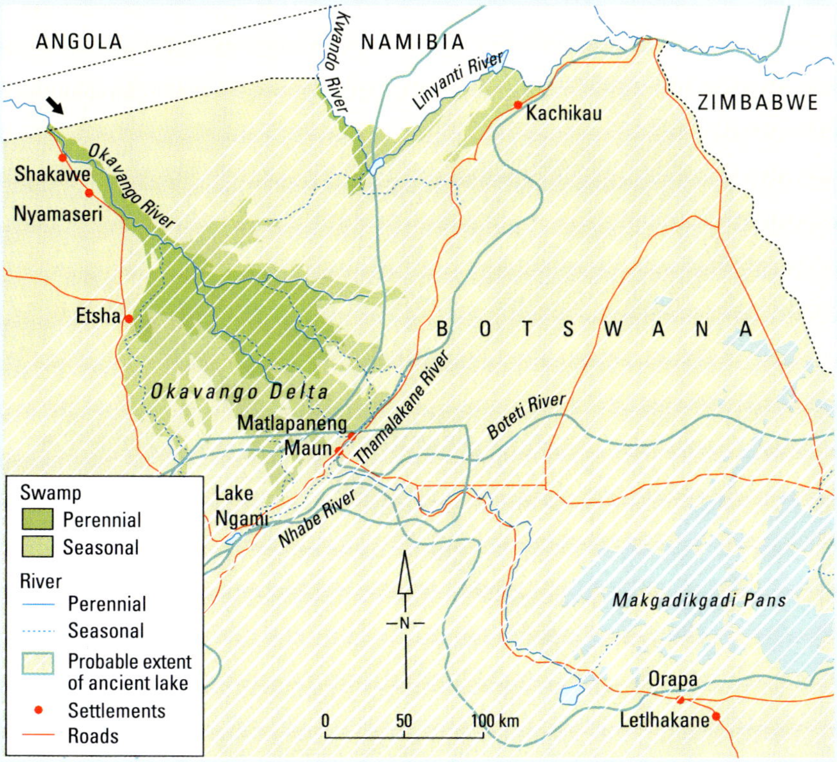

Figure 10.4a The location of the Okavango Delta.

Figure 10.4b Satellite photograph of the Okavango Delta.

Figure 10.4c The Okavango Delta's wildlife and spectacular scenery are major tourist attractions.

These antelope are often hunted by lions, leopards and hunting dogs. Besides the permanent animal inhabitants of the delta, the water attracts many seasonal migrants, such as elephants (see Figure 10.4c, p. 219), zebras and cape buffaloes, and their predators.

Figure 10.4d The people of the Okavango Delta catching fish.

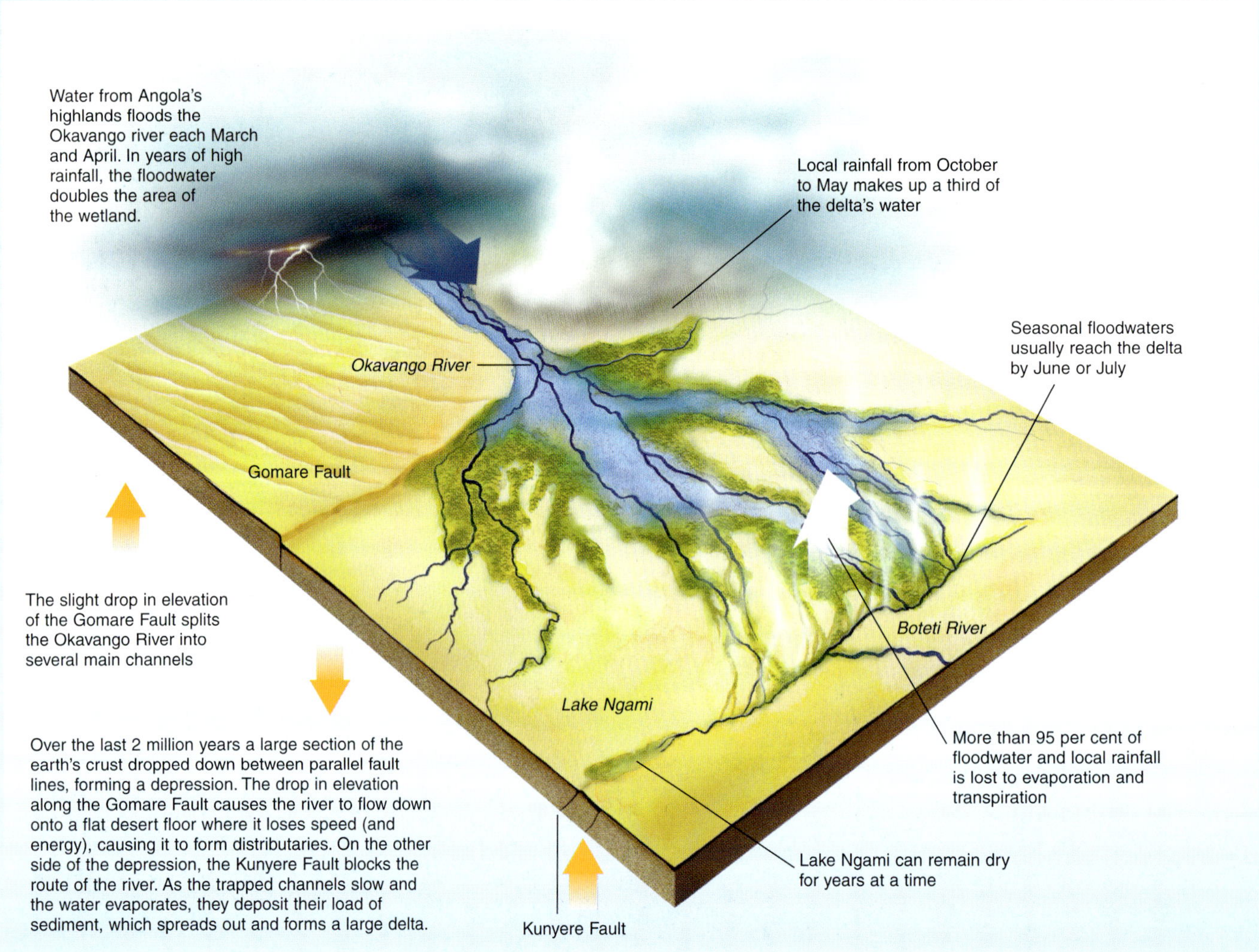

Figure 10.4e How the Okavango Delta was formed.

The people of the Okavango

Five ethnic communities—the Bugakwe, Dxeriku, Hambukushu, Wayeyi and Xanekwe peoples—maintain a self-sufficient subsistence lifestyle within the delta. The Bugakwe and Xarekwe are hunters and gatherers. The Dxeriku, Hambukushu and Wayeyi people practise a mix of subsistence farming, fishing, hunting, collecting of wild plant foods, and cattle and goat herding.

Botswana: a developing country

When Botswana gained its independence from Britain in 1966 it was one of the poorest countries in Africa. It is now one of the continent's wealthiest. The government of Botswana is keen to promote economic development. It especially wants to promote ecotourism (sustainable tourism) as a means of reducing its dependence on diamond mining, which currently accounts for 80 per cent of the country's foreign income. It also has plans to use funds from the European Union and Japan to develop its water resources.

Water schemes: threats from both within and outside Botswana

The Okavango Delta was generally regarded as a useless swamp until about thirty years ago. Since then, various plans have been put forward to drain the water and put it to use in a country where water supplies are very scarce. The government of Botswana has also been very keen to increase the area of farmland in Botswana because the country has a fast-growing population and a shortage of good agricultural land. The first investigations into how parts of the delta could be drained were made in the late 1980s. But conservationists, angered at the possible loss of the wetlands, put international pressure on the Botswana Government. The government agreed not to undertake any drainage schemes until the environmental impact was fully investigated. There have also been pressures to use the water in the Okavango to supply surrounding towns and a nearby diamond mine. At present, these pressures are being resisted.

Botswana's neighbour, Namibia, is short of water. One solution being put forward is to build a 250 kilometre long pipeline from the Okavango River to a large reservoir at Windhoek.

Figure 10.4f outlines some of the reactions to Namibia's proposal to divert part of the Okavango River's flow.

Ecotourism

The fastest-expanding industry in the Okavango is **ecotourism**. It accounts for half the region's employment. Tourism brings in much-needed income, while at the same time providing an incentive to maintain the Okavango wetlands. But any tourist development will have some impact on the environment. There are a growing number of luxury camps, safari lodges and specialist fishing camps in the region (see Figures 10.4g to 10.4i, p. 222).

Tourism in the Okavango targets the well-off traveller from developed countries, such as Britain and Germany. Many of the lodges and luxury camps are set in spectacular sites near the water or overlooking areas where animals are often seen. Tourists mostly buy package deals of accommodation, safari drives, boating expeditions and meals. Despite the high cost of these, the number of tourists is continuing to increase, and the management of numbers has already become a problem for the Botswana Government.

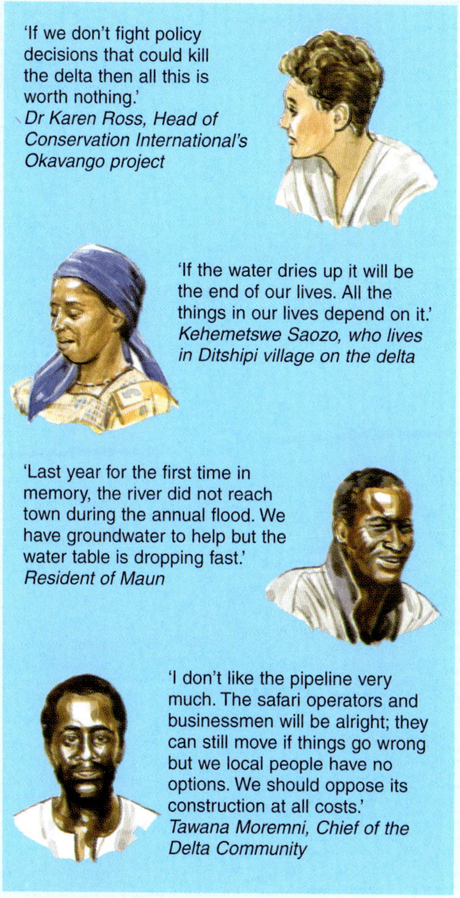

Figure 10.4f Views from Botswana.

Activity 2

1. **Using atlas maps** Study Figure 10.4a (p. 219). Use an atlas to locate Botswana and the Okavango Delta. Write a paragraph describing the location of Botswana in Africa and the Okavango Delta in Botswana.
2. **Interpreting maps** Study Figure 10.4a (p. 219), then complete the following tasks:
   a. Use a dictionary to find the meaning of the terms 'perennial' and 'seasonal'.
   b. What evidence is there to show that river flow varies throughout the year in the delta? What does this suggest about rainfall?
   c. How can you tell that the area mapped was once much wetter?

Figure 10.4g Ecotourism is vital to the future of both Botswana and the Okavango.

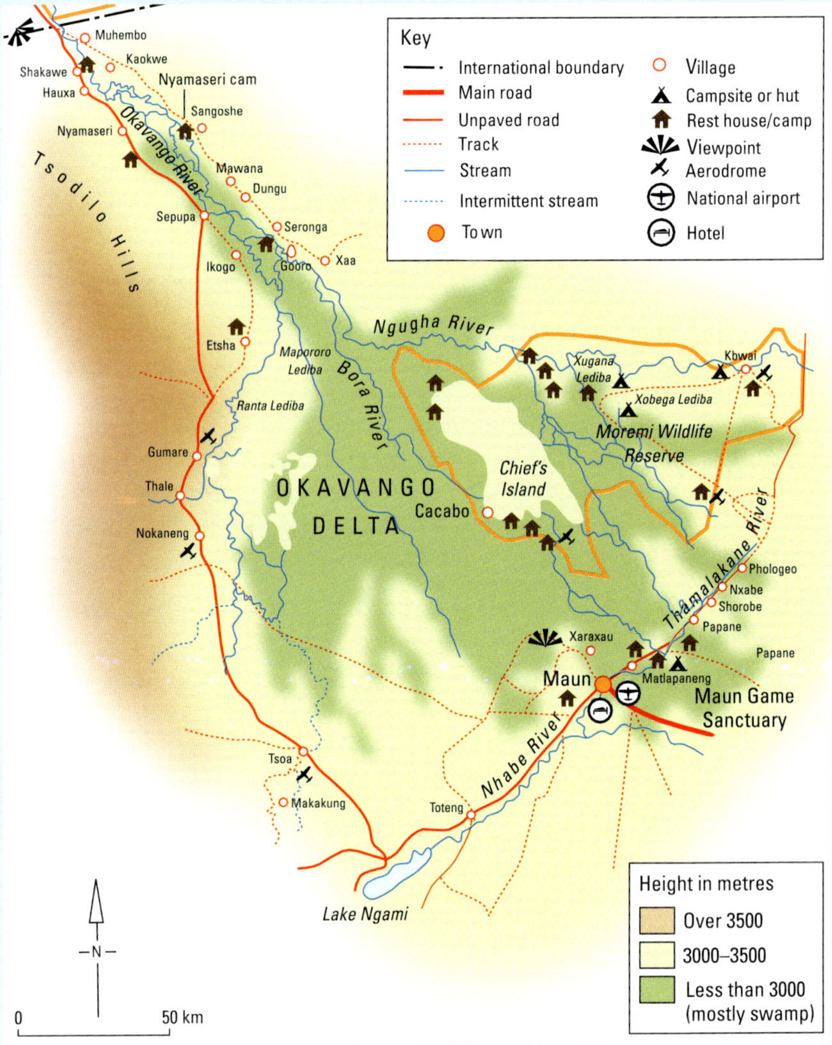

Figure 10.4h Tourism-related developments within the Okavango Delta.

Managing the wetlands

The Moremi Wildlife Reserve (see Figure 10.4h) is the centrepiece of the Okavango Delta. It is the only protected part of the wetlands area. Like other protected areas carved out of larger regions, it suffers from having boundaries that don't take into account environmental considerations and the effects of what happens outside them.

It was declared a reserve in 1963 and has been expanded since then. It contains examples of all the major types of landscapes of the Okavango: savanna woodlands (tall grass with scattered trees), flood plains, reed beds, forests and permanent swamps.

There are a number of tourist lodges on the edges of the Moremi Wildlife Reserve. Part of the management strategy is to limit their location to areas near the edges of the reserve. Tourists are encouraged to take the package deals for accommodation and sightseeing so that there are controls on where they travel.

To limit the number of tourists and the damage to the environment they cause, the management of the wildlife reserve has increased the cost of entering the reserve. This does not seem to have had the desired effect, and instead has shifted the environmental problems elsewhere. Small operators offer tourists trips to areas outside the wildlife reserve: areas that are not under any control and cannot be policed by park authorities.

Understanding the text

1. Describe the landscape of the Okavango Delta.
2. Describe the lifestyle led by the ethnic communities living in the Okavango Delta.
3. Explain how people's views about the Okavango have changed over the last thirty years.
4. Outline the advantages and problems that tourism has brought to the Okavango.
5. Outline the management strategies used in the Moremi Wildlife Reserve. How successful have they been?

UTT worksheet 10.4

Figure 10.4i Tourists on safari in Botswana's Okavango Delta.

Extension worksheet 10.3

Working geographically

1 **Interpreting photographs** Study the photographs in this unit. Write a paragraph describing the physical environment of the Okavango.

2 **Interpreting block diagrams** Study Figure 10.4e (p. 220), then complete the following tasks:

- **a** Explain why the Okavango River splits into distributaries at the Gomare Fault.
- **b** Why does the river deposit its sediment on the flood plain?
- **c** List the sources and the time of year that the Okavango Delta receives water from the following.
  - **i** rainfall
  - **ii** river flow
- **d** Explain why more than 95 per cent of water entering the delta disappears.

3 **Letter writing** Read Figure 10.4f (p. 221), which outlines the views of some people in Botswana regarding Namibia's plans to divert part of the Okavango River's flow. Write a letter or email to the government of Namibia explaining how the proposal may affect the Delta and its people.

4 **Group work: Class debate** Study the range of views expressed in Figure 10.4f (p. 221). In groups, list the arguments for and against plans to drain parts of the Okavango to increase the amount of land available for farming, and Namibia's plan to divert water from the Okavango River. Conduct a class debate. Topic: Exploiting the waters of the Okavango Delta is the price we have to pay for progress.

5 **Writing task: Using software** Study Figures 10.4g and 10.4h. Imagine you are a writer for a travel magazine. You take a guided trip down the Okavango River from Nyamaseri Camp to Chief's Island. Make notes and then write up your travels. Include reference to distance, direction and sights, smells and feelings you may experience. Use desktop publishing software to present your work as a newspaper article. Include at least one copyrifht-free photograph sourced from the Internet.

6 **Challenge: Group work** In groups, brainstorm how you think the Okavango Delta should be managed in the twenty-first century. Share the key points raised in your group's discussion with the rest of the class.

7 **Challenge: Internet research** Using the Internet and information obtained from your local travel agent, plan a holiday to the Okavango Delta. As part of your planning, find out how you would get there, the cost of travel and accommodation, the activities you can participate in while there, the best time of year to go, the climate at that time of year and what you need to take with you. Present your information as a desktop published travel brochure.

8 **Challenge: Group work** An important difference between the Everglades and the Okavango Delta is their location relative to highly populated areas. The Everglades marshland is very close to large cities, such as Miami, whereas the Okavango is surrounded by a sparsely populated area. Work in groups to complete the following tasks:

- **a** Discuss the advantages and disadvantages of each of these locations for tourism, the management of the environment and pressure for other uses.
- **b** Suggest how the difference in distance to large cities has created differences in the way tourism operates in these two areas.

10.5 Review and reflect

Chapter summary

Wetlands are now recognised as one of the earth's most important environmental resources. Given their importance, they need to be managed carefully. If this can be achieved, the benefits wetlands provide will continue into the future. The Everglades of Florida and the Okavango Delta of Botswana enable us to contrast the ways people in the developed and developing worlds interact with and manage wetland ecosystems.

Activity 1

Hypothetical: You be the judge

A developer wishes to construct a large resort on land now partly occupied by a freshwater wetland. The resort will include a hotel, golf course, marina and housing estate, and will create 300 new jobs in the local community, which has high levels of youth unemployment. Local environment groups object to the development on the grounds that it will destroy a valuable wetland ecosystem. They are using the legal system to achieve their objectives. You are a judge of the Land and Environment Court. Will you allow the development to go ahead?

Read the statements below, then complete the following tasks:

1. List the statements that are in favour of building the resort and its facilities. Then list the statements that are not in favour of it going ahead.
2. Which set of views do you agree with? Why?
3. In small groups, discuss the statements about the proposed development. Reach agreement on what you think should happen. Be prepared to defend your group's viewpoint when you report to the class.
4. Examine both sides. Have the people on each side of the discussion in activity 3 present the case for the other side, using exact arguments.
5. Conduct a class debate. Topic: The resort should go ahead.

Activity 2

Interpreting topographic maps

Study the Cairns topographic map extract opposite, then complete the following tasks:

1. What type of wetland ecosystem lines Trinity Inlet and Smiths Creek in the southwest quadrant of the topographic map extract?
2. What type of vegetation is found in the area between Murray Prior Range and Grant Hill (AR8428)?
3. Identify the feature of they physical environment found at each of the following grid references.
   a 822327 **b** 847284
   c 773278 **d** 880322
   e 773341 **f** 741295
4. Identify the feature of the built environment found at each of the following grid references.
   a 790312 **b** 803276
   c 744306 **d** 802278
5. What is the direction of Rocky Island (AR8232) from the summit of Mount Murray Prior (AR7727)?
6. What is the difference in elevation between Mount Murray Prior (AR7727) and Grant Hill (AR8428)?
7. What is the aspect of Oombunghi Beach in the southeast quadrant of the map extract?
8. Estimate the area of Admirality Island.
9. What is the density of buildings in AR8123?
10. Name the landuse activity found in:
    a AR7327 **b** AR8123.
11. What is the density of buildings in AR8123?

SCALE 1:100 000
CONTOUR INTERVAL 20 METRES
kilometres
0 1 2 3 4 5
LEGEND
Built-up area; Divided highway; Metropolitan route marker
Recreation reserve with oval; Drive-in theatre; Underpass
Sealed road two or more lanes
Sealed road one lane; Cutting; Embankment
Unsealed road one lane; Approximate position (AP)
Vehicle track; Road bridge; Gate; Stock grid
Foot track; Foot bridge
Administrative boundary
Mine; Building; Ruin; Church; Windpump; Yard
Fence; Horizontal control point; Spot elevation
Contour with value; Supplementary contour
Depression contour; Sand ; Distorted surface
Levee; Sand ridge
High cliff; Escarpment
Vegetation; Dense; medium; scattered
Rain forest; Pine
Watercourse with flood limits; Area subject to inundation
Swamp; Swamp definite boundary
Perennial lake; Watercourse
Tank or small dam; Waterhole
Saline coastal flat; Intertidal flat; Rock bare or awash
Navigation light; Intertidal ;edge or reef
Exposed wreck; Submerged wreck
Submerged reef; Submerged rock
Indefinite watercourse; Shoreline; Mangrove swamp
Cape Grafton
False Cape
MISSION BAY
WIDE BAY
PORT OF CAIRNS
CAIRNS HARBOUR
Rocky Island (ABORIGINAL LAND)
Palm Beach
Bullburra Beach
Yarrabah Beach
Gribble Point
Lyons Point
Sturt Cove
Bessie Point
Giangurra
Turtle Bay
Deception Point
King Beach
Oombunghi Beach
Oombunghi
YARRABAH ABORIGINAL LAND
Yarrabah Aboriginal Community
MOUNT YARRABAH 630
GRANT HILL 399
MURRAY PRIOR RANGE
MOUNT MURRAY PRIOR 774
MOUNT GORTON 798
NISBET RANGE
MAY PEAK 832
STATE FOREST
Kieta Estate
Amaroo Gardens
Timbertop
Admiralty Island
TRINITY INLET
Stafford Point
Smiths Creek
Koombal
Coolibah
Bessie Falls
sugarcane

Chapter 11

Coral reefs

Introduction

Coral reefs are one of the most important ecosystems in the world. They are very diverse—they are the home to huge numbers of amazing plants and animals. Many scientists refer to them as the 'tropical rainforests' of the sea because of their biodiversity. Although coral reefs cover less than 1 per cent of the earth's surface, over 25 per cent of fish species live in, or close to, coral reefs. Coral reefs are very fragile ecosystems; even small changes in the environment can cause widespread destruction. This means that the reefs must be managed carefully if they are to survive for the benefit of future generations.

In this chapter we investigate the geographical processes that form and transform coral reefs. We also look at how the communities of coastal Queensland and the Caribbean interact with and manage these environments.

Key questions

1. What are the geographical processes that form and transform coral reefs?
2. Why are coral reefs such fragile environments?
3. How do the activities of people in Queensland and the Caribbean affect coral reefs?
4. How can we protect coral reefs?

Finding Nemo

Finding Nemo, the computer-generated animated film, is one of the most successful movies of all time. Produced by Pixar Animation Studios (the creators of *Toy Story*, *A Bug's Life* and *Monsters Inc*.) for Disney Pictures, the film centres on the adventures of Nemo, a clown fish.

Clown fish are bright orange with distinctive white stripes. They are found in the Red Sea and tropical Pacific Ocean and on Australia's Great Barrier Reef, where they live on the ocean floor in a very close relationship with the anemone.

The clown fish, which is unaffected by the anemone's poison, lets the anemone kill other fish first, and then eats the leftovers. It also eats plankton, shellfish and dead tentacles of the anemone. Of the 1000 species of anemone, only ten act as a host for the clown fish.

There are twenty-eight species of true clown fish, which has few predators. The largest threat comes from humans who try to catch clown fish in order to keep them as pets in fish tanks.

Glossary of key terms

Biodiversity Biological diversity. The variety of different species of plants and animals in an ecosystem.

Cnidarians The group of invertebrates that include coral polyps and anemones.

Continental shelf The area of relatively shallow, submerged land surrounding the earth's continents. Beyond this lies the deeper waters of the world's oceans.

Coral Material formed from the hard outer skeletons of animals called coral polyps.

Deforestation The removal of natural vegetation.

Fragile ecosystem An ecosystem in which even small changes can have a major impact.

Infrastructure Features of the human environment that allow a community to function, such as roads, public transport, airports, bridges, sewers, water supply, schools and hospitals.

Interdependence The relationship that exists between elements of the physical and human environments; for example, the relationship between plants and animals.

Larvae An early stage in the development of an animal.

Photosynthesis The production of food in plants using the radiant energy of the sun.

Plates Large, mobile sections of the earth's crust.

Polyps Primitive organisms that build coral reefs.

Sedimentation The deposition of sediment that occurs when water velocity (speed) decreases.

Sustainable development Development that will not affect the ability of future generations to meet their own needs.

Symbiotic A relationship beneficial to two organisms.

Turbidity The muddiness of water.

Zooxanthellae A specialised type of algae that lives in the body tissue of a coral polyp.

cd eGlossary

cd GeoToolkit

cd ICT Toolkit

11.1 Coral reef environments

Figure 11.1a Coral reefs are the most spectacular and fragile of the marine ecosystems.

Coral reefs are the most spectacular of all the marine ecosystems. Formed by massive colonies of small animals called **polyps**, coral reefs provide a home for an amazing variety of plants and animals. For their beauty alone, coral reefs are one of the earth's greatest treasures.

The geological record shows that coral reefs have existed on earth for at least 350 million years. Those that exist today started growing 50 million years ago. Most established reefs are between 5000 and 10 000 years old.

Importance of coral reefs

Coral reefs cover less than 1 per cent of the ocean floor, but are one of the earth's most productive ecosystems (see Table 11.1a). They support at least one-third of all fish species.

Reefs also help to support life on land. They provide the foundations on which thousands of islands have formed and they give a protective barrier against storm waves. They also support the fishing and tourism industries, which provide food, jobs and income for some of the world's poorest countries.

Reef organisms also produce chemicals useful for the treatment of cancer and AIDS. Australian scientists have used chemicals produced by corals to develop sunscreens.

Table 11.1a The productivity of selected ecosystems

Ecosystem	Productivity* (grams)
Coral reefs	2500
Tropical forests	2200
Temperate forests	1250
Savanna grasslands	900
Cultivated land	650
Open ocean	125
Semi-desert	90

*The amount of plant material produced per square metre per year

Threats to coral reefs

Coral reefs grow very slowly and are easily disrupted by even small changes in their environment. Because of this, they are called **fragile ecosystems**. In many parts of the world, coral reefs are under pressure from the activities of people. The main threat to coral reefs is the

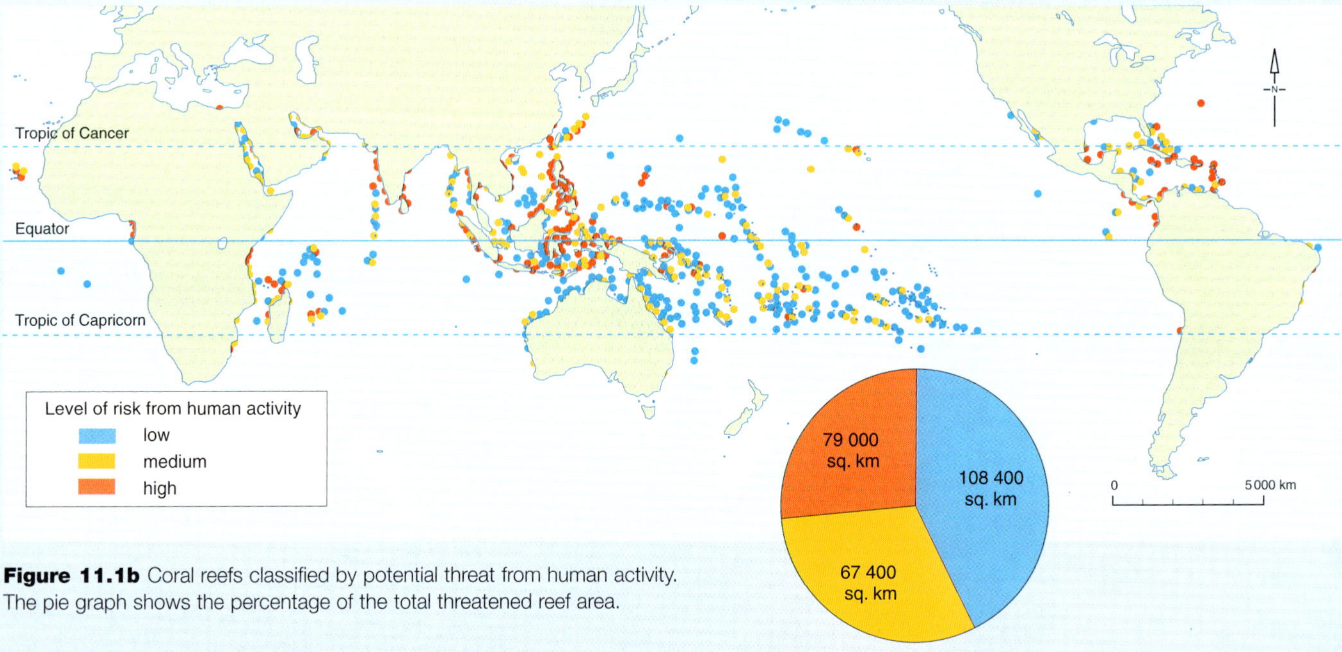

Figure 11.1b Coral reefs classified by potential threat from human activity. The pie graph shows the percentage of the total threatened reef area.

deposition of eroded soil caused by **deforestation**, construction, agriculture, mining, dredging and poor land management along an increasingly crowded coastline. The sediment that washes down rivers and into the sea smothers coral polyps or blocks their sunlight.

Other threats include chemical pollution, oil spills, mining of the **coral** (limestone) for building, damage caused by tourists and recreational divers and nutrient-rich runoff from fertilised fields and sewage treatment plants. There is also a fear that global warming (see Unit 16.3) could destroy what remains of these unique ecosystems.

Scientists estimate that humans have directly or indirectly caused the death of 10 per cent of the world's coral reefs (especially those in Southeast Asia and the Caribbean). Another 30 per cent are in a critical condition, and 30 per cent are threatened. Only 30 per cent remain unaffected. In Indonesia, 86 per cent of coral reefs have been severely damaged by overfishing, **sedimentation** and pollution. Unless people act now to protect the world's coral reefs, another part of the earth's vital **biodiversity** will be greatly reduced. Unlike rainforests, there has been little publicity given to the plight of these important ecosystems.

Location of coral reefs

Worldwide, coral reefs cover an estimated 284 300 square kilometres. The location and distribution of these reefs is determined by the special conditions needed for the survival of reef-building corals. These special conditions include:

- *water temperature*—Coral reefs will only develop in waters warmer than 18°C and they grow fastest in waters around 26°C. The upper limit is about 29°C. If temperatures are sustained at 32°C for a period of time then coral bleaching will occur.
- *sunlight*—Although corals have been found to a depth of 100 metres in clear ocean water, they are more commonly found in waters less than 50 metres deep.

Coral reefs are therefore limited to the clear, shallow tropical seas found on either side of the Equator. These are the same latitudes in which the earth's tropical rainforests are found.

Two additional factors are important in areas close to the shoreline:

- *water clarity*—The sediments that rivers transport to the sea cloud coastal waters and may smother corals and destroy coral reefs.
- *salinity levels*—Corals need levels of salinity close to those found in the open ocean. They cannot develop in waters that receive freshwater runoff.

For these reasons, coral reefs are rarely found near the mouths of large river systems.

Investigating coral reefs

ICT

Use the Internet to gather information about coral reefs. A good place to start is the website of the Great Barrier Reef Marine Park Authority. You will find the authority's multimedia site to be especially useful. Other useful websites include:

- the Department of the Environment and Heritage
- Jean-Michel Cousteau's Ocean Futures Society
- International Coral Reef Information Network

In groups, select one of the sites listed above. Investigate the site and list the types of information available on the site. Share your findings with the rest of the class.

Understanding the text

1. What are coral reefs formed by?
2. Explain why coral reefs are so special.
3. Why are coral reef ecosystems described as being fragile?
4. Outline the threats to coral reef ecosystems.
5. Describe the state of the world's coral reefs.
6. Outline the conditions under which coral reefs may develop.
7. Why are coral reefs not found near the mouths of large river systems?

UTT worksheet 11.1

Working geographically

1. **Challenge: Interpreting maps** Study Figure 11.1b, then complete the following tasks:
   a. With the aid of an atlas, write a paragraph describing the global distribution of coral reefs.
   b. What proportion of the world's coral reefs are at a medium to high level of risk from human activity?
   c. With the aid of an atlas, identify the parts of the world where coral reefs are at a high level of risk from human activity.
2. **Constructing graphs** Using the information in Table 11.1a, construct a column graph showing the productivity of selected ecosystems.
3. **Constructing graphs** Use the information in the section dealing with threats to coral reefs to construct a pie graph illustrating the state of the world's coral reefs.

Types of coral reefs

The distinctive landform features of the coral reef environment are shown in Figure 11.1c.

Barrier (ribbon) reefs

Barrier or ribbon reefs (see Figure 11.1c) run parallel to the shoreline but are separated from it by water. They are often found along the edge of a **continental shelf** and form a barrier between the water near the shoreline and the open sea. These barriers are rarely continuous. In many places they are broken by channels of deeper water that separate the individual reefs. Some channels are large enough to allow large ships to pass through.

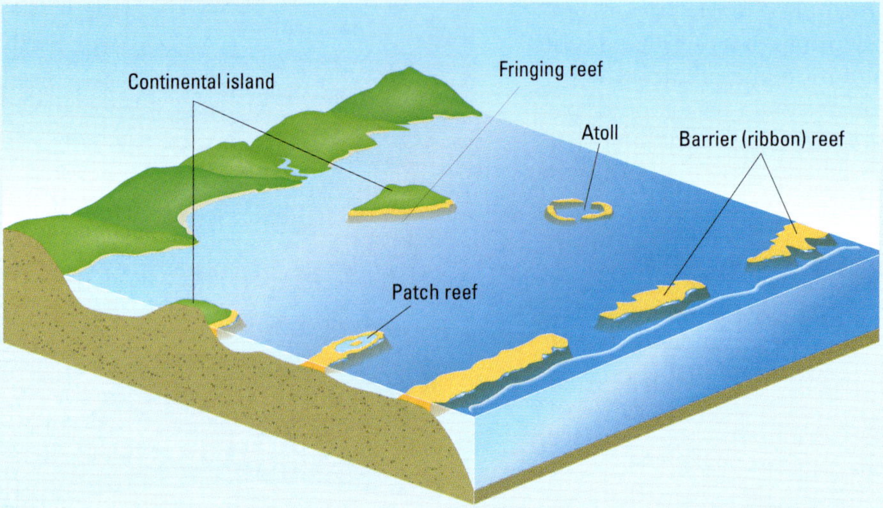

Figure 11.1c Types of coral reefs.

1 A fringing reef develops around a volcanic island.

2 As the island sinks, the coral reef widens and continues to grow upwards.

3 Eventually the island disappears completely beneath the surface, and a circular atoll encloses a shallow lagoon. The lagoon is connected to the open sea by channels of water.

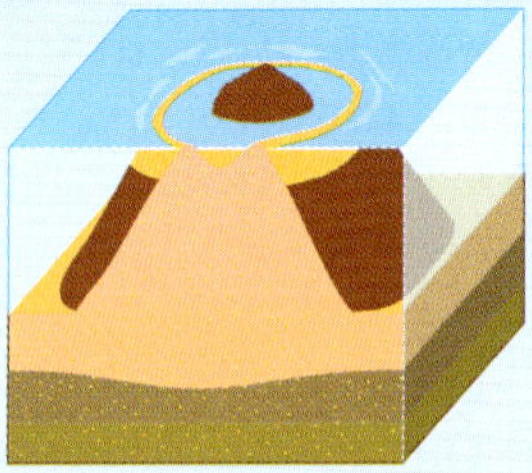

The formation of an atoll.

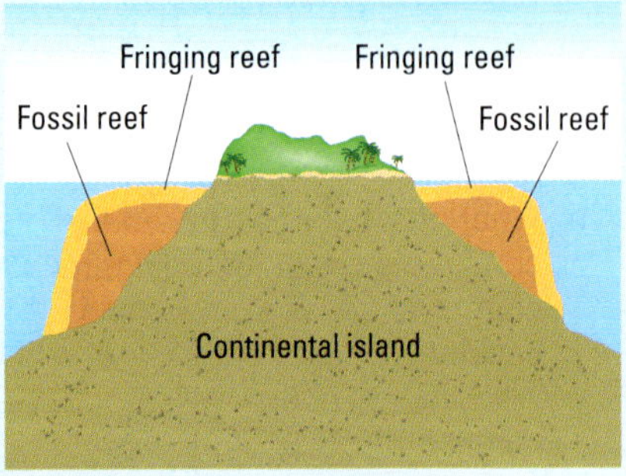

Cross-section of a fringing reef.

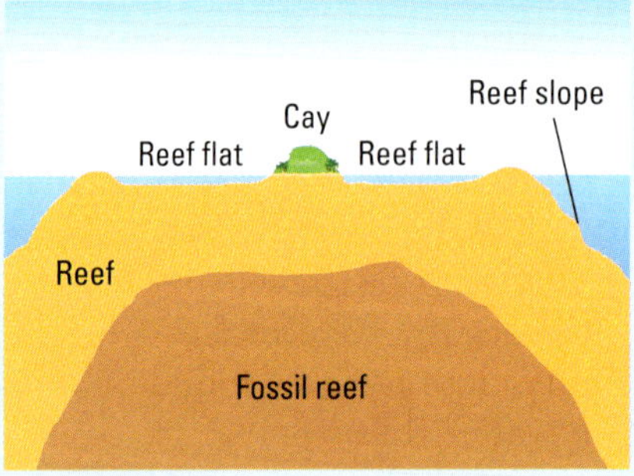

Cross-section of a patch reef and coral cay.

Coral cays

Coral cays (see Figures 11.1c and 11.1d) are low islands formed when eroded reef material is swept into a particular part of the reef by wave action. In the early stages of development, the coral cay is little more than a sandbank, changing its position and shape as weather conditions change. As it grows in size, the cay's position on the reef becomes more stable and there are fewer changes to its shape.

Birds nest on developing cays and introduce the seeds of plants, either in their droppings or attached to their feathers. As the plants grow, they stabilise the sandy surface and add decaying plant matter to the soil. Gradually, a soil able to support larger plants develops.

On some of the larger cays a small natural reservoir of fresh groundwater may form beneath the cay. This enables even larger plants, particularly trees, to grow. Coral cays are sometimes swept away during tropical cyclones.

Patch reefs

Patch reefs (see Figures 11.1c and 11.1d) develop in areas of clear, shallow water. They are generally oval in shape and grow outwards. Some patch reefs have shallow lagoons in the centre and some support small coral cays.

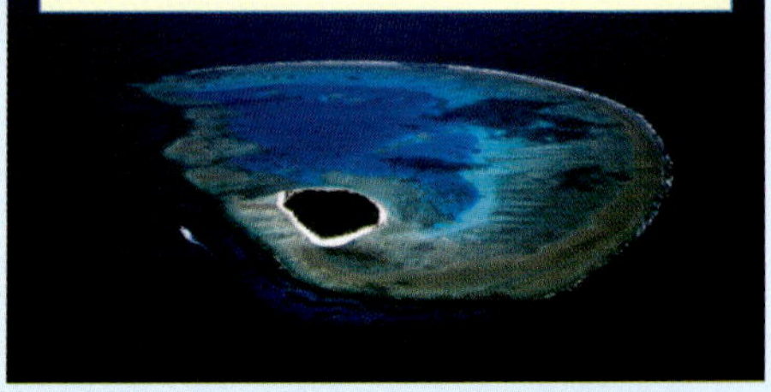

Figure 11.1d A patch reef and coral cay, Great Barrier Reef, Australia.

Atolls

Atolls are ring-shaped coral islands found in the open ocean (see Figure 11.1e). They are formed when coral builds up on a rim of the crater of a sunken volcano (see Figure 11.1c). Atolls enclose a body of water called a lagoon, which is connected by one or more channels to the open sea. Many of the islands of the South Pacific are atolls.

Figure 11.1e Kayangel atoll, Palau Islands, Micronesia.

Fringing reefs

Fringing reefs are coral formations linked to the mainland or to continental islands. Those surrounding continental islands (see Figures 11.1c and 11.1f) are usually the most spectacular. The conditions for coral growth are better there than near the mainland. The water is much clearer because it is less affected by the quality of water flowing from continental areas.

The greatest variety of corals and other reef organisms is found on the reef slopes rather than on the more extensive reef flats.

Figure 11.1f Fringing reef at Hook Island, Great Barrier Reef, Australia.

Foundation worksheet 11.1

Extension worksheet 11.1

Understanding the text

1 List the different types of coral reefs.
2 Where are barrier and ribbon reefs found?
3 Where do patch reefs develop?
4 Why are the fringing reefs surrounding continental areas more spectacular than those attached to the mainland?
5 Explain how atolls are formed.
6 Describe how the more complex types of vegetation develop on coral cays.
7 Explain how coral cays form.

UTT worksheet 11.1

Working geographically

1 **Constructing diagrams** Draw a block diagram illustrating the types of coral reefs described in this unit.

2 **Photo sketching** Construct a photo sketch of Figure 11.1f (see Unit 2.9). Label the key features of the physical environment.

3 **Building models** Construct a model of a coral cay or coral atoll.

4 **Challenge: Internet research** Use the Internet to collect information on coral reefs around the world. Draw up a three-column table with the following headings:
- location of coral reef
- main features/description of coral reef
- main threats to coral reef

Complete the table in order to compare the coral reefs you have researched.

11.2 Life on the reef

Figure 11.2a Coral reefs support a great diversity of life forms.

The coral reef ecosystem

Coral reefs support a large community of plants and animals that have a high level of **interdependence**. For this reason, they are often compared to the earth's tropical rainforests. Unlike the rainforests, coral reefs have fewer highly localised species; most species can be found on reefs throughout the world.

Coral reefs are built by millions of tiny animals called polyps, which form enormous colonies (see Figures 11.2b and 11.2c). The polyps are primitive organisms that largely consist of a digestive sac or stomach and a skeleton of calcium carbonate (limestone). Surrounding the animal's mouth is a ring of tentacles that pulls in food from the seawater. The coral polyps get their brilliant colours from **zooxanthellae** (pronounced zoe-zan-THELL-ee), which is a special type of algae that lives in the body tissue of the polyp. The polyps and the algae have a **symbiotic** relationship; that is, they have a relationship that benefits both of them. The polyps provide the algae with nutrients (food). The algae supply the polyps with sugars and oxygen, the products of **photosynthesis**, which help the polyps to grow at a faster rate. Some coral polyp species receive more than 60 per cent of their food from algae.

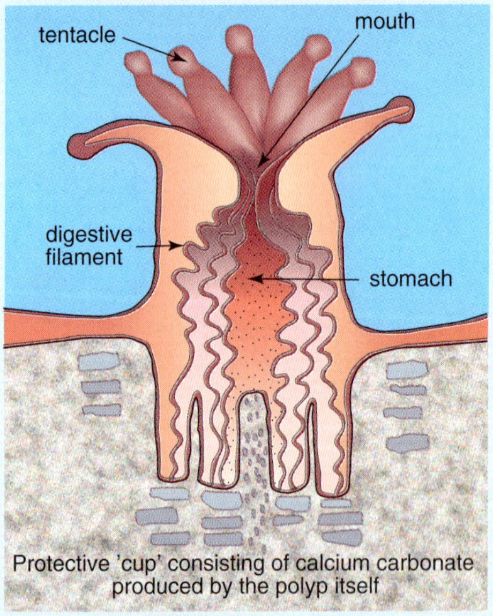

Figure 11.2b Cross-section of a coral polyp.

Formation of colonies

Each coral colony begins life as a single polyp, which then reproduces itself by budding or by dividing. Budding happens when the parent forms an outgrowth, which is a smaller copy of itself. As the polyps multiply, the reef expands upwards and outwards. When the polyps die, their limestone skeletons remain as a platform for more reef growth. Some of the common types of coral formations or colonies are shown in Figure 11.2c.

The rate at which corals grow varies depending on water temperature, salinity, oxygen level, the amount of turbulence and the availability of food. The massive corals are among the slowest-growing species, adding between 5 and 25 millimetres a year. Branching colonies can grow much faster, adding as much as 20 centimetres to their branches each year.

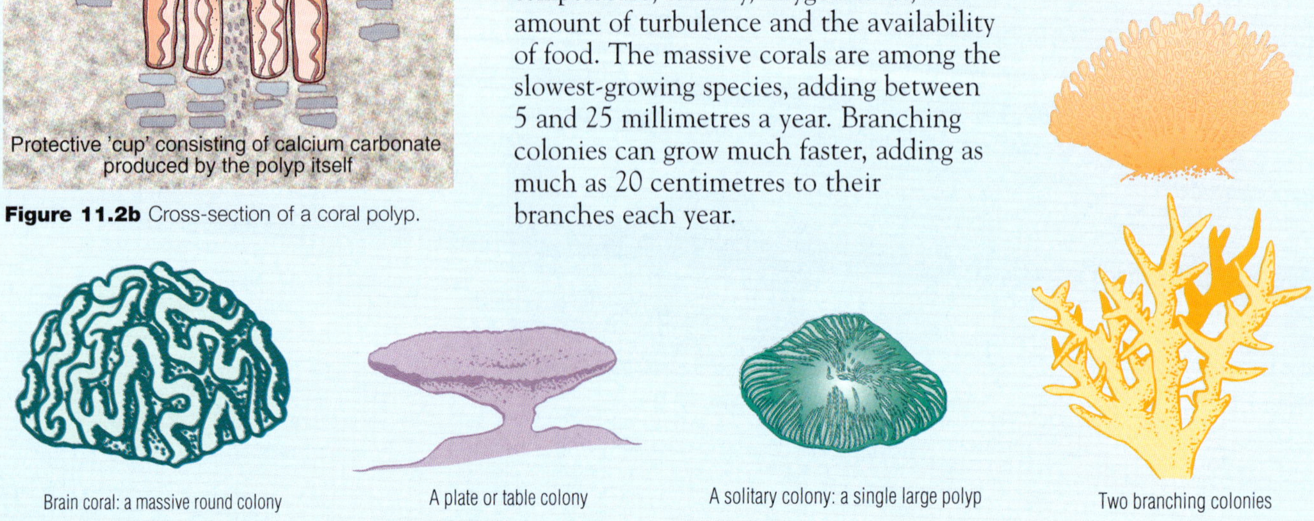

Figure 11.2c Coral polyps and colonies.

Reproduction

Corals reproduce in a way that is unique in the animal kingdom. Every year in late spring or early summer, as the waters of the reef begin to warm, the corals release their eggs and sperm in a spectacular synchronised event (see Figure 11.2d). The eggs that are fertilised by sperm begin to divide rapidly, forming **larvae**. Some of these larvae will settle on the reef where they develop into new polyps. As they do, they start to build their own limestone skeleton. This is the beginning of a new coral colony.

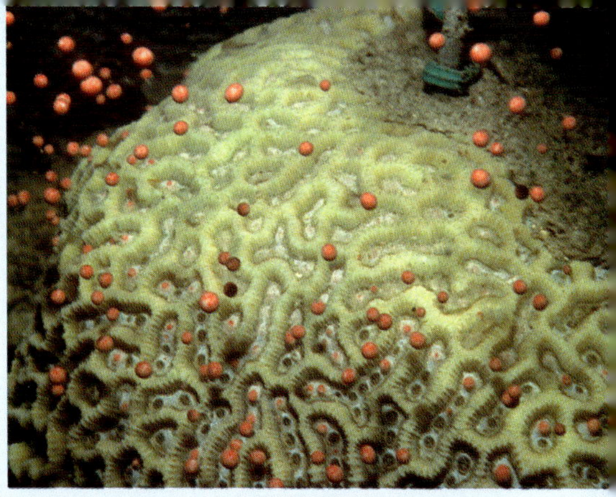

Figure 11.2d Coral spawning.

Biodiversity

A coral reef's biological diversity (variety of life forms) includes thousands of different species of fish attracted by the rich supply of food (see Figure 11.2a). Some fish feed on the tiny marine animals washed in from the open sea, while others graze on the reefs themselves—eating algae and the living coral polyps. Sharks and other large predator fish, at the end of the food chain, eat smaller fish. Other animals that make their home on coral reefs include giant clams, sea turtles (see Figure 11.2m, p. 235) and marine mammals, such as dolphins and whales (see Figure 11.2k, p. 234).

Animals of the coral reef

The world's coral reefs are teeming with animal life. Unlike plants, which make their own food, these animals have to find their own food. The ways they do this are truly amazing.

Cnidarians

Cnidarians are invertebrates (animals without backbones). There are two basic types of cnidarians: those that move around and those that do not:

- Coral polyps and anemones (see Figure 11.2e), which cannot move around, spend their life attached to rocks or, in some cases, other animals.
- Jellyfish are propelled by ocean currents and a pumping action that allows them to move up and down. Most jellyfish are predators. Some have poisonous venom that paralyses prey, while others use their tentacles to trap prey (see Figure 11.2f).

All cnidarians have stinging cells, which they use for defence and to catch prey. Anemones, which can be quite large and brightly coloured, use their stinging cells to paralyse their food (fish, crabs and other invertebrates).

Figure 11.2e Anemones are large, brightly coloured creatures that use poison to paralyse their prey.

Crustaceans

Crustaceans (invertebrates with jointed legs) include prawns, crabs (see Figure 11.2g, p. 234) and lobsters. Most have hard shells and powerful claws, which they use to catch and crush their prey.

Molluscs

Molluscs (soft-bodied animals) include sea slugs, octopuses and clams. Some molluscs (including sea slugs) use poisons for defence, while others (including clams) have a hard, protective shell. Octopuses (see Figure 11.2h, p. 234) release a dark, ink-like substance as a form of defence, and one species —the blue-ringed octopus—has a deadly poison for which there is no known antidote.

The box jellyfish

ICT

The box jellyfish, which lives in the shallow coastal waters of northern Australia, is one of the world's most dangerous (and sometimes deadly) marine animals.

Using the ThinkQuest, list the precautions you should take to avoid being stung and the actions you can take if you are stung.

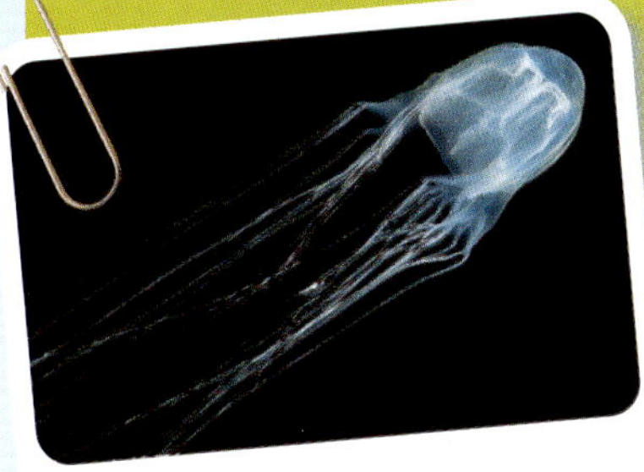

Figure 11.2f The box jellyfish.

Figure 11.2g The hermit crab is a crustacean: an invertebrate with jointed legs.

Figure 11.2h The octopus is a mollusc.

Figure 11.2i In plague numbers, the crown-of-thorns starfish can devastate whole reefs.

Echinoderms

All echinoderms have three distinguishing characteristics: tube feet, a body divided into parts and an armour-like skeleton of plates. Examples include starfish and sea urchins. The coral-eating crown-of-thorns starfish (see Figure 11.2i), which can grow to 80 centimetres long and can have up to twenty-one arms, can have a devastating impact on coral reefs if their numbers suddenly increase.

Fish

Thousands of fish species of all sizes, colours and shapes live on the world's coral reefs. Some of the most spectacular are the clown fish and blue tang of *Finding Nemo* fame, the parrotfish, and the sea horse (see Figure 11.2j). Sharks and stingrays are at the top of the coral reef food chain. Most of the sharks on the reef are fish eaters and, therefore, don't pose a threat to swimmers. The most common species are white tip reef sharks and black tip reef sharks.

Figure 11.2j Sea horses are among the world's most amazing creatures. The male is the one that gets pregnant. The female deposits its eggs into the male's pouch, where they are fertilised.

Figure 11.2k The skin of whales is very sensitive and smooth. Under the skin, a thick layer of blubber insulates the whale against the cold.

Mammals

Mammals are warm-blooded animals. Marine mammals (including whales, dolphins and the dugong) must surface to breathe. Whales travel to the warmer waters of the tropics to breed during the cold polar winters (see Figure 11.2k).

The dugong (see Figure 11.2l) is a herbivore. It grazes on sea grass, which it locates with the sensitive bristles that cover its upper lip.

Reptiles

Reptiles have scales covering their bodies and lay soft, leathery eggs. Turtles are one of the most common reptiles found on coral reefs (see Figure 11.2m). Each summer, female turtles leave the sea and bury several batches of eggs. They then return to the sea. Once they hatch, the baby turtles dig their way out of the nest and head towards the sea. Many don't survive because they are eaten by crabs, gulls, fish, sharks and crocodiles. Only a few survive to adulthood.

Figure 11.2m A green sea turtle.

Figure 11.2l Dugongs can grow to 3 metres in length and can weigh up to 400 kilograms.

Understanding the text

1. Explain why coral reefs are sometimes compared to the world's tropical rainforests. In what way are they different?
2. What builds coral reefs?
3. Describe the coral polyp.
4. What is a symbiotic relationship? Describe the relationship that exists between coral polyps and algae.
5. How are coral colonies formed?
6. Outline the unique way corals reproduce.
7. Describe the food chain of the reef ecosystem.

UTT worksheet 11.2

Working geographically

1. **Sketching** Draw a sketch of the different types of coral, using Figure 11.2c (p. 232) as a guide.
2. **Challenge: Writing task** Write a report describing the coral reef ecosystem (see Unit 2.15).
3. **Research: Oral report** Select one of the animals pictured in this unit and prepare a short, research-based oral report (see Unit 2.14). In your presentation, make reference to the animal's physical appearance, habitat, unique characteristics and place within the food chain.
4. **Constructing a food chain** Use the information contained in the text to construct a simple food chain of reef organisms (see Unit 5.5).

Foundation worksheet 11.2

Extension worksheet 11.2

11.3 Threats to coral reef ecosystems

Figure 11.3a A Greenpeace activist takes a look at the worst coral bleaching ever reported on the Great Barrier Reef. The death of the coral coincided with Australia's hottest January–March on record: 1998.

The conditions required for the growth of reef-building corals give us important clues about possible threats to these ecosystems and how they can be protected and managed.

Runoff

The quality of the water flowing from the land is critical to the health of coral reef ecosystems. The reefs closest to the mainland are the most easily damaged by human activities. The landuse activities of people in coastal river catchments can increase levels of freshwater runoff and the build-up of silt. As more land is cleared of its protective layer of natural vegetation, runoff increases and more soil is eroded (see Figure 11.3b). Agricultural fertilisers, sewage and other pollutants are often part of stormwater runoff and can have a direct impact on reefs. They encourage the growth of algae that cloud the water, reducing the amount of sunlight reaching the corals.

Because coral reefs are found in the same latitudes as tropical rainforests, the destruction of these forests often affects coral reef ecosystems. When the forest is cut down, the soils are exposed to the high levels of rainfall that occur in these areas. Large quantities of topsoil are washed into river systems and flushed into the sea. This sediment clouds the water (causes **turbidity**) and may eventually settle on reefs, destroying the living corals (see Figure 11.3c).

Did U know?

- Corals are very sensitive to human activity. Even the slightest touch can damage them. Some are so sensitive that the sunscreen worn by swimmers will harm them.
- Each year, 11–14 million tonnes of sediment are carried by rivers into the waters of Australia's Great Barrier Reef.

Foundation worksheet 11.2

Extension worksheet 11.3

Extension worksheet ICT 11.5

Oil spills

Many of the world's busiest shipping routes pass through coral reefs. Shipping disasters remain a constant threat. Oil spills from supertankers can destroy entire marine ecosystems. Offshore oil platforms are also a major source of pollution. Accidents, equipment failures and leaking pipelines all contribute to the problem.

Figure 11.3b Silt spreads out from the mouth of a river, smothering corals.

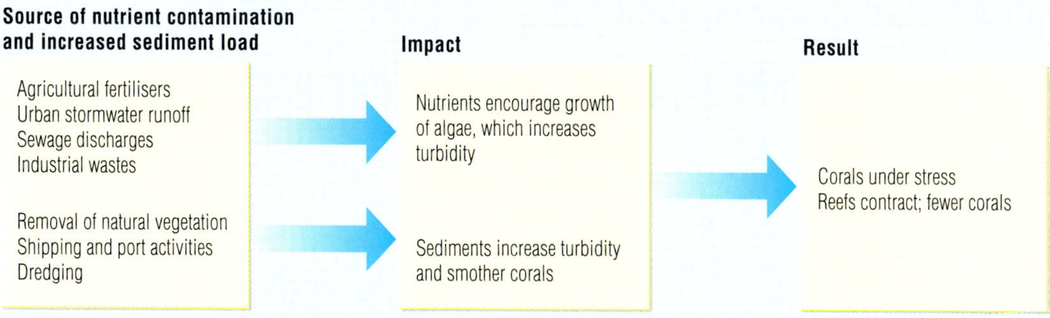

Figure 11.3c The impact of declining water quality on coral reefs.

Tourism

Coral reefs throughout the world are attracting tourists in ever-increasing numbers. While individually their impact may be small, the total impact from their sewage, anchors, walking, specimen collecting, snorkelling and diving is starting to damage or degrade some reefs.

Crown-of-thorns starfish

The crown-of thorns starfish (see Figure 11.2i, p. 234) occurs naturally on coral reefs, but usually in such small numbers that it does not represent a threat to the coral community. Occasionally, for reasons not yet fully understood, its numbers increase rapidly. Each female starfish can produce up to 60 million eggs in a single spawning season, but usually only a very small number survive. If conditions change and allow more of the larvae to survive to adulthood, there is a population explosion. When this happens the starfish can destroy large areas of coral.

The crown-of-thorns starfish is a predator. It eats living coral polyps. It feeds by pulling its stomach out through its mouth, covering the coral polyps and then digesting the flesh of the polyps, leaving only a white coral skeleton.

Global warming and coral bleaching

If global temperatures increase by 1°C or 2°C as predicted, the consequences for coral reefs could be disastrous. Corals are very sensitive to changes in water temperature. They normally thrive at temperatures between 25°C and 29°C, depending on their location. This narrow temperature range is very close to the upper lethal temperature. An increase of just a few degrees above the usual summer maximum can be deadly.

Under stress, the fragile balance between the coral polyp and its symbiotic algae is destroyed. The resulting loss of algae and algal pigment (the natural colouring of plant tissue) leaves the tissue almost transparent. Only the white calcium skeleton can be seen. The coral has been bleached.

Incidents of bleaching have increased throughout the 1980s and 1990s. During 1982–83, the waters of the eastern Pacific Ocean exceeded the seasonal average by 3°C to 4°C. As a result, between 70 and 90 per cent of corals in Panama and Costa Rica were destroyed. In the Galapagos Islands, to the southwest of Panama, the level of destruction reached 95 per cent. In the Caribbean, scientific studies have found that episodes of coral bleaching appear to be most consistently related to increased sea temperatures. The devastating impact of coral bleaching is shown in Figure 11.3a.

Understanding the text

1. Explain how human landuse activities affect the quality of water entering the sea.
2. Using the information contained in the text and in Figure 11.3c, outline the effect that pollutants are having on living corals.
3. Outline the effect that the destruction of the earth's tropical rainforests is having on coral reefs.
4. What is the crown-of-thorns starfish? How does it damage coral reefs?
5. Outline the relationship between episodes of coral bleaching and increasing global temperatures.

UTT worksheet 11.3

Working geographically

1. **Challenge: Using the media online** Using the online archives of a major newspaper, collect newspaper and magazine articles that relate to issues affecting coral reefs. Write a summary of each and develop a noticeboard display.
2. **Research** Use the library and Internet to find out about the crown-of-thorns starfish. Summarise this information in your workbook.

11.4 SAMPLE STUDY

The Caribbean: coral ecosystems under threat

Figure 11.4a The combined impact of thousands of tourists has an impact on coral reefs.

Figure 11.4b Many poor communities in the Caribbean rely on tourism for their income. For them, positive attitudes regarding the protection of the environment are a luxury they cannot afford.

In many parts of the world, coral reefs are under great stress and some have been destroyed. Most coral reefs are found in the developing parts of the world where high rates of population growth, poor environmental management, lack of resources and damaging landuse practices have degraded many reefs. The most vulnerable coral reefs are in the Caribbean. Reefs are being degraded by silt and sewage, by oil spills and by the range of activities associated with fishing and tourism.

The region's spectacular scenery—sandy beaches and clear tropical water—attract millions of tourists from many parts of the world. Many of the communities within the region now depend on tourism for their economic well-being. Any threat to the quality of the physical environment could discourage tourists and undermine the economy of many of the region's island countries.

Threats to the coral reefs of the Caribbean

Tourism

Because of their location, tropical climate and scenic beauty, it is not surprising that the islands of the Caribbean have become a popular destination for wealthy, sun-seeking holiday-makers from North America, Japan and Europe. In 2002, over 140 million tourists visited the islands of the Caribbean. They spent more than US$6.5 billion. Tourism employs half the labour force in the Bahamas, and almost a quarter in Antigua-Barbuda. The money earned from tourism is used to pay for imports and to repay debts.

Some people now argue that the environmental and social costs of this level of tourism are too high. They argue that the region should reduce its dependence on tourism. Tourism has created a demand for luxury beach hotels, resorts, marinas, golf courses, shopping malls and airports (known as **infrastructure**). Much of this development has been uncontrolled and poorly planned. It also tends to be concentrated in areas of great beauty (see Figure 11.4e, p. 240). The rapidly growing number of tourists may well destroy the sites and experiences that brought visitors to the region in the first place.

The infrastructure needed to support tourism can be expensive to build and maintain. The cost of treating sewage is one example. Because it is expensive to treat sewage wastes, they are often pumped directly into the sea, polluting beaches, reducing water clarity and gradually degrading nearby coral formations, mangroves and sea grasses.

The impact of individual tourists is small compared with other threats to the reef, but the combined impact of all tourists is large. Divers can easily damage the fragile coral formations (see Figure 11.4a), as do the anchors of cruise ships and other smaller vessels. Tourism also creates a demand for the resources of the reefs, including seafoods and coral and shell souvenirs.

The geography and people of the Caribbean

The Caribbean is a large (2.75 million square kilometre) basin occupying one of the earth's smaller **plates**: the Caribbean Plate. The edges of the basin are a chain of mountains pushed up by pressures from deep within the earth.

Most of the islands on the eastern and northern boundary are volcanic peaks pushed up from the ocean floor. Others are coral and limestone formations.

Many of these islands are among the world's poorest countries. Population densities are high and they have few natural resources on which to base their economic development.

The islands of the eastern Caribbean are known as the West Indies. The West Indies consists of three main island groups. These are the Bahamas in the north, the Greater Antilles in the centre and the Lesser Antilles in the southeast.

The Caribbean lies almost entirely within the tropics. Average temperatures are high, as is rainfall. Tropical rainforests were once common throughout the region. The destruction of these forests is a major environmental concern because it increases rates of soil erosion and runoff, and degrades water quality in nearby coastal areas.

The people of the region have African, European or mixed African and European ancestry. Many of the ancestors of the Africans were bought to the Americas as slaves.

At least twenty-five countries and territories border the Caribbean Sea. This makes a coordinated approach to environmental management very difficult to achieve.

The Caribbean is linked to the Pacific Ocean by the human-built Panama Canal, one of the world's busiest shipping routes.

Figure 11.4d The tropical beaches and coral reefs of the Caribbean are a major tourist attraction.

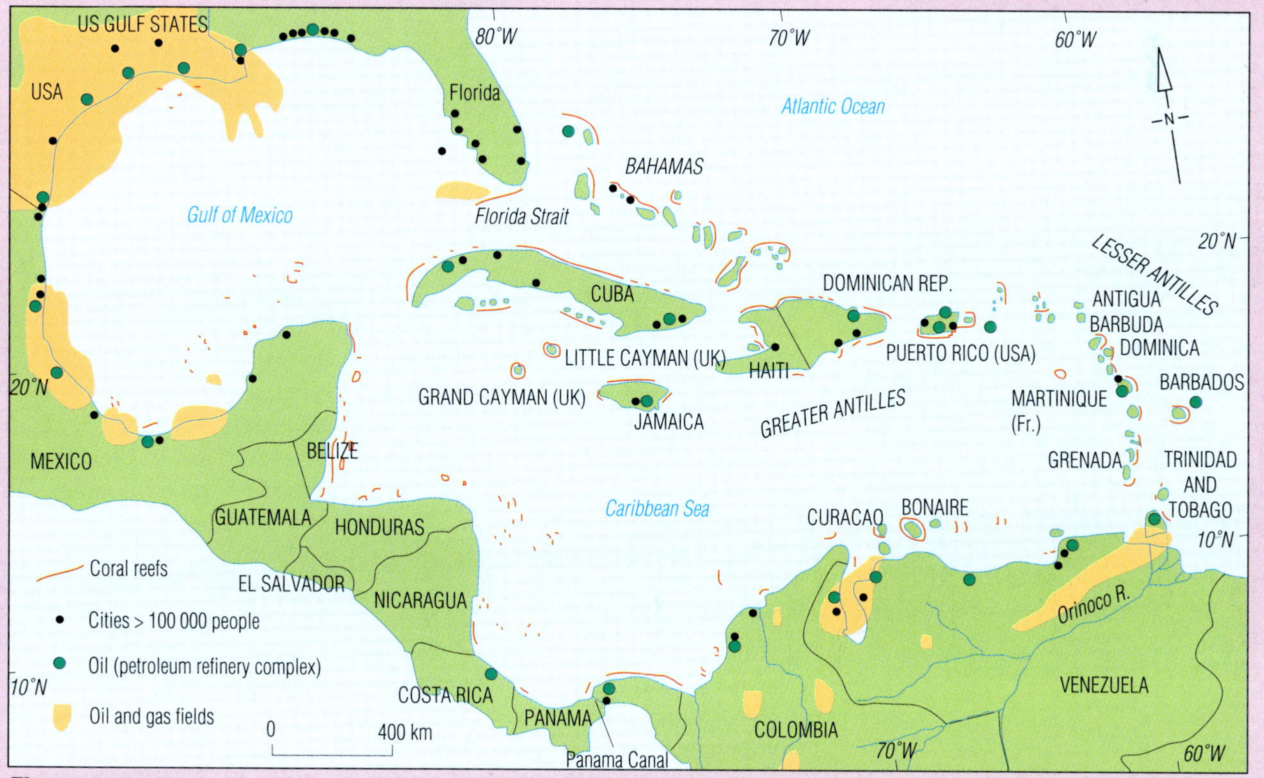

Figure 11.4c The Caribbean.

Caribbean coral reefs in steep decline

The Caribbean is losing coral reefs at a horrific rate, British scientists say.

A team from the University of East Anglia reported in the journal *Science* yesterday that the average amount of hard coral cover on the reefs had fallen from 50 per cent to 10 per cent in the past 30 years.

Tropical coral reefs are among the world's richest habitats, and are at risk everywhere, chiefly from overfishing, pollution, storms and sedimentation.

Experts have warned repeatedly that corals are sensitive to temperature. Reefs in the Indian and Pacific oceans have suffered dramatic bleaching during cycles of warming. But in the Caribbean the problems have been of a different kind …

Isabelle Cote, a tropical ecologist, said: 'The good news is that there are some areas in the Caribbean that appear to be recovering. The bad news is that the new coral communities seem to be different from the old ones. We don't know how well these will be able to face the challenges of rising sea levels and temperatures.'

Sydney Morning Herald, 14–20 July 2003

The Caribbean Environment Programme: challenge task

ICT

For more detailed information about the activities of the Caribbean Environment Programme (CEP) you can access its website.

For more information on tourism's impact on coral reefs you can download the PDF file *Tourism Impacts on Coral Reefs* published by the United Nations Environment Programme. It can be located in the Marine Issues section of the CEP website.

Figure 11.4e Tourism developments are often poorly planned and present a threat to the environment and the social well-being of local people.

Fishing

More than 3 million tonnes of fish are taken from the Caribbean Sea each year. Scientists say that this level cannot be continued into the future. A number of species, including several species of sea turtle, are now endangered and close to extinction. Turtles get tangled in fishing nets and drown; their nesting sites on beaches are disturbed; they are hunted for food; and they are affected by various forms of pollution.

Pollution

Oil spills are a major source of pollution throughout the Caribbean. Venezuela, Colombia, Trinidad and Tobago, Mexico and the Gulf States of the United States are all major oil producers. Their combined production almost equals that of the Middle East. Offshore oil platforms are a particular problem. Oil may spill from broken pipelines, blowouts, overflows and damaged equipment. It has been estimated that up to 7 per cent of the total offshore production is lost into the sea where it affects coral reefs and other marine ecosystems.

The Caribbean is one of the world's busiest waterways. Shipping is often limited to narrow reef passages, so collisions and groundings are a constant threat. A major spill from a tanker could destroy large areas of reef and cause economic hardship through its impact on tourism.

Large amounts of untreated sewage are released directly into coastal waters throughout the region. This increases the levels of nutrients in the water and encourages the growth of algae. Agricultural fertilisers add to this problem and pesticides are absorbed by the food chain. The illegal dumping of dangerous toxic (poisonous) wastes is also a cause for concern throughout the region.

Sedimentation

Sedimentation, caused by land clearing, is a growing problem. Each year more than 2 million hectares of tropical forests are cleared in the areas surrounding the Caribbean. The rate of soil erosion has increased rapidly. Heavy tropical rains strip the soil from the exposed slopes and wash it into river systems and, eventually, into the sea, where it increases turbidity (the muddiness of water) and smothers the living coral formations.

Managing the reefs of the Caribbean

In 1996, the United Nations sponsored the establishment of the Caribbean Environment Programme. The aim was to encourage cooperation between the countries of the region. It stressed the need to study pollution, respond cooperatively to oil spills, manage water catchments, increase environmental awareness, and improve people's access to clean drinking water and proper disposal of sewage and other waste.

Despite the program's good intentions, environmental problems continue to grow. They are all linked to how the resources of the region are used and developed.

Effective environmental management in the Caribbean region is made difficult by:

- a lack of knowledge and concern about environmental issues—in poor countries, education levels are low and many people are more concerned with meeting the basic needs of their family for food and housing than thinking about environmental issues
- the difficulty of working with so many governments—each country tries to protect its own particular interests, which makes cooperation difficult
- governments not standing up to the oil and logging companies
- the lack of trained people to manage the environment.

Possible solutions include:

- creating a powerful organisation to develop ways to protect the environment across the region
- using the aid from rich countries to improve the well-being of people and reduce the region's dependence on tourism and more destructive landuse activities, such as logging
- educating people about environmental issues.

Understanding the text

1. What attracts tourists to the Caribbean?
2. Outline the environmental threats to the coral reef ecosystems of the Caribbean.
3. Explain why tourism is so important to the region.
4. Outline some of the social and environmental costs of tourism.
5. Outline the aim of the Caribbean Environment Programme.
6. Explain why the management of the Caribbean's marine environment is so difficult.

UTT worksheet 11.4

Working geographically

1 **Group work: Interpreting photographs** Study the photographs in this unit. In groups, brainstorm the reasons why tourists might find the region an attractive tourist destination.

2 **Using the media** Study the newspaper article 'Caribbean coral reefs in steep decline', then complete the following tasks:

- a What is the extent of coral reef decline in the Caribbean?
- b List the risk factors that threaten coral reefs.
- c How do the problems faced by reefs in the Caribbean differ from those found elsewhere?

3 **Photo sketching** Contruct a photo sketch of Figure 11.4e (see Unit 2.9). Label the sketch, highlighting the range of possible impacts that developments such as this have on the physical environment.

4 **Using the media online** Use the archive search functions of major newspapers to locate newspaper articles dealing with coral reefs in the Caribbean. Write a one-paragraph summary of the issues addressed in one of these articles. Share your findings with the rest of the class.

5 **Challenge: Debate** Conduct a class debate. Topic: The environmental and social costs of tourism outweigh the economic benefits that it brings to the countries of the Caribbean.

6 **Writing task** Following the debate you conducted for the previous activity, decide whether you agree or disagree with the topic of the debate. Write an exposition outlining the arguments you would use to justify your position on the issue.

11.5 SAMPLE STUDY
The Great Barrier Reef

Figure 11.5a Australia's Great Barrier Reef.

Australia's Great Barrier Reef is the largest single collection of coral reefs in the world. The reefs provide the habitat for thousands of different life forms, many of which have developed unique roles and relationships. It is useful to compare the management of the Great Barrier Reef with that of reefs in the Caribbean.

The Great Barrier Reef was added to the World Heritage List in October 1981. Under the conditions of the United Nations World Heritage Convention, Australia is required to do all it can to protect the reef for the benefit of future generations.

Threats to the Great Barrier Reef

Human activities, if not managed carefully, pose a threat to the fragile ecosystem of the Great Barrier Reef. Some of these threats are shown in Figure 11.5b.

World Heritage Listing

ICT

Access UNESCO's World Heritage Convention website. Use the WH List and Operational Guidelines sections of the site to identify the criteria used to grant the Great Barrier Reef World Heritage status. Outline Australia's responsibilities under the terms of the convention. Which level of government has primary responsibility for the protection of this great global asset?

Did U know?

Great Barrier Reef: biodiversity 'hot spot'

Scientists consider the Great Barrier Reef to be one of the most ecologically important and diverse ecosystems on earth. The thousands of plants and animals living on the reef do not exist in isolation; they interact with each other. This makes the reef one of the world's most complex food webs. A change in any part of the food web will ultimately affect all other parts of the ecosystem.

The reef features at least 360 species of hard coral, including ten that are found nowhere else on earth. It is also home to one-third of the world's soft coral species.

In addition, the reef supports:

- 4000 species of molluscs
- 1500 species of fish
- 215 bird species
- thirty species of marine mammals, including whales, dolphins and dugongs
- fifteen species of sea snakes
- six of the world's seven species of marine turtles.

Protecting the Great Barrier Reef

Many environmentalists believe that the management of the Great Barrier Reef could be used as a model for protecting the earth's other fragile ecosystems.

During the 1960s and 1970s, Australians became concerned about plans to open up the reef to oil exploration and limestone mining. Following public protests and a royal commission, the federal government took control of the sea bed from the states and passed the *Great Barrier Reef Marine Park Act 1975*. The Act is important because it was the first law in the world to apply the concept of **sustainable development** (see Unit 16.2) to the management of a large natural area. The Great Barrier Reef Marine Park Authority's task is to find a balance between protecting the reef for the future and allowing human access and use.

The Great Barrier Reef Marine Park is not a national park. It is a multiple-use protected area where a range of human activities are allowed but managed so that they can be sustained forever without damaging the physical environment. The park is divided into a number of zones. These zones are used to control human activities, to set aside areas for scientific research and to exclude activities

Working geographically

Interpreting photographs Study the photographs in Figure 11.5b. Describe the activities taking place in each photograph and use your knowledge to write a paragraph on how each of these activities could have an impact on the reef ecosystem.

Figure 11.5b Some of the threats to the Great Barrier Reef.

Indigenous history

Aboriginal people have lived along the Great Barrier Reef for at least 40 000 years. In addition to supplying food for their subsistence lifestyle, the reef played a major role in the cultural and spiritual life of Aboriginal people. While many Aboriginal people now live a modern way of life, some maintain traditional cultural practices, including the hunting of turtles, dugong, shellfish and reef fish. Some forty tribal groups lived along the coast of the Great Barrier Reef.

Torres Strait Islanders, who have lived on the islands found between Australia and Papua New Guinea for at least 10 000 years, also relied on the resources of the reef to support their traditional subsistence lifestyle. The Torres Strait Islanders travelled up and down the coast, trading goods with coastal communities.

Figure 11.5c An Aboriginal Australian with a green turtle.

considered unacceptable. Oil exploration and mining are prohibited throughout the park.

The authority can approve or reject proposals for developments within the park. Its zoning powers can override almost all conflicting state and federal laws. Despite this, the authority relies heavily on the goodwill and cooperation of park users. It is advised by a committee that includes representatives of the groups with an interest in the reef.

The success of this type of environmental management depends on the government and the general public being committed to the sustainable development of natural resources. Could this model be used elsewhere in the world? Some experts say it is not suitable for areas where the reefs are used intensively by people; for example, in Asia and the Caribbean.

Managing the Cairns section of the reef

The Cairns section of the Great Barrier Reef is a small, much-used part of the park. It covers an area of 35 000 square kilometres and extends for more than 400 kilometres along the Queensland coast, offshore from the towns of Tully, Innisfail, Cairns, Mossman, Port Douglas and Cooktown (see Figure 11.5a, p. 242).

The construction of an international airport at Cairns has led to a boom in the number of tourists visiting this section of the reef. To meet the needs of these tourists a large number of hotels, resorts and associated facilities had to be developed. Job-seekers from many parts of Australia have been attracted by the prospects of gaining employment. Cairns is now one of the fastest growing areas in Australia. This development and growth is placing new demands on the resources of the reef.

Despite the success of the authority in managing the park, conflict still arises between the various users of the park. Conflict also arises between those who wish to exploit the attractions and resources of the reef and adjacent mainland and those who wish to see the reef maintained in its natural state. A range of views are shown in Figure 11.5d.

Figure 11.5d Some views on managing the reef.

Managing the Great Barrier Reef: challenge task

ICT

Access the Great Barrier Reef Marine Park Authority's website and complete the following tasks.

1 Access the About GBRMPA page. What is the goal of the Great Barrier Reef Marine Park Authority?

2 Access the Critical Issues: Conservation, Biodiversity and World Heritage section of the site and complete the following tasks:

  a Outline the natural and cultural values for which the Great Barrier Reef is famous.

  b Outline the authority's responsibility under the World Heritage Convention.

  c What do the terms 'critically endangered', 'endangered' and 'vulnerable' mean in relation to threatened species?

  d How many species are threatened on the Great Barrier Reef? Name three of these species.

  e How can individuals help threatened species?

Download copyright-free images from the site to illustrate any project work you may complete on the Great Barrier Reef. Look for Reef Snapshots.

Did U know?

The Great Barrier Reef includes:

- 2904 coral reefs
- 600 continental islands
- 300 coral cays.

Working geographically

1 **Research: Using presentation software** Undertake library and/or Internet research into endangered species found on the Great Barrier Reef. Report on your research using the following headings:

- name of the endangered species
- habitat of the species
- human activities that pose a threat to the species
- strategies being used to protect the species.

Present your research findings using presentation software, such as PowerPoint (see Unit 2.16).

2 **Debating issues** Examine the statements in Figure 11.5d. As a class, divide the statements into those that are proconservation, those that are prodevelopment and those that seek a balance between the conflicting demands placed on the resources of the reef ecosystem. Now form three groups and each select one of the sets of comments. Develop a series of arguments to support the particular view. Conduct a three-way debate.

Extension worksheet ICT 11.4

Extension worksheet ICT 11.6

Understanding the text

1 Explain why the Great Barrier Reef is such an important part of the physical environment.

2 According to the United Nations World Heritage Convention, what are Australia's responsibilities regarding the Great Barrier Reef?

3 Explain why the Great Barrier Reef Marine Park Act is significant.

4 Outline the task of the Great Barrier Reef Marine Park Authority.

5 Explain what is meant by the term 'multiple-use protected area'. What makes it different from a national park?

6 What is the purpose of dividing the park into a number of zones?

7 List the activities banned in the park.

8 What powers does the Great Barrier Reef Marine Park Authority have to carry out its task?

9 What other factors are important to the success of this type of environmental management?

UTT worksheet 11.5

11.6 Review and reflect

Chapter summary

The photographs in this chapter show just how special the world's coral reefs are. These spectacular and very productive ecosystems are among the world's most fragile. Even a small change in the environment can have a devastating impact on reefs. In recent years rising global temperatures have resulted in widespread coral bleaching. The impacts of tourism, the siltation caused by land clearing, oil spills and the use of agricultural fertilisers have also taken a heavy toll on coral reefs. Successfully managing these threats will be crucial if people are to protect coral reef ecosystems for the benefit of future generations.

The Caribbean sample study not only highlights the threats faced by coral reefs, it also shows how the protection of these ecosystems is made more difficult when cooperation between countries is required. This cooperation is made more difficult because some countries in the region are poor and struggle to meet the basic needs of their people.

The partnership between the Great Barrier Reef Marine Park Authority and the various communities and interest groups of coastal Queensland is an excellent example of what can be achieved when governments and local communities work cooperatively to promote sustainable development.

Activity 1

Writing task: Managing coral reefs

Write a report that contrasts the management of coral reefs in the Caribbean with those in Australia.

Activity 2

Challenge: Developing an action plan

In small groups, develop an international action plan to protect the coral reefs of the Caribbean. Use the understandings gained in your study of the Great Barrier Reef to assist you in this task. Present your action plan to the rest of the class and allow them to evaluate it.

Activity 3

Interpreting topographic maps

Study the Whitsunday (extract 1) and Green Island (extract 2) topographic map extracts, then complete the following tasks.

Extract 1

1. Identify the feature of the physical environment located at each of the following grid references.
   - **a** 196593 **b** 132578
   - **c** 106533 **d** 238611
2. What type of coral reef is found in the area shown on the map extract?
3. Name the type of vegetation lining Hill Inlet.
4. Which waterway separates Whitsunday and Haslewood Islands?
5. What is the direction of:
   - **a** Harold Island (GR250605) from Workington Island (GR215571)
   - **b** What is the direction of Whitsunday Craig (AR1053) from Pallion Point (AR1959)?
6. What is the straight-line distance between Whitsunday Craig (GR106532) and Haslewood (GR181543)?
7. What is the height of Whitsunday Craig?
8. What is the elevation of
   - **a** the land at GR121550
   - **b** the hill at GR094606?
9. State the difference in elevation between Whitsunday Craig (AR1053) and the spot height on Nicholson Island (AR1853).
10. In what direction is the stream flowing in AR1755 and AR1654?

Extract 2

11. What type of coral reef is found in the area shown on the map extract?
12. What type of island is found on the topographic map extract?
13. Identify the feature of the built environment located at each of the following grid references.
    - **a** 900468 **b** 905466
    - **c** 909466
14. Estimate the area of the reef surrounding Green Island.
15. What is the length of Green Island?

Refer to the Reflection box on page 17.

Extract 1

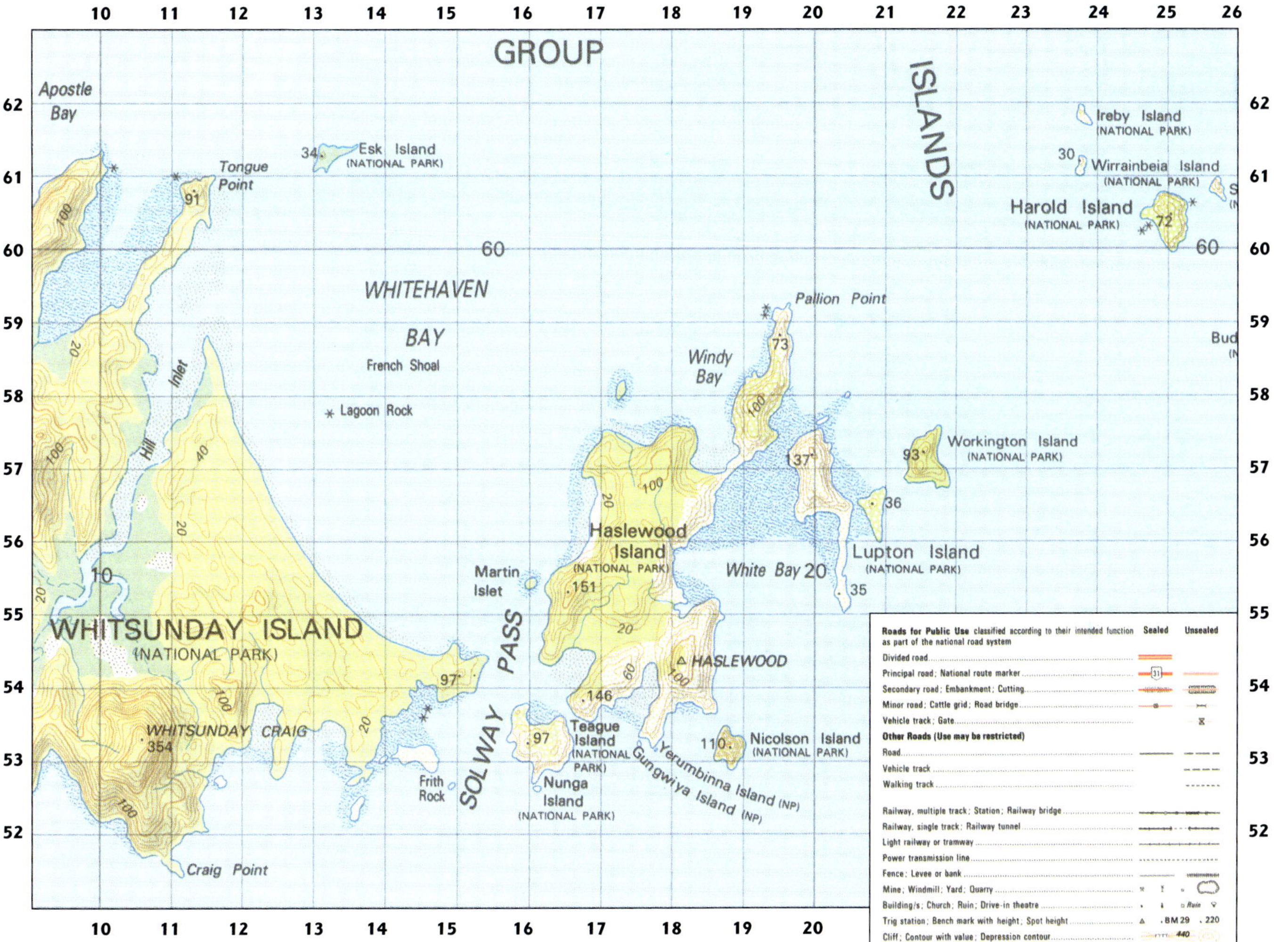

Extract 2

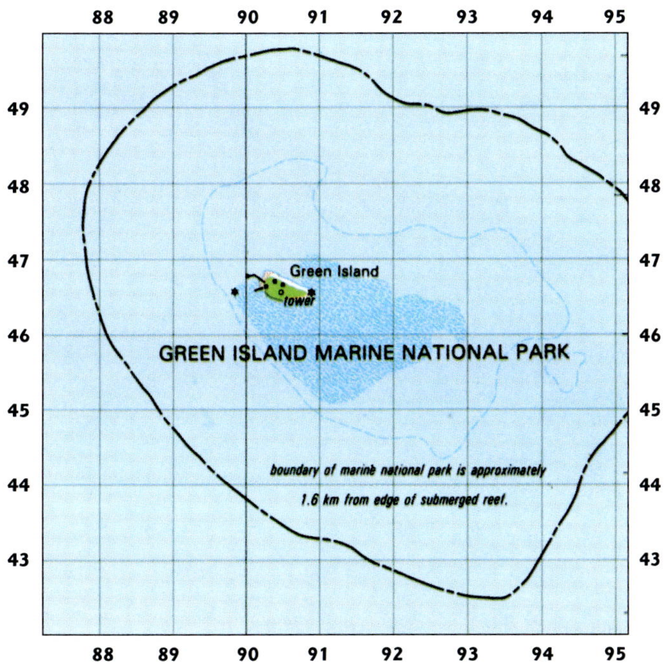

SCALE 1 : 100 000

km 0 1 2 3 4 5 6 7 8km

HEIGHTS IN METRES. CONTOUR INTERVAL 20 METRES

Chapter 12

Deserts

Introduction

Deserts are among the world's most spectacular landscapes. They are found where precipitation is low and evaporation is high. All deserts have a number of features in common, including very low and irregular rainfall, highly specialised plants and animals and few, if any, people. A desert is not necessarily hot.

In this chapter we study the geographical processes responsible for shaping the desert environment. We will also look at how the people of the Sahara Desert struggle to survive in one of the world's harshest environments and how this battle is contributing to the southward spread of the Sahara, a process we call desertification.

Key questions

1. Why are deserts dry?
2. How are the deserts' distinctive landform features formed?
3. How do plants and animals survive in arid environments?
4. How do people cope in environments with little water?
5. What is desertification?
6. How do the activities of people contribute to desertification?

One man's desert obsession

People become obsessed with the oddest things. In the past few years a lonely phone booth in the Mojave Desert, California, gathered a cult following and eventually fell victim to its own popularity.

In May 1997 Godfrey Daniels from Arizona read about the phone booth in a magazine. A man had reported seeing a small dot with the word 'telephone' next to it 25 kilometres from anywhere on a map of the Mojave Desert. The man drove out to see the phone booth and published its number.

Godfrey became obsessed. He called the phone booth every day, even though no-one answered. Finally, after about a month, his patience paid off. He called the booth and a woman named Lorene answered. Godfrey's obsession didn't end with talking to Lorene. He has since made five trips to the booth.

In July 1999 Godfrey and a band of friends visited the phone booth. In four hours they took seventy-two phone calls from all over the United States and Canada and as far away as Germany and Australia. Most were from people who had visited Godfrey's website.

The phone booth (and Godfrey) became minor celebrities. They have received coverage in *The New York Times*, *The Los Angeles Times*, through CNN and in newspapers around the world. Then it happened: the phone booth fell victim to its own popularity.

On 23 May 2000 the *San Jose Mercury* News reported that Pacific Bell and the National Park Service had removed the booth because it was attracting too many curiosity seekers.

Glossary of key terms

Abrasion The wearing down of rocks by friction.

Alluvial fan A low, cone-shaped deposit of sand and rock formed when a stream deposits its load on a low-lying plain as a result of an abrupt change of slope.

Aquifer Layers of rock through which water can flow.

Arable Able to be cultivated.

Bolson An inland desert basin surrounded by mountains.

Butte A flat-topped landform feature that is taller than it is wide.

Deflation The process whereby material is removed from a surface by wind.

Desert Very dry environments where evaporation is greater than precipitation or where precipitation is less than 250 millimetres a year.

Desertification The process by which productive land in arid areas is changed into desert as a result of poor landuse practices.

Environmental refugees People forced to leave their homeland due to the damage caused to the physical environment.

Ephemerals Plants capable of completing their full life cycle in just a few weeks following rainfall.

Erg A desert surface covered with sand dunes.

Escarpment A steep slope or cliff, often defining the edge of a plateau.

Hamada A desert landscape dominated by exposed bedrock.

Inselberg A large erosion-resistant rock feature surrounded by an eroded plane.

Mesa A flat-topped landform feature that is wider than it is high.

Oasis A fertile or well-watered area within a desert.

Playa A dried-up salt lake found in arid or semi-arid environments.

Reg A stone-covered desert.

Sand dune Accumulations of windblown sand.

Succulents Plants capable of storing water in their tissues.

Transpiration The loss of water vapour from the leaves of plants.

Wadi A watercourse or gully that is dry except during periods of rainfall.

Xerophyte Drought-resistant plants adapted to the dry desert environment.

cd eGlossary

cd GeoToolkit

cd ICT Toolkit

12.1 Desert environments

Figure 12.1a Monument Valley, United States. Deserts are found where rainfall is less than 250 millimetres a year.

Deserts occur where evaporation is greater than precipitation or where precipitation is less than 250 millimetres a year. These areas cover about 30 per cent of the earth's surface. Deserts are found on every continent except Europe.

Deserts are the driest places on earth. They usually have few plants and a hard, wind-blown surface covered with rocks and sand. The range of temperatures experienced each day is often very large. Very high daytime temperatures often give way to very cold temperatures at night. There is no cloud cover, so heat is lost into the atmosphere very quickly. The lack of moisture in the air (combined with the lack of vegetation) also allows the surface of the desert to radiate heat rapidly after the sun goes down.

Where are deserts located?

All the major deserts are located in the interior of continents or on their west coasts. There are two reasons for this. First, on the western side of the continents, in the mid-latitudes, the winds blow mainly across the land towards the coasts, taking hot, dry air across the deserts (see Figure 12.1b). Second, there are cold ocean currents off the west coast of most continental landmasses. Evaporation rates from cold water are relatively low. This limits the amount of moisture in the air and the amount of precipitation (see Figure 12.c).

The deserts in North America are different from the others. They exist as a number of separate deserts, each surrounded by mountain ranges that prevent moisture from reaching them (see Figure 1.12d). The plants in North American deserts are different from those found in other deserts. The cactus is a well-known symbol of the desert, but is, in fact, only found in North American deserts (see Figure 12.1e). In southern African deserts, aloes are a widespread plant. In northern African and Middle Eastern deserts, date palms are one of the typical plants.

Table 12.1a Large deserts

Desert	Area (km^2)
Sahara	8 600 000
Arabian	2 330 000
Gobi	1 200 000
Patagonian	673 000
Great Victoria	647 000
Great Basin	492 000
Chihuahuan	450 000
Great Sandy	407 000
Kara Kum	350 000
Sonoran	310 000

Air near the earth's Equator rises into the atmosphere because it is hot. This air then travels towards the Tropic of Cancer and the Tropic of Capricorn. As it does so, the temperature of the air decreases and it sinks back towards the earth. This sinking air creates an air of high pressure. There is little chance of precipitation in these areas because air must be rising before precipitation can develop.

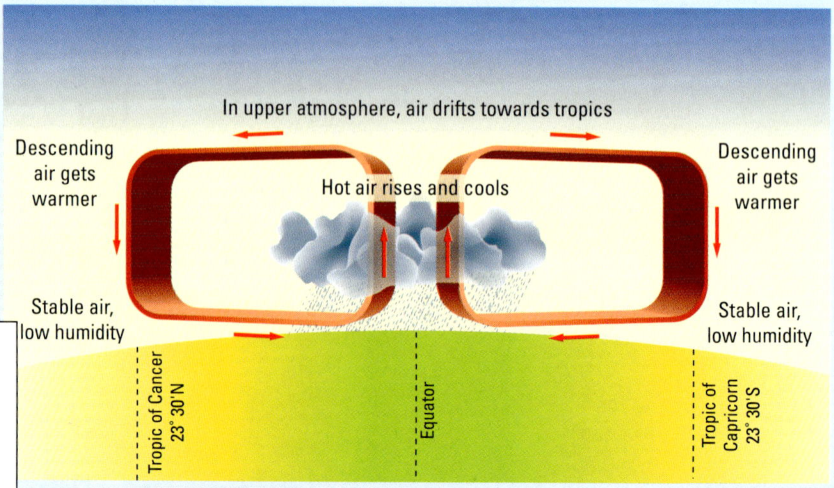

Figure 12.1b Deserts occur in areas where the climate is dominated by high-pressure systems.

It might surprise you that Antarctica (and the Arctic regions) is also classified as a desert. Although covered with a thick layer of ice, Antarctica is, in fact, a very dry place. The continent's average annual snowfall equals just 50 millimetres of rainfall. (The dry polar lands are examined in detail in Chapter 6.)

Figure 12.1g (p. 252) shows the location of the world's main deserts.

Desertification

Since the early 1970s, there has been a growing body of evidence to show that deserts are increasing in size. Semi-arid areas on the edges of deserts (such as the Sahel, south of the Sahara Desert) are getting drier and changing into full deserts. This process is called **desertification**.

There are two main theories about these changes: one theory is that they are the result of natural causes; the other is that they are the result of human causes. Those who support the theory of natural causes argue that climate change has resulted in lower rainfall and a shorter wet season, particularly in the Sahel region of Africa.

Figure 12.1e The cactus is a well-known symbol of North American deserts.

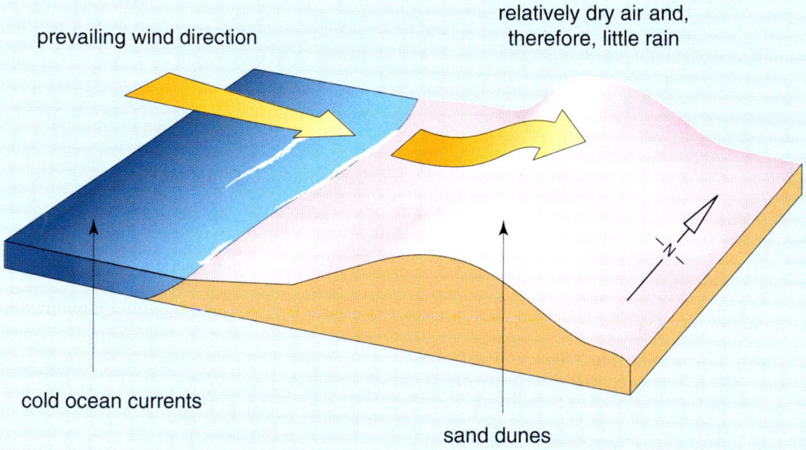

Figure 12.1c Large bodies of cold water result in low rates of evaporation. As a result, the air moving onshore is dry.

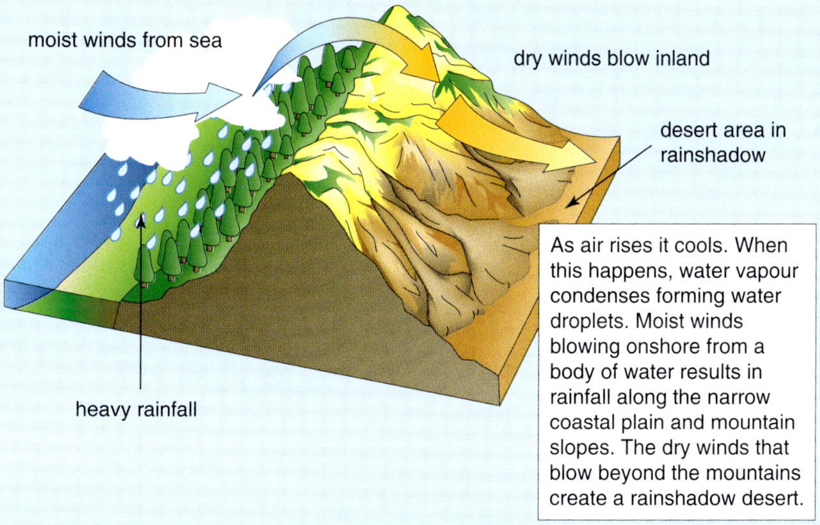

Figure 12.1d Mountain ranges can block the inland movement of moisture, producing desert environments.

Understanding the text

1 What is a desert?

2 What proportion of the earth's surface is covered by desert?

3 Explain why deserts are often very cold at night.

4 a Where are most of the world's deserts located within each continent?
  b Explain why desert-like conditions are found in these areas.

5 Under what conditions do deserts occur?

6 Why are the deserts of North America different from other deserts?

7 What types of plants are common in the deserts in the following locations?
  a southern Africa
  b northern Africa and the Middle East
  c North America

cd UTT worksheet 12.1

Desert mirages

Mirages are often seen in the world's hot deserts. They occur when a shallow layer of warm air next to the ground is trapped by cooler air above. Light bends towards the horizontal line of vision, and eventually travels upwards: the mirage is an upside-down 'virtual' image.

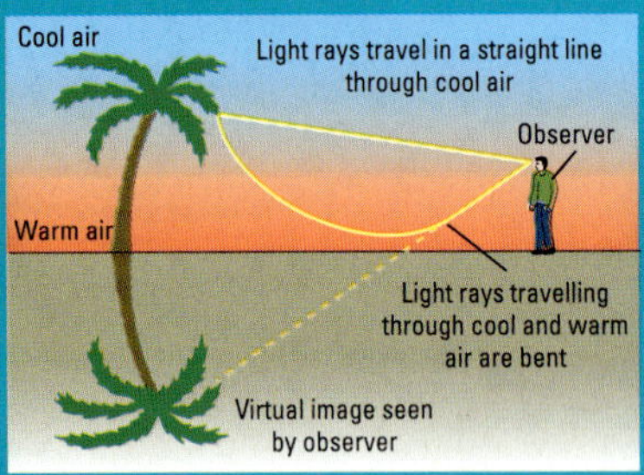

Figure 12.1f A mirage is an optical illusion.

Did U know?

- An estimated 6 million hectares of productive land are lost every year because of desertification and land degradation.
- Drought and desertification threaten the livelihood of more than 1.2 billion people in some 110 countries, with 135 million around the world at risk of being displaced.
- **Arable** land per person is shrinking throughout the world. It has declined from 0.32 hectares per person in 1961–63 to 0.21 hectares in 1997–99 and is expected to drop further to 0.16 hectares by 2030.
- In India, dry spells and deforestation turn 2.5 million hectares to wasteland every year.

Those who argue that desertification is the result of human activity say that population pressure and the overuse of the land are the main causes. They point to examples all over the world where deserts and semi-desert land have deteriorated because of poorly managed landuse on the edges of deserts. People have made many mistakes that seem to cause desertification. In some cases, human greed has led to too many cattle grazing the land, or crops have been grown on land that is not really suited to agriculture. In other cases, it is the result of desperation: the very poor have tried to survive in an extremely difficult environment. Many people, for example, need to collect firewood to cook their food and keep warm at night, although the land cannot survive such a loss of vegetation.

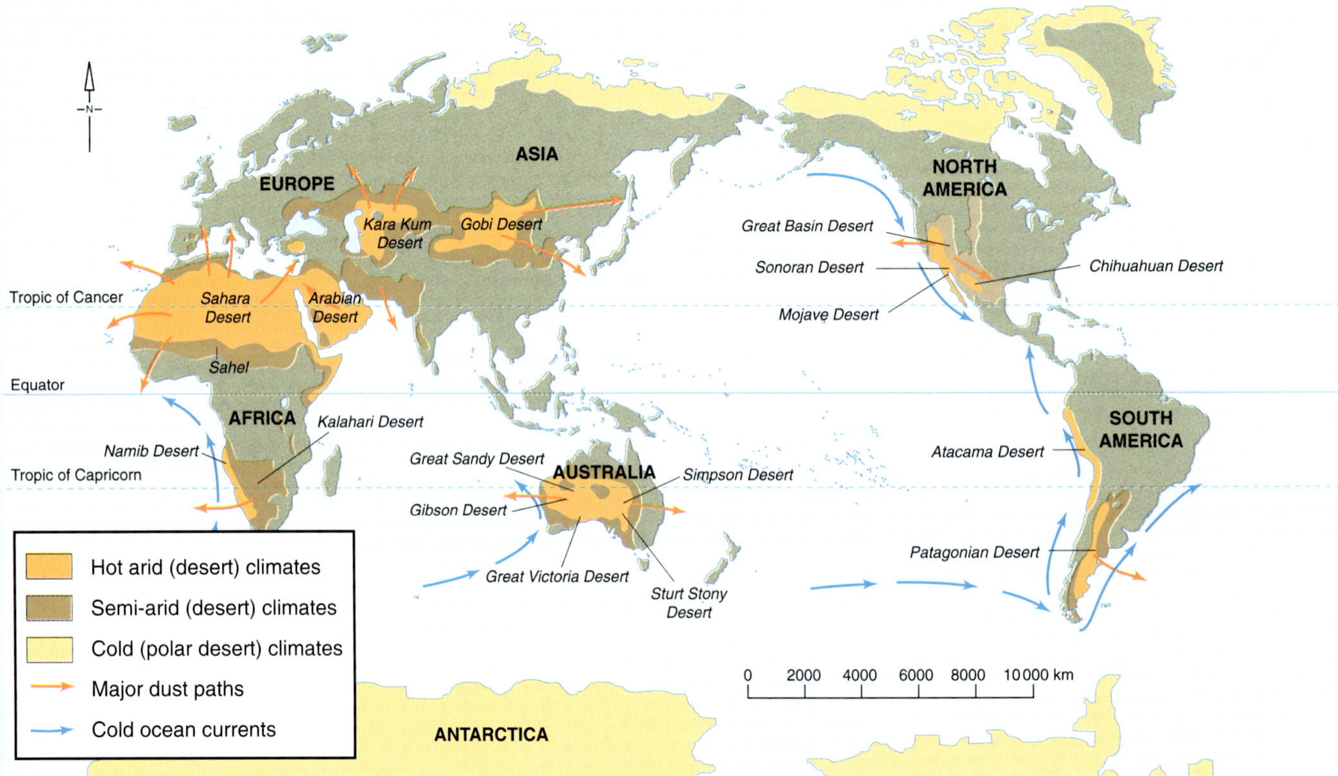

Figure 12.1g The location of the world's deserts.

Foundation worksheet 12.1 | Foundation worksheet 12.2 | Extension worksheet 12.6 | Extension worksheet 12.1 | Extension worksheet ICT 12.5

Figure 12.1h The process of desertification turns semi-arid grasslands into desert.

Some scientists argue that desertification is caused by a combination of both natural and human factors and may also be linked to the process of global warming (see Unit 16.3).

An estimated 8.1 million square kilometres worldwide—an area the size of Brazil—has been affected by desertification in the last fifty years. If this continues, the well-being of at least 1.2 billion people could be threatened.

The most effective way to slow desertification is to drastically reduce overgrazing, deforestation and excessive cultivation. Reforestation (tree-planting) programs will help to bind the soil and hold water while slowing the process of desertification.

Did U know?

- Thirteen per cent of the world's population live in deserts.
- Evaporation rates in deserts are often twenty times the annual precipitation.
- A temperature of 58°C has been recorded in the shade at Azizia in Libya.
- No rain fell for over forty years in the Atacama Desert in Chile.
- Night-time temperatures in some deserts can fall below freezing.
- Sand dunes can reach heights of up to 300 metres.
- Sand covers less than 20 per cent of the world's desert areas.
- If someone spent a day in the desert with no shade, food, water or clothes, their temperature would be about 46°C by sunset, and they would have lost 2–3.5 litres of water. By nightfall they would be dead.
- In sub-Saharan Africa the number of **environmental refugees** is expected to rise to 25 million in the next twenty years.

Working geographically

1 **Mapping: Using an atlas**

a Using Figure 12.1g and an outline map of the world, locate and name the world's major deserts.

b Using an atlas, identify the country or countries in which each of these deserts is located.

2 **Interpreting diagrams: Writing task** Study Figures 12.1b to 12.1d (pp. 250–1). Write an explanation outlining the factors responsible for the location of deserts.

3 **Evaporation experiments**

a Use two shallow bowls filled with water to measure the rate of evaporation. Place one on a sunny windowsill and the other in a cool location. What happens to the water after a day or so? Which dries up first? Why?

b Place an equal amount of water in a shallow bowl and a glass jar. Stand the two containers next to each other on a windowsill. What happens to the water after a day of so? Which dries up first? Why? Where has the water gone?

4 **Challenge: Research** Do some library research. The Namib Desert on the coast of Africa and the Atacama Desert on the coast of South America share an unusual characteristic. Although they are just as dry as other deserts in terms of rainfall, they have frequent fogs and mists. Find out the reasons for these fogs in the Namib and Atacama Deserts. Find out some other facts about these deserts.

Understanding the text

1 What is desertification?

2 Outline the two theories used to explain why desertification is occurring.

3 How much land has been affected by desertification worldwide in the last fifty years?

4 How can the process of desertification be slowed?

UTT worksheet 12.1

12.2 Desert landforms

Figure 12.2a Sandy desert or **erg** surface.

Figure 12.2b Stony desert or **reg** surface (known as a gibber plain in Australia).

Figure 12.2c Rocky desert or **hamada** surface.

Figure 12.2d Pedestal rocks are formed by the abrasive action of wind-blown sand.

Desert landforms are among the most spectacular found anywhere on the surface of the earth. The agents of erosion responsible for shaping these landforms are wind and running water.

The desert surface

When most people think of deserts they think of sand dunes. But sand dunes cover only about 25 per cent of the world's deserts. The remaining 75 per cent are either exposed rock or stone-covered plains. The rocks of the desert surface are usually quite smooth, having been polished by the wind-blown sand. This process is known as **abrasion**.

The three main types of desert surface are shown in Figures 12.2a to 12.2c.

Landforms shaped by wind

The erosion of fine surface sand by wind is known as **deflation**. Once airborne, sand can act as an abrasive tool, wearing down and shaping exposed rock. *Pedestal rocks*, for example, are formed when wind-blown sand cuts away the base of rock structures but leaves their tops intact (see Figure 12.2d).

When the wind-blown material is deposited it accumulates and forms **sand dunes**. The shape of these dunes varies according to the strength and direction of the wind, the amount of sand available and the type and extent of vegetation cover in the area. Dunes are named according to their shape and direction. Some of the more common types are described below and shown in Figure 12.2e.

- *Barchan dunes* are crescent-shaped dunes produced by a strong wind blowing across a level desert. Some barchan dunes can be 30 metres high.
- *Longitudinal dunes* (sometimes called seif dunes) are formed in areas where a strong wind blows in one general direction with a slight seasonal shift in direction. The dunes run parallel to the prevailing wind. Some longitudinal dunes can be more than 60 kilometres in length.
- *Transverse dunes* are formed where there are large amounts of sand and steady winds from a constant direction. The dunes are at right angles to the wind direction.
- *Star dunes* are star-shaped dunes shaped by shifting winds. They have multiple ridges spreading out like the points of a star around a high central peak.

Landforms shaped by water

Water is the most important factor in the development of desert landforms. Although it does not rain often, when it does, the rain is frequently very heavy and results in flash flooding. Because there is no vegetation, runoff is extremely rapid and can erode large amounts of weathered material.

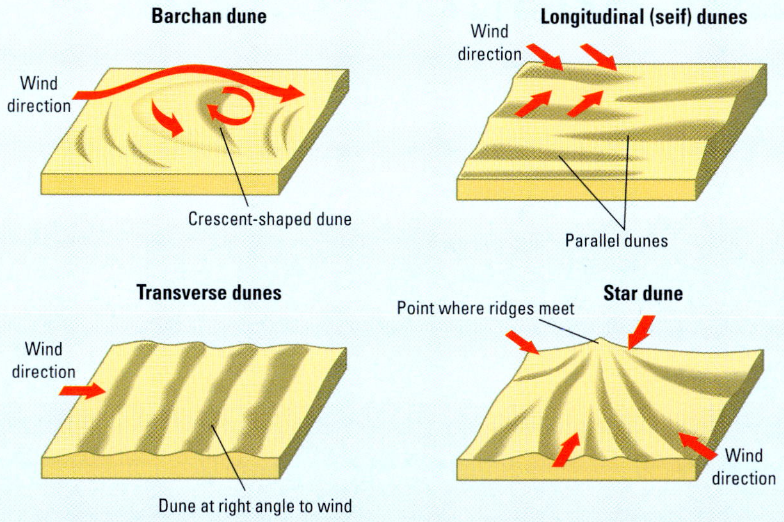

Figure 12.2e Different types of sand dunes.

Surface runoff is channelled into dry river beds (**wadis**) that cut through plateaus, forming canyons. As plateaus are eroded, **mesas** and **buttes** are left isolated from the retreating **escarpment**. Mesas are wider than they are high, while buttes are higher than they are wide.

The eroded material is carried by the water through the wadis. It is eventually deposited on to the lowlands, forming **alluvial fans**. These spread out across the desert basin, or **bolson**, where the fine particles can be shaped into dunes by the wind.

Where water flows into a desert depression, **playa lakes** form. When the water eventually evaporates, *salt pans* or *clay pans* are formed (see Figure 12.2f).

Inselbergs are large masses of resistant rock that rise abruptly from the surrounding plain. They are exposed when the softer surrounding rock material is eroded. Uluru, in central Australia, is probably the world's best-known inselberg.

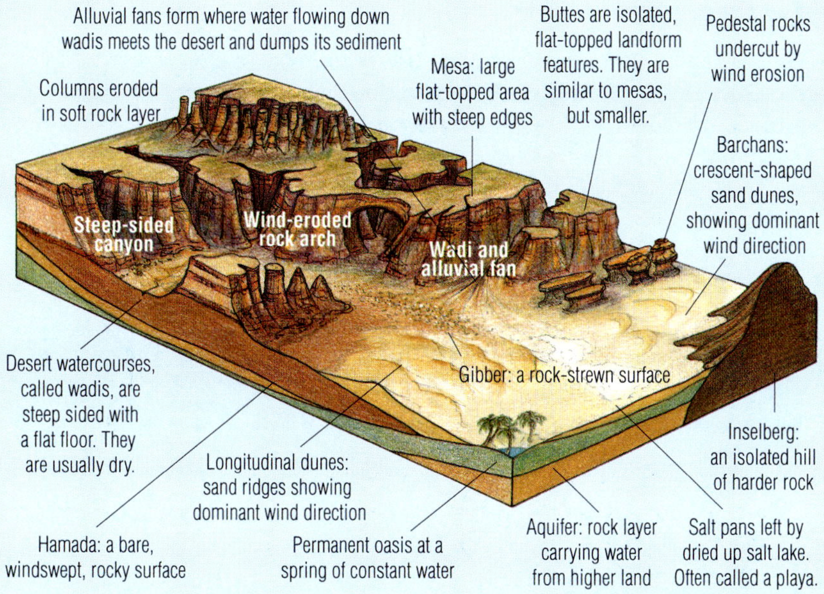

Figure 12.2f Landforms of the desert.

Understanding the text

1. Name and describe the three types of desert surface.
2. What is abrasion? What impact does it have on rocks?
3. What is deflation?
4. Describe the conditions under which longitudinal, transverse, barchan and star dunes develop.
5. Why is rainfall such an effective agent of erosion in desert environments?

UTT worksheet 12.2

Working geographically

1. **Interpreting photographs** Study Figures 12.2a to 12.2c. Describe the different types of desert surface shown. What name is given to each type?
2. **Writing task** Study Figure 12.2d. Write an explanation of how pedestal rocks are formed.
3. **Challenge: Research** Do some library research. Select one of the landform features shown in Figure 12.2e. Investigate how it is formed. Draw a series of sketches to illustrate its development. Present your research as a poster. Display your posters on the classroom wall.
4. **Photo sketching** Construct a photo sketch of Figure 12.1a (p. 250). Refer to Unit 2.9 to assist you. Label the prominent features of the desert landscape.

Foundation worksheet 12.2

Extension worksheet 12.2

12.3 Plants and animals of the desert

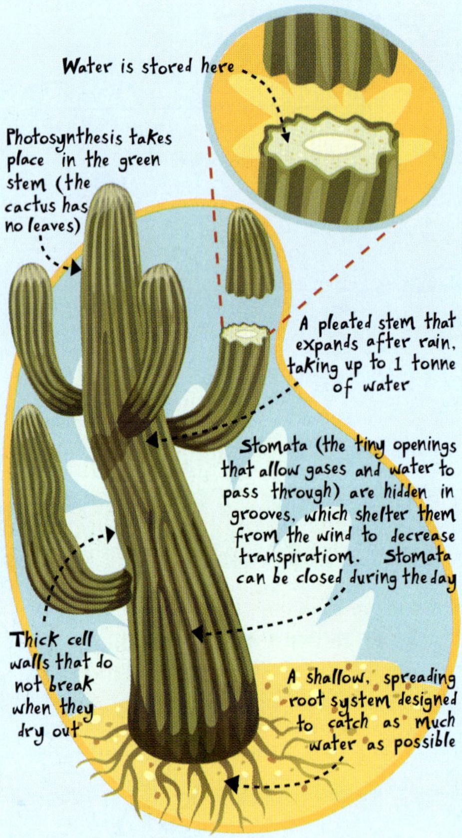

Figure 12.3a The saguaro cactus.

Figure 12.3b Ephemeral plants can complete their full life cycle in just two or three weeks.

Desert plants and animals have developed an amazing range of adaptations that enable them to tolerate very high temperatures and capture and conserve what little water there is available.

Plants

Drought-resistant plants are known as **xerophytes**. Many xerophytes are **succulents**. This means that they are able to store water in their tissues. Cacti, for example, absorb large amounts of water following rainfall. Their fleshy stems swell up, then slowly shrink as moisture is lost through **transpiration** (the loss of water vapour from the leaves of plants). Many succulents further reduce the amount of moisture lost by only transpiring at night (see Figure 12.3a).

Most desert plants, including cactus and thornbush, have small leaves that are spiky or wax-coated. This reduces transpiration and deters animals. Some send their roots deep into the earth to tap into groundwater. The roots of the acacia can be more than 15 metres long. Others, including most cacti and the creosote bush, spread their shallow roots wide to take advantage of any rain or dew. Bushes are widely spaced to avoid competition for water. Some plants have bulbous roots for storing water.

Following a storm, the desert blooms. Many plants are **ephemerals** and can complete their full life cycle in just two or three weeks. The seeds of these plants usually have a thick outer covering that protects them until the next rain falls (see Figure 12.3b).

Some plants, such as the saltbush, are able to survive in very salty soils. Others, such as the date palm, can only survive where the water table is high enough to form an oasis.

Animals

Because of the lack of vegetation, there are very few food chains in deserts. There is not enough plant food to support large numbers of animals. This is why desert ecosystems are described as fragile: animals

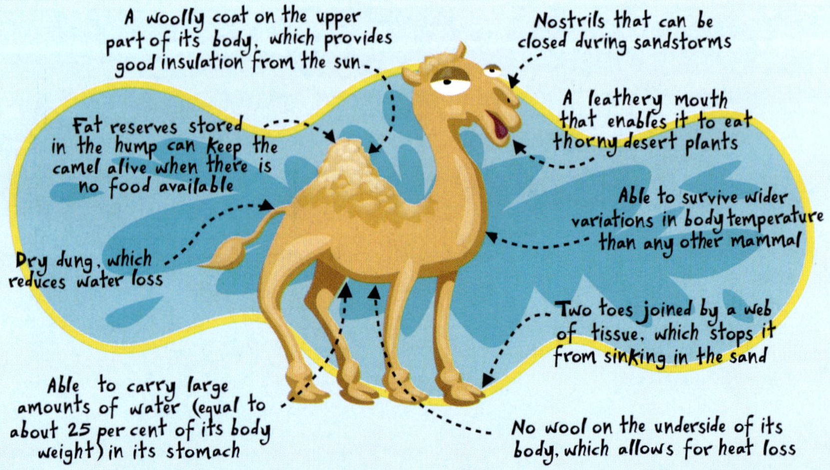

Figure 12.3c Camels are one of the few large animals found in desert environments.

do not have the alternative sources of food that are available in more complex ecosystems.

Most desert animals are small, which keeps heat gain and loss to a minimum, and nocturnal. Most avoid the heat by hiding in burrows or under rocks by day and being active during the night or early morning. Some desert animals also have adaptations for conserving water. Insects and reptiles have thick outer coverings so that they lose as little water as possible through evaporation. Some desert animals become dormant (or inactive) during periods of extreme heat or drought.

Figure 12.3d Scorpions are carnivores (meat-eaters) and have pincers with which to seize their prey while they inject a deadly poison from the stinger in their tail.

The kangaroo rat

The nocturnal kangaroo rat of the Californian desert is an expert in water conservation. As a seed-eater it plays an important role in supporting other desert species and keeping the desert scrub from being replaced by grasses. It distributes the seeds of native plants via its droppings.

The small mammal comes out of its burrow at night (when the air is cool and evaporation is low) to collect dry seeds, which it stuffs into pouches in its cheeks. It empties the seeds into its cool burrow, where they soak up water vapour exhaled in the rat's breath. When it eats the seeds, it gets this water back.

The kangaroo rat does not drink water; its water comes from the recycled moisture in the seeds. Some of the water vapour in the rat's breath also condenses on the cool inside surface of its nose and passes back into its body. Kangaroo rats have no sweat glands, so they don't lose water by perspiration. In addition, they save water by passing hard faeces and thick, nearly solid urine produced by its very efficient kidneys.

Figure 12.3d The kangaroo rat is an expert at water conservation.

Understanding the text

1 What general term is used to describe drought-resistant plants? What characteristics do they have?
2 What are succulents? How do they reduce the amount of water vapour they lose through their leaves?
3 List the various adaptations desert plants have developed to gather water and minimise moisture loss.
4 How do ephemerals cope with the lack of regular rainfall?
5 Why are desert ecosystems described as fragile?
6 How have animals adapted to the harsh desert climate?

UTT worksheet 12.3

Working geographically

1 **Writing task** Study the box describing the kangaroo rat. List the adaptations that enable the kangaroo rat to cope with the harsh desert climate. Use this list to write a report describing the kangaroo rat and its water-conserving strategies. Use the library or Internet to find out more about the kangaroo rat. Find out whether it is an endangered species.

2 **Challenge: Internet research** Study Figures 12.3a and 12.3c. Select a plant and an animal found in the desert. Undertake research to find out the adaptations the selected plant and animal have that enable them to survive in the desert environment. Download a copyrght-free image of each from the Internet. Annotate these images with the adaptations you have identified.

3 **Challenge: Research** Do some library research. Using the box describing the kangaroo rat, write a report describing a desert animal of your choice. Present the findings of your research to the class. Develop a wall display of your research findings accompanied by sketches or photographs of the animals.

Foundation worksheet 12.2

Extension worksheet 12.3

12.4 SAMPLE STUDY

The Sahara Desert

Figure 12.4a The River Nile, which flows through Egypt, provides irrigation water for a narrow strip of the Sahara Desert.

The Sahara is the world's largest desert. It covers almost one-third of the area of Africa and is about as large as the area of Australia. It is a very difficult environment for humans and animals to live in because there are extremes of temperature, frequent sandstorms, little vegetation and few sources of water.

What is the Sahara like?

One-quarter of the Sahara consists of sand dunes (called ergs; see Figure 12.2a, p. 254). Only a small amount of rain falls and, in this sandy landscape, it quickly soaks into the sand. Few animals and plants survive here, but some, such as camels and jerboas, have adapted to this harsh environment. The Tuareg nomads live in the sandy areas. They move their herds of animals around the desert, following the pattern of the small amount of rain that does fall, and moving from one source of water to another. Other indigenous groups of the region include the Fulani, Dinka, Nuer, Shilluk, Oromo, Somali, Tigrayan and Eritrean.

Figure 12.4b Map of the Sahara Desert region of North Africa.

In the other parts of the Sahara there are large areas of stony plains (called reg; see Figure 12.2b, p. 254) and high, rocky plateaus and mountains. At one point, the Qattara Depression, the land dips to 133 metres below sea level.

Water in the Sahara

In the Sahara there is very little water for plants, animals or humans. Some plants and animals are able to make use of the rainwater that filters through the sand or collects briefly on the rocky surfaces. But humans can only find permanent water supplies in rivers or underground water-bearing rocks. The only major rivers are the Niger and the Nile. The Nile River dominates the northeastern part of the Sahara. For thousands of years it has provided irrigation water for agriculture.

The most widespread source of water in the Sahara is in underground water-bearing rocks (called **aquifers**), which are in layers below the sand and surface rocks. In places where these water-bearing rocks reach the surface of a depression in the desert, an **oasis** is formed (see Figure 12.4d).

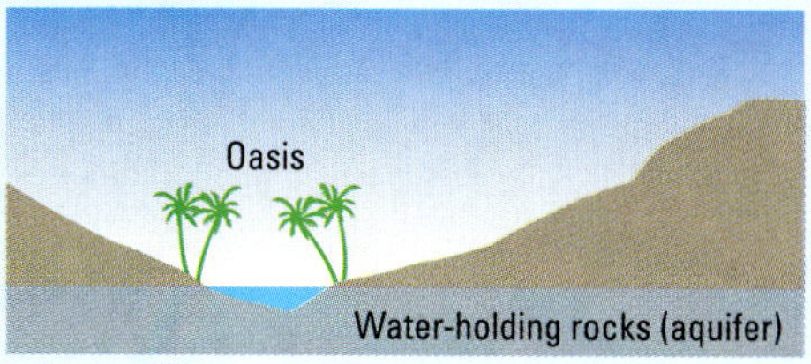

Figure 12.4d A palm tree oasis, Sahara Desert, Algeria. An oasis develops when an underlying aquifer (a saturated layer of rock) meets a depression in the desert surface.

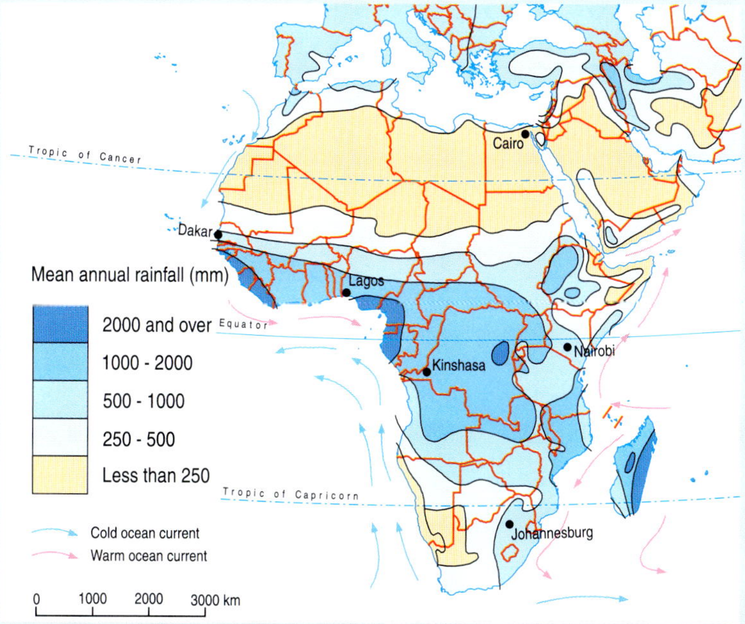

Figure 12.4c Rainfall map of Africa. Source: *Heinemann Atlas*.

Understanding the text

1 Why is the Sahara such a difficult environment for humans and animals?

2 Describe the landscape of the Sahara. In your answer explain the difference between an erg and a reg.

UTT worksheet 12.4

Working geographically

1 **Comparing maps** Compare Figure 12.4c with an atlas map showing the population distribution of northern Africa. Write a paragraph commenting on the relationship between the density of population and the availability of water. Outline what this relationship is.

2 **Interpreting maps** Study Figure 12.4c. Write a paragraph describing the rainfall pattern of Africa.

Working geographically

1 **Photo sketching** Construct a photo sketch of Figure 12.4a (p. 258) or the photograph in Figure 12.4d (p. 259). Refer to Unit 2.9 to assist you.

2 **Interpreting photographs** Study Figures 12.4a (p. 258) and Figure 12.4e. Write a paragraph describing the differences between the Nile Valley and the rest of the Sahara.

3 **Writing task** It is sometimes said that 'Egypt is the gift of the Nile'. Use Figure 12.4a (p. 258) to write a paragraph explaining what this means.

4 **Challenge: Using software** In groups, select another world desert and do some research. Organise your information under the following headings: 'landscapes', 'plants and animals', 'water availability', 'mineral resources' and 'settlement'. Communicate your findings using presentation software (such as PowerPoint).

5 **Challenge: Internet research** Select one of the indigenous peoples listed on page 258. Undertake Internet-based research using a search engine (such as Google). Write a sample study of the indigenous peoples you researched.

6 **Interpreting stimulus material** Study Figure 12.4f. Describe the climate of Tripoli. Suggest why water supply might be a problem in Libya. Make reference to climate, the environment and population.

7 **Writing task** Using the information in the Did U Know? box, write a statement outlining the infrastructure required to support such an ambitious project and the benefits to be gained.

Extension worksheet ICT 12.4

Because of increasing use of underground water, the supply is declining, causing some springs to dry up. Some aquifers now have little water in them.

Wealth beneath the sands

The most important mineral resources that have been exploited in the Sahara are oil and gas. Libya has explored its area of the Sahara for these underground deposits, drilling many wells to tap both oil and gas deposits. The sale of oil to other nations has increased Libya's wealth considerably. Some of this wealth has been used to solve the country's water shortage (see the box: 'Libya: breaking the drought').

People of the Sahara: the Tuareg

Tuareg is a term used to identify the diverse groups of nomadic people living in parts of the Sahara (see Figure 12.4e). The Tuareg share a common language and a common history.

For thousands of years, the livelihood of the Tuareg revolved around trans-Saharan trade. There were five main trade routes that crossed the Sahara from the Mediterranean coast of Africa to the great cities on the southern edge of the Sahara. Tuareg merchants were responsible for transporting goods from these cities to the north. From there they were distributed throughout the world. Because of the nature of transport and the limited space available in caravans, Tuareg usually traded only luxury goods: items that took up little space and on which a large profit could be made. Many Tuareg settled in the communities with which they traded, serving as local merchants.

Tuareg camel caravans continued to transport goods across the Sahara until the mid-twentieth century when European trains and trucks took over. Today, many Tuareg live in the cities bordering the Sahara.

Historically, Tuareg society was divided between those who tended the land and those who did not. Tilling the land was once considered the work of the lower classes, while the upper classes reaped the benefits of trading. As time passed, however, the farmers were able to accumulate wealth while the trans-Saharan trade routes decreased in importance. Nevertheless, Tuareg society remains very hierarchical, with a class of nobles at the top of the social ladder.

Figure 12.4e Tuareg tribespeople leading a camel caravan across the dunes of the Sahara Desert.

In Tuareg society it is the men, not women, who wear a veil in public but this has more to do with practical needs than with religion; because more Tuareg men than women travel in the desert, the men have more need to cover and protect their face.

Libya: breaking the drought

While drilling for oil in Libya in the 1960s, engineers discovered huge reserves of water in aquifers beneath the Sahara Desert. This vast store of water had accumulated over some 70 000 years, much of it from a time when rainfall in northern Africa was much higher.

To develop its economy Libya needed to use this water. In the 1970s the country had made huge profits from exporting oil to the countries of the developed world. Much of this money has been invested in the Great Man-Made River Project. This is the world's largest civil engineering project. Construction started in 1983 and is still going on. When completed the project will improve access to water for over 5 million people and will irrigate dry areas so that the country can become self-sufficient in terms of food. The project will also generate electricity, which will help to promote industrial development.

Some parts of the project have been completed and water has started flowing from the well fields through 750 kilometres of pipelines beneath the Sahara Desert to the north coast.

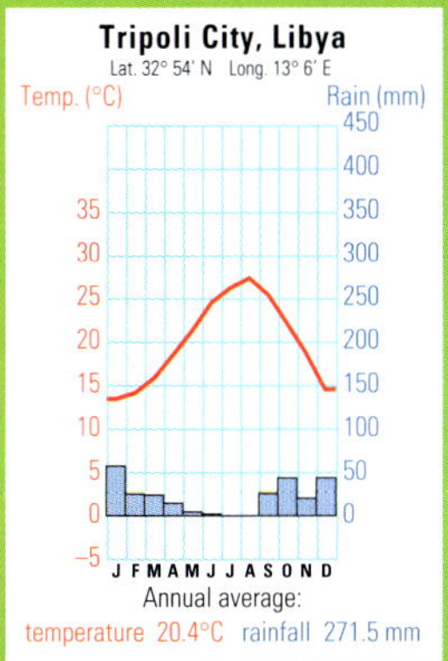

Figure 12.4f Climate graph for Tripoli.

> Libya is a hot, dry country. The rainfall that does fall is limited to a narrow coastal zone. Seventy per cent of Libya's 5 million people live in the coastal cities of Tripoli and Benghazi.

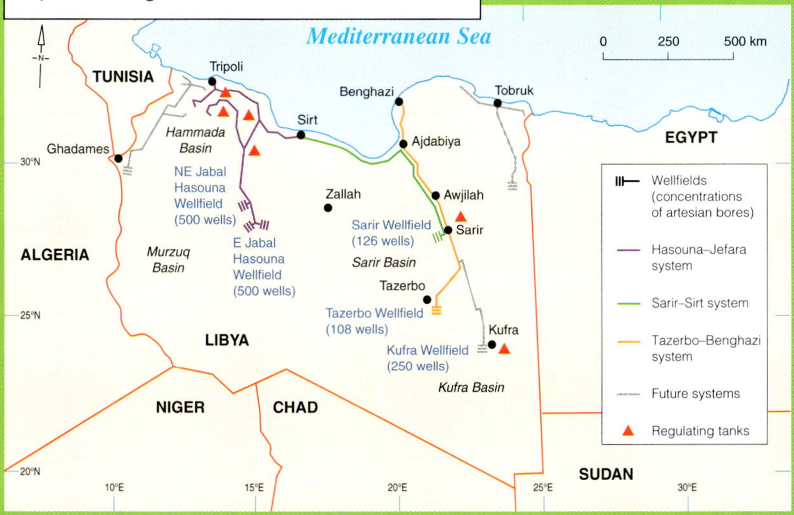

Figure 12.4g Libya's Great Man-Made River Project.

Did U know?

Fact file

Infrastructure

- The sands of the Sahara hold 120 000 cubic kilometres of water—two-thirds of that held by the Black Sea.
- More than 100 wells, most over 500 metres deep, have been dug.
- A 3500-kilometre network of 4-metre diameter pipes is being laid. It will carry 5 million cubic metres of water per day.
- Three major reservoirs (one each at Ajdabiya, Sirt and Benghazi) store 35 million cubic metres of water.
- A 90-megawatt power station is being built at Sirt together with 4000 kilometres of transmission lines.

Benefits

- In urban areas 2 million residents in Tripoli, Sirt and Benghazi now have high-quality water. This has improved their quality of life.
- In rural areas each family has been given 10 hectares of land, a tractor, a house, tools and access to irrigation water. Wheat, barley and maize can now be grown.
- The project has made 135 000 hectares of land available for production. Large quantities of fruit and vegetables, as well as 270 000 tonnes of crops and 760 000 tonnes of fodder, are now grown on irrigated land.

Understanding the text

1. What is an aquifer? What is created when an aquifer reaches a depression in the desert?
2. What resources have been discovered in the Sahara?

UTT worksheet 12.4

12.5 Review and reflect

Chapter summary

In this chapter we investigated the geographical processes responsible for the formation of desert environments. We learned that deserts have a number of features in common, including very low and irregular rainfall, highly specialised plants and animals and few, if any, people. We also discovered that deserts are not necessarily hot places, just very dry.

We looked in detail at the Sahara Desert, the world's largest desert, and the issue of desertification: the process responsible for turning desperately needed agricultural land into desert.

Activity 1

Cloze passage: Desert environments

Test your knowledge and understanding of desert environments. Copy and complete the following passage using the words below.

driest, evaporation, wind-blown, buttes, temperatures, succulents, moisture, ephemerals, sand, cold, range, xerophytes, radiate, mesas, large, precipitation, depositional, plants, rocks, Europe, atmosphere

Deserts are found in places where ________ is greater than precipitation. This is usually where ________ is less than 250 millimetres a year. Deserts are found on every continent except ________ .

Deserts usually have few ________ and a hard, ________ surface covered with ________ and ________ . The ________ of temperatures experienced each day is often very ________ . Very high daytime ________ often give way to very ________ temperatures at night. There is no cloud cover, so heat is lost into the ________ very quickly. The lack of ________ in the air allows the surface of the desert to ________ heat rapidly after the sun goes down.

Drought-resistant plants are called ________ . Plants that store water in their tissue are called ________ . ________ are plants that can complete their life cycle in the few weeks following rain.

Sand dunes and alluvial fans are examples of ________ landform features found in arid areas. ________ and ________ are examples of erosional landform features.

Activity 2

Identifying landforms

Study Figure 12.5a, which shows desert landform features, and identify the numbered features. Select from the list below.

plateau	alluvial fan	mesa
longitudinal dunes	gibber plain	canyon
playa lake	butte	bolson
escarpment	wadi	salt pan
barchan dunes	inselberg	star dunes
transverse dunes		

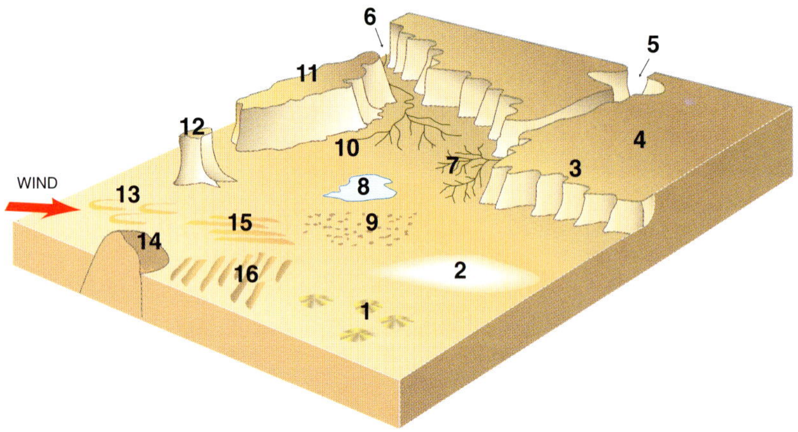

Figure 12.5a Desert landforms.

Refer to the Reflection box on page 17.

Activity 3

Constructing cross-sections

Copy the two cross-section grids in Figure 12.5b. Using the contour map in Figure 12.5b, construct the two cross-sections: A-B and C-D. Label each cross-section as either a mesa or a butte.

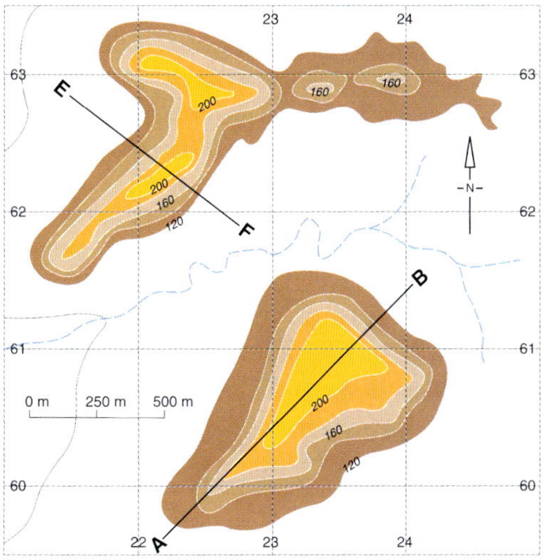

Figure 12.5b A contour map of desert landforms.

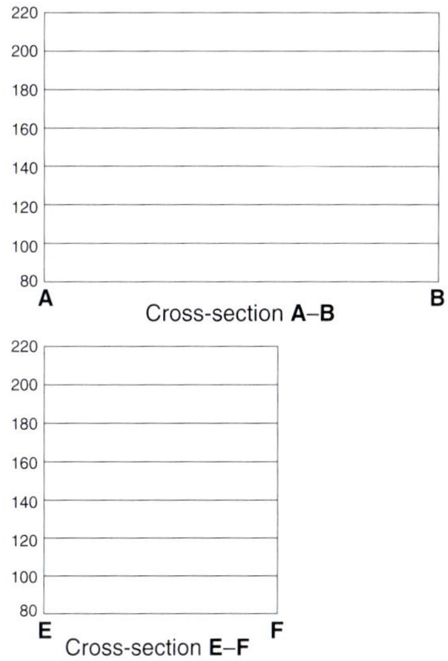

Activity 4

Constructing a three-dimensional model

Aim

To construct a three-dimensional model of a mesa and butte.

Materials required

Thick cardboard; scissors; yellow, orange, light-brown, mid-brown and dark-brown paint; glue; plywood suitable for the base; and light-yellow paint or sand.

Procedure

Follow these steps to create a three-dimensional model of Monument Valley:

1 Enlarge the map in Figure 12.5b onto a sheet of A4 paper. Copy this enlargement five times: one for each contour height on the map.

2 Cut around each set of contour lines to create templates.

3 Using the templates, trace each set of contours on to a piece of thick cardboard. Carefully cut around the shape of the contour layer you have traced onto the cardboard. Paint each shape a different colour, starting with the lightest colour for the largest-shaped pieces through to the darkest for the smallest.

4 Using glue, assemble the mesa and butte and arrange them on the plywood base so that they are located in the same position as in the map. Paint the base a light-yellow colour or sprinkle sand onto a thin coating of glue. Refer to Figure 12.5c to see what the finished model should look like.

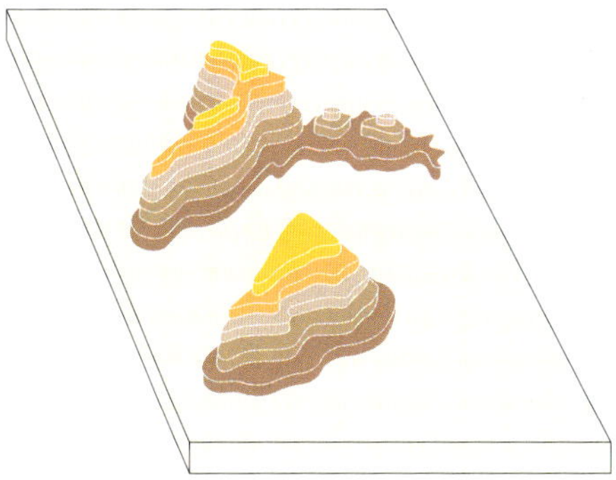

Figure 12.5c A completed model.

Chapter 13

PART C **Global change**

Our changing world

Introduction

The world in which we live is being transformed in ways that we don't yet fully comprehend. Driving these changes is the revolution in information and communication technologies. Just think of how the Internet and mobile phones have changed the ways people access information, buy goods and services and communicate with each other. These technologies hardly existed a decade ago. We now live in a truly global society. The clothing we wear, the food we eat, the sports we play, the television shows we watch and the music we listen to all show how our economy and culture is becoming increasingly integrated with the economies and cultures of other countries.

In this chapter we focus on the processes of economic and cultural integration or what we refer to as globalisation.

Learn about:

- globalisation
- changing global relationships
- global inequalities
- variations in the access of people to the essential aspects of life
- variations in the distribution, access and use of natural resources
- different life opportunities and quality of life throughout the world
- global organisations involved in reducing global inequalities and promoting ecological sustainability

Learn to:

- outline the process of globalisation
- recognise the role of technology in the globalisation process
- identify examples of economic and cultural factors that are shaping the world today as part of globalisation
- identify the impact of globalisation at a variety of scales
- describe changing global relationships as a result of globalisation
- identify global patterns of poverty and wealth
- describe global variations in the access of people to a range of essential aspects of life
- identify global patterns of resource use
- explain the link between resource use and sustainability
- describe different variations in quality of life, including those based on gender
- discuss methods used by groups to influence the global community

Key questions

1. What is globalisation?
2. How has technology transformed the ways people interact?
3. How is economic and cultural integration affecting the way communities interact?

Global teens

He watches
- NBL basketball via satellite TV—USA
- *Friends*—USA
- *Home and Away*—Australia
- *The Bill*—UK
- American and British movies

Plays

Plays basketball, loves skiing and snowboarding and hopes to complete a ski instructors' course in Canada when he finishes the HSC

Listens to
- Metallica—USA
- Eminem—USA
- Ja Rule—USA
- Blink—USA
- POD—USA
- Grinspoon—Australia

Preferred fast foods

McDonald's and KFC—USA

She watches
- *The Bold and the Beautiful*—USA
- *Friends*—USA
- *The Secret Life of Us*—Australia
- *Home and Away*—Australia
- American and British movies

Plays

Practises martial arts, plays touch football and plans to go on a surfing holiday in Hawaii

Listens to
- Eminem—USA
- Red Hot Chili Peppers—USA
- Craig David—USA
- Destiny's Child—USA
- George—Australia

Preferred fast food

McDonald's

Glossary of key terms

Cultural integration The increasing linkages and similarities between world cultures.

Culture The way of life of a people, including their traditions, customs, languages and belief systems.

Economic integration The growing number of commercial links between countries and firms.

Franchising Purchasing the rights to use the trading name, knowledge, methods and procedures of another business.

Global village A term used to describe how the world appears to be getting smaller through advances in technology, especially technologies that allow the transfer of information. What happens in one corner of the globe can rapidly and significantly affect people elsewhere.

Globalisation The integration of the world's economy and culture through the mass consumption of mainly Western culture, technology and trade.

Infrastructure The facilities needed for the effective functioning of a community. It includes education and health care services, water and power supplies, road and railway transport networks as well as communication systems, such as telephone and computer networks.

Intergovernmental organisations (IGOs) International bodies or organisations that are established and sponsored by a number of governments, often via the United Nations. Examples include the World Trade Organization, World Bank and International Monetary Fund.

International trade The movement of goods and services from one country to another.

Mass consumer culture A world dominated by the consumption of the products of popular culture.

Popular culture Mainstream culture; usually associated with 'lighter' forms of entertainment, such as sporting events, television programs, movies, comics and rock concerts.

Sovereignty The idea that a nation has complete autonomy (freedom) to determine its own affairs; government free from external control.

Transnational corporations (TNCs) Large companies that operate in a number of countries but generally have their headquarters in one of the countries of the developed world.

eGlossary

GeoToolkit

ICT Toolkit

13.1 Globalisation

Figure 13.1a Riot police confront antiglobalisation protestors.

What is globalisation?

Globalisation is the term used to describe the way countries are becoming more interconnected, both economically and culturally. It means that it is possible to produce a product anywhere, using resources from anywhere, by a company located anywhere to be sold anywhere. It also means that cultures around the world are being influenced by the **popular culture** (such as books, magazines, television, movies, music and fashions) of other countries, especially the United States. As a result, the world's cultural interests are also becoming more interconnected. The factors driving the process of globalisation are:

- advances in transport and communications technology
- the growth of transnational corporations (TNCs)
- expansion of world trade
- international investment flows.

Foundation worksheet 13.1

Extension worksheet 13.1

What is driving globalisation?

Advances in transport and communications technology

Over the past twenty years there have been significant developments in both communications and transport technologies. The introduction of specialised bulk carriers, oil tankers and container ships has helped to reduce the cost of transport and greatly increase the volume of world trade. Similar advances in aviation, especially the introduction of the Boeing 747, have greatly reduced the cost and time involved in international travel. This, in turn, has led to a growth in international tourism and the movement of people to other countries for services, such as education and health care. Recent developments in communications technology (especially the development of the Internet and email) enable people anywhere on earth to have access to and distribute vast amounts of information. (See Unit 13.2.)

The growth of transnational corporations

The production and distribution of goods and services is increasingly dominated by very large companies known as **transnational corporations (TNCs)**. These are businesses that operate in a number of countries but generally have their headquarters in one of the countries of the developed world. The business links of TNCs create a more integrated world economy where decisions made in one country can affect people in other parts of the world. (See Unit 13.3.)

Expansion of world trade

The movement of goods and services between countries is called **international trade**. Nations import those goods and services that they are unable to produce themselves or can obtain more cheaply from other places. They pay for these imports with the money that they earn from exporting the goods and services that they produce. Because more and more countries are becoming integrated with the global economy, the volume of world trade is also increasing. (See Unit 13.3.)

International investment

Money flows more rapidly around the world today than it has at any other time in history. This is largely due to developments in technology and the relaxing of government controls on the international flow of finance. Money moves both into and out of countries as individuals, businesses and governments invest in offshore assets (such as factories, hotels and office developments), lend money or repay debt. (See Unit 13.3.)

Figure 13.1b Container ships have greatly increased the volume of world trade.

Impacts of globalisation

The evidence of globalisation is everywhere, but it is important to recognise that not everyone is in favour of it. Some environmental groups, for example, argue that TNCs are responsible for many of the world's environmental problems. These problems include global warming, the depletion of natural resources and the production of harmful chemicals. Some groups also claim that TNCs take advantage of developing countries by locating polluting industries within their borders, logging their tropical forests and exploitating their labour. Other concerns include the loss of local culture, the tendency for developed countries to interfere in the affairs of developing countries, and the reduced power of governments to control economic activity. (See Units 13.3–13.5.)

Those who support globalisation suggest that it benefits both individuals and the global community. These groups claim that globalisation results in faster economic growth, quicker access to new technology, cheaper imports and greater competition. In addition, they argue that globalisation will make the world economy more efficient and will continue to create hundreds of millions of jobs, mainly, but not only, in developing countries. This, in turn, it is claimed, will generate an upward spiral of employment and wealth. A summary of the 'globalisation winners and losers' is provided in Table 13.1a.

Figure 13.1c Globalisation is changing the world in ways we don't yet fully understand.

Table 13.1a Globalisation winners and losers

Globalisation winners	Globalisation losers
Those who are able to master new technologies	Those unwilling to update processes or use the new technologies
Those who are educated and able to adapt	Those with limited education
Workers who are willing to change jobs and learn new skills	Unskilled and semi-skilled factory workers in developed countries at risk of losing their jobs to cheap labour in developing countries
Consumers, as they have greater choice	Heavily protected industries
The environment—if globalisation increases economic activity (and tax collections) governments are better able to fund programs that protect the environment	The environment—if TNCs shift polluting industries from developed to developing countries in order to avoid strict environmental regulations
The community through increased cultural understanding	Communities in developing countries—if TNCs exploit workers, ignore workplace safety issues and pollute the environment
Firms with an understanding of the international marketplace	Firms without the drive to innovate and find new markets

Understanding the text

1 Define the term 'globalisation'.
2 What is a transnational corporation?
3 Explain why the number and influence of TNCs has grown in recent years.
4 Explain why countries export and import goods and services.
5 Why does international finance flow so rapidly around the globe? Explain the purpose of these financial flows.
6 Summarise the arguments for and against globalisation.

UTT worksheet 13.1

Working geographically

1 **Interpreting cartoons** Study Figure 13.1c. Write one paragraph explaining the point being made by the cartoonist.

2 **Group work** In groups, list the recent developments in transport and communications technology that have promoted gobalisation.

3 **Research** Select at least ten goods and services that you have purchased recently; for example, food, shoes, clothing and accessories. Try to find out where the goods were made.

4 **Group work** In groups, list the arguments for and against globalisation. Which of these arguments are the most/least valid? Explain your answer.

5 **Challenge: Report** Imagine you are a newspaper journalist. Prepare a short report in which you examine the factors shaping the speed and extent of globalisation over the past fifty years.

13.2 Technological change

Did U know?

- The world's largest container ship, the *Shenzhen*, is 322 metres long and carries 8063 containers. The ship has a 93 120-horsepower engine, the world's most powerful diesel engine. The 100 000-tonne ship's top speed is 46.6 kilometres per hour.
- The world's largest oil tanker, the *Jahre Viking*, weighs in at 564 763 tonnes and is 458 metres long.

The number of computers connected directly to the Internet (Internet hosts), 1991–2003. Source: Internet Software Consortium.

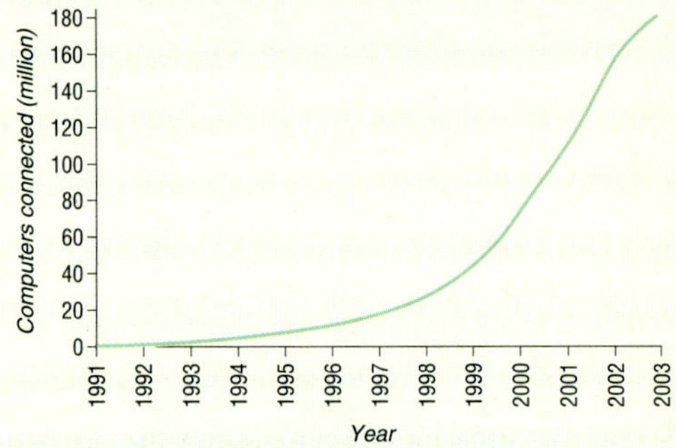

Recent developments in communications and transport technologies have transformed the way that economies operate and cultures interact. These developments have helped to break down many of the barriers that once divided the world, such as the great distances between countries and the high cost of communications.

The shrinking of time and space, which has been brought about by the development of new technologies, has created a more closely linked world, forming what some geographers now refer to as a **global village**. People in developed countries travel more than ever before, communicate with others more often and use the Internet to purchase goods and services from suppliers on the other side of the globe. This unit looks at some of the technological developments that have made these changes possible.

Communications and computer technologies

The Internet

Networked computers make it possible for individuals to transfer large amounts of information around the world twenty-four hours a day, at high speed and at a low cost. The number of Internet users worldwide is expected to increase from 182 million in the year 2000 to more than 765 million by 2005 (see Figure 13.2a). The Internet is an important tool in the promotion of the globalisation of trade, investment and culture. This technology has, for example, enabled many small businesses to market their product to a global audience twenty-four hours a day. (See Unit 2.11.)

Satellite technology

Today we are dependent on satellites for many aspects of our daily lives. They relay and transmit much of the information we use every day,

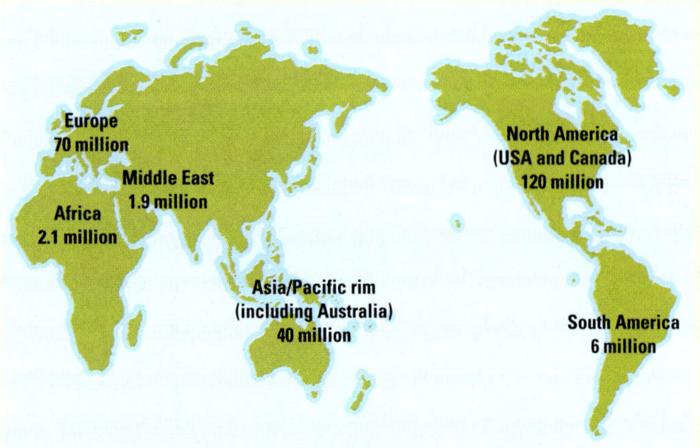

Estimate of the worldwide Internet population, 2000. Source: CommerceNet; Australian Bureau of Statistics.

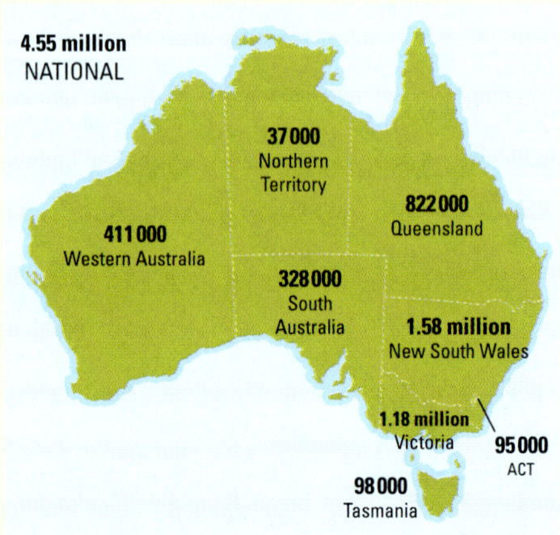

Number of Internet users in Australia, 2002. Source: Internet Activity, September 2002; Australian Bureau of Statistics.

Figure 13.2a An Internet connected world.

including television transmissions, telephone calls, weather information, military intelligence and much more. Until the early 1990s most satellites launched into orbit were used for military purposes. Since then, however, the number of satellites orbiting the earth has increased significantly and the cost of using them has decreased.

Transport technologies

Air transport

Developments in aviation technology, especially the introduction of the Boeing 747, have helped to lower travel costs and increase the volume of international tourism and business activity. This, in turn, has had an impact on our cultural identity. When we are exposed to new customs and traditions, we often integrate aspects of these into our own way of life.

Land transport

Increased levels of investment in rail and road **infrastructure** have made land transport faster and more competitive over longer distances. The introduction of high-speed rail systems and new cargo handling equipment has, for example, cut delivery times and increased efficiency.

Sea transport

Technological developments in shipping and cargo handling have been central to the expansion of international trade. As ships have increased in size, the cost of transporting goods has declined. Specialised bulk carriers, oil tankers and container ships lower costs and reduce the amount of time that ships spend in port being loaded and unloaded. Containerisation has revolutionised the way cargo is handled. Containers are capable of being carried by road, rail or ship. This eliminates the need for the multiple handling of goods.

The monsterbus

The aviation industry is about to take a technological leap forward with the introduction of the giant Airbus A380. The new double-decker aircraft will be capable of carrying 550 passengers: 25 per cent more than the Boeing 747. The 73 metre long aircraft, which will have a range of 14 800 kilometres, comes with a price tag of about US$400 million.

Figure 13.2b The Airbus A380.

Understanding the text

1. Explain how recent changes in technology helped to create a global village.
2. Explain how the Internet has helped small business.
3. How has the availability and cost of satellite communications changed over time?
4. Describe the impact of recent developments in transport on the cost of transporting both freight and passengers.

UTT worksheet 13.2

Working geographically

1. **Hypothetical** What do you think international transport and communications will be like in 2050? Prepare a talk, poster or comic strip outlining your vision.
2. **Constructing graphs** Use the information provided in Figure 13.2a to construct a column graph showing the distribution of world Internet users in year 2000. Which continents have the least/most access to the Internet?
3. **Challenge: Research** Undertake library or Internet research. Find out about current developments in the following areas of transportation: lightweight, fuel-efficient cars; high-speed and light rail systems; passenger ferries; and air transport.
4. **Challenge: Interview-based research** Interview three older people to find out about changes in transport and communications technology over time. In small groups, create a time line to illustrate your results.

Foundation worksheet 13.1

13.3 Economic integration

Where does my Holden come from?

Holden's range of cars shows just how integrated the world economy has become.

Table 13.3a Source of Holden-badged vehicles

Source of Holden-badged vehicles
Barina: manufactured in Spain
Astra: manufactured in Germany (convertible in Italy)
Vectra: manufactured in the UK
Zafira: manufactured in Thailand
Cruze: manufactured in Japan
Commodore: manufactured in Australia; exported to markets in the Middle East, Brazil, Southern Africa, Brunei, Fiji and New Zealand
Monaro: manufactured in Australia; exported to the Middle East, New Zealand, Brunei and the USA
Caprice/Statesman: manufactured in Australia; exported to the Middle East and New Zealand
Holden ute: manufactured in Australia; exported to southern Africa and New Zealand
Rodeo: manufactured in Japan
Jackaroo: manufactured in Japan

What is economic integration?

The term **'economic integration'** refers to the growing number of links between firms and economies across national borders. Examples of these links include flows of goods, money, information and the movement of workers between countries.

The linking of economies is not new. Trade has taken place between distant civilisations for centuries. But these links expanded rapidly during the last half-century due to changes in technology, consumer tastes, governmental regulation and the growth of transnational corporations (TNCs). The four key elements of economic integration are international trade flows, international financial flow, international investment and the global migration of workers (see Figure 13.3a).

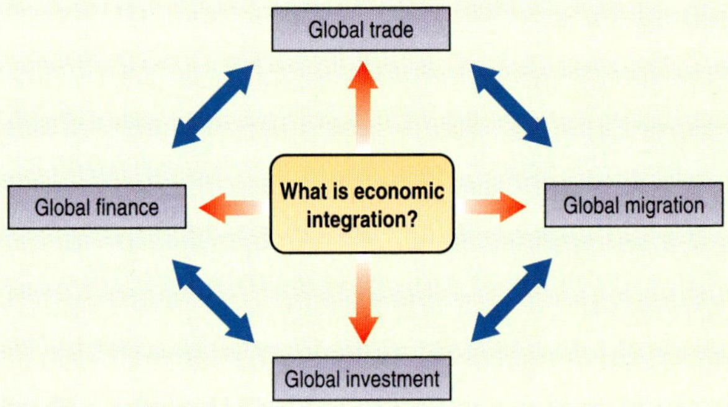

Figure 13.3a What is economic integration?

International trade flows

World trade is an important economic link between countries. The rate of change in international trade has been much faster than the rate of growth in world economic activity. The increasing influence of TNCs has been largely responsible for this trend. TNCs (such as Nike, General Motors, Shell and Sony) play a central role in the global economy. Firms such as these now account for around 25 per cent of all goods and services produced globally. In addition, current estimates suggest that about one-third of all world trade involves the movement of partially manufactured goods within these large companies.

Financial flows

Another important indicator of increasing economic integration has been the rapid growth in foreign investment between countries. This investment usually involves individuals, businesses and governments buying overseas assets, including factories, hotels, office buildings or shares in companies. It is important to note, however, that around 80 per cent of the flow of investment funds is between developed countries. The forty-nine poorest countries of the world received less than 3 per cent of these funds.

The movement of workers between countries

Developments in transport technology have made it easier for individuals to move from one country to another in search of employment. These migrations are of two main types: the movement of highly skilled, highly paid professionals (often employees of TNCs); and the movement of poorly paid, low-skilled workers. Often referred to as 'guest workers', these people (numbering some 90 million) work in countries with labour shortages and send money back home to their families.

Figure 13.3b Cartoon by Nicholson from *The Australian*. www.nicholsoncartoons.com.au

The inequalities of economic integration

In recent years there has been increasing concern about many of the inequalities created by economic globalisation. A number of individuals, interest groups and non-government organisations are campaigning to raise public awareness of these issues using the Internet and public protests. Recent targets of these protests have been the meetings of the World Trade Organization (WTO), which promotes free trade between countries, and the International Monetary Fund (IMF) and World Bank, which give countries loans when their economies are in crisis. One common argument presented by protest groups is that these **intergovernmental organisations (IGOs)** have undermined local decision-making in developing countries by allowing outside companies and agencies to exercise too much control. National **sovereignty** (the power of a country to control its own destiny) is seen as key to protecting local cultures and traditions.

Understanding the text

1 Explain what is meant by the term 'economic integration'.

2 International trade has grown faster than world economic activity. What does this say about the relative importance of international trade?

3 Explain how TNCs help to integrate/link world economies.

4 What is foreign investment?

5 Distinguish between the two main types of international migration.

6 Explain why some groups in society are opposed to global economic integration.

7 Explain the role intergovernmental organisations play in the promotion of closer international economic relationships between nations.

8 Outline one of the criticisms of the role of intergovernmental organisations in developing countries.

UTT worksheet 13.3

Working geographically

1 **Interpreting models** Study Figure 13.3a. Write a paragraph describing the factors that contribute to global economic integration.

2 **Internet research** Study Table 13.3a. Select another make of car. Use the Internet to find out where each of their models is manufactured.

3 **Class discussion: Intepreting cartoons** Study Figure 13.3b. As a class, discuss the message Nicholson is trying to communicate.

4 **Challenge: Internet research** Access the website of at least one organisation concerned about the negative effects of globalisation. Outline the issues that concern the organisation and the strategies it uses to achieve it objectives. Present an oral report outlining your findings.

Extension worksheet 13.2

13.4 Cultural integration

Did U know?

- Most radio airtime in Australia is devoted to bands from the United States, Britain and Ireland.
- Half of all the music bought in Australia is American.
- Australia's share of the global music industry is just 1.5 per cent.
- One-quarter of all music purchased in Australia is recorded in Australia.
- The world's largest music publishing company—Universal—controls over 1 million copyrights, including songs by Prince, U2, Shania Twain and No Doubt, as well as some of the world's most popular songs.
- Sixty-two Universal albums each sold more than 1 million copies in 2001.

Figure 13.4a The symbols of the mass consumer culture are all around us.

The term **culture** refers to the way of life of a group of people, including their traditions, customs, languages and belief systems. **Cultural integration** describes the way in which changes in technology, the growth of transnational corporations (TNCs) and global media/entertainment companies are creating increasing similarities and links between world cultures.

The mixing of cultures is not a new trend. Since the first migrations of people across the globe, local traditions, languages and customs have mixed with and influenced each other. Cultural change continues today but at a much faster rate. Recent developments in communications (including the telephone, television, the Internet and satellites) and expansion in world trade and long-distance travel mean that the way of life of one culture can quickly influence others on the other side of the globe.

Evidence of cultural integration is all around us. Brand names such as McDonald's, Coca-Cola, Disney, Starbucks, Nike, Kodak, IBM and MTV are now found all over the globe. Because of their global popularity and influence, these brands, and their related products, have made a major contribution to the development of a **mass consumer culture**. Two of the best examples of the spread of a mass consumer culture are the global music industry and world sport.

The global music industry

Every year, performers and musicians from around the world record music in a variety of styles ranging from hip-hop, funk, rap and heavy metal to popular music and jazz. Despite the varied backgrounds of these artists, and the diversity of the music they create, the majority of their work is owned and managed by six large US-based multinational recording companies. The enormous power of these companies means that they have control over the type of music played on the radio and available for purchase in stores.

Another important force promoting global cultural integration is music television (MTV). Because of its wide appeal with young people, MTV has become a very effective method for marketing mass consumer products to teenagers.

Sport

The globalisation of sport is another good example of the increased links that exist between cultures worldwide. Sport is an important part of the Australian national identity. As a nation we take great pride in our sporting achievements and look up to our sports stars as popular heroes.

It is important to recognise, however, that the mix of sports played in Australia has changed over time. Historically, colonisation and international migration have played an important role in the spread of sports across the globe. Many of the teams involved in the Cricket World Cup, for example, are former colonies of Great Britain. Events such as the Olympics have introduced Westerners to a range of sports from non-Western nations, including tae kwon do and judo, and have made more sports accessible to people from a variety of backgrounds.

More recent developments include the rising popularity of American sports, such as baseball and basketball, in Australia. This is largely due to the influence of TNCs, the media and pay/satellite television in the marketing of sports worldwide. Today, players of the US National Basketball Association (NBA) are recognised worldwide. Slick marketing campaigns have been used to sell the game to a worldwide audience. The game's stars are featured in Hollywood movies and on everything from licensed sportswear to bubble gum packets and trading cards (see Figure 13.4b). The merchandising (selling of goods) associated with these sports has become popular among Australian teenagers, who now wear clothing and caps featuring the name, logo and colours of their favourite American basketball or football team.

The increased popularity of sportswear is not only related to the culture of sport but to the mass marketing of fashion around the world. Large US TNCs own most of the international brand names in fashion, such as Levi's, Nike, Hanes and Calvin Klein. These companies target the youth market in order to influence the brand of sportswear, shirts and designer jeans we buy.

Another excellent example of the increased links between cultures is the fast-food industry (see Unit 13.5.).

Figure 13.4b An e-card downloaded from the UK Pepsi Football website. British football stars, including David Beckham, dressed as Roman gladiators and promoting Pepsi.

> People, goods and ideas move. And cultures change. The difference now is the scope and speed of these changes. It took television 13 years to achieve 50 million viewers; it took the Internet just five...
>
> The huge number of teenagers—800 million in the world, the most that there have ever been—with time and money to spend, is one of the powerful engines of cultural integration. Kids travel, they hang out, and above all they buy things.

Extension worksheet 13.3

Working geographically

1 **Internet research** Undertake Internet research into one of the following sports: soccer, rugby union, hockey, tennis, baseball, basketball or cricket. Find out:
   - **a** when and where the game originated
   - **b** when the game was first played in Australia
   - **c** how the game has been adapted for different contexts/localities
   - **d** an interesting fact about your choice that illustrates the changing nature of this game.

   Present your findings in the form of a multimedia presentation or oral report.

2 **Internet research** Access the websites for the National Rugby League, Australian Football League and Australian Rugby Union. Make a list of the names of the sponsors and types of merchandise marketed through these sites. Who do you think is the target market for these products? Compare these sites with the home page of the US National Basketball Association. What differences and similarities in the marketing approaches do you notice?

3 **Class discussion** As a class, discuss the likely impact of cultural integration on local customs, traditions and language. Use your ideas to conduct a class debate. Topic: Globalisation destroys local cultural differences.

4 **Internet research: Wall display** Study Figure 13.4b. Use the Internet to locate examples of celebrities who promote global brands to an international consumer market. Mount a wall display of these images.

Understanding the text

1 Define the terms 'culture' and 'cultural integration'.
2 List the factors that have promoted global cultural integration.
3 Outline the extent to which TNCs in the music industry control the type of music played on the radio and made available for sale to customers. Why is this the case?
4 List the factors that have helped to spread sports across the globe.
5 Explain how the mix of Australian sports has been influenced by sports from other countries.

UTT worksheet 13.4

13.5 SAMPLE STUDY

Golden arches: fast food, mega bucks

Figure 13.5a Images of global fast-food culture.

> Today's kids eat American fast foods, wash them down with American carbonated beverages [soft drinks], play or at least watch American sports and wear American clothes. And increasingly they think American thoughts and dream American dreams.
>
> *Philip Adams*

McDonald's: a case study of economic and cultural integration

One of the most obvious examples of globalisation has been the rapid growth of fast-food retailers, such as McDonald's, Burger King, KFC, Pizza Hut and Starbucks. These businesses are examples of transnational corporations (TNCs). While many of these companies have their headquarters in countries of the developed world (often the United States) their shop fronts, products and advertising are found in cities, towns and suburbs all over the world.

As these businesses expand they create important economic and cultural links between countries. The opening of new outlets spreads the influence of Western consumer culture and has an important impact on the lifestyles of local communities by exposing them to new food products (such as Big Macs), new business practices (**franchising** and casual employment) as well as Western ideas and lifestyles. This case study of McDonald's looks at the influence of a fast-food TNC on the economies and cultures of countries around the world.

Golden arches: a brief history

The McDonald's Corporation had its beginnings in 1955 when salesman Ray Kroc walked into a takeaway burger outlet in California and was impressed with what he saw. He convinced the owners of the store (the McDonald brothers) to allow him to open new stores using their name. In return he agreed to pay the brothers 0.5 per cent of the gross sales from each store. Today, the business has expanded to include more than 30 000 stores in over 120 countries on six continents. These stores serve an average of 45 million people worldwide every day. This is equivalent to serving lunch to the entire population of Australia and New Zealand twice over!

The global distribution of McDonald's stores is shown in Figure 13.5d. This map shows that the majority of McDonald's restaurants are located in North America. It is only since 1990 that McDonald's has opened stores in Eastern Europe and the Middle East.

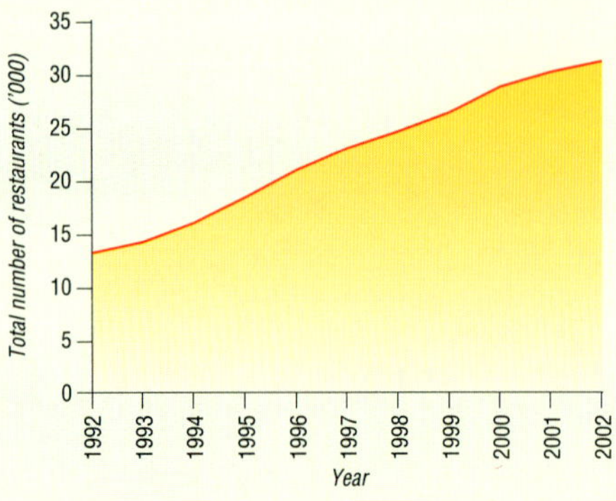

Figure 13.5b Total number of McDonald's restaurants worldwide, 1992–2002. Source: McDonald's.

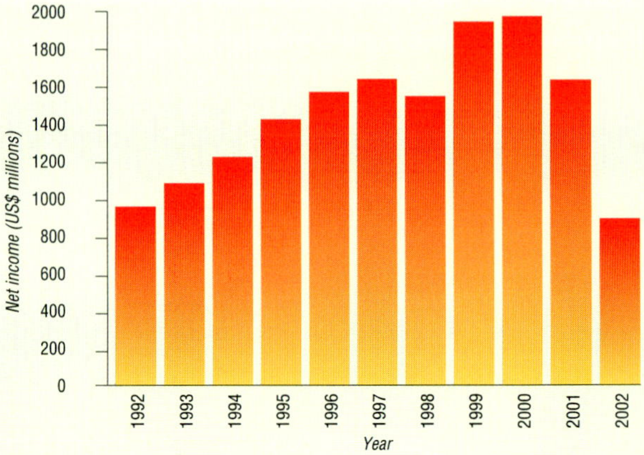

Figure 13.5c McDonald's global net income (profit), 1992–2002. Source: McDonald's.

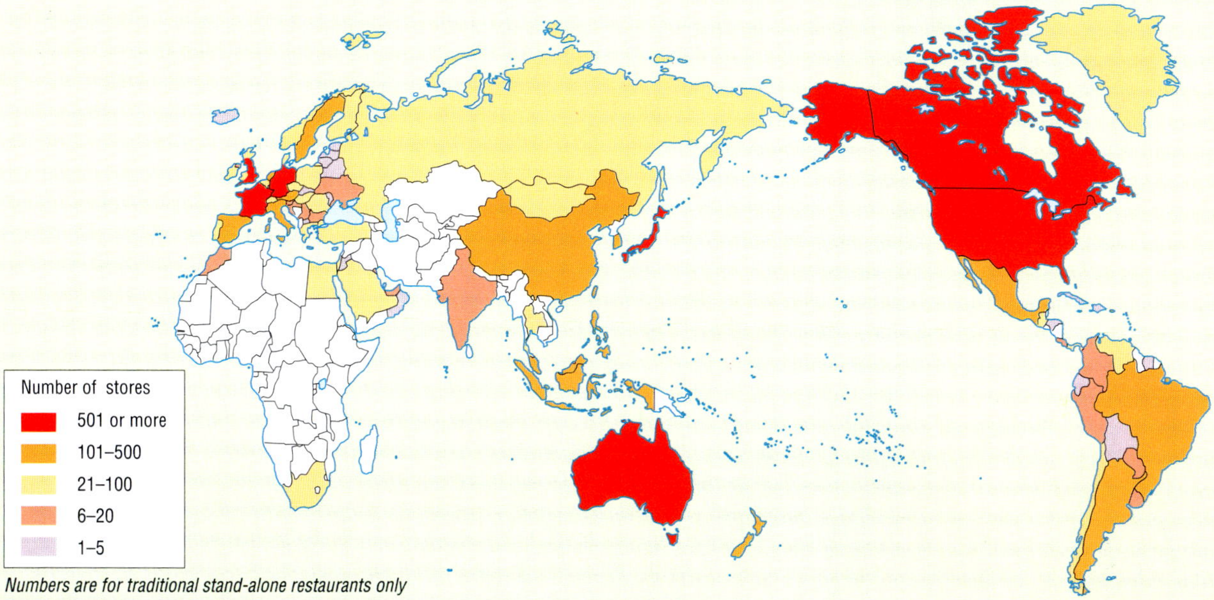

Figure 13.5d The global distribution of McDonald's restaurants.

Economic links

The economic expansion of McDonald's has been rapid. In 1984 McDonald's was opening a new store every seventeen hours. By year 2000, the number of new stores was increasing at three times this rate: a new store was opening somewhere in the world every five hours! McDonald's is aware that this rapid rate of growth cannot continue forever. Competition in the fast-food industry is intense and new retailers enter the market every day. This increased competition has reduced profit levels and forced McDonald's to start closing stores in locations where profits were low. A total of 175 outlets in ten countries were closed following a profit downturn in late 2002.

McDonald's and culture

When we think of McDonald's, two of the images that often come to mind are the golden arches and the company's catchy TV advertisements. These marketing strategies have been so successful that the golden arches is now one of the best recognised symbols in the world. Recent surveys show that the McDonald's logo is now more widely recognised than the Christian cross and that the number of Americans who consume McDonald's now exceeds the number who attend church. One in fifteen Americans have worked for McDonald's.

In many countries of the world, the opening of a McDonald's restaurant is celebrated as an important economic achievement. In these countries, McDonald's is viewed as a symbol of middle-class prosperity, economic efficiency and social progress. When the first Russian store was opened in Moscow in 1990, for example, excited Russians queued for two nights in order to make their first McDonald's purchase. In the first twenty-four hours the store served tens of thousands of people. McDonald's in Moscow's Pushkin Square is now the busiest store in the world.

Not everybody, however, is happy with the continuing global spread of McDonald's products and marketing. Some groups in society argue that fast-food companies, such as McDonald's, put profits before both people and the environment. Over the past few decades fast-food TNCs have been accused of everything from environmental

Did U know?

- In 2002 McDonald's had revenues (total sales) of US$15 406 million and total assets of US$23 971 million.
- McSpotlight is an interest group that is devoted to highlighting the activities of McDonald's and other TNCs.
- McSpotlight claims that McDonald's spends US$2 billion a year promoting its products and corporate image.

Working geographically

Brainstorming task As a class, compile a list of TNCs in the fast-food industry that you are familiar with.

Figure 13.5e Some groups in society disapprove of the strategies used by fast-food retailers, and launch public protests to voice their point of view.

Figure 13.5f Anti-McDonald's cartoons used by protest groups.

destruction and animal cruelty to the exploitation of labour and manipulation of children through advertising (see the ICT box).

As a symbol of Western capitalism and American values McDonald's is a popular target for antiglobalisation protestors across the globe. Many of these protestors argue that the expanding influence of American culture is causing the extinction of many local beliefs and traditions. Recent attacks on restaurants in North America, Australia, Western Europe, China, India, Indonesia, Lebanon, Poland, Russia,

The McLibel trial: Internet-based research activity

ICT

The arguments against multinational companies were highlighted in a recent British High Court Case where two demonstrators, Helen Steel and Dave Morris, were taken to court for distributing pamphlets outside McDonald's restaurants in the United Kingdom. The pamphlets, titled 'What's wrong with McDonald's', made a number of claims about the company's global activities and their impact on both people and the environment. McDonald's argued that these pamphlets contained information that was untrue and 'highly damaging' to their reputation. The trial that followed ran for more than two and a half years: the longest case in British High Court history.

Access the McSpotlight website and complete the following tasks:

1. Write a summary of the claims made in the 'What's wrong with McDonald's' pamphlet. Classify these claims as being either economic, environmental or social/cultural.
2. Go to the link titled 'Story'. Describe the legal resources used by both McDonald's and the two demonstrators, Helen and Dave, to fight this case.
3. Go to the link titled 'Judgement'. Write a summary of the judge's verdict in this case. Which claims about McDonald's were Dave and Helen able to prove?
4. Read the leaflet distributed by McDonald's to its customers before the trial. What was McDonald's point of view about the claims made in the 'What's wrong with McDonald's' leaflet?

Figure 13.5g McDonald's adapt their menus and store architecture in order to cater for local needs.

Saudi Arabia and the United Kingdom demonstrate how widespread these anti-American and anti-globalisation movements are (see Figures 13.5e and 13.5f).

Adapting to local cultures

Despite the use of standardised systems, McDonald's does not have identical restaurants in every country of the world. The architecture of McDonald's restaurants is often adapted to reflect the unique characteristics of local areas. For example, outlets located in historic urban centres or resort locations are given a different appearance to better suit the local character of the area.

There are also local differences in the types of products offered by McDonald's. In the Netherlands, for example, you can buy a vegetarian burger and in Japan you can buy a chicken tatsuta sandwich. It is important to note, however, that the American menu staples (such as Happy Meals, Big Macs, fries and a Coke) are still offered and remain the most popular orders worldwide. The introduction of McCafés and 'New Tastes' menu in Australia represents an attempt by McDonald's to appeal to a broader market and cater for changing consumer tastes.

McDonald's: catering for diversity — ICT

McDonald's corporation is keen to promote the fact that it caters for diversity both in its menu structures and employment policies. Visit the McDonald's website to find out more about the menu items that have been developed to suit the cultural preferences of individual host countries. The website also outlines the company's employment policies. Access the McDonald's website for further information.

Working geographically

1. **Using the media** Collect examples of fast-food advertising from television, radio, newspapers and magazines, then complete the following tasks:
   - a Identify the strategies and images that are used in these marketing campaigns to appeal to particular cultures and communities in Australia.
   - b Outline the extent to which these advertisements promote American ideals and values.
2. **Collage: Class discussion** Use magazines, newspapers and the Internet to put together a photographic collage of different fast-food store designs and menus from around the world. Annotate (label) the important adaptations shown in the photographs. As a class, discuss the extent to which fast-food retailers cater for differences in local cultures and traditions.
3. **Internet research: Group work** Use the Internet to find out more about the history of McDonald's or another fast-food chain of your choice. In small groups, create a time line and a map/wall display showing the geographical expansion of this company over time.
4. **Class survey: Using software—Fast food** Conduct a survey of students in your class to find out how often they visit fast-food outlets and which types of fast food they consume. Graph your results using spreadsheet software (such as Excel). Write a paragraph explaining your survey results.

Foundation worksheet 13.2

Understanding the text

1. Explain how TNCs help to create economic and cultural links between countries.
2. Describe the changing distribution of McDonald's stores over time.
3. Describe the economic expansion of McDonald's over the past twenty years. Explain why some groups in society are unhappy with this trend.
4. How successful has McDonald's advertising been? Provide evidence to support your answer.
5. How has McDonald's adapted its menu selection and store appearance to better suit local cultures?

UTT worksheet 13.5

13.6 Review and reflect

Chapter summary

In this chapter we have examined the process of economic and cultural intergration or what is commonly referred to as globalisation. Many people find it difficult to to understand what globalisation is all about. In reality it is all around us. Consider the following experience of one Australian teenager:

> My mate is back from a visit to the Phillipines, the country his parents migrated from fifteen years ago. He is wearing the latest Phatfarm Classic joggers. I'm impressed. Later that day, while munching on a McDonald's cheeseburger, I access the Internet and find Eastbay: one of the many US-based online retailers of sportswear. With dad's permission, I order a pair of Phatfarm Classic joggers using his American Express card. The shoes, which sell for more than $200 in Australia, cost me just US$49.99 plus US$36.99 in postage and handling: a total of US$86.98 (A$136.35). Five days after placing the order the shoes are delivered, via FedEx, to the front door of my home in suburban Sydney.

This is what globalisation is all about. Economies and cultures becoming more integrated. Technology (in this case the Internet) is what makes this type of commercial activity possible. Governments find it increasingly difficult to control and regulate this type of activity. The joggers, for example, are GST-free. Sites such as Eastbay allow teenagers from around the world to buy the lastest US fashions.

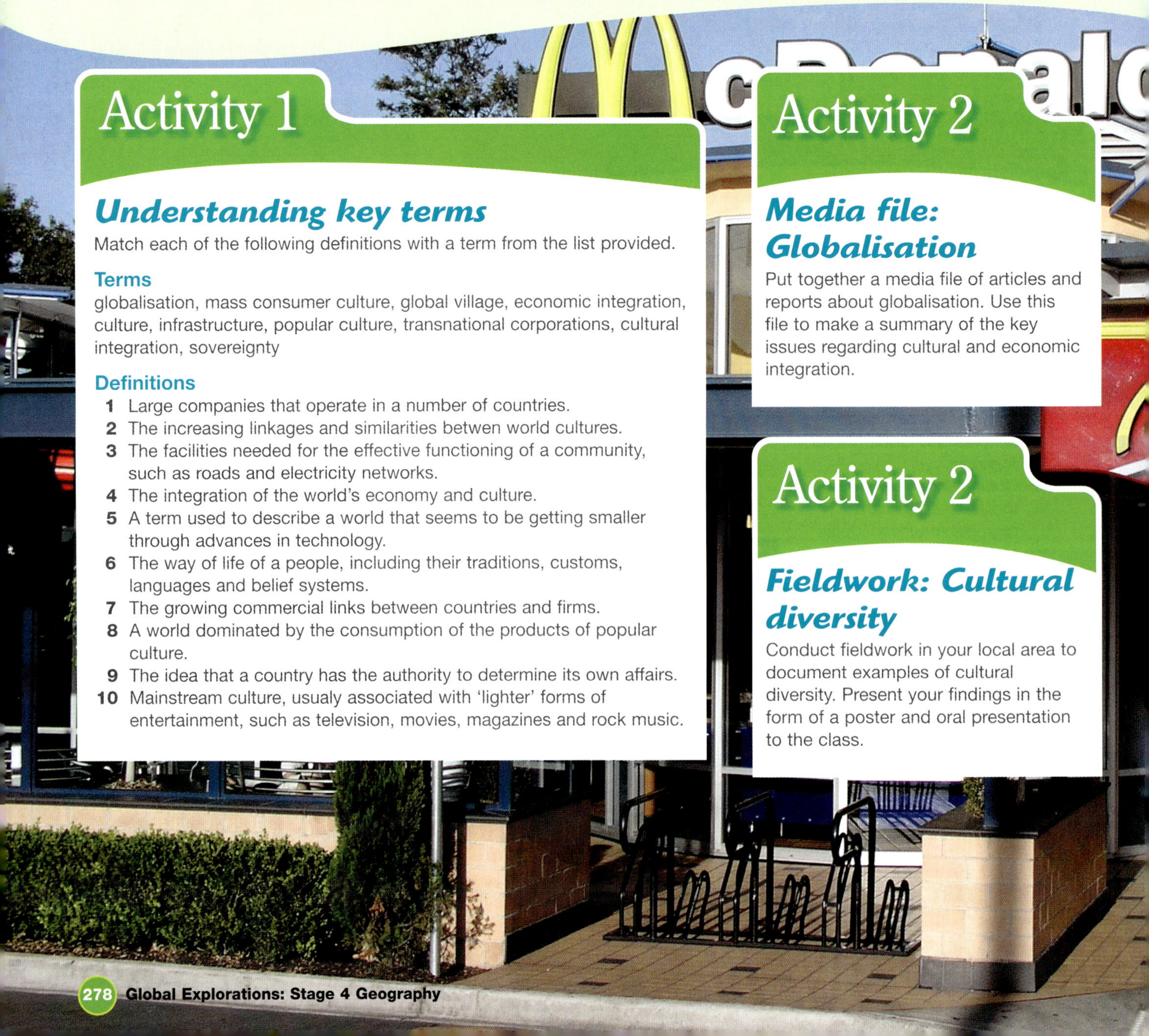

Activity 1

Understanding key terms

Match each of the following definitions with a term from the list provided.

Terms

globalisation, mass consumer culture, global village, economic integration, culture, infrastructure, popular culture, transnational corporations, cultural integration, sovereignty

Definitions

1. Large companies that operate in a number of countries.
2. The increasing linkages and similarities betwen world cultures.
3. The facilities needed for the effective functioning of a community, such as roads and electricity networks.
4. The integration of the world's economy and culture.
5. A term used to describe a world that seems to be getting smaller through advances in technology.
6. The way of life of a people, including their traditions, customs, languages and belief systems.
7. The growing commercial links between countries and firms.
8. A world dominated by the consumption of the products of popular culture.
9. The idea that a country has the authority to determine its own affairs.
10. Mainstream culture, usualy associated with 'lighter' forms of entertainment, such as television, movies, magazines and rock music.

Activity 2

Media file: Globalisation

Put together a media file of articles and reports about globalisation. Use this file to make a summary of the key issues regarding cultural and economic integration.

Activity 2

Fieldwork: Cultural diversity

Conduct fieldwork in your local area to document examples of cultural diversity. Present your findings in the form of a poster and oral presentation to the class.

Refer to the Reflection box on page 17.

Activity 4

Interpreting cartoons

Cartoons are a very effective form of communication. They can be both informative and entertaining and may relate directly to geographical issues or address issues that have geographical implications. The ability of a cartoon to communicate information lies in the quality of the idea, not the quality of the drawing. The ability to interpret a cartoon depends on the reader having an understanding of the issue being addressed by the cartoonist.

Types of cartoons

An *editorial cartoon* is a sketch relating to a particular topic. They are usually found on the editorial or features page of a newspaper. All the cartoons shown here are editorial cartoons. *Strip cartoons* are more likely to entertain, but are still capable of communicating information about important contemporary issues.

1. Study the cartoons shown here. Identify the issues being addressed by each cartoon and write a brief explanation of each. Working in groups, see if other students agree with your interpretation. In your group, reach agreement on the meaning of each cartoon. Share your group's views with the rest of the class.
2. Select one of the cartoons. Research the issue and write a one-page report summarising your findings.
3. Select an issue from this chapter and design a cartoon to illustrate the issue. Share your cartoons with other members of the class.
4. Collect cartoons about geographical issues from newspapers, magazines and textbooks. In small groups, sort the cartoons according to the types of geographical themes each addresses. Display your cartoons on the wall of your classroom.

Figure 13.6b

Figure 13.6a Cartoon by Nicholson. From *The Australian*. www.nicholsoncartoons.com.au

Figure 13.6c

Chapter 14

Global inequalities

Introduction

The quality of life experienced by people largely depends on whether they live in one of the world's developed countries or in one of its developing countries. In Australia, for example, a child born today can expect to live to around 80 years of age, attend school and have enough to eat. But a child born in Ethiopia can expect to live to just 41 years and 57 per cent will never be able to read and write. Many Ethiopian children will go to bed hungry each night and may eventually die of starvation or from waterborne diseases.

In this chapter we focus on the variations in the quality of life experienced by people around the world.

Key questions

1 What is development?
2 How does people's access to the essentials of life vary from place to place?
3 What is natural resource?
4 How does the production and consumption of natural resources vary on a global scale?
5 How does poverty affect women in developing countries?

If the world were a village

If we could shrink the world's population to a village of just 100 people it would look something like this.

58 Asians, 15 Europeans, 12 Africans, 9 South Americans
5 North Americans, 1 would come from elsewhere, including Australia

52 would be female

48 male

30 people would be below the age of 15

3 would be aged over 65

70 would be non-white

30 would be white

33 people would be Christian

19 would be Muslim

13 would be Hindu

17 people would speak Chinese

9 would speak English

8 would speak Hindi or Urdu

20 people would control 85 per cent of the village's wealth

20 people would use 80 per cent of the village's resources

20 people would consume 45 per cent of all the energy used

7 would own a car and only 20 would ever have made a telephone call

20 people would be undernourished, 1 would be dying of starvation, while 15 would be overweight

25 would not have shelter to protect them from wind and rain

40 people would be without basic sanitation

18 people would not have clean water to drink

27 would be unable to read and write

1 would have a university education

2 would have a computer

Glossary of key terms

Absolute poverty Coping without the resources (food, clothing and shelter) necessary for life. People living in absolute poverty are barely surviving.

Development A process of change that results in an improvement in the quality of life of a community. It usually involves reducing poverty.

Development indicators Aspects of development that can be measured.

Fossil fuels Energy-producing materials—oil, coal and natural gas—formed from the remains of long dead plants and animals.

Global commons Resources that no individual or country owns or has legal responsibility for.

Inequalities The differences that exist in people's standard of living or quality of life.

Infrastructure Features of the human environment that allow a community to function, such as roads, public transport, airports, bridges, sewers, water supply, schools and hospitals.

Non-renewable resource Any part of the physical environment that cannot be replaced once it has been used.

Private wealth The income and savings of individuals.

Public wealth The infrastructure of a community; often supplied by government

Quality of life A term used to describe the way in which people live their daily lives, not just how poor or wealthy they are.

Recyclable Able to be used more than once.

Relative poverty The situation where some people are poorer than others in the community but still have access to adequate food, clothing and shelter.

Renewable resource A resource that can maintain and/or replace itself if managed carefully.

Reserve The unused supply of a non-renewable resource.

Resource Any part of the physical or human environment used to meet the needs of people.

Slum A permanent dwelling that has fallen into a state of disrepair.

Squatter settlement An unplanned settlement dominated by makeshift dwellings that are often built from scrap timber, iron and cardboard.

Standard of living A term used to describe the economic well-being of people.

Sustainable The wise use of natural resources so that people in the future can still use them

eGlossary

GeoToolkit

ICT Toolkit

14.1 Rich world, poor world

Getting technical

A world divided

What is development? The process of **development** involves improving the quality of people's life through increasing per capita income, reducing poverty and enhancing individuals' economic opportunities. It is also sometimes defined to include better education, improved health and nutrition, conservation of natural resources, a cleaner environment and a richer cultural life.

Developed world The developed world includes Australia, New Zealand, Japan, Canada, the United States and the countries of Western Europe. These countries have high levels of industrial development and most of the population enjoys a high standard of living.

Developing world The developing world includes most of the countries in Asia, Africa and South America. These countries are poorer than the developed countries. Most of the people support themselves and their families by farming the land. In some of these countries people are denied the political and personal freedoms we take for granted: the rule of law; freedom of speech, movement and religion; and the right to vote.

The differences in the **quality of life** experienced by people largely depend on whether they live in one of the world's developed countries or in one of its developing countries. However, variations can also be found within a single country. For example, a homeless person living on the streets of Sydney or a disadvantaged Aboriginal Australian living in a remote outback community may have much in common with people living in developing countries. Similarly, a wealthy business owner living in Ethiopia may enjoy a quality of life as good as that experienced by people living in a developed country. Geographers call these differences **inequalities**. In this unit we focus on the variations in access to life's essentials—food, health care, education, shelter and clean water—at a global scale.

Figure 14.1a There are great variations in the quality of life experienced by people in different parts of the world.

Working geographically

1. **Interpreting photographs** Study the photographs in Figure 14.1a. Decide whether each photograph is typical of a developed or developing country. List the factors that helped you decide.
2. **Group work: Interpreting photographs** Photograph 1 in Figure 14.1a shows the Philippines. In groups, discuss the inequalities that the Filipinos may experience.
3. **Group work** In groups, list the inequalities that exist in your own community. Find or take a photograph to illustrate these inequalities.
4. **Group work: Mindmapping** In groups, use the ideas from activities 3 and 4, brainstorm the causes of such inequalities and show these in a mindmap.

Development indicators

Different aspects of development can be measured using **development indicators**. Many different indicators can be used. The pattern of development will vary depending on which indicator is selected.

The most widely used indicator is *gross domestic product (GDP) per capita*. Another commonly used indicator is the United Nations Development Programme's *Human Development Index (HDI)*, which takes into account life expectancy, income and access to education.

What is wealth?

How would you define wealth? Is it having money in the bank? Is it having many possessions? Is it having a high income? All these are often seen as part of the **private wealth** of individuals. Some countries are also much wealthier than others. In wealthy countries the majority of people have a higher **standard of living**, and they benefit from what we call **public wealth**. Public wealth includes **infrastructure**, such as good roads, public transport, schools and hospitals and a range of entertainment and recreational facilities.

How do we compare the wealth of countries? As mentioned above, it is often measured using GDP: the total value of the goods and services produced in a country each year. When this statistic is divided by the population of a country we calculate the country's GDP per person, or per capita. This measure has been used to determine the list of the world's ten richest countries shown in Table 14.1a and the information shown in the world map in Figure 14.1b (p. 284).

What is poverty?

How can we define poverty? Is it the opposite of wealth? Is it just a lack of money, having few possessions or having a low-paying job? Or is it more complex than this? Is it having no prospect or hope of these, and having no chance of ever getting a permanent job?

GDP can also be used to rank the world's poorest countries, but as with wealth, this gives us only part of the picture. Before we can make a judgment about the overall level of a country's development we need more information about the way that people in that country live.

Global patterns

Tables 14.1a and 14.1b show the extremes of wealth and poverty. The GDP per capita of all countries is shown in Figure 14.1b (p. 284). This map shows the global distribution of rich and poor countries. Most of the world's wealthiest countries are found in North America and Western Europe. Other wealthy, or developed, countries include Japan, New Zealand and Australia.

An even better way of looking at the difference between the rich and poor worlds might be to analyse people's access to basic needs, such as food, health care, education, shelter and clean water.

Food

Having enough to eat is the most basic of all human needs. This can be measured by calculating the kilojoules consumed per person each day. When this is compared with the amount of food that is considered necessary for a basic diet, the differences between rich and poor countries become clear. The average American consumes 16 329 kilojoules per day, while the average Ethiopian makes do with just 6950 kilojoules per day. The number of kilojoules considered necessary for a healthy lifestyle is 9630 per day.

Table 14.1a World's ten richest countries, 2001*

Rank	Country	GDP per person (US$)
1	Luxembourg	53 780
2	USA	34 320
3	Ireland	32 410
4	Iceland	29 990
5	Norway	29 620
6	Denmark	29 000
7	Switzerland	28 100
8	Netherlands	27 190
9	Canada	27 130
10	Austria	26 730

*In 2001 Australia was ranked twelfth with a GDP per capita of US$25 370

Source: UN Development Programme

Table 14.1b World's ten poorest countries, 2001

Rank	Country	GDP per person (US$)
1	Occupied Palestinian Territories	<470
2	Sierra Leone	470
3	Tanzania	520
4	Malawi	570
5	Dem. Rep. of the Congo	680
6	Burundi	690
7	Zambia	780
8	Yemen	790
9	Ethiopia	810
10	Mali	810

Source: UN Development Programme

Understanding the text

1. Outline the ways in whichthe comparative, or relative, wealth of countries is measured.
2. Explain how gross domestic product per capita is calculated.
3. Explain how the HDI differs from GDP per capita as a measure of development. Which do you think is the best indicator? Justify your answer.
4. Distinguish between 'private' and 'public' wealth.

cd UTT worksheet 14.1

At what cost a war?

The US invasion of Iraq in 2003 is reported to have cost US$90 billion (plus another US$50 billion to rebuild Iraq). What could this amount of money achieve if it was used to address the needs of the world's poor?

Table 14.1c Meeting the needs of the poor

Activity	Cost (US$ billion)
Cancelling 10% of the foreign debt of all African countries	$30
Reducing worldwide infant mortality by 66%	$20
Providing education for all	$10
HIV/AIDS prevention, treatment and support for a year in low–middle-income countries	$7
Removing all land mines from affected countries in Southeast Asia	$5.5
Providing universal access to water and sanitation	$5
Doubling direct foreign investment into the 49 least developed countries	$2.7
Eliminating polio from sub-Saharan Africa and southern Asia	$1
Funding the activities of the International Red Cross for a year	$0.6
Total cost	**$81.8**
Change	**$8.2**

Source: *Guardian Weekly*, 11–17 September 2003

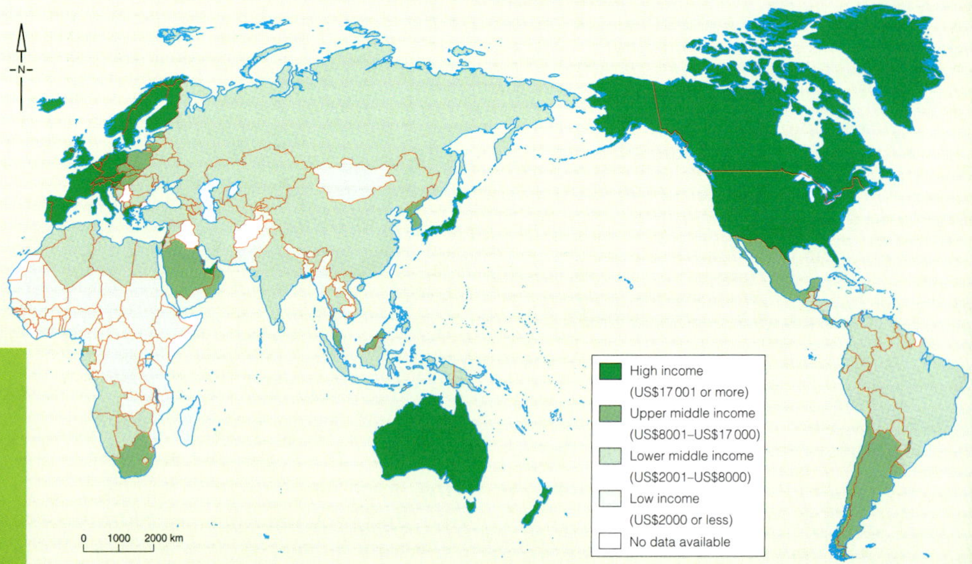

Figure 14.1b Gross domestic product per capita, 2001. Source: UNDP.

Just measuring the amount of food is not enough. The quality of the food must be considered. A diet that does not include a balance of fresh produce does not promote good health. Many people in the developing world survive on a diet featuring a limited range of foods, many of which are low in nutritional value.

Health care

Access to health facilities is a sign of a wealthy country. Educating doctors and building hospitals is very expensive. In developed countries governments spend a lot of money building and staffing health facilities, and buying the latest high-tech medical equipment and drugs. In developing countries this money is not always available. As a result, there are fewer doctors and hospital beds and a shortage of medical equipment and medicines.

In addition to lack of medical resources, many developing countries do not have enough money available to provide safe drinking water and the resources needed to stop disease from spreading. This means that life is more hazardous, and becoming dangerously ill is more likely. The figures for life expectancy are shown in Figure 14.1c.

Education

Most of you have been reading and writing since you were 6 years old. If you were growing up in a poor country, you might never have learned those important skills. You probably also hope to get a good

Did U know?

Even the cows live better

The livestock in rich countries get more money than poor people in developing countries. In Japan, farmers receive a subsidy of US$2555 a year for each cow they own. In the United States the figure is US$660. Meanwhile, 81.9 per cent of Ethiopians survive on less than US$1 a day. In Uganda the figure is 82.2 per cent. In Zambia it is 63.7 per cent.

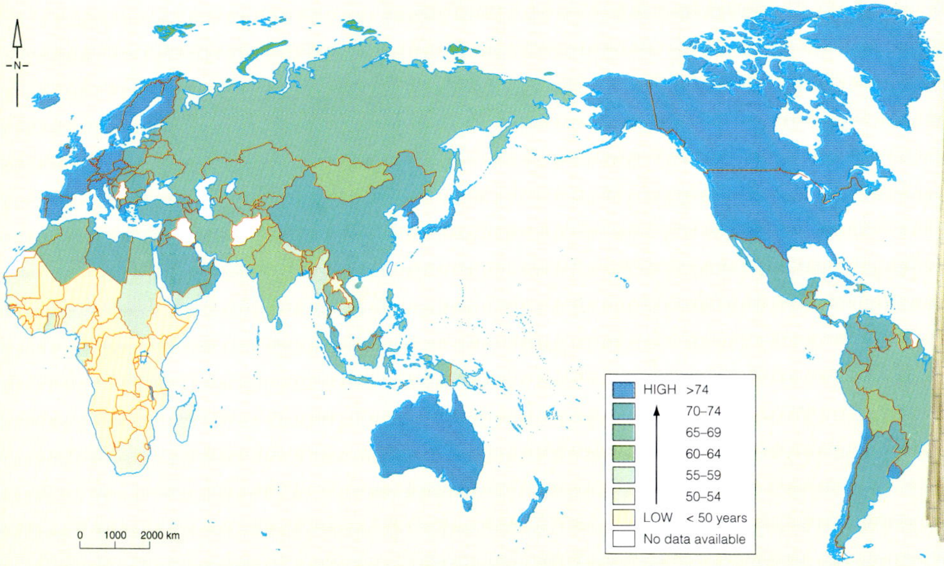

Figure 14.1c Life expectancy, 2001: how long can people expect to live? Source: UNDP.

job as a result of your education. In the poorest countries this would be impossible. It is likely that you would have completed all of your schooling by now—if you were ever able to attend school at all.

The difference between education levels in countries is shown in the percentage of people who are illiterate (unable to read and write). It is also shown in the percentage of people who reach Year 12 or go to university. Education opportunities only become available if governments have enough money to spend on schools.

Shelter

Rapid rates of urbanisation (see Unit 3.5) and poverty have made it almost impossible for developing countries to meet the housing needs of their growing urban populations. As a result, many of the urban poor have been forced to find shelter in squatter settlements.

Squatter settlements are roughly built dwellings located on unused land in the cities of developing countries. **Slums** are permanent dwellings that are in a very poor state of repair. The size of the problem is staggering. Forty per cent of the population of Karachi, Pakistan, live in slum and squatter settlements. In Manila, the capital of the Philippines, the figure is 32 per cent. In Mexico City, it is over 50 per cent. In Cairo, the capital of Egypt, more than 1 million people live in the city's cemeteries. In Lima, Peru, around half the city's population lives in inner-city slums, and another quarter in squatter settlements. Around half a million people live and sleep on the streets of Calcutta.

Water

During the lesson in which you read this material, 160 children will have died because they didn't have access to clean water or sanitation facilities. On just this one day, 9300 people (equal to 3.4 million a year) will have died from diarrhoea, cholera or another disease spread by contaminated water or poor personal hygiene resulting from water shortages. Most of these people will have lived in Asia and Africa, and most will have been under the age of five. (The issue of access to clean water is examined in more detail in Unit 14.2.)

Understanding the text

1 Explain why we can't determine whether people are receiving proper nutrition just by knowing how much food they eat.

2 In what ways is health likely to be affected by poverty?

3 List the ways in which variations in the level of education between countries can be measured.

4 Explain the difference between squatter settlements and slums.

5 What factors have contributed to the growth of squatter settlements in developing countries?

6 Outline the link between good health and access to clean water.

7 Why is access to good health and education facilities a sign of a wealthy country?

UTT worksheet 14.1

Working geographically

1 **Group work: Comparing opinions** In groups, discuss what you consider to be the basic minimum of food, education and health facilities. Draw up a list as a result of the discussion. See how much agreement there is between individuals and groups.

2 **Class discussion** Discuss what you consider poverty to be. Compare your ideas and make a statement based on everyone's views.

3 **Challenge: Interpreting maps** Study Figures 14.1b and 14.1c, then write a paragraph outlining the relationship between GDP per capita and life expectancy.

4 **Drawing conclusions** Using all the information in this unit, identify the regions of the world that have a high, medium and low level of development.

Foundation worksheet 14.1

Foundation worksheet 14.5

Extension worksheet 14.1

Extension worksheet ICT 14.4

14.2 SAMPLE STUDY
Access to clean water

A woman lowers a bucket into a dry well in Chad. A Chinese family watches as their home disappears below a new reservoir. An Australian farmer kicks the salt crust slowly ruining his field. In all parts of the world people face trouble with water. It is the link that binds every living thing, as vital to life as air.

A clean supply of fresh water is vital for good health. Like many of the earth's resources, however, it is unevenly distributed. Over 1 billion people live in parts of the world that experience water shortages and between 5 and 10 million people (mostly children) die each year from water-related illness. The most serious of these are hepatitis, typhoid, cholera, hookworm, malaria and trachoma. The World Health Organization (WHO) says that each person needs a minimum of 5 litres of water per day to survive. A further 25 litres per day is needed to stay clean and healthy.

Did U know?

More than two-thirds of the earth's surface is covered by water. But, accessible fresh water accounts for less than one-tenth of 1 per cent of all the earth's water. People have tapped half of these freshwater sources already, and many of the world's river systems now suffer from overuse and pollution. Unfortunately, fresh water is rarely found where it is needed most.

Some 97 per cent of liquid fresh water is stored underground in aquifers. These aquifers are being depleted faster than they can be recharged (see the extract opposite).

Poor suffer as world's water seeps away

By Tim Radford

Underground water, the unseen source of life for 2 billion people, is diminishing rapidly almost everywhere…

This [is] threatening the drinking water of millions of people and compounding the effects of drought and famine…

Across Africa, Asia and Latin America, groundwater levels are dropping as much as three metres a year. As aquifers [dry] up, sea water [is] seeping into the water table in coastal areas, causing irreversible pollution…

Twelve cities of more than 10 million people—including Bangkok, Shanghai, London and Calcutta—rely on underground water reserves … in rural India 50 per cent of irrigation water and 80 per cent of drinking water comes from underground, through 3 million hand-pumped wells…

About 450 million people in 29 countries live with chronic water shortages,… One person in six cannot rely on safe drinking water.

The Guardian, Associated Press (*Sydney Morning Herald*, 7–8 June 2003)

Access to water

One-third of the world's people live where water supplies don't meet demand and 1 billion lack access to clean water altogether. These numbers will increase significantly over the next half-century as the world's population increases from 6.3 billion in 2003 to 9.1 billion in 2050.

People in developing countries pay, on average, twelve times more per litre of water than those connected to municipal systems in developed countries. Up to one in four people living in the cities of the developing world buy water from vendors—spending 10–20 per cent of their income on water.

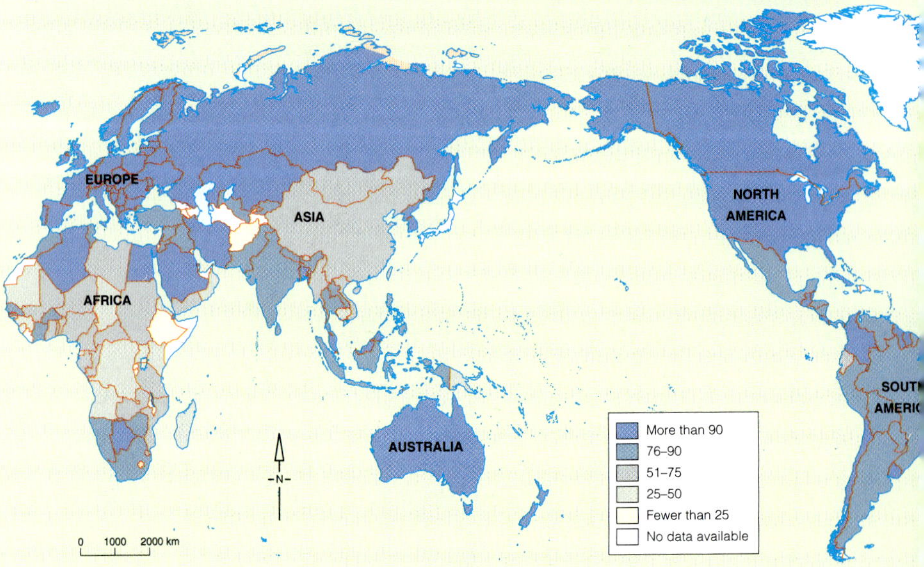

Figure 14.2a The percentage of the world's population with access to improved (treated) drinking water, 2000.

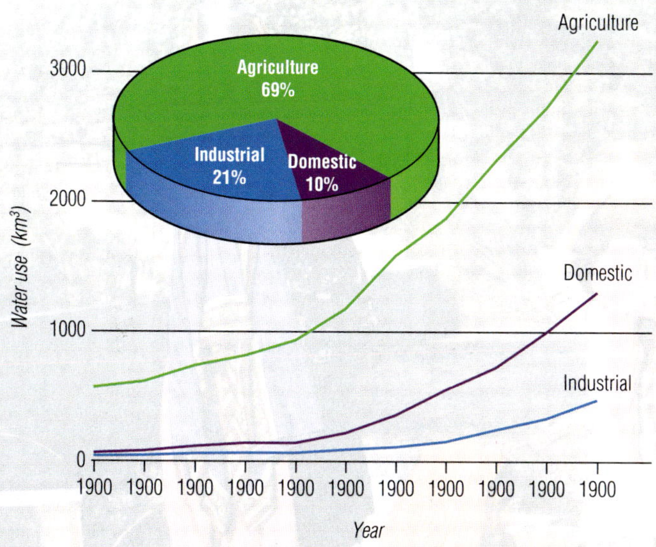

Figure 14.2b Global water use by sector, 2000.

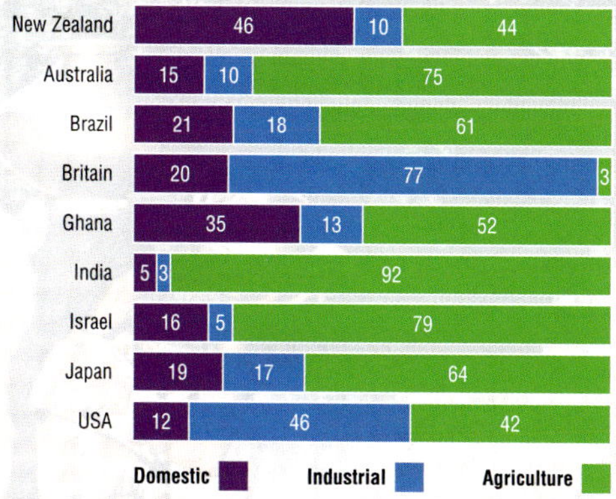

Figure 14.2c Water use, selected countries, 2000.

Global water use

On average, it takes at least 2000 litres of water to produce enough food for one person per day. In Asia, irrigation of water-greedy crops, such as rice and cotton, are responsible for most of the water taken from rivers.

The average African family uses about 20 litres of water a day. The average Australian household more than 450 litres.

Working geographically

1 **Research** Keep a detailed diary of the amount of water you use in twenty-four hours. Compare your data with others in your class. The following data will assist you in this task.
   - bath—90 litres
   - shower—30 litres
   - toilet flush—8 litres
   - glass of water—0.5 litres

2 **Challenge: Internet research** Select one of the following water-related diseases: malaria or bilharzia. Investigate the causes and symptoms of the disease. How can it be treated and/or prevented?

3 **Interpreting maps** Study Figure 14.2a. With the aid of an atlas, identify the countries where less than 50 per cent of the population has access to improved drinking water. Name the regions of the world that enjoy greater than 90 per cent access to improved drinking water.

4 **Interpeting graphs** Study Figures 14.2b and 14.2c, then complete the following tasks:
   - a Estimate the amount of water used in agriculture in 1960 and 2000.
   - b Estimate the amount of water used for domestic and industrial activities in 2000.
   - c Write a paragraph outlining the trends in water consumption.
   - d Write a paragraph contrasting the use of water in India with that in Japan and Britain.

5 **Using the media** Study the extract on page 286, then answer the following questions:
   - a What issue is highlighted in this extract?
   - b Outline the statistical data used by the journalist to highlight his concerns. Does that data support what you have learned through your interpretation of Figures 14.2a to 14.2c?

Foundation worksheet 14.2

Extension worksheet 14.2

Progress?

While the situation remains critical, some progress has been made. In percentage terms, both water supply and the availability of sanitation improved during the 1990s. However, the actual number of people in need has barely changed due to the growth in world population.

Table 14.2a Progress in water supply and sanitation

Access to	1990 (%)	2000 (%)
Water supply	79	82
Sanitation	55	60

Source: *New Internationalist*

Understanding the text

1 Outline the nature and extent of the world's freshwater crisis.

2 What problems have resulted from people's overreliance on water stored in aquifers?

3 Explain how people in developing countries are disadvantaged in terms of access to water.

UTT worksheet 14.2

14.3 Natural resources

Figure 14.3a Natural resources include the air, water, soil, the minerals in the ground and most plants and animals.

A **resource** is any part of the physical or human environment used to meet the needs of people.

What are natural resources?

Most of the earth's natural resources (including the air, water, soil and most plants and animals) have been available for use in the past and may always be available because they are renewed naturally. Other natural resources, however, are being used faster than they can be replaced. These include most minerals, fossil fuels, tropical rainforests, groundwater supplies, those plants and animals threatened with extinction and soils in some areas. Natural resources can, therefore, be classified as either renewable or non-renewable:

- **Renewable resources** are those that can maintain and/or replace themselves if managed carefully.
- **Non-renewable resources** are those that cannot be replaced once they have been used.

Who owns natural resources?

Some resources (for example, coal, gold and bauxite ore) are found in fixed locations. This means that the landowner, the government or a company can decide how and when it is used. Other resources (including the atmosphere, the open oceans and the polar lands)

Recycling

Some resources are **recyclable**. This means they can be used more than once. People in developing countries are efficient at making use of everything because resources (or the money to buy them) are often in short supply. In developed countries people tend to throw more away. Many minerals can be used time and time again, and steel and aluminium are often recycled. In many developed countries, paper, glass, metals, plastics and garden waste are now being recycled.

In Australia, state governments set targets for recycling, local governments put policy into practice and environmental non-government organisations work to raise public awareness about the need to recycle. Companies make a profit from the processing and resale of recycled materials.

In the cities of most developing countries groups of people work around landfill sites sorting and recycling waste materials.

Recycling reduces waste disposal costs, saves energy, conserves resources and raises public awareness about resource use.

Sustainable resource use

Sustainable resource use involves using resources wisely today so that people in the future can still use them. To be sustainable, renewable resources must be allowed to regenerate, and alternatives must be found for non-renewable resources.

Eventually humans will exhaust the earth's non-renewable reserves of oil, natural gas and coal. Sustainable sources of energy include solar energy, wind power, tidal power, hydroelectric power and wave power. The use of these resources would reduce the world's reliance on fossil fuels and help address the problem of global climate change.

Figure 14.3b The wind, tides, waves and the sun are sources of renewable energy.

Figure 14.3c The exploitation of the world's forests continues at an unsustainable rate.

are part of what we call the **global commons**, a term used to describe those resources that no individual or country owns or has legal responsibility for.

What is the difference between a resource and a reserve?

A **reserve** is a non-renewable resource that exists in a finite quantity (that is, there is not an endless supply) in the crust of the earth. We do not know the full extent of these reserves because as technology changes, previously unknown reserves may be discovered and exploited.

Are natural resources evenly distributed?

Some continents and countries have more resources than others. Some places lack basic resources (such as water and soil), which makes life difficult for people in those areas. Other countries have more resources than they can use. Australia, for example, has large reserves of several renewable and non-renewable resources, and can export these to other countries. Income from the sale of natural resources is vital to the economic well-being of many poor countries.

Working geographically

1 **Class discussion: Mindmapping** Study Figure 14.3a. As a class, brainstorm the issues associated with the exploitation of the earth's natural resources. Build up a mindmap of the issues identified.

2 **Challenge: Research** Investigate one of the renewable sources of energy listed in the box 'Sustainable resource use'. Construct a diagram showing how the source is converted into electrical energy. Annotate (label) your illustration.

Extension worksheet 14.3

Unequal access to natural resources

People in different parts of the world do not have equal access to the world's natural resources. Consider the following:

- the richest 20 per cent of the world's population use 80 per cent of the resources
- the richest 20 per cent of the world's population control 85 per cent of the wealth
- 80 per cent of the world's population live in developing countries.

One reason for this unequal access is that natural resources are not found evenly throughout the world. Another is that wealthier countries have the power and money to gain a bigger share of the world's resources through trade. For example, wealthy countries with few natural resources (such as Japan) buy resources from poorer countries with more resources. The population of the United States uses more of the earth's resources than any other country. Unlike Japan, however, it has many resources of its own.

Understanding the text

1 What is a resource?
2 Explain the difference between a renewable and non-renewable resource.
3 Explain what is meant by the terms 'global commons' and 'reserves'.
4 Account for the unequal distribution of access to natural resources.
5 What condition must be met for the use of a renewable resource to be considered sustainable?

UTT worksheet 14.3

Oil as a natural resource

Getting technical

Fossil fuels When burned, fossil fuels release energy, which is used to generate power. Fossil fuels are non-renewable energy sources, because they will eventually run out.

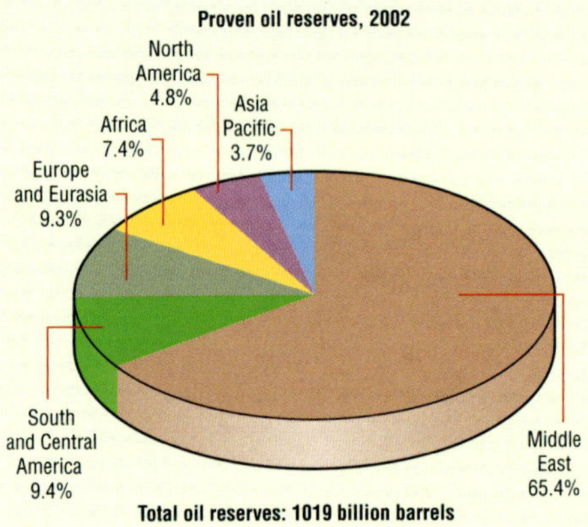

Figure 14.4a

Oil is a **fossil fuel**. Together with coal and natural gas, oil provides the vast majority of the developed world's energy needs.

How is oil formed?

When marine plankton dies it is eaten, decomposed by bacteria or sinks to the ocean floor. Over millions of years, layers of sediment cover these remains. Heat and pressure then transform the plankton into oil. As the process continues the oil gradually forms a gas.

Oil and natural gas are found trapped under a dome-shaped layer of gently folded rock strata. Advanced technologies are used to locate oil reserves and drill deep wells to extract oil from far below the sea bed.

Oil production and consumption

The large-scale production of oil is confined to just a handful of countries. These are shown in Figure 14.4b. The world's top ten oil-consuming countries are shown in Figures 14.4c and 14.4d.

Together, these maps show there is a poor match between the big producers and consumers. Of the top ten oil consumers, only two—Canada and the Russian Federation—produce more than they consume and over half do not have any significant oil production of their own. The United States alone accounts for one-quarter of total world consumption. Despite being the world's largest producer it is still the world's largest importer.

The global trade in oil is shown in Figure 14.4b.

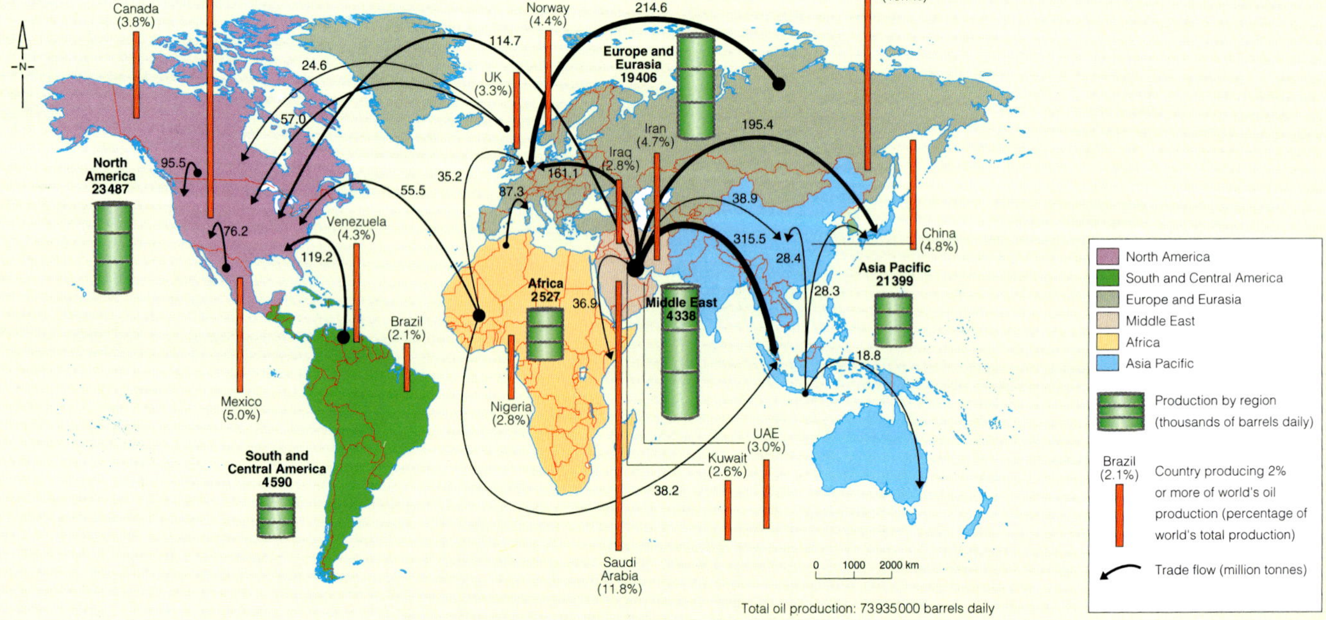

Figure 14.4b The world's oil production and the major oil trade movements, 2002.

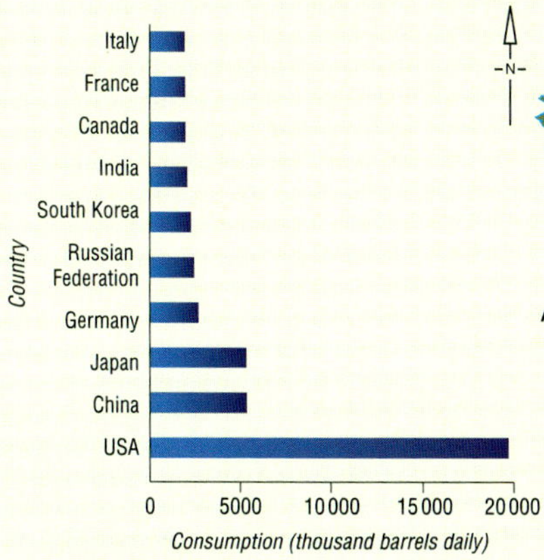

Figure 14.4c Top ten oil consuming countries, 2002.

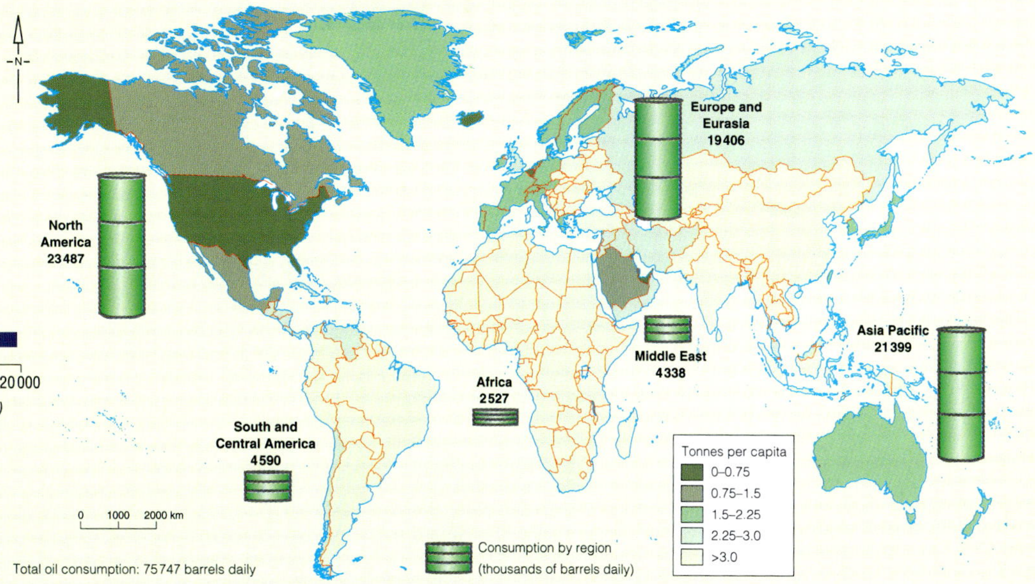

Figure 14.4d The world's oil consumption, 2002.

Working geographically

1 **Writing task** Write a paragraph explaining how fossil fuels are formed.

2 **Interpreting maps and graphs** Study Figures 14.4c and 14.d, then complete the following tasks:

- **a** With the aid of an atlas, identify the countries that have a per capita consumption of oil greater than 2.25 tonnes.
- **b** Which regions of the world have a per capita consumption of 0.75 tonnes or less?
- **c** Calculate the proportion of the world's total oil production consumed by North America and Eurasia.
- **d** Which top ten oil-consuming nations are also represented among the top ten oil producers (see Figure 14.4b)?

3 **Interpreting maps and graphs** Study Figures 14.4a and 14.4b, then complete the following tasks.

- **a** Name the world's ten largest oil producers.
- **b** How much oil was produced by the United States in 2002?
- **c** What proportion of the world's oil reserves are located in the Middle East?
- **d** What are the total oil reserves of the Middle East?
- **e** State the volume of oil shipped from the Middle East to:
  - **i** the United States
  - **ii** Japan.
- **f** From where does Western Europe import the majority of its oil?
- **g** What proportion of the world's oil supply is produced by:
  - **i** North America
  - **ii** Central and South America?

4 **Challenge: Writing task** Using the information gained in activities 2 and 3, write a paragraph describing the global pattern of the production and consumption of oil.

5 **Challenge: Internet research** Use the Internet to research the risks of transporting oil by ship. Write a half-page report outlining the risks. Include information relating to a recent oil spill.

Transporting oil

The point at which oil is consumed is often many thousands of kilometres away from where it is extracted, and so it needs to be transported. Supertankers and pipelines are the most common forms of transport, with which there are associated risks. Tankers can sink or run aground, spilling their load into the ocean. Pipelines can rupture, threatening fragile ecosystems. In Alaska and northern Russia special pipelines have had to be constructed to protect the fragile tundra.

Figure 14.4e The oil spilling from this wrecked tanker poses a risk to the environment.

14.5 Women and equality

It is possible to compare the differences between the lives of men and women for individual countries. This can be done by comparing development indicators, such as life expectancy, educational opportunity and literacy rates. When we study such data some clear worldwide patterns emerge (see the box 'Women's lives' and Table 14.5a).

Did U know?

- Half a million women die each year during childbirth. Of these, 99 per cent are in developing countries.
- At least one-quarter of women still don't have access to birth control.
- Of the 960 million illiterate people in the world, two-thirds are women. Over 75 per cent of girls in Burkina Faso, Burundi, Mali, Niger, Nepal, Pakistan and Yemen receive no education at all. In Bangladesh, Guinea, Morocco and Senegal it is over 50 per cent.
- Women work two-thirds of the world's working hours and produce half the world's food, and yet earn only 10 per cent of the world's income and own less than 1 per cent of the world's property.
- Only 8 per cent of the world's cabinet ministers are women.
- Although women make up half the electorate, they held just 14 per cent of seats in the world's parliaments in 2001. In many countries in northern Africa and southern and western Asia, women hold fewer that 10 per cent of seats in parliament. In Sweden, women hold 43 per cent of seats. In Australia the figure is 26.5 per cent.

Women's lives

- On average, women in developing countries live twenty-seven years less than women in developed countries. Women in Australia and Japan, on average, live to 83 years; the *life expectancy* of women in Uganda is just 40 years.
- The average age at *marriage* for women in Mali and Niger is 16; in Australia it is 27.
- In Senegal, women spend about 2.5 hours a day gathering *fuel wood*.
- The global average wage for women is about three-quarters of that for men. It ranges from 92 per cent of the male wage in Belgium, Germany and the United States to 42 per cent in Bangladesh.
- In nearly every country, women work more hours than men—when paid and unpaid *labour* is taken into account.
- In many African countries, women contribute up to 80 per cent of total *food production* yet receive less than 10 per cent of the financial help given to small farmers.
- In South America and the Caribbean, 85 per cent of women can read and write; the female *literacy* rate in South Asia is 34 per cent; in the Arab states, 41 per cent.
- Every year, about 1 million children, mostly girls, are forced into *prostitution*.
- Of the 1.3 billion people living in *extreme poverty*, about 70 per cent are women.

Table 14.5a Women of the world

Development indicator	World	Developed countries	Developing countries
Women per 100 men	99	106	97
Life expectancy at birth	69 [65]	79 [72]	66 [63]
Average number of children	2.8	1.6	3.2
Death of mother during child birth (per 100 000 live births)	400	21	440
Percentage of women aged 15 + who are able to read and write	69 [83]	98 [98]	66 [81]

[...] Male data supplied for comparison

Source: Population Reference Bureau

Figure 14.5b Women returning home with water from a well in Niger. Collecting water is very time-consuming and physically demanding.

Fetching water: a women's burden

For millions of women around the world the fetching and carrying of water is part of their daily routine. Men rarely help because it is seen as women's work.

Women in rural Africa often walk 6 kilometres a day, fetching water (see Figure 14.5b). In times of drought the walk may be much longer. When they reach the well the women often must wait in a long line before they can fill their containers, which usually hold about 20 litres of water and weigh 20 kilograms.

Carrying such heavy water containers on their head, back or hip often results in serious health problems. Curved spines and deformed pelvic bones can cause complications during childbirth. Pregnant women often keep fetching water until the day they give birth.

Traditional wells are often little more than water holes dug deeper and deeper as the dry season advances. They can be difficult to reach, their sides are steep and sometimes the walls collapse, killing women and their children.

The water collected is often dirty and polluted. Polluted water causes illness, such as dysentery: diseases that kill thousands of children under 5 years of age each day.

WaterAid: making a difference

WaterAid is an international non-government organisation dedicated to helping people escape the stranglehold of poverty and disease caused by living without a safe water supply and sanitation. It works with communities in fifteen African and Asian countries, helping them build and maintain safe, sustainable water supplies and sanitation facilities close to home. Since its formation in 1981, WaterAid's work in developing countries has helped over 7.5 million people. The assistance provided includes building tubewells with hand-operated pumps.

WaterAid sees women as important to the success of its projects. It makes sure that women are involved in the design, implementation and ongoing management of their projects. Their knowledge of local water resources is especially valuable. They know, for example, where the nearest, cleanest water sources are and in which months they dry up.

Once a safe, easily accessible water supply is available, the health of the community improves and women have time to devote to other activities.

Understanding the text

1 List the indicators that can be used to compare the differenced in life opportunities of women and men.

2 Using examples, outline some of the ways women are disadvantaged.

UTT worksheet 14.5

WaterAid

ICT

Access the WaterAid website. Collect case studies highlighting the role of WaterAid in addressing the needs of people living in developing countries. Prepare a short oral presentation outlining one of WaterAid's projects. Make sure you address the way in which the project has improved the quality of life, and especially that of women.

Figure 14.5a WaterAid's logo.

Working geographically

1 **Class discussion: Mindmapping** Study the box 'Women's lives'. As a class, discuss the ways in which the quality of life for women living in developing countries differs from that experienced by women in developed countries. Construct a mindmap highlighting the main points raised in the discussion.

2 **Simulation** Fill a large container with 20 litres of water and see how far you can carry it. Reflect on the effort required by women collecting water in developing countries.

3 **Internet research** Use an Internet search engine to locate a sketch of a tubewell. Download a copy of the sketch and glue it into your workbook.

14.6 Review and reflect

Chapter summary

We only have to watch the news on television to realise that there are huge differences in the standard of living experienced by people living in different parts of the world. These images often give us the impression that all people in the same country have the same quality of life. There are, of course, rich and poor in all countries. Their standard of living is usually linked to income; the problem in some countries is that higher incomes are limited to just a small minority whereas the majority of people have a very low income and quality of life. When people talk about these differences they often describe countries in terms of being either 'developed' or 'developing'.

In this chapter we studied the global inequalities in the access to food, health care, education, shelter and clean water. We also looked at natural resources, with a special focus on oil.

Activity 1

Hypothetical: Thinking about development

A groups of nine students have just returned from a visit to Southeast Asia where they participated in a cultural exchange program sponsored by the United Nations. The students hold a reunion where they exchange their ideas about development (see the illustration opposite).

Read each of the statements made by the students attending the reunion, then complete the following tasks:

1. a Select the view that you agree with most and give a reason for your decision.
   b Select the view that you disagree with most and give a reason for your decision.
2. Kurt gave some examples of basic human needs. What other human needs would you add to this list?
3. Some people have a rather narrow view about what development is. Others think the definition should be based on a large number of factors. Divide the views of the nine people into two columns based on whether you think they have a narrow or broad view of development. The table has been started for you.
4. Develop a mindmap showing all the factors that could be used to define development. Use the 'development compass rose' below as the basis of your mindmap.
5. Drawing conclusions: what is a developed country? Imagine that you were at the reunion. Write down what you would have said after hearing all nine opinions. Try to develop what you think is the best definition of a 'developed country'.

Broad view of development	Narrow view of development
Simon	

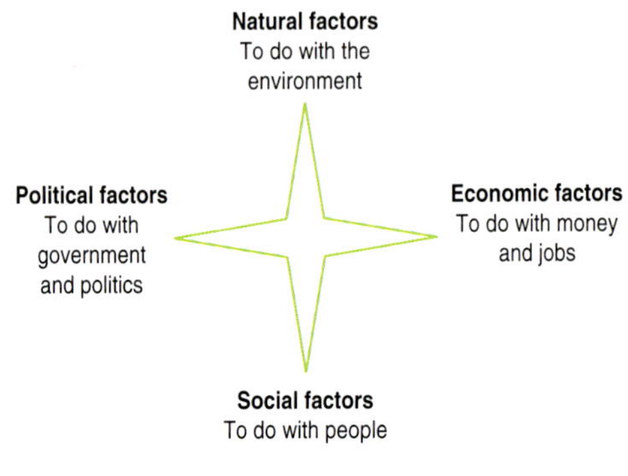

GeoMatch

GeoWords

GeoQuiz

Chapter test

Refer to the Reflection box on page 17.

Activity 2

Challenge: Investigating indigenous peoples

As mentioned in the introduction, comparing one country with another often hides the huge differences in the quality of life experienced by people within a country. Indigenous people, for example, are often among the world's most disadvantaged people and have a much lower standard of living than their fellow, non-indigenous citizens.

1 Access the UN's education website (Cyberschoolbus) to investigate the world's indigenous people. Use the following questions to develop a word-processed report.
   a Who are the world's Indigenous people?
   b Where are they found?
   c What is meant by 'indigenous knowledge'?
   d Outline the collective rights of indigenous peoples.

2 Undertake library and/or Internet research on one of these indigenous peoples:
   - Inuit of northern Canada
   - Navajo, Crow, Cheyenne or Comanche of the North American plains
   - Yanomani, Mapuche or Ayamara of South America
   - Maoris or Tahitians of the South Pacific
   - Penan, Dyak or Karen of Southeast Asia
   - Dinka, Tuareg or Masai of Africa
   - Ainu of Japan.

   Use presentation software (such as PowerPoint) to develop a presentation of five slides addressing the following themes:
   a traditional lands
   b traditional way of life
   c relationship with nature
   d level of development compared with non-indigenous population
   e recognition of indigenous rights.

Activity 3

Internet research: Natural resources

Investigate the uneven pattern of production and consumption of a non-renewable resource.

1 Locate an atlas map showing the global distribution of mineral ores. Select one and map its pattern of production and consumption.

2 Use the Internet to locate data about the production and consumption of the selected mineral. Enter the data for the ten largest producer countries and the ten largest consumer countries into a spreadsheet program and use the graph creation function to produce two column graphs. Write a paragraph explaining what the graphs show about the pattern of production and consumption of the resource.

Activity 4

Investigating issues in global inequality: Child labour

According to the International Labour Organization, sixteen out of every 100 of the world's children are child labourers. Twelve are involved in the worst forms of child labour.

Of the 246 million child labourers in the world today, most are found in developing countries. Some (186 million) are under the age of 15 years of age. One hundred and seventy million children are employed in the most hazardous forms of employment: working with dangerous tools and machinery, in mines and on construction sites and exposed to toxic chemicals. Eight million children are subject to the worst forms of human exploitation: slavery, forced labour, armed conflict and prostitution.

1 Use the Internet to investigate the issue of child labour.

2 Develop a PowerPoint presentation, of no more than six slides, educating the public about the extent of the problem. Give at least one example of child labour and the steps that non-government organisations, such as UNICEF, are taking to address the problem.

Foundation worksheet 14.2

Chapter 15

Global organisations: making a difference

Introduction

As we watch the television news each night we are confronted with images of human suffering and environmental decline. As individuals we often feel powerless to do anything about these problems. But there is much that we can do to make sure we leave a better world for the generations who will follow us. There are actions we can take individual responsibility for, such as reducing our consumption of fossil fuels by turning off the lights when we leave a room or by using public transport. We can also join with other like-minded individuals to achieve collective goals. Our lifetime achievements won't be measured in terms of the material wealth we accumulate but by the contribution we make to the society and environment in which we live. Each of us should strive to make the world a better place. In this chapter we focus on what it means to be a good global citizen.

Key questions

1 What is global citizenship?
2 What are the rights and responsibilities of global citizens?
3 What is the role of non-government organisations?
4 How do non-government organisations promote sustainability and reduce global inequalities?

Ian Kiernan: making a difference

Ian Kiernan, founder of the Clean Up Australia campaign, was born near the shores of Sydney Harbour and grew up learning to swim, fish and sail. Throughout his life, Ian has been a passionate yachtsman. It was during the 1986/87 BOC Challenge (a solo around-the-world yacht race) that he saw, and was appalled by, the amount of rubbish choking the world's oceans. He committed himself to do something about it on his return, starting in his own backyard: Sydney Harbour.

With the support of friends, Ian organised a community event, Clean Up Sydney Harbour, in January 1989. The organisers were overwhelmed by the response from Sydney residents, with 40 000 volunteers turning out to lend a hand.

In 1993 Ian signed an agreement with the UN Environment Programme to manage and promote Clean Up the World. Each year some 40 million people from more than 120 countries take to the streets, beaches, river banks and parks to clean and conserve their local environment.

To find out more about Clean Up Australia go to the organisation's website.

Ian Kiernan

Glossary of key terms

Active citizenship Taking seriously our responsibilities as citizens by becoming actively involved in the political process.

Culture The body of traditions, beliefs, attitudes, skills and tools by which communities organise their way of life and interact with the environment.

Ecological sustainability The ability to meet the needs of the present generation without affecting the ability of future generations to meet their own needs.

Global citizenship A term used to highlight the idea that we are citizens of the world. Responsible global citizens think about the impact of their activities on the world as a whole. They also attempt to protect and improve the physical and human environments.

Global community A term used to describe the way the world seems to be becoming more integrated. Actions of people in one corner of the globe can rapidly and significantly affect people elsewhere.

Globalisation A term used to describe the way the world (and peoples) are becoming more interconnected, both economically and culturally.

Human rights The rights to which all people are entitled.

Non-government organisations (NGOs) Organisations, made up of like-minded individuals, which seek to achieve a collective goal. They operate at a variety of scales to promote social and ecological sustainability.

Quality of life The happiness, well-being and satisfaction of a person. Among the many factors that influence quality of life are the person's family, income and access to services.

Sustainable Capable of being maintained over time for the benefits of future generations.

Sustainable development Development that meets the needs of the present generation without affecting the ability of future generations to meet their own needs.

Transnational corporations (TNCs) Large businesses that operate in a number of countries but generally have their headquarters in one of the countries of the developed world.

- eGlossary
- GeoToolkit
- ICT Toolkit
- Foundation worksheet 15.1
- Extension worksheet 15.1
- Extension worksheet 15.2
- Extension worksheet 15.3

15.1 Practising global citizenship

Developing a plan of community action

Become actively involved in a geographical issue affecting your local community. Develop your own campaign by following the steps below.

1. Become informed about the issue.
2. Develop strategies to increase community awareness about the issue. For example, you could make up posters that explain or illustrate the issue. Display these around the community. You could also seek publicity for your campaign by contacting the local media and write letters to the editor for publication in your local newspaper.
3. Try to influence decision-makers. Write letters or emails to local members of parliament and members of the local council. Outline your views on the issue and ask for their support.
4. Evaluate your campaign. What was successful and what changes would you make if you were to be involved in another campaign?

Foundation worksheet 15.1

Extension worksheet ICT 15.5

Almost every part of our lives is affected by the process of **globalisation**, including the types of jobs we do, the clothes we wear, the food we eat, the music we listen to, and the religions and cultures we interact with in our communities.

The term globalisation describes the increasing economic and cultural links between countries. Some of these links include trade, aid, tourism, information and communications technology, finance, migration and employment. In this fast-changing and interconnected world it is important that we see ourselves as being part of a **global community**, where our actions can influence the lives of people in other countries and the state of the global environment.

Global citizenship involves people everywhere thinking about the impact of their activities on the world as a whole—and then attempting to protect and improve the physical and human environment. Global citizens may decide to act as individuals or express their views with other like-minded people, perhaps through membership of a **non-government organisation (NGO)**, such as Greenpeace or Amnesty International (see Units 15.2–15.5). NGOs aim to ensure the highest possible **quality of life** and availability of resources for the global population, today and in the future.

As active global citizens we have two important responsibilities. First, we need to understand the social and environmental issues that impact on the world in which we live. Many of these issues (such as overcrowded cities, land degradation, climate change and access to fresh water) are discussed in detail in Chapter 16. Secondly, as global citizens we need to be willing to take an active role in *protecting the **human rights*** of others and *promoting **sustainable** practices* in order to preserve the global environment for future generations. Some of the strategies for achieving this are discussed below.

Strategies for active citizenship

While many of us feel powerless when we think about the number of social and environmental problems facing the planet, it is important to remember that it is the collective actions of individuals, working with their local communities, that offer the best hope for the future. There

Our rights as global citizens

ICT

All humans are born free and equal in dignity and rights.

Article 1, Universal Declaration of Human Rights

As a world community we should act to protect the basic human rights of all people. These rights are set down in the UN's Universal Declaration of Human Rights.

Visit the UN website and access a copy of the declaration. List what you consider to be the ten most important rights. Compare your list with those of other class members. Discuss the reasons for your choice.

are many possible solutions to the problems facing the earth and its people. Here are some things we can all take responsibility for:

- Respect all life and learn as much as you can about global environmental and social issues.
- Respect the culture and beliefs of other people.
- Learn and care about and protect a part of your local environment
- Work with others to improve the local environment and community.
- Consider the impact of our lifestyle on the environment and other people.

Taking the last suggestion as an example, we can make a difference by reducing the environmental impact of our consumption decisions. We can achieve this by living more simply and consuming fewer resources. Every year, Australians throw out 14 million tonnes of rubbish (that is 800 kilograms per person, each year). This level of consumption is not **ecologically sustainable**; that is, it cannot be continued into the future without significant damage to the environment. To improve this situation, we need to consider the environmental impact of our purchases. As environmentally aware consumers it is important to ask ourselves the following questions: Does any part of the production or distribution process cause harm to the environment? Will the disposal of this product damage the environment? Is the product recyclable? Some practical steps that we can take are given below:

- Minimise the social impact of our consumption decisions by boycotting (refusing to buy) goods produced by companies that exploit people; for example, through the use of child labour.
- Write a letter or email to a newspaper editor or major political leader expressing your point of view about a social or environmental issue.
- Support political parties and interest groups that promote appropriate social and environmental values and policies.

Remember the following important points:

- Don't expect immediate results; progress may be slow.
- Avoid the use of guilt or fear to change the behaviour of other people and don't allow others to do this to you. A more effective strategy is to lead by example so that you can demonstrate to others that they can also make a difference.
- Don't try to do everything. Focus on what you care about most.
- Take time to enjoy life.

Figure 15.1a Some negative attitudes about global citizenship.

Understanding the text

1 Define the term 'global citizenship'.

2 Outline the responsibilities of global citizens.

3 Outline the steps consumers can take to minimise the environmental and social impact of their consumption decisions.

UTT worksheet 15.1

Working geographically

1 **Group work** In small groups, discuss the reasons why it is important to act as a good global citizen. Present your top ten reasons to the class.

2 **Group work** As a group, work through the list of actions that you can take personal responsibility for (see the first list above). Give examples of how you could put each of these suggestions into action.

3 **Interviewing: Oral report** Find someone in the community who you think is a good global citizen. Interview the person and present an oral report to the class describing the person's qualities and outlining the contribution the person makes to the well-being of society and/or the environment.

4 **Class debate** Conduct a class debate. Topic: Can we make a difference? Make notes during the debate and write a discussion to summarise your findings.

5 **Challenge: Writing task** Write a discussion. Topic: As global citizens we should recognise that there is more that unites us than divides us. Consider the importance of this statement in your life and in the life of your friends.

15.2 Non-government organisations: making a difference

Amnesty International and Guantanamo Bay

ICT

In the months following the 2001 September 11 terrorist attacks on New York and Washington DC, the military forces of the United States and its allies invaded Afghanistan. Their aim was to overthrow the Taliban-led government, which had provided refuge to Osama Bin Laden's al-Qaeda network.

During the invasion a number of 'prisoners of war' or what the Americans referred to as 'unlawful combatants' were captured. They were transferred to a prison camp at Guantanamo Bay Naval Base, in Cuba—beyond the reach (and protection) of the US legal system.

By mid-2004, some 600 suspected members of the Taliban and the al-Qaeda network (including two Australian citizens) had been held for more than two years in what Amnesty International called a 'legal black hole' without access to lawyers and families.

Visit the Amnesty International website and write a brief update of this report. In preparing your report try to answer the following questions:

1. What happened to those imprisoned?
2. Why would Amnesty concern itself with the right of suspected terrorists?
3. What were Amnesty's main concerns?
4. What strategies did it adopt in its campaign to have the human rights of the prisoners protected?

Over the last twenty years there has been a growing awareness of the need to protect the global environment and to defend the human rights of individuals and communities. Of particular concern are the growth in global population and the impact that human activities are having on the environment. Likewise, the growing number of world conflicts, acts of terror, and incidents of cruelty, persecution and torture have many people worried about the type of world that their children and grandchildren will grow up in.

One indication of this growing concern is the large number of non-government organisations (NGOs) that have been formed in recent years to address these issues.

Why do people join NGOs?

People join NGOs because they believe they can achieve more by working with others to influence the decision-making processes of governments and large corporations. Some groups operate internationally and are concerned with global issues, such as environmental protection, climate change, human rights, social justice, and self-determination for indigenous people. Such groups include Greenpeace, Amnesty International and the World Wide Fund for Nature. Other groups (such as the Australian Conservation Foundation, the Wilderness Society, Aidwatch and the National Trust) operate within one country but often focus on broader issues. Many of these organisations rely on membership fees, fundraising and donations from the public to support their campaigns.

Working geographically

1. **Internet research** Conduct an Internet and/or media search to identify the names of as many NGOs as you can. Describe the types of issues that these groups are concerned with. Categorise these issues as social or environmental.
2. **Class discussion** As a class, discuss the ways in which NGOs act to increase public awareness of particular issues and influence decision-makers.
3. **Class discussion** Conduct a class brainstorm. Topic: Why would I want to join an NGO?
4. **Challenge: Oral report** Contact a major NGO. Prepare a short oral report outlining the origins of the organisation, structure, the main issues it deals with, its past successes and its current campaigns.
5. **Using software** Design a sticker that highlights the issues addressed in this topic. Use design or desktop publishing software for a professional finish.

Amnesty International

Amnesty International is an independent NGO with over 1 million members in 150 countries and territories. Amnesty plays a very specific role in the international protection of human rights by focusing its activities on prisoners. Amnesty:

- works to secure the release of prisoners of conscience. These are people detained for their beliefs, colour, gender, ethnic origin, language or religion and who have not used or encouraged violence
- works for the fair and prompt trials of all political prisoners. It also works on behalf of people who have been detained without charge or trial
- opposes the death penalty, torture and other cruel, inhumane or degrading treatment or punishment.

Amnesty International seeks to mobilise public opinion by having its supporters participate in letter-writing campaigns. Written appeals calling for the release of specific prisoners of conscience are sent to the government leaders accused of suppressing the prisoners' human rights.

All these actions are examples of **active citizenship**. This involves people taking seriously their responsibilities as citizens and becoming active participants in the political process.

Figure 15.2a Amnesty International's logo.

Foundation worksheet 15.1

Extension worksheet ICT 15.4

Extension worksheet ICT 15.6

Amnesty and the 2003 Gulf War

During the 2003 Gulf War, Amnesty International, fearing for the safety of Iraqi citizens, campaigned to stop the use of cluster bombs. These bombs spread death and destruction over large areas rather than destroying specific targets. Amnesty International claims that hundreds of civilian lives were lost when these weapons were used in heavily populated areas of the country. During the conflict, Amnesty called on the Iraqis to end the tactics that violated international humanitarian law and endangered civilians. This included the use of suicide attacks and fake surrenders by Iraqi soldiers.

As part of their Iraq campaign, Amnesty International encouraged members to send faxes, letters and emails to government authorities to insist on the following humanitarian safeguards:

- Civilians must not be attacked.
- Weapons that kill and injure indiscriminately should not be used.
- Civilian detainees should be treated fairly and humanely.
- Captured soldiers must be treated according to the Geneva Convention.
- The basic needs of the Iraqi people must be catered for.
- Refugees and people who are internally displaced (homeless within their own country) must be protected and helped.
- Those who commit crimes under international law must be brought to justice.
- All parties should allow independent investigation of their conduct.
- All parties must support the UN's humanitarian and human rights work.

In addition to the above, Amnesty International also encourages members to donate money to help NGOs relieve the humanitarian crisis in Iraq.

Understanding the text

1. How has the level of environmental and social awareness changed over the past twenty years? Why have these changes occurred?
2. What is an NGO? Why have the number of these organisations grown in recent years?
3. Who is Amnesty International? What are the aims of this organisation?
4. How did Amnesty International act to protect human rights during the 2003 Gulf War?

UTT worksheet 15.2

Figure 15.2b During the 2003 Gulf War, Amnesty International worked to protect civilians caught in the crossfire.

15.3 NGOs and the media: getting the message across

Figure 15.3a This Greenpeace balloon makes a point at the 2002 Winter Olympics in Utah, United States. Global warming threatens the future of winter sports.

The media (including radio, newspapers, television and the Internet) have become an important resource for global organisations in the twenty-first century. Many of the campaigns of non-government organisations (such as Greenpeace, Community Aid Abroad and Amnesty International) rely on the use of 'people pressure' to influence governments. For people to be concerned about an issue, however, they need to be aware that problems exist. For this reason, NGOs often use the media to raise the public's awareness of issues. Some of the ways in which international organisations use the media are summarised below.

Interviews, press conferences and press releases

Television and radio interviews can provide an opportunity for representatives of NGOs to increase public awareness of their campaigns and rally public support.

NGOs use press conferences regularly to communicate with the mass media. During these short presentations organisations can present information to journalists about their campaigns and highlight the importance of global issues.

A press release is a short statement providing the details of an event or the progress of a campaign. Journalists can use the summary of key facts and figures provided within a press release to prepare a newspaper

Bono: rock icon and social activist

From icon to humanitarian activist, U2 singer, Bono, in 2003 embarked on a four-nation African tour with the then US Treasury Secretary Paul O'Neill. In doing so, he demonstrated that the image of 'rockers without a conscience' is false. Few singers have put so much passion and enduring commitment into politics while continuing to thrive on artistic merits. U2 scooped four coveted Grammy awards in 2002.

Like fellow Irish rocker Bob Geldof, who was the inspiration for the 1985 Live Aid fundraisers for Ethiopian famine victims, Bono has become a tireless champion of the world's underprivileged. The frontman for the successful Irish group has focused primarily on the fight against poverty and HIV/AIDS in the developing world.

Before heading to Africa, Bono said the trip was an opportunity to exploit his celebrity by focusing attention on some of the world's most appallingly poor places and the urgent need of inhabitants for health care, schools and clean water.

'My job is to be used. I am here to be used,' he told the *Washington Post*. 'It's just, at what price? As I keep saying, I'm not a cheap date.'

If the trip helps advance progress on cancelling debts, boosting a global fund for fighting AIDS and lowering trade barriers to African products in markets of rich countries, 'Then I'm very, very happy to be used,' Bono said.

Figure 15.3b Bono, the lead singer of U2, meets with US President George Bush in an attempt to reduce the pressures of debt on developing countries.

or television report. International organisations need to think carefully about the way they present information so that the media will pick up their message and promote it to a wider audience.

Email and the Internet

The Internet has changed the way NGOs provide information to the public and the methods they use to lobby governments. Most NGOs have a website that provides information about its aims, structure and current campaigns. This material can be read by anyone across the globe with access to the Internet. Many of these organisations also provide an e-bulletin service to keep their members and the media up to date on the progress of campaigns. These sites also encourage members to send emails to government departments and businesses requesting changes to government policies and corporate practices.

Publicity campaigns

During the 1980s and 1990s many NGOs focused on 'headline-hitting' campaigns to attract media attention to global issues. Some people refer to these campaigns as 'publicity stunts' because often they are designed to generate maximum media attention and provide dramatic images that capture the attention of the public. Examples of these campaigns are shown in Figures 15.3a and 15.3c.

Other media strategies involve collecting video and photographic evidence of human rights abuses and of animals and environments under threat. The images of slaughtered whales and seals used in environmental campaigns are examples of this strategy in action. Often celebrities and pop stars lend their support to these types of campaigns, which helps to attract further media attention to the cause. Rock stars such as Bono from U2, Sting, Peter Garrett and Bob Geldof have a reputation as effective global campaigners (see the box 'Bono: rock icon and social activist').

Figure 15.3c Protest groups, including the Australian Conservation Foundation (ACF), were active in opposing the Jabiluka Uranium Mine in the Northern Territory.

Understanding the text

1. What role does the media play in the activities of international organisations?
2. Outline the ways in which NGOs use the media.
3. Why is it important for NGOs to think carefully about the way they present information?
4. What impact have changes in technology had on the campaigning methods of NGOs?

UTT worksheet 15.3

Working geographically

1. **Class debate** Conduct a class debate. Topic: Media stunts by lobby groups are annoying and ineffective.
2. **Challenge: Research** In groups of two or three, select an NGO with which you are familiar. Use library or Internet research to answer the following questions:
   - a How does the NGO use the media in its campaigns?
   - b How effective do you think its media strategy has been? Explain your answer.
   - c How could the NGO use the media more effectively?
3. **Active citizenship** Design a media campaign to support an environmental or social cause that you believe in. As part of your campaign you should design a press statement and a plan for your campaign in the form of a poster or wall display. Using the class as an audience, conduct a mock press conference outlining the details of your campaign strategy.
4. **Research: Oral report** Find out about the involvement of pop stars and other celebrities in social and environmental issues. Why are these individuals passionate about their particular causes? Present your research to the class in the form of an oral report (see Unit 2.14).
5. **Internet research: Writing task** Select Figure 15.3a or 15.3c. Use the Greenpeace or ACF website to find out more about the role of the media in the campaign shown in the photo. Write a short report summarising your findings.

Oxfam Community Aid Abroad: promoting human rights

Oxfam Community Aid Abroad

Figure 15.4a The logo of Oxfam Community Aid Abroad. (Reproduced with permission from Oxfam Community Aid Abroad.)

Oxfam Community Aid Abroad is the Australian-based member of Oxfam International. Oxfam Community Aid Abroad is an independent, not-for-profit, secular, community-based aid and development organisation that works to eliminate poverty, achieve social justice and promote ecological sustainability by addressing the underlying causes of these problems: inequality and powerlessness.

Oxfam Community Aid Abroad works towards its aims by:

- supporting self-help projects in over thirty countries
- campaigning against injustices and educating people about the causes of poverty
- promoting community involvement by offering Australians the chance to be part of building a better world
- supporting business practices that are socially and environmentally responsible
- publishing a wide range of magazines, papers and books
- sharing information with other government and non-government organisations.

Oxfam Community Aid Abroad's perspective

ICT

The Oxfam Community Aid Abroad website contains a very useful Frequently Asked Questions facility (which can be accessed via the About Us button) and an entertaining Doonsbury Nike comic strip, which can be used to promote classroom discussion.

Table 15.4a Checklist of NGO campaign strategies

- *Petitions* to parliaments or company executives
- *Deputations* (issues-based, organised visits) to members of parliament or company executives
- *Direct appeals* to ministers or heads of large corporations
- *Letter-writing campaigns*
- *Advertising*—such as T-shirt slogans, posters and bumper stickers
- *Talkback radio*—used to promote community-wide discussion about issues
- *Protests and demonstrations*—effective for gaining the attention of the media
- *Public meetings*—used to educate the public about an issue
- *Direct political action*—standing candidates in elections or trying to influence the political outcome in marginal electorates (those most likely to be won or lost only narrowly at an election)
- *Legal action*—pursuing an issue through the legal system

NikeWatch

One of Oxfam Community Aid Abroad's campaigns is 'NikeWatch'. The home page for the campaign features the slogan 'Just Stop It'. The aim of the campaign is to get Nike to ensure respect for the basic rights of people who produce their labelled shoes and clothing. Oxfam Community Aid Abroad would like to see Nike upgrade its code of conduct to include a requirement that workers be paid enough to provide for their basic needs and those of their children. Since 1996 Oxfam Community Aid Abroad has produced numerous reports on working conditions in Nike's factories and those of other sportswear companies. A summary of just some of these statistics is provided below.

Nike facts: who are the winners and losers?

According to Oxfam Community Aid Abroad, during peak periods workers in factories producing Nike clothing can be expected to work up to seventy hours a week. Employees are harassed or threatened with dismissal if they refuse overtime.

Basic wages for workers in the factories of Nike's Indonesian suppliers vary between A$3.10 and A$4.66 per day. Although overtime income and bonuses are added to the basic wage, Oxfam Community Aid Abroad reports that these wages are still inadequate to meet the basic needs of a family. The majority of those Indonesian Nike workers who are parents are forced, by their financial circumstances, to live apart from their children. Workers whose home villages are within a few hundred kilometres of their factory are usually able to see their children once a month. Workers from more distant villages are only able to see their children three or four times a year.

According to *Business Review Weekly* (2001), Nike's profit for the 2001 financial year to 31 May was US$589.7 million. Adidas's net income

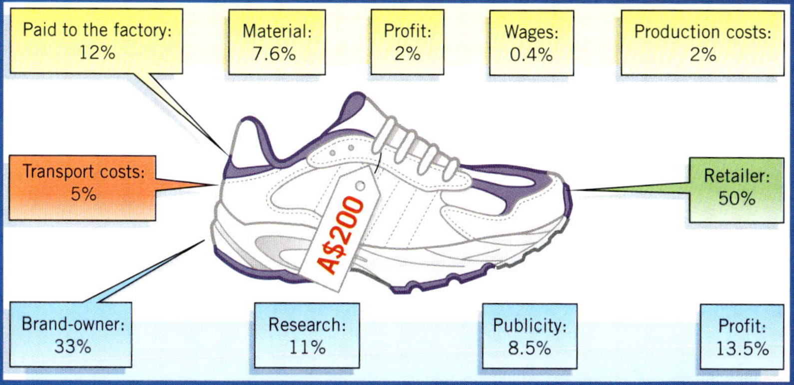

Figure 15.4b A fair share? Who gets what?

for the year 2000 was US$160 million. Both can be very generous when it comes to athlete endorsements. According to *the Los Angeles Times* (2001) Nike has a US$100 million five-year endorsement contract with US golfer Tiger Woods, and another with Australian tennis star Lleyton Hewitt worth US$15 million for the same period.

Strategies used in the NikeWatch campaign

As a part of its NikeWatch campaign, Oxfam Community Aid Abroad is promoting the following demonstrations of active citizenship:

- The NikeWatch website has been set up so that people from around the world can access up-to-date information about work practices in Nike's supply chain and the progress of the campaign.
- Supporters of the campaign are encouraged to 'let Nike know that you don't like sweatshops' by sending them a letter, email or postcard.
- The NikeWatch website contains links to other antisweatshop campaigns, which supporters are encouraged to join.
- Oxfam Community Aid Abroad provides educational resources for teachers and students.
- Oxfam Community Aid Abroad has also organised peaceful protests and publicity campaigns to highlight the plight of workers making Nike goods.

It is important to note that many of the strategies and actions listed above are also used by other NGOs to lobby governments and other organisations. Table 15.4a provides a summary of the techniques commonly used by NGOs.

Nike fights back

ICT

Nike is keen to demonstrate that it is a responsible corporate citizen. Check out its website to see how it counters the anti-Nike campaign mounted by organisations such as Oxfam Community Aid Abroad. Take particular note of the material that can be accessed via its Responsibility button. The company addresses issues such as its manufacturing practices and the environment. What does the company say about its record in these areas?

Foundation worksheet 15.2

Understanding the text

1 What are the aims of Oxfam Community Aid Abroad?
2 What are the aims of the NikeWatch campaign?
3 List the strategies used by Oxfam Community Aid Abroad in its NikeWatch campaign.
4 What other strategies can NGOs use to promote human rights and ecological sustainability?

UTT worksheet 15.4

Working geographically

1 **Library and Internet research** Find out about the working conditions in the textiles, clothing and footwear industry. Make a list of the other NGOs involved in campaigns about this issue. What strategies do these organisations use to attract attention to their cause?

2 **Internet research** Access Oxfam Community Aid Abroad's website. Use this site to find out about the campaigns that this NGO is involved in. Present your results to the class in the form of a poster or PowerPoint presentation.

3 **Challenge: Internet research** In pairs, discuss what should be included in an employer's code of conduct for workers producing clothing and shoes. Compare your points with those listed by others in the class. Now check your list against the code of conduct published on Nike's website.

15.5 *SAMPLE STUDY*

Greenpeace: promoting sustainability

Greenpeace's mission statement

Greenpeace is an independent, campaigning organisation that uses non-violent, creative confrontation to expose global environmental problems, and force solutions for a green and peaceful future. Greenpeace's goal is to ensure the ability of the Earth to nurture life in all its diversity.

Source: Greenpeace website

Figure 15.5a A Greenpeace activist helps to block an Esso petrol station from carrying out business in Esch, Luxembourg.

Accessing NGOs online ICT

You will find Internet Resources for Australian Activists a useful site for accessing the websites of major NGOs.

Greenpeace is a global non-profit-making organisation that campaigns to promote a sustainable environmental future for the planet. **Ecological sustainability** involves meeting the present needs of the world's population without affecting the ability of people in the future to meet their own needs.

With a presence in over forty-one countries Greenpeace is able to focus its attention on important environmental issues wherever they occur in the world. It achieves this through the use of non-violent protests and by lobbying corporations and governments. Greenpeace's campaigns focus on:

- stopping climate change
- protecting ancient forests
- saving the oceans
- stopping whaling
- saying 'no' to genetic engineering
- stopping the nuclear threat
- eliminating toxic chemicals
- encouraging sustainable trade.

Greenpeace maintains its independence by relying on more than 2.8 million individual members for financial support. Hand-outs from governments, political parties and corporations are neither asked for nor accepted. The organisation takes this issue very seriously and carefully screens every cheque it receives. Donations from corporations and political parties are marked 'return to sender'.

Greenpeace has been campaigning for a better global environment since the early 1970s when a small boatload of volunteers and journalists sailed into an area north of Alaska in an attempt to stop the US Government from conducting underground nuclear tests. Greenpeace refers to these types of actions as *bearing witness*. This means taking non-violent direct action to voice opposition to activities that are environmentally destructive. Greenpeace members continue to use the idea of bearing witness in their campaigns around the world today.

Greenpeace campaigns have played an important role in the following environmental achievements:

- the banning of toxic waste exports to less developed countries
- a halt to commercial whaling
- the UN convention providing for better management of fisheries
- the establishment of the Southern Ocean Whale Sanctuary
- a fifty-year ban on mineral exploitation in Antarctica
- the banning of radioactive and industrial waste dumping at sea
- an end to high-sea, large-scale driftnet fishing
- the banning of all nuclear weapons testing.

Greenpeace maintains a 'press centre' on its website that provides journalists and other media representatives with photographs and up-to-date reports about the progress of its campaigns. For each campaign, the website provides a list of recommendations for individual action.

Using the media: Greenpeace shuts down ESSO

Greenpeace has for a long time been concerned about the impact on earth's climate of burning fossil fuels (such as oil, coal and gas). According to Greenpeace the world's largest petroleum producer, ESSO (also known as EXXON or Mobil), has blocked international efforts to stop global warming, which is worsening the problem. The Greenpeace website claims that ESSO uses its financial strength to try to ensure it can keep polluting the atmosphere with greenhouse gases without any limitations: 'Esso has been a key player in the USA's decision not to be part of the Kyoto Protocol—the only international agreement aimed at controlling the greenhouse emissions that are hurting our climate. Esso denies climate change is a real problem and it doesn't invest a single cent in renewable energy.'

On 25 October 2002 Greenpeace took action against ESSO by closing down its petrol stations in the European nation of Luxembourg. The campaign, which lasted twenty-four hours, was an enormous media event involving more than 600 volunteers from thirty-one countries. Greenpeace targeted all of ESSO's twenty-eight petrol stations in Luxembourg by blocking their entrances with 'caution' tape, displaying 'closed' signs and chaining up the petrol pumps. Greenpeace International Executive Director, Gerd Leipold, appeared at Wasserbillig, the world's largest petrol station, dressed in a costume of the Exxon Tiger mascot. He explained to passersby and to the media why Greenpeace had targeted Esso. The protest gained widespread media attention and was reported in both the electronic and print media.

Figure 15.5b Esso was a key player in the US's decision not to ratify the Kyoto Protocol: the only international agreement aimed at controlling greenhouse emissions.

Understanding the text

1. How does Greenpeace promote ecological sustainability?
2. What is the source of Greenpeace's funding? Explain why this is significant.
3. When was Greenpeace founded and what did its first campaign focus on?
4. Explain why Greenpeace launched a campaign against ESSO.
5. a What strategies did Greenpeace use to draw media attention to the activities of ESSO?
   b Do you think this strategy was successful? Explain your answer.

UTT worksheet 15.5

Working geographically

1. **Group work: Brainstorming** In small groups, brainstorm strategies that could be used to promote ecological sustainability. Present your findings in the form of a mindmap.
2. **Research: Oral report** Use the Internet or library to make a list of NGOs concerned with protecting the environment. Select one of these organisations and research the following questions:
   a What are the aims of this organisation?
   b What issues are of concern to this organisation?
   Present your findings in the form of an oral report.
3. **Challenge: Research** Select one of the campaign achievements listed on page 306. Use library and/or Internet research to find out about the history of this campaign. Present your findings as a poster display or PowerPoint presentation.

15.6 Review and reflect

Chapter summary

Being a good global citizen involves more than just being aware of the impact our activities have on the physical and human environments. It involves doing something about it. One way individuals can make a difference is to join or support a non-government organisation. These are groups of like-minded people who believe they can have a greater impact on decision-making processes by acting collectively. NGOs have become very skilled at using the media to promote their campaigns.

In this chapter we have focused on two of the most effective non-government organisations: Greenpeace and Oxfam Community Aid Abroad. These organisations play a major role in promoting ecological sustainability and human rights.

Activity 1

Internet research: Non-government organisations

Select one of the organisations whose logo appears in Figure 15.6a or another NGO you may be interested in, such as the World Wide Fund for Nature or Australian Conservation Foundation. Use an Internet search engine (such as Yahoo!) to locate the NGO's home page, then answer the following questions:

1. Outline the origins and history of the organisation.
2. Make a list of the organisation's aims.
3. Identify the main issues addressed by this NGO. Classify these issues as being either environmental or social.
4. Write a brief summary outlining the various campaigns undertaken by this organisation.
5. Select one of these campaigns and investigate it in greater detail. Use information on the website to describe the following:
   - **a** What is the issue of concern?
   - **b** Where is the issue located?
   - **c** Why is this issue a concern?
   - **d** What strategies is the NGO using to resolve these issues?
6. Summarise the major successes and failures of the NGO.

In activity 2 (opposite) you will have the opportunity to present your findings.

NATIONAL TRUST

THE WILDERNESS SOCIETY

Australian Red Cross BLOOD SERVICE

Figure 15.6a Logos of selected non-government organisations.

Activity 2

Presenting your research findings

When you have completed your Internet-based research of an NGO (see activity 1, opposite) prepare a presentation of your findings. Use presentation software (such as PowerPoint) and follow the guidelines below:

- Limit your presentation to ten minutes.
- Develop a worksheet that students can complete during your presentation.
- Include no more than ten to twelve slides in your presentation. Include a range of multimedia resources, including copyright-free photographs downloaded from the Internet.
- Use bullet points to provide a brief summary of your findings.
- Use your talk to provide further detail on each point. Do not read from your presentation; use it as a guide.
- Don't overuse colour, photographic images and animations. Use them sparingly so that they have an impact.

See Unit 2.14 for advice on how to present an effective oral report and Unit 2.16 for advice on multimedia presentations.

GeoMatch GeoWords GeoQuiz Chapter test Refer to the Reflection box on page 17.

Activity 3

Hypothetical: Active citizenship

A large UK-based transnational corporation (TNC) has expressed an interest in relocating its Asia Pacific headquarters from Hong Kong to Australia. In addition to being its administrative headquarters, the new centre will handle the TNC's telephone-based marketing for the region. Australia is the TNC's preferred location because of its multicultural population and excellent telecommunications infrastructure. There is, for example, a ready supply of people able to speak the range of languages required by the TNC.

The NSW Government is keen to have the TNC locate its headquarters in the state. It has offered the TNC a number of taxpayer-funded incentives. One of these incentives is the long-term lease of government-owned land in your local community. It is anticipated that the new headquarters will employ 500 employees when it is fully operational.

The land offered by the state government is one of the few remaining areas of native bushland in the community and home to an endangered species of sugar glider. It is also a valued recreational resource.

The state government's proposal has split the local community. Some people support it because of its potential economic benefits. Others, including the recently formed Save Our Bush group, oppose the proposal because of its environmental impact. Figure 15.6b outlines a selection of the views expressed by members of the local community.

Local environment groups, including the Save Our Bush group, have decided to oppose the government's decision because of the impact it will have on the environment. These groups are planning a political and legal campaign to force the government to abandon its plan.

Read each of the statements in Figure 15.6b, then complete the following tasks.

1 List the statements that are in favour of the state government's proposal. Make a separate list of the statements that are not in favour of the state government's proposal.
2 In groups of four or five students, discuss the different statements about the proposal. Reach agreement on what you think should happen. Prepare to defend your group's viewpoint when you report back to the class.
3 Conduct a class debate. Topic: The proposed development should go ahead. After the debate, conduct a secret ballot to determine whether the class will recommend that the development should go ahead.
4 Determine which point of view you agree with. Write an exposition outlining the arguments you would use to justify your position.
5 In groups of four or five students, brainstorm the strategies or methods you could use to influence public opinion and the government's decision-making processes. Share your group's list with the rest of the class.
6 As a class, role-play one of the methods or strategies identified in activity 5.

Figure 15.6b Members of the local community express their views about the proposed development.

Extension worksheet ICT 15.7

Chapter 16

PART D Global issues and the role of citizenship

Global issues

Introduction

At the beginning of the twentieth century there were 1.6 billion people on earth. Pollution and environmental degradation were common, but the problems were mainly local. The world still seemed vast, and large areas remained virtually untouched by the activities of people.

Just over 100 years later the world's population is heading towards 7 billion and the environmental problems that have resulted from this rapid growth now affect the whole planet.

In this chapter we focus on climate change, threatened habitats, land degradation and the use of ocean resources. Other global issues have been addressed throughout the text. Confronting such issues represents the greatest challenge facing humanity.

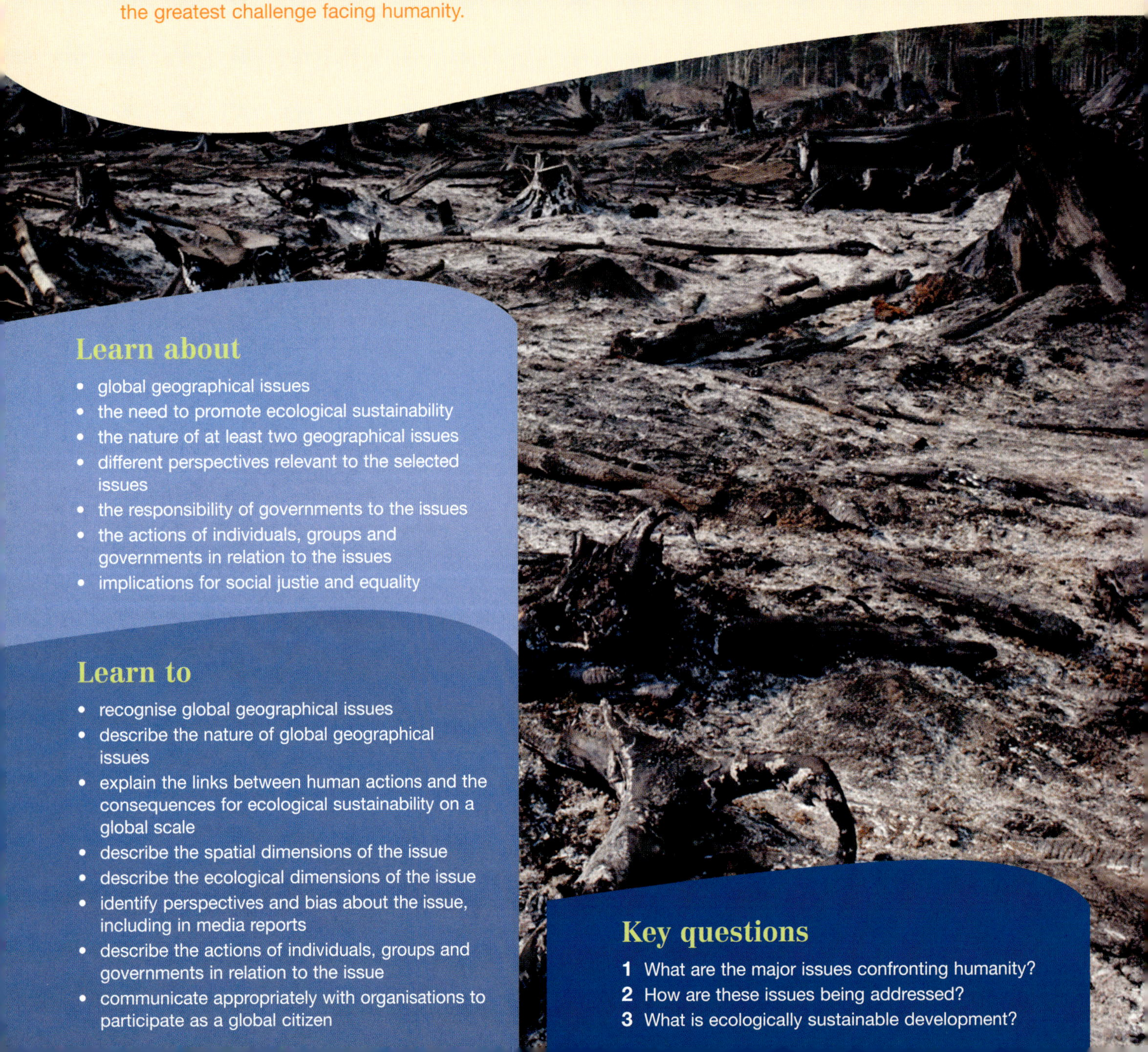

Learn about

- global geographical issues
- the need to promote ecological sustainability
- the nature of at least two geographical issues
- different perspectives relevant to the selected issues
- the responsibility of governments to the issues
- the actions of individuals, groups and governments in relation to the issues
- implications for social justie and equality

Learn to

- recognise global geographical issues
- describe the nature of global geographical issues
- explain the links between human actions and the consequences for ecological sustainability on a global scale
- describe the spatial dimensions of the issue
- describe the ecological dimensions of the issue
- identify perspectives and bias about the issue, including in media reports
- describe the actions of individuals, groups and governments in relation to the issue
- communicate appropriately with organisations to participate as a global citizen

Key questions

1. What are the major issues confronting humanity?
2. How are these issues being addressed?
3. What is ecologically sustainable development?

Deadly chain reaction

Jim Estes, a US researcher, has helped solve the mystery of why the population of Alaskan sea otters is declining. The clue that helped solve the mystery was the 'invasion' of sea urchins Estes had seen in waters off Alaska. Normally rare except in deep waters, the sea urchins had eaten right through the underwater kelp forest—the home of many marine creatures.

Jim's study revealed that an ecological chain reaction, which started with the large-scale hunting of whales fifty years ago, led to the widespread decline in the number of seals, sea lions and otters and the explosion in the population of sea urchins.

Estes believes that the hunting of the 'great' whale caused a collapse in the food chain. Killer whales that once preyed on the larger 'great' whales had to look for other food to eat. Some turned to seals, but it was not long before most of the seals were eaten and the killer whales turned their attention to sea lions. Then, when those grew scarce, they went for the otters.

So, one of the longest, most complex ecological chain reactions ever investigated had been set off by commercial whaling some fifty years ago. Without the otters to eat them, the sea urchin population exploded. Urchins, in turn, took a heavy toll on the kelp forests. The loss of the kelp caused a decline in the number of marine creatures that depend on kelp.

The lesson here is that the earth's food webs are incredibly complex. When a species is taken out it has an effect throughout the ecosystem.

Adapted from 'Whaling starts deadly chain reaction' by Robert McClure, *Sydney Morning Herald*, 27 September 2003

Alaskan sea otters.

Glossary of key terms

Biological diversity (biodiversity) The term used to describe the variety of life forms (species) found on earth.

Desertification The spread of deserts.

Ecologically sustainable development (ESD) Any development that satisfies the needs of the present population without affecting the ability of future generations to meet their own needs.

Endangered species A species with so few members that urgent action is required to make sure it survives.

Environmental degradation The problems that arise when an environment is altered or destroyed by the activities of people. Environments affected by these activities are described as having been degraded.

Extinct species A species of animal or plant that no longer exists.

Global warming The gradual rise in average temperatures brought about by an increase in the heat-absorbing gases present in the atmosphere.

Greenhouse effect The atmospheric processes that maintain an average surface temperature of 15°C.

Greenhouse gases Atmospheric gases that help retain heat; for example, carbon dioxide.

Habitat The physical environment in which a community of plants and animals lives.

Human rights The rights to which all humans are entitled.

Indigenous A person who is descended from the original inhabitants of a country.

Land degradation The downgrading of the productive capacity of land due to the activities of people.

Self-determination The power to make decisions about one's future.

Threatened species A species showing a pronounced drop in numbers but still reproducing with some success.

Vulnerable species A species that is not yet endangered but, while the population of the species may still be quite large, its numbers are falling rapidly.

eGlossary

Foundation worksheet 16.1

GeoToolkit

ICT Toolkit

16.1 Global issues: an overview

In this unit we outline some of the key global issues confronting humanity.

Climate change

Over the last 200 years, the amount of carbon dioxide present in the atmosphere has increased by 25 per cent. The main cause of this increase is the burning of fossil fuels (oil, coal and natural gas) and the cutting down of trees, which convert carbon dioxide into oxygen. Increasing global temperatures, rising sea levels and the retreat of ice caps and glaciers have all been linked to the impact of people on the atmosphere. (See Unit 16.3.)

Figure 16.1a The activities of people have altered the composition of the atmosphere. This, in turn, is changing the earth's climate.

Energy use

As noted at left, the burning of fossil fuels, which are used to meet the energy needs of communities, has had a major impact on the earth's atmosphere. Finding alternative sources of energy is one way people's reliance on fossil fuels can be reduced. Alternative sources of energy include solar energy, wind power, tidal flow and hydroelectricity. These issues were examined in Units 14.3 and 14.4.

Figure 16.1b Solar power : promoting alternative sources of energy is a way to tackle the problem of climate change.

Figure 16.1c Salinity: an example of land degradation.

Land degradation

The removal of natural vegetation (the result of deforestation, overgrazing and farming) is the main cause of **land degradation**. When trees are removed the land is exposed to the agents of erosion: wind and running water. (See Unit 16.5.)

Human rights

The idea that all humans have equal rights has taken centuries to develop. In many countries laws have been passed to protect people's rights. The extent to which such laws are observed and enforced varies from country to country. The UN's Universal Declaration of Human Rights (1948) (see Unit 15.1, p. 298) sets out the basic rights to which all people are entitled.

The abuse of **human rights** is widespread. Children are exploited, people are imprisoned because of their political views and persecuted because of their religion, while others are tortured or executed. In Unit 15.4 we examined the role of Oxfam Community Aid Abroad in protecting the human rights of workers in developing countries.

Figure 16.1d Gorillas, the largest of the great apes and humanity's closest relative, face extinction due to hunting and loss of habitat.

Threatened habitats

A **habitat** is the physical environment in which a community of plants and animals lives. As habitats are destroyed, the communities of plants and animals that depend on them are displaced, with some facing extinction. (See Unit 16.4.)

Figure 16.1e Child labour. Unfortunately, human rights abuses are still widespread. These young girls live and work sorting rubbish at the massive rubbish tip in Pune, India.

Extension worksheet ICT 16.1 | Extension worksheet ICT 16.5 | Extension worksheet ICT 16.6 | Extension worksheet ICT 16.7

Indigenous people and self-determination

An **indigenous** person is someone who is descended from the original inhabitants of a country. Examples include Aboriginal Australians, the Inuit of northern Canada (see Unit 6.5), the Dyaks and Penan of Borneo (see Unit 7.4), the Tuareg of the Sahara (see Unit 12.4), the Sherpa people of Nepal (see Unit 8.6) and the Yanomani of the Amazon. Indigenous people have their own distinctive language, spiritual beliefs, traditions and technology.

The world's 250 million indigenous people are among its most disadvantaged citizens. Much of this disadvantage can be traced back to the period in which the European powers invaded and occupied North and South America, Africa, Australia and New Zealand, and much of Asia and the South Pacific. As European migrants spread out across these lands the original inhabitants were forced off their traditional lands. Many met a violent death as they struggled to defend their way of life. Others died from the diseases brought by the invaders. Many more died because they could no longer follow their traditional way of life.

Today, many of the world's indigenous people are fighting back. They want access to their traditional lands and **self-determination**: the power to make decisions about their future.

Figure 16.1f Men of the Wodaabe group, Africa.

Access to fresh water

As we saw in Unit 14.2, access to fresh water is a major issue for more than 1 billion people, especially those living in developing countries. Without a clean, reliable source of drinking water it is almost impossible to avoid catching waterborne diseases. These cause great human suffering.

Figure 16.1g Waterborne diseases account for millions of deaths in the developing world.

Tourism

Each year, nearly 700 million people travel internationally for leisure, business and to visit friends and relatives. Many more people travel within their own countries. Today, tourism is one of the world's largest and fastest growing industries, but there are risks associated with this growth. Increasing tourist numbers threaten to overwhelm the features that attract people in the first place. **Environmental degradation**, for example, may reduce the pleasure that visitors receive from visiting a place. Undesirable social impacts (such as child exploitation, prostitution and loss of traditional values), which often accompany the growth of tourism, may have a negative impact on communities.

Figure 16.1h Sex-related tourism in Bangkok. If not managed carefully tourism can have undesirable social and environmental impacts.

Figure 16.1i Overcrowded squatter settlements, such as this one in Caracas, Venezuela, are one of the impacts of rapid urbanisation.

Urbanisation

The migration of people from rural areas to large cities has created many problems. The rapid growth of cities, especially in developing countries, has overwhelmed the ability of authorities to meet the basic needs of the urban population. Overcrowding, pollution and the growth of squatter settlements are all results of rapid urbanisation. We looked at the process of urbanisation and its impacts in Unit 3.5.

Figure 16.1j Fishing trawlers are used to harvest the world's oceans.

Use of ocean resources

The world's oceans are an important natural resource. Of particular importance are the world's fisheries. These supply vast amounts of food. Unfortunately, the rate at which this resource is being exploited is unsustainable. Pollution is another major problem affecting oceans. If oceans are to be used sustainably they must be carefully managed and there needs to be international cooperation. (See Unit 16.6.)

16.2 Ecological sustainability

Getting technical

Ecological The relationship between living things (including people) and their physical environment.
Sustainable Able to be carried on into the future.
Development Changes that create a better quality of life for people.

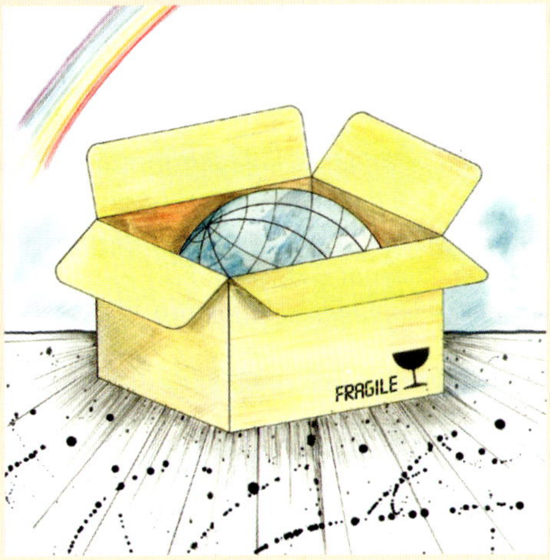

Figure 16.2a Handle with care.

One answer to the questions and issues outlined in Unit 16.1 is an idea called **ecologically sustainable development (ESD)**. Ecologically sustainable development is development that satisfies the needs of the present population without affecting the ability of future generations to meet their own needs. Examples of this include not cutting down forests at a rate faster than they can regrow and using farming methods that maintain and improve the fertility of the soil.

The aim of sustainable development is to achieve improvements in people's *quality of life* while protecting the environment. Sustainable development and good environmental management go hand in hand. If we are to put sustainable development into practice we must:

- Improve the quality of life experienced by the world's poorest people. Experience has shown that as people's quality of life improves (especially their health care, education and access to clean water) they tend to have fewer children. This, in turn, reduces the demands placed on the earth's resources.
- Use the earth's renewable resources (especially its fresh water, soil, forests and fisheries) in ways that do not reduce their usefulness for future generations.
- Avoid making decisions that limit the prospects for maintaining or improving future living standards.
- Involve people in decisions that affect their lives, their children's lives and their environment.
- Develop technologies that are cleaner, use less energy and require fewer natural resources.
- Make products that last longer and are easy to recycle and repair.
- Reduce the waste we produce and the amount of energy we use.
- Encourage the development and use of renewable energy from the sun, wind and flowing water.
- Take steps to prevent further environmental damage.
- Evenly share the benefits of economic growth.

cd Foundation worksheet 16.1 | cd Extension worksheet 16.2 | cd Extension worksheet 16.3

Understanding the text

1 What is meant by the term 'ecologically sustainable development'?
2 List the ten steps that need to be taken if we are to put ecologically sustainable development into practice.

cd UTT worksheet 16.2

Working geographically

1 **Challenge: Mindmapping** As a class, brainstorm the concept of 'ecological sustainability'. Develop a mindmap highlighting the main points raised in the discussion. Use the mindmap to write your own definition and explanation of 'ecological sustainability'.

2 **Writing emails** Email the Australian Prime Minister with suggestions about how the government could promote ecologically sustainable development.

16.3 Climate change

Life has existed on earth for nearly 4 billion years. During this time, the climate of the planet has undergone great change, from ice ages lasting tens of thousands of years to long periods of steamy heat. With each change some species of plants and animals have flourished, others have adapted and some have become extinct.

During the past century **greenhouse gases**, such as carbon dioxide (CO_2), have trapped enough heat in the atmosphere to raise the average temperatures by half a degree Celsius (see Figure 16.3a). This may not seem like very much, but if present trends continue it could significantly alter the earth's climate—melting glaciers, increasing sea levels, increasing rates of **desertification** and shifting vegetation zones. In this unit we look at the process of climate change and how it will affect life on earth.

Investigating climate change ICT

The are many excellent websites dealing with the issue of global warming. One of the best is the United Nations Environment Programme's: Climate Change site. Check out the site's great graphics under the heading 'Vital Climate Graphics'. Use them to illustrate any project work you do on this topic.

Investigate the UN Framework Convention on Climate Change and its Kyoto Protocol. Write a summary of the protocol's objectives and strategies for reducing CO_2 emissions.

Global warming

The main cause of climate change is **global warming**: the gradual rise in average temperatures brought about by an increase in the heat-absorbing gases present in the atmosphere. The gases that make up the earth's atmosphere help trap and retain some of the heat radiated from the earth's surface. Without the atmosphere the earth's surface temperature would average about –18°C instead of the present 15°C.

Thanks to the atmosphere, only a fraction of the sun's energy (heat) makes it directly back into space. The rest is trapped in the lower

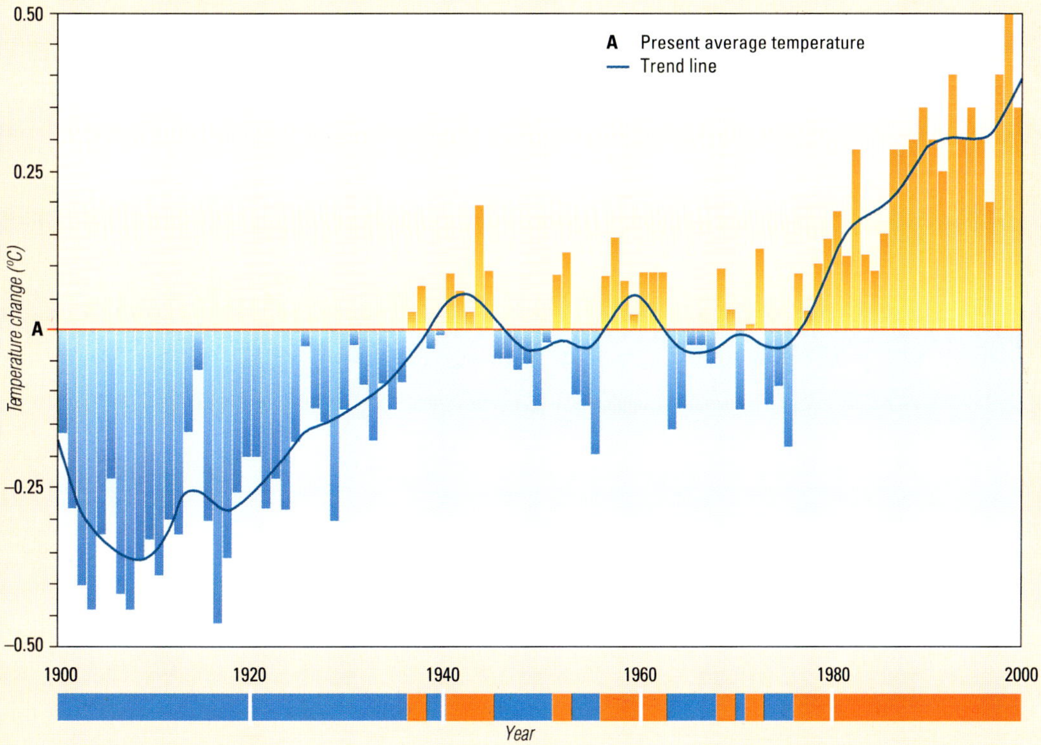

Figure 16.3a Global temperature change since 1900.

Figure 16.3b

Table 16.3a Concentration of CO_2 in the atmosphere, 1960–2003	
Year	**Concentration (ppm*)**
1960	316.91
1965	320.03
1970	325.68
1975	331.15
1980	338.69
1985	345.90
1990	354.19
1995	360.88
2000	369.40
2002	372.95
2003	379.00

*Parts per million

Lake's fish hit by global warming

Scientists are blaming global warming for falling fish harvests in Africa's Lake Tanganyika, threatening the diets of several developing nations.

Warming air and water and decreasing wind have cut the amount of mixing between the lake's surface water and deeper, nutrient-rich layers. The changes have cut algae growth, reducing food for several important fish species.

The Guardian, 14 August 2003

Getting technical

Ozone layer A layer of the atmosphere between 10 and 40 kilometres above the earth's surface where ozone molecules absorb dangerous ultraviolet radiation from the sun.

Ultraviolet rays Invisible rays in sunlight that cause suntan, sunburn, premature skin ageing and most cases of skin cancer.

layers of the atmosphere, which contain various gases that absorb the heat and then radiate it back towards the earth's surface. This process is known as the *natural* **greenhouse effect** because it is similar to what happens in a greenhouse or glasshouse. The natural greenhouse effect raises the average temperature of the earth by about 33°C (that is, from –18°C to +15°C)

The most important greenhouse gases are water vapour, carbon dioxide, methane, nitrous oxide and chlorofluorocarbons (CFCs). Water vapour is by far the most important of these gases because it is able to absorb large amounts of heat. Humans have very little direct control over the volume of water in the atmosphere. They do, however, influence the amount of carbon dioxide, methane and CFCs in the atmosphere. These, in turn, intensify the effect of the water vapour. The hotter the atmosphere gets, the more water vapour it can hold, thereby increasing the amount of heat trapped. This is called the *enhanced* greenhouse effect and is thought to be the main cause of global warming.

Estimating the actual rate of global warming is made difficult by the natural variability of the climate from place to place and from time to time. There are also other unknown factors that might significantly influence global temperatures. One of these is the effect of the oceans. The ability of a large body of water to retain its present temperature for a long time might slow the atmospheric temperature rise for many years. Because so little is known of this effect, it is difficult to predict accurately the rate at which temperatures will increase.

Figure 16.3c illustrates the enhanced greenhouse effect and how it is contributing to global warming. Figure 16.3d shows the sources of these greenhouse gases. Table 16.3a shows the build up of carbon dioxide in the atmosphere between 1960 and 2003.

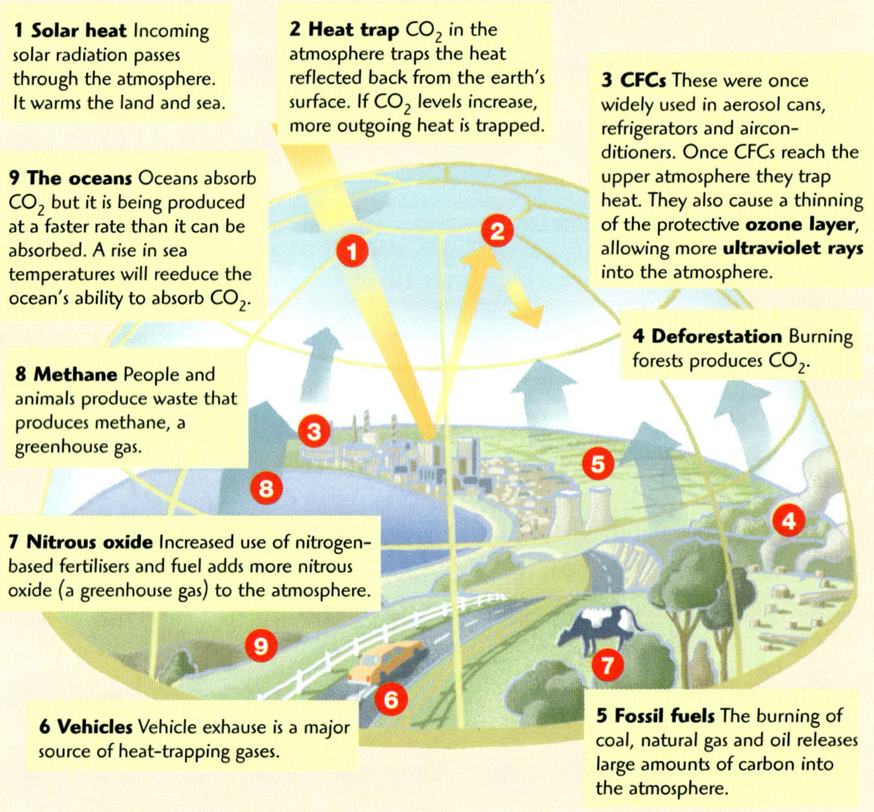

Figure 16.3c The enhanced greenhouse effect.

1 Nitrous oxide
This is a naturally occurring gas. Its supply has increased by 15% since 1800 due to the use of fertilisers and fossil fuels.

2 Carbon dioxide
The amount of carbon dioxide (CO_2) in the atmosphere today is about 30% higher than it was before the Industrial Revolution. Most of this increase is due to deforestation and the burning of fossil fuels: coal, oil and natural gas. If the current rate of increase (0.3% per year) continues, the amount of CO_2 in the atmosphere will be 400% higher than preindustrial levels by the end of the twenty-first century. CO_2 is though to account for as much as 60% of the warming observed since 1850. Per capita emissions of CO_2 are highest in developed countries (see Figure 16.3e).

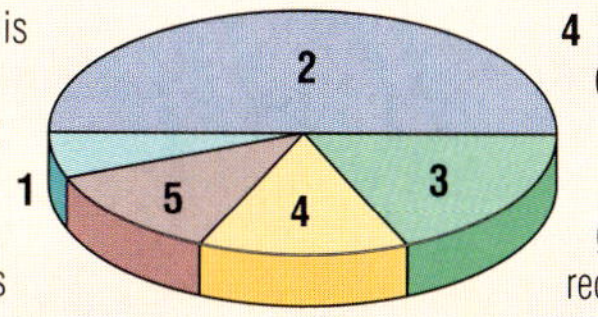

3 Methane
There is now about two and a half times more methane in the atmosphere than there was in the eighteenth century. Methane is produced by bacteria in rice fields, by decomposing garbage and by livestock (such as cattle). Methane is thought to account for about 15% of global warming in modern times.

4 Chlorofluorocarbons (CFCs)
CFCs are not naturally occurring gases in the atmosphere. They are artificial chemicals produced for industrial use. As well as destroying ozone in the upper atmosphere they have also been found to be greenhouse gases. The amount of CFCs in the atmospophere has been reduced since an international treaty banned their production.

5 Ozone
A molecule containing three atoms of oxygen. It is an important part of the upper atmosphere because it protects the earth from harmful ultraviolet radiation.

Figure 16.3d The contribution of different gases to the greenhouse effect.

Impacts of global climate change

Now that scientists have accurately recorded the increasing concentrations of greenhouse gases in the atmosphere, they are turning their attention to the long-term impact of these gases on climate. While predictions vary, most scientists agree that the average temperature of the lower atmosphere will increase by between 1°C and 3.5°C over the next century.

This increase is likely to affect environments and communities all over the world. The expected impacts are discussed below.

Changes to weather and climate

Temperatures

The predicted increase will produce temperatures that were last experienced 100 000 years ago. Any increase, however, will not be even across the globe. Continental landmasses are likely to experience a greater temperature increase than ocean areas, because land absorbs heat faster than the sea. There would be a greater temperature increase in regions in the high latitudes (that is, nearer to the poles) than near the Equator. Heatwaves would also become more frequent and last longer.

Islanders consider exodus as sea level rises

By David Fickling

Faced with the prospect of being swamped by rising sea levels, the Pacific island nation of Tuvalu is considering evacuating its 9300 residents.

With a highest point just five metres above sea level, Tuvalu is one of the world's most low-lying countries. Half its population is crammed on the 30 hectare Funafuti atoll, which is only three metres above the waves.

With global sea levels predicted to rise by more than 80cm over the next century, Tuvaluans are living on borrowed time. The only solution, according to the government, is to transport the entire population overseas.

The Guardian, 19 July 2003

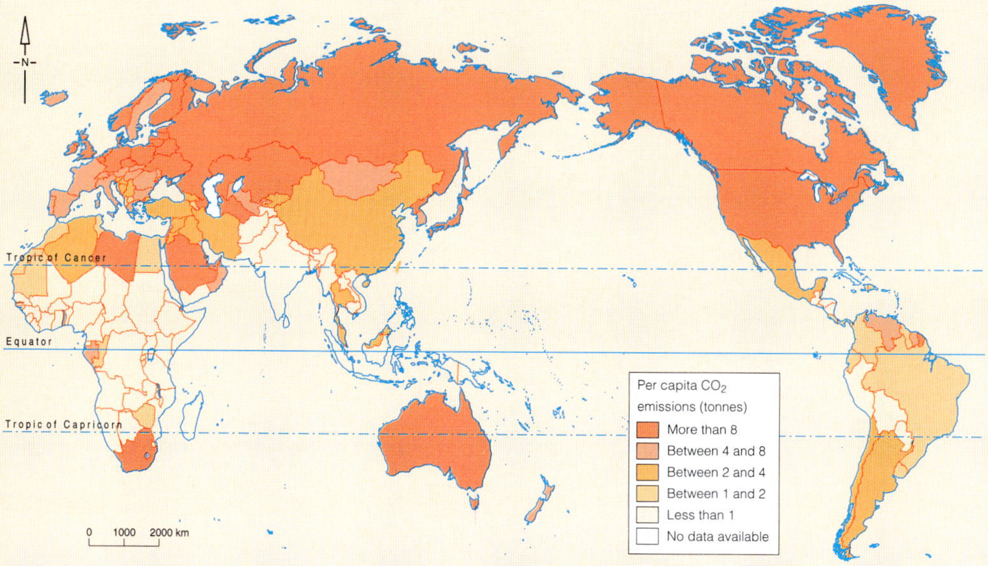

Figure 16.3e Per capita carbon dioxide emissions.

Warming warning for Antarctica

By Tim Radford

The face of Antarctica will change in the next 100 years as ice melts, glaciers retreat, penguins move south and green plants begin to colonise bare rocks of the Antarctic peninsula, researchers warned yesterday.

'We know parts of Antarctica are warming, and they are warming very rapidly,' [said] Andrew Clarke of the British Antarctic Survey.

The Guardian, 9 September 2003

Rainfall

Higher temperatures will result in much more water vapour in the air: about 6 per cent more for every 1°C increase in temperature. In some places this will mean more intense rainfall and flooding. Increases in sea and land temperatures will produce complex changes in wind patterns and, in turn, precipitation patterns.

Storm patterns

The combination of increased sea and air temperatures will affect the storm belts (areas of frequent storm activity) across the globe. At present, tropical cyclones are confined to particular latitudes (8°–25° north and south of the Equator) where water temperatures are high enough to support the evaporation rate necessary for storms to form. With global warming, the storm belts will spread from the Equator. As a result, places on the same latitude as Brisbane could regularly experience tropical cyclones, whereas they are presently out of range.

Not only will the area affected by tropical cyclones expand, the warmer oceans will also create more intense storms. One estimate is that global warming could increase the intensity of tropical cyclones by 50 per cent.

Melting ice sheets and glaciers

Scientists have recorded the retreat of the world's glaciers over the last century. There is growing evidence that the ice shelves surrounding Antarctica are beginning to break up and melt.

Changes in sea level

Rising sea levels could have a devastating impact on coastal communities. It is predicted the polar regions will experience the greatest warming. If these predictions are correct, then the melting of

Indian Ocean 'heatwaves' spell disaster for coral

By Tim Radford

Vast areas of coral reef could perish within the next few decades in a procession of cyclic 'heatwaves' in the Indian Ocean, a marine biologist warns today.

Charles Sheppard, of Warwick University, reports in the journal Nature that in 1998, unusually high sea temperatures killed more than 90% of the corals on shallow Indian Ocean reefs, and such events in future could finish the job.

'In 1998, there was a huge wipeout of corals,' Dr Sheppard said. 'The global figure seems to have been about 16% of all corals, but the Indian Ocean was the worst affected.'

'I have dived on reefs there for a whole hour, and not seen one left alive.'

The Guardian, 18 September 2003

Will Venice really disappear within 100 years?

By Alok Jha

If nothing is done to stop the encroaching sea, then yes. The land is sinking while, thanks to global climate change, the sea is rising.

Flooding may well be a way of life for the Venetians but they do recognise that the situation is deteriorating. In 1900, the central area of the city around St Mark's square flooded around 10 times a year. Nowadays, that figure is closer to 100… And it's only going to get worse. Climatologists agree that global sea levels are likely to rise by up to 60cm by the end of the century…

The Guardian, 18 September 2003

Foundation worksheet 16.1

Foundation worksheet 16.1

Extension worksheet ICT 16.4

Figure 16.3f Venice, one of the world's architectural treasures, is threatened by rising sea levels. Plans are in place to build a series of floodgates to regulate sea level in Venice's lagoon.

polar ice caps could be so great that it would add a significant amount of water to the oceans. In addition, water expands as it warms, forcing sea levels higher still. Average sea levels have risen by 10–25 centimetres during the twentieth century.

The areas most at risk from a rise in sea level are the low-lying areas of the Pacific and Indian Oceans.

Combating global warming

At the 1997 Climate Change Conference held in Kyoto, Japan, the countries of the industrialised world agreed, in principle, to cut their emissions of greenhouse gases. But what about the countries of the developing world? In the face of worldwide demands to reduce emissions, developing countries are torn between going along with the plan or trying to lift the *standard of living* of their people. In the long run, the well-being of all the world's people will require greater cooperation between countries and a commitment by individuals to a more sustainable lifestyle. We will, for example, need to:

- reduce the amount of fossil fuels used
- use alternative sources of energy, such as wind and solar power
- stop cutting down forests, especially rainforests
- conserve energy.

Understanding the text

1 What is global warming?
2 What is the natural greenhouse effect? Why is it important?
3 Explain how people have increased the effectiveness or intensity of the greenhouse effect.
4 Outline the factors that make it difficult to estimate the actual rate of temperature increase.
5 Explain how global warming will affect the world's climate.
6 What will cause sea levels to rise?
7 What actions has the international community taken to address the problem?

UTT worksheet 16.3

Working geographically

1 **Interpreting graphs** Using data from Figure 16.3a (p. 315), describe the trends in global temperature over the course of the twentieth century.

2 **Interpreting cartoons** Study Figure 16.3b (p. 315). Write a sentence or two outlining the issue that Wilcox addresses in the cartoon.

3 **Challenge: Writing task** Use the information in Figure 16.3c (p. 316) to write a report outlining the operation of the natural and enhanced greenhouse effects.

4 **Interpreting graphs** Study Figure 16.3d (p. 317), then complete the following tasks:
   a What are the main sources of the additional CO_2 in the atmosphere? What contribution have these made to global warming?
   b Where does the additional methane in the atmosphere come from?
   c Why are CFCs unlikely to be a major contributor to the problem in the future?

5 **Constructing graphs** Use the data in Table 16.3a (p. 316) to construct a line graph (see Unit 2.13) showing the concentration of CO_2 in the atmosphere between 1960 and 2003.

6 **Interpreting maps** Study Figure 16.3e (p. 317). With the aid of an atlas, complete the following tasks:
   a Identify the countries with CO_2 emissions greater than 9 tonnes per capita.
   b Identify the regions of the world with annual CO_2 emissions of less than 1 tonne per capita.
   c Using your knowledge of global inequalities, comment on the relationship between CO_2 emissions and level of economic development.

7 **Writing task: Research** Write a report outlining the likely impacts of global warming. Add to the information contained in this unit by undertaking research.

8 **Using the media: Wall display** Study the newspaper extracts on pages 316–318. List the impacts of global warming discussed in each article. Can you think of any others? Use the archive facility of major international newspapers to find your own newspaper extracts on this topic. Add these to a wall display headed 'Impacts of global climate change'.

16.4 Threatened habitats

Big cats face extinction

The fate of the world's big cats shows the impact that habitat loss is having on species. African lion numbers have decreased by 90 per cent since the mid-1980s. There are only about 23 000 alive today. The tiger is also endangered (see Figure 16.4a). There are probably fewer than 15 000 cheetahs in all of Africa and the Iberian lynx is down to about 800.

Figure 16.4a There are now fewer than 8000 tigers living in the wild.

Habitat and species loss

As the world's population grows, so does the demand for food, products for clothing and shelter, and space for living and playing. As a result, whole habitats are lost. On the island of Borneo, for example, orang-utans could be extinct within ten to twenty years if the current rate of rainforest destruction continues. In China, fewer than 1000 giant pandas survive. (See the box 'Big cats face extinction'.) While, sadly, some species are already **extinct** an alarming (and growing) number of species are classified as **endangered, vulnerable** or **threatened**.

This unit looks at the link between habitat destruction and species loss, and the strategies people are using to protect the habitats of endangered species.

Causes of species loss

The main reason why so many species have become endangered or extinct in the last 100 years is *loss of habitat*. The clearing of land for housing, logging and farming is the main cause of this habitat destruction. Other causes include the introduction of non-native species and hunting. The known causes of animal extinctions are shown in Figure 16.4b.

Introduced species of plants and animals can be an important factor in the decline of established native species. Rabbits, foxes, camels, goats, blackberry, prickly pear, cane toads and cats are some of the species introduced to Australia that have gone feral. They now compete with native species and often eliminate them from wide areas. Many small species, such as the short-tailed hopping mouse and the numbat, have become endangered because of hunting by introduced species.

Hunting is a significant cause of species loss and endangerment. Animals are hunted for food and skins. In the Caspian Sea, fishing for the highly valued beluga sturgeon's eggs, used to make caviar, has pushed the fish species close to extinction.

Why does species loss matter?

The earth has been losing species for millions of years. So why does it matter if more species become extinct? It is not just the possible loss of magnificent creatures such as the North American bison, the Bengal

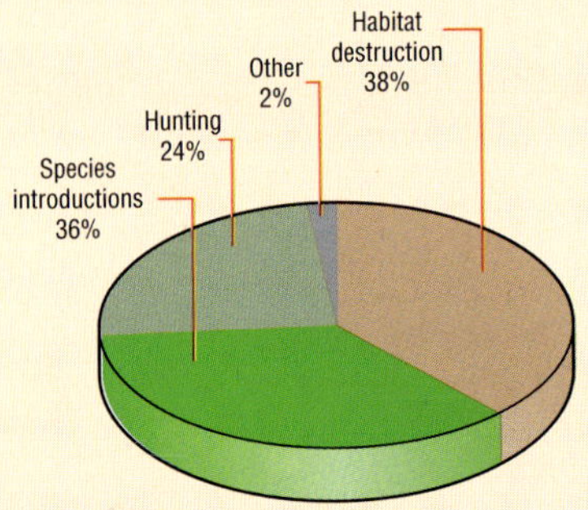

Figure 16.4b Known causes of animal extinctions.

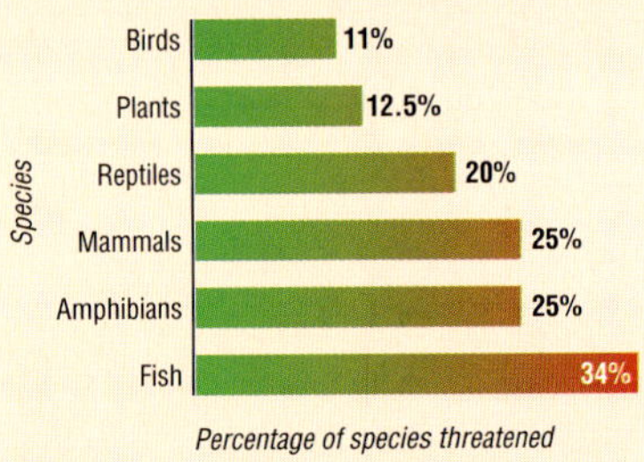

Figure 16.4c Species under pressure. Source: *Time* magazine.

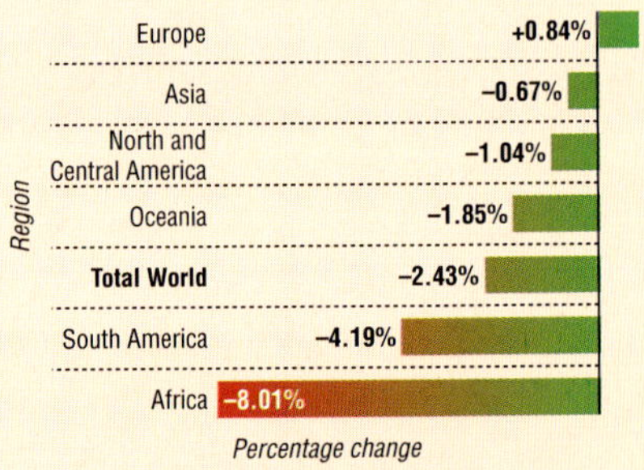

Figure 16.4d Forest loss/gain by region (percentage change), 1990–2000. Source: *Time* magazine.

Africa's black rhino: on the brink of extinction

The magnificent animals in Figure 16.4e may be extinct in a few years. The numbers have declined from 65 000 in 1970 to just 3100 in 2001. The black rhino can weigh up to 1350 kilograms and stand 1.7 metres tall. Its larger horn can grow to a length of 1.3 metres. These horns have been a major cause of the rhino's declining numbers. Some traditional Chinese medicines use powdered rhino horn as an ingredient, while in some Middle Eastern countries the horn is carved into decorative dagger handles. Despite a worldwide ban on the rhino horn trade for over twenty-five years, poachers have slaughtered huge numbers of black rhinos—just for their horns.

Some African governments have gone to extreme methods to protect their declining populations of black rhinos. Dehorning the rhino makes them less attractive to hunters. Zimbabwe has a more extreme measure: game rangers have the power to shoot poachers on sight. Breeding programs in protected areas are one possible solution. But reproduction rates are naturally low.

A special rhino breeding program based at Dubbo's Western Plains Zoo is part of a worldwide effort to protect the black rhino from extinction.

You can find out more about the rhino by visiting the International Rhino Foundation website.

Figure 16.4e Endangered black rhinos at Dubbo's Western Plains Zoo.

tiger, the gorilla or panda. All these species are part of different ecosystems. A full variety of life forms—**biological diversity**—in ecosystems allows these ecosystems to function better. They can purify water, maintain the quality of the air we breathe, recycle nutrients and waste, provide food and shelter for other species and keep the population of some species from dominating an environment.

Plants and animals also supply many of the medicines that are used to cure human diseases. The medical potential of many species is yet to be fully realised.

Strategies for maintaining biodiversity

Attempts to protect habitats and biodiversity range from setting aside and protecting large areas of land to the preservation of species in zoos, botanical gardens and seed banks. None of the actions will, however, be sufficient to save many species from extinction.

Protected areas

Protected areas are national parks, wilderness areas, nature reserves and World Heritage sites. The first national park was established in 1872. Since then, an area of 13 250 000 square kilometres has been set aside to provide protection for threatened habitats and to maintain biodiversity. This area is roughly the size of India and China combined or 8.8 per cent of the earth's surface. A much smaller area (just 1 per cent) of the world's seas are protected.

Working geographically

1 **Interpreting graphs** Study Figures 16.4b, 16.4c and 16.4d, then complete the following tasks:
   a Write a paragraph outlining the causes of animal extinctions.
   b Which species are under greatest pressure?
   c Which continents have experienced the greatest rate of forest loss in the period 1990–2000.

2 **Planning campaigns** Study the box 'Africa's black rhino: on the brink of extinction' and then complete the following tasks:
   a Explain the rapid decline in black rhino numbers.
   b In a group, plan two campaigns to help save Africa's black rhino. Your first campaign targets Australia, while the second campaign targets people and organisations in Africa. Decide what form your campaign will take (for example, a letter-writing campaign, advertisements and/or meetings with politicians).

Investigating endangered species ICT

There are a number of excellent websites featuring information about endangered species. Try these:

- Bagheera
- United Nations Environment Programme World Conservation Monitoring Centre
- World Wide Fund for Nature
- Convention on International Trade in Endangered Species of Wild Fauna and Flora (CITES).

Understanding the text

1 Outline the main causes of habitat destruction and species loss.
2 Outline the impact that introduced species can have on established native species.
3 Explain why we should be concerned about the loss of species.
4 What conditions need to be met if the protection of an area is to be successful?
5 How are zoos helping to save endangered species?

UTT worksheet 16.4

To be successful, protected areas need to:

- be large enough to protect whole ecosystems and allow evolutionary processes to continue into the future
- have boundaries that are based on environmental rather than political considerations; for example, taking in an entire catchment area that might span more than one country
- take into account the interests of the local people by not, for example, banning traditional hunting practices, which would only encourage poaching
- be surrounded by a buffer zone, which is an area surrounding the protected area where human activity is carefully managed
- be well managed and adequately funded.

Zoos, botanical gardens and seed banks

Zoos play an important role in captive breeding programs for endangered species, scientific research and public education. Animals bred in zoos are being used to repopulate their original homelands. Przewalksi's horse, for example, has been reintroduced into northern China and Mongolia from animals reared at the San Diego Wild Animal Park in the United States and the Western Plains Zoo in Australia.

Botanical gardens carry out similar programs for endangered plant life. Seed banks have been established to store genetic material for future study and use.

International agreements

International agreements between countries can make a great difference to the future of endangered species and threatened habitats.

The Convention on International Trade in Endangered Species of Wild Fauna and Flora (CITES), for example, aims to protect named species by limiting or banning international trade in particular items. It has successfully banned the trade in ivory to protect African elephants from poachers. Helped by breeding programs, the number of African elephants has increased significantly in Namibia, Botswana and Zimbabwe.

A side effect of trade bans has been the growth of illegal trade, especially in smaller birds and reptiles. Private zoos, for example, are willing to pay thousands of dollars for pairs of Australian parrots and lizards. Birds are usually drugged, put into narrow tubes and packed into suitcases. Sometimes dozens of birds die on their way to their destination overseas.

Working geographically

1 **Group discussion** In groups, discuss why zoos in the past contributed to species becoming endangered. In what ways have zoos and animal parks now become essential elements in the survival of endangered species?

2 **Class discussion** As a class, discuss whether habitat protection is a more successful method of saving endangered species than a breeding program conducted in a zoo or animal park.

3 **Internet research** Use the Internet to locate the CITES website. Summarise a case that shows how one of its decisions has worked. Mention the plant or animal involved and which countries have an interest in its decision.

16.5 Land degradation

Land degradation means the downgrading of land so that it is not as productive as it once was. If land is degraded, it loses its ability to produce the quality of vegetation or crops that it once did. Land degradation is one of the most important environmental problems in the world because it is so widespread and so difficult to reverse.

Figure 16.5b Soil erosion.

Types of soil degradation

Soil can be damaged, or degraded, in four main ways.

Soil salinity

Increasing levels of salt in soils is common in some parts of the world, including Australia. It is caused by salty *groundwater* (water that is stored in rock and soil below the surface) reaching the surface of the soil. Normally this water level is controlled by large trees, which pump water from the soil as they transpire. But when trees are cut down, salty water may rise to the surface. The water evaporates, leaving a salty crust (see Figure 16.5a).

Soil erosion

Soil erosion is the removal of topsoil by water or wind (see Figure 16.5b). This happens wherever the soil is unprotected by plant cover. Once the original plant cover is removed, soil can be carried away easily by strong winds or heavy rain. Winds can strip the land of its topsoil and carry it hundreds of kilometres. Heavy rain and runoff can cut deep gullies in the soil (see Figure 16.5d, p. 324).

Figure 16.5a Salinity.

Figure 16.5c Loss of vegetation.

Table 16.5a	Land degradation of cropland in Australia
Type	**Area ('000 km^2)**
Total	**443.0**
Undegraded land	142.0
Degraded land	301.0
Degraded by water erosion	206.0
Degraded by wind erosion	52.0
Degraded by combined wind and water erosion	42.0
Degraded by salinity and water erosion	0.9
Degraded by other means	0.5

Source: Eswaran, Lal, Reich, *Land Degradation: An Overview*, Oxford University Press, 2001

Figure 16.5d Gully erosion.

Landcare Australia ICT

Investigate the work of Landcare Australia by accessing its website. Make a note of the aims of Landcare, and investigate one of the organisation's project. Report your finding to the rest of the class.

Figure 16.5e Landcare's logo.

Table 16.5b Estimates of degraded lands in dry areas

Continent	Total dry area (km^2)	Degraded area (km^2)	Degraded area (%)
Africa	14.3 billion	10.5 billion	73
Asia	18.8 billion	13.4 billion	71
Australia	7.0 billion	3.8 billion	54
Europe	1.5 billion	0.9 billion	65
North America	5.8 billion	4.3 billion	74
South America	4.2 billion	3.0 billion	70
Total	**51.6 billion**	**35.9 billion**	**70**

Source: Eswaran, Lal, Reich, *Land Degradation: An Overview*, Oxford University Press, 2001

Compaction

Soil can be compacted by the weight of heavy machinery or the trampling of hard-hooved animals. Both of these can compress the air spaces in the soil so that it develops a hard layer on top. This reduces infiltration and makes it difficult to use the land for crops or pasture.

Acidification

Soil can be made acidic by the overuse of chemical fertilisers. Often the use of some fertiliser is essential to ensure the soil keeps producing crops. When used over a long period of time, however, fertilisers can also harm the soil.

Causes of soil degradation

The activities of people that contribute to soil degradation include *overclearing* of the natural vegetation (which contributes to both soil salinity and erosion) and *overgrazing* by animals. When too many cattle or sheep are put onto an area of land, they eat all the grass and bushes, leaving nothing to hold the soil together. Their hard hooves compact the top layer of the soil.

These causes of soil damage are examples of poor *land management*. Usually this is unintentional, but may be caused by greed.

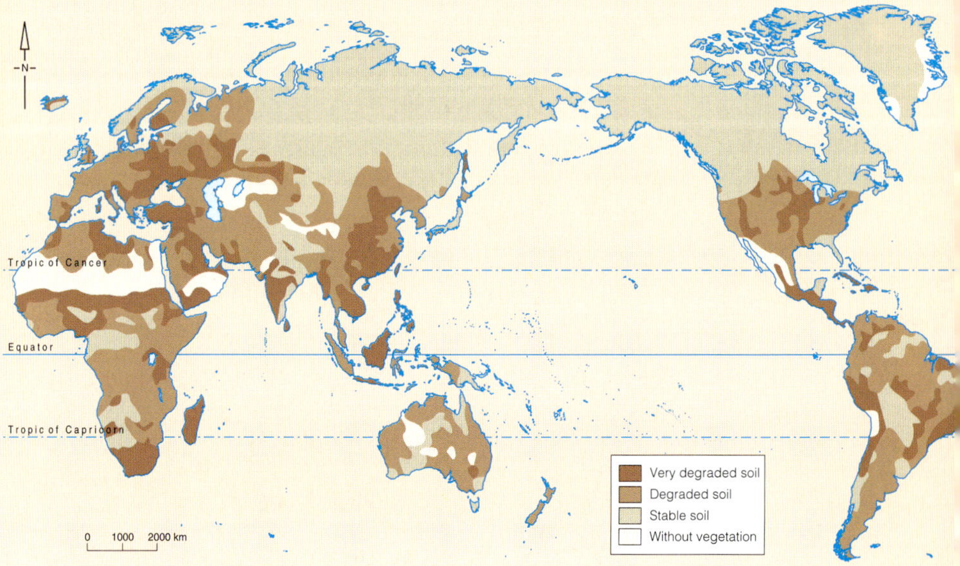

Figure 16.5f Map of world soil degradation. Source: UNEP.

Vegetation degradation

Natural vegetation can also be degraded. A natural ecosystem of plants can be changed in a number of ways. For example, vegetation can be affected by introduced plants. These can upset the natural balance of the ecosystem and spread uncontrollably.

Fires can also change the vegetation greatly. Although fire can be a natural part of the environment, it has a major effect on some species. It can remove some species, and encourage the growth of others.

Weed infestations often occur when vegetation is disturbed. Weeds are plants that have run wild (like animals gone feral) and have taken over from other species. Plants turn into weeds when they find conditions that are ideal, leading to their domination of an ecosystem.

Desertification

One of the most serious forms of land degradation in the world is desertification, which means the creation of deserts. Desertification is a problem in parts of Africa where the desert is steadily advancing over what used to be good farming land.

Desertification in northern Africa has occurred on the edges of the Sahara Desert (see Units 12.2 and 12.4). These marginal lands have variable rainfall and can only be used with great care. A mixture of overuse and periodic changes in the rainfall has destroyed the productive ability of the land. The results are creeping desert sands and salty water holes.

Fighting land degradation

Land degradation can only be reversed by the combined action of individuals working on their own properties or in their communities. In Australia this is done by Landcare groups, which have been set up all over the country. Table 16.5c gives three examples of projects sponsored by the United Nations to deal with land degradation.

Table 16.5c Examples of UN projects to fight land degradation

Location 1: a ranch in Namibia, southern Africa	
Problems	Soil erosion; bush encroachment; reduced livestock production; degradation of vegetation cover
Solutions	Division of the land into smaller paddocks with rotated grazing; control of soil erosion; use of fewer chemicals
Achievements	Increased cattle production; improved soil structure; improved vegetation; increased farm income
Location 2: western China	
Problems	Movement of sand dunes over productive land; salinity; water shortages in some seasons
Solutions	Planting of tamarix over large areas (tamarix is a well-adapted plant that anchors sand, grows in saline land and can protect oases)
Achievements	Increased fodder and cattle production; more jobs
Location 3: an arid region of Pakistan	
Problems	Extremes of climate; severe wind erosion; moving sands; waterlogging (saturation of the soil that occurs when the water table rises close to the surface) and salinity
Solutions	Planting of windbreaks; planting of woodlots (tree plantings to provide a supply of fuel wood) to soak up the water that is causing salinity and waterlogging
Achievements	Doubling of crop production; fewer sandstorms

Understanding the text

1 What is land degradation?
2 Outline the various types of soil degradation.
3 Outline the causes of soil and vegetation degradation.
4 What is desertification?
5 Outline the strategies used to fight land degradation.

UTT worksheet 16.5

Working geographically

1 **Interpreting statistics** Study Tables 16.5a and 16.5b, then complete the following tasks:
- a Which continent has the largest area of degraded land?
- b Which continent has the smallest area of degraded land?
- c Name the continent with the largest percentage of degraded dry lands.

2 **Challenge: Fieldwork** Conduct a survey of the school grounds or an area nearby to evaluate the amount of land degradation.
- a Draw up a base map of the site.
- b Look for evidence of damage to soil: erosion, compaction, waterlogging and salinity.
- c Map the areas where nothing grows
- d Map the areas of plants. If possible, label them as native or introduced.
- e Use this information to make a list of steps that could be taken to improve that particular area of land.

16.6 Use of ocean resources

Did U know?

- The average annual consumption of fish in developed countries is 9.2 kilograms per person. In developing countries it is 27.0 kilograms. Therefore, any depletion of world fish stocks would have a greater impact on those living in developing countries.
- The number of people engaged in aquaculture (fish farming) has doubled since 1970.
- Worldwide, more than 21 million people are full-time fishers and 200 million depend on fishing for their livelihood.
- In 2000 there were 3.5 million operational fishing vessels.
- Fishing is a dangerous industry. More than 24 000 fishers are killed each year.
- Is it worthwhile? The world's fishing industry spends US$124 billion each year to catch US$70 billion worth of fish. The difference (US$54 billion) is made up of government subsidies.

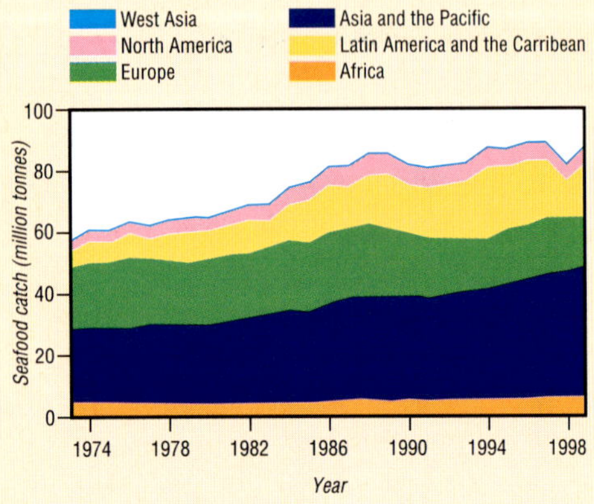

Figure 16.6a Global seafood catch by region, 1974–2000. Source: UNEP.

The oceans

The earth is sometimes referred to as the 'blue planet'. This is because two-thirds of its surface is covered by water: its four great oceans and smaller seas. People have used these oceans and seas for centuries with little consideration of the long-term impact of their activities. Some of these impacts are the:

- overexploitation of the world's fisheries
- dumping of toxic pollutants, which enter the aquatic food chain and cause genetic damage
- increased flow of nutrients (such as agricultural fertilisers and sewage) into the sea. These encourage the growth of algae, which can turn the water green and slimy
- dumping of plastics and other solid wastes. Marine mammals, such as seals and dolphins, can get tangled in plastic and may drown or starve to death
- oil spills, which can smother the sea floor, killing plants, aquatic animals and birdlife.

Just as people are now beginning to think about how their activities are affecting the atmosphere (see Unit 16.3) there is a growing interest in, and concern for, the impact people are having on the world's oceans. Environmental groups such as Greenpeace have played an important role in drawing the public's attention to the issue. The success of Greenpeace's 'Save the whale' campaign (see Unit 15.5) is one example of how public opinion can be used to bring about international cooperation on environmental issues.

Harvesting the world's oceans

More than 3 million fishing vessels now sift the world's oceans for seafood—twice as many as in 1970. The global catch exceeds 85 million tonnes a year (see Figure 16.6a). This level of activity cannot be sustained. Fish populations are declining at an alarming rate.

In an effort to protect their fishing grounds, many countries have extended their territorial control from 12 to 200 nautical miles (300 kilometres) beyond their coastline. As a result, nearly 40 per cent of the world's oceans have now been claimed as exclusive fishing zones by countries who then restrict the access of foreign fleets to these waters. This has been a source of ongoing conflict between some countries. Military forces are often used to detain the crews of boats caught fishing illegally within the 200 nautical mile limit.

In some regions fish species have been exploited close to extinction. In other areas fish yields are in serious decline. One such area is the Grand Banks of Newfoundland, Canada. In the mid-1990s the Canadian Government became so concerned with the rate of decline that it ordered a stop to fishing in the region. The impact on local communities was dramatic—40 000 people were put out of work. But distant-water trawlers operating out of Spain, Portugal and other nations continued to fish the edges of the Grand Banks just outside Canada's territorial waters.

The problem is just as serious in the developing world. Having reduced fish numbers in their own waters many rich countries are now buying access to poor countries' waters. This disadvantages local fishers who are unable to afford the technology used by the larger foreign-owned factory ships, where the catch is processed on board. In the waters off Senegal in western Africa, for example, locals must now travel farther and farther to get the same catch. Large long-range trawlers from China, South Korea, Spain, Japan and France are depleting Senegal's local fish stocks.

International efforts to regulate the industry have not yet met with much success. Because the oceans are so vast it is difficult to make sure that operators comply with international agreements.

The Patagonian toothfish

The Patagonian toothfish (often referred to as sea bass) plays an important part in the Southern Ocean ecosystem. It can live for fifty years and does not breed until at least ten years old. While it grows only slowly, the toothfish can reach a length of more than 2 metres. As with most deep-sea creatures, little is known about the species. What is known, however, is that the toothfish forms an important part of the diet of sperm whales and elephant seals.

The poaching (illegal fishing) of the toothfish threatens the future of the species. The main importers are Japan and the United States. A single fish can fetch up to US$1000.

Figure 16.6b Royal Australian Navy personnel boarding a Uruguayan trawler suspected of illegal fishing of Patagonian toothfish.

The bluefin tuna

Japan has the world's biggest appetite for fish. Its large fleet harvests nearly 8 million tonnes of fish each year. The most prized fish is the bluefin tuna, a sushi delicacy. A single fish can sell for as much as 1 million yen (A$12 700).

According to Greenpeace, the southern bluefin tuna is now critically endangered. Despite this the Japanese continue to exceed the quota of fish they are allowed to catch. Greenpeace has called on the Australian and New Zealand Governments (in whose waters much of the harvesting of the bluefin tuna takes place) to nominate the species for protection under the Convention on International Trade in Endangered Species of Wild Fauna and Flora (CITES).

Understanding the text

1. What actions have countries taken to protect their fishing zones?
2. How have people in developing countries been affected by the worldwide growth of the fishing industry?
3. Why have international efforts to regulate the industry met with little success?

UTT worksheet 16.6

Working geographically

1. **Internet research: Using software** Study the boxes 'The bluefin tuna' and 'The Patagonian toothfish'. Use the Greenpeace website to further investigate the issues raised in this unit. Develop a presentation using appropriate software (such as PowerPoint) outlining:
   - a the ocean-related issues on which Greenpeace campaigns
   - b the arguments used by Greenpeace to justify its interventions
   - c the strategies used by Greenpeace to bring issues to the public's attention
   - d Greenpeace's successes.
2. **Challenge: Writing task** Write a report outlining the impact people have had on the world's oceans.

Foundation worksheet 16.2

16.7 Review and reflect

Chapter summary

The environmental issues examined in this chapter can be looked at in terms of a conflict between the short-term benefits that individuals and groups receive from the use of resources and the long-term welfare of the whole human population. Should we, for example, continue to maintain a way of life that relies on the burning of fossil fuels (coal, oil and natural gas) when we know that their use adds to the greenhouse gases that are changing the planet's climate?

Fortunately, many people are now beginning to realise that international cooperation will be essential if we are to sustainably manage and protect the environment for the benefit of future generations. The most effective forms of management seem to involve countries reaching an agreement on how the environment is to be used or protected. They then sign a formal agreement or treaty and try to prevent other countries from breaking them. Unfortunately, not all countries agree to sign treaties or cooperate.

Activity 1

Research: Global issues

Select one of the issues listed in Unit 16.1 but not addressed in Units 16.2–16.6. Undertake library or Internet research into the selected issue. Communicate your findings in a presentation created using appropriate software (such as PowerPoint). Use the following points to structure your presentation:

- the nature and geographical extent of the issue
- different perspectives relevant to the issue
- the responsibility of governments in relation to the issue
- the actions that individuals, groups and governments could take to address the issue
- the implications for social justice and equity (if relevant).

See Unit 2.16 for advice on how to develop an effective multimedia presentation

Activity 2

Challenge: Internet research—Threatened habitats

Study the following list of endangered 'flagship' species sourced from the website of the World Wide Fund for Nature:

- giant panda
- African and Asian elephants
- tigers
- whales
- white, Sumatran, Javan and Indian rhinos
- the great apes (western and eastern gorilla, chimpanzee, bonobo and orang-utan)
- marine turtles (leatherback, loggerhead, green and hawksbill).

1 Carry out library or Internet research into one of these endangered species. Use presentation software (such as PowerPoint) to develop a series of slides on the species. Use the following points to structure your research and presentation:
   - name the species
   - locate a copyright-free image of the animal and download it into a slide
   - provide a brief description of the animal and identify its original and current distribution
   - outline the reasons why the species has been listed as endangered
   - outline the actions that are being taken to protect the species
   - evaluate the effectiveness of these actions.

   See Unit 2.16 for advice on multimedia presentations.

2 In groups, develop a recovery plan for one of the endangered species listed above. Justify the particular features of your plan.

Activity 3

Interpreting cartoons: Global warming

1 In groups, study the cartoon opposite and brainstorm the issue Nicholson is addressing. Share your group's findings with the rest of the class. Use this information to write a paragraph explaining the point Nicholson is trying to communicate in his cartoon.
2 Conduct a class debate. Topic: People in developed nations must accept a lower standard of living as part of their contribution to global reductions in greenhouse gas emissions.
3 In groups, brainstorm what you and your family could do to reduce greenhouse gas emissions. Make a list of the suggestions and share them with the rest of the class.

Cartoon by Nicholson from *The Australian*. www.nicholsoncartoons.com.au

Activity 4

Understanding key terms: Land degradation and ocean resources

Match each of the following definitions with a term from the list provided.

Terms

acidification, introduced species, erosion, ecological sustainability, groundwater, desertification, land degradation, compaction, endangered species, global commons

Definitions

1 The downgrading of the productive capacity of the land as a result of the activities of people.
2 Water stored in rock and soil below the surface.
3 The compression of the air spaces in the soil by the weight of heavy machinery or the trampling of hard-hooved animals.
4 An increase in the acidity of soil due to the overuse of chemical fertilisers.
5 The removal of topsoil by water or wind.
6 The creation of deserts resulting from poor land management practices.
7 Those parts of the global environment that everyone shares and which no individual or country owns or controls.
8 A non-native species of plant or animal.
9 Meeting the needs of the present population without affecting the ability of future generations to meet their own needs.
10 A plant or animal species in need of urgent action to make sure it survives.

Index